# Out of Darkness—Light

# Out of Darkness—Light
# A History of Canadian Military Intelligence

# Out of Darkness—Light

## A History of Canadian Military Intelligence

### Volume 2,
### 1983-1997

## *Major Harold A. Skaarup*

iUniverse, Inc.

New York  Lincoln  Shanghai

# Out of Darkness—Light
## A History of Canadian Military Intelligence

iUniverse books may be ordered through booksellers or by contacting:

iUniverse
2021 Pine Lake Road, Suite 100
Lincoln, NE 68512
www.iuniverse.com
1-800-Authors (1-800-288-4677)

Many significant elements of the history of Intelligence in the Canadian Forces remain classified and cannot be included here. The material found within this collection of stories, reports and articles generally reflects the activities of past and current members of the CF Intelligence Branch within the experience of the author. Much of the information found here is based on the personal observations of a handful of past and presently serving Intelligence Corps and Intelligence Branch veterans, some of whom have passed on, and therefore much of it is only as accurate as collective memories can provide.
E Tenebris Lux.

ISBN-13: 978-0-595-35928-8 (pbk)
ISBN-13: 978-0-595-67298-1 (cloth)
ISBN-13: 978-0-595-80382-8 (ebk)
ISBN-10: 0-595-35928-0 (pbk)
ISBN-10: 0-595-67298-1 (cloth)
ISBN-10: 0-595-80382-2 (ebk)

Printed in the United States of America

Out of Darkness—Light, Volume 2, is dedicated to the men and women who have served with the Canadian Forces Intelligence Branch, past, present and future.

Because what we do makes a difference.

"*Good combat intelligence and its proper use enabled Hannibal to cross the Alps and invade Italy. The lack of combat intelligence helped defeat Napoleon Bonaparte at Waterloo and General Robert E. Lee at Gettysburg. It was through the proper use of intelligence on weather and terrain that General Gerd Von Runstedt succeeded, at first, in the Battle of the Bulge. General Patton's use of counterintelligence enabled him to change the direction of an entire field army and help eliminate the Bulge without disclosing to the Germans the serious weakening of the lines in another area. Proper appreciation of the enemy, weather and terrain enabled the First Canadian Corps to successfully storm Vimy Ridge with all troops fully briefed on details of the enemy and Canadian objectives.*"[1]

*The Canadian Forces and its predecessors have required useful intelligence and battlefield information throughout its history. "Meeting the intelligence needs of the CF of the future will require a wide spectrum of sources ranging from technologically sophisticated aerial sensors to conventional ground reconnaissance formations employing time tested methods. Some new sources and agencies will be prolific in providing and disseminating information and intelligence."*

*"Multiple sources will produce large volumes of information which must be filtered, processed and disseminated to the ultimate user. The speed of the modern battlefield and the vast quantities of information or intelligence available creates a requirement for dedicated intelligence units supported by Automated Data Processing to manage collection, process data and to display and disseminate intelligence. The intelligence system [must] provide a filter to ensure that commanders and staff are not inundated with extraneous and unnecessary information."*

---

1.  FMC 2910-CFP 315 (2), 2 Aug 1988, p. 1-8.

*To be able to move faster, achieve surprise and strike the enemy a decisive blow, commanders will require increasingly accurate and timely information of all activity within a widely expanded area.*[2]

*"Tell me what you know...tell me what you don't know...tell me what you think...always distinguish which is which."*[3]
General Colin Powell

---

2. FMC 2910-CFP 315 (2), 2 Aug 1988, p. 1-12.
3. General Colin Powell, Chairman of the Joint Chiefs of Staff, USA, quoted in JP 2.0, p. IV-7.

# Contents

## Volume 2, 1983-1997

# List of Illustrations

# Foreword

This book is neither amusing nor entertaining; but then it is not intended to be amusing or entertaining. It is intended to be an accurate factual account of the history of Military Intelligence and the people involved in it in Canada for most of the 20th Century. And that is what it is; complete and in detail. It is in fact a work of reference.

Major-General (Retired) Reginald J.G. Weeks
Ottawa, 12 February 2005

# Preface

## *Intelligence Branch History*

The collection of Intelligence Reports, Intelligence Summaries and many other writings on the subject of the Canadian Forces Intelligence Branch found in Out of Darkness—Light, Volume 2, have been derived from a great many sources and agencies. These include *Canadian Intelligence and Security Association* and *Intelligence Branch Newsletters,* which have recorded the developing story of Intelligence in the Canadian Forces. The author can only claim a partial role as writer and editor of this reference work, because of the extensive number of valued contributors to our story.

The various volumes of Out of Darkness—Light! are primarily written for those of us who have been 'in the trade,' so to speak, but they should also open a window for the interested reader on Canada's Military Intelligence history. E Tenebris Lux.

# Acknowledgements

Virtually everyone who has served in Canadian Military Intelligence has an incredible a story to tell, many of which you will find in these and subsequent volumes. The story would be almost impossible to tell by just one person, since there are so many different viewpoints, particularly at decision-making times both in crisis and in peacetime. The author is therefore indebted to his colleagues in the trade, and hopes the details and the contents of this collection of intelligence reports is seen through the collator and analyst's discerning eye in an understanding light.

Much of the information found here has been extracted from various Intelligence Branch Journals, unclassified Intelligence news bulletins, and from people who have forwarded their stories, observations and comments based on their career experiences within the Intelligence Branch. It would be difficult to name all of them, but I would particularly like to thank those who offered valuable advice or shared the specific stories that you find in the pages that follow:

Major-General Reginald J.G. Weeks, Brigadier-General James S. Cox, Brigadier-General Patricia M. Samson, Colonel Victor V. Ashdown, Colonel Gordon S. Graham, Colonel Jeff S. Upton, Colonel Patrick D.R. Crandell, Colonel R. Geoff St John, Colonel C.S. Hamel, Lieutenant-Colonel William "Bill" Tenhaaf, Lieutenant-Colonel David M. Robb, Commander M. Josh Barber, Lieutenant-Colonel Susan F. Beharriell, Lieutenant-Colonel Ray J. Taylor, Lieutenant-Colonel J.R.Y. Mike Foucreault, Lieutenant-Colonel Greg W. Jensen, Lieutenant-Colonel Mike R.J. Ouellette, Lieutenant-Colonel Rhedegydd ap Probert, Lieutenant-Colonel David W. Wiens, Lieutenant-Colonel Robert S. Williams, Major Gerry C. Mayer, Major Rick A. Mader, Major Ivan J. Ciuciura, Major J.A.E. Kent Dowell, Major Stephen P. Desjardins, Major S. Robert Elliot, Major Mark D. Godefroy, Major James

D. Godefroy, Major Gary W. Handson, Major John "Pappy" MacKinnon, Major Alex C. Chambers Major Pericles Metaxas, Major Ron Roach, Major Elaine E. Mellor, Major Colin A.J. Kiley, Captain Alfred G. De Boda, Captain William D. Ellis, Captain Lisa Elliott, Captain Andrew Morrison, Captain Rick G. Stohner, Captain Penelope Whiston (Noble), Lieutenant E. Bruce Worrall, Chief Petty Officer 1 William J. Lindsay, Chief Warrant Officer Collin "Ed" Affleck, Master Warrant Officer John Paul Michael Parsons, Petty Officer 1 J.L. Dennis Goulet, Petty Officer 2 S.A. Irskine, Warrant Officer R. Grant Oliver; Warrant Officer Andrew J. "A.J." Krause, Warrant Officer Chris K. Buczynski, Sergeant Anna Marie Langlois, Master Corporal S.P. Prendergast, Leading Aircraftman Don Detweiler, Marilyn McLellan, Robert Neilson, Dan R. Jenkins, Melissa Parsons, Edmond Cloutier, Doctor Joel J. Sokolsky, Doctor David A. Charters, and Doctor Marc Milner.

# Introduction

*"The role of the G2 is to provide the commander with the intelligence he requires to plan and conduct operations. The G2's primary task is the timely determination of the enemy's location, activities, capabilities and intentions."*[1]

*Out of Darkness—Light, a history of Canadian Military Intelligence, Volume 1*, concluded with the inauguration of the Canadian Forces Intelligence Branch in 1982. This year was also the 40th Anniversary of the Canadian Intelligence Corps. *Out of Darkness—Light, Volume 2*, is a direct continuation of the history, from 1983 to 1997.

Major Harold A. Skaarup
G2
Land Forces Atlantic Headquarters
Halifax, Nova Scotia
01 June 2005

---

1.   FMC 2910-CFP 315 (2), 2 Aug 1988, p. 3A-1.

# Volume 2

# 1983-1997

# 1

## *1983, Intelligence Branch, the First Year*

Int Branch personnel have been involved in the mainstream of many military operations worldwide since the Branch's inauguration in 1982. Intelligence Branch members at that time were employed overseas with the CDLS in London and in Washington; with SHAPE in Belgium, with the CFAs in Beijing, Belgrade, Warsaw, Prague, Moscow and Tel Aviv. There were also many undergoing training at the CF Language School (CFLS) in Ottawa. Int Branch personnel were serving at Canadian Forces bases in Germany with 1 Canadian Air Group at Baden-Söellingen and with 4 Canadian Mechanized Brigade Group in Lahr when they put up their new branch badge on 29 October 1982 along with their Intelligence counterparts in other locations in Europe and Canada.

The years since the formation of the Intelligence Branch have demonstrated that "change" is constant factor in the current events and conflicts that continue to unfold throughout the world. Intelligence reports of concern to all members of the CF continue to be generated and pumped out to commanders at all levels, and virtually every member of the CF Int Community has been affected by the world events that have taken place during the "Cold War" and its aftermath. The chapters that follow tell the story through the end of the Cold War to the beginning of the era of rapid CF expansion in the world of peacekeeping.

## 1983, CISA Member News

The CISA Academic Award program is open to dependent children of either members of the Association, MPs, Int Ops, Security or Intelligence Officers. The award is normally to one candidate for $600, but last year was divided between two equally qualified candidates, Ms Elaine Marion of Ottawa and Ms Vivianne Vella of Montreal.

CISA Regional Representatives for 1983 are: Ottawa, Regular Force, LCol Victor V. Ashdown; Ottawa, Retired and Militia, Maj Howard Mansfield; Ontario, Maj Fred E.G. Jones, Oshawa; Maritimes, Regular Force, Capt Carl R. Delaney, B Secur O, CFB Shearwater; Maritimes, Retired and Militia, Maj Sherman R. Veinotte, Halifax; Quebec, LCol Al R. Wells, FMC HQ, St Hubert; Prairies, Maj Al A. Bell-Chambers, Winnipeg; BC, Capt R.H. Yeomans, East Surrey; Overseas, Capt Harold A. Skaarup, HQ CFE G2 Ops.

A full-page review of Scarlet to Green appeared in the Nov 82 issue of the Army Association of the USA publication "Army." The review by MGen Edward B. Atkeson was entitled "Monumental Account, a Model for Americans; and "Good Plots for Spy Thrillers." The book was summed up as follows:

"Scarlet to Green will find a respected place in many military libraries around the world, particularly those serving Intelligence agencies. It is a monumental accounting of the birth, life and disappearance of scores of Canadian Intelligence Units, together with an exhaustive listing of the men who staffed them. It remains now for an American to step forward with a comparable chronicle of US Army Intelligence."

Capt W. Doug Whitley reported that he is the chairman of an Intelligence Branch Historical Committee that has been established to promote any activity designed to enhance understanding of the Canadian Military Intelligence history. Maj Sherman R. Veinotte is CISA's historical collator and coordinator. Reports from all areas indicate that the re-badging ceremonies on 29 Oct 1982 went very well. Capt Yvon Cousineau, a very popular Regular Force Intelligence officer, passed away in the fall of 1982.[1]

---

1.   CISA Newsletter, Vol. 14, No. 1, January 1983, pp. 1-2.

# 1983, Canadian Forces Europe Intelligence Community

Maj Gordon S. Graham, SO2 Int HQ CFE, successfully gained additional Int personnel by transferring positions from 1 CAG in Baden to Lahr. In Feb 1983, the HQ CFE Int Section included Capt Harold A. Skaarup, Sgt Mike E. Higgins and Sgt W. Ken Spike. This is to change with the loss of one Sgt and the gain of 4 MCpls in the summer rotation. Capt John "Jack" W. Nixon will turn over his position as SO3 Int for the 4 CMBG Fd Security Section to Capt George Johnstone. Maj K.A.W. Peter Mackenzie from NDHQ will replace Maj John W. Sullivan who works in HQ AFCENT in Brunsuum, Holland.[2]

Capt Skaarup reports Prime Minister P.E. Trudeau and one of his son's visited Lahr for the 11 Nov 1982 Remembrance Day ceremonies (16-jet fly-past and full parade with 4 CMBG), along with our DG Int, RAdm Rodoca-nachi and Ambassador Goldshaub.

From 18 to 19 May 1983 Major Gordon S. Graham and Capt Skaarup visited the British Joint HQ at Rheindahlen by Monchengladbach. Over the next two days both officers were made welcome and visited the both the Army and RAF Int Sections, where they were shown British examples of "real-world real-time Int."

# 1983, Intelligence Branch Advisor Update

Int Branch Advisor *LCol Victor V. Ashdown* provided an update on items of interest to members of the Branch in the 1st edition of Scarlet and Green as follows:

*Classification/Trade Specifications.* Branch Boards wrote mobilization Speci-fications for MOC 82 and Int Op 111 in Jan 1983. They were subsequently used as a basis for new Reserve Specifications, which were prepared by FMC HQ in Feb 83. Eventually, the Int Branch Mobilization Specs and Regular Force Specs will become one and the same. A Branch Board sat in Trenton 14-18 Mar to sort out all the Imagery Specs and CTSs. The only fuzzy area is CI.

*CI Study.* A revised draft of this major study is now complete and should be out for review and comment about mid-Apr. Basically, Int retains the overall Intelligence function while Secur conducts counter-HUMINT operations.

---

2.  Author's letter to CISA, 21 Feb 1983.

We will need an officer CSQ (HIS Analyst) and probably a TSQ as well to cover collation and analysis of "security" Intelligence. Operations Security (OPSEC) is a closely related program.

*Combat Intelligence 1985-95.* This is a somewhat futuristic study, which we have been working on for two years in support of the Army Combat Development (CD) process. The CD process is quite complex and extensive. Suffice it to say that our study, which hopefully will be approved in Apr, will give us a good idea of the Intelligence organization needed if we for a division or even a corps. It will be a big help in our mobilization planning and, more important, will allow us to organize, train and employ the Militia in direct support of the mobilization plans.

*Organizational Changes CIS OP&T.* With an OSMER now going on in CIS, there have been many rumours concerning the future of OP&T. Few would disagree that the Int and Secur Branch Advisors should be responsible for "Branch" matters and have small staffs to assist them; even the OSMER agrees! Beyond that, however, there is a requirement for a CIS "Plans and Requirements" organization manned by both Int and Secur personnel. OSMET options show this organization ranging in size from sub-section to directorate. The OSMER will be completed in early Jun and then CIS has to decide.

*FMC HQ I&S Section.* Long-time plans have finally come to fruition and this Section has now been split into separate Intelligence and Security Sections. The Int Section remains under COS Ops and the Secur Section goes to COS Adm. Three TFHQ Int Op positions have been recalled from the Brigades to augment the new Int Section and an Int Capt position has been added. The shared LCol SSO I&S position becomes SSO Secur so the SSO Int will be a Major.

*HQ CFE Int Section.* Raising CFE to Command status has placed an extraordinary workload on this Section. Three Int Op positions from 1 CAG (one from each squadron) have been transferred to HQ CFE. Another Int officer (Capt) is essential and efforts are being made to find an officer.

*Hat Badges.* Approval has been granted for the loom-embroidered badge (for wear on the beret) in Jan. A Supply issue of this badge and the metal badge should be available in May. The prototypes of the Officer/CWO metal-embroidered badge have not yet been received.

*Belt Buckles.* A request is in the mill to the Director Ceremonial (DC) for authorization to wear the Branch brass buckle with star.

*Award to Colonel Commandant.* Later this year, Sir William S. Stephenson will receive the Donovan Award by direction of US President Ronald Reagan. This Award is named for General "Wild Bill" Donovan, head of the wartime OSS (forerunner of the CIA) and is given to OSS veterans. The only non-US citizens to have received it are Lord Louis Mountbatten and Margaret Thatcher (UK PM). It is a singular honour and most appropriate since Sir William, as head of BSC during WWII, provided valuable assistance to General W.J. Donovan during the formation of the OSS. The USN is pulling out all the stops for the occasion and is making the USS Intrepid available for the presentation. Sir William is understandably thrilled by this honour, and [LCol Victor V. Ashdown] has sent him congratulations on behalf of the Branch. He remains in good health and keenly interested in all aspects of the Branch.

*Alliance—UK Intelligence Corps.* The paperwork on the Alliance is progressing on schedule. Both governments have agreed, we now await approval by our Governor-General and, finally, Her majesty. The Intelligence Corps is planning to host suitable ceremonies at Ashford on 28-29 Oct 83 to mark the Alliance.

*Branch Advisory Council.* The Terms of Reference of the Council have been drafted, and will be released when finalized shortly.

*Branch Numbers.* CWO Fred L. Juett provided the "joining dates" for all Regular Force Int Ops. The joining dates for officers are more difficult to determine because of the various policy changes over the last 15 years, and this problem is causing a delay. Each case will have to be determined after consultation between the Int Branch Advisor and the Career managers, and a master list will be prepared. A Militia list will also be drafted (volunteers to assist were requested). Int Branch scrolls and retirement plaques are also being prepared.

*Branch Historical Committee.* Capt W. Doug Whitley has formed a small Historical Committee to oversee the location, cataloguing and preservation of Branch memorabilia. A historical column will also be a regular feature of Scarlet and Green.

*Canadian Intelligence and Security Association (CISA).* All officers are urged to consider joining the CISA. It is the only way that the Int Branch can provide a balanced input to CDA on defence matters related to Intelligence.

*Branch Day—Ottawa.* The third Friday of each month is "Intelligence Day" at the Army Officer's Mess, Somerset Street, Ottawa.

*Retirements.* LCol John O. Dendy, Maj G.G. Rowlandson and WO D.E. Richardson have retired since the Branch was formed in Oct 82.

*Female Int Ops.* Up to 13% of the trade PML could be women (at the MCpl rank), although the authorization to remuster women into the trade has not yet been received because we are at PML. Women will be remustered into the trade as Int Ops, but when and how many will depend on the vacancies available and the qualifications of the candidates relative to all the remuster applications received.

*New Positions.* The Int Op Career Manager position is an MWO. One additional Capt will be at FMC HQ, an IO is being added at CFB Shearwater and another of the DIAC Int Capt positions at CFB Greenwood are being converted to hard Int; a Capt slot in CFTS HQ is now changed to hard Int; the Maj (any) exchange position at DIA is annotated as hard Int, and the Branch is looking at other exchange positions; there are several areas where the Branch has been asked to consider either an Int LCol or Maj. Air Command is expanding its requirements for Branch personnel quite rapidly and will ask for up to five Int Capts for the new CF-18 squadrons, one Int Op in each tactical helicopter squadron and probably an officer and an NCO at ATG HQ, plus others. More exchange positions, particularly at the Senior NCO level, are receiving very positive attention. Commanders and senior operations staffs, not the Branch, have initiated most of the requests. This bodes well for the future effectiveness of the Intelligence function in the CF, and of course, for the Branch itself.

## CDS Commendation

Lt (N) W. Burns MacDonald has been awarded the CDS Commendation for his excellent effort prior to and during the 1982 Falklands crisis. He was serving in the NDIC at the time.[3]

## Historical Committee

Capt W. Doug Whitley is the Chairman of the Int Branch Historical Committee. The purpose of the committee is to promote any activity designed to enhance understanding of Canadian Military Intelligence History, to include: the collection, cataloguing, preserving and displaying of any and all items of historical Intelligence interest; the promotion of significant dates in Canadian

---

3.   Extracts from *Scarlet to Green*, Apr 1983, LCol Vic Ashdown, Editor, pp. 2-8.

Intelligence history (i.e. Corps of Guides, C Int C etc.); and, the sponsorship of activities designed to encourage research into Canadian Military Intelligence history (i.e., essay competitions, etc).

## *Acorn's Corner*[4]

Col Felix H. Walter, Deputy Director Military Intelligence Overseas authored a document entitled the After Action Intelligence Report of the Canadian Military Headquarters (CMHQ) London, produced 27 December 1945. This document reviewed the organizational, operational and training responsibilities of the Military Intelligence Section CMHQ. While CMHQ, and in particular, the DDMI, was subordinate to DMI in Ottawa, it was found that the latter was too far away from the European theatre to effectively supervise the Intelligence function in detail. DDMI, therefore, was for all intents and purposes the focal point for all technical and operational matters relating to Intelligence in the Canadian Army Overseas. As such, much fell upon the shoulders of Col F.H. Walter, his small staff and the Intelligence Company Number 1 Canadian General Reinforcement Unit (CGRU).

Prior to the winter of 1942-43, the operations staffs largely handled Intelligence matters as an afterthought. Many Intelligence duties were performed by British officers on behalf of or on loan to the Canadian Army. That winter, however, several things happened which propelled the establishment of a functioning Intelligence effort in the Army.

The first development was the establishment of Headquarters First Canadian Army. This boosted the requirement for various types of Intelligence personnel to a new degree. Not only did the requirement to train Combat Intelligence and Counter Intelligence (Field Security personnel remain, but specially qualified personnel were then needed such as interrogators, order of battle specialists, captured document analysts, radio intercept analysts, and Photo Interpreters.

The second event, which was largely prompted by the first, was the formation of the Canadian Intelligence Corps as a vehicle to standardize and consolidate Intelligence organization and training.

---

4.   The term Acorn is used as the radio appointment title of the Intelligence representative in any Army field Unit or organization.

The third event was the assumption by the Intelligence staffs of Intelligence training from the operations (G) staff, which occurred concurrently with the initiation of Intelligence Corps personnel into actual operations.

Last, but not least, the Intelligence staff at CMHQ and elsewhere finally rid itself of many functions, which had nothing to do with Intelligence (such as public relations). It is probably notable that the winter of 1982-83, forty years after the winter of 1942-43, heralds the rededication of Intelligence in the Canadian military.[5]

## 1983, Intelligence Personnel News

Maj Tom F. Davie promoted to LCol, 18 Mar 83; Maj K.J. Radley promoted to LCol, 30 June 83; MWO William "Bill" L. Dickson promoted to Capt, 1 Feb 83.

WO J.P.A. Norm Lefebvre promoted to MWO, 1 Feb 83, Sgt P.R. Berikoff and Sgt Jim R. Fysh promoted to WO, 2 Jan 83, Sgt J.C. Cotton promoted to Sgt, 1 Feb 83.

The following are promoted to Sgt: MCpl Collin "Ed" Affleck, 2 Jan 83; MCpl Barry E. Beldam, 2 Jan 83; MCpl J.J. Dionne, 2 Jan 83; MCpl J.F. Gauthier, 2 Jan 83; MCpl Dan J. Haslip, 2 Jan 83; MCpl Mike E. Higgins, 2 Jan 83; MCpl M.E. Malcolm, 2 Jan 83; MCpl J. Ron Martineau, 2 Jan 83; MCpl Pierre Michaud, 9 Mar 83; MCpl J.A. Réjean Montmarquet, 2 Jan 83; MCpl Robert W. Moug, 2 Jan 83; MCpl Tom W. Pieroway, 2 Jan 83; and MCpl Armado Santos, 2 Jan 83.

The following are promoted to MCpl: Cpl Jeff A. Collings, 2 Jan 83; Cpl R.N. Cooper, 3 Feb 83; Cpl R.G.G. Fournier, 2 Jan 83; Cpl J. Pierre Murret-Labarthe, 2 Jan 83; Cpl Tom C. O'Brien, 2 Jan 83; Cpl Bruce E. Smith, 2 Jan 83; and, Cpl D.B. Smith, 2 Jan 83.[6]

## 1983, Canadian Land Forces Command and Staff College Course

Capt Robert M. Parsons completed completed the CLFCSC course in December 1983.

---

5.    Scarlet to Green, Apr 1983, Capt W. Doug Whitley, pp. 14-15.
6.    Scarlet to Green, Apr 1983, pp. 32-33.

## Intelligence Branch Inauguration Ceremony and Rededication Ceremony for Security Branch

The inauguration ceremonies for the new Intelligence Branch and the rededication of the Security Branch took place at CFB Borden on 29 Oct 1982 in the presence of a large number of present and former Intelligence and security personnel. The Chief of Defence Staff, General Ramsay Withers, took the salute, gave a brief address, and performed the re-badging ceremony for the Intelligence personnel on parade. Capt Margaret R. Prentis, immediate past President, attended the ceremony on behalf of CISA. She commented, "The pervading atmosphere throughout the entire two days was one of happiness. Both Intelligence and Security people seemed to be pleased by the formation of the new Branch, while at the same time emphasizing that the close working relationships of past years would continue unchanged." (Capt Margaret R. Prentis served with the British Army from 1941 to 1946, No. 2 Int Trg Coy, Toronto from 1956 to 1965 and qualified Major and LCol).

## 1983, CISA AGM

The CISA AGM was held at CFB Montreal, Longue Pointe Garrison, 15-16 Sep 1983. Present were: Maj H.F. Andrew, Maj Al A. Bell-Chambers, LCol Emile Berger, Maj A.G. Cameron (Treasurer), LCol Pierre J.F. Couture, Maj Patrick D.R. Crandell, Maj G. Robert Corbeil, Maj Robert C. Dale, LCol G. Wally Field, Col Robert T. Grogan, Maj D.E. Guyatt, Col Robert W. Irvine, Maj Jan A. Jezewski, Capt J. Keeler, Maj Fred E.G. Jones, Maj Terry B. Kelly, LCol Alf J. Laidler (Director), Maj Franz F. Laizner (Director), Capt Nils E. Lindberg, Maj John "Pappy" MacKinnon (Secretary), Maj J.H. Mansfield (2nd VP), Maj Elaine E. Mellor, Capt Stephen D. Moody, Maj Ian A. Nicol (Director), Maj P. Denis Pelletier, 2Lt Paul R. Perchaluk, Maj Wilf S. Puffer, Capt Peter T. Patton, Lt T.J. Reilly, LCdr Sherry J.Y. Richardson, Lt Kostas P. Rimsa, Col Andrew F. Ritchie (Director), Capt David A. Rubin (Director), LCol Ed D. Sanford, Maj Bruce K. Smith, Capt Harold F. Smith, Capt Kelly E.M. Stone, Maj Merrick K. Szulc, LCol William "Bill" Tenhaaf (Director), Capt D.H. Neil Thompson, Capt James "Jim" P.K. Van Wynen, Maj Sherman R. Veinotte (Director), Maj Richard J. Vella, Maj William "Bill" L. Watt (Director), Maj Dale M. Watts (Director), and LCol Al R. Wells. Present as an observer was BGen J.R. Genin, Vice-Chairman (Québec) of the Conference of Defence Associations (CDA).[7]

## 1983, CISA Member News

LCol Victor V. Ashdown is posted to Washington in August 1983 as the A/ CFDA (CFILO), replacing LCol Bill Vallevand who is leaving the service to accept a civilian job offer "he couldn't refuse." Col Robert W. Irvine replaces Vic as Int Branch Advisor. LCol Ed D. Sanford is posted to FMC as SSO Security, and LCol George L.R. Bruce is posted to London as the CFILO. Sgt Tom Maddox received the Order of Military Merit (OMM) for his work as a Collator. CISA member Capt A.E. "Bert" Altherr and Maj Ernie Ofenheim, former OC of 2 Int Trg Coy in Toronto, passed away a few months past.[8]

## 1983, CFSIS

The first Basic Intelligence Officer's Course (BIOC 8301) to be run at CFSIS following the inauguration of the Int Branch began on 9 Aug 1983 and was completed on 23 Nov 1983. The newly qualified officers and members of the Int Branch included: Capt William "Bill" L. Dickson, Capt Gordon R. Teale, Lt G. Allan Grant, Lt J. Kent Peebles, Capt Lloyd W. Hackel, Capt J.G.A.J. Christian Rousseau, Capt Clark J. Beamish, Capt Tim A. Larson, Lt Jay G. Mercer, Lt Larry T. Grandmaison, Lt Brian E. Hamilton, Lt Mike R.J. Ouellette, and Lt Harold A. Skaarup.

7.   CISA Newsletter, Vol. 14, No. 4, December 1983, p. 1.
8.   CISA Newsletter, Vol. 14, No. 2, June 1983, pp. 3-4.

BIOC 8301, CFSIS, 23 Nov 1983.
Rear Row: 2Lt B.E. Hamilton, 2Lt J.G. Mercer, 2Lt H.A. Skaarup,[9] Capt
L.W. Hackel, Lt M.R.J. Ouellette.
Centre Row: Lt J.P.A. Tremblay, Capt G.R. Teale, Capt W.L. Dickson,
Lt G.A. Grant, Capt C.J. Beamish, Lt L.T. Grandmaison, Lt J.K. Pee-
bles, Lt T.A. Larson, Capt J.G.A.J.C. Rousseau.

9.  The author was sworn into the Regular Force as a Direct Entry Officer
(DEO) on 19 Jul 1983. He took down his Militia Captain's rank and
put up 2Lt slip-ons again, only this time as a Regular Force officer,
while serving as the SO3 Int, HQ CFE Ops, Lahr, Germany. Shortly
afterwards, he was posted to CFSIS to attend BIOC 8301, which ran
from 9 Aug to 23 Nov 1983. From graduation until 07 Mar 84, the
author served as CFSIS Staff Projects Officer, and instructed on Combat Int Course 8401. Shortly into the New Year, he was promoted to
Lt, backdated to 21 Jul 1983, plus two year's seniority. On 8 Mar 1984
he was posted to Ottawa as the Attaché Training and Coord Officer,
NDHQ/CIS/DDI-6, Tunney's Pasture.

Front Row: WO R.K. Bushe, Capt J.E.H.B. Lemieux, Capt G.C. Mayer, LCdr C.S. Hordal, Capt J.H. Newman, Sgt G.T. Izzard.

1983 Intelligence Operator 6A Course 8301
Rear Row: MCpl J.O. "Rick" Limoges, MCpl Ray O. Toovey, MCpl R.G.G. Fournier, MCpl Rolf F. Overhoff, Sgt Jean Guy H.E. Martineau, MCpl William A. Mitchell, Sgt J.J. Dionne, MCpl Lynn J. Brooks, Sgt Ed A. Knobelsdorf, MCpl M.P. Paquin, MCpl M.B. Mahoney, MCpl Robert W. Moug, MCpl Rick L. Gill, MCpl Peter A. Maillet, MCpl Gordon P. Ohlke, MCpl Sgt Richard E. "Dick" Hurst.
Front Row: Sgt Terry W. Fader, WO John E. Cranston, Maj Christopher S. Hordal, Capt William "Bill" L. Dickson, WO Brian M. Noble.

1983, Militia TQ 4 Course 8301
Back Row: Sgt Phillip A. Dawes, Sgt Maj Barry A. MacDonald, Lt Kostas
P. Rimsa, Sgt J.M. Lauzière.
Front Row: Sgt Wes von Papineau, Maj Christopher S. Hordal, MCpl
J.L. Dawes.

## *1983, CISA Member News*

VAdm James Andrew Fulton, CMM, CD, former Commander MARCOM
was appointed Colonel Commandant of the Security Branch. His opposite
number in the Intelligence Branch, Sir William S. Stephenson, received the
Donovan Award for his contribution to the defence of freedom in New York
on 23 Sep 1983. The presentation took place onboard the USS Intrepid. Previous recipients of the award include British Prime Minister Margaret
Thatcher and Lord Louis Mountbatten. Sir William is the only Canadian to
receive it.

Several CISA members were in the Int Branch contingent that took part in
a visit to Ashford, England on 29 Oct 83 for a ceremony to mark the alliance

between the CF Int Branch and the British Int Corps. MGen Al Pickering, Col Robert W. Irvine and Maj Sherman R. Veinotte took part in the ceremony marking the establishment of an alliance similar to one established in 1982 between the CF Security Branch and the British Military Police.

It was noted that Bill C-157, which was to set up a civilian "Canadian Security and Intelligence Service"(CSIS) died on the House of Commons order paper on the dissolution of Parliament in 1983. It was anticipated that a similar bill, with amendments, would appear during the next session of Parliament. (CISA took no stand, publicly or privately, on the creation of a CSIS).

Col Craig B. MacFarlane was made an Honorary Life Member of CISA. Honorary Life Member Col Len H. Nicholson, Maj F. Burrard-Creasy and Capt J.A. Yvon Cousineau passed away in the past year.

Maj William "Bill" L. Watt stated that some improvements had been made in the Int sections, but problems continued to exist concerning command and control, equipment deficiencies (particularly vehicles), unrealistic training, career development, and mis-employment of RSS. He suggested Branch Study and action could solve many of the problems. Competitions and concentrations are needed. A proposal was put forward to reinstate Int Militia competitions; to ascertain annually the most efficient Unit; and to acquire an appropriate trophy to reward that Unit. A proposal was also put forward to have annual national Intelligence concentrations. Both proposals were accepted.

The following resolution was proposed for presentation to the CDA Jan 1984 AGM: "Whereas Int specialists will be required to meet forecast War Establishment (WE) Int Specialist requirements, therefore be it resolved that specialist Int training be made part of the Militia Int training program, with sufficient priority and support to meet requirements. The resolution was carried.[10]

## WO R. Grant Oliver—Combat Intelligence Report

WO R.G. Oliver responded to the author's request for personal observations of his service in the C Int C and Int Branch with the following report:

"I would like to offer my views from the ranks. In 1961 I remustered from 2 RCR into the C Int C. Prior to this remuster, I had attended a Combat Int/ Photo Reader course at CSMI. This was the genesis of my conversion. Capt

---

10.   CISA Newsletter, Vol. 14, No. 4, December 1983, pp. 1-4.

Jeff S. Upton taught the air photo and SSgt Jerry Martyn handled the Combat Int. This experience was a far cry from the repetitious training common to an infantryman. All ranks including students took coffee in the library, and heavens, we could wear low shoes instead of boots and puttees. The staff certainly looked us over and we were more than a little curious. The atmosphere plus the subject matter sealed my fate. At this juncture, I was a Battalion Int Sgt with no aspirations to be a drill stick. I requested a remuster to C Int C and upon acceptance I had to revert to the rank of Cpl.

Within days I was posted to Target Area HQ London and worked with my former Bn Int Sgt, John H. Newman. The primary focus of this job was to collect data for disaster planning. The possibility of a nuclear exchange was taken seriously. Our morning ritual was to do a fallout prediction from a 20 KT [nuclear weapon] using current weather conditions. For the most part, this was not an exciting pastime but collection/collation skills were put to work. Some months after remuster, I was promoted back to Sgt as the Corps was expanding with this new responsibility. Life seemed to involve an endless stream of courses. Every other rank (OR) had to qualify Gp 1 collator, assistant photo interpreter and CI investigator before specializing. All were given a modern language aptitude test to ferret out Sig Int candidates. Specialization was supposed to be by aptitude, but in practice was influenced by vacancies. A special National Survival Int course was part of the menu at this time. The Corps held a major influence over who was accepted and by and large they came from the Combat Arms. A few who had failed Officer Candidate School also joined us. For me, it was easy to transfer my loyalty from the Regiment to my Corps. I was pleased if not a little proud to be C Int C. Although there was the odd strange case wearing silver and green, I was pleased with my new associates.

In 1964 I was posted to DG Int/CFHQ. This was expensive territory on a Sgt's pay. I was given the task of collating data on Indonesia and Malaysia as a territorial conflict became low intensity warfare. I was pleased to have John H. Newman beside me on the China desk. To cover Asia and Latin America, we had a Maj, Capt, SSgt and three Sgts. Only the Ors were Int. There was no in-house training, little direction and a daily influx of material that would choke a horse. We had some contact with Air Force Int in Beaver Barracks, but never saw a sailor. Their focus was elsewhere. Regardless, I enjoyed my job, quickly learning streamlined collation skills and selective reading habits. It was frustrating not being able to answer problems that confronted me. As a small example; troop strength in this confrontation was problem, e.g.: during the rainy season a delivery of 500kg of rice was to be delivered upstream to [a site] on the border area. When was the last shipment? How many workers would it feed? Was some given to local tribesmen? Have a small staff with a million questions will always be our lot.

If life was busy, it became chaotic in 1964 when the three service directors physically integrated. To my knowledge, the people at my level cooperated well. In a matter of a week, we were up and running in our old digs in A Bldg. As expected, there was the odd friction over areas of responsibility. We now saw RCAF Clerk Intel and RCN RS (Radio Specialty) [operators], but little changed concerning the job at hand. At this time a staff study was circulated suggesting the amalgamation of Int and MP into one branch. As it made no sense trade-wise, little attention was paid. Oh how the thin air of DG Int dulls one.

Shortly after integration, I was made a watchkeeper in the indications centre (Current Indications/Int Briefings). Shift work stunk, but handling incoming traffic was interesting. At times I felt out of my depth. Our staff consisted of a SLdr and Lt (N) for briefing and four Sgt/SSgts as watch-keepers. We spent the evening hours reading incoming messages and if needed could call the duty officer at home. Periodically we had the thrill of sending a test FLASH message to Washington and London on the signature of a Sgt C Int C. On day shifts I was given a close look at the Defence Council for morning prayers. Not much concern was expressed over Paul T. Hellyer's plans and in my small circle morale seemed to be fine.

The JIC met weekly in an adjoining room and we would table the UK product for them to digest before preparing ours. XA (DL2) chaired the meeting and often called in desk officers to clarify submissions. You are no doubt aware of our primary focus. I thought our weekly was reasonable. Did it serve decision-makers? Was everyone happy with Int early warning/troubling indications resting with a C Int C Senior NCO? Our indications list was periodically updated. At times we were asked to look for specific information in trouble spots.

In 1966 I was offered a plum and found myself posted to CFILO (L). For the first time in my service life I wore civilian clothes and was more than pleased with my generous allowances. The staff consisted of LCol Jeff Williams (PPCLI), SLdr Bill McNair and LCdr Blackburn. To assist, we had a Sgt Clerk Admin and a female secretary. We had a good office in the main building between DIA (L) and CIA (L). In addition, we had a LCdr exchange officer in the Navy Shop. I was the only Int body. Each morning required a trip to Canada House to pick up traffic and ask our JICLO for release of any XA traffic. I was tasked with the job of searching out items of interest in the XA traffic as the officers were quite busy. I was only involved in minor liaison tasks and releasing the odd message. If anything, I was impressed by the experience of British desk officers. A good number were retired and had intimate knowledge of their area of interest. Their product contrasted greatly in style and poignancy when compared to other neighbour. The 1967 Arab/Israeli conflict was high drama. There was much to learn by being silent.

In 1969 I was posted to the Canadian Airborne Regiment in Edmonton. As I was already qualified Advanced Para (Jump Master) this should not have been a shock. It was, trade-wise, two wasted years. We collated airfield data in the north as our primary role was defence of Canada.

In 1971 I was posted to CFSIS, Borden and happy to be near family. This was my first encounter with the Security Branch. I was still in C Int C uniform. The Int NCOs in those early days operated like a cell in a foreign land. Hence, Silver and Green Productions was created and little acorns appeared in all our products. It proved to be an aid to sanity. At this time we were an Int Platoon in the Advanced Training Company and commanded by MPs. The whole school was dominated by MPs. The officers had the unholy task of making this work. As we shared the same facilities and resources, it says much that there was no open warfare. Rumours were rife with branch politics, which detracted from the job at hand. Trade specifications were in turmoil and much of course content was flavoured by the experience of the four WOs in staff.

Frustration was largely directed at limited resources, poor specifications and limited time to prepare the complex exercises that would truly test an Int Op. I was happy with most courses but was puzzled by some of the [unsuitable candidates] the Personnel Selection Officers (PSOs) sent for remuster.

In 1975 I was posted to 4 CMBG and found the varied operational procedures in use within CENTAG very interesting. Interoperability was much in vogue. The job held no great Int challenge as we were low in the feeding chain. It was difficult to acquire the information that I thought necessary for a tactical formation. Our own sources were useless. Some help was forthcoming from a friend in the UK. Seems we operated on the old boy network quite often. Maybe we still do?

In 1977 I requested my release to pursue a new adventure. After three years of letting my hair grow long, I was offered a Class C Callout at CFSIS. They specifically needed me to run an interrogator's course and I was the only warm body within reach. I remained instructing and with standards until 1983. During these three years, two highlights stand out. First, I was to see my son remuster to Int and this was followed by the rebadging of the Int Branch. What a good ending to 28 years of service.

Although I have offered few specifics, I will gladly attempt to answer any of your questions. I would suspect that you have collected much and all I offer is a personal note. Good soldiering in Kabul and environs." Aye ready aye, Grant Oliver.[11]

## 1983-2004, LCol Mike Ouellette Observations on Service in the Intelligence Branch

LCol Mike R.J. Ouellette had some interesting observations on this period in our Int Branch History. "Since joining the Branch in 1983 as a new Direct Entry Officer (DEO), my service in the CF has been characterized as a continuous adventure. Service as an Int officer since the early 80s has meant that I have participated in a great deal of international missions. Specifically, Intelligence officers, myself included, have been involved in operationally focused Intelligence, including war and peace support operations for the past 20 years. In my case, one year after I became a commissioned officer I was posted to 5e GBMC and began Intelligence planning for the defence of Northern Norway in case of a "Soviet" attack against NATO. During my four years at "5e Bde" from 1984 to 1988, I made six trips to northern Norway, including many a long reconnaissance by foot along valleys and fjords, estimating potential Soviet avenues of approach.

From 1988 to 1990, I was posted to Cyprus as the UNFICYP "Ops-Info" officer, where I was able to hone my skills collecting, analyzing and disseminating Intelligence on the Greek and Turkish sides of the island. From 1990 to 1994, I was a strategic analyst in DG Int where my task was to analyze the

---

11. Letter from Grant Oliver, 18 June 2004, and Telecon, 12 July 2004. In December, Grant's son MWO Rick Oliver was medically evacuated from Kabul with an illness likely brought on by the dust and foul air conditions in Afghanistan. Six months later he was operated on and is doing well. Those of us still in Kabul at the time of writing are following his treatment and recovery with serious interest. The author had the privilege of serving with Grant at CFSIS, and with Rick in the Canadian Airborne Regiment in Cyprus and again with 4 CMBG in Germany.

changes in the Soviet Armed Forces as it transitioned from a Soviet to a Russian force. This also included six trips to Russia, this time as an Arms Control Verification inspector, where teams of inspectors from NATO countries would arrive in the former Soviet Union (FSU), with very little notice and request to be taken to an Army Garrison somewhere in the FSU. This allowed us to not only count and inspect Russian military equipment, it also allowed to us to compare previous military assessments with reality. These trips were truly fascinating, as we were, for the first time, able to discuss issues with our former "enemies." Past differences completely forgotten, much camaraderie and many friendships were made during these visits."[12]

## CFILO London

Major Alex C. Chambers was the D/CFILO London, UK, serving under LCol Darcy J. Beatty and LCol David M. Robb. He reported, "My office windows were blown out by an IRA car bomb, my regular train from Harrow-on-the-Hill was firebombed, & getting to work was sometimes an adventure when bomb threats were called into several train/tube stations at once."[13]

---

12. LCol Michael Ouellette, E-mail 29 September 2003.
13. Maj Alex Chambers E-mail 5 Sep 2003.

# 2

## 1984, Intelligence Branch

### 1984, CISA Member News

Honorary Life Member Capt Thorolf Desmond Ingall (Tom to many of his friends, Dinty to his many other friends) passed away on 2 June 1984. Tom was a past President of CMIA, served for a long time with the Bank of Montreal and its Caribbean subsidiary, his fine WWII service in the United States as part of Sir William S. Stephenson's team and among many other notable achievements, for his service with No.1 Int Trg Coy in Montreal. Intelligence Branch Advisor Col Robert W. Irvine was reported to be retiring in the summer of 84.[1]

### 1984, Ex Coelis, Airborne Jump Bivouac

Whiles posted to DDI-6, the author had the opportunity to participate in Ex Coelis, the annual Airborne Jump Bivouac held at CFB Petawawa (160 km North of Ottawa) on 8 Aug 1984, making six static-line jumps with other like-minded soldiers using C-130 Hercules transports and a CH-147 Chinook helicopter. During the bivouac, the author ran into Major Kent White, who had assisted him in getting a shot at competing for a position on the Army Parachute Team when he was still in the Militia in Halifax. He also

---

1. CISA Newsletter, Vol. 15, No. 1, June 1984, p. 2.

jumped with Capt Roy Thomas who served with him in Lahr; Capt Sandy Robertson, who was also on the Parachute Team for a period; Capt Collin Mombourquette, who had also taken Phase I ROUTP; and Maj John Hasek, who also served on the Para Team, and many others. Good adventure training and all were in very high spirits.

## 1984, CISA Member News

Maj Patrick D.R. Crandell reported that another officer position had been added to the SSO Int & Secur Staff at Mobile Command in St Hubert. He will work exclusively on Militia Int matters. Maj Crandell is posted to Toronto.[2]

## 1984, Canadian Land Forces Command and Staff College Course

Capt Clark J. Beamish and Capt D.H. Neil Thompson completed completed the CLFCSC course in December 1984.

---

2.   CISA Newsletter, Vol. 15, No. 2, August 1984, p.2.

# 1984, CFSIS

CFSIS Staff, December 1984.
Front Row: WO J.R. Fysh, Mrs Marilyn McLellan, Capt R.C. Arm-
strong, Capt G.C. Mayer, LCdr C.S. Hordal, Capt J.H. Newman, Capt
J.E.H.B. Lemieux, WO R.K. Bushe.
Centre Row: Sgt, Sgt J.V.W. Leclair, Sgt A.C. Lawrence, Sgt M.B.
Mahoney, Sgt A.E. Sibley, Sgt R.L. Gill.
Rear Row: Sgt G.T. Izzard, Sgt C. Aucoin, Sgt J.R. Shaver, Sgt T.H.
Maddox.

# 1984, FMC

The 1984 FMC Intelligence Section included WO J.G. Nadeau, Mme
Cerutti, Cpl J.RP. Turcotte, Sgt J.P. Bissonette, MCpl Ron K. Townsend,
Capt D.H. Neil Thompson, Maj Patrick D.R. Crandell, WO J. Ron Martin,
and WO Mike V. Marsh.

# 1984, CISA AGM

The CISA AGM was held at Longue Pointe 20-22 Sep 1984, with Col Robert T. Grogan presiding over the meeting with the following members in
attendance: LCol William "Bill" Tenhaaf, Maj. A.G. Cameron, Maj Terry B.
Kelly, LCol Alf J. Laidler, Maj William "Bill" L. Watt, Maj Sherman R.

Veinotte, Maj Merrick K. Szulc, Capt Doug R. Bennett, Maj Franz F. Laizner, Lt D. Egglefield, Lt E. Bruce Holmes, Capt Peter T. Patton, Maj Al A. Bell-Chambers, Maj Dale M. Watts, Capt W. Doug Whitley, LCdr Sherry J.Y. Richardson, Maj J.H. Mansfield, Maj Jan A. Jezewski, Maj Christopher S. Hordal, Capt James "Jim" P.K. Van Wynen, Capt Gordon R.B. Panchuk, Capt M.A. Kulba, Maj Wilf S. Puffer, 2Lt Paul R. Perchaluk, LCol Emile Berger, Maj Elaine E. Mellor, Maj Nils E. Lindberg, Capt James L. Downey, Lt Wes B. von Papineau, LCol Al R. Wells, LCol Ed D. Sanford, LCol Darcy J. Beatty, Capt Margaret R. Prentis, Maj Bruce K. Smith, Col A. Hall, Maj A. Cannons, LCol David M. Robb, Capt Gary W. Handson, Maj A. Copeman, Capt F. Michael Halloran, Lt P.I. Jackson, Maj Marie Louise "Tony" Guyon, Capt David A. Rubin, MGen Al Pickering, BGen J.R. Genin, Maj Stanley H. Winfield, Maj Paul F. O'Leary, Maj Robert C. Dale, Maj H.H. Samson, LCol Pierre J.F. Couture, Lt Harold A. Skaarup, Maj Richard J. Vella, Maj G. Robert. Corbeil, Maj D.E. Guyatt, and LCol A. Jeddry.[3]

In the discussions held at the CISA AGM, several concerns were voiced in the Intelligence session of the conference. The following two were the most important:

The role of women in the Int Militia Units. The restriction on employment of women in the Int Militia was expressed in Mobile Command regulations, but reflected government policy that women were not to be employed in war areas, to which Int personnel could be assigned in time of emergency. The policy was being reviewed and FMC was optimistic that there would be a return to the previous policy of no such restrictions.

There is a lack of competitions and trophies for Int Sections. LCol David M. Robb was queried on this and on the lack of a national Militia Int concen-

---

3. The author attended the CISA Mess dinner at Longue Pointe Garrison in Montreal held on 21 Sep 1984. It was an excellent reunion with Edmonton and Halifax Militia Int cohorts and Int colleagues, including Dale M. Watts, Sherman R. Veinotte, Elaine E. Mellor, Robert C. Dale, David M. Robb, Wes von Papineau, W. Doug Whitley, Gary Handson and many others as well as a number of familiar names and faces and in many respects historical figures in the Int world both regular and reserve. He spent the night in a room on base after the dinner with a group of Russian speaking Int officers.

tration. He replied that it was up to FMC to arrange competitions. Concentrations can be organized on an area basis, and Capt F. Michael Halloran had arranged one for the past two years in Central Ontario. LCol Al R. Wells said the Int and Security Branch Funds could be approached to donate trophies, but more resources are required to finance a system of examining Units in a competition. Capt Gary W. Handson remarked that many trophies are held at CFSIS; however, the Crerar Trophy for the best Int Section is now the property of the Winnipeg Int Section, so a new one had to be acquired. Maj John "Pappy" MacKinnon suggested that the Colonel Commandant of the Int Branch, Sir William S. Stephenson, might like to donate a trophy, since the previous such trophy had been donated by the then Colonel Commandant of the C Int C, General Harry D.G. Crerar and so bore his name. It was proposed (and carried) that the President of CISA write to Sir William concerning the matter.[4]

LCol W. Tenhaaf was elected President of CISA. The matter of a trophy for CISA was later solved by his signing of the letter drafted by Maj John Mackinnon which produced the trophy. At this time it was also decided that the practice of subsidizing Regional Representatives as well as Directors from Regions to annual meetings was too expensive. Henceforth, Regional Directors did the job.

---

4.    CISA Newsletter, Vol. 15, No. 3, December 1984, pp. 1-3.

# 3

## 1985, Intelligence Branch

### CISA Member News, 1985

Shortly after the beginning of the year, the President CISA received a telegram from Sir William S. Stephenson from his home in Bermuda stating that a draft for $500 was on its way "to purchase a superior trophy" for competition among our Intelligence Units in the Reserve, to replace the Crerar Trophy.

CISA President LCol William "Bill" Tenhaaf, 1st VP Maj Howard Mansfield, Director LCol Jack S. Dunn and Secretary Maj John "Pappy" MacKinnon hosted a luncheon on 10 May 85 for outgoing CIS MGen Al Pickering and incoming CIS, MGen C. William "Bill" Hewson, Security Branch Advisor Col Bert N. Hall and former Int Branch Advisor LCol David M. Robb (subbing for newly-appointed Col George L.R. Bruce, just back from England).

WC Ted Atherton, former Director of Air Force Security Services, and Capt John Depew, formerly with Intelligence passed away in 1985.

Frank C. Muldoon, a lawyer and former Lt in the Winnipeg Int Section has gone from being Chairman of the Law Reform Commission of Canada to becoming a judge in the Federal Court.[1]

---

1.    CISA Newsletter, Vol. 16, No. 1, May 1985, pp. 1-2.

## 1985, Canadian Land Forces Command and Staff College Course

Capt Brad N. Hall completed the CLFCSC course in June 1985 and Capt W.A. "Tony" Rennett completed the course in Dec 1985.

## Intelligence Branch Advisor, Col George L.R.Bruce

I am very pleased as your Branch Advisor to have this opportunity to bring you up to date on developments over the past year, which have highlighted the work of the Intelligence Branch as an integral part of the Canadian Forces. We are more than ever conscious that the provision of Intelligence is first and foremost an operational support function and this confers on us the responsibility to continuously identify those areas where a need for innovation exists or improvements are required in our capability to deliver this vital service.

Conscious of these responsibilities, in April of [1985] my predecessor convened an Intelligence Branch Workshop at National Defence Headquarters for the purpose of reviewing the current status, problems and success of the Branch. Following the tradition of previous Branch workshops, an overall theme was set, in this case "Policy." As this was by far the most significant event in recent months of general interest to the Branch as a whole, much of what follows will be based on the deliberations of the Workshop and how they reflect current thinking among Intelligence staffs throughout the structure of the Canadian Forces. Within this general context I intend to touch upon recent Canadian Forces Policy Initiatives as they affect the Branch.

*Personnel Challenge.* Requests for Intelligence Branch officer and NCO positions continue to challenge our personnel resources. Wherever possible, we have filled these positions: however, a "quantity over quality" philosophy is being resisted, because we are endeavouring to maintain the professional standards of the Branch, which have so judiciously been established over the past several years. We will undoubtedly suffer shortfalls in the manning of some operational positions in the short term, but will at the same time continue to ensure that in the long term, we sustain our capability to maintain required standards. As one response to this challenge, SSOs INT have been advised to search for, advertise and interview potential candidates for reclassification and remuster.

*Intelligence Mobilization and the Reserves.* The concept of viable reserves has been an item of general interest both in the military and elsewhere, not only from a political perspective, but also as a result of recent Canadian Forces exercises such as BOLD STEP. In this regard the Chief Intelligence and Security wishes to see an Intelligence and Security Reserve Force in being to support his operations.

The problem of increasing the number of reserves is force-wide and is prioritized in favour of the environmental commands. It hinges, however, as much on organizational constraints as it does on financial resources and political considerations. Intelligence Reserve shortfalls. For example, as enunciated by the Director of Force Structure, approach 363 Army slots for FMC alone, whereas Army Intelligence Militia currently numbers only 40 personnel.

Many of you will be familiar with Capt W. Doug Whitley's draft paper on The Revitalization of the Intelligence Reserve Component of the Canadian Forces. Apart from its reflection upon the foresight of the author, Capt Whitley's paper received close scrutiny at the Branch Workshop in April, and this was subsequently followed by correspondence and liaison with the Director General Reserves and Cadets. LCol David M. Robb is now our representative on the D Reserve Study Team. It should of course be recognized that Government Defence Policy is now under review, and that the resultant Cabinet White Paper will be a keystone document regarding any subsequent decisions concerning all components of the reserves, including Intelligence.

Relevant to this discussion on reserves is the recent FMC decision to authorize recruiting of female personnel for up to 20% of Militia Intelligence Company manning levels. Basic guideline is that no females will serve at echelons below division level. It has been recommended that FMC Intelligence staff determine which positions within the FMC war establishment are suitable for this purpose (considering the stated constraint).

*Canadian Forces Intelligence Branch Association.* On 01 May 1985, the Intelligence Branch Fund was discontinued, and in its place the Canadian Forces Intelligence Branch Association was formed. Maj Ray J. Taylor has been appointed as President of the new association, and other officers of the executive committee include CWO Barry Toomer as Vice President; Capt Gary W. Handson as Secretary; and, Capt Brian E. Hamilton as Treasurer. Capt W. Doug Whitley fills an ex-officio position as Chairman of the Historical Committee. Membership on the Executive Committee will total eight in all, including three WOs/NCOs, and as practicable a serving reserve member of the Branch. Maj Ray J. Taylor will report in detail.

*Branch Dress.* Policy regarding the adoption of three different uniforms (Army, Navy and Air Force) for Intelligence Branch personnel has become a reality and a special effort will be required to preserve a sense of Branch Unity once the new uniforms become available. From this arises the need to retain the Intelligence Branch badge as a mandatory step towards the preservation of Branch Unity, and by personal example to instil a sense of cohesiveness and clear direction throughout the Branch.

Environmental commanders have been directed by the CDS to be responsible for the dress criteria of their commands. For FMC, representations are being made to equip Branch personnel with their own uniform button design, brass shoulder titles, Garrison smock shoulder flashes, shirt slip-ons, combat hat badge, and a stable belt. I have made representation to the commanders of MARCOM and AIRCOM respectively to ensure their Int Branch personnel wear Branch insignia with their respective orders of dress.

## 1985, Branch Highlights, Canadian Forces Europe (CFE)

The most significant highlight in CFE over the past years was the growth of Intelligence Branch positions for Air Force Units. The Base Intelligence Section at Baden received a second Branch Officer to plan targeting, and each of the three squadrons is replacing its Navigator Intelligence Officer position with an Intelligence Branch Capt. The second of the three squadrons completed that conversion this summer.

For the first time an Intelligence Section has been established at CFB Lahr. Preliminary manning over the summer months included one Branch officer, one senior and one Junior NCO. A new Branch Capt position has also been established at 1 Canadian Air Group Headquarters. Within Europe as well this year, a new Lt Col position was established at NATO Headquarters; a Major provided to HQ AFNORTH in Oslo, and a Capt has been added to the HQ CFE Intelligence Staff. Overall, the size of the Intelligence Branch in Europe has increased to 46 personnel.

## 1985, Branch Highlights, Air Command

From a shortfall in AIRCOM manning totalling four Branch officers and five NCOs has been the recent authorization of an additional Capt/Lt SO Int position within the ATG HQ establishment.

With assistance of AIRCOM a Unit Air Intelligence Officer course has been designed for those officers/NCOs who have assumed a secondary duty appointment as Unit Intelligence Officer. The course conducted at CFSIS is intended to provide prospective Unit Int Officers with the wherewithal to cope with the fundamentals of Intelligence and security at their respective level. The course is 20 working days in duration and will be held once per year.

## 1985, Branch Highlights, MARCOM

In MARCOM over the past year, effort has been centred on determining the most productive position for Int Branch positions within MARCOM. The MARPAC Int organization has also been evaluated, with the recommendation of a significant increase in staff including at least one Int Branch Capt and several Int Ops.

Another recommendation originating from MARCOM is to seek more positions dedicated to Naval Intelligence interests in the Directorate of Defence Intelligence at NDHQ as a counter-balance to the few operational billets now open to Int Branch Officers within MARCOM itself. Implementation of this recommendation is contingent upon future adoption of internally generated personnel Resources Management Study (OSMER), which applies to the total peacetime manning structure of the Canadian Forces.

## 1985, Branch Highlights, FMC

FMC has stated a requirement for a viable tasking for the Militia and as a start has recommended the formation of Intelligence Platoons for 5e GBMC (CAST Bde Gp) and 4 CMBG. It is intended to conduct a feasibility study on this measure based on the recently approved Required War Structure and if successful, to seek formalization of such a tasking and to obtain the necessary equipment.

In the meantime, planning continues on the formation of a Reserve Electronic Warfare Squadron to be based at CFB Kingston. The squadron will incorporate an Intelligence component, which comprises three officers and 26

ORs, with one Regular Force training assistant. The primary function of Intelligence Branch personnel will be analytical support to the squadron.

Finally, an FMC-produced handbook of Soviet TO&E was distributed in late April.

The 1985 FMC Intelligence Section included Sgt J. Michael Poulin, Cpl J.RP. Turcotte, MCpl Al H. Dickie, Mme Monette, MCpl Arsenault, WO Mike V. Marsh, Sgt William E. Hamilton, Sgt Ivo J.M. Schoots, MCpl Ron K. Townsend, WO J. Ron Martin, Maj Paul F. O'Leary, LCol Darcy J. Beatty, Capt D.H. Neil Thompson, Lt Wes B. von Papineau.

## 1985, Branch Highlights, CFSIS

The provision of training programs to meet the professional requirements of the modern Intelligence Officer and Intelligence Operator continues as a top-level Branch priority. Current courses being conducted by the Intelligence Training Company at CFSIS (as well as their duration) include Int Officer 82A, Int Op TQ5A, Int Op TQ6A, Int Op TQ6B, Interrogator, Combat Intelligence Officer, Combat Intelligence NCO, Air Intelligence and Reserve Int courses.

In the field of training development, a CTS Board was held last January, which produced Mobilization Training Standards for both Intelligence Officers and Int Ops.

CFSIS, NCO Militia Course, summer 1985.
Front Row: WO J.M. Lauzière (Montreal), LCdr Christopher S. Hordal,
Lt Wes B. von Papineau, Sgt Marlowe (Montreal).
Rear Row: MCpl K.D. Zoroneck (Winnipeg), MCpl W.E.B. Young
(Halifax), MCpl K. Boutin (Halifax), Sgt N.L. Gordon (Vancouver), Sgt
Kozak (Edmonton), MCpl J.A.E.K. Dowell.

## MWO Richard "Dick" Bushe, CD

Members of the Int Branch share my distress over the tragic death of MWO
Dick K. Bushe, CD, in a cycling accident at Camp Borden on 31 July 1985.
MWO Bushe was born in Marylebone (London), England on 10 August
1953. He began his military career with the British Army, serving with the
Royal Engineers from 1954 to 1957. He enrolled in the RCAF in November
1957, serving until 1962. He left the service, rejoining the RCAF in 1965 as
an Instrument Engineer. In March 1971 he remustered to the Canadian
Intelligence Branch. After serving at CFB Shearwater from 1971 to 1974, he
was promoted to Sgt and posted to CFSIS. While at CFSIS he was promoted

to WO in September 1978, then posted to 1 CAG in July 1979. He was promoted to MWO in January 1982 while at CFB Baden, and then posted back
to CFSIS in July 1983 as the MWO Intelligence Training Company. His
hobbies were predominated by running and cycling activities. His wife Dinah,
his daughter Susan and son John survive Dick.

(On 1 Aug 1985 Col George L.R. Bruce, Col Jeff S. Upton, Capt Harold
A. Skaarup and Lt H. Wayne Nightingale visited Mrs. Bushe at her home to
pay their respects. All attended MWO Bushe's funeral on Saturday 2 Aug at
CFB Borden).

Plans are underway to establish a trophy in memory of MWO Bushe to be
presented to the top student of the TQ6B course. This will complement the
Oliver Trophy, sponsored by CISA and awarded to the top student of the
TQ6A Course.

## MWO Joseph Paul Antoine Normand Lefebvre, CD

MWO J.P.A.N. "Norm" Lefebvre died on 14 December 1985. He was born
in Quebec City on 13 January 1943. He began his military career with the
RCAF on 21 February 1961. He remustered to the CF Intelligence Branch in
January 1970. He served with the 1st Canadian Signal Regiment, 2 EW
Squadron from August 1973 to July 1975. Following a tour of duty to New
Delhi, India as a CFA Clerk from July 1975 to July 1977, he returned to
Kingston for a second tour with 2 EW Squadron. While serving with 2 EW
Squadron he was promoted to the rank of WO. He attended the Canadian
Forces Language School in Ottawa from August 1980 to June 1981 and stud-
ied the German Language. Following his language training, he was posted to
Canadian Forces Europe in June 1981 and was employed with the Field Secu-
rity section of 4 CMBG. While serving in Germany he was promoted to
MWO in February 1983. Norm was posted to FMC HQ Intelligence Section
in June 1985. Normand is survived by his wife Jean, a son Robert and two
daughters, Lorri and Chantal.

Col George L.R. Bruce delivered a eulogy to MWO Lefebvre at St
Michel's Chapel, CFB St Hubert, on 18 Dec 1985. "I think the most difficult
and painful thing for a soldier to do is to say goodbye to a comrade. Indeed, it
almost seems as though we go out of our way to avoid having to say goodbye,
and I am not sure why. It may be superstition, or it may be that we know that
in saying goodbye we are saying something more final. We go on course

together, we are posted together, we work together and we socialize together and at the end of all those things we shake hands, mumble something and go on about our business. Our friends, that is our brothers and sisters whose native language is French, very sensibly have two words for a leave taking. One word is "au-revoir" which means until we meet again, and the other, and more final word, is "adieu"—a going to God. We have said au-revoir to Norm Lefebvre on many occasions, for example when he and his family left for their posting to New Delhi as an Attaché's assistant and again when he left the Signal Regiment and most recently when he left Europe to come to this Headquarters. Saying au-revoir we do not find difficult. Today, though, we must say adieu.

The Intelligence Branch of the Canadian Forces is very small, indeed, a quite small part of the Canadian Forces, as a whole. With their smallness, however, comes a certain uniqueness in that we all know one another, we are indeed a family and the loss of one member of our family is felt by all. We all knew Norm as a soldier, a colleague, and a friend and in all those things he was greatly respected and admired. His loss for us is tremendous but pales totally in comparison with the loss of husband, companion and father that Jean, Robert, Laurie and Chantal have suffered. Yet, in the midst of all that sadness there is joy, and hope and thanksgiving for the life of a good man. Today the Intelligence Branch mourns, whether it is in the Maritime Forces in the Pacific, here in this Chapel, in Europe, Cyprus or the Middle East. Indeed, as we sit in this Chapel Norm's colleagues and friends from the Branch and the Forces are gathered in the Chapel in Lahr to celebrate a service of thanksgiving for the life of Norm Lefebvre.

In the context of that sadness and joy we should not be afraid or ashamed to say goodbye, but it should be in the context of its original English meaning—goodbye, God be with you."

The author served with MWO Norm Lefebvre in Germany. A full 40-pax bus took Int Branch representatives from Ottawa to Montreal for the funeral in stormy, bitterly cold (minus 20º) winter weather. He was buried with full honours in a cemetery high on the Mount Royal hillside. Many who had known and served with him in Germany were in attendance, including MGen A. John G.D. de Chastelain (later to become our Chief-of-Defence and Ambassador to Washington), LCol David M. Robb, WO Mike V. Marsh (Honour Guard Commander) and many former members of 4 CMBG. The church was packed, and included many long-time colleagues, Capt Robert T.

Greyeyes, CWO Rolf F. Overhoff, Capt H. Wayne Nightingale, CWO Barry Toomer, WO David James Sundberg and many from the SIU and NDHQ in Ottawa as well as Intelligence personnel from Valcartier, Borden, North Bay and FMC.

## 1985, MGen R.J.G. "Reg" Weeks, CD Appointed Intelligence Branch Commandant

The term of office of Sir William S. Stephenson, CC, MC, DFC, as Colonel Commandant of the Canadian Forces Intelligence Branch has drawn to a close. Sir William indicated that it would be appropriate for another person to take up the appointment, but graciously consented to act in the unofficial capacity as Honorary Patron of the Branch for an indefinite period.

Ministerial permission was granted to offer the post of Colonel Commandant for a three-year term to MGen R.J.G. "Reg" Weeks, CD. MGen Weeks accepted, and assumed the appointment on 10 Oct 1985.

From the above, I am certain that you will agree that the Int Branch on its third birthday is well established, growing, and is receptive to the changing needs of the user formations. The important aspects of Branch esprit de corps and morale are being addressed, and we continue to build on the historical traditions so well established by our predecessors.

I would like to extend to you all my best wishes to you and your families for the New Year. E Tenebris Lux.[2]

## 1985, Commodore J.C. Slade, CD, Director General Intelligence

Although born in Portsmouth, UK, of a naval family, Commodore Slade completed his high school education at Lisgar Collegiate, Ottawa, before being accepted for ROTP and attending the Royal Military College of Canada in 1955.

After graduation in 1959, Commodore Slade attended the University of Toronto for a further year to complete his degree in Electrical Engineering. This was followed by the completion of junior officer courses and a first seagoing appointment in HMCS Ottawa in January 1961. His next series of seagoing appointments—Navigating Officer of HMCS Saskatchewan in 1963,

2.    Intelligence Branch Journal, Number 1, 1985, pp. 2-4.

Operations Officer of HMCS Yukon in 1965 and Executive Officer of HMCS Terra Nova in 1969, were interspersed with a one-year Operations "long course" in 1964, and a one-year post-graduate course in Operations Research, again at the University of Toronto, in 1966. This latter was followed by a tour in the Operations Research Establishment, Ottawa, and by participation on the 1968 Officer Development Board.

Following Terra Nova, Commodore Slade spent two and a half years ashore in Halifax, NS, working first in the Operational Test and Evaluation force office, then as the Maritime Command coordinator for the DDH 280 program. His only "foreign" posting occurred for a 6-month period in 1972 when he attended the Armed Forces Staff College, Norfolk, Virginia, before returning to his previous appointment in Halifax.

In 1973, as a Lt Commander, Commodore Slade was appointed in Command of HMCS Gatineau in Esquimalt, BC, and was promoted Commander shortly before returning to Halifax as Senior Staff Officer, Sea Systems Readiness, in 1975.

In 1976, Commodore Slade took command of HMCS Athabaskan for two years, prior to spending two years at NDHQ in the Directorate of Maritime Requirements as Section Head of the C3 section. In 1980 he was promoted to Capt (N) and was appointed in Command of the Second Canadian Destroyer Squadron in Esquimalt. This was followed in 1982 by another tour in Halifax as DCOS Plans on the Maritime Commanders staff, and one year later, Commodore Slade returned to NDHQ as the Executive Assistant to the CDS.

In 1985 Commodore Slade was promoted to his present rank and was appointed to his present rank and was appointed as the Director General Intelligence.[3]

## RV 85, CFB Wainwright

During the past year, FMC HQ has conducted a number of exercises, which included the RITE SIMPLE and RITE DOUBLE series as well as RV 85. All regular and most Militia sections participated in these CPX's and FTX. The major event, however, was Ex RV 85, which included the first tactical deployment of a Divisional HQ in the field for many years. The Div HQ G2

3. Intelligence Branch Journal, Number 1, 1985, p. 6. Commodore Slade achieved the rank of Rear Admiral before retiring from the CF.

staff consisted of 14 Int Branch all ranks, which ranged from the G2 himself, LCol Paul F. O'Leary, to several Militia Cpls. The exercise was a great success and focussed much attention on the current state of Militia training with FMC. Members of the FMC Int Staff deployed to RV 85 on 6 April and the last member returned on 12 June 1985. Also during RV 85, the Int Branch Advisor and the Int Branch CWO conducted a successful visit to all elements of the Branch deployed on the Ex. The visit was topped off by a BBQ, which saw the Div Commander, MGen A. John G.D. de Chastelain, and 58 members of the Int Branch assembled in the same place at the same time.[4]

## 1985, Intelligence Personnel News

The following Intelligence Branch members have been promoted to the rank indicated: Col George L.R. Bruce, 25 Feb 85; LCol Christopher S. Hordal, 29 Jul 85; LCol Paul F. O'Leary, 15 May 85; Maj K.F. Binda, 1 May 85; Maj D. Rick Douglas, 1 May 85; Maj Gerry C. Mayer, 1 May 85; Maj John H. Newman, 1 May 85; Capt J.A. Grant, 1 May 85; Capt Brian E. Hamilton, 1 Jan 85; Capt Tim A. Larson, 16 Jun 85; Capt J.P. André Tremblay, 1 May 85; Lt Barry S. Alexander, 1 May 85; Lt Richard A. Derkson, 14 Aug 85; Lt Terry W. Procyshyn, 1 May 85; Lt J.R.R.R. Sylvain Robidoux, 11 Apr 85.

MWO R.A. Mader, 6 May 85; MWO Jean Guy H.E. Martineau, 1 Aug 85; WO Paddy Hatfield, 12 Aug 85; WO George T. Izzard, 27 Oct 85; WO T.H. Maddox, 12 Aug 85; WO Rick M. Milne, 1 Aug 85; WO Ivo J.M. Schoots, 6 Aug 85; WO Terry J. Thompson, 4 Oct 85; Sgt R.N. Cooper, 3 Feb 85; Sgt L.D. Crosby, 2 Jan 85; Sgt Robert A. Deleau, 2 Aug 85; Sgt David A. Gelsinger, 27 May 85; Sgt J.M. Letellier De St Just, 24 Jun 85; Sgt J.O. "Rick" Limoges, 12 Aug 85; Sgt P.A. Maillet, 1 Aug 85; Sgt Tom C. O'Brien, 13 May 85; Sgt E. Bruce E. Smith, 27 May 85; Sgt Mike R. Tracey, 6 Aug 85; MCpl D.D. Campbell, 2 Aug 85; MCpl G.D. Chaisson, 24 Jun 85; MCpl Al H. Dickie, 2 Jan 85; MCpl K.L. Dyer, 1 Aug 85; MCpl Terry W. Fader, 13 May 85; MCpl Darrell L. Gammon, 12 Aug 85; MCpl J.L.S. Gauvin, 22 Oct 85; MCpl William "Bill" D. Kean, 12 Aug 85; MCpl E.L. Larocque, 27 May 85; MCpl J.L.A. Martineau, 4 Nov 85; MCpl D.A. McCoy, 4 Oct 85; MCpl W.A. Morgan, 3 Feb 85; MCpl Robert J. O'Gorman, 2 Jan 85; MCpl Joseph Jean Pierre Paquette, 15 Oct 85; MCpl Greg S.

4. Intelligence Branch Journal, Number 1, 1985, p. 13.

Smith, 11 Aug 85; MCpl Manuel A. Thibault, 27 May 85; MCpl Ron K. Townsend, 6 Aug 85; and, MCpl J.P.G. Vinetti, 1 Aug 85.

The following Int Branch members have been released, retired or remustered: Col Robert W. Irvine, 29 Nov 85; Col Jeff S. Upton, 10 Oct 85; Capt John Antaki, 6 Nov 85; Capt Roy C. Armstrong, 24 Jun 85; Capt C.J.T. Dodd, 16 Sep 85; Capt J.E.H. Bernard Lemieux, 3 Apr 85; CWO W. Richard "Dick" Ulm, 6 May 85; WO E.H. Brogan, 4 Oct 85; WO R.T. Dicks, 30 Sep 85; WO William "Bill" R. Jones, 6 Aug 85; WO Trevor R. Palmer, 27 Oct 85; WO D.W. Renwick, 18 Aug 85; Sgt D.A. Butt, 27 May 85, UTPM; Sgt R.N. Cooper, 13 May 85, UTPM; Sgt Pierre Michaud, 214 Jun 85, UTPM; Sgt Gary Rung, 4 Nov 85; and, MCpl R.B. Adye, 11 Aug 85.[5]

## 1985, CISA AGM

The CISA AGM held at CFB Montreal, Longue Pointe Garrison was presided over by the President, LCol William "Bill" Tenhaaf on 19 Sep 85. The following members were in attendance: MGen Reginald J.G. Weeks, LCol Paul F. O'Leary, LCol Ed D. Sanford, Maj Dale M. Watts, Maj J.H. Mansfield, Capt James L. Downey, Maj Nils E. Lindberg, Maj Elaine E. Mellor, Maj Robert C. Dale, LCol Al R. Wells, Maj Merrick K. Szulc, Maj Sherman R. Veinotte, Maj G. Robert Corbeil, Capt M.A. Kulba, Capt Harold F. Smith, Capt Doug R. Bennett, 2Lt R. Lapointe, LCol Alf J. Laidler, Maj Terry B. Kelly, Maj Ian A. Nicol, Capt Peter T. Patton, Maj John H. Newman, LCol Christopher S. Hordal, LCol Jack S. Dunn, Col Robert T. Grogan, Maj William "Bill" L. Watt, Col Jeff S. Upton, Maj Fred E.G. Jones, Col Andrew F. Ritchie, Lt William "Bill" B. Iler, Capt Eugene Slonetsky, Maj Jan A. Jezewski, Capt James "Jim" P.K. Van Wynen, 2Lt Paul R. Perchaluk, Lt E. Bruce Holmes, LCol Emile Berger, Maj Wilf S. Puffer, Lt Wes B. von Papineau, Capt John A. Lauer, Capt Harold F. Smith, Capt W. Doug Whitley, LCol A.G. Cameron, Maj Franz F. Laizner, Lt Harold A. Skaarup, Capt J.R. Sparling, Capt F. Michael Halloran, Lt J. Mullen, Maj Richard J. Vella, Lt J.K. Pineau, MGen C. William "Bill" Hewson, Col George L.R. Bruce, Col A.H. Sam Stevenson, and Maj John "Pappy" MacKinnon.

LCol William "Bill" Tenhaaf had attended the AGM of the CDA in Jan 85, and reported on resolutions of interest to reserve Units included: a call for

5.   Intelligence Branch Journal, Number 1, 1985, p. 22.

a mobilization plan; CPP for Reservists; Identity cards; increased ceilings in budget; reactivation of Reserves; and, Identity cards for Retired Members.

CISA members LCol Ted Atherton, Maj Ed L. Babcock, Maj Gunnar J. Ramslie and Capt Jake Yakmission passed away in 1985. Col Charles Chaveau was appointed as an Honorary CISA Lifetime Member. Michele Bailey was the recipient of the $600 academic award for 1984-85. CISA members of the Regular Force mugged out in the Army Officer's Mess in Ottawa in Sep 85 included Col Bert N. Hall, Col Jeff S. Upton, Col Robert W. Irvine, LCol Ronald E. Gladstone and LCol Peter A.H. Dupille. Former CIS RAdm John Rodocanachi and former CIS MGen Al Pickering also attended the event. LCol William "Bill" Tenhaaf, Col Robert T. Grogan, Maj J. Howard Mansfield and Maj Marie Louise "Tony" Guyon were to represent the CISA at the CDA AGM in Jan 86. Int Branch Colonel Commandant MGen Reginald J.G. Weeks and Int Branch Advisor Col George L.R. Bruce were also to attend the AGM.[6]

The CISA President attended the Council Meeting of the Conference of Defence Associations (CDA) on 12 April 1985 and reported there was still no White or Green Paper on defence policy. Nevertheless, the government was considering the purchase of new equipment; the updating of destroyers with a complete air defence system; and, the exercising of the Canadian Air Sea Transportable (CAST) Brigade Group in its entirety (5,500 Troops), complete with aircraft. LCol William "Bill" Tenhaaf also reported CISA member Maj Raymond S. Shelley passed away in March 1986.[7]

## 1985, Intelligence Collection and Analysis Centre

*Introduction.* The first trial of the Intelligence Collection and Analysis Centre (ICAC) was conducted at CFB Valcartier between 20 Oct and 1 Nov 1985 as part of a series of Brigade Group and Division-level Command Post Exercises (CPX) called Ex RITE SIMPLE XIII and RITE DOUBLE III. The trial was conducted in a realistic field environment, which included tactical deployment and movement.

This trial was the most important initiative in Canadian Army Combat Intelligence operations in many years. For the first time, the ICAC allowed the G2 to present to the commander a detailed estimate of the enemy's inten-

6.   CISA Newsletter, Vol. 16, No. 3, December 1985, pp. 1-2.
7.   CISA Newsletter, Vol. 17, No. 1, June 1986, pp. 1-2.

tions based on a coordinated all-source assessment. Another major benefit of this trial was the creation of an effective collection and tasking management system at the tactical level. These achievements were due partly to the introduction of computers into the tactical Intelligence area as they greatly enhanced the ICAC ability to rapidly cross-reference and collate data.

This ICAC field trial was designed to operationalize the ICAC concept as presented in the Combat Development Combat Intelligence Study, and used the Required War Structure of the Task Force Intelligence Company. The ICAC was deployed tactically throughout the trial in temperatures ranging from -15°C to +12°C. In addition, this trial saw the first use of computers in the field for Combat Intelligence applications. This ADP support was provided by operators using three Apple IIe computers utilizing a combination of Canadian software and software developed by the Military Intelligence personnel of the XVIII AB (US) Corps.

*Aim.* The aim of this trial was to field deploy an ICAC and using a series of CPXs, develop policies, procedures and detailed SOPs to enable the ICAC to become an integral part of the Task Force/Div Intelligence Company of the future.

*Conduct of the Trial.* The trial was conducted in three phases as follows:

Phase I: This phase was conducted 20-22 Oct 1985, and was used to conduct training of all ICAC personnel and to review the G2/ICAC relationships;

Phase II: This phase was conducted 23-27 Oct 1985, and allowed the ICAC to become a player on a Brigade Group Command Post Exercise, Ex RITE SIMPLE XIII. During this time, procedures were modified and ADP training commenced; and,

Phase III: This phase saw the ICAC become a full player in Ex RITE DOUBLE III. This exercised the FMC Division HQ for the period 28 Oct-1 Nov 1985, and included tactical deployment and several night moves of the ICAC.

*Background.* The requirement for the G2 to provide the commander with all-source Intelligence has long been recognized. In addition, the number and complexity of sensors available to formations has recently grown dramatically. In an effort to improve the Intelligence provided, the Combat Intelligence Study and the FMC Required War Structure recognized the requirement for an Intelligence Company at the division or Task Force level. For purposes of the trial, only the ICAC was exercised in the field, however, during Ex RITE

DOUBLE, there were lower controllers playing the Intelligence Company platoons and higher controllers representing the corps ICAC.

*Conceptual Framework.* One of the most important aims of the trial was to validate the doctrinal framework of the relationship between the ICAC and the G2 staff. This relationship was developed and refined and the following is the currently agree relationships and responsibilities.

*G2 Staff.* In general, the G2 himself has the responsibility as the commander's principal Intelligence staff officer. He alone advises the commander and staff of the enemy's location, capabilities and most importantly the enemy's most likely intentions. The G2 also provides direction on the commander's behalf to the CO of Intelligence Company supporting that Division. The detailed relationship between the G2, G2 Staff and the Intelligence Company is dealt with below. Although the CO of the Company in his capacity as CO of one of the division Units has access to the commander for various matters, he does not have access on Intelligence matters, as the G2 remains the commander's principal advisor on all elements of Intelligence support to the division.

*The Division G2 Branch* has three main sections: the G2, G2 Operations; and the G2 Estimates. The G2 provides the overall direction and coordination of the entire Intelligence system within the division. He personally advises the commander on the selection of the Priority Intelligence Requirements and then provides direction to the G2 estimates for the preparation of the Intelligence estimate.

*The Division Intelligence Company.* The Company provides the G2 staff with its current Intelligence. This allows the G2 Operations to keep the HQ and formations up-to-date on the enemy picture, the G2 Estimates to maintain a data base so he may prepare the estimates and long term studies; and the G2 himself so he may direct and coordinate the total Intelligence system. It is important to note that the staff is neither receiving nor analyzing raw information or Intelligence, nor directing the minute-to-minute activities of any collectors. All this collection and analysis is done by the elements of the Intelligence Company.

*Intelligence Company Organization.* The Company is tasked to provide the commander with the first line acquisition and exploitation of tactical information from imagery, human and all other non-electromagnetic sources. This organic capability provides the commander through the G2 with timely, reliable Intelligence on which operational decisions can be based. The collection elements of the Company are found within the Intelligence Operations Platoon and are as follows:

*Imagery Exploitation Section (IE).* The IE Section is tasked to exploit all available imagery. This includes not only processing, printing and interpretation of conventional air photographs to support the Division, but also could include SLAR or FLIR forwarded from other sources or agencies. In addition, they will conduct second phase interpretation of RPV imagery, as the RPV section has its own imagery exploitation detachment for the initial phase of exploitation. The IE Section has two laboratory detachments, which provides a printing and storage facility.

*Interrogation Section.* The Interrogation Section has three teams plus an HQ and is tasked to acquire information from prisoners of war and refugees.

Counter Intelligence (CI) Section. The CI Section has three teams and their major task is to identify and neutralize/exploit agents of hostile Intelligence services. This data forms the human Intelligence input to the ICAC where the all-source Counter Intelligence analysis is conducted. This includes Signals Intelligence and Human Intelligence.

*Remotely Piloted Vehicle (RPV) Section.* The RPV Section maintains two RPV launchers and ground control stations and is capable of conducting first phase imagery exploitation of the RPV imagery.

*Intelligence Collection and Analysis Centre (ICAC).* As can be seen in this discussion, the roles and responsibilities of the G2 staff and the Intelligence Company are quite different. The G2 staff is advising and disseminating Intelligence while the Intelligence Company is actually part of the collection and analysis process. The organization that provides the bridge between these two groups is the ICAC. This is where the G2's Intelligence collection requirements are turned into operational taskings. These taskings are then issued to the Electronic Warfare Coordination Centre, RPV Section, air recce, etc. The raw data is then received, collated, analyzed and checked with all other sources, and finally finished Intelligence is produced. This finished all-source product is passed back to the G2, who in turn informs the commander, staff and formations. In return, the G2 will issue new priorities to the ICAC and the cycle starts again. Therefore, the G2 establishes the priorities and keeps them updated; the ICAC tasks the collectors; receives the data; does the detailed analysis and then passes the finished Intelligence to the G2.

The trial was extremely successful. This was due to the positive attitude displayed by all members of the ICAC team. This team was made up of both regular and reserve members of the Intelligence Branch who not only had to understand a totally new system but also had to learn how to use the new computers. The training period was short and the results were most successful.

This trial represents the crossing of the first threshold in providing the commander with an all-source Intelligence assessment. Moreover, the lessons learned apply equally to the Intelligence Company within the Divisional context or to the Intelligence Platoon provided to Brigade Groups. To continue the development of the ICAC, it is considered that the next full-scale ICAC deployment should be during RV 87. This would see a three-phased exercise, which would include an ICAC training phase followed by an Ex RITE SIMPLE followed by a Divisional CPX RITE DOUBLE. The continuation of ICAC deployments will ensure that when the first Intelligence line Units are fielded, the ICAC will be an effective element of those Units.[8]

## *From the Intelligence Branch Advisor, Col George L.R. Bruce*

The Intelligence Branch is gaining a new Branch Advisor. He will not be a stranger to that job having performed in that capacity temporarily between the retirement of Col Robert W. Irvine and my appointment as DDI. I am sure that you will all give LCol David M. Robb the same degree of loyalty and cooperation that you have given me. At the same time our Branch Chief will be changing, as the present incumbent is being commissioned, and will be succeeded by CWO Barry Toomer. I cannot over-emphasize the vast amount of behind the scenes work that CWO Fred L. Juett has done on all your behalves, and I wish him the very best of good fortune as his career takes a new direction. I am sure I speak for all of you in extending to him your congratulations.

This year so far, and it is only April, has been a banner year for promotions in the Branch. To date we have had one promotion to LCol, five to Major, three to Capt, one to CWO, two MWOs and the number of Sgts and MCpls seems almost too many to count. They are well-deserved and in many cases, in my opinion at least, long overdue. My congratulations to all of you.

In the last issue, I explained to you, at some length, where the Branch had gone over the past 12 months, and where it would be going in the future. That future is now yours. The Branch is and can become exactly what you make of it and, from the safety and sanctuary of my retirement, I can only watch as

8.    Intelligence Branch Journal Number 2, 1986, pp. 9-11.

changes occur. I would be remiss, however, if I did not offer you all a word of warning. The switch to three distinctly coloured environmental uniforms bears within it the seed of destruction for the Intelligence Branch. That unique sense of identity, which we all shared from the moment the Branch came into existence in 1982, was based on our ability to perform the tasks required of us in all three environments. While we wore one uniform that uniqueness of identity was not questioned either by the operators for whom we worked or more importantly by ourselves. Now, unless we exercise extreme care, we face the possibility of internecine bickering, which can only work to all of our detriments. Be proud of the new uniform that you will wear regardless of its colour but remember that you are a part of a specialist profession in which all of us work together to ensure that we bring light from darkness to our masters.

I have tried in this article to avoid either sentimentality or to fall victim to the urge to reminisce but I find it difficult in fact to say goodbye to you all without reflecting briefly on the large number of skilled and thoroughly professional people of all ranks that I have encountered in 27 years in the Intelligence business. We are a different breed of service person. Most of our qualities do not fit the mould envisaged by most people when they think of uniformed members of an armed force. That uniqueness or perhaps eccentricity, is, I believe, essential if we are to do our job to the best of our ability. We must be sceptical but honest; innovative and willing to try new ways, and not willing to accept things because that is the way they were done last year; outgoing and extroverted. All of those are main attributes of the Intelligence professional and as I look back over my career I can recall a great many who fall into that category and I see a new generation of Junior NCOs and officers who look set to follow in that tradition. I have enjoyed my military service and would not trade a day of it for anything. I wish you and your families the very best of good fortune and prosperity and hope that through membership in the Int Branch Association I can watch your careers. My best wishes to you all and God speed.[9]

## *Intelligence Branch Prayer*

Almighty God, by whose grace we are called upon to positions of trust and responsibility! We ask for your blessing upon all who serve in the Intelligence

---

9.  Intelligence Branch Journal Number 2, 1986, p. 2.

Branch of the Canadian Forces, at home and abroad. Inspire us with the courage to always seek the truth, and the wisdom to give proper counsel to our comrades. Give us the strength to persevere in the face of doubt and adversity, and clarity of vision that we may always know the light when it is revealed from the darkness; that by serving others honourably and with wisdom, we may serve you well and be worthy of our calling. Amen.[10]

10.  Intelligence Branch Journal Number 5, Fall 1987, p. 7.

# 4

## 1986, Intelligence Branch

### 1986, Capt Jean Pierre Rose, CD

Capt "JP" Rose passed away on 29 January 1986. JP was born in Quebec City on 24 Dec 1944. He began his military career with the RCAF in November 1965, enrolling as a photo technician and later remustering to the Canadian Forces Intelligence Branch in 1972. He was commissioned as an Intelligence Officer from the rank of Sgt in December 1976. He was posted to 434 Sqn at Cold Lake in May 1977. In July 1980 "JP" assumed the duties of Base Coordinator of Official Languages. He continued his operational role in the performance of his secondary duty of Base Nuclear Defence Officer. His voluntary contributions to the Cold Lake Community led to his appointment as Mayor of the Medley Community Council from June 1980 until May 1981, earning him a well-deserved Community Service Award. His wife, Louise and two daughters, Nathalie and Christine survive Jean Pierre.

### 1986, WO Robert Melrose Steedman, CD1 ·

WO Robert "Bob" M. Steedman passed away in Ottawa on 15 January 1986. He was born in Edinburgh, Scotland, on 13 August 1937. He began his military career with the Royal Canadian Artillery on 27 August 1954 and served with them until 31 August 1962. WO Steedman remustered to the C Int C in August 1962. He began his new career as an Int Op with the Target Headquarters in Windsor, NS, from 1962 to 1964. Afterwards he completed a tour of duty with CFPIU in Ottawa from 1964 to 1967. He was then posted to 439 Sqn in Germany from 1967 to 1971. He returned to Canada in 1971 and served with 403 Sqn in Petawawa and Gagetown until 1974. While at Petawawa he was promoted to the rank of Sgt. He then returned to Germany for a second tour with 439 Sqn. He was promoted to the rank of WO in May 1977 while at CFB Baden, and then posted to the Group Intelligence Section in Baden until 1978. He returned to Canada in 1978 serving with 1 Combat Group, Calgary, Alberta, until 1980. Bob was then posted to NDHQ/CIS/DDI-6 in July 1980. While serving with DDI-6, Bob was a very active member of the Unit. Bob's main hobby was painting. His wife Marie-Louise, two sons, Robert Junior and Richard, and two daughters Brenda-Marie and Deborah Ann survive Bob.

The author had the privilege of serving with WO Robert "Bob" M. Steedman while working at DDI-6 at Tunney's Pasture. When WO Steedman realized he was terminally ill, the medical officer recommended that he stay home. Not comfortable with the idea of just sitting at home "waiting for the end," Bob felt his work and his skills were still of great value and that he could still be useful as a Master Photo Interpreter. He spoke with Col George L.R. Bruce, requesting that he be allowed to continue in his work at DDI-6, even if only for a few hours a day. His request was granted, and he continued to work until shortly before his death in Ottawa early in the new year. Bob is one of many examples of the high calibre of people who have served in the Intelligence Branch family.

## TAC SIGINT—Acorn's Corner
## Extracts from an article by Capt W. Doug Whitley

Do you remember when the "Intelligence business" was simple? The Intelligence officer of a battalion, ship, or air squadron read the newspapers, marked "the old man's" map, and tried to convince everyone else that all their plans were in vain if they didn't anticipate the enemy or potential enemy. The pioneers of yesterday seem to have succeeded in the latter activity as today, the Intelligence function in any command is more recognized than ever before. The modern battlefield is not only fluid and complex but is also changing at a rapid pace. New weapons systems are matched by counter measures even more devious. Any commander worth his salt now uses his Intelligence specialists to keep track of what the enemy is doing more than ever. These weapon systems, and the means used to find out about them, have one thing in common: they all use electronics.

The term "electronics" is used in the broadest sense in that all of the radio frequency (RF) spectrum is considered including visible light. These electronics are used to control fighting Units and weapon systems. They are used for "illuminating" battle areas and possible battle areas. They are also used to stop an enemy from doing the same thing. Electronics are ubiquitous and the Intelligence specialist must know what and how the enemy uses them and how to use them himself to achieve his aim of anticipating the intentions of the opposing forces.

The generic term for all this activity is Electronic Warfare (EW) and the Intelligence function in EW is termed either Electronic Warfare Support Measures (EWSM) or Tactical Signals Intelligence (TAC SIGINT) depending upon the purpose of the activity. EWSM is the collection of information electronically for immediate targeting purposes whereas TAC SIGINT is the collection of information electronically for longer-term purposes. Indeed, some Intelligence collected electronically may be of use to strategic military planners in which case it simply becomes known as SIGINT. In TAC SIGINT terms, all environments have a requirement to detect, locate and analyze enemy forces electronically in order to prepare tactical plans. However, due to the different nature of each service and their varying time requirements, the product is acquired and processed differently. What they all have in common is the same purpose.

How the TAC SIGINT process varies between operational environments may be better understood by examining the shorter term EWSM function.

In an air engagement, the primary concern in the EWSM or targeting function is to detect a hostile aircraft in order to take either an evasive or attack action. A prime example of the tool used is the radar-warning receiver (RWR) mounted in the aircraft. Modern aircraft such as the CF-18 Hornet contain a reprogrammable RWR in which the electronic characteristics of enemy aircraft can be changed as fast as the supporting Intelligence organization can get the changes into it. Changing the electronic signature of a hostile aircraft is an example of an Electronic Counter-Counter Measure (ECCM).

In the land battle, EWSM is not quite so immediate or automatic. An enemy battlefield radar, which is detected by a mobile radar intercept detachment, is identified and located semi-automatically (the soldier is still in the loop). It can be decided whether to take an electronic counter measure (ECM) such as electronically jamming it, or shoot at it with artillery or otherwise destroy it. The principle is the same but more dependent upon the overall tactical scenario than in the air environment.

The naval EWSM function is a hybrid of that found in the air or land environments. A ship at sea has the immediate problem of electronically detecting incoming missiles similar to the air situation but also has a requirement to detect enemy vessels, which aren't directly threatening it such as in the Army's case. Once again, the factors determining the requirement vary.

Many good books and magazines can be found in your library on the subject of EW and more specifically EWSM and TAC SIGINT. For a real example we will turn to the summer of 1943, when the Luftwaffe introduced a devastatingly effective new weapon for use against capital ships: the FRITZ-X, a 3,000-pound armour-piercing bomb which could be guided by radio signals to its target.

Carried by Dornier 217s, the FRITZ-X scored its first success off Sardinia, on two Italian ships on their way to Malta to surrender. Two bombs struck the battleship ROMA, which sank with a heavy loss of life; another damaged her sister-ship, the ITALIA. During the week that followed, FRITZ-Xs inflicted severe damage on the British battleship WARSPITE, the cruiser UGANDA, and the US Cruiser SAVANNAH.

The initial Allied reaction was to provide fighter cover when their ships were within range of the Dorniers. But the FRITZ-X was vulnerable too, once its control frequencies were discovered using EWSM techniques. At first, allied ships used improvised jammers as an ECM reaction; later, they quickly developed a specialized jammer to counter the threat. After September 1943, the FRITZ-X achieved virtually no hits against allied vessels.

Today, Electronic Warfare cannot be left to improvisation and reaction to events weeks after they occur. "The Battle of the Beams" as Sir Winston Churchill called it, is more intense than ever, and the Intelligence Community plays a vital role.[1]

## 1986, Intelligence Personnel News

The following Int Branch personnel have been promoted: Col Victor V. Ashdown, 20 Jun 86; LCol Gordon S. Graham, 27 Jun 86; Maj Gary W. Beckman, 1 Jul 86; Maj Susan F. Beharriell, 1 May 86; Maj Brad N. Hall, 1 Jun 86; Maj Robert M. Parsons, 1 May 86; Maj D.H. Neil Thompson, 1 Jan 86; Lt

---

1.    Intelligence Branch Journal Number 2, 1986, pp. 18-19.

(N) Darren W. Knight, 1 Jan 86; Capt Jay G. Mercer, 1 May 86; and, Capt Harold A. Skaarup, 1 Jan 86.

CWO Jean G. Charette, 1 Jun 86; MWO William "Bill" J. Lindsay, 1 Jun 86; MWO J. Ron Martin, 16 Dec 85; MWO Barry W. Sweeney, 1 Jun 86; WO Hans J.G. Kroemer, 1 Jun 86; WO J.R. Claude Morin, 1 Jun 86; WO Dean E. Smith, 16 Dec 85; Sgt W.C. Campbell, 1 Jun 86; Sgt Jeff A. Collings, 1 Jun 86; Sgt Ed C. Denbeigh, 1 May 86; Sgt Henry E. Doucette, 14 May 86; Sgt J.J.P.M. Fournier, 1 Jun 86; Sgt R.G.G. Fournier, 1 May 86; Sgt J.J. Girard, 1 May 86; Sgt Dave D. Turner, 14 May 86; MCpl Rick M. Chaykowski, 1 Mar 86; MCpl P. Cost, 1 Mar 86; MCpl T.D.G. Graham, 1 Mar 86; MCpl Dave L. Howarth, 18 Apr 86; MCpl J.P.S. Knight, 1 Mar 86; MCpl Daryl W. Monk, 1 Mar 86; MCpl R.G. Oliver, 1 Mar 86; MCpl Alex D. Radzion, 1 Mar 86; MCpl Chuck J. Spillane, 1 Mar 86; and, MCpl J.RP. Turcotte, 16 Dec 85.

## 1986, Canadian Land Forces Command and Staff College Course

Capt J.A. Grant completed completed the CLFCSC course in June 1986, and Capt Greg W. Jensen completed completed the course in December 1986.

## 1986, Int Branch Activities and Development, Air Command Intelligence Policy

*General.* The planning and successful conduct of any military operation is largely dependent upon the provision of timely and accurate Intelligence. Air Command Intelligence staffs are to provide Intelligence required by commanders to enable them to carry out the varied missions assigned to them. The large number of missions that may be undertaken by Air Command requires that commanders and staffs at all levels plan for as many contingencies as possible.

Air Command Intelligence staffs at all levels must be prepared to provide both basic and current Intelligence as well as Intelligence advice to commanders during training and planning for contingency tasks. In addition, when required, Intelligence staffs must provide Combat Intelligence in the field during actual operations and training exercises.

*Aim.* The aim of this order is to outline Air Command policy on Intelligence requirements, procedures, capabilities and resources.

*Air Command* Intelligence Policy. The Air Command Intelligence Section will collect from appropriate agencies and disseminate as required information and Intelligence relating to those geographical areas where Air Command has a direct commitment or may have a future commitment.

The following factors are basic to the Air Command Intelligence policy:

Commanders of Units under command or operational control of Air Command will define their own Intelligence requirements based on their operational tasks. The resulting Intelligence requirements will be coordinated by the Air Command Headquarters Intelligence Section;

The Intelligence interest of Commanders and staffs will be considerably broader in scope during peace-time multiple tasking that during actual operations; and Because of the requirement for Intelligence support it is imperative that professional Intelligence organizations, capable of performing the whole range of Intelligence services, to be established and maintained at all levels with Air Command.

*Intelligence Priorities.* The highest priority task of an Intelligence Section is the maintenance of a basic foreign Intelligence data bank based on the Commander's areas of Intelligence interest and the provision of current Intelligence for those areas. The Air Command Intelligence Section will disseminate Intelligence information in order to facilitate normal planning by Air Command HQ staff and subordinate formation and Unit commanders and staff in support of their assigned operational roles.

Intelligence staffs are required to perform key functions during operations and exercises and Intelligence support during operation planning. These staffs are also employed carrying out a mixture of ongoing and short duration projects and any priority assigned to such tasks must be based on:

The type and content of the Unit Intelligence requirements as stated in the annual submission to AIRCOM/NDHQ/CIS;

The present assigned tasks of Air Command; and

The factors listed above as basic to the Air Command Intelligence policy.

Intelligence training of subordinate formation and Unit Intelligence staffs shall be given the highest priority. In general terms this will include contact, refresher and continuation training of personnel employed in Unit Intelligence sections and Intelligence related training of all ranks at formation and Unit level.

The collection, reporting and briefing system for information of an internal security nature within the scope of DND responsibilities is outlined in

NDHQ instruction. Security staff and not Intelligence staff will handle this information.

The above priorities apply to Air Command as a whole; however, there could be specific instances when priorities have to be reallocated due to international situation changes or other short-term taskings. In any case Intelligence training will continue to have the highest priority within formations and Units.

*Intelligence Requirements.* Changes in tasking priorities and changes of commanders cause variations in the Intelligence requirements of Air Command formations and Units. It is essential that these changes be identified to Air Command Headquarters so that action can be taken to meet new requirements. All Air Command formations and Units will review their Intelligence requirements annually and submit their needs to the Air Command Headquarters Intelligence Section for inclusion in the annual Air Command Statement of Intelligence Requirements to NDHQ/CIS. The formation/Unit commander is to personally approve each submission and forward it to Air Command Headquarters by 1 October each year.

Intelligence requirements will vary between formations and Units and it is imperative that no significant requirements are left unidentified. Formations and Units are to develop intelligence training of the type and scope required to support planning and operations for assigned tasks. Commanders are to ensure that all ranks receive Intelligence-related training on a regular basis. Intelligence training must include, but not be limited to: reporting of information; conduct after capture; handling of prisoners of war; air photo reading; task-related familiarization briefings; intelligence-related security; and equipment recognition training.

*Scope and Responsibilities.* The Air Command Headquarters Intelligence Section is responsible to the Commander Air Command for initiating, interpreting and monitoring of the Command's Intelligence plans, policies and procedures. Air Command Headquarters will coordinate all aspects of Intelligence within the Command and formations and Units shall not approach non-Air Command agencies without prior approval from Air Command HQ. This does not apply to the provision of operational Intelligence to 10 TAG by FMCHQ, to MAG by MARCOM/MARPAC or to FG by NORAD. The Air Command Intelligence Section responsibilities are outlined in broad scope and include:

a. the provision of Intelligence to the Commander regarding foreign and potential enemy capabilities against North America, NATO and other areas where Air Command resources could be employed;

b. maintaining an orderly and timely flow of Intelligence material and information to Air Command formations and Units to meet operational training requirements;

c. development and implementation of Air Command Intelligence policy; and,

d. staff assistance visits and operational evaluations of Air Command formation or Unit Intelligence section functions and capabilities.

The production of foreign Intelligence within Air Command must be centralized at this HQ. Air Command HQ staff with necessary assistance from NDHQ/CIS staff will disseminate as much foreign Intelligence as resources and security restrictions permit. This dissemination is intended to provide enough Intelligence automatically to enable formations or Units to make specific requests to fill any perceived missing information requirements. The program will consist of sending daily INTSUMs, periodic INTREPS, pertinent briefings, reports, estimates, studies and include replies to specific requests from formations or Units.

Air Command subordinate Intelligence sections should not attempt to maintain extensive files on countries other than those in which their formation has a direct interest due to current tasking. Generally, Intelligence sections should continue their information production to dissemination of finished Intelligence material received from Air Command HQ and to the preparation and delivery of briefings to their commander and staff. This should allow Intelligence staffs to concentrate on both professional advancement training and continuation training of non-Intelligence Unit personnel. Deficiencies in Intelligence training now being conducted within Air Command or in other commands for Air Command must be brought to the attention of this HQ. Air Command HQ is the sole authority for stating such deficiencies to NDHQ or CFSIS.

Within Air Command, formation and Unit Intelligence staffs may freely communicate with each other and with the Air Command Headquarters Intelligence Section in order to foster the free exchange of ideas, information and Intelligence estimates. Subjects having policy implications will be staffed through the appropriate chain of command to Air Command Headquarters prior to any final action being taken.

To ensure that the provision of Intelligence services is not jeopardized, personnel employed in Intelligence sections are not to be assigned any secondary duties, which could inhibit the performance of their Intelligence functions. This policy is not designed to restrict local commanders but to assist them in ensuring that their Intelligence staffs receive the maximum degree of training and practical experience. Dedicated Intelligence personnel are not to be employed as operations staffs, administrative staffs, COMSEC inventory holders, historical diary keepers, mess steward, projectionist, duty driver, runner, escort, sentry, or in other non-Intelligence related duties. The employment of subordinate Intelligence staffs will be a prime item of review during operational evaluations and staff inspections by subordinate formations or Air Command Headquarters.

*Intelligence Standardization.* NATO nations have collaborated in the development of standardization agreements (STANAG). Certain of these agreements cover Intelligence planning and procedures in NATO. Air Command Intelligence staff will follow the direction and guidance provided by appropriate STANAGs and other operational agreements when functioning directly within NATO.[2]

## 1986, Chapitre Saguenéen, Int Branch Personnel at CFB Bagotville
## Article by Capt J.P. André Tremblay

Capt J.P. André Tremblay reported on the activities of Int Branch personnel at CFB Bagotville, Quebec, and the reason for their presence on the Base. Bagotville is an Airbase located in the Saguenay-La St Jean valley, 240 km north of Quebec City. Its primary roles are to support two squadrons, a rescue flight and a Technician Training School for helicopter maintenance. The Int Branch personnel include: Base, Sgt Joe V. Million; 433 Sqn/433e ETAC, Capt J.P. André Tremblay, WO J.G. Berrigan, Sgt Jean Guy .H.E. Martineau, Sgt J.P. Bissonette & MCpl J.R. Marc A. Paradis; 425 Sqn, Lt J.R.R.R. Sylvain Robidoux, Sgt J.O. "Rick" Limoges, MCpl Manuel A. Thibault, and Cpl R.G. Oliver.

Sgt Joe V. Million, at Base level, is responsible for providing strategic military Intelligence to the Base Commander and his staff so they can carry out

---

2.    Intelligence Branch Journal Number 2, 1986, pp.7-8.

their missions and maintain the Base roles. He is presently in the process of establishing a dissemination program for the base at all levels, which will touch many people on the Base.

433 Sqn/433e ETAC is a Tactical Fighter Sqn equipped with the CF-5A Freedom Fighter. Its primary role is to participate within the NATO family to defend the European Northern Flank in Norway, where the Sqn deploys approximately twice a year. Its secondary role is to provide fire support and reconnaissance for ground forces on exercise. The section is involved with mission planning and a training program for the pilots. All this is done without neglecting the collation, interpretation, and dissemination of "Intelligence." The training program is a continuing effort that includes the creation of scenarios, recognition training of enemy equipment, and maintaining an aerial recce role. From February, 433 Sqn/433e ETAC had begun its conversion phase from CF-5A to CF-18 Hornet. In the summer of 1986, apart from two Int Ops, all the section personnel will be posted; to be replaced only in the summer of 1987 to prepare for the squadron taking up its operational roles in December the same year.

425 Sqn is an Air Defence Sqn working in coordination with NORAD to defend Canada's airspace. The Int Section at 425 Sqn was formed in the summer of 1985 and is predominantly occupied with briefing and debriefing missions. They also follow a training program similar to 433 Sqn/433e ETAC and the section manages daily manages daily Intelligence requirements that are necessary to the Squadron's mission.[3]

## From the Intelligence Branch Advisor, LCol David M. Robb

I am very pleased to have the opportunity as your new Branch Advisor to include this "state of the union" editorial in our Intelligence Branch Journal. As was the case with my predecessor, I value it as a means to keep you abreast of significant Branch developments and to highlight certain items, which are important to all of us. The time and effort required to ensure the regular publication of such a Journal is indeed considerable, and I would like to express my appreciation to the editor, MWO J.R. Ray LeCavalier, for making this possible.

---

3.　Intelligence Branch Journal Number 2, 1986, pp. 15-17.

It is gratifying to report that the Intelligence Branch continues to be in demand at all levels of the Canadian Forces and in all three environments. The efforts of all of our serving members, both Regular and Reserve, are in large part responsible for this high profile posture and I commend you on your dedication. Further, the Branch has made great strides towards resolving many of the contentious issues of policy which come as part of the bag and baggage of a fledgling organization. I would like to acknowledge the sagacity and leadership of my predecessor, Col George L.R. Bruce, and the practical advice of our former Branch CWO, CWO Fred L. Juett, as being essential elements in this achievement.

In the last issue, my predecessor observed on the number of promotions in the Branch this year. Complimentary to this, we have had a number of new positions accrue to us, including a Capt at NORAD HQ, Colorado Springs, a Major as CFLO at the US Army Intelligence Center and School, Fort Huachuca, Arizona, a Major with the AFCENT Collection Management cell and a major with the recently established Chief of Review Services, NDHQ. At the time of writing, I expect that final approval will be granted for four more Capts in the DG Int Division of CIS. I am also advised that ECO action has been taken to harden those Brigade SO3 Int posts in Canada, which were previously annotated for other MOCs. Finally, although the position has been established for some time, this was the first year that we were able to provide an SSO Int at Air Command HQ Winnipeg, in the person of Maj Susan F. Beharriell.

Lest I appear to dwell excessively on new officer positions, it is because the number of new Int Op posts has so far not kept pace with the rapid increase in officer vacancies. This trend is however, I expect, a temporary one as I am counting on our officers to examine closely the Intelligence function at each of these new locations and to press for the Int Op positions required to make things work as they should. As said many times before, Intelligence is a commodity that sells itself if tailored to the Commander's needs and delivered professionally. The consequent demand for more and better product should thus be used to secure the necessary infrastructure, including personnel, required for the task.

As mentioned earlier, the Branch continues to grow in numbers and despite the demands upon us for more positions, we have so far managed to keep up fairly well. The requirement for new Int Ops and Int Officers to replace losses of various types will however, continue, and I encourage all of you to actively recruit those CF members who appear to be interested and suitable to join our ranks. It is only by having a reasonably large inventory of applicants from which to choose that we will be able to maintain the standard of the Branch that we and those whom we serve have set for ourselves. On this note, I would like to mention that, keeping step with CF policy, the Branch will be seeking 90 percent of its officers from those holding University degrees. For our Int Ops, we will continue to seek out the most qualified candidates from those remuster applicants who come to our attention, and are particularly looking to recruit bilingual Francophone members to the Branch.

While the Intelligence Branch has included a number of females as officers for some time, the Int Op trade has until recently been closed to them. This has now been changed by the ruling that both Int 82 and Int Op 111 have been designated as minimum male component MOCs. No ceiling for females in either has yet been promulgated; it would be premature on our part to open up the Int Op trade on a wholesale basis at this time. I do believe however, that this development will allow us to select female candidates in competition with their male peers so as to employ the best of both, to the betterment of the whole Branch. In anticipation of this, I have asked the Branch CWO to seek advice from Commands as to which Int Op positions they consider suitable for members of either sex.

Although Col George L.R. Bruce previously addressed the issue, I would like to highlight my views on Branch Unity. As we grow nearer to the time when separate environmental uniforms will be taken into wear, the challenge to our sense of Branch identity becomes all the more acute. Although a strong case was put to the CF Uniform Committee for the retention of the midnight blue mess kit by all support classifications including Intelligence, this appeal was rejected and we were directed to adopt mess kits of all three environments. Intelligence Branch members will therefore be wearing three different uniforms, for all orders of dress and unless we make conscious effort to remember that we are members of a unified Branch, we could be at risk of devolving into three separate organizations. To guard against this, it will remain Branch policy that our members be cross-employed in environments other than which they have been assigned. This in itself however, will not be sufficient to preserve our cohesion, and it will be incumbent upon all of us to actively maintain our ties to the Branch and not ourselves to be drawn into the inter-environmental confrontations, which occur on occasion.

In closing, I think you can see that the Branch is continuing to grow and expand into new areas of activity. This fact, however, is a mixed blessing and will require active participation on your part to seek out new members for our

Branch and to maintain your links with your comrades serving in other environments. If we can achieve this, and successfully pass through this period of turbulence and transition, we will be in an even better position in the years ahead. In anticipation of success in these objectives, I wish all of you and your families the best wishes for the holiday season and a Happy New Year.[4]

## *1986, Branch Activities and Development—Professional Intelligence in Our Navy?*
## *Article by Lt (N) Darren W. Knight*

Which came first, the chicken or the egg? The dilemma is an ancient one that has never quite been solved. How about this one: Is the Navy going to ask for professional Intelligence personnel to fill more of their naval Intelligence billets, or is the Intelligence Branch going to have to prove to the Navy that they need more of what our branch has to offer? Not as simply stated as the chicken or the egg parable, but still a dilemma. The difference between the two is that the Intelligence Branch is in a position to solve the naval Intelligence dilemma if it chooses to make the effort.

We are infants at the dawn of the information age. The computer and associated technologies have sprung up around us and left us struggling to keep up with a volume of information greater than we could previously imagine. Concurrent with the rise of computers has been the increase in sophistication of weaponry and war-fighting capability. Modernization, specialization, and team integration have become the keys to success. People in the operational branches are starting to realize that Intelligence is no longer a secondary duty, but a full-time profession—a valuable part of a good team. For some reason it seems the Navy has been slow to catch on to this. Navies are reputed to be very conservative organizations, but they have also bee surprisingly innovative from time to time. When our Navy sees it can get the kind of solid, timely, professional Intelligence it needs, then no doubt they will demand it. When that time comes, as it surely must, the Intelligence Branch must be ready to meet the requirement. In the mean time, the "Branch" should be working to convince the Navy that this is the right route to follow. We are selling the product—the onus is on us to make it attractive, effective, and available.

---

4.    Intelligence Branch Journal Number 3, 1986, pp. 2-3.

We are a tri-service branch, a fact that will be difficult to hide when we are all in distinctive uniforms. As such, we have a responsibility to each service to provide the best support we possibly can. We have a relatively small number of "Naval" Intelligence personnel who are constantly being told that the Navy wants little or nothing to do with the "Branch." If this is so then it could be our fault for not providing the right product or not selling it hard enough. This brings us back to the chicken or the egg: We cannot afford to train and dedicate people for a Navy that does not want our services, yet the Navy refuses our services because we do not have enough well-trained people to replace the existing system. Of course the Navy is protecting their own REMAR positions, but they do have a point. Unless the "Branch" can prove to the Navy that we can offer something better than they already have, why should they be asking for more of us? The answer for the "Branch" is to find ways to train our people in disciplines required by the Navy, make ourselves indispensable, and let the Navy know it.

With respect to training, I am referring to the following areas:

*Acoustics.* In an ASW Navy, we must know the language and the Intelligence requirements for this art.

*Computer Training.* Officers and Int Ops alike must receive training in computer applications to the Intelligence cycle, not just for Naval purposes, but also for all environments. If we do not accept the computer and use it to our advantage, it could eventually replace us in many of our functions. The Navy has created an officer sub-specialty just for computer work.

*At-Sea Employment.* The Navy does have a sea-going Intelligence requirement from time to time. Intelligence personnel should be part of augmentation teams. There are many shore stations and organizations that can aid us in training for this mission. We already fulfill a similar role with our Unit in Kingston, so why should it not be our business elsewhere?

Language Training. The Navy gets close to the threat on a regular basis. We have access to good language training programs and have many trained personnel, so why don't we get involved?

*Tactical Training.* Our people must have a good grounding in naval tactics, not so they can do the operator's jobs, but so they can interpret threat tactics in a manner operators relate to. There is not reason Intelligence personnel cannot participate in at least portions of courses such as the CCO course.

*Exchanges.* The USN has a corps of professional Intelligence personnel from which we can learn a great deal. Operational or training exchanges would help us fill short-term requirements and allow us to better design our own training for the long-term.

*Post Graduate Training.* This training is available to officers and can be of great value to the "Branch." On the naval side the USN degree in "Naval Intelligence" would not only have a practical use, but would also be a good ticket to prove we have something our Navy does not.

In no way would any of this training threaten Branch Unity, no more than the "Foxhole U" does. The goal is simply to get a better foothold in the Navy so that our personnel can find reasonable career progression if they wear a Navy uniform. If we can get some positions for senior officers then we will improve career progression and enhance on-the-job training for NCOs and junior officers. If we can establish a presence onboard HMC ships our credibility can only improve, and we will have a true tri-service image. Why shouldn't the MARCOM/MARPAC SSOs INT and the head of the new DDI Navy Shop be Intelligence Branch officers? We should be content with nothing less and even push further for a position as part of an afloat staff. However, nothing is free, so we will have to work very hard to prove we are worthy.

All other considerations aside, our "Branch" must remember that it is our duty to give the best service we possibly can to each of the three services. If we don't take steps to provide it for the Navy, they will turn elsewhere.

(The Int Journal Editor commented: This article has been written to take advantage of the unique forum for discussion provided by the Intelligence Branch Journal and is not intended to represent or criticize current Branch policy. It is further realized that some of the solutions proposed may not be practicable, at least for the time being. The concerns expressed are however, of significant import to both the Branch and the Navy, and it is hoped that this article will promote initiatives which will see us contributing more fully to the Naval Intelligence function).[5]

## 1986, Intelligence Personnel News

The third Annual Intelligence Branch Workshop was held at Canadian Forces Headquarters Europe, Lahr, Germany, 4-5 May 1986. Many Int Branch members flew in from Canada via Ramstein to participate. Those in attendance included Col George L.R. Bruce, Maj Gordon S. Graham, Lt (N)

5. Intelligence Branch Journal Number 3, 1986, pp. 7-8.

Frank W. Keating, MWO Jean G. Charette, Maj John H. Newman, CWO Barry Toomer, Cdr Christopher S. Hordal, CWO Fred L. Juett, LCol K.J. Radley, Capt Pat A. Renaud, Maj Ray J. Taylor, LCol David M. Robb, Maj K.A.W. Peter Mackenzie, Capt Alex C. Chambers, LCol Darcy J. Beatty, and LCol Paul F. O'Leary.[6]

The following Int Branch Personnel have been promoted: Capt Fred L. Juett, Oct 86; Capt J. Kent Peebles, May 86; Capt Andrea L. Siew, Mar 86; Lt Ed C. Denbeigh, Sep 86; Lt J.P.S. Knight, Sept 86.

WO J.P.R. Goguen, Jul 86; WO Armado Santos, Aug 86; WO W. Ken Spike, Aug 86; Sgt Tim G. Armstrong, Jul 86; Sgt Lynn J. Brooks, Jul 86; Sgt Jack G.W. Campbell, Jul 86; Sgt D. Garry Kohinski, Oct 86; Sgt M.B. Mahoney, Jul 86; Sgt J. Pierre Murret-Labarthe, Jul 86; Sgt J.R. Marc A. Paradis, Aug 86; Sgt Dean B. Smith, Aug 86; MCpl J.D. Bouchard, Aug 86; MCpl J.R. Michel "Mike" Labossiere, Aug 86; MCpl Eric P. Grehan, Aug 86; MCpl Nick R. Procenko, Aug 86; and, MCpl R.K.H. Wood, Aug 86.

The following have been released or retired: Col George L.R. Bruce; Capt A.W. Catherwood; MWO R.A.T. Hawkins, Mar 86; MWO Mervin B. Michener, Jul 86; Sgt R.J. Herman, Mar 86; and, Cpl R.O. Hill, Apr 86.

The following have remustered to the Int Branch: Capt Rhe Ap Probert, Inf; Capt J. Michel Bédard, Inf; Capt Ward A. Sweet, Inf; Lt Wes B. von Papineau, Reserve Int; and, 2Lt Chione M.B. Hughes, Reserve Comm.[7]

Capt Rhe Ap Probert was recently awarded the CDS Commendation for exceptional service in Beirut, Lebanon with UNTSO. On behalf of the CDS, BGen Jim Hansen, the Base Commander CFB Borden, presented the clasp to Capt Rhe Ap Probert while he was undergoing Intelligence Classification training at CFSIS on BIOC 8701.[8]

## *1986, FMC*

The 1986 FMC Intelligence Section included Sgt William E. Hamilton, Sgt Robert W. Moug, MCpl J.RP. Turcotte, MCpl Don B. Powers, Sgt J. Michael Poulin, MCpl Ron K. Townsend, Mme Cerutti, WO Mike V. Marsh, Maj A. George Johnstone, LCol Paul F. O'Leary, Maj Donald H. Neil Thompson, WO Jean Pierre Caron.

---

6.  Intelligence Branch Journal Number 3, 1986, pp. 8-9.
7.  Intelligence Branch Journal Number 3, 1986, p. 23.
8.  Intelligence Branch Journal Number 4, Spring 1987, p. 11.

# *1986, CFSIS*

Participants in the Reserve Intelligence Operator TQ4 Course 8601 included MCpl Wes E.B. Young, WO J.M. Lauzière, MCpl R. Cipro, Sgt Dave J. Bruton, and Capt Clark J. Beamish.

Participants in the Reserve Intelligence Officer Block 4 Course 8601 included 2Lt Jason, 2Lt A.F. Berdais, 2Lt S.I. Squire, Capt (W) MacGarin, and 2Lt.

Participants in the Reserve Intelligence Officer Block 5 Course 8601 included 2Lt A.F. Berdais, 2Lt Jason, OCdt Colin A.J. Kiley, 2Lt S.I. Squire, 2Lt J.A.E. Kent Dowell, Sgt Dave J. Bruton, 2Lt J.L. François Messier, Capt Clark J. Beamish, MWO E.M. Dziepak.

Participants in the Reserve Intelligence Officer Block 9 Course 8601 included Maj James L. Downey, 2Lt Kostas P. Rimsa, Sgt Dave J. Bruton, Lt S.L. Bullock, and Maj Brad N. Hall.

1986 Intelligence Operator 6B Course 8601
Rear Row: WO Ivo J.M. Schoots, WO Arthur E.B. "Bert" O'Brien, WO
Rick M. Milne.
Centre Row: WO Robert A. Lavalle, WO Phil R. Berikoff, WO W. "Bill"
Goodland, WO Jim R. Fysh, WO J. Charles Cotton.
Front Row: WO Art E. Sibley, MWO Rick A. Mader, Maj John H. New-
man, Capt Ivan J. Ciuciura, WO Carl R. Keenan.

## 1986, CISA Member News

Col George L.R. Bruce retired as the Int Branch Advisor in order to study for
the Anglican priesthood. Capt Margaret R. Prentis moved from her post on
the Canadian Import Tribunal in Ottawa to Queen's University in Kingston
to work in the Economics Department. She also vacated her appointment as
Treasurer of the Conference of Defence Associations—the first from Intelligence or Security, and the first woman to have served on CDA's executive.

LCol George Wilkinson, LCol Reg F. Bornor, Lt J.T.A. Wilson and 2Lt David H. Schimmelpenninck van der Oye are mentioned along with Capt Carl Ian Walker, LCol Robert H. "Tex" Noble and C Int C "original" Honorary Col George B. MacGillivray. Capt Harold A. Skaarup, the new Regt Int O with the Canadian Airborne Regiment is off to Cyprus for six months. Maj Al A. Bell-Chambers, the Provost Marshal at Nicosia, Cyprus, reported on the signs of spring approaching on the island and noted it must be time to pay his CISA membership dues.[9]

## 1986-1987, UN Duty in Cyprus with the Canadian Airborne Regiment

The author had been working as an Intelligence Analyst in DDI-6 covering the Russian Far Eastern Military Districts when he was promoted to Capt on 1 Jan 1986. Having a set of jump wings may have been a factor in the posting to the Canadian Airborne Regiment (CAR) at CFB Petawawa as the Regimental Intelligence Officer on 16 June 1986. The CAR was part of the Special Service Force (SSF), and the Regiment's Intelligence Section came under the unit's HQ and Signals Squadron. The author had the privilege of serving with the CAR until July 1989.

Shortly after his arrival in Petawawa, the author was handed a message which read, in part, "you are hereby warned for United Nations Duty, OP SNOWGOOSE, Cyprus, etc." The notice was short, as the author was flown out of Ottawa to Germany within a few weeks, and he arrived in Larnaca, Cyprus on 19 Aug 1986 after a six-hour C-130 Hercules flight from Lahr. The author replaced the RCR Int O who had to return to Canada early, and thus found himself serving under Col James Cox, who has contributed a number of articles on the Int Branch history to this project. The author remained in theatre when the RCR was rotated out and replaced by the Canadian Airborne Regiment under the command of Col J.J.M.R. Gaudreau.

Nicosia was a one-hour drive north of Larnaca, and since it was August, the author found the ancient city to be hot, congested and very interesting, much like Athens. The author was billeted in the Ledra Palace, a partially damaged hotel located in the centre of the green line downtown and between the Turkish and Greek belligerent factions. The tour stated off with an abrupt "stand-to" as there was a flare-up over movement of flags and markers at a site

---

9.    CISA Newsletter, Vol. 17, No. 2, August 1986, pp. 1-2.

called "Beaver Lodge." One side moved markers forward, the Canadians moved them back, guns were pointed and people became agitated. The situation was resolved after some tense interaction between RCR officers and their counterparts to the north.

The UN was intensely adverse to the use of anything having to do with military intelligence. The author, therefore, was the Ops B Information Officer (Ops B IO), Canadian Airborne Regiment, Nicosia, Cyprus (CCUN-FICYP). During his handover with the members of the RCR Ops B Information Section, the author visited the "Blue Beret Camp" (BBC), and was shown the ground from West to East on the island in the buffer zone between the Greeks and the Turks. The enormous waste and destruction of buildings and property in the zone had changed little since the war following the Turkish invasion of the northern part of the island in response to Greek declarations in 1974. Capt Tim A. Larson, who had been the Airborne IO before handing over to the author, was also serving in Cyprus, but on the one-year accompanied tour at Blue Beret Camp.

The author took part in routine morning briefings to the CO and his staff, and participated in meetings with other UN Ops B Information representatives. In August he was taken across the Turkish line in an Iltis by WO Gilmore, the RCR Int WO, to attend a UN Ops B Info Conference in the Austrian Contingent's Camp based near Famagusta, a large old Venetian walled city and fortress sited on the East coast of the Island. WO Gilmore then took the author South through the Sovereign Base Area (SBA) that belongs to the UK, and on down to Larnaca along the coast, passing through several Greek, UN, and Turkish checkpoints. The Swedish guards at these checkpoints put on a spectacular salute twirling their rifles high in the air as they drove back to Nicosia for the 5 PM briefing.

During the Turk-Canadian confrontation, later referred to as the "Beaver Lodge" incident which took place on 22 Aug 86, the author was flown on a reconnaissance flight over Sector 4, Nicosia in a British Alouette helicopter to get an overhead view of the situation. The RCR CO expected an interesting and perhaps difficult day, with a crisis on the line over a change to the status quo boundaries. The situation calmed down after a great deal of discussion. The following day, the Ops B team went on a patrol in an Iltis with a Recce team to Kyrenia via the NW route through the mountains. Several Turk sentries waved, some saluted, but one pointed his rifle at them, which was interesting. In the evening the unit held a dining-in at the mess with General

Douglas Yuill, who was at that time Canada's Military representative in Damascus, Syria, and an active CISA member.

In spite of a great deal of negotiation and talk, the confrontation on the Green Line in the Canadian Sector continued to fester, forcing the RCR's Col James Cox to put the Turks on the defensive again after they decided to push their luck on 28 Aug. Armed Canadian soldiers reoccupied the Beaver Lodge site, and shortly afterwards, the Turkish Commander agreed to remove the Turk flags from the Canadian position. Shortly afterwards, the vanguard of the CAR began to arrive in theatre. Tension was still high on the Greek side of the line, and following a conference at BBC on 4 Sep, the author and WO Dean J. Dunlop, drove over to observe a Greek Union rally at the PEO building in downtown Nicosia, then back to the Joint Operations Centre. MCpl Chuck J. Spillane and MCpl Rick G. Oliver, and the author also participated in a recce West to the Astromeritis Gate, up to Morphou and then West to DANCON HQ and Liminitis.

In September, the British Contingent sent a representative from the "Red Devils" to coordinate a number of UN jumpers for the British Medals parade. The author represented Canada. When the other countries declined to participate, it was determined that all jumpers would become "Red Devils" and thus the author donned their uniform & parachute equipment, very much reminding him of his "Skyhawk" days. The team made five practice jumps from an HC-5 Wessex helicopter at BBC, but also had one emergency landing with the helicopter. There is something unsettling about being in a hovering helicopter and seeing smoke emanating from the instrument panel, but the machine was duly landed intact and the problem was "fixed." Shortly after the repair, the group went back into the air for the show, where the author had the honour of jumping into the parade flying the Canadian flag.

Also in September, the CAR Acorns took part in an Ops/Info conference in Sector 2 HQ at the UK Contingent's St David's Camp, with representatives attending from the Swedish, Danish, Austrian, British, Australian and Canadian contingents. In October, the conference took place at DANCON HQ's "Viking Camp," located at the West end of the island's buffer zone. The Danes took their visitors out to Kokkina, on the other side of a Turkish held enclave separated from the North, in a Greek area. The UN Commander, Canada's BGen MacInnes, flew in via Alouette helicopter to brief the group on points of concern. Capt Tim A. Larson, WO Dean J. Dunlop, WO Mike E. Higgins and the author represented the Canadian Contingent. In December, Ops/Info conference was held at BBC. Afterwards the group visited FIN-

CON with the Finnlanders and Austrians, and were invited to enjoy their sauna. While we were enjoying the sauna, members from the Swedish contingent swiped everyone's clothing, then had their UN police order us out of the hut by loudhailer for not having our identification cards. There were a few unhappy campers over the incident.

On 6 Dec 86, BGen Ford from the UK Int Corps visited the CAR for a line tour. Unfortunately, this day the Regiment lost a soldier when MCpl Mark MacRae was killed in a climbing accident while touring St Hilarion castle. The evening was a sombre one for the contingent, as every soldier is well known to each other. The Regimental Chaplain, Capt Reg Gilbert, spoke to everyone in the HQ and Signals Sqn about the accident.

Early in January the author took part in another Alouette helicopter recce flight over the Sector 4 area of the Buffer Zone, with Capt Randy Kemp and Capt Mike Beaudette to check on Turk construction activity. WO Dean J. Dunlop and the author participated in an Ops B Conference at Camp Duke Leopold V, AUSCON, near Famagusta, and then later in January visited DANCON and Camp Xeros for another conference. On 19 Jan 87, BGen Douglas Yuill, the CFA in Lebanon, gave the Canadians a brief on events across the water from Cyprus.

Although the end of the tour seemed to take its time in coming, the author turned in his 9 mm pistol at BBC on 24 Feb 87. Shortly afterwards, he and his chalk cleared customs and boarded a bus for the trip to Larnaca and marched straight onto the B-707. As the aircraft lifted off the island from Larnaca headed for Lahr, everyone onboard cheered. After a 1½-hour stop in Lahr, the cheer was even louder when the aircraft lifted off for the second time and headed back to Canada, and home.

## 1986, CISA AGM

The CISA AGM took place at Longue Pointe, on 18-20 Sep 1986. Present were: LCol A.G. Cameron, Col Robert T. Grogan, LCol William "Bill" Tenhaaf, LCol Jack S. Dunn, Maj Marie Louise "Tony" Guyon, Lt E. Bruce Holmes, Capt James "Jim" P.K. Van Wynen, Maj Merrick K. Szulc, Maj William "Bill" L. Watt, Capt Peter T. Patton, Maj Terry B. Kelly, Col Jeff S. Upton, Maj Sherman R. Veinotte, Maj Robert C. Dale, Maj J.H. Mansfield, Maj Elaine E. Mellor, Maj Wilf S. Puffer, Maj Fred E.G. Jones, Maj Nils E. Lindberg, Capt David A. Rubin, LCol Paul F. O'Leary, Maj A. George Johnstone, Capt P.W. Clare Lagerquist, LCol Al R. Wells, Maj John H.

Newman, Capt Chuck C. Bamlett, LCol Dale M. Watts, Maj Gordon R.B. Panchuk, Capt Carl R. Delaney, Cdr Christopher S. Hordal, LCol Ed D. Sanford, Lt G. Piper, Maj P. Clouthier, MGen C. William "Bill" Hewson, LCol David M. Robb, Col A.H. Sam Stevenson, 2Lt J.A.E. Kent Dowell, Maj Franz F. Laizner, Maj Richard J. Vella, Capt J.R. Sparling, Maj P. Denis Pelletier, Capt Gary W. Handson, LCol Pierre J.F. Couture, Capt M.A. Kulba, LCol Emile Berger, 2Lt Paul R. Perchaluk, Capt Charles Hillman, Lt William "Bill" B. Iler, BGen P. Boucher, Lt John M. Heinrichs, and Maj John "Pappy" MacKinnon (Secretary).[10]

President LCol William "Bill" Tenhaaf reported Maj Raymond S. Shelley, Maj Murray Paulin and Maj Gordie Huff had passed away during the past year. Maj Cyril Nelson "Bud" Cowan of the Security Branch passed away on 8 Nov 1986. Col the Honourable Peter E.R. Wright, the last Colonel Commandant of the C Int C, a retired judge of the Supreme Court of Ontario, and an Honorary Life Member of CISA, died in Toronto on 26 Nov 86.

LCol William "Bill" Tenhaaf reported on the meeting of the Executive Council of the CDA in Ottawa at which a number of resolutions were passed, including one for a definition of the defence mandate; a position paper calling for the Government to more publicly support the Militia; and, a resolution calling for a more visible assertion of sovereignty in the Arctic. Other resolutions included the raising of the paid ceiling of Primary Reserve Units; insurance for reserves; a more active approach to industrial preparedness; overcoming delays in enrolment; increasing the enrolment of females in Militia Intelligence, logistics and communications Units; an increase in compensation in accordance with the Reserve Force Compensation Study completed in 1985; and, a call on the Government to stay the implementation of a policy recommending females for combat trades and the enrolment of aged, handicapped and homosexual persons in the Forces. The AGM for the CDA in Feb 1987 will be the 50th.

The Regular Forces are receiving some financial support and improvements, including: search and rescue equipment (SARSAT); updating of the Tribal Class Destroyers; the marriage of civil air search and rescue resources to that of DND; and, an early warning system for ships and an air defence system. The Northern Europe Exercise finally involved 5,500 soldiers.

---

10.   CISA Newsletter, Vol. 17, No. 3, December 1986, p. 1.

The CISA proposed the following resolution for presentation to the Jan 87 CDA AGM: "That the percentage of female personnel in Int work remain at the present level in the Reserves...unless there is a change in the policy on employment of women in Int work in the Canadian Forces. The proposal was carried.

Maj J.H. Mansfield became the new CISA President. The winner of the 1986 CISA Academic Award is Kristine Dawn Hensel.[11]

## From the Intelligence Branch Advisor, LCol David M.Robb

Since last writing to you in this column, there have been a number of developments on which I would like to comment. In December 1986, the candidates of the first Int Op TQ6B course at CFSIS, CFB Borden, elected to purchase a trophy to be awarded to the top candidate of future course serials. This prize, named the MWO Dick Bushe Memorial Trophy, will commemorate the service and professionalism of our comrade who was so tragically taken from us in a traffic accident during the summer of 1985. On your behalf, I took it upon myself to write Mrs. Bushe and provide her with photographs, both of the first TQ6B course candidates and the trophy itself. Her reply:

"Dear LCol Robb,

I should like to thank you for your letter and the two photos you enclosed of the trophy in honour of Richard's memory. I was deeply touched to know the high regard in which my husband was held by everyone who knew him, and I really appreciated your taking the time to write and let me know about it, and to thank all the people who contributed towards the design and the award of such a trophy.

The tribute you pay him makes me realize just how much he had contributed towards his living a successful life, in his career as well as his personal life. It is comforting to know that he has made such a significant contribution.

Yours sincerely, Dinah Bushe."

---

11.   CISA Newsletter, Vol. 17, No. 3, December 1986, pp. 1-6.

More recently, you were all informed of the decision to remove branch collar dogs from wear with the new Air Force and Naval environmental uniforms. This development was of great concern to me, as it represented yet another step in the growing pressures to de-unify the support branches. We have tried to partially compensate for this loss by submitting for approval an Intelligence occupational badge for wear by naval NCMs, and FMC is developing a similar trade badge for Sgts, MCpls and Cpls of the Army. In each case, the central device will be the Branch star, which has now progressed to the point where it is generally accepted as the functional symbol of Intelligence in the CF.

One problem, which I hesitate to mention, but which I nonetheless feel requires comment is our propensity to engage in gossip and rumour-mongering. While an active interest in Branch affairs is certainly encouraged, unchecked rumours often cause confusion and unnecessary tension, which can demoralize our members. I have therefore opted to use the vehicle of our Branch AIG 1883, in addition to this forum, to pass on to you developments which I believe are of general interest to our members. I trust that regular use of this measure will serve to keep you better informed, as well as scotch many of the more wild rumours in circulation for which you may be seeking confirmation.

I should at this point remind you that in almost all of the CF major commands there is now a senior Intelligence officer with whom my office communicates frequently. If you have some question or concern regarding Branch matters, which you cannot resolve locally, I would encourage you to use the technical chain of command to consult with that officer. Her or she should be able to provide you with the needed answer on the spot, or else seek direction from me, as I am only a telephone call away.

In the last issue of the Journal, I noted that it would be Branch policy to put a premium on those reclassification applicants holding degrees. In concert with this general emphasis on higher academic profile within the CF, DPED has been conducting a study into the degree requirements of the various classifications. You may be interested to know that while the right percentage of Intelligence Branch officers now possesses degrees, the mix of degree specialization is generally out of tune with the requirement. To redress this imbalance and for the guidance of those seeking to be officers in our Branch, I believe that for the foreseeable future, we will have to place emphasis on the following degree programs: Soviet and East European studies; Middle East/Islamic studies; and General Science. Related to the first two is also the requirement for foreign language capability, which has been allowed to decline over the post-war years. We at the Branch office are looking into means by which we can rectify this deficiency among our current members, as well as the question of advanced training, but this will in no way reduce our search for new candidates with the foregoing qualifications.

Regarding officer career progression, I would like to reiterate some points emphasized on numerous occasions by PCO/INT. OPDP is a prerequisite for Staff College Toronto, and CFCSC in my opinion is a prerequisite for advancement beyond Major in our Branch. For those officers designated as Army, FOE and CLFCSC Kingston are intermediate steps, which also have to be mastered in order to reach the top.

For the guidance of our NCMs, I understand that there is some discussion as to whether it is better to take steps to upgrade your education or to under-take the OPDP program in order to gain merit board credits. At the risk of second-guessing the merit board, my counsel would be to go for the academic upgrading first. Depending on what you now hold, this will increase your potential points for promotion and if you pursue your formal education beyond senior matriculation, it could well open the door to the possibility of commissioning through UTPM or the Special Commissioning Plan. OPDP on the other hand may be nice to have but does not in my opinion confer a particular benefit to the NCM.

By now you will have heard that CIS has adopted a new organization with two Divisions: DG Int and DG Secur. DG Int retains DDI, DSTI, DISA and PPC, but now includes Director of Current Intelligence (formerly DDI 5), and Director of Imagery Exploitation (formerly DDI-6). DDI sections have been renumbered and CIS OP&T has been renamed Director Intelligence Plans and Doctrine. These changes, recommended by the 1983 OSMER, call for an increase in personnel subject to the availability of accru-als. For this fiscal year, DG Int has been allotted 16 Int positions from Cpl to Maj rank and I regard this as a very significant increase in view of the overall scarcity of personnel. In addition to these positions, we now have another Capt at NORAD HQ, a Capt at NORAD in Alaska, a Capt as instructor and RPV Trial Officer at CTC, CFB Gagetown, a Capt at CFCC HQ, Ottawa, and a Capt upgraded to Maj at FMC HQ. It is evident that the Branch has not yet ceased its recent pattern of growth.

Our Reserves are also making significant progress. There are now three reserve officers serving on Class C contracts in DG Int, and one of them has taken on the duties of Intelligence Branch Association Secretary. The Militia officer/NCM specifications are being rewritten along with the associated Course Training Standards so as to support the mobilization specifications and the MITCP 85 program. Efforts to recruit and train Intelligence personnel for the Reserve Electronic Warfare Squadron in Kingston are also underway. Having heard the Minister's address to the Conference of Defence Associations in January, I anticipate even further growth for the Reserves following the publication of the Defence White Paper.

Despite these increases, however, I hope that you will have appreciated from my prior comments that even as we grow larger, progression in our Branch will become more competitive. Those who reach the top will not only be solid performers with a wide variety of functional experiences but will also have taken the initiative to improve their potential profile through military and academic upgrading. We are now on a course to build a bigger and better Intelligence Branch so that all may recognize us as the undisputed experts of the CF Intelligence function. I invite all of you to join with me in this great purpose.[12]

---

12. Intelligence Branch Journal Number 4, Spring 1987, pp. 2-3.

## 1986, FMC *Intelligence Branch* Workshop

FMC Intelligence Workshop, October 1986
Rear Row: Capt G. Grant, Sgt N.L. Gordon, Lt J.A.E. Kent Dowell, WO
J.M. Lauzière, Sgt Ed J. Granger, Sgt Gary E. Fox, Sgt Herb C. Bond,
Capt Brian E. Hamilton, WO Rick M. Milne.
Centre Row: WO Ivo J.M. Schoots, MWO Barry M. Gardner, WO W.
"Bill" Goodland, Sgt Dave J. Bruton, Lt Mike R.J. Ouellette, Capt
Théberge, Lt J.L. François Messier, Capt F. Michael Halloran.
Front Row: CWO Jean G. Charette, Maj Robert M. Parsons, Maj A.
George Johnstone, LCol Paul F. O'Leary, Maj Robert C. Dale, Maj James
L. Downey, Lt John M. Heinrichs.

# 5

## 1987, Intelligence Branch

### 1987, Intelligence Branch Reserves
### Extracts from an article by Maj James L. Downey

The Intelligence Branch Reserve is relatively small in comparison with other organizations found with the Militia establishment, but nevertheless they provide valuable support to the Reserves in general, and to the Int Branch in particular. This article's purpose is to familiarize all Intelligence Branch members with our Reserve Units.

The first question that obviously comes to mind is, "what Units do we have in the Reserves and where are they located?" At the present time, the only active Reserve Units belong to FMC and therefore are Militia Units. They are called Intelligence sections and we have six at the following locations: Vancouver, Edmonton, Winnipeg, Toronto, Montreal, and Halifax.

The next question has to be, "to whom do they report?" Generally, each section reports to its respective area headquarters: Pacific, Prairie, Central, Secteur de l'Est, and Atlantic. The exception is the Edmonton Intelligence Section, which reports to Northern Alberta Militia District since its Area Headquarters is a thousand miles away. Some sections are co-located with their headquarters while others are located in buildings in the same city to provide adequate space for their activity. The sections provide a staff officer (SO2 Int) to each of their respective headquarters to give Intelligence expertise to the commander and his staff. You will also find a Militia staff officer with the SSO Int at FMC whose job is to act as a technical interface between the Intelligence Staff at FMC HQ and the Intelligence Sections (Militia) spread across the country.

Now that we know where they are and what their chain of command is, "what is their role and taskings?" At the current time their role is pretty fuzzy and is based on the role of the old Intelligence Training Companies, although greatly reduced. They are to conduct training in Combat Intelligence to the brigade Intelligence section level. Fortunately this general role has allowed a wide degree of flexibility, which allows their personnel to be used in many tasks for both the Militia and the Regular Force.

What kind of taskings do the Militia Intelligence Sections normally carry out? The obvious ones come from their training role. Being small organizations, General Military Training is done either in conjunction with larger Units or at a "battle school." They also conduct trades training at the Militia TQ1 and TQ2 level for their NCMs. Quite often members of other Units are included to make the small student numbers more worthwhile and at the same time spread the "Intelligence Gospel." The Intelligence Sections also conduct collective training simulating a brigade Intelligence section in operations. Here, practice in maintaining collation systems, analysis, dissemination and section step-up drills are carried out. In addition, the Sections are tasked with providing support to the Headquarter staffs through briefings on the Threat, Threat lectures to various Units, and support to training and operational staffs in developing and conducting CPXs and TEWTs.

The Intelligence Sections do not have a standard organization, yet have tended to be set up along the same lines. Usually there is a very small headquarters cell, consisting of the OC and a couple of other personnel, whose basic job is to provide direction to the section and to fight the "paper war" to allow the rest of the staff to carry on their Intelligence jobs. The Section is then broken down into two groupings. The larger one is for Combat Intelligence and training where the unclassified database is maintained and day-to-day training of members is carried out. They usually conduct the unclassified level lectures and training for other Units, a large task, since most Militia do not hold security clearances. The smaller grouping is tasked with maintaining the classified database and the preparation of classified briefings and training for commanders and staff who do have clearances. Bear in mind that this description of section breakdowns is general and that there are many variations on this main theme.

Having had a look at the way Militia Intelligence is organized, we should now have a look at the Intelligence Reservist. An Int Reservist tends to have a very high level of education on average compared to Militiamen and women in other Units. Almost all have completed or are in the process of completing some form of post-secondary education. Although they come from a wide variety of disciplines they almost all have a fascination for the way things are done by a potential "enemy" force. Most have a strong interest in history or military/foreign policy, and pursue both formal and informal study in these areas. I have noted that there are many war-gamers in the Militia Intelligence Trade and it does produce personnel with a good grasp of tactical principles.

What do these people do for a living? Most of the younger members are either students or are in the process of establishing a career. The Militia provides them with part-time earnings to support their efforts and often-valuable education for those that are pursuing studies in an Intelligence related field. Those that are working come from a wide variety of careers. Aside from those employed in Intelligence and security positions, we will find teachers, managers and accountants, civil servants, businessmen, technicians and a variety of others. Very often these different backgrounds produce Intelligence Operators with unique and, quite often, very effective solutions to the problems that bedevil us. The normal Intelligence Reservist is between 19 and 25, with the NCOs and officers being a little older. This makes them older than most Reservists, although many have remustered from other trades or have come in from outside after acquiring training in some civilian field. This is an advantage though, because they tend to be retained much longer than the normal period young Reservists stay (usually less than two years). This tends to create a high degree of cohesion.

The next question is, "what are the men and women in the Army Intelligence Reserve trained to do?" At the present time, the training specifications are being re-written at FMC, although there are a number of broad parameters that have been adhered to. Generally, both the NCMs' and officers' mobilization specifications will be the basis of the Militia specifications. The NCM training specifications are based on the existing Intelligence Operator 111 courses at CFSIS, while the officers are based on the 82A Course.

In addition to the Recruit and GMT courses, the Reservist has four Intelligence Trade Courses at the NCM level. These are produced from the Regular TQ5 and TQ6 courses, with most of the non-Army components removed, as Militiamen are Land Operators. Inter-spaced among these trade courses will be command and leadership training courses at the various NCO and WO levels. In addition, most Intelligence Reservists will have other trades training in Administration, Supply or Vehicle Tech, or they may already be a trained Infanteer, Armoured Crewman or Artilleryman.

The officers are also trained in line with the Regular Force courses, with concentration on the Land environment. The Basic and Intermediate Classification Training is drawn from the Regular Int 82A Course, which should produce a Capt capable of being an SO3 Brigade Staff Officer. The Advanced Classification Training should produce a divisional level Intelligence staff officer at the SO2 level, capable of running an Intelligence sub-Unit. In addition to the Intelligence training, officers also receive staff and leadership training.

The Militia Intelligence Sections have made significant contributions to the Armed Forces, quite often out of proportion to their numbers. As mentioned before, they provide briefings on all aspects of the land threat and extensive support to CPXs and TEWTs, both for courses and Unit/headquarter collective training. A major impact in training is their involvement in training our Militia Troops to fight Threat tactics, rather than against our own tactics. Various other forms of assistance to Militia Units has been given to liven up their training and to provide a vital element of realism in their exercises. Support to the Regular Force has been strong, with Reservists giving Intelligence assistance to staffs in the formations and commands, as well as providing personnel for various exercises such as Final Drive, Stalwart Warrior, the RVs, Rite Simple and Right Double.

Aside from the various examples of short-term support given previously, there are a number of Reservists in the Branch filling positions at NDHQ and FMC on a Class B or C basis. The Brigade Intelligence Officer for 4 CMBG during FALLEX has been a Reservist. Unlike many other Militiamen, they do not stick out as they wear the same badge and have been trained in the same school. We Reservists also like to think that our work and knowledge is good enough that we can fill the bill as well as our professional counterparts.

The intent of this article was to educate the interested reader in the Intelligence Branch Reserve and to provide some insight into how it works. Although small in size, the Int Reserves aim to make up the shortfall in quantity with quality. The one common complaint often heard is that there are not enough of them to support FMC in all its taskings, let alone other Units and organizations. There will be an even greater requirement to expand the numbers of Int Reservists with the commitment to support the Electronic Warfare Squadron (Comm Reserve), but if Communication Command follows the pattern shown in the past, it is unlikely that these people will be permitted to serve independently. It is to be hoped that the recent studies for an expanded Reserve will include the members of the Intelligence Branch. All indications are, both from the Regular and Reserve forces, that our Reserve Intelligence Branch personnel are a valuable addition to the military.[1]

## 1987, The Tactical Command, Control and Communications Project and its Impact on Military Intelligence. Extracts from an article by Capt. G. Grant, PMO TCCCS

"How nice it was to be once more among my brave Troops, with my finger on their pulse, so to speak, instead of sitting in my office at Headquarters and waiting with uncontrollable impatience for every telephone or aeroplane report. The commander of modern times is denied the part assigned to a Frederick or a Napoleon on the battlefield." Crown Prince Wilhelm of Prussia, May 1918.

Wilhelm lacked what a technological era had removed from 18th and 19th century battlefields—the ability to "see" the ebb and flow of battle. The "pulse" he spoke of, may be understood as the intimate knowledge of battlefield activity required by commanders to support decision-making. Frederick the Great could actually watch and control the precise movements of his battalions, and, until his armies grew fat with manpower and spread irresistibly over the European landscape, so could Napoleon. Instant knowledge of enemy movements allowed them to react immediately to changes in almost every sector of the battlefield.

Wilhelm and his contemporaries were faced with battlefields of far greater complexity, covering larger geographical areas and involving hundreds of thousands of combatants employing weapons of unheard of lethality. Commanders of late 20th century armies are confronted with most of the same problems. However, the pace of battle is faster and the senses of the commander and his staff are being bombarded with information and Intelligence at increasing rates. More significantly, the time available for decision-making has decreased while the speed, mobility and lethality of weapon systems have increased dramatically.

---

1.    Intelligence Branch Journal Number 4, Spring 1987, pp. 7-8.

The commander at every level, therefore, requires a system that supports and enhances his ability to plan, direct, control and coordinate the battle. There should be no sensation of "light from darkness" occurring as this fact is absorbed. Everyone knows it, whether intuitively or through direct exposure to military operations. So what is being done about it?

The Army decided some years ago to address the problem of an obsolescent command and control information system (CCIS). The failings of a manual staff system supported by elderly communications in an age of automation and Electronic Warfare have been obvious to soldiers for some time. In the late seventies a project called Army Command and Control System 85 (ACCS 85) was formulated. As the complexity of the problem and the scale of the solution became better understood, the project evolved to its present stage—PMO TCCCS. Its mandate is to provide the Army with a reliable, secure, rapid and cost-effective system to support the tactical command and control process.

This tactical CCIS, to be fully deployed during the 1995-2004 time-frame, is a major element in the Defence Services Program. A significant amount of time and money will be expended to develop and field its component parts, the Combat Communications System (CCS) and the Automated Combat Information System (ACIS). The intention is to do it well and to get it right the first time, avoiding much of the waste that occurs when the estimate of factors, option analysis and planning process are circumvented.

It is essential that Army Intelligence personnel develop some awareness of the ACIS and its application to the provision of tactical Intelligence to commanders. Project officers at PMO TCCCS, in conjunction with their colleagues in the field, are conducting a detailed analysis of Operations, Intelligence, Fire Support, Air Defence/Airspace Control and Combat Service Support functions. Staff professionals, information system analysts, computer scientists, industrial advisors and soldiers will pool their talents to provide the best possible automated support to the Army.

The ACIS will "provide such common capabilities as formatted message generation and dissemination, data-base updating, report generation, word processing and file transfer, graphic display of spatial data and other planning aids such as spread sheets and staff planning applications." Support to the Intelligence process will be evident throughout. The commander's estimate, the Intelligence estimate, the collection plan and various Intelligence annexes and paragraphs will be prepared and updated more rapidly using a computer's word processing capacity. Tasking and coordinating collection assets will be made easier using formats and automatic alerting of incoming reports and source availability.

Critical stages of the processing function will be simplified using an internal mail feature that allows the collator to quickly transfer relevant messages or parts of messages to an analyst's working file. Analysts will be able to exchange information and ideas without generating unwanted, time-consuming paper reports. Graphic displays will be updated automatically using pre-arranged formats. Intelligence reports will be integrated rapidly into the section database supporting the maintenance of a consistent and coherent assessment of the enemy situation.

Intelligence reports and summaries will be generated using standard formats, and under certain conditions might be disseminated automatically by the system. Large screen displays will assist in the oral briefing process. Graphic overlays can be generated and sent to Units and formations without the time consuming manual operations currently employed. This will release Intelligence staffs from mechanical tasks and enable them to concentrate on Intelligence work.

Intensive evaluation and training will have to take place prior to the actual fielding of ACIS. In addition, a knowledge of manual operations must be retained—computers have breakdowns, too. Intelligence staffs, among others, will have to be educated about the potentials and pitfalls of automation. As a tool it can make the job easier in today's combat environment; as a crutch it will cripple the objectivity of Intelligence staffs and make them no more than mouthpieces for bits and bytes.

This brief overview covered the progress being made at PMO TCCCS. It is hoped that you in the Army will begin thinking seriously of the value of automation as a tool in anticipation of the time when a tactical CCIS joins DIAC and MCOIN as useful complements to human reasoning and knowledge.[2]

## *1987, Intelligence Personnel News*

The following Int Branch personnel have been promoted effective the date shown: LCol Patrick D.R. Crandell, 13 Jul 87; Maj Alex C. Chambers, 1 May 87; Maj John "Jack" W. Nixon, 1 Jul 87; LCdr W. Burns MacDonald, 1 Jul 87; Maj Pat A. Renaud; Capt P.R. Campbell, 1 Jan 87; Capt J.M. Richard

---

2.    Intelligence Branch Journal Number 4, Spring 1987, pp. 9-10.

Larchevesque, 1 Jan 87; Capt Mike R.J. Ouellette, 1 Jan 87; WO J.V. William "Bill" Leclair, 1 Jan 87; and, Sgt Ed A. Knobelsdorf, 1 Jan 87.

The following personnel have remustered to the Int Branch: Cpl J.B.F. Allard, LS J.J. Charbonneau, Cpl Richard C. Gow, LS David H. Kushmier, Cpl Luc J.A.M. Leroy, Cpl Rick F. Luden, Cpl D.G. McNulty, Cpl D.H. Mitchell, Cpl P.M. Palahicky, Cpl J.E. Paul Pellerin, Cpl J.A. Chris Pelletier, Cpl Jacques M.A.D. Verbrugge, Cpl Mel A. Wilkerson, and, Cpl Ron T.A. Wulf.

The following Int Branch personnel have been released: Maj Gary W. Beckman, 23 Apr 87; and, Capt Jay G. Mercer, 1 Jun 87.[3]

## 1987, Canadian Land Forces Command and Staff College Course

Maj John F. Cruse and and Capt Stan L. Carr completed CLFCSC in June 1987; Capt Brian E. Hamilton, and and Capt J.G.A.J. Christian Rousseau completed the course in December 1987.

## 1987, CISA Member News

Capt W. Doug Whitley reported that the Intelligence Branch's 5th Anniversary and Reunion would be celebrated at CFB Borden between 30 Oct and 1 Nov 87. The Sir William S. Stephenson Trophy to be awarded annually to a Reserve Intelligence Unit for general proficiency had been purchased. It is a very handsome silver cup with Int Branch badges mounted on its walnut base. President Howard Mansfield and Secretary Maj John "Pappy" MacKinnon presented the CISA Academic Award in the form of a cheque for $600 to Kristine Dawn Hensel on 18 Dec 1986. Col Charles Chaveau forwarded a copy of La Citadelle, the magazine of the Royal 22ème Régiment Association to CISA. Capt Gary W. Beckman retired to become an investment executive in Ottawa, along with Capt J.R. Sparling. Col George L.R. Bruce, former Int Advisor at CIS was ordained to the Anglican deaconate, witnessed by Col Jeff S. Upton and Col Robert W. Irvine.[4]

Two CISA members, Capt Charles Hillman and Maj Gordon R.B. Panchuk, passed away. Maj Al A. Bell-Chambers retired from the Int Branch in

3. Intelligence Branch Journal Number 4, Spring 1987, p. 25.
4. CISA Newsletter, Vol. 18, No. 1, June 1987, pp. 1-2.

Winnipeg in June 87. A luncheon was held as the Base Officer's Mess with Maj Willy Williamson, LCol Dale M. Watts, LCol G. Cecil W. Dawkins, Maj Susan F. Beharriell, and Lt Brad J. Smith in attendance. Other members of the Winnipeg Int crew include LCol Ron J. Donovan, Capt Bev Dawkins, Maj Robert P. Haier, Maj Nils E. Lindberg, and Capt Jack B. Martin. Maj Elaine E. Mellor handed over the duties of CISA Membership Secretary to Lt Paul G. Rivard.[5]

## 1987, CAR, RV-87, Wainwright

On 13 Apr 1987 members of the Canadian Airborne Int Section were flown by B-707 to Edmonton, Alberta from CFB Trenton, Ontario. We got off the aircraft at Namao and walked almost straight on to a Hercules for another flight to Wainwright, where we were bussed to the bivouac area, arriving about 3 AM on 14 Apr. All moved into tents or hooches for the next six weeks of field exercises. The weather was sunny but cool, with spring coming on. From 13 Apr to 22 May 87 we participated in RV-87, a Division FTX at CFB Wainwright, Alberta. During the work-up exercises we were taught how to rappel from buildings, towers and helicopters. We had field showers set up, worked out of excavated, dug-in, underground CPs and participated in an interesting exercise. All were required to throw hand grenades on the pairs range, and we worked with a great number of our Int counterparts taking part with other Units on the exercise. We were back in Petawawa in time to take part in Exercise Final Drive, held at CLFCSC in Kingston from 11 to 17 Jun 87.[6]

## A Birthday Message from the Colonel Commandant, MGen Reginald J.G. Weeks

The Canadian Intelligence Corps came into being on 29 October 1942, to provide a home for all the administrative odd-balls who had been seconded, borrowed, purloined, bribed or otherwise cajoled from other Units. I was one of them. Our ranks included interrogators, photo-interpreters, wireless intercept analysts, map makers and markers, linguists, field security investigators,

---

5. CISA Newsletter, Vol. 18, No. 3, August 1987, pp. 1-4.
6. From 8 Sep 87 to 6 Nov 87, the author was a student on the Canadian Forces Staff School Course (# 69), held in Toronto, Ontario.

Intelligence staff officers and NCMs with an infinite variety of skills, all of whom were involved in some way with producing the Intelligence needed by forces in the field.

The British Army already had an Intelligence Corps and it made sense for our organizational structure to follow their pattern; both Canadian Corps went into action as parts of British formations. Our formal Alliance with the British Intelligence Corps was renewed and reaffirmed ceremonially in 1983.

The existence of a Canadian Intelligence Corps (C Int C) also helped to protect, preserve and enhance the expertise which nearly all the wartime members of the C Int C came to possess through specialized training and unique experience. It was a fact, however, that C Int C members rarely, if ever, held Intelligence appointments below the Divisional level. This was because it was considered then that battalion and brigade commanders should select their own Intelligence officers from their own Units. They should be combat arms officers and NCMs with Intelligence training rather than the other way round.

Consequently, the C Int C was very small, most were serving only "for the duration" and long-term career considerations were irrelevant. In the Navy and in the Air Force, the same view of the primacy of operational experience was apparent to such an extent that a career in Intelligence was not possible.

After the Second World War, the demand for photo-interpreters, wireless intercept analysts and other kinds of operational expertise diminished and most, but not all, members of the C Int C who went into the Regular Army had been engaged in field security operations (i.e., Counter Intelligence). That function was carried over to meet the continuing requirement for security clearance investigations and other Counter Intelligence investigations within the military establishment.

When the Intelligence functions of the three services were combined at NDHQ in 1966, the subsequent formation of a single Branch to bring together the people concerned seemed logical, and when the three services were unified in 1967, the Security Branch inherited all the Security, Intelligence and Counter Intelligence duties common to the former three services.

This combination of duties and people did not last, and in 1982 the Intelligence Branch came into separate being, bringing together, initially in a common uniform, those individuals with expertise in the accurate and timely analysis of vast amounts of often conflicting information. The amount of raw information to which focused thought would have to be applied was characterized as an information explosion. This information is increasingly technical, increasingly specialized, and increasingly sophisticated on topics ranging from missiles to mines and from the ocean floor to outer space. Expertise is needed and that is the challenge, which the Intelligence Branch must face to bring such a measure of order and clarity to the massive quantities of information available as will permit Intelligence and informed decisions to be made on a basis of knowledge rather than intuition. It was no accident that the motto of the C Int C was "Action from Knowledge."

The Intelligence Branch (or, in its absence, something similar would have to be invented) is needed because once again there is a demand for the unique expertise of its members to ensure that optimum use is made of limited resources. It will survive only so long as it provides that expertise. It should, therefore, be part of the function of the Intelligence Branch to anticipate what those needs for expertise will be and to keep up with them, not only technically, but also by ensuring that the right people, properly trained, are available to practice the profession of Intelligence within the Armed Forces.

Having been a member of the C Int C and of the Security Branch and now as an honorary member of the Intelligence Branch, I can perceive a continuity of curiosity on the part of those whom we serve to know "what is on the other side of the hill," an expression attributed variously to Wellington or Napoleon depending on your point of view. In principle however, the demand for Intelligence tends to be more or less perfunctory until the need for it becomes paramount; until the possession of Intelligence spells the difference between success and failure.

Historically, forces on the defensive and with limited resources need Intelligence far more than a numerically superior attacker. Or, to put that another way—you don't crave Intelligence when you are winning. This was the case from about 1944 following the landings in Normandy until about 1949 when the NATO Alliance came into being as a defensive Alliance with limited resources facing a numerically superior potential enemy.

The years after 1949, therefore, and even more so after 1957 when the first Sputnik was launched, should have been the years of wine and roses for the Intelligence Community; and in many ways this was so, especially in the United States which carries the lion" share of our common defence. One of the consequences of this, however, has been that those of us, as it were on the periphery of power and without significant responsibility, have been able to enjoy the luxury of having our cake and eating it. Consequently it has often been the case that very narrow domestic political interests seem to have governed decisions about equipment purchases and force deployments, to give only two examples and a gulf has often yawned widely between the Intelligence available and the responses to it.

This, of course, is as it should be because there are no rules which say that a Commander's decision must be and be seen to be a response to Intelligence. He can choose deliberately for other reasons to ignore the Intelligence which he has been given and set his own course. It is his responsibility. What he must not do is seek to change the Intelligence conclusions to match the course of action he wants. That is known as directed Intelligence and it is anathema. It is the duty of every Intelligence officer to keep the faith in that respect.

It is clear, I think, that the Intelligence Branch has a role to play in the unfolding of events and the perception of them, which is out of all proportion to its size. Although in its present manifestation it only five years old, it has inherited a long and proud tradition going back nearly a century. It has a responsibility to be the custodian of its own history as well as the trustee of its own future.[7]

## 1987, Retirement of CWO Barry Toomer

CWO Barry Toomer began his career in the Canadian Forces in 1957 when he joined the 1st Bn PPCLI. He served with the Patricias in Victoria, Germany, Edmonton, Cyprus and Calgary, until remustering to Intelligence in 1969. He then pent some time at HQ 1 Cbt Gp in Calgary before going to 4 CMBG in 1971.

Barry returned to Canada in 1973, serving in Ottawa as an Imagery Analyst a job in which he appeared to have found his calling. His next posting to 434 Sqn at Cold Lake, Alberta in 1977, reinforced his knowledge in this area before he returned to Ottawa in and DDI-6, where he was promoted to MWO in June 1980.

Over the next seven years, Barry was promoted to CWO (May 1985), and took on the tasks of Branch CWO, Chief Imagery Analyst and Vice President of the Branch Association's National Executive. At DDI-6 and later DIE, Barry established what can only be called a tradition: one of continuity in our operations and training that has enabled us to move ahead. Those who worked with him or studied under him are well aware of the benefits he passed on both professionally and personally.

---

7.    Intelligence Branch Journal Number 5, Fall 1987, pp. 2-3.

Barry was given a proper send off at a retirement dinner held in August in Ottawa. MGen C. William "Bill" Hewson presented CWO Barry Toomer with his retirement certificate. The Branch wishes Barry and his wife Gwyn all the best in his retirement.[8]

# Y Service, Acorn's Corner
# Extracts from an article by Capt W. Doug Whitley

In the 1986 issue of the CF Communications and Electronics Newsletter a Special Wireless Edition was produced and devoted to describing Canadian Signal Intelligence (SIGINT) efforts during WWII.

Capt Norman Weir put the story together from information related to him by Major R.S. Grant, an officer who built what was known as the "Y" service from absolutely nothing. Major Grant observed that the Intelligence staff exercised control of the Y service, with field command being the responsibility of the signal corps staff. Y field Units (vice static Units in Canada) had a unique organization in that there was an Officer Commanding Special Wireless Section (a signal officer) responsible for the general administrative state of the Unit and an Officer Commanding Wireless Intelligence Section who was responsible for all aspects of the main Unit function, Intelligence production. Consequently, the OC Wireless Intelligence provided the OC Special Wireless Section with direction on the administrative, maintenance, and movement requirements.

For security purposes, the primary concern was to ensure the enemy did not become aware of the Unit's operations and subsequently begin deception operations. The handling restrictions imposed on the Intelligence material produced of course had its effect on its timeliness.

Major Grant commented on intercept operations, noting that a successful tactical operation must be backed by a sound database collected before the operation begins. The Germans targets his Unit was working against were very methodical in their signal procedures, thereby making his Unit's code-breaking task easier.

There were many different tradesmen in the Unit, including dispatch riders, drivers and cooks. The intercept personnel carried out a variety of work and a great deal of skill and dedication was required to do their tasks. The

---

8.    Intelligence Branch Journal Number 5, Fall 1987, p. 18.

Unit had an interesting history of activity during WWII, making it a part of the Int Branch history as well.[9]

## 1987, Intelligence Personnel News

The following Int Branch personnel have been promoted: Capt H. Wayne Nightingale, 1 May 87; Capt J.R.R.R. Sylvain Robidoux, 11 Apr 87; Lt R.N. Cooper, 1 May 87; Lt Paul W. Hope, 16 Jul 87; Lt Chione M.B. Hughes, 17 Jun 87; Lt Robert J. McCutcheon, 7 May 87; 2Lt J.C. Hill, 1 May 87.

CWO Rick A. Mader, 1 Aug 87; MWO Brian M. Noble, 1 Aug 87; MWO David James Sundberg, 1 May 87; WO Collin (Ed) Affleck, 1 Jul 87; WO Barry E. Beldam, 1 Jul 87; WO J.J. Claude Fradette, 1 Jul 87; WO M.E. Malcolm, 1 Jul 87; WO Robert W. Moug, 1 Jul 87, WO J. Eric C. Savoy, 1 Jul 87; Sgt Al H. Dickie, 1 Aug 87; Sgt Terry W. Fader, 1 Jul 87; Sgt J.L.S. Gauvin, 22 Oct 87; Sgt E.L. Larocque, 1 Jul 87; Sgt W.A. Morgan, 1 Jul 87; Sgt Joseph Jean Pierre Paquette, 14 Oct 87; Sgt Greg S. Smith, 1 Jul 87; Sgt Manuel A. Thibault, 1 Jul 87; Sgt Ron K. Townsend, 1 Dec 87; MCpl G.R.A. Gauthier, 1 Dec 87; MCpl D.H. McLaren, 1 Dec 87; MCpl R. Hal Pugh, 1 Jul 87; MCpl J.R.M. Ross, 1 Jul 87.

The following personnel have remustered to the Int Branch (Jun 87): Cpl P. Murray Campbell, Cpl J.M.A. Stéphane Chartrand, Cpl J.J.L. Dennis Chercuite, Cpl J.L. I. Dallaire, Cpl D. Mike Donahue, Cpl John A. Dooley, Cpl A. Bruce Fenton, Cpl Tim L. Hagel, Cpl Mike H. Hurley, Cpl Alex D. Mackenzie, Cpl Dan B. McQuinn-Legér , Cpl Brian K. Mudge, Cpl Kris E. Pedersen, Cpl John C. Penner, Cpl R.D. Sammons, Cpl J.A.N. Tremblay, and, Cpl R. Jack Wilson.

The following personnel have been released from the Int Branch: CWO Barry Toomer, WO Mel C. Barlow, WO A.C. Lawrence, Sgt C.K. Hansen, Sgt Tom W. Pieroway, Cpl L.W. Bradt, and, Cpl B.I. Schimmen.[10]

## 1987, CISA AGM

The CISA AGM was held at CFB Montreal, Longue Pointe Garrison, 17-18 Sep 1987. Present were: Maj J.H. Mansfield, Capt David A. Rubin, Maj Sherman R. Veinotte, Maj Robert C. Dale, Maj Terry B. Kelly, Col Robert

9.   Intelligence Branch Journal Number 5, Fall 1987, pp. 19-20.
10.  Intelligence Branch Journal Number 5, Fall 1987, p. 27.

T. Grogan, Maj Fred E.G. Jones, Col the Hon J.R. Matheson,[11] Lt Grant Campbell, LCol Ian A. Nicol, Maj Jan A. Jezewski, Col Charles R. Raefe Douthwaite, Lt William "Bill" B. Iler, MGen Reginald J.G. Weeks, Lt C.E. Burley, Capt Chuck C. Bamlett, Maj D.E. Guyatt, Maj James "Jim" P.K. Van Wynen, Maj Merrick K. Szulc, Col E. Laroche, LCol Alf J. Laidler, Maj P. Clouthier, LCdr W. Burns MacDonald, Maj Nils E. Lindberg, Maj Brian Kent, LCol D.A. Henderson, Capt Ed D. Kirby, 2Lt Paul R. Perchaluk, Maj W.D. Weames, Maj Wilf S. Puffer, LCol Emile Berger, Capt Doug R. Bennett, LCol William "Bill" Tenhaaf, LCol Pierre J.F. Couture, MGen C. William "Bill" Hewson, Col A.H. Sam Stevenson, LCol David M. Robb, Maj P. Denis Pelletier, Lt Paul G. Rivard, Cmdre Eric F. Gaskell, LCol J.W.G. MacDougall, MGen Al Pickering, Maj Franz F. Laizner, LCol Ernest Skutezky, Lt J.A.E. Kent Dowell, Maj A. George Johnstone, 2Lt R. Nickerson, Capt Eugene Morosan, and Maj John "Pappy" MacKinnon (Secretary).[12]

CISA AGM 1987 participants.
Front Row: LCol Emile Berger Maj Fred E.G. Jones, Lt Grant Campbell, LCol Ian A. Nicol; Col E. Laroche, MGen C. William "Bill" Hewson, Maj J.H. Mansfield, MGen Al Pickering, Col A.H. Sam Stevenson, Col Robert T. Grogan, Col the Hon J.R. Matheson, Col Charles R. Raefe Douthwaite, LCol Ed D. Sanford
Centre Row: Maj W.D. Weames, 2Lt J. Vallée, Maj Brian Kent, Maj Wilf

11. The Honourable John R. Matheson is a former MP who was known as the father of the present Canadian flag, and Honorary Colonel of the Artillery Branch. During WWI, he was a Battalion Intelligence Officer. CISA Newsletter, Vol. 23, No. 1, Jan 1993, p. 1
12. CISA Newsletter, Vol. 18, No. 4, December 1987, p. 1.

S. Puffer, Maj Terry B. Kelly, Capt Chuck C. Bamlett, Maj D.E. Guyatt,
Maj Robert C. Dale, Maj Jan A. Jezewski, Maj A. George Johnstone, Maj
John "Pappy" MacKinnon, Maj James "Jim" P.K. Van Wynen, Maj Sher-
man R. Veinotte, LCol Alf J. Laidler;
Back Row: 2Lt R. Nickerson, Capt M.A. Kulba, Maj Nils E. Lindberg,
Capt Doug R. Bennett, Lt Mailhot, Lt Paul G. Rivard, Lt C.E. Burley,
2Lt Paul R. Perchaluk, LCdr W. Burns MacDonald, Maj P. Denis Pelle-
tier, Capt J.L. François Messier, Maj P. Clouthier.

## *1987, CISA Member News*

MGen Al Pickering, former CIS, was appointed Colonel Commandant of the
Security Branch, succeeding VAdm James A. Fulton. Capt Jack B. Martin,
former Membership Secretary for CMIA and an active member of CISA
passed away in Winnipeg. During the CISA AGM held at Longue Point in
Montreal 17-18 Sep 87, tributes were paid to Honorary Lifetime Member
Col the Hon Peter E.R. Wright, and members Maj Bud Cowan, Capt
Charles Hillman, Maj Gordon R.B. Panchuk and former member LCol Robert I. Luker who had passed away during 1987. A minute's silence was
observed in their memory.

At the last CISA AGM, a resolution for presentation at the 1987 CDA
AGM was passed, "That the percentage of female personnel in Int work
remain at the present level in the reserves; that this be the recommendation
unless there is a change in the policy on employment of women in Int work in
the Canadian Forces." Discussions took place with both the Int Branch Advisor at CIS and the SSO Int FMC on this matter. As there has been a change
in policy, allowing for women to be employed in Int work up to, but not
including, front-line combat roles, and ensuring full involvement of women in
the reserves, no further action was deemed necessary on this resolution. The
Int Branch Advisor and the SSO Int indicated that they were satisfied with
this and with the policy.

The CISA Academic Award went to Mr. Kenny Richard, son of WO R.L.
Richard. MGen Reginald J.G. Weeks recommended that an inventory of wartime active service personnel be compiled by CISA to assist in identifying
those who might be nominated to represent the former C Int C, C Pro C and
RCAF Security at anniversary events. Carried.

CISA will make the following recommendation to the Jan 88 CDA AGM:

"Acknowledging with satisfaction that the Government of Canada has tabled its White Paper on Defence in the House of Commons on 5 Jun 87; and agreeing with the priorities and objectives of Canada's defence and security policy contained therein; the Canadian Intelligence and Security Association expresses accord with the general thrust and direction of the policies contained in the White Paper; and urges the provision of funds required to implement those policies."

CISA President Maj Howard Mansfield reported the White Paper was of great significance to CDA as the new policy statement had addressed many of the resolutions CDA had made in recent years. Policy with regard to the Reserves is to move towards a Total Force Concept with the Reserves increasing in the long term to 90,000. An early interpretation of this by CDA suggests that the Primary Reserves would increase from its present paid ceiling of 21,494 to 65,000 over the next 15 years, requiring an annual increase of 3,000 recruits with a greatly increased RSS. The creation of additional brigades, mainly from the Reserves, for operations in the defence of Canada was also referred to. The impact on Security and Intelligence Units is of prime interest to CISA and it was hoped that CIS, the Branch Advisors and FMC would provide more information at the AGM.[13]

# RV 87 Intelligence Analysis and Collection Centre Article by Lt J.A.E. Kent Dowell

In late October 1985, a small group of Regular and Reserve Intelligence officers and NCMs formed the first ad hoc Intelligence Analysis and Collection Centre (ICAC) during Ex RITE SIMPLE XIII and Ex RITE DOUBLE III in Valcartier, Quebec. Seventeen months later, on 11 Apr 1987, a much smaller group surveyed a piece of snow-covered ground in Wainwright, Alberta, and tried to remember how it was done.

A three-section modular was chosen as the optimum size. Any larger and there were serious doubts about the ability to move it under tactical conditions. Smaller was preferred but lacked the required working area. Once erected and shovelled out, the operators began to search for the furnishings required to operate. After much initiative, tables, chairs, power cables and a much-valued heater were acquired and the ICAC began to take shape. Two 5/

---

13. CISA Newsletter, Vol. 18, No. 4, December 1987, pp. 1-5.

4-ton vehicles were attached to the ICAC, one for the Electronic Warfare Coordination Centre (EWCC) and the other for the Terrain Analysts.

The first challenge faced by ICAC 87 was the training of personnel in operating techniques, not the least of which was the often-complicated relationship between the ICAC and the Division G2. The G2 is the commander's principal Intelligence staff officer and he alone is responsible for advising the commander on the enemy's location, capabilities and intentions. He is also responsible for determining the Intelligence collection requirements and for the dissemination of Intelligence to higher, flanking and lower formations. What then was the ICAC's position in the scheme of things? The answer was found to be quite simple. In response to the G2's Intelligence collection requirements, the ICAC coordinated the full spectrum of Intelligence assets and available sources in the ICAC to provide finished all-source Intelligence to the G2. This process would continue with the G2 revising the collection priorities in accordance with the ongoing operational situation and passing them to the ICAC.

Another problem facing the smooth operation of the ICAC was computer training. The ICAC made use of computers to generate report formats, maintain a sensor-tasking database, and maintain the enemy order of battle (ORBAT). The first real use of computers by many of the ICAC personnel was with two venerable Apple IIe holdovers from the first trial. To compound the problem, the computers immediately developed idiosyncrasies of behaviour brought about by the dusty Wainwright air and extremely variable temperatures. Notwithstanding these problems, those present conquered computer phobia and all from Private to Capt were able to operate the computer to accomplish word-processing, database management, and spreadsheet functions.

Exercise RITE BASIC II saw the ICAC deploy tactically in a CPX scenario. No real Units were deployed and higher and lower controllers drawn from the Brigades generated all Intelligence play data. The ICAC on this exercise practiced basic operating procedures and concentrated on developing an effective ICAC/G2 relationship. The practical side of ICAC deployment was also exercised with both day and night moves and operations in various NBCW states. Additional vehicles had been procured for this exercise and for the first time the provisional ICAC was able to lift itself and its personnel as a packet without external assistance.

In the Division FTX BOLD WARRIOR, the ICAC adopted a static role while still tactically deployed. This was a unique opportunity to experience the frustrating realities and limitations of real sensor management. Air reconnaissance was available and used extensively in all phases of the exercise. Some problems existed with the timeliness of imagery dissemination as bottlenecks occurred in bringing the imagery forward to the formations. Data facsimile was not available. This was sometimes solved in novel fashion. On one occasion, the ICAC personal actually flew forward in a light observation helicopter (LOH), in the middle of the night to one of the brigades to provide timely Intelligence. It was found particularly useful to have the imagery delivered forward to the Division for additional exploitation by the ICAC terrain analysis team. This allowed continuous monitoring of the terrain conditions showing any modifications caused by enemy engineers or weather.

A team of defence research scientists from Suffield along with Intelligence and artillery personnel were present to test an RPV ground control station (GCS). This provided the ICAC with two missions a day from a simulated RPV sensor package mounted on a Cessna aircraft. While the imagery was of poor quality, the experience gained in the use of real-time information flow was invaluable. A data link was set up using two grid-portable tempest laptop computers to pass RPV reports as they developed during the mission. This was found useful in minimizing the time required to format, verbally send and recopy the RPV reports by hand. The GCC recorded the data on their terminal in a computerized format, called the ICAC and once communication was established sent the data. A hard copy result could be obtained in the ICAC using the printer.

For the second time a valuable Intelligence asset was available to the division on an RV, the Interrogation centre, first deployed during RV 81. Manned by a small team of Intelligence personnel and operating at the division prisoner of war cage, this organization produced Intelligence throughout the FTX. The presence of the Interrogation centre also increased the useful exploitation of captured enemy documents (CED) as proper CED handling procedure was enforced throughout. Many items of Intelligence value were gathered from soldiers, communicators, officers and the occasional dispatch rider. In one instance, a captured dispatch rider was found to be carrying an infantry battalion's plan including positions, flanking Unit locations, armour defence plan, and surveillance as well as the locations of all division engineer demolitions.

The major success of the ICAC at RV 87 was accomplishing a greater understanding by all involved of the concept and operation of the all-source collection and analysis centre. While problems were identified with the flow of information within division Intelligence, these are currently being addressed by the drafting of new operating procedures. Hopefully, the future will see the implementation of a divisional Intelligence radio net with secure voice/data transmission devices to alleviate information bottlenecks and subsequent time delays. The incorporation of TCCCS in the late 1990s will see the continued development of the ICAC with a quantum increase in its ability to handle real-time Intelligence data. A division ICAC has been added to the Canadian Land Forces Command Staff College (CLFCSC) Kingston Command Post Exercise FINAL DRIVE on an ongoing basis. This latter development will assist in developing doctrine and identifying the limitations of the ICAC in fulfilling the Intelligence requirements.

When you hear the term ICAC, think Army Intelligence potential, now and in the future.[14]

## 1987, Intelligence Troop, EW Squadron

On 4 Sep 1987 four new members joined the Int Branch at CFB Kingston. They are graduates of the Int Op Basic Trade Training Course 8701, the first Int Ops trained for a Communication Reserve Unit: The Intelligence Troop, Electronic Warfare Squadron, 763 Communication Regiment.

LCol David M. Robb, CD, reviewed the parade and rebadged the graduates. In his speech he welcomed the new members pointing to their position in the vanguard of developments planned for the Branch and the Reserves. LCol Robb also noted with appreciation, the presence on parade of the EW Sqn's Radio/Teletype Operator Course currently in progress.

The Intelligence Troop has an authorized establishment of 29 all ranks. Staff and graduates were WO Phillip A. Dawes (Course Officer), WO N.L. Gordon (Course WO), Pte M.D. Keates, Pte T.P. Burke, Pte C.A. Isbell, and Pte D.E. Hueglin. Pte Hueglin was the Top Student for the course.[15]

## 1987, FMC

The 1987 FMC Intelligence Section included Cpl P.G. Manuge, Cpl D.H. Mitchell, WO Robert W. Moug, WO Jean Pierre Caron, Sgt J. Dan Galley, Sgt P.M. Gallant, Cpl J.G. Chartier, Cpl A.J. Lane, Sgt J. Michael Poulin,

---

14.  Intelligence Branch Journal Number 6, Spring 1988, pp. 11-13.
15.  Intelligence Branch Journal Number 6, Spring 1988, p. 8.

WO A. Paul Grant, MWO Barry M. Gardner, Lt J.L. François Messier, Maj A. George Johnstone, LCol Paul F. O'Leary, Capt Greg W. Jensen, Lt K.A.V. Sutton, Lt J.A.E. Kent Dowell.

## 1987, CFSIS

1987 Intelligence Operator 6A Course 8701
Top Row: MCpl MWO Rick G. Oliver, Sgt D. Garry Kohinski, MS William D. Kean, MCpl Eric P. Grehan, MS Daryl W. Monk, PO2 Campbell, MCpl P. Murray Campbell
Centre Row: MCpl Al H. Dickie, MCpl D.J. Rankin, Sgt Dan J. Haslip, MCpl Chuck J. Spillane, MCpl MWO J.L.A. Martineau, MCpl Hayes, MCpl Joseph Jean Pierre Paquette, MCpl J.L.S. Gauvin, Sgt Smith.
Front Row: PO2 Harry V. Delorey, CWO Rick A. Mader, LCdr W. Burns MacDonald, PO1 F. Vance Gordon.

# From the Intelligence Branch Advisor, LCol David M. Robb

29 Oct 1987 marked the fifth anniversary of the Intelligence Branch. A number of us were able to make the journey to renew ties with our brothers and sisters in Borden, while others marked the event in their home areas. A birthday is a celebration both of creation and continuing life. Five years ago, Intelligence was created as a separate and unique Branch, after a hiatus of some fourteen years following unification. This new identity gave the Branch a renewed vitality and we have grown rapidly as a result. Furthermore, we have broadened our profile from essentially a Corps of the Army to a Branch serving all three environments and the national level. The Defence White Paper has now given us a new direction in that we must expand and integrate with our Intelligence Reserves over the next dozen years, in order that a total force Intelligence component of twice our present size may be created. Indeed, the Intelligence Branch is alive and well, and can look forward to an exciting and challenging future in the years ahead.

Now for some updates on recent developments. As I advised in an Intelligence AIG message, Commodore J.C. Slade was promoted to Rear Admiral and moved from DG Int to Chief of Maritime Doctrine and Operations last September. His successor, Commodore J.B. O'Reilly took over the post of DG Int in October.

In view of Rear Admiral Slade's experience as head of Intelligence at NDHQ, I see his move to CMDO as a positive development, which may hold some promise for further Branch involvement in the area of naval Intelligence. We are building a significant inventory of both officers and NCMs with naval backgrounds, and the time could well be drawing near when the Navy decides that it wishes to follow suit with the other environments—namely to have Intelligence performed by Intelligence personnel.

I am pleased to report that the new Reserve EW Squadron of 763 Communications Regiment in Kingston is doing well. Last September I attended the graduation parade of the first four reserve Int Ops qualified and was informed that more would be undergoing training this winter. All the graduates impressed me by their keenness and deportment. They will indeed be prime assets for the Branch and models for the many more we will need to fulfil our new tasks.

Now I should like to say a few words regarding the Defence White Paper. As you all know, its publication last June gave the Canadian Forces a new direction with a number of different and expanded roles. As a result of the White Paper, both the NDHQ and environmental staffs are still in the process of defining specific taskings, peace and war establishments to accomplish these missions, and implementation plans to achieve them by the end of this century. At this time it would appear that the land forces, including their Intelligence component, will expand to a larger degree than those of the other two environments. Some of our members in the sea and air environments have therefore expressed concern at this prognosis, feeling that they will be passed by in career progression as a result. I would like to reiterate a number of points, which I hope will ease this concern. First, the final establishments have yet to be determined and there is still scope for increased involvement by our Branch in all environments.

Next, while the size of the CF total force is to double under the White Paper, most of the personnel expansion will be by the Reserves. This growth in Reserve strength may result in some redistribution of resources among Regular Force MOCs, but should not affect Intelligence adversely. Lastly, Intelligence will remain a unified Branch supporting all three environments. Although I see a trend emerging wherein our people, and especially the officers, will be identified more with their parent environment, there will still be a sufficient quantity of hard Naval and Air Force positions as well as "open" billets for each to progress according to his or her merit. To conclude, I would counsel all of you to do your best and let the chips fall where they may. Any tendency to lie awake at night worrying over who may gain some advantage under force restructure will only degrade your performance and earn you a classic case of ulcers.

As I write this, the annual merit boards are about to begin here at NDHQ. One of the results of this year's boards for the officers will be increased offers of IPS to compensate in part for the acute shortage of general service officers now plaguing the CF. Some will have received IPS offers by the time you read this. In any event, I must be candid and inform you that like most things in life, revised OCDP is likely to prove a mixed blessing. On the one hand, it will probably slow down promotion to Major, which is any case could not have been maintained at the rate we have experienced over the past three years. This, however, will prove a much needed stabilizing influence which will better allow us to grow into the many and varied jobs which we have been assigned. On the other hand, several officers who would have had to leave at age 40 or slightly after will have the opportunity to serve until age 55. While the effects will be more immediate for the officers, our NCMs will experience similar results when revised ORCDP (Target 93) takes hold early in the next decade. In view of these changes, some of us will have to change our expectations regarding quick promotion in the Branch and put an increased emphasis on job satisfaction while we wait our turn.

I have previously given advice in this column as to measures that our officers and NCMs could take to increase their chances of promotion. While these still stand, I would like to add another to the list: French language. Bilingualism in the CF has now reached a point where it is virtually a prerequisite for promotion to General Officer grade. The word has new descended from on high that this will soon be extended to the rank of Lt-Col, and I would speculate for our NCMs, even to CWO. This past year, the Branch had to scramble to provide a DC Int Major who was capable of briefing in French, and one can project that such high-profile requirements will continue into the future. I therefore advise all of you who have attained functional grading to "keep your numbers up." Those of you who have not, but still aspire to the highest ranks in the Branch should indicate your desire for French language training in your PER. Please remember however that there are numerous other means to obtain the same objective if you don't get loaded on the yearlong course.

I hope that all of you will take these remarks in the spirit, which they were intended: guidance for realistic self-assessment and personal planning. We have come a long way in the five years since the Branch was formed, and that success is due to the professionalism of each and every one of you at all levels. Such performance, however, creates the expectation of continued excellence and thus it falls to all of us to represent the Branch to the best of our ability. I therefore wish you all success in this objective and both health and happiness in the year ahead.[16]

## From the Intelligence Branch CWO, CWO Jean G. Charette

First off, I would like to say how pleased an honoured I am to have been appointed Branch Chief. I will try and fulfill the obligations and responsibilities of this appointment to the best of my ability. We are not a large Branch, and therefore we cannot afford the luxury of a Branch CWO who is responsible solely for Branch matters. I wear two hats: branch Chief and a full time staff job as a member of the Directorate of Intelligence Plans and Doctrine.

---

16.  Intelligence Branch Journal Number 5, Fall 1987, pp. 4-5.

Many personnel feel that the Branch Chief should do nothing else but travel. But, there is another problem—that of finances. There is a very limited TD budget for Branch Advisor/Branch Chief. The monies allocated must be used wisely and where possible trips must be coordinated to visit several Units in the same area at the same time. Despite these constraints, I will try to meet as many of you as possible wherever and whenever we have a gathering of Intelligence per personnel whether that be at a conference, an exercise or a Branch social activity. I would like to visit each Command at least once annually.

Often bases and/or Units may have funding available and in such circumstances when Intelligence personnel are celebrating a special occasion or Branch function, it is simply a matter of a formal invitation and letting me know what finances are available to cover TD costs. I would like to visit Int Ops in their working environment and, having said that, I hope I have not discouraged anyone from communication by other means. As the old saying goes, one is never further than a phone call away. I appreciate the contacts that many of the senior NCMs in the Branch maintain with me on a more or less regular basis. If you have anything at all pertaining to the Branch that you would like to make me aware of, please speak to your Warrant or senior Branch NCM at your Unit. They will be in contact with me. Naturally, if the matter impinges on Branch policy it is necessary to involve the SSOs through your Intelligence Officer at the onset, but otherwise, anything else pertaining to Branch matters is fair game. The Branch Advisor and myself have an open door policy and if he requires advice on NCMs he asks me. Likewise if there is some matter which I cannot answer, the Branch Advisor is there for advice and/or guidance.

By the time you read this article, the Branch 5th Anniversary celebrations will have come and gone. Each anniversary is special for me because I have seen this organization grow from a fledgling Branch just five years ago to the Intelligence Branch we know today. There has been growth in numbers and there will be more. More significantly, however, there has been an increase in the loyalty, devotion and esprit de corps in the Branch. Our people are proud of what they can do and what the Branch has achieved.

Some of our members however, overly concern themselves as to what they can get from the organization when they should be asking what they can do to promote it. Some feel they do not wish to belong or associate with fellow-Branch members after work. I find that hard to understand. What I have always liked about the Armed Forces is the feeling of belonging to something. Identifying with a Branch is belonging to a small part of a bigger organization.

I am certain, whether you wear an Army, Air Force or Navy uniform, you are all deeply proud to be serving.

I have noticed at Branch functions in the Branch Association, and in the individual Branch Chapters, the relatively large number of ex-military and former Intelligence personnel participating, and in some cases, even more actively than our currently serving members. The reason for this is obvious as any one of them will say—they miss the "association"—the camaraderie. Most of these individuals are well established in the civilian sector, some are embarked upon successful second careers, but they still miss that feeling of belonging, the lasting friendships and bonds formed during their active military service. A point to contemplate is that someday we will all be in the same situation. If we, the serving members of the Branch do not help to develop and support such organizations as the Branch Association, where will we be later on? Look at it as an investment for the future but with fringe benefits for today!

It is my intention to write a message for the Branch Journal periodically—let us call it the Branch Chief's Corner. Up to now I have been told that the AIG messages on Branch matters have been much appreciated. Hopefully, we have responded to Branch concerns quickly and effectively. This column will therefore be in addition to those messages, another media by which to address Branch matters. So, until the next article—E Tenebris Lux.[17]

---

17. Intelligence Branch Journal Number 5, Fall 1987, pp. 6-7.

# 6

## 1988, Intelligence Branch

### Spring 1988, LCol David M.Robb, Intelligence Branch Advisor

One of the difficulties in writing a column [for the Intelligence Branch Journal] such as this is the need to "aim off" by about four months from the time of the first draft until the article finally appears in print. In the last edition, I predicted that one of the likely effects of revised OCDP would be a decrease in the rate of promotion to Major. As you know by now however, I have since been proven wrong because I had not calculated on the ever-increasing demand for Branch officers at all rank levels.

Now that the dust has cleared for this year, we have already had one promotion to LCol, four to Maj, seven to Capt, and there may even be one or two more by Christmas. Furthermore, I see no end in sight to this expansionary trend, which was confirmed by a recent ADM (Per) Group study. Looking back over the past six years since our formation, the PML of Intelligence Branch officers has grown from 66 to 124, or 87%. For your information, that makes us the fastest growing officer MOC in the CF!

Our NCMs have also done well this year with one promotion to MWO, eight to WO, 15 to Sgt, and 16 to MCpl. As for their rate of expansion, our Int Ops have gone from 184 in 1982 to 234 this year. This represents an increase of 27%, which, while not spectacular, is still a respectable growth rate during a period of tight resources.

This year, we have made a significant breakthrough by finally being given the opportunity to put one of our people, namely LCdr D. Rick Douglas, into the job of SSO Int-MARPAC. This was a momentous development, as we had tried since our formation to get well established in the naval Intelligence function, but were tuned off at each try. Now that the precedent has been set, I feel confident that senior representation in MARCOM and the Navy Shop of DDI will follow.

I am gratified to see that the high performance of our people is finally receiving formal recognition. Recently, the Branch office was informed that two of our people had received prestigious awards: Maj K.A.W. Peter Mackenzie having been presented the Meritorious Service Cross for his work on BICES at AFCENT HQ and Sgt Barry R. Eddy, the Order of Military Merit for his performance with 1 CAG.

Maj K.A.W. Peter Mackenzie was posted to AFCENT Headquarters at Brunsuum in July 1983 as the Intelligence Plans Staff Officer. It was in this position that he conceived a new design for the Central European Intelligence Community, creating a new concept for NATO Intelligence; participated in the cementing of international agreements to automate Intelligence sharing by allied central European nations; and was a key motivator in the creation of an international Intelligence network both in the operational and experimental fields. The formal investiture was performed in June by the Governor General at a ceremony at NDHQ, Ottawa. Sgt Barry R. Eddy was appointed to the Order of Military Merit in the degree of Member on 14 Dec 1987.[1]

I have always maintained that it is through the performance of our people in various Commands and HQ that the Branch has gained respect and acceptance and these awards are indicative of that recognition.

While I would prefer to be able to tell you that all is bright on the horizon for the Branch, there are of course some problems which continue to plague us. Chief among them is the requirement to produce more officers and NCMs to fill the new billets which are accruing to us. As I write this, we are still well below our objective in candidates for the next BIOC course, and the Branch Chief is beating the bushes for remuster candidates. As I stated earlier, this appears to be a continuing requirement for the foreseeable future. I would therefore urge you to keep a watch for prospective new members for our Branch and attempt to recruit all who appear both interested and suitable.[2]

---

1.    Intelligence Branch Journal Number 6, Spring 1988, p. 22.

## *Spring 1988, CWO Jean G. Charette, Intelligence Branch CWO,*

For this edition [of the Intelligence Branch Journal] I have two topics which are loosely related and which I would like to address. The first concerns members of the Branch (officers and NCMs) who are admitted to NDMC. The Branch Advisor and I would ask Branch personnel to please notify the Branch office (DG Int/DIPD) when you have an Int member of your staff admitted to NDMC. Unless that person is admitted to hospital as a result of an accident and is placed on the serious or very seriously ill list, we have no way of knowing that they are in the hospital. If we are advised then we will make an effort to visit them and advise others of their admission. Hopefully, if they are in hospital for several days they will receive some visits from Branch members in the Ottawa area.

My next topic concerns medical categories, employment restrictions, and Career Medical Review Boards (CMRBs). This is quite a broad subject and one which I do not claim to be an expert. Certainly I would recommend to those who are interested in this matter to refer to Personnel Newsletter 12/87, which featured an excellent article on CMRBs. In addition, I would like to add a few points in the context of how it affects this branch specifically.

Many times I have been asked, "Why does the Int Branch carry so many sick, lame and lazy?" The truth of the matter is that this is simply not the case. Let us look at the figures in detail. At present, there are only seven NCMs with permanent medical categories. There may be others with temporary categories. A temporary category may result in restrictions; however, these restrictions will only apply for a short duration of time—usually six months to a year. In such circumstances, sections have no alternative but to suffer the loss by having other members of the team "take up the slack." All sections or Units have probably experienced this at one time or another, and there is little else that can be done.

Now let us consider personnel with permanent categories. These individuals have had certain restrictions placed on them as a result of CMRBs. CMRBs are chaired by a medical officer who is thoroughly familiar with the medical history of the case and three other staff officers who are career managers. The restrictions that they decide upon which are more likely to affect us

---

2.    Intelligence Branch Journal Number 6, Spring 1988, p. 2.

albeit indirectly—are those restrictions of a geographic or occupational nature. Tow of our seven restricted Int Ops have no specific limitations on their employment and can be posted anywhere. Of the remaining five, two have more serious cases. They do have limitations and as a result, these personnel have been restricted in rank. In other words, they are "paying the penalty" because of their limited employability. The last three cases, although relatively minor, do have some degree of restriction on their employment. In these cases, there are controls built into the decision-making process, which ensure no injustice occurs to others because of their restrictions.

CMRBs use, as a guideline, the criteria that if an individual is employable in at least 80% of the established positions at any given rank level, there is no need to consider career restrictions, occupational transfers or release. Our last three cases fall into this category. As one can see the 80% employability rate is a valuable safety valve. There are no exceptions to the 80% rule in this Branch at this time, but even if there were, these exceptions would be only in the interest of humane treatment. They would certainly have only a minimal affect on the Branch. The problem is therefore not as monumental as may originally have been perceived.

In conclusion, CMRBs provide us with job security. It is nice to know that should our physical fitness and health deteriorate, or should we develop a certain medical problem which may restrict us in some aspect of our employment, we will not simply be released without first taking into consideration our service history, personal and domestic circumstances and the recommendations of our COs and PSOs, not to mention the requirements of the Branch. All factors are given serious consideration before any decision is taken. I feel that the system is as fair as it can possibly be without causing undue hardship to others.[3]

## 1988, Exercise Maple Flag, CFB Cold Lake

Twice a year the four-week Exercise MAPLE FLAG XX has been conducted at CFB Cold Lake Air Weapons Range in Alberta. The exercise is now in its tenth year of operation. For 1988, there is one six-week session beginning at the end of April and lasting until mid-June. This will allow Cold Lake to make better use of its resources in training and housing two Canadian-based

---

3.    Intelligence Branch Journal Number 6, Spring 1988, pp. 3-4.

operational CF-18 squadrons, in addition to carrying out its many other train-ing missions.

According to the exercise's Canadian Director, Major Rick Martin, an 18-year veteran fighter pilot, there are lots of operational benefits in each MAPLE FLAG. "It's not only excellent training but it's also an extremely important part of our force readiness," he said. "MAPLE FLAG is the largest, most comprehensive air exercise in Canada. Canadian fighter pilots, Hercules pilots, air weapons controllers, Intelligence staffs and others have an opportu-nity to work with other Allied forces, operate with state-of-the-art equipment, fly against realistic surface-to-air and air-to-air missile threats and opportuni-ties to command and plan large-scale offensive and defensive forces. We stress self-discipline, leadership, tactics and initiative in our missions."

Major Martin says that MAPLE FLAG trains fighter pilots and other air-crew to survive those first ten combat missions, which cost the United States 90% of all losses in the Vietnam War. Canadian flyers exchange and observe tactics, concepts, techniques and operating procedures from which ideas are gained which enhance Canada's defences.

But Canadian pilots aren't the only ones who learn from MAPLE FLAG, Cpl R. Jack Wilson, an Int Op From CFB North Bay, pointed out a new enemy position to USAF Sgt Gary Gravelle during the exercise. Staff Sgt Gravelle is a member of the 49th Tactical Fighter Wing at Holloman Air Force Base (AFB) in New Mexico. "It's been interesting," Cpl Wilson said. "It's the first time I've worked with the Americans and also in a fighter envi-ronment. There's a lot to learn."

Sgt Jim H. Rasmussen, Base Int Sgt at CFB Cold Lake, briefed fellow Int Sgt, Tech Sgt Doreen Blumhagen of Nellis AFB, Nevada, and pilot Capt Mark Stevens of Holloman AFB New Mexico, on the next mission. "It cer-tainly is different," said Sgt Jim H. Rasmussen. "It's also a lot of work keeping the briefings up-to-date and accurate."

Planning a fighter mission takes time, patience, skill and information. USAF F-15 pilot Capt Mark Stevens got that information from Capt Dan A. Climo and the other members of the MAPLE FLAG XX Intelligence section throughout the four-week air combat operation. Partisan reports, satellite reconnaissance, other aerial reconnaissance photos, maps and weather Intelli-gence were all used to plan successful attacks and defensive actions.[4]

4.   Intelligence Branch Journal Number 6, Spring 1988, pp. 6-8.

## 1988, 12-Plane Airborne Mass Drop

From 20 Jan to 8 Feb 1988, members of the Airborne Int Section participated in Ex Lightning Strike, flying from Petawawa to Edmonton in this Defence of Canada Exercise. A few soldiers slept on the hood of the of the trucks en route in a very slow C-130 Hercules flight. During the exercise the HQ elements operated out of the old hospital quarters at Lancaster Park, and worked with the Reserve Int Section, meeting many members of the Edmonton militia crew at the officer's mess. The author ran into many familiar faces. The Int Section gave lots of briefings, built terrain models, photo mosaics, maps and conducted an enormous amount of exercise preparation. Unfortunately there were no jumps this time, and since it was cold (minus 30°) few objected.

The HQ and Signals Squadron returned to Petawawa, and then went to shoot at the Connaught Ranges just outside Ottawa. At the end of the firing exercise, the busses were sent away, and the HQ & Sigs Sqn members marched back to base between 15 and 20 Apr 1988, on "Exercise Capitol Stroll," a 142 km march from the ranges to Petawawa. Of course it had to snow and turn nasty, but on Wednesday, 20 Apr at 0730 in the morning the group marched through Pembroke to Petawawa. Pipes and Drums met them at the town outskirts and piped them all the way to building L-106. The Regimental Commander met the group at the gate with the march complete. We turned in our weapons, had a BBQ in the Z lines, and then most of us went home to soak our feet.

From 2 May to 27 May 1988 the Airborne Int Section took part in PET-CON 88, an SSF Field Exercise in Petawawa, including Exercise Pegasus Venture, an Airborne Battle Group Jump/Exercise into CFB Borden, which was carried out between 19 and 23 May 88. On 22 May 88 we departed CFB Trenton to participate in a 12-plane C-130 Hercules Mass Drop putting 450 of us on the DZ. The loading and boarding of the 12 Hercules (plus two more as standby/backup) was one of those impressive memories that the author will carry with him for the rest of his life. One can really see the organization coming to its pointed end going into a field job with that many people involved in a jump. The aircraft came in waves of three at a time from four different directions within a few minutes of each other. The Regiment dropped onto the airfield at Borden, dumped their parachutes in small piles and carried out the assault as planned. They had two hours to get to the objective, release a group of hostages, take prisoners and board the aircraft or get left behind to hike back to Petawawa the hard way. When it came time to pick the paratroops up, all boarded the first nine planes to land and three aircraft didn't have to come in. The paratroops then flew back to Petawawa to debrief after a very professionally rewarding exercise.

## *Standardization*
## *Extracts from an Article by Maj Gary W. Handson*

Imagine coming under fire, running low on ammunition and being resupplied by an ally, only to find the wrong calibre of ammunition has been delivered. The results can be disastrous. This illustrates the need for standardization between cooperating forces on a battlefield. The requirements for standardization not only involve ammunition but equipment of all kinds as well as common doctrine and procedures. All environments have a need for standardization and at all command levels from national down to the individual soldier, sailor and airman. Intelligence is the most influenced by standardization in the areas of doctrine and procedures. Agreements have been concluded between control planning and operations staff so that cooperating forces clearly understand one another and exchange Intelligence.

There are two international standardization arenas which involve Canada and hence involve members of the Int Branch: one is NATO and the other is the cooperative efforts of the ABCA (1) programs.

Each one has two specialist organizations, which deal with Intelligence related doctrinal and procedural subjects. These fora, which are called either a Working Party or Working Group, conduct their work by correspondence and meet approximately every 14 months to consolidate their previous efforts and plan their activities for the next year.

*Standardization in NATO.* The overall aim of NATO standardization is to increase the effectiveness of the military forces of the Alliance. This overall aim has interacting military and economic (including industrial) components, and its attainment depends on political will:

The military aim of NATO standardization is to increase the combined operational effectiveness of the military forces of the Alliance.

The economic aim of NATO standardization is to increase overall efficiency in the use of available Alliance defence resources. This includes, among other things, increasing cooperation and eliminating unnecessary duplication among Alliance nations in research.

The Military Agency for Standardization (MAS) is the principal agency for military standardization in NATO. The main functions of MAS are:

a.  To initiate standardization proposals in conformity with the Military Committee (MC) standardization policy;

b.  To assess proposals for standardization studies arising primarily from military considerations;

c.  To sponsor and promulgate all NATO allied publications (AP)/Standardization Agreements (STANAGs) and reports;

d.  To arrange for the exchange of equipment for test and evaluation;

e.  To coordinate demonstrations of equipment; and,

f.  To maintain liaison with NATO commands, the International Staff, and appropriate organizations of the North Atlantic Council.

MAS consists of three Service Boards—Naval, Army and Air—each functioning under a chairman appointed by the MC and supported by a Secretariat. Each Service Board carries out the functions of MAS in respect of that particular service and in coordination with the boards of other services. Further, each Service Board establishes and directs working parties and panels as appropriate to negotiate standardization agreements.

Working parties are the principal study groups of the Service Boards and are convened to study subjects covering a wide field of military interest of a continuing nature requiring the knowledge of experts and specialists. Panels are created to assist working parties and may be directed to report either to the working party or directly to the Service Board concerned.

The Intelligence Interservice Working Party (INTWP) is a tri-service working party tasked to initiate and develop essential intelligence and security standardization within the Alliance. The Chairman of the INTWP is assigned from the SHAPE Intelligence staff. Members are Belgium, Canada, Denmark, France, Germany, Greece, Italy, Netherlands, Norway, Portugal, Turkey, United Kingdom, and the United States. SHAPE. SACLANT and CINCHAN. This Working Party is assigned to the Army Board for direction but operates in support of all three services.

Intelligence and Security standardization has been developed within three primary spheres:

a.   The Intelligence process (6 agreements);

b.   Handling and exploiting captured personnel and materiel (3 agreements); and,

c.   Security (including Counter Intelligence) (3 agreements).

The Intelligence Process

| a. Doctrine | 2936 (AINTP-1) |
|---|---|
| b. Request | 2149 |
| c. Nomenclature of Weapons and Equipment | 2097 |
| d. Designation of Aircraft and Guided Missiles | 3236 |
| e. Report | 2022 |

Handling & Exploiting Captured Personnel and Material

| a. Dealing with PW | 2044 |
|---|---|
| b. Exploitation of PW Handling, and | |
| c. Exploitation of Captured Enemy Equipment and Documents | 2084 |

Security

| a. Doctrine | 2363 (AINTP-2) |
|---|---|
| b. CI | 2844 |
| c. Aircraft Security | 2952 |

The Intelligence Working Party held its 34th meeting in February 1988 and it is currently reviewing the Intelligence request through to reporting areas of standardization with a view to creating more useful and timely procedures.

They are also readying messages in these subject areas for ADP formatting. Member nations are reviewing the current requirements for handling and exploitation of captured personnel and materiel to see if the existing agreements require amending.[5]

*Standardization (Part II).* The previous article emphasized the need for standardization in general, reviewed the NATO forum and detailed the Intelligence Interservice Working Party (INTWP) activities and standards. The INTWP with the Director Intelligence Plans and Doctrine (DIPD) as Canadian Office of Primary Interest (OPI) is the cornerstone of Intelligence doctrine and procedural standardization. An equally important, specialized standardization working party in NATO is the Imagery Reconnaissance Interpretation Working Party (IRIWP). Two other standardization forums outside of NATO are the ABCA Armies and the Air Standardization Coordinating Committee (ASCC) programs.

*IRIWP.* The IRIWP is a tri-service working party entrusted with the development of essential procedural standardization in the Imagery interpretation field. The IRIWP is concerned only with the requesting, reporting and Intelligence value of reconnaissance products while other working parties consider interoperability and standardization within recce aircraft, related equipment, films and processing.

There are currently 13 agreements or studies controlled and under development by the IRIWP. Two of these agreements are Allied Tactical Publications:

a. ATP-26 (STANAG 3483) Air Recce Intelligence Reporting—Nomenclature of Equipment's and Installations. This is a working Imagery Interpreter's guide to the written descriptions of military equipment's and various military and civilian installations.

b. ATP-47 (STANAG 3920) Handbook for Air Recce tasking and Reporting. This handbook contains the contents of all IRIWP Agreements as an Annex, some basic tactical reconnaissance doctrine and also has sections where nations insert their particular recce fitments and unique requirements or procedures.

---

5.    Intelligence Branch Journal Number 6, Spring 1988, pp. 14-16.

The IRIWP held their 19th meeting in Ankara, Turkey, in September 1988. Canada's OPI is the Director Imagery Exploitation (DIE).

*Other NATO Forums.* There are many other NATO forums of importance to the Intelligence field such as the Army, Navy and Air equipment panels of the Council of NATO Armaments Directors, the NATO Advisory Committee on Special Intelligence (NACSI) etc. The advent of automated Command Control and Information systems within nations and the need to maintain interoperability has forced the creation of a NATO agency (ADSIA) to control and rationalize the development of character and bit-oriented standardization for messages and communications data links.

*ADSIA.* The Allied Data Systems Interoperability Agency (ADSIA) has several specialized working groups, one of which, Working Group 7, is assigned the task of formatting Intelligence related reports and messages. ADSIA WG 7 receives requests for formatting from NATO Working Groups such as the INTWP, IRIWP or NACSI and attempts to prepare formats in accordance with established rules which satisfy both the user and the inter operability requirements for ADP.

ADSIA WG 7 meets four times a year and members are currently involved Imagery interpretation reporting requirements from the IRIWP and in preparing new ORBAT and enemy activity reports. Canada, with the Director Land Command and Information Systems (DLCIS) as OPI, became an active participant in WG 7 in 1988.

*ABCA.* Three of the NATO nations, namely Canada, the United States and the United Kingdom, are partners with Australia in a dynamic standardization venture away from the NATO forum. Canada, the US and UK realized the importance of retaining the high level of importance of retaining the high level of standardization that had been achieved by the end of WWII, and they also recognized that their combined requirements for operations in areas other than Europe would often be different. Army, Navy and Air Force and industrial standardization programs were developed which eventually included Australia as a full partner and New Zealand as either a participant or an observer. The two forums of direct interest to Intelligence are ABCA Armies QWG Int and the ASCC.

*ABCA Armies.* The Armies of the US, UK, AS and the CF, as signatories of the Basic Standardization Agreement 1964 (BSA), are members of the ABCA Armies Standardization Program. The NZ Army became associated in 1965. The aims of this program are to:

a. Ensure the fullest cooperation and collaboration among the ABCA Armies;

b. Achieve the highest possible degree of interoperability among the signatory Armies through material and non-material standardization;

c. Obtain the greatest possible economy of the use of combined resources and effort.

*Combat Development Guide.* The ABCA Armies have produced a Combat Development Guide for up to the year 2005. This Guide lists the General Capabilities (GCs) and the Quadripartite Objectives (QOs) which have been agreed as required for various types of conflicts. NATO concerns are primarily for high-level conflict and the ABCA Armies standardization work has no wish to duplicate the work of the MAS Army Board and its working parties. The direction and concentration of efforts within ABCA Armies is on the development of standardization and programs concerning mid-level, low-level conflicts and peacekeeping.

*Quadripartite Working Groups* (QWGs). The aim of a QWG is to identify and recommend to Armies how standardization and/or interoperability should be achieved within its area of interest. Each QWG identifies and Armies agree to specific objectives toward which its work is directed. These objectives are incorporated in each QWG's Terms of Reference (TOR) which are reviewed at each meeting. There are currently 19 ABCA Army Working Groups.

*QWG Intelligence.* QWG Int is the youngest QWG and the inaugural meeting was held in Canada during July 1987. A hierarchy of Concept Papers mirroring the phases of the Int Cycle was agreed to and these papers are currently being written. The Concept Papers are intended to review the current status of Intelligence and security (I&S/CI) standardization within the ABCA Armies, identify shortfalls and make recommendations for improvements. This review includes considering the validity and usefulness of:

a. Existing QSTAGs (ABCA Armies equivalent to a NATO STANAG);

b. Working papers on Intelligence, related Electronic Warfare (EW) and Battlefield Surveillance, Reconnaissance and Target Acquisition (BARSTA); and

c. Existing SOPs in the ABCA Armies SOP (QSTAG 831).

The ABCA Armies' goals of being able to operate together on the battle-field by 1995 appear, in most cases, to already have been achieved by Intelligence. An examination of Intelligence requirements in an automated C3 battle management system in the year 2005 is also being considered in the working group's concept papers.

A review of all NATO Intelligence agreements (STANAGs) is currently being made by the four Armies to determine their acceptability and usefulness as QSTAGs.

ABCA Armies' Intelligence will probably require a couple of years to complete their design and framework of Standardization requirements through to the year 2005.

The second meeting of QWG Int took place in February 1989 at the Intelligence School in Canungra, Australia. Canada's OPI (called national point of contact (NPOC)) is the Director Land Command and Information Systems (DLCIS).

Air Standardization Coordinating Committee (ASCC). After the experience of WWII, the United States Air Force, the Royal Air Force and the Royal Canadian Air Force agreed on the need for a better capability to conduct combined operations and to provide each other with certain essential services. Therefore, in 1948, they formed the Air Standardization Coordinating Committee (ASCC). Membership was extended in 1964/65 to the Royal Australian Air Force and Royal New Zealand Air Forces. Naval air has since been included and now the Royal Navy, the United States Navy, the Royal Australian Navy and the UK Ministry of Defence (Procurement Executive) are represented on the Management Committee and working parties.

The objective of the ASCC is to achieve sufficient standardization among the Air Forces of the ASCC to:

a.   Ensure that in the conduct of combined operations there will be a minimum of operational and technical obstacles to full cooperation;

b.   Enable essential support facilities to be provided for the aircraft of the other ASCC Air Forces;

c.   Enable justifiable logistic support; and,

d.   Promote economy in the use of national resources.

The ASCC recognizes that there are practical levels of standardization ranging from total commonality descending to interoperability or to merely a reduction of alternatives. The decision on the level to which the ASCC or individual nations should aspire is based on an assessment of necessity and worth; thus effort and expense is tailored to need.

There are currently 17 Working parties responsible for all of the work of standardization. The Working Party of direct interest to Intelligence is WP 101—Imagery Interpretation.

*WP 101—Imagery Interpretation.* WP 101 has not only adapted NATO MAS (Air) IRIWP Imagery Interpretation Standards (STANAGs) for use as Air Standards, but have developed standards for use in areas such as titling of hand-held film and reporting of data for use in dimensional analysis of Imagery. There are currently 11 Air Standards controlled and under development by WP 101.

WP 101 is a valuable specialized forum for the exchange of ideas and the stabilization of procedures in Imagery interpretation. The Intelligence Community benefits through formal and informal contacts on subjects as diverse as insight into new Imagery interpretation equipment/systems being developed by Air Forces through to materials to aid in training future interpreters and analysts. The OPI for WP 101 is the Director of Imagery Exploitation (DIE).

*Conclusion.* This two-part article has examined only in the briefest terms, the extensive work being conducted internationally to support a survivable and winning presence on a future battlefield through common procedures and doctrine.

The next time you are on an exercise with Units from another NATO or ABCA nation and discover that your report formats are the same or that radio power packs or ammunition is interchangeable, just remember the on-going efforts of your standardization representatives. When something doesn't fit, or a procedure is out of synchronization, or the information needs from a Unit are not understandable, is also the time to remember your standardization rep, and to give him your problem and recommendation to make it work![6]

# *1988, CFSIS*

From 12 Jun to 12 Aug 1988, the author was tasked by FMC to be the course-conducting officer (CFSIS Incremental Staff) for the summer militia courses in Borden. He worked with the CO, LCdr W. Burns MacDonald and Capt Lloyd W. Hackel. He set up the course with Capt J.A.E. Kent Dowell, three WOs and a number of militia instructors, and proceeded to get on with the task. For a brief period, he was also made acting OC of the Int Trg Coy while the LCdr was on leave. He commuted back to Petawawa on the weekends for the nine-week tasking.[7]

---

6.  Intelligence Branch Journal Number 7, Fall 1988, pp. 25-27.
7.  On Saturday, 17 June 1988 the author had the privilege of being invited to participate in a parachute demonstration jump for the opening ceremonies for the Canadian Air Museum in Ottawa, with Prime Minister Brian Mulroney, MND Perrin Beatty and Col Marc Garneau (Canada's first astronaut, and commentator) in attendance.

Intelligence Operator 6A Course 8801.
Rear Row: MCpl Byron K. Mackenzie, MCpl Turcotte. J.R.P. Turcotte
Third Row: MCpl R. Hal Pugh, Sgt Dave L. Howarth, Sgt Alex D. Radz-
ion, MCpl Robert P. Conway.
Second Row: MCpl T.D.G. Graham, MS H.W. Glover, MS Dan A.
McCoy, MCpl Darcy H. McLaren, Sgt R.K.H. Wood, Sgt Rick M.
Chaykowski, MS J.R. François Bouchard, MS J.R. Michel Labossiere.
Front Row: PO2 Harry V. Delorey, CWO Rick A. Mader, LCdr W.
Burns MacDonald, Capt J.M. Richard Larchevesque, WO Barry E. Bel-
dam, Sgt Henry E. Doucette.

## Intelligence Personnel News, 1988

The following Int Branch members have been promoted: LCol Peter W.M.
Wilson, 1 Jul 88; Maj G.W. Jensen, 1 Jan 88; Maj Gary W. Handson, 1 May
88; Maj Jean E.T. Bigras, 1 Jul 88; Maj J. Mike Gauvin, 1 Jul 88; Capt Linda
P. Knie, 1 Jan 88; Lt (N) Brian E. Watson, 1 Jan 88; Capt Lois J.C. Hart, 1
May 88; Capt Terry W. Procyshyn, 1 May 88; Capt Barry S. Alexander, 1

May 88; Capt Brad J. Smith, 1 May 88; and Capt Richard A. Derkson, 1 Jan 88.

WO Joe V. Million, 1 Jul 88; WO Rolf F. Overhoff, 1 Jan 88; WO Yves Levesque, 1 Jan 88; WO E. Meril Crane, 1 Jun 88; Sgt Kevin N. Rowe, 1 Apr 88; Sgt Glen B. Hupe, 1 Jun 88; Sgt A. "Tony" Wyver, 1 Jun 88; Sgt R.K. Wood, 1 Jan 88; Sgt Dave L. Howarth, 1 Jan 88; Sgt P. Cost, 1 Jan 88; Sgt Alex D. Radzion, 1 Jan 88; Sgt William "Bill" D. Kean, 1 Jan 88; Sgt J.P.G. Vinetti, 1 Jan 88; MCpl D.D. Campbell, 1 Jan 88; Sgt Richard E. "Dick" Hurst, 1 Jul 88; Sgt Eric P. Grehan, 1 Jul 88; Sgt Rick M. Chaykowski, 1 Jul 88; Sgt G.D. Chaisson, 1 Jul 88; Sgt K.S. Rankin, 1 Jul 88; MCpl Richard C. Gow, 1 Jan 88; MCpl Michael M. Glover, 1 May 88; MCpl J.P. Tetu, 1 Jan 88; MCpl J.D. Roy, 1 Jan 88; MCpl David H. Kushmier, 1 Jan 88; MCpl Sgt J.G. Chartier, 1 Jan 88; MCpl William "Bill" M. Flanagan, 1 Jan 88; MCpl P.W. Young, 1 Apr 88; MCpl D. Mike Donahue, 1 Apr 99; MCpl John A. Dooley, 1 May 88; and, MCpl G.M. Chartrand, 1 Jul 88.

The following personnel have reclassified or remustered to the Int Branch as of 17 June 1988: Capt Mike J. Popovich, 2Lt S.R. Bruyea, Capt Ron J. Ruiters, Capt Dan A. Climo, Capt D.J. Arsenault, Capt Robert G. Nash, 2Lt Phil J. Drew, Capt W.A. "Tony" Rennett, Lt (N) F.W. Parkinson, A/SLt Dave S. Peterson, Lt (N) R. Paul Grimshaw, Lt K.A.V. Sutton, Capt J. Michel Bédard, Lt Robert J. McCutcheon, Lt R.N. Cooper, and 2Lt J.C. Hill.

The following personnel have reclassified/remustered to the Int Branch as of April 1988: Cpl Marie M. Hudson, Cpl J.C. Tony Gagnon, Cpl J.F.J.M. Tremblay, Cpl Greg C. Collins, Cpl J.M.R. Dan Jacques, Cpl Reginald J. McAuley, Cpl G.A. McGuire, Cpl John Paul Michael Parsons, Cpl George P. Houston, LS David G. Maxim, Cpl Mark H. Figge, Cpl J.D.H. Jodoin, Cpl P.G. Manuge, Cpl William "Bill" R. Lorimer, and, Cpl Dean G. Hyde.

The following Int Branch personnel have been or are expected to be released: Capt W. Doug Whitley, Capt William "Bill" L. Dickson, Capt W.H. Vouriot, Capt D.G. Carr, WO A.A. Hiscock, WO M.V. Marsh, WO Roger E. Oderkirk, WO Art E. Sibley, Sgt E.L. Larocque, Sgt E.S. Burke, PO2 M.B. Hayes, and, MCpl Chuck J. Spillane.[8]

---

8. Intelligence Branch Journal Number 6, Spring 1988, p. 26.

## 1988, Canadian Land Force Command and Staff College

Capt Ward A. Sweet completed CLFCSC in June 1988, and Maj R. Geoff St John completed the course in December 1988.

## 1988, CISA Member News

Maj Sherman R. Veinotte, former OC of the Int Coy in Halifax died of a heart attack in late January. Sherman was always very involved in the affairs of CISA. FLt (Ret'd) Eugene Morosan, Ph.D. was working on a project to recognize the part played by Air Intelligence in the past, including the collection of information and personal experiences, plus documents, memorabilia and artefacts which could be placed in museums.[9]

CISA members Maj G. Robert Corbeil and Capt J.M. Grady passed away. Col A.H. Sam Stevenson and Maj Gary W. Beckman retired from the Regular Force in June. It was noted that BGen Walter J. Dabros was the first ex-C Pro C officer to attain general officer rank. MGen C. William "Bill" Hewson is leaving Ottawa in the summer for a senior Intelligence posting at SHAPE HQ in Belgium. MGen Al Pickering and MGen Reg Weeks as well as members of the CISA Executive attended a farewell dinner in his honour.[10]

## From the Intelligence Branch Advisor, LCol David M.Robb

I would like to continue my theme of recruiting and personnel production, which I touched on in previous issues. While you may think by now that this all sounds like a broken record, I can assure you that it is most necessary if we are to meet the continuing new commitments, which are being levied upon us. Although the bookwork is currently being worked on to establish new positions for 1989, indications are that both our officers and NCMs will continue to benefit from this ongoing expansion.

To meet our commitments, recruiting new members for both officer and NCM ranks will have to be an ongoing priority for all of us. Some of you have been particularly diligent in this regard as evidenced by the fact that BIOC

9.  CISA Newsletter, Vol. 19, No. 1, April 1988, pp. 1-2.
10. CISA Newsletter, Vol. 19, No. 2, July 1988, pp. 1-2.

8901 and two QL5 courses for 1989 are now both fully booked. For this, I give you my sincere thanks. We are in a far better position now for new members than we were a few months ago, but must continue our combined efforts at recruiting until we reach a steady state, which will allow us to progress in a more even fashion.

This year, I have again urged the NCM's merit board to keep a watch for prospective UTPM candidates, as they have been a very useful source of new officers. For those of you contemplating UTPM, I would urge you to enrol in those courses of study most applicable to the Branch, namely a BSc or BA in Soviet and East European Studies. At present, the Branch is overborne with officers holding a General BA, and the UTPM program is the major means we have available to draw upon those degrees we really need.

As for the UTPO program, although we remain short of officers, it is my policy to encourage those within striking distance of an undergraduate degree to apply for it. CF policy is to eventually establish a bilingual, degree-holding officer corps and I think we must "get with the program" as much as we can. That being said, I do not favour thinning the ranks of our officers in pursuit of various postgraduate degrees unless each qualification can be definitely shown to benefit Branch interests.

Soon we should have the first Direct Entry officer candidates for our Branch completing the first step of the production pipeline. These members, both civilian and reservist, have varied backgrounds which will prove of value to the Branch in the future. It remains our policy however, to judiciously select such candidates on a case-by-case basis, rather than opening up the Branch to them in a wholesale fashion.

While on the subject of policy, I would like to address what appears to be a source of some confusion as to when a new member is authorized to wear the Intelligence Branch badge. When new members are occupationally transferred to us, they are awarded the MOC designator 82U for officers and 111U for NCMs. This takes off the books of the MOC from whence they came. As they are not MOC qualified until they complete the BIOC or QL5 course, however, what badge should they then wear? Our policy is that new members wear the badge they have previously earned until they become MOC qualified in their new profession. Those rare individuals having no MOC qualification, such as civilian Direct Entry candidates, should wear the CF general service badge. Only after having passed their CFSIS course are new members authorized to wear the Intelligence badge. I believe this policy to be in harmony with other MOCs, which accept OT candidates, and it accords formal recognition to the standards we have set for ourselves.

To keep you all informed of Branch senior appointments, I am pleased to report that the CDS has extended MGen Reginald J.G. Weeks (Ret'd) as our Colonel Commandant for a further two years. MGen Weeks represented us extremely well during his initial tour, and I am gratified that he has seen fit to accept this post for another cycle.

Finally, I expect that this coming year will be another banner one for promotions, particularly as the White Paper begins to take hold in the Army. This trend should offer much promise to all of you, no matter what uniform you wear. This is indeed a great time to be in the Intelligence Branch![11]

## From the Intelligence Branch CWO, CWO Jean G.Charette

I would like to give you an update on the Intelligence Branch manual. This publication has been a long time in coming due mainly to a lack of personnel. In August of this year, Lt (N) R. Paul Grimshaw (DIPD 2-2), was assigned the task of completing this project. At present, the final touches are being added and it is hoped to have it produced and distributed to all Commands early in the New Year. The manual will form the basis for the performance checks on Branch history for both the Basic Intelligence Officer's course and the Int Op QL5 course. It is hoped the publication will grow as our history grows and will serve to preserve and pass on our Branch customs and traditions. Suggestions for improvements or additions for future editions should be forwarded to the Branch office.

Another matter of interest, particularly for NCMs is the Intelligence Branch cap badge. Many complaints have been received since the current cloth badge was first authorized for wear on berets and wedge caps. The badge gets dirty quickly and soon the symbol becomes indistinguishable. It is interesting to note that no one from the Intelligence Branch, to our knowledge, has submitted an unsatisfactory condition report (UCR) on these badges; nonetheless, your verbal complaints have been heard by the Branch and we are attempting to do something about the situation. Firstly, I should mention that the Army is developing a subdued badge for field wear with combat clothing. Also, although an unsatisfactory solution, the metal cap badge is still autho-

---

11. Intelligence Branch Journal Number 7, Fall 1988, pp. 2-3.

rized for wear on berets and wedge caps. The Branch policy regarding the wearing of the gold embroidered hat badge only by officers and CWOs has recently been reviewed by the Branch Advisor in consultation with senior Branch members and it was decided to retain the present policy for two reasons:

*Unit.* It is desirable to have as much standardization as possible in items of dress. The Branch Advisor was reluctant to authorize another item of kit that might be worn by some NCMs but which was not "free issue," and,

*Tradition.* In both the Air Force and the Army it has been traditional for officers and CWOs to be dressed or issued with different items of kit not necessarily authorized for wear by all ranks.

However, having said that, I would like to apprise members of new initiatives, which the NDCDC is taking in regard to CF headdress badges forces-wide. At a recent meeting of the NDCDC it was recommended that a new policy be approved authorizing each Branch a maximum of two badges (combat badge not included). There would be one full size metal or J metallic badge for Service Dress cap/hat and a reduced size rayon loom embroidered or J metallic badge for berets and wedge caps. Where it is technically feasible due to shape and size of the badge and agreed by the Branch Advisor, only the one size need be approved. Other comments were sought from Branch Advisors. The comments from our Branch to NDCDC were that the one size badge would suffice. As for the J metallic badge, this badge appears to be of much higher quality than the present cloth badge. In fact, it is very similar to the gold wire embroidered badge for officers, except that the j metallic is perhaps brighter than the gold embroidered thread. Nonetheless, the Branch Advisor prudently reserved judgement until an actual sample was provided. If the J metallic badge produced with the Intelligence Star is of sufficiently high calibre and compatible to the present badge authorized for officers, he may be receptive to changing the policy so that all personnel (officers and NCMs) would be authorized to wear the same cap badge. We are awaiting a sample from DC and will keep members posted of new developments.

A lot of personnel have been asking me about a naval occupational badge for Intelligence. Yes, the Branch has developed a badge which is approved and being produced in the near future. The badge consists of a gold star within the framework of other naval occupational badges, i.e., same size and shape and topped with a gold maple leaf. The star is gold vice silver because of the naval requirement to standardize all naval occupational badges. The first production of badges was for the hard sea trades. DC is now negotiating to obtain a contract for the other occupational badges. The badge will be authorized for wear as soon as it is available for issue through the supply system.

While we are on the subject of dress, I would like to voice my disapproval to those NCMs who are still wearing the web belt without the Branch buckle or with buckles of other Branches. I would like to remind personnel that our policy calls for the wearing of the web belts with Intelligence Branch buckles. I am sure that all personnel should be proud enough to purchase and wear this occupational symbol. The buckles may be ordered through the Kit Shop and I have been assured that there are plenty in stock.

In conclusion, and to end on a bright note, I would like to extend best wishes to you and your families for a happy and prosperous new year. May 1989 be a successful year in your careers and other endeavours.[12]

## 1988, News from the Reserves, Army Intelligence Training

The final confirmation exercise for Militia Intelligence Basic Classification and Intermediate Trade courses, Ex KALEIDOSCOPE KAPER was the conducted at the Intelligence Training Company, CFSIS, CFB Borden in the summer of 1988. Militia Intelligence courses have been conducted on base since 1948, and although the numbers of participants has fluctuated greatly over the years, the numbers are once again on the way up. Up until 1967 there were six Militia Intelligence Training Companies across Canada, one in each area headquarters and an additional company in Edmonton, Alberta. Then all companies were reduced to section strength. Now it's on the rise again in support of Army 2002 and the Intelligence Companies are coming back.

This summer, after a one-year hiatus in training to rewrite course training standards and plans, national Militia Intelligence training was back. To support the four courses being run, augmentee instructors were drawn from the Militia, the Regular Support Staff, the Canadian Airborne Regiment, Mobile Command Headquarters and 1st Canadian Division to form the directing staff. Instructors provided additional support when available from the Intelligence Training Company.

An Intermediate Trade Training (ITT) course 8801 was run for four master-Cpls, including one air reservist with the Intelligence section at 1 Tactical Air Wing. The objective was to qualify them as senior collators at the brigade

---

12.   Intelligence Branch Journal Number 7, Fall 1988, pp. 3-4.

level. The two-week course covered such topics as potential enemy force structure, equipment, doctrine, tactics and operational art up to Army level, Canadian Intelligence doctrine, security, prisoner of war handling and the use of automated data processing (ADP). The top candidate of ITT 8801 was MCpl M.V. Hubley from the Atlantic Militia Area Intelligence Section in Halifax.

The Basic Classification Training (BCT) course was run as two three-week courses, BCT I 8801 and BCT II 8801. BCT trained seven Second Lts to perform the duties of a junior Intelligence staff officer in a battle group or brigade Intelligence section. Such topics as potential enemy force organizations, equipment, uniforms, doctrine and tactics up to Division level, Canadian Intelligence doctrine, basic Canadian tactical concepts, prisoner of war handling, patrol briefing and debriefing, ADP use, air photo reading, the conduct of Intelligence training, military symbols, security and Counter Intelligence were covered. Capt Harold "Hal" A. Skaarup, Cdn AB Regt Int O, Lt J.A.E. Kent Dowell, WO Jean Pierre Caron and WO Robert W. Moug were course officers and instructors.

To better understand the tactics of one potential threat, candidates examined enemy force Regimental tactics in depth on a series of tutorial exercises as commanders and staff of a Motor Rifle Regiment. They were responsible for the planning and presentation of a regimental operation as part of a tank division. Such categories of combat action as the meeting engagement, the attack against a defending enemy from the march, the attack against a defending enemy from a position in contact, the pursuit, the hasty defence, the prepared defence and the withdrawal were conducted.

The BCT top candidate was 2Lt Norman A. Sproll from the Prairie Militia Area Intelligence Section in Winnipeg, Manitoba. In recognition of this, 2Lt Sproll was the first recipient of the "Lieutenant's Cup," donated by this year's staff of the two courses to be awarded to the top Candidate of the Militia Intelligence Lieutenant's Qualifying Course.

The Intermediate Classification Training (ICT) course 8801 was run to qualify six candidates to perform the duties of an Intelligence officer in the brigade. This two-week course covered such topics as potential enemy force organizations, equipment, uniforms, doctrine and operational art up to Front level, Canadian Intelligence doctrine, Canadian tactical concepts, prisoner of war handling, ADP use, the conduct of Intelligence exercises, security and Counter Intelligence. The ICT course was "treated" at one point to a demonstration of prisoner of war handling techniques, as prisoners, to better understand conduct after capture. The top candidate of ICT 8801 was Lt Don M. Stedeford of the Pacific Militia Area Intelligence Section in Vancouver, BC.

Two of the officers attending the training at CFSIS, CFB Borden, were part of the Intelligence Reserve Entry Scheme Officer (RESO) program. In accordance with the new standards implemented in the fall of 1987, one candidate, who attended the BCT, augmented the SSF Intelligence Section for a period of six weeks to complete his required on the job training (OJT) experience. The other candidate completed ten weeks OJT at the Combat Training Centre (CTC), CFB Gagetown with the Enemy Doctrine section.

Next summer will see a repeat of these courses as well as the addition of the Advanced Trades Training and Advanced Classification Training courses.[13]

Intermediate Trades Training Course 8801, 25 Jul–5 Aug 1988.
Top Row: MCpl .J.D. Pete Boutin, MCpl M.V. Hubley, MCpl C.B. Temple-Unger, MCpl P.D. Chartrand.
Front Row: WO Jean Pierre Caron, Sgt Dave J. Bruton, Capt S.L.C. Carr, Capt H.A. Skaarup, Lt J.A.E.K. Dowell, Lt P.A. Wilson, WO R.W. Moug.

13.  Intelligence Branch Journal Number 7, Fall 1988, pp. 13-14

Basic Classification Training 2 Course 8801, 18 Jul 15 Aug 1988
Top Row: 2Lt R.B. MacRae, 2Lt P.G. Rivard, 2Lt Colin A.J. Kiley.
Centre Row: 2Lt J. Lefebvre, Lt B. Boily, 2Lt N.A. Sproll, 2Lt K.F. Herman.
Front Row: Sgt Dave J. Bruton, Lt J.A.E.K. Dowell, Capt H.A. Skaarup, Lt P.A. Wilson, WO R.W. Moug.

Intermediate Classification Training Course 8801
Top Row: Maj David A. Haas, Lt P.A. Wilson, 2Lt Arnold S. Neumann,
Maj Pierre D. St Amant, Lt André F. Berdais, Lt Don M. Stedeford.
Front Row: Sgt Dave J. Bruton, Capt Lloyd W. Hackel, Maj Greg W.
Jensen, Lt J.A.E.K. Dowell, WO R.W. Moug.

## The Intelligence Function and the Fleet of the Future
## Article by Lt (N) Darren W. Knight

*Introduction.* The fleet of the future is evolving now—and it will be substantially different from the present. Gone will be the single-purpose ASW Navy. Instead we are planning for a balanced naval force capable of operating independently or as part of a larger formation in a multi-threat environment. Certainly alterations will have to be made in our C3 structure. But of course, C3 has now evolved to the point where Intelligence is inextricably linked (C3I). Enhancement of Canadian sovereignty, particularly in the Arctic, and the possible acquisition of nuclear submarines will require real-time, all-source, accurate, and timely Intelligence support for all operational missions; something we do not currently possess. The infrastructure, facilities, and most importantly, the personnel to provide such Intelligence support cannot be created overnight.

The purpose of this discussion is to demonstrate the need to start thinking about the Intelligence requirements for the Navy we are building. Providing Intelligence support for fleet operations, both in the Arctic and elsewhere, will be a complex and demanding task. A broad plan for development of future Intelligence support should be progressing hand-in-hand with plans for the employment of SSNs. This discussion first looks at Intelligence in general, then examines the existing naval Intelligence structure, and finally offers one version of a future plan for Intelligence support to the fleet.[14]

*General.* Consider the faculties in use by a boxer when he is engaged in a fight: his arms provide the striking power; his brain judges where and how to deliver that power; and finally, his eyes feed crucial inputs to the brain to assist in decision-making and in guiding the arms. The boxer relies on the integration of all these faculties to win fights, and would indeed be at a loss without any one of them. By analogy, one could compare a naval fleet to the same boxer. Ships, submarines, and aircraft are the striking power, the arms. Command staffs, both ashore and afloat are the brain, directing the blows and counterblows. Intelligence then, is the eyes of the fleet. Through the Intelligence function we learn the disposition, capabilities, and intentions of potential threats, and can therefore decide how to most effectively deploy our forces in defence.

The Intelligence Function. The best way to convey a clear, general understanding of the Intelligence function is to use another analogy. Everyone knows what a jigsaw puzzle is and how to assemble one. The puzzle comes in a box with a picture on it and a set number of pieces to recreate the picture. Intelligence work can be likened to assembling a puzzle, but with a few added twists; in the Intelligence puzzle there is no final picture for guidance, or even a box to start from. Pieces are scattered all around, and new pieces arrive continually. Some pieces are actually puzzles in themselves. Several boxes must be created to organize all the pieces. Each box has a picture of its own, and a

---

14. The word "fleet" as used herein, is meant to represent ships, submarines, and maritime aircraft, while the "future" refers to the mid-1990s-2000. Lt (N) D.W. Knight.

combination of several boxes taken together might form a larger picture. All this is done without really being sure that we have construed the correct picture, and of course no picture is ever complete. The task is truly formidable.

*The Threat.* The Intelligence cycle and the three types of Intelligence derived from it allow threat assessment to be made of potential enemies. In mathematical form the threat can be expressed in a simple equation: Capability + Intentions = Threat.

Every Intelligence target is assessed on this basis. If basic Intelligence indicates a capability to pose a threat and strategic Intelligence ascertains an intention to pose a threat, then a target does pose a threat. Conversely, a target lacking either the capability or the intention to threaten does not pose a threat (try the USA and the USSR in the equation). Once a threat has been established, current Intelligence completes the picture by monitoring activity. It is only through the rigorous application of the Intelligence function that a reasonably clear and honest assessment of the threat can be maintained.

*Intelligence Sources.* It is impossible to discuss Intelligence sources without going into problems of security classification. However, some insight can be offered in abstract, general terms. Consider how daily news reaches you. Various media such as radio, TV, magazines and newspapers provide news. Some news may also be conveyed by word-of-mouth in conversation, phone calls, or letters. Each of these could be called a source of news. Most sources are usually right, but not always—you cannot believe everything you read! Consciously or unconsciously we do tend to seek confirmation of news from a single source in other sources. It takes considerable time and experience to understand the many single sources and to make an independent judgement based on all the sources. The situation is exactly the same way in the Intelligence world. There are a variety of sources available, all of which are accurate most of the time. Of course the best Intelligence assessments are made in consideration of all-sources. Intelligence gathered from many sources, both foreign and domestic, is known as all-source Intelligence as opposed to single source Intelligence. The goal in Intelligence work is to have many single sources operating independently and then synthesizing their reporting through an all-source agency. The resulting product should be the best assessment available to the user.

*The Present Naval Intelligence Structure.* At the present time, Naval SSO(s) INT and fed by NDHQ, Allied agencies, single sources and naval Forces. The fleet is provided with current and basic Intelligence from several sources. The offices of SSO INT in MARCOM and MARPAC provide the best current

Intelligence they can, given manpower constraints, and pass on what basic Intelligence they consider relevant. The fleet also receives direct support from certain source organizations, much of which is never seen by SSO Int. The problem is that the deployed Units are receiving fragmented, uncoordinated, and sometimes contradictory Intelligence. Such a situation is acceptable if there is plenty of expertise available and lots of time for all-source analysis, as might be the case with basic Intelligence, but it is not at all for real-time current Intelligence. This, although the existing system is adequate, if not entirely efficient, for supporting of present naval force, an improved system will be required for the fleet of the future.

*Proposed Future Naval Intelligence Structure.* The fleet of the future in general, and nuclear submarines in particular, will require many innovations in C3I. This is especially true as we attempt to gain control over the Arctic. Certainly many of the requirements are already well under consideration, no definite plans appear to have been made for improved Intelligence support. The main concern is that deployed Units and operational decision-makers ashore must be able to receive truly current, all-source, near real-time Intelligence from one and only one agency. It is proposed that an Intelligence "fusion centre" be located within the C3 infrastructure to provide such support on a 24/7 basis. One fusion centre could support operations on all three coasts and overseas if required. Existing sources would feed current Intelligence into the fusion centre, which in turn would conduct a quick and effective all-source analysis before dissemination. The SSOs Int in the commands would continue to function in the capacity of coordinating basic Intelligence support for MARCOM/MARPAC. The idea of a fusion centre does not radically alter the face of Intelligence, it just makes better use of existing resources and offers a viable goal in trying to determine how best to support the fleet of the future.

The first question that comes to mind when discussing the idea of creating a so-called Intelligence Fusion Centre is that of manpower. For the most part the fusion centre would only seek to redistribute existing personnel, but some increase in establishment will be essential. The optimum personnel mix in Intelligence work is based on a fine blend of long-term Intelligence background and operational experience. In an ideal situation, professional Intelligence Branch officers would provide the depth, and operational officers posted periodically to Intelligence duties would provide current knowledge of fleet requirements. Thus continuity is maintained without becoming stale. In order to properly support deployed forces with all-source, near real-time, current

Intelligence, the fusion centre would have to be organized along the following lines:

The Commanding Officer would have to be at the rank of Cdr/LCol, and be from the MARS, AIROPS, or Int classifications. The CO should be suitably experienced in all-source Intelligence analysis/reporting.

The Executive Officer would serve in the capacity of shift supervisor, running the day-to-day operation of the centre. A rank of LCdr/Maj would be required. The classification of the XO should be one of the same three listed for the CO, either the CO or the XO should be from the Intelligence Branch. Of course the XO should also have suitable Intelligence experience.

There should be five watch teams, each headed by a Lt/Capt of the Intelligence Branch with all-source Intelligence experience. The remainder of the team would consist of five NCMs; one representing each of the major Intelligence sources and one as a collator.

A small administration, training and research staff would be required to support the operation, probably not more than five people, some or all of whom could be civilians.

What would become of the SSOs Int in MARCOM and MARPAC? Some increase in overall strength would be required if these offices are to properly provide basic Intelligence support to their respective commanders and maritime forces. The SSO himself should be a Cdr/LCol of the INT, MARS, or AIR OPS classifications. The SSO should have at least five officers working as analysts and up to six NCMs providing collation support. The senior analyst would be a LCdr/Maj, who would supervise the day-to-day analytical and collation effort. The senior analyst should be from one of the same three classifications as the SSO, but at least one of them should be an Intelligence Branch officer at any given time. The remainder of the analysts should be drawn from the same classifications at the Capt/Lt (N) level, with due consideration to maintaining a healthy balance of operational and Intelligence expertise. Other single source Intelligence cells within the commands would be required to report through SSO Int, so that basic Intelligence going to maritime forces will have gone through an all-source filter. Personnel with basic Intelligence experience (all-source and/or single source) at the command and/or national level, would be suitable candidates to draw on for manning the current Intelligence fusion centre, and likewise those with experience at the fusion centre could return to occupy senior positions at the basic Intelligence level.

The fusion centre and modified SSO Int organization would provide a sufficient number of positions, in addition to those already in existence elsewhere, to offer a meaningful and interesting career pattern to anyone. Intelligence Branch personnel would develop a structure large enough to breed real, in-depth expertise, and operational personnel would have challenging shore/ground jobs that are directly related to their classifications. Of course the primary beneficiaries, the operational forces, stand to gain the most by receiving the best Intelligence support possible.

*Conclusion*. The fact is that if Canada is going to build a modern and very capable naval force for the future, then that naval force must be properly supported. If the job is worth doing, it is worth doing right. Intelligence support should be one of the main considerations in planning for the needs of the fleet of the future. If other aspects of support are now being planned, then Intelligence is already behind and must move immediately to get on track—the future will not wait. The task is largely a matter of reorganizing existing resources and building in accordance with a common plan towards a common goal.[15]

## Future Intelligence Support in Naval Establishments
## Extracts from an article by Lt (N) Ted Parkinson

It has been well established that Naval Intelligence played an important—if not crucial—role in the success of the Battle of the Atlantic. This veracity has been aptly described in such works as *Room 40*, *Very Special Intelli*gence, and *The RCN in Retrospect*. Twice in the lives of so many at the time, the Intelligence Division of the Royal Navy and the Royal Canadian Navy grew from very humble establishments (in terms of size) and rose to the difficult task of defeating the enemy.

What of the future? The current Int establishments at MARCOM have been described elsewhere; however, some support is growing within naval Establishments other than Headquarters or MAG bases. One such establishment is the Canadian Forces Maritime Warfare Centre, located in Halifax, Nova Scotia.

*History of CFMWC*. The Maritime Warfare Centre was established in 1950 as a joint RCN/RCAF school tasked with providing training in Maritime

---

15. Intelligence Branch Journal Number 7, Fall 1988, pp. 17-20.

operations. Its responsibilities were grouped under four functional areas: training, formal courses, operational analysis, and maritime tactical development.

The present staff at the Centre comes from a variety of backgrounds. The CO is normally a MARS officer who has had command of one of HMC Ships as in the case of the incumbent, Capt (N) D.E. Miller, the former CO of HMCS Nipigon. The Deputy CO is normally a LCol in the Air Force, having previously been in command of either a Maritime Patrol (MP) or Helicopter Squadron (HS), but always from Maritime Air Group (MAG). The current deputy, LCol R.B. Sutherland, was the CO of MP 407 in Comox before being appointed to the Centre.

The remainder of the staff are brought from the Fleet (including submarines), MP and HS squadrons as well as officers on exchange from the Royal Navy and from the United States Navy. The complement is approximately 40 all ranks, and civilians.

*Training, Courses and Analysis.* The Warfare Centre has two areas of activity related to training, one of which involves exercises at sea for ships, aircraft and submarines. These are Maritime Command Operational Training (MARCOT) exercises, which are conducted twice annually on the East Coast and, less frequently, on the West Coast. A MARCOT is particularly aimed at exercising the Officer in Tactical Command (OTC) and command-level personnel in tactical decision-making and resource management in a multi-threat environment. The second area of training centres on tactical games in the Action Speed Tactical Trainer (ASTT). Detailed Intelligence is required within the software of the ASTT to support each game.

Four courses are conducted at CFMWC, which vary in complexity from Introductory to Advanced. Int officers have attended some of these courses, which are run several times annually and require a significant Intelligence input.

Another important function carried out by the Centre is operational analysis. CFMWC is the Naval Analysis Centre for maritime operations; therefore the centre analyzes actions and responses of particular Units, and thus tactics evolve from this analysis. As one can imagine, Int has an important role at CFMWC, and indeed Capt (N) D.E. Miller has stated "Intelligence features in every aspect of the Centre's activities."

In 1988, the CFMWC organization consisted of CANMARCOM with the CO, Capt (N) D.E. Miller, Deputy CO LCol R.B. Sutherland, and six sub-sections: Admin O, OIC Tactical Maritime Publications, OIC Trg, SO Int, OC Operational Analysis, and, OIC Trainer Visual Aids.

Although there is always an officer on the staff designated as the "Intelligence Officer"—a secondary duty—he does not have the pleasure of specific Int training other than what he might have received as a MARS or AIR OPS officer. This officer gave a weekly Int briefing to the CO and senior members of the staff. As a result of a number of factors, this situation was deemed cumbersome and inefficient, and SSO Int in MARCOM now provides this service. More importantly though, is the question of whether or not the needs of the Centre can best be served by direct support from SSO Int or perhaps by an Int officer who is a bona fide member of the staff? Capt (N) D.E. Miller was recently asked if he perceived a need for Int personnel at the Centre, and his reply was that, "an Intelligence officer would certainly benefit from the operational training and analysis responsibilities at CFMWC. Conversely, CFMWC could well use an Intelligence officer as a valuable contributor to all the areas mentioned above, that is to say, training, courses, OPANAL and so on. At present, the operator staff provide the Intelligence requirements at CFMWC with assistance from SSO Int...There is definitely a full-time job for an Intelligence officer, should one be available."

As can be seen, a need does exist for an Int officer at CFMWC. Where he would belong in the organization of the Centre would be in the group of six sub-sections as the SO Int. Two Int Ops would support the SO Int. Duties he would perform include course lectures, support for the ASTT, Int input for MARCOTs, and in addition he would deploy with the Officer Conducting the Exercise (OCE) for each MARCOT as the OCE's Intelligence Officer. Thus, Intelligence personnel could provide dedicated support to CFMWC in the best interests of its activities.

*Conclusion.* In conclusion, as the Canadian Navy looks toward the 21st century, the current Int positions in various Naval Establishments should be re-examined, especially when the government's decision to purchase SSNs reaches the next stage. These submarines will introduce a new element for our national Intelligence Community to consider, and in Capt (N) Miller's words, "real-time dissemination of Intelligence is a must." The importance of having people in place at the right time is as important now as it was in 1939.[16]

## 1988, Status Report on Project L1225, Unmanned Airborne Surveillance and Target Acquisition System

16. Intelligence Branch Journal Number 7, Fall 1988, pp. 20-21.

## *(UASTAS). Extracts from an article by Capt W.A. "Tony"Rennett*

To win on the battlefield of the future, the commander must have the capability to see and understand the battlefield to accurately acquire and destroy the enemy. The increasingly mobile nature of the battlefield makes it critical that this information be provided to our commander in real or near real time. Therefore assets designed to provide him that information must be as flexible and dynamic as the battlefield upon which hi is expected to fight.

Unmanned aerial vehicles offer great potential to satisfy many of these battlefield requirements. In particular they provide our forces with access to enemy airspace without risking manned aircraft. The Canadian Army, like many of its NATO allies, is currently involved in developing the doctrine and requirements for such a system and this article will provide a brief description of our Remotely Piloted Vehicle (RPV) project known as Project L1225 UASTAS.

The aim of Project UASTAS is to provide for the Land Forces, under the Army 2002 structure, a real time unmanned airborne sensor covering the Canadian Division's area of influence. The number of complete systems required is not yet fully defined, but will likely include one system for the Canadian division in Europe and one system to meet training needs. Although many studies, CPXs, and war games have used the Canadair CL-227 air vehicle (the flying peanut), the project is not restricted to purchasing this vehicle, and other systems will be considered for procurement.

*System Description.* The system will be designed with a day/night and limited visibility capability to acquire a variety of targets in real time for reconnaissance, surveillance, and target engagement tasks. The complete system will form the RPV Troop in its parent military organization and will consist of the following elements:

*The Sensor.* The "eyes" of the system, the sensor will provide real time Imagery which will in turn provide a capability to detect, recognize, and identify targets on the battlefield as well as to conduct artillery engagements;

*The Data Link.* The two-way data link will provide communications between the Ground Control Station (GCS) and the RPV in flight which includes an uplink for passage of commands to the RPV and the capability for autonomous or commanded flight;

*The GCS.* This command post will provide the capability to conduct the mission. This includes detailed mission planning, control of the sensor package and air vehicle during flight, and providing a means of recording and dis-seminating the gathered information to the necessary user. The GCS will also have the capability to conduct real time indirect fire target engagement should the operational situation so warrant; and,

*The Troop Command Post.* The Troop Command post will contain the command and control element of the RPV Troop and will include the neces-sary resources for deployment, mission planning and reporting.

*Doctrine For Use.* The specific doctrine for the employment of RPVs within a Canadian formation is currently being developed, however, the general con-cept of employment and tasks for the RPV have been identified and they are consistent with our current staff doctrine on command and control. The RPV Troop will be a divisional resource controlled by the Operations staff. Depending on the commander's priorities, RPV missions could be allocated to subordinate Formation Commanders or their respective staffs, i.e., the G2 staff at Brigade. Regardless of who gets the mission, the requirement for close coordination between the Operations, Intelligence, and Fire Support Coordi-nation Cell staffs will be required to ensure the most effective use of this resource.

*Current Status of the Project.* Project L1225 is seeking Statement of Requirements (SOR) approval by December 1988. It is estimated "in-service" date is January 1994. Money allocated for project definition has been used in a number of ways that would allow the Canadian military to gain some expertise in the development and use of unmanned airborne platforms. These include studies contracted to civilian firms to determine the availability of "off the shelf" systems. An RPV Troop has been formed at CFB Gagetown to deter-mine operating procedures as well as the skill level required to operate the sys-tem. Units will participate in various exercises such as RV 87, and the Defence Research Establishment Suffield (DRES), Alberta, will conduct RPV testing. Finally, joint Canadian/US evaluation of the CL-227 system will be con-ducted.

In conclusion, Project L1225 will provide the Canadian Forces with a cost-effective method of enhancing our war fighting capability. It will redress some of our most critical battlefield shortfalls by providing real time information that will enhance the functions of surveillance, target acquisition, target engagement, and reconnaissance.[17]

---

17.  Intelligence Branch Journal Number 7, Fall 1988, pp. 22-23.

## 1988, CFSIS Int Trg Coy

Sgt Matt McCann was the first recipient of the MWO Dick Bushe Memorial Trophy. It was presented to him at CFSIS by LCol Bernie N. Wright, Commandant CFSIS, following the graduation of the QL6B course. The trophy is presented to the student who meets the requirements of "overall leadership, academic achievement and professional attributes (respect, cooperation and motivation).

Another first for the Int Branch in 1988 was the graduation of the first female NCM into the Branch. Cpl Marie M. Hudson remustered from the Security Branch on Int Op QL5 course 8802. Cpl Hudson's husband was also at CFSIS on a MP QL3 course after remustering from the Infantry to the Security Branch.[18]

## 1988, Intelligence Personnel News

The following Int Branch personnel have been promoted:

Maj Rudy Vanderstoel, 1 Oct 88. MWO Dean J. Dunlop, 1 Aug 88; MWO Arthur E.B. "Bert" O'Brien, 1 Aug 88; WO G. Wayne Ivey, 1 Aug 88; WO J.H. Yves Labarre, 1 Aug 88; WO Barry A. MacDonald, 1 Aug 88; MCpl R.P. Conway, 1 Aug 88; MCpl J. Guy Foisy, 1 Aug 88; MCpl J. Patrick D. Knopp, 1 Aug 88; and, MCpl Byron K. Mackenzie, 1 Aug 88.

The following personnel have been released from the Int Branch:

Capt Tim A. Larson, Capt Russel H. Hensel, MWO David James Sundberg, WO John E. Cranston, WO R. Shaver, WO J.J. Claude Fradette, Sgt J.P. Bissonette, Sgt P. Cost, Sgt G.E. Fox, Sgt Brian D. "Jake" Gallipeau, and, Cpl J.A. Carr.[19]

## 1988, CISA AGM

The CISA AGM was held at CFB Borden 25-26 Aug 1988. Present were: Maj J.H. Mansfield (President), Maj John "Pappy" MacKinnon (Secretary), LCol A.G. Cameron (Treasurer), LCol Peter W.M. Wilson (FMC), Maj Pierre D. St Amant, Maj Fred E.G. Jones (Director), LCol Alf J. Laidler, Col Robert T. Grogan (Director), Maj William "Bill" L. Watt (1st VP), Lt Paul G. Rivard (Membership Secretary), LCol Robert H. "Tex" Noble, Capt

18. Intelligence Branch Journal Number 7, Fall 1988, p. 28.
19. Intelligence Branch Journal Number 7, Fall 1988, p. 29.

David A. Rubin (Director), LCol William "Bill" Tenhaaf (Past President), LCol Jack S. Dunn (2nd VP), LCol Dale M. Watts (Director), Capt Peter T. Patton, Maj Wilf S. Puffer, LCol David M. Robb (CIS Int), LCol D.A. Henderson, Capt D. Burnett, Maj Peter W. Sloan, Maj Franz F. Laizner (Director), Capt James "Jim" P.K. Van Wynen, LCol Ed D. Sanford (FMC), Maj Stanley H. Winfield, LCdr W. Burns MacDonald (CFSIS), Maj Terry B. Kelly (Director), Maj Robert C. Dale, Maj Nils E. Lindberg (Director), Maj D.E. Guyatt, LCol G. Wally Field, MGen Al Pickering (Security Branch Col Comdt), Capt Ed D. Kirby, Col W. McCullough (CIS-Secur), LCol Jim E. Parker, LCol Bernie N. Wright, Lt J. Leigh Cullen, Mr C. Carruthers, Capt J.D. McKenna, and Maj Greg W. Jensen (FMC).[20]

During the AGM, Maj William "Bill" L. Watt, assisted by LCol Robert H. "Tex" Noble, Maj Franz F. Laizner, Maj J.H. Mansfield and Maj John "Pappy" MacKinnon, paid tribute to deceased members Maj Sherman R. Veinotte, Capt Alexander C. Kinnear , Maj G. Robert Corbeil, Capt Jack B. Martin and Capt J.M. Grady, and to former Int Branch officer LCol Tom F. Davie. Regrets were also expressed at the loss of the wife of Capt D.R. Cole and the son of Capt W. Doug Whitley.

Maj John "Pappy" MacKinnon reported that LCol Paul F. O'Leary, the outgoing SSO Int at FMC, said that there was no consensus among the Militia Unit OCs on how their Units could compete for the Sir William S. Stephenson Trophy. LCol Dale M. Watts proposed that the incoming SSO Int, LCol Peter W.M. Wilson, be requested to find a solution satisfactory to all, and the executive agreed to proceed with this approach.

Mr. Daniel Johnson was the recipient for the 1988 CISA Academic Award.

LCol Jack S. Dunn served as moderator of a panel, comprising Col W. McCullough, LCol David M. Robb, LCol Ed D. Sanford and Maj G.W. Jensen, which focused on the future of Security and Intelligence in the Canadian Forces in the light of the 1987 Defence White Paper. Proposed organization charts and tasks were presented and discussed.

The following resolution was proposed and carried for presentation to the ADM of the CDA: "Whereas the present Intelligence training facilities at the Canadian Forces School of Intelligence and Security, CFB Borden, are inade-

---

20.  CISA Newsletter, Vol. 19, No. 3, December 1988, p. 1.

quate to train the increasing number and variety of Intelligence personnel pursuant to the 1987 Defence White Paper, be it resolved that the Conference of Defence Associations urge the Department of National Defence that these facilities be expanded in accordance with the latest School project application and the 1985 manpower review."

The following was also proposed: "That the CISA Executive contact senior officers of CIS and the environment components with the object of formulating additional resolutions in order to prepare for an improved position for Intelligence and Security in the Canadian Forces in the year 2002, and to present any appropriate resolutions to the Annual General Meeting of the Conference of Defence Associations."

The new slate of CISA officers includes: President, Maj William "Bill" L. Watt; 1st VP, LCol Jack S. Dunn; 2nd VP and Alberta-Saskatchewan Regional Rep, LCol Ian A. Nicol; Past President and Director, Maj J.H. Mansfield; Treasurer, LCol A.G. Cameron; Membership Secretary, Lt Paul G. Rivard; Secretary, Maj John "Pappy" MacKinnon; Director Ottawa Region, Maj Terry B. Kelly; Director Quebec Region, Maj Franz F. Laizner; Director Maritime Region, Maj Robert C. Dale; Director Ontario Region, Maj Fred E.G. Jones; Director Manitoba Region, LCol Dale M. Watts; Director BC Region, Col A.H. Sam Stevenson; Director Academic Program, Maj Nils E. Lindberg; Director Regional Affairs, Col Robert T. Grogan; Director Historical and Legal Affairs, Capt David A. Rubin; Director-at-large, Maj D.E. Guyatt; and, Director-at-large, Col Jeff S. Upton.[21]

## 1988, Award of the Nobel Peace Prize to UN Peacekeepers

Canada continues to send intelligence personnel with various units assigned to NATO and UN duties overseas. The Canadian Airborne Regiment, accompanied by its Regimental Intelligence Section, went to Cyprus in 1986 for example. At the time of writing, one Canadian Intelligence Branch member is still on duty at UNFICYP in Nicosia, Cyprus.

On Friday, 30 September 1988, it was announced in Oslo, Norway, that the 1988 Nobel Peace Prize was awarded to all United Nation's peacekeepers. Committee chairman Egil Aarvik said the UN forces have made "a decisive contribution" to peace around the world, and the award citation noted that

---

21.  CISA Newsletter, Vol. 19, No. 3, December 1988, pp. 1-4.

they have done so "under extremely difficult conditions." In New York, UN Secretary General Javier Perez de Cuellar told the General Assembly, "The award is a tribute to the idealism of all who have served this organization and in particular to the valour and sacrifice of those who have contributed, and continue to contribute, to our peacekeeping operations." Since 1948, more than 500,000 UN personnel from 58 nations have been involved in the peace-keeping forces (including virtually all serving members of the Int Branch). More than 733 persons have been killed over the years (and of these, more than 150 of them have been Canadian). Under the Nobel charter, the prize is awarded "for the best work for fraternity between nations, for the abolition of standing armies and the holding and promotion of peace congresses."[22]

In Central America, Canada participated in two UN peacekeeping missions. The United Nations Observer Group in Central America (ONUCA) operated in five countries, particularly in Nicaragua from November 1989 to January 1992. Team members serving with ONUCA verified the cessation of foreign military assistance to the Nicaraguan rebels known as the Contras, and ensured the non-use of one territory for attacks on others, and demobilized the rebels.[23]

## *1988, Electronic Warfare Course, UK*

On 13 Oct 1988, the author was loaded on a two-week course in Electronic Warfare held in the UK, flying to London with Capt Yung Gin Hou, and Capt Michel Bédard and LCdr W. Burns MacDonald who were to attend the same course. Between 17 and 27 Oct they were trained on the Electronic Warfare-Land Specialist Course (EL), at Loughborough and Blandford, UK. On Thursday, 27 Oct, they were notified that Princess Anne needed the Mess for the evening, so they finished the course at 5 PM and headed back to London via bus to Salisbury and train to Waterloo Station, staying in the Strand Hotel. While there, the author was notified that he would be required to stay in the UK for another two weeks to attend a Psy Ops course at the UK Intelligence School in Ashford. He was to report to CDLS in London the next day. From 2 Nov to 11 Nov 88 he attended the Staff Psy Ops Course (RJ), at Ashford, with Capt W.A. "Tony" Rennett and Maj Greg Jensen. In the evenings

---

22. Fred Kaplan, *Boston Globe Online*, Internet: www.boston.com, 30 Sep 1988, pp. 1-2.
23. Internet: www.thememoryproject.com.

they walked around the town of Ashford, finding an old WW I tank on display in the centre of the town square, where it had been parked since 1919.

# 7

## 1989, Intelligence Branch

### 1989, Airborne Casualties

The author received his posting message on 19 Jan 89, which indicated he was going back to Germany to be the Brigade G2 Ops in 4 CMBG HQ and Signals Squadron. From 23 Jan to 9 Jun 89 the author attended the Canadian Land Force Command and Staff College (Foxhole U) in Kingston, Ont. Between 10 and 11 Feb 1989 there was a terrible series of accidents back in Petawawa. A Trooper from 1 Commando was killed on the grenade range, another died in a motorcycle accident. Five soldiers from 2 Commando died in a car accident on Friday, then on Sunday 14 soldiers were killed including nine from the Canadian Airborne Regiment, in a Hercules crash in Alaska during Exercise BRIMFROST. MCpl P. William MacKinnon was one of them from the Regiment's HQ, and WO Arsenault from the Med Section, two from the RCHA, two from 1 Cdo, and three from Edmonton. It is bad enough to lose one, but so many at once was very hard on all who had served with them

### 1989, CISA Member News

MGen Reg Weeks, Colonel Commandant of the Intelligence Branch, notified CISA that he had nominated Capt Gerald "Gerry" A. Mendel to the Department of Veterans Affairs to represent the former C Int C at the forthcoming 45th Anniversary ceremonies to commemorate the Normandy landings, (6 June 1944). Gerry landed on 7 June 1944 with a C Int C Interrogation Team attached to 3 Canadian Infantry Division.

LCol Robert H. "Tex" Noble acquired a copy of The Intelligence Service within the Canadian Corps, 1914-1918, written by James E. Hahn, DSO, and MC in 1930.[1] Col Noble reported the 263-page book covered "in some considerable detail, the organization, functioning and disposition of the Intelligence services in-so-far as a WWI Infantry Division was concerned." The book dealt chiefly with "Front Line Intelligence and how it was obtained, digested, disseminated and acted upon. The organization etc., of the Intelligence Service in formations senior to divisions was dealt with in outline only. Intelligence Summaries, reports, maps and air photos, etc., were included." LCol Noble added, "It is interesting to note that this book was only "discovered" by the Canadian Army's Intelligence organization in 1942, at which time it was studied very thoroughly at the Intelligence School, then located at RMC in Kingston. And, as one of the instructors remarked to me in 1953, 'had we had a copy of the book in 1939 we could have saved a lot of the time we wasted on trial and error.' The main value of the book is perhaps historical—but much of the material in the book reveals that the principles have remained constant; only the application has to be updated. [It is] a damned good book to read and studied by the really interested Intelligence professional."[2]

## 1989, CISA Member News

Three CISA members passed away, LCol John "Jack" Platt, Maj David G. Kerr and Capt Michael Wormley. 1 Canadian Division Int Company (1 Cdn Div Int Coy) will stand-up on 27 Oct 1989 at CFB Kingston, Ontario. Former members of the wartime 1 Cdn Div Int were invited to attend.[3]

---

1.  James E. Hahn, DSO, MC. The Intelligence Service Within the Canadian Corps, 1914-1918, (MacMillan Co. of Canada, 1930). Hahn was the founder of a pioneer company in radio, and his company, Inglis, manufactured the Czech-designed Bren gun. He served as an Intelligence officer in WWI, and also "designed, developed and put into operation the first Mobile Laundry and Bath Unit in the allied armies." James E. Hahn, DSO, MC. For Action—The Autobiography of a Canadian Industrialist (Clarke-Irwin Co., 1954), pp. 23-87.
2.  CISA Newsletter, Vol. 20, No. 1, May 1989, pp. 1-4.
3.  CISA Newsletter, Vol. 20, No. 2, July 1989, pp. 1-2.

LCol Kam Len Douglas was the most decorated, highest-ranking Chinese-Canadian officer in history, a veteran of RCAF 426 Thunderbird Squadron, fighting in the Malay States, and Chief Intelligence Officer at Immigration in the B.C/Yukon Region. As an RCAF Staff Officer, Intelligence, he maintained liaison with high-level U.S., British, and NATO agencies including Pentagon and Central Intelligence Agency (CIA) Headquarters. He died in Vancouver, B.C. on July 3, 1989.

## 1989, CLFCSC Kingston, (Foxhole U)

During the author's training at CLFCSC, the students were flown on 26 Feb 1989 by C-130 Hercules from Trenton, Ontario to Lawson AFB and then on to Fort Benning, Georgia, USA, where they were billeted in a huge troop complex. Over the next few days the "Rangers" gave the students a series of lectures, tours and a demonstration. They were also given a live fire demonstration by the M-1 Abrams tank and the Bradley armoured fighting vehicle. The highlight of the display came when the students were given the opportunity to actually get into the Bradley turret and fire the 25-mm cannon for several bursts down range. Each student took the opportunity to fire the M-19 grenade launcher, the M-16A2 rifle (very accurate—at least the targets fell down that were shot at), the 9-mm Berretta pistol, and the Minimi machine-gun. The class fired approximately $1 million worth of ammo during the demo, before flying back to Trenton and being driven from there by bus to Kingston.

On 30 Apr 1989, the staff college course was flown from Toronto to Frankfurt, Germany for additional training. While in Lahr, the author took the opportunity to meet his future German landlord, and to visit the Kaserne to meet with Capt J. René Gauthier and Capt Clark J. Beamish at 4 CMBG to discuss the new job. The author also sent some of his paperwork forward for processing into 4 CMBG. He ran into the men at the CFE Int Section where the author had worked from 1981-83. On 3 May 89 the Staff College was taken as a group to a German Leopard II tank base. The students were given a briefing on this unit's mission, then all loaded onto three big Sikorsky CH-53 Super Stallion helicopters and flown up to Hof to do a 30-km ground tour of the Inter-German Border (IGB). The East German guards photographed the group photographing them etc. The dog runs between the barbed wire were disturbing to see. The students were then loaded back onto the two helicopters and were flown back to a field training area near Amberg to view a dynamic weapons display in the field, which included Leopard II tanks in heavy camouflage and Marder recce vehicles providing a route-clearing exhibition. They were also allowed to clamber onboard each of the vehicles, AAA Gepard systems, MRLS etc. One of the helicopters was grounded, so there was a delay while the students had to wait for a third to arrive. They ate lunch in the field with the German Troops. In the evening the Germans hosted the students to a Bayerisherabend, and brought in a really good band (ohm-papa music), beer and pork.

On 4 May 89 the students were bussed from Amberg to Nurnberg, stopping briefly at the sports stadium to view the scene of the famous Nazi rallies (and trials), then went on to the train station. The group went by train to Frankfurt, then changed trains for Paris, arriving about 1130 PM. From there the group immediately loaded onto buses for the three-hour drive to Caen in Normandy. On 5 May 89 they left the Climat Hotel in Caen and took a bus to St Aubin-sur-Mer and the Normandy beaches with a group of Canadian and German veterans. The author's group hosted Col Helmut Ritgen of the Panzer Lehr Division. All visited Bernières-sur-Mer and Courseulles-sur-Mer, both invasion beach-landing sites, then drove on to Creully, Putot-en-Bessin, Buron, and Villons les Buissons. The students were given a French box lunch, which included a bottle of red wine, then moved on to Marcelet, Carpiquet and later in the evening into Caen.

On 6 May 89 the bus drivers took the group to battlefield sites, with lectures and briefings on site at Hill 112, St André, Troteval Farm, Bourgebus, "Tilly" and the area concerning "Operation Totalize." The tour ended with a visit to one of the Canadian cemeteries containing many unknown Canadian soldiers. In the evening the group went to the Memorial museum in Caen, with a very rare Hawker Typhoon fighter-bomber suspended from the ceiling and a great amount of information displayed. On 7 May they took the bus to Carpiquet airport, where a C-130 Hercules flew them to back to Lahr. They were later taken by bus to Frankfurt airport for the flight back to Toronto.

Between 1 and 8 June all of the students took part in Ex Final Drive, the last CLFCSC Div CPX, with course graduation on 8 June 1989. The author drove back to Petawawa, took some leave, and then turned in his airborne jump smock and kit at base clothing stores on 22 June. He was mugged out at the Airborne Officer's Mess on 23 June, closing with the words (from the heart), "Gentlemen, it has been a privilege to have served with you."

The author and his family flew to Lahr on 8 July 1989, to take up his new job as G2 Ops at 4 CMBG, part of 1 Cdn Div Fwd, under BGen J.J.M.R.

Gaudreau (his former Airborne Commander, present Brigade Commander and future Division Commander). The author would serve in this Unit until June 1992, the year before it was disbanded as 4 CMB (1993).

## *From the Intelligence Branch Advisor, LCol David M. Robb, Fall 1989*

When I took up the appointment of Branch Advisor five years ago, I was told that it would be only temporary. Due to the short tenure of Col George L.R. Bruce who followed me, I found myself in the job once again in 1986, and have held the appointment since. All things come to an end however, and by the time you read this, Col Victor V. Ashdown will have returned to Canada to take up both the post of Director Intelligence Warsaw pact and the appointment of Branch Advisor. He is no stranger to either since he has worked in DG Int before and was Branch Advisor during the creation of the Intelligence Branch. I therefore anticipate a smooth transfer of Branch administration.

As I leave this appointment, I do so with a good deal of satisfaction. In the seven years since our inauguration, I believe that our Branch has indeed confirmed its identity and is well on the road to achieving recognition as the acknowledged expert in the Intelligence function. As you all know, this was not always so. During our formative years, however, we have doubled the size of our officer corps and increased the number of our Int Ops by over 25%. Our growth has been so rapid that we cannot keep up with the demands for new Sgts. In all the operational Commands, we have been assigned the responsibility for providing the senior Intelligence officer. I believe all these to be positive indicators that our Branch is now recognized and its product valued in the CF.

I have said it before but believe that it bears reiteration that most of this recognition is due to your individual and collective efforts. You have all been salesmen for our Branch and it is evident to me that Commanders have liked what you have shown them. At the risk of singling out one agency, I would especially like to thank the staff of Intelligence Training Company, CFSIS, CFB Borden for this achievement. Despite being short staffed and over tasked, they have succeeded in moulding the students sent to them into the Intelligence officers and NCMs who are eventually sent afield to be our representatives. To my mind, the results quoted above prove that they have done a praise-worthy job, which merits the thanks and support of all of us.

These achievements however, are only the beginning. As we enter an era of gradually warming relationships between East and West, it will behove us even more to carefully monitor and assess the present and future capabilities of the Warsaw Pact, so as to allow our government to respond appropriately as we move towards arms control. More specifically for our Branch, we will have to increase the environmental specialization of our training if we are to provide Commanders with the Intelligence detail they deserve. ADP is now with us, and our older generation especially will have to come to terms with its use as a processing tool. Finally, if we are ever to truly become "masters of our own house" as the Colonel Commandant would say, we must continue to demonstrate that we are indeed the best in the business. Only then can we expect to be given the responsibility at all levels of directing the conduct of our function.

In closing, I would like to thank all of you for the support you have given me during my tour of duty. Having been in many cases "primus inter pares," it has not always been easy and without your help and advice I could not have done the job. I wish you all the best in your careers and urge you to keep the light shining from the darkness.[4]

## *Intelligence Branch Advisor, Col Victor V. Ashdown, CD, Fall 1989*

Col Victor V. Ashdown enrolled in the Canadian Army in 1960 and joined the Canadian Intelligence Corps in 1962. He graduated from the Royal Military College in 1965 with a degree in Politics and Geography. Following a few months as Area Security Officer for Alberta Area and Brigade Intelligence Officer at 1 Brigade, Calgary, he was posted to 1 Battalion, Canadian Guards, Picton, Ontario, for a two-year tour as an infantry platoon commander.

In 1967, he returned to the Canadian School of Military Intelligence, CFB Borden, completed his advanced Intelligence training and remained as an instructor. He was promoted to Capt in September 1967, and became Adjutant of CFSIS in 1969. In October 1970, he served with FMC HQ in Montreal and subsequently was posted to 2 Combat Group, Petawawa as the Intelligence Officer in December of that year. In October 1972, he was promoted to Major and posted to FMC HQ as Intelligence Staff Officer.

---

4.    Intelligence Branch Journal, Number 8, Fall 1989, p. 2. (Last of eight editions of the IBJ)

The year 1975 saw another move, this time to NDHQ in Ottawa for analyst duties in the Directorate of Intelligence Production. After a few months, he was tasked to establish the National Defence Intelligence Centre (NDIC). This done, he was selected to attend the Canadian Forces Command and Staff College (CFCSC), Toronto, in the fall of 1976.

On graduation from CFCSC in 1977, he was promoted to LCol and returned to Ottawa to command the NDIC for one more year. Subsequently, he served two years as a Section Head in the Directorate of Defence Intelligence and three years in charge of the Operations, Plans and Training Section in the Intelligence and Security Division. During this latter employment, he was closely involved in the formation of the CF Intelligence Branch, and became the first Branch Advisor in October 1982.

In August 1983, he was sent to Washington as the Senior Canadian Forces Intelligence Liaison Officer for a three-year tour. He returned to Ottawa in the summer of 1986, and was promoted to Col and completed language training in preparation for a tour as CF Attaché, Warsaw, Poland, commencing in 1987. Col Victor V. Ashdown was posted to NDHQ in August 1989, and assumed the appointments of Director Intelligence Warsaw Pact (DIWP) and Intelligence Branch Advisor.

Col Victor V. Ashdown is married and he has two children. His hobbies include electronics, music, woodworking, current affairs, military history and bicycling.[5]

## *1989, Out of Service Training*

Once a year, usually in April, the Director of Individual Training (DIT) will issue a message to Command SSOs Training calling for out-service training (OST). This covers specific specialized training for the CF including Intelligence training, which is coordinated directly through DIPD in NDHQ. Although out-of-service courses are not tailor made for Canada, quite often they can be the only means of obtaining a course not practically available due to cost in Canada.

The qualifications that have been obtained by Int Ops on such courses include:

5.    Intelligence Branch Journal, Number 8, Fall 1989, pp. 4-5.

a. Soviet Operational Doctrine—Intelligence;

b. Basic/Operation Imagery Interpretation;

c. Strategic Imagery Analyst;

d. Land EW Analyst—Basic;

e. Land EW Analyst—Advanced;

f. Typing (RPO);

g. 111.13      PW Handling & Tactical Questioning Methodology;

h. 111.TBA    Kinesic Interviewing Techniques;

i. 8A         Combat Ops Air/Ground Familiarization;

j. US         Soviet Awareness.

Qualifications obtained through out-of-service training for Int 82 officers include:

a. 82.A6      Electronic Warfare—Int Analysis;

b. 82.A8      Instructor Soviet Operational Doctrine;

c. 82.A9      PW Handling & Tactical Questioning Methodology;

d. 82.TBA     Kinesic Interviewing Technique;

e. EJ         ATO Air Staff Officer;

f. EK         EW—Land Basic;

g. EL         EW—Land Specialist;

h. EQ         EW—NATO Advanced;

i. ET         EW—NATO Orientation;

j. EO13       NATO Air Ground Operations Course;

k. RG         Joint Staff Intelligence;

l. RJ          Psy Ops Staff Officer;

m. RT         Soviet Awareness;

n. UM        Ace Targeting Procedures;

o. 4E         Combat Ops Air/Ground Familiarization.[*]

    *   Intelligence Branch Journal, Number 8, Fall 1989, pp. 6-7.

## *1989, CFSIS*

Intelligence Operator 6A Course 8901.
Rear Row: MCpl Donald M. Gallaher, MCpl J.M.A. Stéphane Chartrand, MCpl Ron T.A. Wulf, MCpl J.C. Mario Roy, MS William M. Flanagan, MS David H. Kushmier, MCpl D. Mike Donahue, MCpl J.H.D. Gauthier.
Centre Row: MCpl John C. Penner, MCpl J.P. Tetu, MCpl Nicholas R. Procenko, MCpl J.R. Mario Ross, MCpl Keith M. Young, MCpl Sgt J.G.

Chartier, MCpl Richard C. Gow.
Seated: PO2 Jeff A. Collings, WO Barry E. Beldam, Capt J.M. Richard
Larchevesque, Maj Robert M. Parsons, CPO Brian Noble, Sgt N.L. Gordon.

## 1989, Militia Intelligence Summer Training, CFSIS Article by Lt André. F. Berdais

Summer 1989 was another busy period at CFSIS, CFB Borden. Militia personnel from Reserve Intelligence Sections received extensive training on a variety of Combat Intelligence-related courses. The instructors were a mixed group of Regular and Reserve Force officers and NCOs from across Canada. Capt Gord P. Ohlke, CTC, CFB Gagetown and Capt J.L. François Messier, FMC HQ, St Hubert, and the Intermediate Classification Training (Capt Qual) course. Lt Arnold S. Neumann, Edmonton Intelligence Section and 2Lt R.B. MacRae, CFSIS, took care of the Basic Classification Training (Lt Qual) course. Lt Colin A.J. Kiley, AMA Intelligence Section, with the help of the other instructors was kept busy with the Intermediate Trade Training (Sgt Qual) course. Lt André. F. Berdais, Section des Renseignements de Secteur de l'Est, instructed on all these courses and was responsible for their proper coordination. PO2 A. "Tony" Wyver, 1 CBG G2 staff, and Sgt David A. Gelsinger, CFSIS did magnificent work in handling the sometimes-frustrating course administration. In addition, the instructional staff from CFSIS assisted the instructors. In particular, Cpl Reginald J. McAuley 's lectures on equipment recognition, WO Terry J. Thompson's lectures on Soviet-related subjects, and Capt J.M. Richard Larchevesque's lecture on friendly and enemy air operations were very informative. At the CFSIS Coordination cell, Sgt F.V. Gordon was more than helpful in dealing with our "much too often" last minute requests.

The curriculum on all courses was quite heavy, and included extensive lectures on Canadian and Soviet Forces organization, doctrine and operations, PW handling, military security and Unit training. Of course, Intelligence doctrine, organization and operations were also taught in great detail.

Because of the heavy course load, students were only able to survive by working hard, working smart and exercising careful time management. To supplement their in-class lectures, reading and homework assignments to be done for the next morning became a way of life for the students. Their newly acquired knowledge was tested through the use of written PO checks, Tutorial

Exercises, Command Post Exercises and Tactical Exercises Without Troops (TEWTs).

To conclude, although working through a hot and humid summer, students left CFB Borden having gained more knowledge and experience which will be helpful in their continuing part-time careers with the Intelligence Branch.[6]

## News from the Reserves, Basic Classification Training Intelligence Course 8901
## Article by 2Lt James P. Terfry, AMA Int Section

The Basic Classification Training (BCT) Intelligence Course 8901, commenced on 3 July 1989. The BCT course is separated into two phases, BCT 1 & BCT 2, for a total of six weeks. The course is coordinated through the CFSIS Intelligence Training Company, but instructed primarily by Reserve force personnel. Upon the successful completion of BCT 1 & 2, the candidates will be qualified to the rank of Lt in the Army Intelligence occupation.

Being a basic qualifying course, the BCT Intelligence course covers a very wide range of subjects such as military security, PW handling, Canadian Land Forces organization and doctrine, Intelligence organization and doctrine, enemy organization, equipment and tactics. Due to the short duration of the course, the workload can be described as heavy at the best of times. The lessons include several in-class/home assignments, special projects, and readings on related material.

This year, there were five candidates attending BCT 1 & 2. These candidates were reservists from all across Canada and were instrumental in providing the framework for the total force expansion program. Lt Sandra Gordon and 2Lt James P. Terfry of the Atlantic Militia Area Intelligence Section in Halifax, NS, 2Lt Brian A. Werner and 2Lt Charles Buffone of the North Alberta Militia District Intelligence Section in Edmonton, Alberta, and Lt Liam Robertson of the Central Militia Area Intelligence Section in Toronto, Ontario, were the students on this course.

The BCT Intelligence course is laid out so as to familiarize and exercise the student in carrying out the varied duties and responsibilities within a brigade

---

6.    Intelligence Branch Journal, Number 8, Fall 1989, pp. 8-9.

group Intelligence section. On completion of the course the student will be able to perform the duties of an officer with a brigade G2 staff.[7]

Basic Classification Training Course 8901.
Rear Row: Lt Colin A.J. Kiley, 2Lt Brian A. Werner, 2Lt Charles Buffone, Lt Sandra Gordon, Lt Liam Robertson, 2Lt James P. Terfry, Lt Arnold S. Neumann.
Front Row: WO B.E. Beldam, Maj Robert M. Parsons, Lt André F. Berdais, PO2 A. "Tony" Wyver, 2Lt R.B. MacRae.

## 1989, Militia Intelligence Training, Camp Aldershot, Nova Scotia

Cpl Danny J. Palmer, 3 Battalion, the Black Watch (Royal Highland Regiment of Canada) won the top candidate's plaque for the Intelligence Opera-

---

7.  Intelligence Branch Journal, Number 8, Fall 1989, p. 8.

tor's Basic Trade Training (BTT) Course that graduated from Camp Aldershot on 11 Aug 1989. Cpl D.J. Palmer is on attachment to the Section des Renseignements de Secteur de l'Est, Montreal.

Pte Nancy L. Mah of the North Alberta Detachment, Prairie Militia District Intelligence Section, won the Veinotte Memorial Trophy as the top candidate on the Specialist Trade Training Intelligence Operator's Course that graduated from the Militia Training Centre (MTC) at Camp Aldershot on 25 Aug 1989. Pte N.L. Mah is a first-year engineering student at the University of Alberta in Edmonton. She joined the Prairie Area Intelligence Section in July 1988.

The officers and soldiers of the Atlantic Militia Area Intelligence Section dedicate the Veinotte Memorial Trophy to the memory of Major Sherman R. Veinotte, CD, on behalf of his family. Maj Veinotte, who died in May 1988, commanded the AMA Intelligence Section from 1976 to 1978. He was among the first recruits to 3 Int Trg Coy in 1951, and served with Militia Intelligence for over 30 years.[8]

## *1989, Intelligence Personnel News*

The following Int Branch personnel have been promoted: LCol K.A.W. Peter Mackenzie, 1 Jan 89; LCol Ray J. Taylor, 1 Jan 89; LCol R. Geoff St John, 1 Jan 89; Maj J. René Gauthier, 16 May 89; Maj Mike R. Rothschild, 15 Jun 89; Maj Lloyd W. Hackel, 1 Jul 89; Maj G. Allen Grant, 1 Jan 89; Maj J.P. André Tremblay, 14 Jun 89; Maj J.G.A.J.C. Rousseau, 15 Jun 89; Maj S.L. Carr, 25 Jul 89; Capt John M. Heinrichs, 1 Jan 89; Capt Peter J. Scales, 1 Jan 89; and, Capt J.L. François Messier, 1 Jan 89.

CWO J.R. Ray LeCavalier, 1 Jan 89; CWO J. Ron Martin, 1 Jan 89; MWO Rick J. Tervo, 1 Dec 89; MWO P.R. Berikoff, 1 Jul 89; MWO Armado Santos, 1 Aug 89; MWO J.R. Claude Morin, 1 Aug 89; WO David J. Whalen, 1 Jun 88; WO Barry R. Eddy, 1 Jul 88; WO J.J. Dionne, 1 Dec 88; WO Mike E. Higgins, 1 Dec 88; WO Rick C. Nickerson, 1 Dec 88; WO Harry V. Delorey, 1 Jun 89; WO J. Dan Galley, 1 Jun 89; WO D.J. Bruton, 1 Jun 89; WO Ray O. Toovey, 1 Jun 89; WO P.A. Maillet, 1 Jul 89; WO William A. Mitchell, 1 Jul 89; WO Roderick L. Gill, 1 Aug 89; WO Dan J. Haslip, 1 Aug 89; WO J. Ron Martin, 1 Aug 89; WO M.G. McCann, 1 Aug 89; Sgt R.G. Oliver, 1 Jan 89; Sgt Steve Mercer, 1 Jan 89; Sgt D.H. McLaren,

---

8.    Intelligence Branch Journal, Number 8, Fall 1989, pp. 9-10.

1 Jun 89; PO2 J.R. Michel "Mike" Labossiere, 1 Jun 89; Sgt Gary R. Hayes, 1 Jul 89; Sgt Daryl W. Monk, 1 Jul 89; Sgt R. Hal Pugh, 1 Jul 89; Sgt J.L.A. Martineau, 1 Jul 89; Sgt J.R.M. Ross, 1 Jul 89; Sgt K.L. Dyer, 1 Aug 89; Sgt J.R.P. Turcotte, 1 Aug 89; Sgt J.R. François Bouchard, 1 Aug 89; MCpl J.M.R. Dan Jacques, 1 Jan 89; MCpl Brian K. Mudge, 1 Jan 89; MCpl J.P. St Pierre, 1 Jan 89; MCpl John Paul Michael Parsons, 1 Jan 89; Maj J.P. André Tremblay, 1 Jan 89; MCpl John C. Penner, 1 Jan 89; MCpl Donald M. Gallaher, 1 Jun 89; MCpl Dennis G. McNulty, 1 Jun 89; MCpl D.M. Wilkerson, 1 Jun 89; MCpl R. Jack Wilson, 1 Jun 89; MCpl J.E. Paul Pellerin, 1 Jun 89; MCpl David G. Maxim, 1 Jun 89; MCpl J.A. Chris Pelletier, 1 Jul 89; MCpl P.G. Manuge, 1 Jul 89; MCpl J.J.L. Denis Chercuite, 1 Aug 89, MCpl T.P. Farnel, 1 Aug 89; and, MCpl J.B. François Allard, 1 Aug 89.

The following personnel have remustered to the Int Branch and completed the Basic Intelligence Officer Course (BIOC) 8901:

Capt T.J. O'Toole, Capt Boris A. Fedoruk, Capt J.C. Chris Gagnon, Capt Kathryn B. Clouston, Lt (N) Doug C. Jantzi, Capt D.D. Nickel, Lt Al Haywood, 2Lt William "Bill" M. Glenfield, Lt (N) W.E. Miller, 2Lt David R. Canavan, Capt G.F. Dow, Capt Chris J. Wallace, Capt Rajeev G. Nath, Capt J.E.S. Lesage, Capt Mike H. Heitmann, Lt (N) Shawn P. Osborne, Lt J.A.E. Kent Dowell, Lt P.M. Kelly, Lt Phil R. Coo, and, 2 Lt R. Stu W. MacAulay.

The following personnel completed the QL 5A Course 8901:

Cpl P.G. Manuge, Cpl M.G. Gillingham, Cpl Neil M. Fletcher, Cpl J.R. Charles Conlin, Cpl Kenneth E. Davies, Cpl Sean T. Dutrisac, Cpl J.J.J. Brun, LS J.U. Serge St Jacques, LS Dan C. Little, LS Richard Lee Fletcher, LS Donald R.A. Wagnell, LS Thomas E. Scott, LS R.R. Given, LS W. Robert "Bob" Murley, LS Don S. Eenkooren, and LS J.L. Dennis Goulet.

The following personnel completed the QL 5A Course 8902:

Cpl L.A. Clarke, Cpl C.M. Fleming, Cpl Lawrence M. Tierney, Cpl Daniel Francis McNeil, Cpl Wayne D. Upshall, Cpl J.L.R. Pelletier, Cpl Serge Laforge, Cpl Richard R.P. Walsh, LS Cliff J. Boyechko, Cpl J.C.M. Toy, Cpl Connie F. Lancaster, Cpl John T. Smola, Cpl Ernest S. Kuffner, Cpl Kevin Toomer, Cpl J. Daniel Garant, and, Cpl J.D. Pete Boutin.

The following personnel have been released:

MWO Barry M. Gardner, Sgt J.G. Malenfant, Sgt M. Paul McNeil, PO2 S.B. Calford.[9]

---

9.    Intelligence Branch Journal, Number 8, Fall 1989, p. 28.

## 1989, Canadian Land Force Command and Staff College

Capt Harold A. Skaarup completed CLFCSC in June 1989.

## Army Intelligence in 2002
## Article by Capt W.A. "Tony"Rennett, Int Journal, Fall 1989

*Background.* The 1987 Defence White Paper concluded that consolidation in Southern Germany was the best way for Canada to better satisfy its NATO defence commitments. It also stressed the requirement for National forces dedicated to the protection of our sovereign territory. While these tasks appear to differ little from previous policy, they initiated a flurry of staff planning which has lead to a major reorganization of Canada's Land Forces and will culminate in the Total Force Army of 2002. As most readers are aware, the restructure has breathed new life for the Intelligence Branch. The aim of this article is to describe the effects that restructure will have on Army Intelligence organizations. In order to understand how Intelligence fits into the new structure, it is necessary to be familiar with Army 2002. This organization will contain a Field Force and Infrastructure.

The major organizational highlights of the Field Force include the formation of 1 Cdn Division, Augmentation and Readiness Brigade Groups, and a Territorial Defence Force. 1 Cdn Div is tasked as the CENTAG Reserve, while the Territorial Defence Force is responsible for Defence of North America. The Augmentation and Readiness (A&R) Brigade Groups will be required to provide support to both our ACE and Territorial Defence Forces. The Infrastructure will provide a stable base for mobilization and expansion even though the Field Force may be committed to other tasks. This means that Land Force HQ (LFHQ) will be responsible for the command, control, training, and administration of all Land Forces in Canada. LFHQ will delegate responsibility for these activities as well as aspects of Regional Operations to four Area Commanders. The Area Commanders will command all Land Forces both Regular and Reserve within their geographic areas of responsibility. This last point is the cornerstone of restructure. In the new Army, there will be no such thing as Regulars and Reserves; rather, full and part-time soldiers will serve together in the same Unit. The percentage of full to part-time personnel will depend in large part to the degrees of readiness required of each Unit.

Army Intelligence 2002 Structure and Tasks. The plan to provide Intelligence support for Army 2002 requires the provision of Intelligence staffs to LFHQ, the Task Force (TF), our ACE committed forces, the A&R Brigades, and the Infrastructure. There will be a substantial increase in Militia Intelligence positions.

The LFHQ Intelligence staff will likely be based on the existing FMC HQ organization. It will include a G2 Estimates, a special material control office, a policy and training coordination cell, liaison teams, and Imagery exploitation section and an administrative support cell. It will be responsible for coordinating all source Intelligence in direct support of the Intelligence requirements established by the Commander Land Forces and Defence of North America Operations will be a high priority. It will also coordinate support for all land Intelligence matters including policy, plans, training and doctrine. Reflecting the Total Force idea, it is significant that over 50% of the War Establishment positions in this organization are Militia.

An Intelligence Company will be formed to support the TF, with a structure that will provide Intelligence support to the TF in Defence of Canada Operations. As with the LFHQ Intelligence staff, this organization's war establishment is approximately 60% Militia.

1 Cdn Div Int Coy is a new Unit in the CF Order of battle that will support 1 Cdn Div with three Int Platoons consisting of an Intelligence Collection and Analysis Centre (ICAC), a Support Platoon and an Intelligence Operations and Training Platoon. The Division G2 will provide direction based on the Divisional Commander's mission to the Intelligence Company. The Company will be responsible for collecting and processing information for the G2 who will then control dissemination. In contrast to the manning of the previously described staffs, the Division Intelligence Company will be primarily manned by Regular Force personnel. This is because the Division has a higher degree of readiness than the TF and therefore requires more full-time soldiers. The Intelligence staffs of the two Brigades that makeup 1 Cdn Division (4 and 5e Brigade), will also be expanded to a platoon with an ICAC and an Intelligence Operations section.

An Intelligence Platoon (-) will provide support to the A&R Brigade Groups. The net result is that the A&R Brigade Group Intelligence Organizations will retain an ICAC facility. The Operations Intelligence Support functions will be provided by resources from either the TF Intelligence Company or by the Intelligence Organizations found in the Area Headquarters. This structure has evolved from the concepts that the Army is developing for dividing the Intelligence responsibilities between the various levels of command supporting Defence of Canada Operations.

As stated earlier, the Infrastructure will provide a firm base for further mobilization and the mechanism by which Regional Operations will be conducted. It will be based on the formation of 4 Area Headquarters: Western, Central, Eastern and Atlantic. The Intelligence staff to support the Area Commanders will contain a G2 staff supported by an Area Intelligence Company. The G2 will assume responsibility for providing Intelligence support to Regional Operations and for coordinating the Intelligence training requirements within his area of responsibility. Except for Eastern Area, the Area Intelligence Companies are co-located with the Area HQs. These Companies will be modeled on the current Militia Intelligence Sections and the proposed locations include Vancouver, Edmonton, Winnipeg, Toronto, Ottawa, Kingston, Montreal, and Halifax. The Companies will have the responsibility to train branch specialists for augmentation to other Intelligence staffs within the Land Forces, and to support the Area G2.

Augmentation means Operational Tasking and depends on three considerations: 1) Op Tasking must recognize the distinction between ACE, TF, and A&R commitments and should be assigned in a manner which serves to promote an even distribution of resources across Canada. 2) Op Tasking will be issued for formed sub-Units so that all Intelligence specialists assigned to each formation are drawn from one parent Intelligence Company. 3) Op Taskings will, as far as possible be assigned to the Intelligence Company which is closest to the support Formation. For planning purposes, FMC Int Op Taskings will ensure each Company has a TF, ACE, or A&R mission. All Militia Intelligence personnel assigned to either a Headquarters or a Combat Intelligence Unit are drawn from a single Intelligence Company and can be deployed as individuals or a sub-Unit.

*Implementation Schedule.* At this point it must be understood that the proposed structures represent Army Intelligence in 2002. The implementation schedule will be tied closely to the Army restructure plan and no one should be surprised if this schedule requires modification during the next decade. In addition, the Intelligence Branch is small and this limits its capacity to absorb and train new members whether Reserve or Regular. As FMC staff checks show, the Branch will have difficulty to cope with more than 60 students each year during the next five years. Therefore it is the Army's philosophy that growth must occur at a gradual rate. However, the increases for 1989 are occurring now. Part of the G2 staff and the ICAC Platoon of 1 Cdn Div will be manned this summer. This also includes the transfer of the three-man CI section now held against 4 CMBG's establishment to the Company. 2 Int Trg Coy in Toronto which is Op Tasked to the Division will be expanded. In addition, it is expected that an Officer and WO position will open this year to form the nucleus of the TF G2 staff. Finally, FMC intends to issue an Op Tasking to the Intelligence Section in Winnipeg to form a cadre to support the TF Intelligence Company ICAC.

1990 and beyond will witness the reactivation of the Militia Intelligence Companies in phases over the next few years. FMC staff checks suggest that it will take approximately three to four years to get each of these Companies through the start-up phase and up to seven years to train and recruit to establishment. The increase in Regular Force positions will also be phased in over a period of years and additional Officer and NCM courses have been scheduled to meet the demand.

*Implications for the Intelligence Branch.* The organizations described in this article are likely to alter the way that Intelligence staffs conduct training and day-to-day operations. Fundamental to the training issue, is the entire philosophy on how the Branch should structure training. Current Army Intelligence Doctrine has evolved faster than the infrastructure required to train the personnel to make it work. For example, the Basic Intelligence Officer's Course (BIOC) has been criticized because it does not provide the staff training necessary for Army Intelligence Officers to function within the ICAC concept of Operations. In trying to be all things to all environments, the BIOC fails to adequately meet the requirements of any of the environments. In addition, the formation of Intelligence Companies place a renewed emphasis for subject matter expertise in training areas long neglected within our Branch. For example, what are we going to do and where are we going in the development of CI training? Even if our courses are not amended, the increasing numbers of land Intelligence positions will strain our already inadequate training infrastructure to the point where the quality of the product will suffer. Given the limitations in training time and resources, it essentially boils down to resolving the conflicting priorities of Canadian Forces green Intelligence training or more comprehensive environmental training.

The division of responsibility for the day-to-day production of Intelligence could also change as a result of restructure. The increased capability for analysis at lower echelons of Command, should result in decentralization for Intelligence production and a corresponding increase in efficiency. For example, might not some of the information now processed at the National level on combat capabilities of Warsaw Pact Ground Forces, be more appropriately conducted by the G2 staff at LFHQ or by the Division Intelligence Company. Would this not allow DG Intelligence to concentrate more on strategic Intelligence matters while leaving Combat Intelligence to those Army Units tasked with combat missions? These are only two examples of how the restructure could affect the Intelligence Branch. However, these changes pose a challenge to all Branches and should not be considered unique to the Intelligence Branch. Ultimately, the litmus test for success will be measured by the resolve of the Intelligence Branch and environments to recognize that changes are necessary and to devise solutions which support the plan.

Finally, the challenges presented above will be surmounted if all personnel foster a positive attitude with the Total Force philosophy. The time to argue whether Regular and Militia can or should operate in Total Force Units is over. Attitudes that hinder the restructure implementation plan based on personal attitudes, ambitions, or parochial Branch positions must be resisted if we are to successfully fulfil our responsibilities in the restructure plan.

(The Int Journal Editor noted that the 27 Apr 1989 Budget would significantly modify the Army 2002 Plan in scope, structure and implementation).[10]

*"A plan, like a tree, must have branches—if it is to bear fruit. A plan with a single aim is apt to prove a barren pole."* Napoleon.

## Intelligence for War: The Challenge in Peace
## Article by LCol R. Geoff St John

The wartime requirement for Intelligence is obvious to Army officers and the application of the Intelligence cycle to gain it is well understood. Simply put, the commander decides what he most needs to know about the enemy, and the G2 gets the answers. There is nothing magic about this process; though actually doing it can be difficult, the steps and the respective responsibilities are straightforward. The peacetime applications of the Intelligence cycle seems to be less effective for a variety of reasons, chief amongst which is an apparent lack of awareness that the process and the responsibilities should be just the same in peace as they are in war.

10.　Intelligence Branch Journal, Number 8, Fall 1989, pp. 11-16.

The aim of this article is to describe how the Intelligence cycle should be applied in peace to better prepare ourselves for war. I will break no new ground; rather, I will stick to basics. It will be of practical use to both line and staff officers in all Army Units and formations.

Intelligence Cycle-Same as Ever. The heart of the matter is the Intelligence cycle. To review briefly (in a wartime context) the cycle comprises four steps:

*Direction.* This step involves determining the Priority Intelligence Requirements (PIRs) of the commander; those key facts and estimates about the enemy he needs to fight and win. The busy commander may not have enough time to fully explore his problem, and therefore calls on his G2 and G3 staffs to aid him. He nevertheless, personally makes the final decision on what the PIRs will be, because establishing them remains a command function.

*Collection.* This involves tasking the sources best suited to collect the raw information which, when analyzed as a whole, results in the intelligence the commander wants. While this is essentially a G2 function, the point is that the G2 is not collecting information for his own benefit, but to produce the Intelligence which satisfies the commander's PIRs. This is worth keeping in mind when considering the allocation of resources. Getting the information necessary to satisfy PIRs requires resources.

*Processing.* Information collected is compared with other information and Intelligence in order to produce the answers, which satisfy the commander's PIRs. This is almost entirely a G2 function that is 90% perspiration and 10% inspiration. Processing is manpower-intensive; it requires a considerable number of analysts to plough through the often vast quantities of information available, separate wheat from chaff, and produce usable Intelligence.

Dissemination. All of this is of course useless if the G2 does not answer the commander's questions. While not the focus of this paper, it is worth emphasizing that the commander is by no means compelled to accept his G2's views. The commander is ultimately responsible for judging what the enemy is doing and is going to do, and will thus properly reserve his right to pass final judgement on these two key questions.

*Direction—the Key.* It bears re-emphasizing that it is the commander's responsibility to give this direction. Hence, CFP 301(1) Land Formations in Battle, lists direction of the Intelligence effort as the first specific task of every commander. While the G2 staff must always strive to anticipate the commander's requirements, and aid him in their formulation, this is not enough. The G2 has enough to do trying to read the enemy's mind, without having to read his own commander's as well! For those who tend to take a "hat badge" perspective of the Intelligence function, do not forget that the G2 is simply an Intelligence staff officer while so employed, regardless of his branch of service. Any claim by him that he knows what the commander wants, and thus does not require direction, be a professional Intelligence officer or an arms officer, is dangerous nonsense. If direction from the commander is not forthcoming, the G2 must seek it, and in most cases this is best done by the G2 and G3 developing recommended PIRs to place before the commander.

However, commanders and their G2 staffs are usually not in a position to acquire all the required information using only the resources available to them. In most cases higher Intelligence staffs will have to provide a portion of the information and Intelligence sought. Getting this help means asking specifically for it, rather than assuming it will be forthcoming. This, too, is part of the direction step of the Intelligence cycle. It is therefore necessary for the commander to ensure that, where his acquisition resources are insufficient, the next superior HQ be approached for it. While this might well be accomplished through the G2 technical chain, the commander must not remove himself from the process once the request has been levied. He must at least manage by exception and personally approach the higher G2 staff or his commander if he is dissatisfied with the initial response.

If the commander is not prepared to request assistance from his own commander, then the importance of the information sought is open to question, and so too, the sense of requesting it in the first place. Perhaps judging its real importance lies in the commander asking himself at the outset if he is prepared to fight for the information, either using his own Troops against the enemy, or himself against the higher HQ.

*Direction in Peace is as For War.* Having established the vital role of the commander in the Intelligence cycle, and the frequent necessity to seek higher assistance, we now turn specifically to the question of Intelligence requirements in peace. There is nothing inherently wrong with the process described insofar as its peacetime use is concerned. What is different is that only in rare circumstances will a commander have his own resources or the authority to gain information about the enemy on his won. What is also different is that while higher HQs will have greater authority, their peacetime resources to collect and process information into Intelligence are usually very limited.

At the present, Intelligence collection and processing are functions, which are almost entirely the province of NDHQ. Army G2 staffs are too small to do much original processing themselves. It follows that Unit COs will have their PIRs satisfied for the most part by the NDHQ Intelligence staff. Naturally, Units would not forward their requirements directly to NDHQ; brigade HQ staffs would consolidate the brigade commander's PIRs with those of the Unit COs, to send up the chain of command. At each level, similar staff action would occur before they arrive at NDHQ.

At all levels, the commander must personally approve the PIRs and sign the correspondence, as he would in war. Otherwise, there is a risk that the PIRs will not be given the attention they are due. And, at all levels, staff involvement in the process must not be restricted to the G2. G3 staffs must review, with G2 assistance, requirements from below in order to develop PIR recommendations for the commander. The G3 involvement, while certainly necessary in war, is probably even more important in peacetime, when busy commanders quite naturally must concentrate on other pressing issues.

*The CO's Role.* The process described above will work, but only if commanders at all levels make it work. Not addressed so far, is the question of how Unit COs determine just what their PIRs are. The past portion of this paper suggests some practical guidelines.

Every PIR should be geared to one of two things: war plans or training for war. The CO reviews his war missions and training plans and then decides, were his Unit to be committed to battle, what he and his Troops would most need to know about the enemy in that situation. Obviously, many questions could not be satisfactorily answered until much closer to the event, but some could be. For example, rather than asking for generalized enemy tables of organization and equipment, the specific organization and equipment of the enemy Units likely to be fought must be known. What kind of tanks, APCs, artillery, etc., are held by X regiment or Y division, and how many of each?

Similarly, PIRs in support of training should be as specific as possible. Which of our weapons systems can kill his armoured vehicles from which aspects and vice-versa? What are the recognition features of these vehicles and weapons systems? Recent examples of reports which provide this sort of Intelligence include the NDHQ Handbook of Soviet/Non-Soviet Warsaw Pact Armoured Fighting Vehicles and Anti-tank Weapons (30 Dec 1987), the FMC HQ Special Intelligence Report, The Threat from Soviet Indirect Artillery Fire (20 Jan 1987).

Often it seems that Units seek information to satisfy the personal interests of a few individuals, or want material for the purpose of general officer education. While wholly understandable, if unrelated to war planning or training, it is a waste of scarce Intelligence resources for NDHQ to satisfy such requests.

They should be weeded out by commanders from PIRs being forwarded to NDHQ.

Do not ask for the enemy's war plans—it is a virtual certainty that they are not held. Avoid too the "cosmic" questions, e.g., "does the enemy's culture and history dispose them to military expansionism?" While important, such questions can rarely be better answered by the G2 staff than by competent scholars writing in widely available open source journals and books.

The PIRs should be in order of priority, to ensure that more pressing requirements are given first attention. The NDHQ Intelligence staff is too small to guarantee that all a Unit's PIRs will be satisfied, and must thus know which are the most important. The form in which the Intelligence is conveyed should also be specified, e.g., handbook, reference work, wall chart, OHP graphics, whiz wheel, or a standard written report. It should be specified whether updating is required, and if so, how often and by what means. Obviously, it should be noted when the Intelligence is required. Lastly, and of prime importance, is the security classification desired. If troop training is the aim, CONFIDENTIAL is probably the highest classification acceptable to the Unit, SECRET for officers and senior NCMs. While it is generally true that the lower the classification, the less that can be said, much useful Intelligence is still available from G2s who know how to write reports without comprising sources. (Note that the aforementioned NDHQ and FMC HQ reports are classified at the lowest level in recognition of the needs of Unit officers, NCMs, and soldiers). In this vein, do not be overly concerned about security. Often, classified documents are so carefully handled in Units as to actually deny Intelligence to those who need to know it.

Before asking for it, make sure that it is not already held. Frequently, G2 staffs are approached for Intelligence they have already disseminated, and which lies in the bottom drawer of the safe in the Unit Intelligence office. Unit Intelligence sections must be properly organized and manned, and the Intelligence officer knowledgeable about what he already holds, if this is to be avoided.

Once dispatched, PIRs should not be forgotten. Insist on feedback, either in the form of Intelligence required, or at least an explanation of why the answers sought cannot be provided. If no response is forthcoming, it is time for the CO to involve himself once more in the process.

*The Staff and Command Challenge.* It should be obvious that while developing PIRs is a challenge for the Army commanders and staffs, it is neither so complex nor time-consuming as to be relegated to the "lowest priority" category. Indeed, the first effort, if carefully and thoroughly completed, should only require minor revisions annually for the next few years, barring major changes in missions or the thrust of training.

The best possible use must be made of the scarce Intelligence resources available, and that it is decidedly not up to G2s to set the priorities. Determining what the G2 staff should focus on, and what Intelligence is to be produced, is the function of commanders, who must direct the Intelligence effort.

*In Summary.* Commanders at all levels must take an active part in the peacetime Intelligence cycle, including personally approving and forwarding their PIRs to higher HQ. G3 staffs must also be intimately involved in the formulation of PIRs. PIRs should be in support of war plans and or training for war, and nothing else. Intelligence must be fought for in peace as well as in war; if not satisfied with the Intelligence he is getting, a commander must take up the issue with his commander and the higher HQ staff. The challenge is therefore to accept the same responsibilities in peace as we would in war.[11]

## *1989, 4 CMBG FALLEX*

On 24 Jul 1989, the 4 CMBG headquarters group loaded up in a convoy of staff cars and drove North West to Weilberg with the Brigade Commander, BGen J.J.M.R. Gaudreau and his staff, to conduct a recce of the exercise area. The group stayed in the Schloßß Weilberg Hotel (the hotel was actually in part of the palace). They then moved on to a German Army Kaserne in Rennerod to liaise with members of the US forces, where the author met Capt Steve Darulla with the US 188th MI Bn.

From 9-19 Aug 89, the 4 CMBG Int Section took part in Ex Agile Swordsman, a Command Post Ex held at Boblingen and Stuttgart, Germany. The Command Post (CP) was set up on a rifle range sighted on the back end of a US Army base. All participants slept in the back of box-bodied 2 ½ ton trucks called sleepers, much better than tents. The Int Section members worked long shifts over six nights.

From 25 Aug-9 Sep 89, the Brigade took part in Ex Royal Safari at a US Army installation in Hohenfels, Germany. All Int staff took part in NBCW Gas hut training. The author received the keys to the American-owned Soviet equipment display on base, which included two T-62's, a T-54 and T-55 and two PT-76 tanks, a BMP, a BRDM-2, MTLB and BTR-152 armoured vehi-

---

11.   Intelligence Branch Journal, Number 8, Fall 1989, pp. 16-18.

cles, a D-30 122 mm gun, a ZU-23 AAA gun, as well as ZIL, Ural and Kraz trucks etc., and a T-80 tank mock-up. In the evening the Brigade Commander invited all of his officers to the city of Nurnberg for an officer's dinner. On 30 Aug 89 the officers were taken on an Inter-German border tour up to Hof. They also explored an interesting museum in the US Army Kaserne at Hof. They were driven in buses along the border and stopped to view the guard towers—quite a contrast to what would be left after the wall fell in the exciting months which lay ahead.

On 2 Sep 89 the Int Section took part in the first of two 4 CMBG two-by-ten mile runs, followed the next day by the second two-by-ten mile run. On 4 Sep 89, Int staff including Major Paul Crober, Capt Clark J. Beamish, WO J.H. Yves Labarre, WO G. Wayne Ivey and the author went to a Gasthaus in Parsberg for an Int "hashing" session. On 7 Sep 89, the HQ staff were transported into the ancient Roman city of Regensburg for an officer's dinner in a very nice Gasthaus booked by the Ops O. From 9-22 Sep 89, the Brigade and its Int staff participated in Ex Caravan Guard, which covered more than 400 kms of cross-country training in Germany. On 13 Sep 89, Capt Peter Benoit from the US MI Bn, dropped in with his HUMMV for a visit with the CP staff. The HUMMV is a very wide vehicle, and although it is a very stable piece of kit, and the Americans really like it, there are places it can't go that the Iltis can.

23 Oct 89, the author drove a staff car up to Baden for a staff inspection of the RCR, and then went back to Lahr to catch a service flight in the afternoon to Trenton to attend an Int conference in Kingston. The author caught an inter-base bus with Capt Clark J. Beamish, Capt Ron H.J. Ruiters, Col Salmon, WO G. Wayne Ivey and Sgt Dave L. Howarth, to Kingston, where they were billeted in quarters at Vimy Barracks. On 24 Oct 89, they visited 1 Division Headquarters Int Company. Major A. George Johnstone, Capt W.A. "Tony" Rennett, 2Lt Clark P. Cornect, 2Lt J.A.E. Kent Dowell, WO Barry A. MacDonald et al were on site. The group took part in the 26 Oct 89 Intelligence Conference chaired by LCol Peter W.M. Wilson. They also participated in the 27 Oct 89 inauguration of 1 Cdn Div Int Coy, with Maj W.A. "Tony" Rennett the first official Officer Commanding. MGen Reg J.G. Weeks spoke and the Division Commander, MGen Jack Dangerfield, presided over the ceremonies. An excellent Mess dinner was held to commemorate the event in the evening. Major Gary W. Handson, Capt W. Doug Whitley (Ret'd), Major Lloyd W. Hackel, Major Christian Rousseau, LCol

Darcy J. Beatty, Capt Brian E. Hamilton and many members of the BIOC class of 1983 attended.

There were many familiar Int faces from the Reserve units in Halifax, Edmonton, Winnipeg, Vancouver, Toronto and Montreal. Large numbers however, were noticeably absent from Ottawa. CSE was well represented, with Tim A. Larson and Kelly E.M. Stone in attendance. Lt Wes B. von Papineau, Lt Paul G. Rivard, Maj David A. Haas, Lt Colin A.J. Kiley, Lt Don M. Stedeford, Lt André. F. Berdais, Maj John Cruse, Sgt Mike E. Higgins, MWO Dean J. Dunlop, 2Lt Judi Hastings and 2Lt Bev Baker, Maj Gerry C. Mayer and Capt Rhedegydd ap Probert , Capt Michel Bédard and Maj René J. Gauthier were there as well.

The author spoke to a WW II veteran who had served in a Div Arty unit who participated in the inauguration. He had called down fire on large concentrations of Germans, which had left a lasting impression on him. The speech at the dinner by MGen Reg J.G. Weeks was far reaching and left a very strong good impression on all of who attended, looking to the future. The author spoke and listened to as many as possible. Well worth the trip.

On 22 Nov 89, Int staff members WO G. Wayne Ivey and Cpl Kenneth E. Davies and the author took a staff car up to visit the British Army Int staff in Sennelager/Paderborn. The team met SSgt Talbot Jones from 733 (UK) Int Trg Coy, in an old SS Kaserne. The training area is huge, with visiting German Marder APC's everywhere. The author met a Capt from Saudi Arabia in the NATO officer's mess, and a Brit officer from Cyprus, as well as a Brit Army Air Corps officer from the same EW course he had attended in Loughborough. He also met two Canadian officers from Petawawa on exchange duty with the Brits. The group later visited the UK Int and Security Detachment. From 27 Nov-08 Dec 89, the author attended the NATO Advanced Electronic Warfare Course (EQ), Oberammergau, Germany.

On 13 Dec 89, Maj Clark J. Beamish and Maj A. George Johnstone and the author took a staff car from Lahr to USAREUR HQ Heidelberg for an Intelligence conference conference. The group spent the night in the Hotel Diana, where Clark and the author pulled George's leg long and hard on what "we almost saw."

## 1989, CISA Member News

Elizabeth Stephenson, adopted daughter of Sir William S. Stephenson, wrote CISA from her home in Bermuda, to say, "Pops was very delighted to have had the opportunity of donating a trophy to the Canadian Intelligence and Security Association...I am so happy that my father's name will continue to live on in the Trophy."

Col André Gauthier, LCol Frank Leigh, Maj David E. Clemis and Capt W. Doug Whitley retired from the Regular Forces with a ceremony at the Army Officer's Mess in Ottawa. Current CIS is RAdm J.C. Slade.

During the CISA AGM held 24-26 Aug 89 at CFB Borden, tribute was paid to members of the association who had recently passed away, including Sir William S. Stephenson, LCol John "Jack" Platt, Maj David G. Kerr, and Capt Michael Wormley. A minute of silence was observed in their honour.

The CISA Academic Award of $600 was made to Mr. Doug Lindberg, a 3$^{rd}$-year Agriculture student at the University of Manitoba.

Maj Fred E.G. Jones reported that Camp X near Whitby, Ontario, which was used by Sir William S. Stephenson to train agents during WWII, was dedicated as "Intrepid Park" on 29 Aug 1989. Six personnel from CFSIS attended the ceremony rededicating the cairn honouring Sir William. Maj Robert M. Parsons, OC CFSIS Int Trg Coy, presented an Int Branch plaque in Sir William's honour.

BGen D.A. Pryer, Vice-Chairman (Ontario) of the Conference of Defence Associations, addressed the CISA AGM, speaking briefly on CDA activities. LCol D.A. Henderson, CDA/LO spoke on CIOR, the NATO reserve officers association. Reports were presented on Militia activity by Maj Robert C. Dale for Atlantic Militia Area; Maj Pierre D. St Amant for Secteur de l'Est Int; LCol Dale M. Watts for Winnipeg Int; Maj Nils E. Lindberg for Winnipeg MP Platoon; Maj David A. Haas for Alberta Int; LCol Ian A. Nicol for Edmonton MP Platoon; and Maj David A. Haas (on behalf of Lt Don M. Stedeford) for BC Int.

A $500 donation was made to the Canadian War Museum to assist in the purchase of armed forces memorabilia, especially, but not limited to, those with an Intelligence or Security connection. LCol Don R. Johnson reported that development plans for the Base Borden Museum had been delayed two years. A new building is to be constructed north of Worthington Park.[12]

The CISA AGM will be held at CFSIS, CFB Borden, 23-25 Aug 1990.[13]

12. CISA Newsletter, Vol. 20, No. 3, December 1989, pp. 1-6.
13. CISA Newsletter, Vol. 21, No. 1, June 1990, pp. 1-3; and, CISA Newsletter, Vol. 21, No. 2, August 1990, pp. 1-3.

## RV 89, Wainright, Alberta

RV 89, Wainwright, Int Branch participants.
Third Row: Capt Brian E. Hamilton, Capt Gord P. Ohlke, Capt Lloyd
W. Hackel, Lt André. F. Berdais, WO J.M. Lauziere, Sgt John T. Mans-
field, WO N.L. Gordon, Sgt Dave J. Bruton, WO Rick M. Milne, and Sgt
Robert R. Belliveau.
Second Row: Lt Don M. Stedeford, Capt J. Michel Bédard, WO Ivo J.M.
Schoots, WO J. Eric C. Savoy, Maj Ward A. Sweet, WO Jean Pierre
Caron, MWO B.M. Gardiner, Capt Ed D. Kirby.
Front Row: Capt L. McGarva, Sgt Roderick L. Gill, Maj A. George
Johnstone, Maj Gerry C. Mayer, LCol Peter W.M. Wilson, Sgt Charles
T. Scott, Maj Robert C. Dale, LCol K.A.W. Peter Mackenzie.

# 1989, NDIC

1989, CIS, RAdm J.C. Slade and the NDIC Staff.
MCpl Alex D.K. Mackenzie, Capt Phil R. Coo, Cpl W. Paul Wehmeier,
Cpl Ian K. Hargrove, Cpl Andrew J. "A.J." Krause, Maj John W. Sullivan,
Sgt Lloyd D. Crosby, RAdm J.C. Slade (CIS), LCol Al G. McMullan, Lt
(N) Mike F.H. Arnoldi, BGen L. Doshen (DG Int), Cpl Larry E. Neil-
son, Capt Alan Haywood, Sgt J. Pierre Turcotte, Capt R. Stu W.
MacAulay, WO Mike E. Higgins.

# 1989, Soviet Military Liaison Missions, Germany Extracts from an interview WO Wayne Ivey and Sean M. Maloney

"Troops operating in the Central Army Group (CENTAG) area of Germany had to contend with the Soviet Military Liaison Missions (SMLM) in the same way that their predecessors had with SOXMIS in Northern Germany." WO G. Wayne Ivey of the 4 CMBG Int Section had the following comments on Warsaw Pact intelligence activity in West Germany:

"Down here we had SMLM, one group located in Frankfurt to monitor the Americans and one located in Baden-Baden to monitor the French. When we or other NATO partners went on exercise, they were out having a look at us, looking for new equipment, how long it would take you to move from point A to point B, how you refuelled, what your logistics were. Logistics to these people appeared to one of the most important things they were after. The rules were that they were not allowed off the Autobahn. If they got off the Autobahn or into a restricted area during exercises or into a permanent restricted area, our job was to find the and "neutralize" them. To neutralize them, all we had to do was let them know we were there and follow them. That in fact is what did the trick. They could not do anything once they knew we were there. If we felt that they were up to something, then we went a little more in depth…"

"Besides SMLM, the Soviets employed other methods of intelligence gathering against 4 CMBG. A favoured method was the *Transport International Routier* (TIR) trucks, roughly 50,000 East Bloc commercial vehicles per year, moving goods around Europe. Not all could be watched or followed. Some of them carried concealed cameras, and many could be seen parked near important NATO installations. Drivers would routinely measure highway underpasses, bridges and other parts of transportation infrastructure, obviously compiling data that would be of use to Warsaw Pact forces invading West Germany. East Bloc barge traffic moving along the Rhine or other rivers also carried intelligence gathering apparatus."[14]

14. Sean M. Maloney, *War Without Battles, Canada's NATO Brigade in Germany, 1951-1993*, (Toronto: McGraw-Hill Ryerson Limited, 1997), pp. 390-391.

# 8

## 1990, Intelligence Branch

### 1990, 4 CMBG

On 5 Feb 1990, a number of Int pers from Lahr including Capt Ron H.J. Ruiters, WO G. Wayne Ivey, WO Marvin J. "Red" Hodgins who was working in Augsburg, and the author, drove down to Berchtesgaden in a base Kleine-bus for the BAOR-USAEUR Intelligence Conference, 5-10 Feb. In April 90 a few members of the same group also attended the Psy Ops Conference at CENTAG, Campbell Barracks, Heidelberg. From 10-17 May 90, the Brigade Int Staff took part in Exercise Snakebite (a Recce Ex), at the Eisberg Kaserne, in the "Canter" area, Germany. In May and June the Int Section took part in another session in the field on Ex Royal Sword, Germany. In June the 4 CMBG HQ & Sigs Sqn staff participated in Officer Professional Development Training with a WW1 Battlefield Tour of Verdun, France. On 18 June 1990, BGen J.J.M.R. Gaudreau took all Brigade HQ Officers to tour the European Parliament in Strasbourg. All were briefed in the Conference Hall, had lunch there then back to Lahr early in the afternoon. Quite an interesting view from the European perspective of the world.

In September 1990, the Brigade added Ex RADOME SCULPTOR, to the list of exercises the Int Section had a part to play in Lahr, this time in the woods up on the Langenhard for three days. Shortly afterwards the Brigade went off to FALLEX, taking part in Ex REBEL SADDLE and Ex ROYAL SWORD, 22 Sep-21 Oct 90, at Hohenfels/RMA, Germany. During

FALLEX participants set all watches on Zulu time, about two hours earlier than our usual time, in order to work internationally for ranges and briefings. During a 400-km running battle, the Brigade moved virtually every night and often twice, hiding in a forest West of Weiher on 10 Oct; then rolling up to Weiher, NE to Hirschau, North to Kohlberg forest, then on to Holzhammer, Kemnath and Trichenrichte. Back to HQ and West via Hainstettin-Wutschdorf and North to a forest hide near Weiher. In the evening the Brigade moved again, to Lintach.

On 12 Oct, the HQ staff trundled into the next hide just in time to observe US forces moving behind them with M1 tanks and M3 Bradleys. The staff later moved the CP to a forest south of Gebenback. During the exercise, the events in Iraq began to unfold at a rapid rate, and the author was tasked to provide situation briefings to each of the Brigade units in the field. On 14 Oct 90 he took an Iltis to B Sqn, 8 CH (equipped with Leopard tanks), and briefed them on the Iraqi situation. The Brigade continued on the exercise to a point West of Schnaitten, behind a huge slagheap, with lots of large mines in the area. Driving west over a hill, the author met a 2-½ ton truck rapidly barrelling up the opposite side of the hill on a single track in the woods. Interesting surprise and quite an adrenalin rush etc. He found C Sqn at the right grid, but it turned out to be the wrong Sqn. He then radioed to A Sqn and then drove back through the woods 10 km. They set up a white sheet for a screen in the back of a 2-½ ton truck and connected the projector to a generator, so the author could brief using the slides showing types of Iraqi kit, which worked well. He then drove back to the CP, then South of Burgstall, then West with an Artillery rep to Sitzenback to give a 1½-hour briefing, then back to Burgstall forest. His throat was pretty dry by then. Back on duty in the CP. The HQ & Sigs Sqn Commander moved the CP West to a forest near Buchelberg, and on 18 Oct 90, ENDEX was called and all headed home.

4 CMB Combat Intelligence Course 9001, Lahr, Germany, May 1990.
Front Row seated: Sgt; Int Sgt J.C. Mario Roy, Sgt Kenneth E. Davies,
Capt Harold A. Skaarup, Major Paul Crober, WO G. Wayne Ivey, WO
J.L.A. Martineau, and WO J.M. Letellier De St Just. Second Row stand-
ing, far right: MCpl John A. Dooley.

## 1990, Canadian Forces Europe Int Branch

Positions for the Int Branch in Europe in June 1990 included: Maj G. Al
Grant, SO2 Int, HQ CFE; Maj Clark J. Beamish, G2 Ops/CI, 1 Cdn Div
Fwd; Capt Ron H.J. Ruiters, SO3 Int HQ CFE; Capt Harold A. Skaarup,
G2 Ops, 4 CMBG HQ & Sigs Sqn; Capt Dan A. Climo, B Int O, CFB
Lahr; Capt Robert G. Nash, Int O, 4 Wing HQ; Capt H. Wayne Nightin-
gale, Int O, 4 Wing HQ; Cdr Christopher S. Hordal, NATO IMS, Brun-
suum; Maj Greg W. Jensen, HA AFNORTH, Kolsaas; Maj Susan F.
Beharriell, HQ AAFCE, Ramstein; Maj Ward A. Sweet, CPA HQ
AFCENT, RMS Brunsuum; Lt William "Bill" M. Glenfield, Int O, 439 Sqn;
Capt J.R.Y. Michel Foucreault, Int O, 409 Sqn; Capt (Ret'd) William "Bill"
L. Dickson, Bde G5, 4 CMB; and, Capt Richard A. Derkson, SO Int 1
CAD.[1]

---

1.  Capt H.A. Skaarup letter to CISA, 13 June 1990.

## 1990, *Arms Verification Course*

In Oct 90, the author flew to Ottawa via Frankfurt for the Arms Verification—On Site Inspection Course (UZ), earning Inspector Number 021. The course took part in several training sessions at Tunney's Pasture, which felt to some extent to the author like being back on the job in DDI-6, although it was now named DIE. He ran into lots of familiar faces, including Capt Robert T. Greyeyes, CWO Rolf F. Overhoff, WO Dean J. Dunlop, and Colin Buckett—a good start to the course.

## 1990, *CISA AGM*

CISA AGM 1990 participants.
The CISA AGM was held at CFSIS, CFB Borden, 23-25 Aug 1990.
Present were: Maj William "Bill" L. Watt, LCol Jack S. Dunn, LCol A.G.
Cameron, LCol Don R. Johnson, Maj J.H. Mansfield, Maj Terry B. Kelly,
Capt James "Jim" P.K. Van Wynen, Lt Paul G. Rivard, Maj David A.
Haas, Capt David A. Rubin, Col A.H. Sam Stevenson, Maj Fred E.G.
Jones, Cdr John C. Macquarrie, Maj Robert C. Dale, Maj D.E. Guyatt,
LCol Bernie N. Wright, Lt E. Bruce Holmes, BGen D.A. Pryer, Capt
Harold F. Smith, LCol Jim E. Parker, Maj Merrick K. Szulc, Col Victor
V. Ashdown, Col Andrew F. Ritchie, Lt Douglas Monk, Capt J.D. Baxter,
Lt D.A. Stolovitch, LCol Alf J. Laidler, Maj Richard J. Vella, Capt J.D.
McKenna, BGen J.E. Pierre Lalonde, MGen Reginald J.G. Weeks, Capt
Eugene Morosan, Maj Peter W. Sloan, Capt Doug R. Bennett, LCol R.F.
Bornor, Capt Y.S. René, Capt R.A. Mader, Capt Wes B. von Papineau,

Maj J. Michel Bédard, Lt J. Humen, Lt Arnold S. Neumann, and Maj John "Pappy" MacKinnon (Secretary).[2]

## *1990, CISA Member News*

Col Charles R. Raefe Douthwaite of Halifax passed away on 29 Oct 1990. Raefe served with distinction in the C Int C with 3 Cdn Inf Div during WWII, becoming the most highly decorated officer to serve in the C Int C. Maj John "Pappy" MacKinnon spoke of working with Raefe as a Maj at DMI post-war, commenting on his fairness and efficiency. He rose to the rank of Col in the Militia after leaving the Regular Force and had been active in several associations in the Halifax area.

Capt Harold Alexander Hunter of St Stephen, NB, died on 24 Mar 1990. Harold served as an Intelligence officer in Canada before being posted to HQ 5 Cdn Armd Div in May 1941, serving in Italy and NW Europe. On his return to Canada, he served with the RCMP until his retirement in 1959.

During the CISA AGM, tribute was paid to Capt John A. Lauer of Kitchener following his passing since the last AGM. Capt Lauer served in Intelligence during WWII and was a member of the CISA.

Maj Hugh Andrew was mugged out at the Army Officer's Mess in Ottawa following his retirement on 30 Nov.

There were two CISA Academic Awards of $600 for 1990, with the first going to Mr. Robert Owen Clark, and the second to Ms. Susan Van Wynen.

DG Int, BGen J.E. Pierre Lalonde, spoke on Intelligence in the CF in the international context. In the panel, (chaired by LCol Jack S. Dunn), Col Victor V. Ashdown, Cdr John C. Macquarrie and LCol Bernie N. Wright spoke on the effects of international and national developments on Security and Intelligence in the Canadian Forces. The SSO Int at FMC, LCol Peter W.M. Wilson did not attend, as he was involved in work related to the events ongoing in the Persian Gulf and at Oka, although his comments were provided to LCol Wright.

BGen D.A. Pryer reported that letters had been sent by CDA to the Prime Minister and the Minister of National Defence on the Oka and Middle East crises; on maintenance of the present level of defence; and on the reintroduction of COTC in Canadian universities.

---

2. CISA Newsletter, Vol. 21, No. 3, December 1990, p. 1.

LCol Don R. Johnson outlined plans for the cenotaph on Stewart Square at CFB Borden, fixed with a bronze plaque on one of its four sides.[3]

## The Canadian Navy Visits Vladivostok, 1990

In June 1990, the Canadian Navy conducted its first-ever visit to Vladivostok in the Soviet Union. This was, in fact, the first visit by a non-Communist Navy to Vladivostok since 1935. The visit gave the participating Canadian a fascinating view of the Soviet Navy close-up shortly before the entire Soviet edifice collapsed—although this imminent collapse was far from obvious to the observers at the time. Viewed close-up (with a surprising degree of openness on the part of their Soviet hosts) it was evident that the Soviet Navy was not quite the fearsome beast that many had thought, but it did have an impressive collection of equipment. Intelligence Major Mike J. Popovich participated as the interpreter for RAdm Cairns and Lt (N) Sam Cowan was also present as the Task Group Intelligence Officer. [Sam had also participated in a goodwill visit to Leningrad in 1976, although he was a MARS officer at that time.][4]

---

3.   CISA Newsletter, Vol. 21, No. 3, December 1990, pp. 1-4.
4.   Cdr M. Josh Barber, E-mails fall 2000.

# CFSIS

Intelligence Operator 6A Course 9001.
Top Row: MCpl Reginald J. McAuley, MCpl Patrick M. Palahicky,
MCpl George Gillingham.
Third Row: MCpl J.M.R. Dan Jacques, MCpl J.A. Chris Pelletier, MCpl
J.P. André Tremblay, MS J.E. Paul Pellerin.
Second Row: MCpl Brian K. Mudge, MCpl R. Jack Wilson, MS T.P.
Farnel, MCpl J. Patrick D. Knopp, MCpl John A. Dooley, MCpl J.S.
Daniel St Pierre, MCpl Tim L. Hagel, MCpl Mel A. Wilkerson.
Front Row: Sgt G. Bruce Scott, WO Barry R. Eddy, Capt J.B.P. Trudeau,
Maj J. Michel Bédard, CPO2 Brian Noble, Sgt David A. Gelsinger.

Intelligence Operator 6B Course 9001.
Top Row: PO2 William D. Kean, Sgt Ronald K. Townsend, Sgt Steve Mercer, Sgt Manuel A. Thibault, PO2 Terry W. Fader.
Third Row: Sgt J. Pierre Murret-Labarthe, Sgt V.S. Keefe, PO2 J.A. Réjean Montmarquet, Sgt D. Garry Kohinski, Sgt Rick M. Chaykowski, Sgt Tim G. Armstrong.
Second Row: Sgt G. Bruce Scott, Sgt Robert A. Deleau, Sgt J.H.D. Gauthier, Sgt M.B. Mahoney, Sgt R.K. Wood.
Front Row: MWO Robert A. Lavalle, Capt Brian E. Hamilton, Maj Robert M. Parsons, CPO2 Brian Noble, WO David J. Whalen.

# Militia Intelligence Training 1990

Intermediate Trades Training Course 9001, Camp Aldershot, Nova Scotia.
Rear Row: Pte Giesbrecht, Pte J.S. Amorin, Sgt Stéphane S. Auger, Sgt Steve J. Goronzy, MCpl S.J. McSherry.
Second Row: Cpl Steve Mullins, Pte P.D. Eves, MCpl Kovacs, Pte David F. Moore, Pte Wlodek, Cpl Ollia Kitash.
Front Row, seated: Cpl Michael C. Wagner, Sgt Robert R. Belliveau, Lt Colin A.J. Kiley, Pte Lawrence G. Willett.

# 9

## 1991, Intelligence Branch

### 1991, 4 CMBG

Most Int Branch personnel were well aware of the 16 Jan 91 deadline set by US President George Bush for Saddam Hussein in the Persian Gulf. When the deadline passed for Iraq, heavy EW jamming began across the forward area. At 0100 hours on 17 Jan 1991, the US and its allies launched their opening attack against Iraq with Tomahawk missiles and aircraft. Outside the Lahr Kaserne there were major protest demonstrations. Although there was a lot of activity within the Brigade, the Int Section did not initially have a great deal of involvement. The HQ staff had been told to get the brigade ready to go to the gulf months ago, but the Department of External Affairs stopped this. All Brigade troops therefore waited and watched. All school buses had armed Troops on-board, and all PMQ residential areas were patrolled 24 hours a day in very cold weather. On 24 Feb 91, as large numbers of protesters outside the Kaserne waved signs saying, "Give Peace a Chance," the US and Coalition forces began their ground war in Kuwait and Iraq. It was over very quickly.

### 1991, CISA Member News

Capt David A. Rubin retired as Chairman of the St. John Ambulance Metro Toronto Branch, and has been appointed to the Canada Memorial Foundation, established to honour the service of 900,000 Canadians who served in the UK during WWI & II. Maj Wady Lehman, Surrey, BC, and LCol Robert H. "Tex" Noble are mentioned. HCol George B. MacGillivray, Phoenix, Arizona, was appointed Clan MacGillivray's Ceann Cath, or Commander of the Clan worldwide.

Dr. Ibrahim Hayani, a former economic development officer with the United Nations in the Middle East, and a professor at Seneca College, would be speaking on "The Arabs and the West" at the RCMI in Toronto in April 1991. The Consul General of Syria was also to attend.

CISA member Lt John Laban of Thunder Bay, Ontario, passed away in Nov 1990.

CISA sent President LCol Jack S. Dunn to the CDA AGM in Ottawa in Jan 1991.[1]

## 1991, Air Command Intelligencer From the SSO

It is indeed a pleasure to write my first letter for the Air Command Intelligencer. I have wanted to initiate this project since my arrival at Air Command but was unable to do so because we lacked the personnel and equipment to sustain its production. I believe a Command newsletter for the Intelligence Branch is long overdue, and I hope that you share my enthusiasm by supporting its production with written contributions.

This past year has been tumultuous for the CF, Air Command and the Intelligence Branch. The rapidly changing world situation, the Gulf War, the budget cuts and the recently announced withdrawal of CFE have affected us professionally and/or personally. I don't believe anyone can accurately assess the full impact of these events. In fact, we should probably anticipate more changes as a result of the recent fiscal cutbacks. The most immediate is our withdrawal from Europe.

A considerable number of Intelligence Branch personnel will be relocated to various locations in Canada commencing this APS. The immediate benefit of the CFE reduction is that a number of Canadian-based Units and headquarters will receive supernumerary officers and NCMs. The appropriate Career Managers have been hard at work finding jobs for those about to be posted from Europe; a few will be posted to newly-established positions within Air Command.

---

1.    CISA Newsletter, Vol. 22, No. 1, March 1991, pp. 1-2.

I suspect that a number of you might be concerned that personnel reductions-may occur within the Intelligence Branch. I cannot allay those concerns, but nor do I have any information to support that contention. Trade reductions largely depend upon the percentage that a trade is overborne. If the Intelligence Branch is sufficiently over the allowable surplus, it is possible that extraordinary measures might be taken to reduce the trade. This year's FRP for some other trades is an example of measures that could be taken. The voluntary response to the recent FRP was so great that not one person in those affected trades was released against his will. So, while I cannot provide you with any definitive answers at this time, I urge you not to become overly concerned. I will be following this very closely and will report to you if anything develops.

As you know, the recent freeze on spending resulted in the postponing of the Air Command Intelligence Seminar. We are in the process of rescheduling this important event. One of the aspects which was to be covered at the seminar, is the Intelligence production within the Command. By now, you should have seen our new bilingual product entitled "The Air Command Intelligence Daily (ACID). This Intelligence Summary is intended to address those items of Intelligence interest to the Commander of Air Command, and as such is geo-political and strategic in nature. It is nonetheless distributed to every group, base and Unit of Air Command.

Group and Unit Intelligence staffs are free to use any item of interest to their commanders; however, we must attempt to reduce redundancy in our products. For example, Fighter Group may wish to re-publish an ACID item for a specific reason, but in the main, Fighter Group's Intelligence summary should provide reports of interest to the "fighter" world. Transport Group's Intelligence production should be aimed at focusing on items of perceived use to transport aircrew.

The Intelligence Operator 111 trade Badge (Air) has finally been accepted. I regret the delay; however, we have not been satisfied with the quality of the embroidered compass rose. After five prototypes, I believe we have a badge that will be worn with pride. The problem has been with the lack of definition in the compass rose and the limitations of the embroidery machine. The accepted badge uses a combination of "new" and "old" gold-coloured thread on the compass rose. Air Command is now proceeding with the badge's procurement through the supply system. It is anticipated that it could take up to one year to get the badges to you.

The same badge is in the process of being approved for wear by air element Int 82 officers. That approval process is some six months behind the Intelligence Operators, but procurement should be expedited by the use of the same badge.

You should be aware that the Air Force Council is also seeking approval of a common Air Force hat-badge. The logic is that the sense of identity is preserved through the "trade badges." All trades in the Air Force will be affected if the CDS approves the application from the Air Force Council.[2]

## 1991, Automation at Air Command HQ

Perhaps the biggest change in the SSO Intelligence Section is the installation of the long awaited local area network. Over the next several months, we will be automating the administrative functions and the Intelligence cycle. For those who are technically minded, the system is a combination of 486 PCs and Macintosh IIfx with a VAX 4200 server and a 5Gb hard drive on an Ethernet backbone. A number of peripherals have also been added, such as: CD ROM drive, OCR and scanners, re-writeable optical drive, colour and grey-scale printers.[3]

## 1991, G-Staff Forms at Air Command Headquarters

Late in 1991, an operational staff or "G-Staff" was formed at Air Command Headquarters. The "G-Staff" shortened from "General Staff" has its roots in the Continental Staff Structure which has been employed in the United States for several decades and was successfully employed by NDHQ during the Gulf War. When more than one service element is controlled (i.e., the Air Force and the Navy), the controlling headquarters is termed a "Joint" headquarters; hence the NDHQ operational staff during the war was called a "J-Staff." The J-Staff exists at NDHQ today. The three commands: Air Command, Mobile Command and Maritime Command, each have their respective "G-Staffs"—since in isolation, they control a single service element.

A "G-Staff" consists of the following groupings: G1 is Personnel; G2 is Intelligence; G3 is Operations; G4 is Logistics; G5 is Civil/Military Affairs;

---

2.    Air Command Intelligencer, Edition 1, Volume 1, 17 March 1991, pp. 1-2.

3.    Air Command Intelligencer, Edition 1, Volume 1, 17 March 1991, p. 2.

G6 Communications. At NDHQ, the "J-Staff" has its equivalent J1, J2, J3 etc.

When an operation is planned or executed, the G-Staff or J-Staff (Command or NDHQ, respectively) is formed depending on whether a single service or multi-services are envisaged. At that time, staff officers, who normally have a day job, group together their expertise to the planning or execution of an operation. For example, the Assistant Judge Advocate General (lawyer) would become part of the G-5 Staff for an impending operation and that lawyer would be able to task (when required) other members of the AJAG staff who continue on in their normal job.

At Air Command, the SSO Intelligence Section is the G2 Staff. As such, when an operation involving only the Air Force is envisaged, Air Command is tasked by the J-Staff at NDHQ to plan and write the Operation Order for the operation. To make a long story short, the G-Staff is formed and its personnel dedicate their time to the planning of the operation. There have been a number of recent examples of this: OP PRESERVE was an operation designed to carry foodstuffs to Ethiopia, and OP BOREAL is the on-going operation to haul medicines to the Commonwealth of Independent States.

The G2 Intelligence Staff at Air Command commences its participation earlier than the others because it is their job to identify all threats to the aircraft or aircrew so that the other experts on the G-Staff can properly plan for any contingencies. Consequently, the staff of SSO Intelligence dons their G2 hats and commence a 24/7 operation, during which they task various sources and agencies to fill in any Intelligence gaps and subsequently write an Intelligence Estimate. This estimate forms the basis of the Intelligence Annex to the formal Operation Order.

When an operation is executed, most of the G-Staff monitors and controls the conduct of the operation. Obviously, the G2 Staff is kept very busy at that time.[4]

## 1991, Capt (Ret'd) J.C. Chartrand and Capt (Ret'd) L.A. Dumais, SOE, visit 4 CMBG

On 3 May 1991, the author was tasked to escort Capt (Ret'd) Joseph C. Gabriel Chartrand and PSM/Capt Lucien A. Dumais, both highly decorated

---

4.   Air Command Intelligencer, Edition 1, Volume 1, 17 March 1991, p. 3.

Canadian WW II veterans of the Special Operations Executive (SOE),[5] on visits to the 1 R22eR, CFN/RFC and the Schwarzwald Stube.

Capt Chartrand had served with the Régiment de Maisonneuve before he became Intelligence (Censorship). He was taken to France by Lysander aircraft in mid-April 1943, with his organizer, Philippe Liewer. They set up in Rouen, but Chartrand later joined another group working the region from Rouen to Le Havre. The Gestapo was active in this area, and he was spotted. He managed to escape, and moved to Paris. His companions were arrested in early September, and Capt Chartrand was withdrawn via one of the escape lines, leaving France on the night of 15 November 1943.[6]

PSM/Capt Dumais conducted himself with gallantry at Dieppe, and made a single-handed escape following the surrender. He was recruited for intelligence work, but because of his strong accent, he was sent to North Africa as an observer with the British First Army. While there, he set up an Intelligence gathering irregular cavalry/private army that was so successful that the decision was made to send him to operate in Brittany. He was landed by Lysander aircraft in November 1943 at Chauny, northwest of Compiegne, where he and Sgt Raymond J. Labrosse, MC, set up the "Shelburne" network to deliver escapees to Anse Cochat beach at Plouha, in Brittany, where they were to be picked up by motor-gunboats from Dartmouth in the UK. Their system was used to successfully evacuate a considerable number of downed Allied aircrew members. On one occasion, however, in July 1944, Dumais, an aide and a group of Bretons had to fight a whole German battalion at Chatelaudren, killing 80 and taking 100 prisoners. During its existence, his organization was responsible for the return of 365 airmen and 7 agents.[7]

The author asked them both to sign beside their names in his copy of Scarlet to Green. They spoke very highly of Major Gustave "Guy" Daniel Alfred Bieler, (mentioned in the articles on SOE in Volume 1). BGen Clive Addy, the new Brigade Commander, picked up the tab.

---

5. Extensive details on the Canadian participation in SOE activity may be found in Volume 1.
6. Maj S. Robert Elliot, *Scarlet to Green*, pp. 389-390.
7. Maj S. Robert Elliot, *Scarlet to Green*, pp. 401-402.

## 1991, CISA Member News

Lt William "Bill" B. Iler retired from the federal public service in Edmonton and is now in Toronto. 2Lt Michael Hertwig-Jaksch, serving with the Edmonton Int Section, had formerly been in service with the Austrian Army. He is currently an administrator and lecturer at the University of Alberta. Col John P. Page reported he is now Vice-Chairman of the Toronto Mayor's Committee on Aging, and a member of the Toronto City Council's Assessment Reform Working Group. Capt W. Doug Whitley has had a business (Trailblazers Technical Writing Inc.) in operation for three years. His sister, Capt Bonnie Whitley, is transferring from the Communications Branch to Public Affairs, and is working as a Public Affairs Officer for the Alberta Militia District in Edmonton. Maj Gary W. Handson and Maj Denis Dumains are mentioned, and Maj Gary W. Beckman, a Financial Advisor with Midland Walwyn Capital Inc., assists the CF SCAN program with presentations on financial planning. Lt Frank Muldoon, a Federal Court judge, has been made an Honorary Member of St. Paul's College, University of Manitoba, as of 25 Jan 1991. Maj Wilf S. Puffer has retired form his job as a psychiatric nurse at the Alberta Hospital, Edmonton. He and his wife are moving to Parksville, BC. Maj David A. Haas (Treasurer), Int, and Lt Alexander Hart Tsang, MP Platoon, Edmonton are mentioned, as well as Capt Robbie A. McColgan, reporting from the Chancery of the Grand Priory of the Military and Hospitaller Order of Saint Lazarus of Jerusalem.

Col Robert T. Grogan reported on the retirements of Capt J.E.H. Bernard Lemieux and Capt Robert T. Greyeyes in Ottawa, with MGen Reg Weeks in attendance. Capt Peter T. Patton retired from his federal public service post as a Dominion Customs Appraiser at Customs and Excise Canada; and, Maj John "Pappy" MacKinnon is running for Ottawa City Councillor in the Nov 91 civic elections.[8]

---

8.   CISA Newsletter, Vol. 22, No. 2, July 1991, pp. 1-6.

# 1991, CFSIS

Intelligence Operator 6A Course 9101.
Rear Row: Sgt Peter G. Manuge, MCpl J.J. Jean Brun, MCpl Mark H. Figge, MCpl George P. Houston, Sgt Dennis G. McNulty, MCpl J.C. Mario Roy.
Centre Row: PO2 David G. Maxim, MS Donald R.A. Wagnell, MCpl Gregory Charles Collins, Sgt John Paul Michael Parsons, MCpl J.L. Dellaire, MCpl J.D. Pete Boutin.
Front Row: Sgt G. Bruce Scott, WO Mike R. Tracey, CPO2 Brian Noble, Maj J. Michel Bédard, Capt J.B.P. Trudeau, WO Barry R. Eddy.

## 1991, CFSIS

1991 Militia QL6A 9101
Rear Row: Cpl Nancy L. Mah, MCpl François Maheux, Cpl Chris W.
Free, Sgt Steve J. Goronzy, Sgt Stéphane S. Auger, MCpl Michael C.
Wagner, Cpl L.A. Beck, MCpl John L. Henderson.
Front Row: Pte Alan W. Wilson, WO Dave J. Bruton, MWO F.V. Gor-
don, C. Moor, WO Dan Galley, 2Lt Oreste M. Babij, WO Jean Pierre
Caron, MCpl Giesbrecht, Cpl Daniel J. Topolinski.

1991 Basic Classification Training Course 1 & 3 9101.
Participants: MWO F. Vance Gordon, Cpl Daniel J. Topolinski, 2Lt Oreste
M. Babij, 2 Lt K.N. Gehman, 2Lt Doug F. Agnew, 2Lt Ziviski, Lt P. Michel
Gareau, OCdt J. Desjardins, Cpl P.D. Eves, WO Cyril P. Aucoin, Cpl
Michael J. Ostafichuck, Capt C.W.E. Moor, and Capt Norman A. Sproll.

1991 Intermediate Classification Training Course 9101.
Participants: Lt Rick G. Stohner, Lt Charles B. Buffone, Lt L.F. Spence, Lt
David H. Hunt, Cpl Daniel J. Topolinski, MWO F. Vance Gordon, Capt
C.W.E. Moor, Lt (N) J. Doug Schweyer, Capt Arnold S. Neumann, 2Lt
Oreste M. Babij, and, Cpl Chris W. Free.

## 1991, 4 CMBG Normandy Battlefield Tour

From 2-5 Jun 1991 the 4 CMBG HQ and Sigs Sqn staff participated in
Officer Professional Development Training in France with a Normandy Bat-

tlefield Tour and an on-site battlefield study. The staff drove via the Paris autoroute, passing through the historic city on a bright sunny day, with the Sacre Couer cathedral and the Eiffel tower visible in the distance, and then on to the city of Caen. They stayed in a moderate Hotel and visited the Caen Memorial Museum, excellent tour, Typhoon fighter-bomber hanging in the foyer, Panther Mk V and Sherman tanks inside, and many very good displays and exhibits dealing with the battles and actions fought in Normandy.

On the first day of the tour they visited Pegasus Bridge, the site of the first French home liberated by paratroopers on the night of the 5/6 Jun 44. The First Canadian Parachute Battalion landed with the 6th British Airborne Division near Ranville/Breville. The Airborne museum was small but well worth the visit, with a half-track carrier, 25-lb gun and Bofors gun on display. They then drove west to Sword Beach via Ouistreham, West again to Lion and then Juno Beach, where a French guide spoke at length in French about the landings. They viewed a Churchill Armoured Vehicle Royal Engineer (AVRE) on display, which had been buried during the landings due to shellfire and only recently uncovered and partially restored.

The group continued west to Bernières-sur-Mer, and onwards to view a Canadian Duplex Drive (DD) tank memorial, where they stopped to take photos. They continued West to Arromanches and the remains of the Mulberry artificial harbours used on D-Day. There is an excellent Museum here with a good display of Canadian memorabilia. South to Bayeux and then NW to Point du Hoc and Omaha Beach, where they examined the enormous bomb craters on the site of the German gun positions. They had a good view of the Atlantic coast from very high cliffs. There is a large US Cemetery nearby, and several châteaus in the vicinity. The group moved East to Bayeux, then East to Beny-sur-Mer and the Canadian cemetery, with 2,000 graves on site including North Nova Scotia Highlanders, North Shore NB Regt and too many more markers for young soldiers (very much like those who were present) who never went home. They continued south to Caen and before returning to the Hotel.

On 4 June they headed south to the Bretteville-sur-Laize Canadian cemetery, with another 3000 graves. There were at least 18 unknown soldiers buried here, other members of the group said that there were many more.[9]

The group continued South past a Polish cemetery, and then drove into the town of Falaise and up to the castle where William the Conqueror was born. It has a very impressive large round keep and may be viewed in the background in a number of WWII photos of the Canadian action in Normandy. William is actually buried in Caen. NE through the battlefield area and then East to St Pierre sur Dives, East into Lisieux, East to Fontaine la Soret, East to Evreux, all very well-known place names to Canadians who fought there. From here the group drove East to the autoroute Chaufour, then E/NE of Paris and on back to Lahr. It was an extraordinary experience being an Int Officer and having the privilege of walking the grounds of our predecessors with other officers now serving in the same Army.

## 1991, Canada Day with 4 CMBG

On 1 July 1991, the 4 CMBG G2, Maj Jacques H. Levesque and the G2 Ops (author) carried out six parachute demonstration jumps for the Canada Day celebrations at the Lahr airfield."[10]

## 1991, Arms Verification Inspection, Northern Germany

From 9-19 July 1991 a number of 4 CMBG officers participated in Arms Control Verification training at HQ CFE, followed by an Arms Verification Exercise with 1 (UK) Corps in Northern Germany during which time the group inspected 14 different Bases. They set off by bus and drove to Olden-

---

9.   The official Canadian Army Historian noted that on D-Day, "the Canadians lost 1,074 killed, wounded and missing, including 113 casualties suffered by the 1st Canadian Parachute Battalion, far less than the price that had been paid for the experience at Dieppe." LCol D.J. Goodspeed, *The Armed Forces of Canada 1867-1967*, DHist, CFHQ Ottawa, 1967, p. 137.

10.  Both the G2, Maj Jacques Levesque and the G2 Ops (author) jumped from a balloon operated by a representative of the Swiss Watch (Swatch) company, who was also a skilled parachutist. At an altitude of 7000' above ground level, the G2 climbed out first, followed moments later by the G2 Ops. We each very carefully placed one foot in the outside "step," dangled the other and then leaned backwards and gently let go. It felt as though one had just stepped off the edge of a very high building. Both parachutists made a successful cross-country glide back to the Lahr airfield and completed their landings intact.

burg in Northern Germany, where their equipment was examined on the German Air Force base at Oldenburg. The next day they headed south to Munster for the first inspection which was conducted on the 1 Queen's Own Highlanders at Buller Barracks, who were equipped with mostly FV-432 armoured carriers etc. From there, they headed south to Dortmund, where they conducted the second inspection on 5 Heavy Artillery Regiment in West Riding Barracks. This unit's equipment consisted of M-107 heavy guns, with most of their removable or spare parts still sitting in the Gulf. The following day they moved on to inspect 26 Engineer Regiment, Corunna Barracks in Iserlohn, which had once been a Canadian base. The group moved North to HQ 33 Armoured Brigade in Alanbrooke Barracks at Paderborn, where we checked HQ equipment, Scorpions, Ferrets, FV-432's etc. They were billeted in the NATO Mess in Sennelager.

The following morning they moved south to Paderborn, to inspect 5 Inniskilling Dragoons in Barker Barracks. Their unit was equipped with 57 Chieftain tanks and 1 Centurion. The inspectors returned to Sennelager for the rest of the evening. On 14 July, the UK representatives organized a tour for the group to visit Schloßß Wewelsburg, 20 km South of Paderborn. It was a 16th century castle which had been blown up and restored several times. It is also the former SS castle redesigned by Heinrich Himmler, with a very spooky history. Swastikas and runes were still very evident in the castle's stonework. The castle is in the shape of a triangle, sited at the end of a long narrow road and laid out in a ground plan designed by Himmler. He wanted the area to be shaped like a spear, in commemoration of the "Holy Lance" said to have been used to pierce Christ's side. The group included Capt William "Bill" L. Dickson, FLt Fletton, Capt Denis Bouillé, Capt Anne Mongeon, and Capt Pat Rechner. The inspectors then returned to Sennelager and the following day departed for Minden, passing by the memorial to Kaiser Wilhelm I on a hill above Porta Westfalica.

Near Minden they inspected the 1st Argyll and Sutherland Highlanders at Elizabeth Barracks, mostly equipped with FV-432's. After the inspection and lunch, they proceeded North to Minden and Kingsley Barracks, where they inspected HQ 11 Armoured Brigade. They were given an aerial familiarization flight of the layout of the barracks in a Westland Lynx helicopter, getting a good low-level view of the UK installations and their Northern training area. The helicopter was equipped with TOW racks mounted on either side. The Lynx is about the size of our Iroquois, but with a lot more vibration. Shortly afterwards, they were visited by the COS HQ 1 (BR) Corps, Brigadier Walker.

The next morning, 16 July, the inspectors headed off to Bielefeld to visit Redcar Barracks, where they inspected 63 Ordnance Company, 4 Division equipped with Abbot self-propelled guns. The group continued on to Herford in the afternoon to visit Harewood Barracks to inspect the 16/5 Lancers, with their AFV-432's etc. They then moved on to a third site at Maresfield Barracks to inspect the 7$^{th}$ Signal Regt. There was a lot of ground to cover on foot, but the unit had interesting security arrangements including electrified fences, video cameras and observers in place. In the evening they went back to Hereford Barracks, where they were confined to quarters for "security" reasons.

That same evening Capt Pat Rechner asked the Brits for permission to go for a run in the morning, but Maj Konyk directed the runners to be in pairs, so he volunteered the author to run with Pat. The UK's LCol Russell challenged Capt Denis Bouillé to go as well, and Denis accepted, with all to participate in the run at 5 AM. At 0445, the author got up, stretched and went down to take part in the run. About eight people turned up, but not Denis! LCol Russell put his finger on the author's chest and smirked. The author immediately ran back up and kicked him out of bed (he had somehow managed to put himself "under the weather" or worse, I'm not sure which). The LCol had also substituted his Physical Training Officer to run in his place (interesting approach to the challenge). The group of runners started off at a healthy trot, but about ½ a km into the run, Denis stepped off a curb and very badly sprained his ankle. Pat and the author quickly hauled him off to the base hospital in an ambulance. It was an interesting start to the day, and of course the Brits were really suspicious of us now.

The inspectors had a long drive East to the town of Hameln, passing by Schloßß Schaumburg near Rosenthal, and arriving in Hameln at Gordon barracks to inspect 35 Engineer Regiment, and 664 Helicopter Sqn equipped with Lynx and Alouettes. In the afternoon they drove over to Tofrek Barracks in Hildesheim to inspect 32 Armoured Engineer Regiment, and a German Medical Unit, then returned to Minden and checked into Assaye Barracks for the night. The next morning they had an early trip West to Osnabruck and drove into Roberts Barracks to inspect 25 Engineer Regt and the 4 Field Arty Regt. In the afternoon, they went on to the 2$^{nd}$ Heavy Engineer unit at Quebec Barracks, equipped with Armoured Vehicle Laying Bridge (AVLB) Chieftains and other heavy equipment. The inspection team finished the inspections, closed with final reports in Minden and headed back to Lahr on 18 July 1991.

## 1991, The Last FALLEX

Author briefing SACEUR General John R. Galvin and LGen George R. Joulwan[11] & BGen J.J.M.R. Gaudreau in the Brigade Headquarters G2 Section's
M-113 "Queen Mary" Command Post, Fallex 91.

---

11. Supreme Allied Commander Europe (SACEUR) General John R. Galvin (US)—appointed June 1987–June 1992. His deputy in the photo, LGen George R. Joulwan, followed him as SACEUR from 1993 to 1997. BGen J.M.R. Gaudreau was the Commander of 4 CMBG.

## 1991, FALLEX 91

The 4 CMB (the Brigade's "Group" status had by now been deleted) Int Section participated in one of the last major exercises with the Brigade in the field in Germany from 19 Aug–27 Sep 1991. FALLEX 91 was conducted in the Hohenfels/RMA, and began with Ex Raiser Celery which ran from 19 Aug–10 Sep 91. This was followed by a move to Gauboden Kaserne near Straubing, about 130 km NE of Munich for Ex Royal Alliance, which ran from 19-27 Sep. II German (GE) Korps tested the Canadian Division, with the HQ of 4 CMB, 5e GBMC, and 10 Panzer Grenadier Brigade (10 (GE) PzGrBde) as the lower control. The author had the opportunity to take part in a Kiowa helicopter recce flight to Straubing and back, flying along the site of the exercise forces and hovering low along the Isar river with Capt Chris Coates (444 Sqn IO) flying, and Capt Simon Kitchener forward.

## 1991, Arms Verification Inspection, Iceland

From 30 Sep–4 Oct 91 the author took part in Ex Upper Crust, an Arms Verification Inspection conducted on the USAF stationed in Iceland. The inspection team flew out of Lahr to Dublin, Ireland on a Cosmopolitan transport, and headed off to the UK, with the scheduled destination being Edinburgh. 70-knot winds blew the flight West of Scotland, and so instead of landing in Edinburgh the team landed in Dublin, Ireland (Eire). Capt J.R.Y. Mike Foucreault also participated as an inspector on this trip. The next day the team flew on to Keflavik, Iceland, and were met at the airport by Icelanders, US Air Force representatives and the press. The team went through a formal introduction and inspection of equipment, which is when (Capt) Arno Sigurdjonssonn, the Icelander who had been a friend and part of our inspection team in Lahr, turned up. It turned out that he was not only there to represent his country, but it also just happened that he was Iceland's Minister of Defence. He welcomed the inspection team, and then the group separated into three sub-teams, with Major Konyk, Major Tepylo and Capt Ray Farrel leading. The author joined sub-team two with Major Konyk, and proceeded to inspect 20 F-15 Eagle fighters on a very cold and gusty day.

The following day the weather turned bad, with rain, sleet and snow etc. The inspectors were all frozen as they spent the morning outdoors inspecting the US installations, radar sites, and aircraft repair workshops etc. In the afternoon, the Icelandic hosts took the team for a drive into Reykjavik, the capital of Iceland. On the drive in, there were plains of black lava and moss as far as the eye could see in every direction, very bleak and in many ways much like the far North in Canada. The sun came out for a few minutes between the wind and rain, highlighting the snow-capped mountains nearby. The first stop was at a huge observatory, followed by a very brisk walk downtown, passing the Thingvelir Parliament buildings. The group was shown the building where President Ronald Reagan and Mikhail Gorbachev met, but they didn't stay long as there was a storm coming, and it was a 47 km drive back to the base. Because all water is heated geo-thermally (volcanic lava is used to heat water which in turn heats the pipes that carry fresh water everywhere), the inspectors had access to unlimited hot water for showers etc. The team left on a very cold windy morning for the five-hour flight back to the comparative warmth and sunshine of Lahr.

## 1991, Life with the ECMM in Yugoslavia
## Sgt Daniel St Pierre

In the summer of 1991, the Canadian government, through its membership in the Committee of Security and Cooperation in Europe (CSCE), was asked to participate in the European Community Monitoring Mission (ECMM) in Yugoslavia. In October 1991, I was shipped over to Yugoslavia to work with the ECMM. There were often vivid reminders of violence and destruction. In December, the Mayor of the City council of Zagreb passed a bylaw which condemned the carrying of automatic weapons in town. The only weapons allowed were sidearms. It was an eerie feeling to travel in Zagreb and see people checking in their 9-mm pistols as you would an umbrella. The nine months that I was in the country added a completely different perspective to my job.[12]

## INTREP, the Newsletter of the CF Intelligence Branch and Intelligence Branch Association, December 1991

The demise of the Intelligence Branch Journal left a gap in the means of keeping Branch and Association members up to date with ongoing events of con-

---

12. Intelligence Branch Association Quarterly Newsletter, Edition 1, 1993, p. 3.

cern, hence the birth of INTREP. This issue contained a series of letters on recent events.

## *From the Branch Advisor, Col Victor V. Ashdown*

As I review the activities of the Intelligence Branch over the past year or so, I feel a deep pride in the manner in which Branch members have performed their duties. Events at Oka and in the Persian Gulf clearly demonstrated the professionalism and dedication of all—for surely events such as these place an extra load on all members of the branch, not just those directly involved. Your efforts greatly enhanced the visibility and credibility of the Branch, and, more importantly, of the military Intelligence function as a whole.

One can conclude from this that we must be doing something right, and perhaps we are. Certainly, we have been blessed in recent years with the excellent quality of personnel entering the Branch, our training, both on courses and on the job, is improving, and our evident professionalism has self-generated new tasks (and new positions) throughout the CF. However, the world is rapidly changing and these changes are directly affecting the future of Canada and the CF. The Int Branch cannot remain immune to these changes. We have had a "good run," but now is not the time to dwell on past glories; the future will present us with challenges more difficult than those we have faced in the past.

So what can we do? Obviously, there is a limit to the effect a small, scattered group of 430 souls can have on the great affairs of state. Nonetheless, we can act and we must! Since many of the challenges we will face are as yet undefined, it follows that we must be "ready for anything." The first and most important step is to put our Branch in order.

History is full of examples of small military Units winning great victories against overwhelming odds. The common factor in all these instances is the indomitable spirit of the people involved, a spirit nurtured by: first, confidence in themselves, in their abilities, in their leaders, and in the rightness of their cause; and, second, the cohesiveness of their Unit, that felling of "belonging," of "family." Measured against history, the Branch is doing pretty well by the first yardstick, if our recent performance is any guide. However, our record on the second is spotty. We must recognize this failing and take action because the Branch morale and "cohesiveness" may well be the deciding factor if one of those future challenges places us face to face against overwhelming odds!

The task is not really all that difficult. We can start with Participation. [All members of the Branch can do more to foster our "family."] Senior NCMs are the "heart" of any military organization—our Int Ops proved that during our "lean years" in the late 1960s and 70s. Officers are the "head" of the Branch and must be prepared to provide leadership by example.

The CF is being reduced in numbers and the Branch will undoubtedly suffer some cuts as a result. To date, our losses do not appear to be serious and I do not foresee anyone losing his or her job. However, even though our senior leaders understand the vital importance of Intelligence, they will be forced to make very difficult choices as the downsizing continues. We are a small Branch widely deployed. Therefore, the work of every Branch member is on display and critical to our overall effort. We must show our leaders that we are able and willing to do more with less by being more efficient. We must also pull together, for as the old saying goes, "United we stand, divided we fall."[13]

## From the Branch CWO, CWO John G. Charette

I regret that the Int Branch Journal will no longer be published. In many respects, it developed to the point where it was not spreading news about the Branch as it was originally intended to do. The news for 1992 is less than cheery, due to the concerns over impending defence cuts and the economic conditions in Canada, although the Int Branch will survive. Let's not forget this and make an even greater effort in 92 to build on the ties that bind.[14]

---

13.  INTREP, December 1991, pp. 1-2.
14.  INTREP, December 1991, p. 2.

1991 CISA AGM participants.

## 1991, CISA AGM

The CISA AGM was held at CFSIS, CFB Borden, 22-24 Aug 1991. Present were: LCol Jack S. Dunn, Capt David A. Rubin, Capt J.D. Baxter, Maj Merrick K. Szulc, Lt M. Motyl, LCol Alf J. Laidler, Capt M.G. Galloway, LCol Dale M. Watts, LCol Ian A. Nicol, Maj Nils E. Lindberg, Capt Ray Bordeleau, Capt J.E.H. Bernard Lemieux, Maj Robert C. Dale, Capt Ed D. Kirby, Lt Don M. Fowler, Maj William "Bill" L. Watt, Maj Peter W. Sloan, MGen Al Pickering, Lt E. Bruce Holmes, Capt W. Doug Whitley, Capt P.W. Clare Lagerquist, Lt P. Liggins, Maj Gary W. Handson, Capt Peter T. Patton, Maj David A. Haas, Maj Franz F. Laizner, Maj Wilf S. Puffer, Maj Terry B. Kelly, Capt James "Jim" P.K. Van Wynen, Maj D.E. Guyatt, Capt Paul G. Rivard, LCol Bernie N. Wright, LCol Ed D. Sanford, Maj J. Michel Bédard, Capt Eugene Morosan, Col Robert T. Grogan, Col A.H. Sam Stevenson, Capt Harold F. Smith, Maj Reginald R. Dixon, Maj Pat R. Ansell, Capt Doug R. Bennett, Maj Fred E.G. Jones, LCol D. Jazey (observer), and Maj John "Pappy" MacKinnon (Secretary).[15]

## LCol Robert H. "Tex" Noble

LCol Robert H. "Tex" Noble passed away in the fall of 1991. Tex served with distinction during WWII, winning the OBE and a number of other medals. He joined the Canadian Army in England at the outbreak of the war, and

15. CISA Newsletter, Vol. 22, No. 3, December 1991, p. 1.

worked his way up through the ranks from Private to Major by 1945. He remained in Germany, serving as a senior officer in the Intelligence Division of the British Control Commission for Germany, then returned to Canada in 1947 to rejoin the Canadian Army, rising to the rank of LCol. After leaving the Army, he joined the Government of Ontario in a senior capacity, and later headed his own consulting firm. He also served as the Executive Director of the Canadian Professional Golf Association. Maj John "Pappy" MacKinnon stated, "Tex made his mark on everyone he met, and with his dynamism, was completely unforgettable."[16]

## 1991, CISA Member News

Maj John "Pappy" MacKinnon was elected as Councillor for Canterbury Ward in Ottawa, ending his 8-year term as full-time President of the Economists', Sociologists' and Statisticians' Association on 30 Nov and being sworn in as Regional Councillor on 15 Dec 1991.

Capt Paul G. Rivard, CISA Membership Secretary, completed all the requirements for his Ph.D.

During the AGM, the President, LCol Jack S. Dunn introduced the Base Commander, BGen J. Tousignant, and the Commandant of CFSIS, LCol Patricia M. Samson. LCol Samson stated that the school would do everything possible to assist in making the meeting a success, with admin support supplied by Capt J.B.P. Trudeau. LCol Dunn also introduced LCol Don Jazey, the Departmental Liaison Officer to the Conference of Defence Associations and new members Maj Pat R. Ansell and Lt M. Motyl.

On 23 Aug 91, members of the CISA assembled at the CFSIS Cenotaph at Stewart Square for the dedication of a plaque honouring fallen members of the Intelligence and Security Branches. MGen Al Pickering and LCol Jack S. Dunn participated in the inspection party.

Ms. Joanna Marie Haney was the successful candidate for the 1991 CISA Academic Award.

DG Int BGen L. Doshen spoke of studies being undertaken in CIS. He discussed changes in East-West relationships and effects on the UN and the Int Community. Because there are few available resources for defence in spite of the continued existence of threats, the Intelligence function is all the more

16.  Acorn INTREP 003, Feb 1992, p. 7.

important. The work of the Int Branch in CIS is respected, but there is a need for an Intelligence reserve.[17]

## Notes from the Branch Advisor, Col Victor V. Ashdown

CWO Jean G. Charette will be leaving as the Branch CWO to take up his new position as the Base CWO at CFB Moosejaw. His posting as a Base CWO is just one example of a very positive trend that is now becoming apparent—the Branch is being asked to fill more "any" positions. For example, Cdr Christopher S. Hordal is posted to NDHQ/ADM Policy/D NATO Pol this summer, joining LCdr Ted Parkinson who went there last year. This trend, along with the establishment of new positions in the Commands, is tending to compensate for some of the slots we lost because of reductions at NDHQ and in Europe. The CPO2 position at MARCOM HQ and CWO Jean G. Charette's posting to Moose Jaw means that we are no longer overborne in MWOs and have a promotion to CWO as well. I expect this trend to continue, thus giving Branch members valuable out-of-Branch experience and keeping the promotion flow trickling along. It is something to keep in mind when you are filling out your future employment "wish list" on your PER.

CPO1 William "Bill" J. Lindsay will be the new Branch CWO as of this summer. Let me explain my policy on the selection of the Branch CWO—it is essential that the Branch CWO be in Ottawa so that he is readily available to the Branch Advisor. It would be ideal in the senior CWO could also be the Branch CWO, but I firmly believe that location is more important than seniority. Therefore, the selection policy is simple—the senior CWO in Ottawa is the Branch CWO.[18]

## Farewell Message from Branch CWO Jean G. Charette

It is with a mixture of sadness and happiness that after six years as the Intelligence Branch Chief, I relinquish this position in order to accept a new and personal challenge. To my knowledge, it will be the first time that the Intelligence Branch fills a Base CWO position. After 30 years in the military, I am both honoured and pleased to be afforded this opportunity. My wife and I will have been ten years in Ottawa this summer. It is the longest time we've ever

---

17. CISA Newsletter, Vol. 22, No. 3, December 1991, pp. 1-8.
18. Intelligence Branch Association Quarterly Newsletter, Edition 2, April 1992, p. 1.

spent in one place and it will be difficult to pull up roots. Equally difficult, will be saying goodbye to my many associates in the Branch with whom I have had dealings and may rewarding experiences in my past 25 years in the Intelligence business. In many ways, I do not feel like I'm leaving the Branch. I will continue to wear, with pride, my Intelligence cap badge. Undoubtedly, my office will be filled with numerous mementos of my days as an Int Op. I will continue to follow, with keen interest, the developments in Intelligence and despite adversities, the continued evolution of the Branch. I wish each and every one of you "bonne chance" and rewarding careers. E Tenebris Lux. CWO Jean G. Charette, Int Branch # 32.[19]

## 1991, 1ˢᵗ *Canadian Division Intelligence Company Total Force Intelligence*

Formed on 29 October 1989, the 1ˢᵗ Canadian Division Intelligence Company (1 Cdn Div Int Coy) currently has a proposed establishment of 45 officers and NCMs. In keeping with the Total Force concept, 24 of the 45 positions are filled with operationally tasked Reserve Int Officers and NCMs from across Canada. Eventually it is intended to open up a number of the 24 restricted positions to Reservists in the Kingston area.

The value of Reserve augmentation on operations was proven during the Oka Crisis. The Commanding Officer of 1 Cdn Div Int Coy, Major Gord P. Ohlke, CD, was eager to exercise a larger portion of his Total Force Unit. The opportunity to do this was created through an initiative nicknamed RADICAL ASSEMBLY conducted between 19 and 23 August 1991.

Exercise RADICAL ASSEMBLY was the first collective training exercise specifically for Reserve Intelligence Troops since the demise of the Reserve Intelligence Training Companies in the early 1970s. It was designed to train and exercise the participants in the functions of an Intelligence Collection and Analysis Centre (ICAC). The ICAC Platoon is a sub-Unit of 1 Cdn Div Int Coy. It is an all source Intelligence "fusion" centre where all tactical information and Intelligence from formation Troops, and the Intelligence products from higher and flanking formations are processed against the Priority Intelligence Requirements of the Commander of 1 Cdn Div. Should 1 Cdn Div Int

---

19.  Intelligence Branch Association Quarterly Newsletter, Edition 2, April 1992, pp. 1-2.

Coy, or just the ICAC Platoon, be detached under command of a Brigade Group, as during the Oka Crisis, it retains exactly the same role.

The aim of the ICAC's operation is to provide the Formation Commander with current Intelligence. Through the refinement of current Intelligence, the ICAC conducts target development for Formation fire support assets.

The objectives of Exercise RADICAL ASSEMBLY were to determine whether enough reservists could be mobilized to support 1 Cdn Div Int Coy; train Reservists in the operations of the ICAC Platoon, in the context of 1 Cdn Div operations in a mid to high intensity conflict, and, fully integrate the full-time and part-time members of the Int Branch in one Total Force Unit.

It was necessary to form five ICAC shifts, which operated simultaneously using the same exercise scenario throughout. Each ICAC shift was composed of Reservists and Regulars. Moreover, the integration of Regulars and Reservists extended to Company Headquarters and to the Exercise Control Staff. The exercise ended with Fantasia being routed, in large part, due to the accurate and timely Intelligence provided by the ICACs. A celebratory BBQ and awards ceremony was held immediately upon ENDEX in order to bask in the glow of victory.

The significance and utility of Exercise RADICAL ASSEMBLY is evident merely by the response and attention that it received. In addition to the Regulars of 1 Cdn Div Int Coy, 37 Reservists from across Canada (equating to 2/3 of the Int Branch Reservists) participated from the Primary Reserve List, the Primary Reserve and the Reserve Electronic Warfare Squadron. The exercise was observed y many distinguished visitors. MGen J.J.M.R. Gaudreau, the Commander of 1 Canadian Division, paid a visit to all elements of the Unit during the final exercise and addressed the Troops at the close. Present also at this time were MGen Reginald J.G. Weeks (Ret'd), Colonel Commandant of the Int Branch; Col Victor V. Ashdown, the Int Branch Advisor; and LCol Rive, the G2 at Land Forces Central Area (LFCA) Headquarters.

In summary, Exercise RADICAL ASSEMBLY was a successful and much-publicized event. All of the objectives were achieved. It was the first such collective training effort in many years, and it highlighted what can be attained through Total Force endeavours. Most importantly, all members of the Exercise RADICAL ASSEMBLY 1 Cdn Div Int Coy had gained knowledge and experience which they could not have acquired otherwise. Both the Reservists and the Regulars are eager to participate in RADICAL ASSEM-

BLY 92 in order to further develop their own skills and the strength of the Total Force.[20]

## 1991, Intelligence Personnel News

Maj Gerry C. Mayer reports the following Int Branch personnel have been promoted in 1991 to the rank indicated: Col Patrick D.R. Crandell, CFLS; LCol J.F. Cruse, DISA; LCol Al G. McMullan, DG Int; Maj Rhedegydd ap Probert , CTC; Maj J.C. Chris Gagnon, Tyndall AFB; Maj H. Wayne Nightingale, DG Int; Maj Gord P. Ohlke, 1 Cdn Div Int Coy; LCdr Ted Parkinson, DG Pol Plan; Maj Mike J. Popovich, SO CIS; Maj Ron H.J. Ruiters, FMC HQ; Capt Phil R. Coo, DG Int; Capt J.A.E. Kent Dowell, 2 EW Sqn; Capt Al Haywood, DG Int; Capt J.C. Hill, DG Int; Capt R. Stu W. MacAulay, DG Int; Lt (N) Dave S. Peterson, DG Int; and, Capt K.A.V. Sutton, DG ADP Svcs.

The following personnel were promoted in 1992: Maj Terry W. Procy-shyn, Air Command HQ; LCdr Dan P. Langlais, MARPAC HQ; Lt (N) Ivan Allain, DG Int; Lt (N) Mike F.H. Arnoldi, DG Int; Capt M.P. Bou-dreau, 433 Sqn/433e ETAC; Capt David R. Canavan, DG Int; Lt (N) A.W. Chester, DG Int; Capt Clark P. Cornect, DG Int; Capt R.B. MacRae, LFCA; Capt Jan L. Malainey, CSE; Capt Pierre Michaud, 1 Div HQ; Capt Robert J. O'Gorman, DG Int; Capt David B. Owen, MARCOM HQ; and, Capt T.A. Quiggin, DG Int.

The following Int Branch personnel were promoted to the rank indicated: CPO1 William "Bill" J. Lindsay, DGPCOR Ottawa; MWO Paddy Hat-field, CFB Cold Lake; MWO Ivo J.M. Schoots DG Int Ottawa; WO Mike R. Tracey, CFSIS Borden; WO M.B. Mahoney.

Promotions to Sgt/PO2: Sgt Brian K. Mudge, CFLS Ottawa; Sgt T.D.G. Graham, 433 Sqn/433e ETAC Edmonton; Sgt J.B. François Allard, 419 Sqn Cold Lake; Sgt Donald M. Gallaher, 439 Sqn Baden; Sgt J. Guy Foisy, CFILO Washington; Sgt J.D. Roy, 1 Cdn Div Int Coy Kingston; Sgt R. Jack Wilson, 416 Sqn Cold Lake; Sgt Dennis G. McNulty, 4 Wing HQ Baden; Sgt J.M.R. Dan Jacques, 433 Sqn/433e ETAC Bagotville; Sgt John Paul Michael Parsons, DG Int Ottawa; Sgt J.P. André Tremblay, 5 GBC Valcart-ier; Sgt T.P. Farnel, DG Int Ottawa; Sgt J.A. Chris Pelletier, 421 Sqn Baden;

20. Intelligence Branch Association Quarterly Newsletter, Edition 2, April 1992, pp. 3-4.

Sgt David G. Maxim, DG Int; Sgt P.G. Manuge, CFSIS Borden; Sgt J.M.A. Stéphane Chartrand, 5 GBC Valcartier; Sgt John C. Penner, 2 Sqn 1 CDHSR; Sgt Nicholas R. Procenko, 1 CDAB & Sigs; Sgt J.E. Paul Pellerin, 1 Cdn Div Int Coy Kingston; Sgt J.S. Daniel St Pierre, DG Int.

Promotions to MCpl/MS: MCpl J.F.J.M. Tremblay, 430 Sqn Valcartier; MCpl J.W. St Jacques, 416 Sqn Cold Lake; MCpl Kevin Toomer, 1 Cdn Div Int Coy Kingston; MCpl Don S. Eenkooren, 408 Sqn Edmonton; MCpl Mark J. Kelly, DG Int Ottawa; MCpl P.D. Cooper, DG Int Ottawa; MCpl Trevor Cave, SSF HQ & Sigs Petawawa; MCpl R.S. Wilkie, HQ CFE; MCpl J.R. Charles Conlin, SSF HQ & Sigs Petawawa; MCpl Richard R.P. Walsh, DG Int Ottawa; MCpl Dave V. Morley, 1 Cdn Div Int Coy Kingston; MCpl Warren L. Lawrence, SSF HQ & Sigs Petawawa; MCpl A. Bruce Fenton, DG Int Ottawa; MCpl Kris E. Pedersen, DG Int Ottawa; MCpl Marie M. Hudson, 4 Svc Bn Lahr; MCpl A.L. Pride, SSF HQ & Sigs Petawawa; MCpl K.J. Ash, DG Int Ottawa; MCpl Connie F. Lancaster, 1 CBG Calgary; MCpl G. Bruce Scott 2 Sqn 1 CDHSR Kingston; and MCpl J.H.D. Gauthier, FMC HQ St Hubert.

The following Int Branch personnel were released in 1991: Maj J. René Gauthier, Maj Brad N. Hall, Maj Gary W. Handson, Capt Robert T. Greyeyes; and in 1992: Maj Alan G. Barnes, Maj Ken F. Binda and Maj John H. Newman.

WO Henry E. Doucette has been accepted to the University Training Program for NCMs.[21]

---

21. Intelligence Branch Association Quarterly Newsletter, Edition 2, April 1992, p. 5-7.

# 10

## 1992, Intelligence Branch

### 1992, Interrogation Course, Ashford, UK

Early in May 1992 the author flew to England to take the British Interrogation Course along with 16 other students, all from the UK Army, Navy and Royal Air Force. He took the subway to Hyde Park, and listened to some interesting speaker's expounding various bits of hype and nonsense then took the Subway to Charing Cross and got on the train to Ashford, about an hour and 20 minutes south of London. He checked into the Int Officer's Mess, while taking note of a captured Iraqi 2S1 122-mm self-propelled gun on display just inside the main gate. The course was a solid three weeks of work, with lots of stress and study, but one of the best and most professionally conducted courses he had the privilege to attend. All classes were conducted with participants wearing only civilian clothing.

The students took part in a number of training exercises, including one in the village of Doddington, where they visited the 500-year old Chequers Inn (which had two ghosts according to the lady innkeeper. One was a Cromwellian soldier and the other was one of the former lady owners). The original Inn on the site is mentioned in the Domesday Book (about 1080+-).

Another exercise called for a five-hour Bus ride North to an exercise area at Catterick up near York. Crossed under the Thames River via the Dartford Tunnel. The fields were bright yellow with ripe rapeseed, and beautiful weather. Rolling country, with uncountable miles of stone walls, somewhat like the area north of Baden. In the evening the students drove past a stone manor where Mary Queen of Scots once hid. The interrogation exercise was done in an old stone built farm, and very professionally conducted. Two groups of PW were brought in after midnight, blindfolded and under escort, and not a sound was spoken during the search. The PW handlers used dogs, not a pleasant exercise for the prisoners. We were introduced to "egg banjo's," (fried egg sandwiches), which all had for breakfast. Back in class, the students were given a presentation by a British police officer named Trevor, who had been taken hostage in the Iranian Embassy, telling us the details of his dramatic and difficult experience. In the evening all went to a pub in Ashford for curry night—more water please!

The next training exercise had all of the students on the course heading off to Pointrilas in Wales, a training site located near the SAS base in Hereford. The exercise involved putting 22 SAS candidates through the final phase of their training, and it was a hard one for them in many respects. The exercise began at midnight. There were a number of interesting encounters and training experiences conducted under very closely controlled supervision as the participants worked their shifts interrogating the PW. This was an extraordinary course, and one that would come in very useful during a number of later operations the author took part in. It was an intense course, and not one recommended for the timid.

## 1992, CISA Member News

CISA sponsored its first annual "CISA Essay Competition" with an award of $250 as the prize. Essays are to be on a current or historical topic related to military Intelligence or security; of 2,000 to 5,000 words in length in either language; and open to members of CISA in the CF, Regular and Reserve.

RAdm John Rodocanachi, Maj Gary W. Handson and Maj Brian Kent retired and were mugged out at the Ottawa Officer's Mess.

MGen Reg Weeks nominated Daniel O'Doheny, a Lt in 5 Fd Regt RCA, assigned to 2 Div HQ as an Int Staff Officer, as the C Int C representative to the 50th Anniversary of Dieppe ceremonies. Lt O'Doheny served with then Maj Peter E.R. Wright, and landed at Dieppe on 19 Aug 1942, was captured and made a POW for the rest of the war. He is a lawyer, QC, and lives in Montreal.[1]

---

1.    CISA Newsletter, Vol. 23, No. 1, June 1992, pp. 1-2.

# 1992, *Yanus*

In 1992, Intelligence Officer LCol Robert S. Williams, then serving as a Capt and Russian linguist, reported that he was, "plucked from within the bowels of Tunney's Pasture to be an interpreter for a series of Humanitarian Relief flights on a CF 707 to the former Soviet Union." He flew out of Lahr, "to various points and in 1993 from Turku, Finland to various points." Rob mentioned, "Each iteration was five to six weeks. Work was exhausting, rewarding and at times humorous. During one stop at a place called Ioshkar Ola, east of the Volga, after we had stopped at a fighter base and unloaded, we had a few hours before takeoff. I wandered about, chatted to various Russian aircrews, and was offered a tour of an ELINT equipped Tu-104. Never one to say no to a tour, I had a good look through the aircraft. The crewmembers were anxious to respond to questions. At one point, I asked what they used to aid in aircraft identification. The Navigator (Sturrman) replied proudly that they used the Yanus system. Never having heard of this, I asked if it would be possible to see it. At that point, still puzzled as to what to expect, I was taken to the cockpit and handed a recent copy of JANES All the World's Aircraft; in Russian, "Yanus." Mystery solved."[2]

# 1992, *Close Out of 4CMB*

From 11 June 1992, preparations were made to host a large number of past serving commanders of 4 Canadian Mechanized Brigade visiting Lahr for the repatriation of 1 Canadian Division ceremonies. As an escort officer, the author wore gold epaulets to the hilt, and with so many secondary taskings it was a madhouse for much of the week. The Russians chose this same time to arrive to conduct an Arms Verification Inspection of the Brigade units in Lahr, and the author was detailed to handle them as well. There were beaucoup visiting Generals, Russians, with their requirements adding to the time taken to go through rotation posting clearances. Murphy was on the loose, and of course there had to be an accident at the jump club just to make things interesting. A formal function was held at the Stadthalle in Lahr, on the following evening with Mayor Dietz and BGen J. Clive Addy exchanging plaques and flags etc. The past and present commanders enjoyed themselves, while a German paratroop band gave a great concert.

---

2.   LCol R.S. Williams, E-mail 10 Sep 2003.

On 13 June, the author gave an Intelligence briefing to the various Generals on the situation in Yugoslavia in the morning. In the afternoon all attended the Division Repatriation parade, the stand down of the Division, and the Brigade Change of Command, with Col Robert "Bob" G. Meating as the new Brigade Commander. Later, MGen Meating would be DG Int.

## 1992, Air Command SSO

In late April 1992, the SSO and MWO Barry W. Sweeney made a long overdue visit to the Maritime Air Group and its eastern bases. They visited Capt Derek Marchbank and PO1 Don B. Powers at CFB Shearwater, Nova Scotia. 434 Sqn is about to be reformed there. The SSO and MWO continued their trip, visiting CFB Greenwood where they spoke with Capt Glen McKay and the Int Section of the DIAC for an interesting overview of their 24/7 operations.

Air Transport is undergoing some significant changes this APS, with Capt Richard A. Derkson arriving from Europe to replace Capt Rajeev G. Nath, who is posted to NDIC in Ottawa. Capt Rob Cooper in Edmonton is posted to NORAD in Colorado Springs and will be replaced by Capt Kathryn B. Clouston. The Int positions in Edmonton have been centralized at Base Ops and one position has been relocated to ATG HQ. Capt Sean Bruyea and MWO Paddy Hatfield worked hard to help bring off a highly successful Exercise Maple Flag in Cold Lake. To those Int Branch personnel in Bagotville and Comox, future visits from the SSO are planned.

WO Dean Smith was presented with the ATG Commanders Commendation for his Int briefings given in Cyprus to ATG aircrew during OP FRICTION. BGen D.N. Kinsman presented him the award.[3]

## 1992, NORAD HQ Colorado Springs Update

This APS will be a season of great change for the Intelligence personnel posted in Colorado Springs. APS 92 will see the departure of Capt J.R.R.R. Sylvain Robidoux, who is bound for AIRCOM HQ; and the arrival of Capt Rob Cooper from CFB Edmonton. Capt Robidoux will be sadly missed, as he was the resident expert for just about everything related to LRA.

---

3.    Air Command Intelligencer, Edition 2, Volume 1, July 1992, p.1.

The biggest change for Int personnel posted in COS is a change of location and the promise of entering the advanced world of automation. In Feb 1992, both the Capt positions moved from Cheyenne Mountain AFB to Peterson AFB. This move was to place all the NORAD/USSPACECOM analysts in the same location, the Combined Intelligence Centre (CIC). The CIC is a state of the art building, but most importantly, incorporates a new CIC LAN computer system. The system has had its growing pains, however, when operational it should take us from the Stone Age into the world of automation.

The long term will probably see the move of the WO position from Cheyenne Mountain AFB to Peterson AFB as well. The WO is presently employed in the Exercise and Evaluation Shop and the move will bring him to the LRA section.

As you can see, NORAD HQ is an exciting and rapidly changing place. The future will probably hold many challenges as we adjust to a changing world and adapt to new priorities and missions. We hope all our comrades in the "North" are doing well. Take care.[4]

## 1992, FG/CANR HQ Int Section Update

Fighter Group/Canadian NORAD Region (FG CANR) Headquarters is unique within the Canadian Air Force in that it is a joint headquarters encompassing both national and international chains of command. To meet this distinctive challenge, the FG CANR HQ Int Section is configured to answer the needs of the Commander in the full range of his responsibilities.

Current Roles. The role of the Int Section is to provide the Commander and his staff with the Int support necessary to carry out both the NORAD and sovereignty roles. In order to fulfill this role, the section is currently split into four cells: SDA/Strategic; Sqn support/NORAD; Production—Management/Briefings; and, Exercise and Counter-Drug Support Cell.

The Strategic Cell monitors all CIS strategic forces, particularly Long Rang Aviation (LRA) and Naval Aviation. This cell is also responsible for the administration matters related to Special material. The Sqn Support Cell is responsible to both Wings and Sqns with assistance in fulfilling both NORAD and sovereignty roles. Production-Management and Briefing Cell coordinates all production, briefings and office administration.

---

4.   Air Command Intelligencer, Edition 2, Volume 1, July 1992, p. 2.

Finally, the Exercise and Counter-Drug Cell provides Int scenario support for both NORAD and Region sponsored exercises as well as Int support to Counter-Drug ops. The latter includes all associated liaison with both national and international Intelligence and law enforcement agencies.

In order to provide full support to the Commander and his staff, the section has a Duty Intelligence Watch Officer (DIWO) on call 24/7. The DIWO is part of the Standby Battle Staff and maintains a continuous on-call readiness for Region response to day-to-day peacetime incidents and for air defence operations.

Evolving Roles. Evolution is a national constant. Like anything else, military organizations must adapt to shifting realities. With the perceived diminishment of NORAD's traditional threat from the former USSR, greater attention is being paid to two evolving areas of responsibility.

As 1 CAD winds down, Commander Fighter Group assumes responsibility for all fighter operations (both nationally and internationally). OP FRICTION demonstrated the need to maintain a capability to deploy fighter assets in support of national and UN goals. In recognition of this, planning to meet future contingency operations in Europe, or anywhere else in the world is currently underway at FG CANR. Accordingly, the Int section is reconfiguring to include a Contingency Ops cell consisting of two officers.

Over the last two years, counter-drug ops have rapidly gained importance in the NORAD sphere. Several international agreements between Canada and the US (such as the current NORAD agreement and the CANUS Land Ops Plan) direct that assistance to law enforcement counter-drug operations will be provided by both the US and Canadian military. Recognizing this reality, a dedicated Counter-Drug Cell will be formed from an already overworked Exercise Cell and be established with one officer and one WO.

We would not be able to fulfill these responsibilities without the cooperation and dedication of all Int staff at Wing and Sqn level. Their professionalism and devotion have directly contributed to the accomplishments of FG/CANR missions and roles and to the excellent reputation of the Air Intelligence with National Defence. You are encouraged to continue to do your best and it is our duty to ensure that you have the tools to do it.[5]

---

5.    Air Command Intelligencer, Edition 2, Volume 1, July 1992, pp. 2-3.

## Message from the New Int Branch Chief, CPO1 William "Bill" J.Lindsay

It is with great pleasure that I assume the role of the Intelligence Branch Chief. There are three parts to my new position. I am responsible to NDHQ for VCDS taskings, in other words, for finding breathing people to do those pesky but important jobs such as Guards of Honour, stocktakings, etc., a very mundane but necessary function. Secondly, in my position as Directorate Intelligence Plans, Coordination and Doctrine (DIPCD) 2-3, I am mainly responsible for out of service Intelligence courses. This also gives me a place to sit, thanks to my Director, LCol Darcy J. Beatty. The third part of my new position is that of Branch Chief. I envision my appointment as requiring that I foster Branch Unity, assist the Branch Advisor on matters pertaining to the NCMs and generally poke around in the best interests of the Branch. I have seen the majority of you over the past two years in my former capacity as Career Manager, and I hope to be able to see all of you in the near future.[6]

## 1992, A View from the Viking Outpost, Norwegian Army Staff College
## Article by Maj Stan Carr

Maj Stan Carr attended two years of formal Norwegian Language training in Ottawa and in the Norwegian Army Staff College in Oslo, Norway. He wrote, "The whole episode has been very rewarding for both myself and my family. It is not very often that an Int Branch officer is afforded the opportunity to broaden his or her horizons in other than the standard CF pattern. The thrill and challenge of learning a foreign language—albeit one not overly popular the world over—is something too few of us officers get to experience. This is made even more challenging by having to put those new sounds to immediate and practical use on a foreign Staff College. In this case, the course is completely conducted in Norwegian, including all written work except a major staff paper.

While it might be taken lightly, the use of a new language on a course should not be. Consider for a moment that the average officer will take

---

6.    Intelligence Branch Association Quarterly Newsletter, Edition 3, 1992, p. 1.

upwards of 15-20 years of experience in our own forces and our operational procedures before he or she is fully prepared by attendance at our staff college. Attending a foreign one on the other hand offers a definite hurdle, having to learn as much about a foreign military as possible in short order. This aspect is exacerbated by the foreign language, which is compounded by the fact that the language course itself is largely "civilian" or "cocktail circuit" oriented. The first few months in Oslo become a new language course in itself in adjusting to Norwegian military terminology. Lastly, one thing that foreign language courses do not teach is the ability for analytical thought in the target language. Its not difficult, it just takes time and practice.

It is in overcoming these difficulties that one finds the challenge and excitement that most of us seek as professional officers. The greatest reward was the personal satisfaction that I completed this unique task while offering the Norwegians the benefit of insights into our training in operations and Intelligence, and the CF system as a whole.

The completion of these courses gives our officers an instant credibility in the AFNORTH HQ staff due in part to the high standard that Canadian Intelligence officers have shown in the past and because the Norwegian staff college course is directed at the Northern European Command's area of responsibility. As Chief of Current Intelligence at HQ AFNORTH, I can see continuous challenges unfold as we attempt to operate an all-source "NDIC" type operation with individuals of different nationalities and of varying experience in Intelligence work. Major Greg W. Jensen left for Canada recently, having left for me a well-organized Current Int Cell. We here in Oslo wish Greg continued success in NDHQ. Here in Oslo, my TED date is July 1995, although my replacement, if we continue with language and Staff College first, will not likely be through the system until 1996.

In any case, I hope someone out there considers this process important enough to keep it going and that someone is considering the challenge. My recommendation is, if the career manager asks you, take it! E Tenebris Lux.[7]

---

7.   Intelligence Branch Association Quarterly Newsletter, Edition 3, 1992,
     p. 4.

## 1992, Coming and Going at CFSIS
## Article by Cpl Ken Saunders

This APS has brought more than the usual cosmetic change at the home of the Branch. Gone this year are Capt Rick Mader and Capt J.B. Pierre Trudeau (both to Ottawa), CPO2 Brian Noble (Halifax), WO Barry R. Eddy (England), WO Henry E. Doucette (UTPNCM), Sgt David A. Gelsinger (Calgary), and Sgt Gary R. Hayes (Kingston).

Arriving this year to command Army Platoon is Capt Harold A. Skaarup. At the helm of Air platoon is Lt (N) Shawn P. Osborne, and our new CSM is MWO Joseph A. Michel White. Other new arrivals include WO Tim G. Armstrong, WO E. Meril Crane and Sgt J.R. Mario Ross.

The postings are not the only changes to take place. To improve overall efficiency, CFSIS and Int Trg Coy were reorganized. All of these changes, which will be implemented over a five-year period, will result in a new organization, which is better suited to our mission and tasks.

The old Land, Air and Sea Platoons have been reduced in size (one officer and one WO) and scope, and will be responsible for teaching TO&E, tactics, and staff duties applicable to their environment. A fourth platoon has been created to teach general Intelligence subjects, and has aptly named the "Generic Intelligence Training Platoon." The Intelligence Standards section has been increased in size to one officer and three NCMs, and is now incredibly busy writing new CTPs and CTSs.

Lastly, our home is expanding. Workers have started construction on an addition to the Intelligence Training Company building, which includes new classrooms and other facilities. It is expected to be ready for December 1992. See you then. E Tenebris Lux.[8]

---

8. Intelligence Branch Association Quarterly Newsletter, Edition 3, 1992, pp. 4-5.

Intelligence Operator 6A Course 9201.
Rear Row: MCpl Mark J. Kelly, MS Dan J.M. Ash, MCpl Dave V. Mor-
ley, MCpl Trevor Cave, MCpl Kenneth E. Davies, MCpl J.J.L. Denis
Chercuite, MCpl Tremblay.
Third Row: Sgt Luc J.A.M. Leroy, Sgt J. Guy Foisy, MCpl Rick F.
Luden, PO2 B.D. Sammons, Sgt J.B. Franck Allard, MCpl Kevin
Toomer, Sgt Glen A. McGuire.
Second Row: MCpl J.R. Charles Conlin, MCpl Connie F. Lancaster.
Front Row: WO Michael R. Tracey, Lt (N) Shawn P. Osborne, Maj J.
Michel Bédard, MWO Joseph A. Michel White.

Intelligence Operator 6B Course 9201.
Rear Row: Sgt Fournier, Sgt .M. Letellier De St Just, Sgt Campbell, Sgt Rick G. Oliver, Sgt Dave L. Howarth.
Centre Row: Sgt John G. "Jack" W. Campbell, WO Smith, WO Michael R. Tracey, Sgt Kevin N. Rowe, WO Dan J. Haslip, Sgt J.J.P. Michael Fournier.
Front Row: WO Barry R. Eddy, Capt Rick A. Mader, CPO2 Brian M. Noble.

Intelligence Operator 6B Course 9202.
Rear Row: Sgt R. Hal Pugh, Sgt J.R. Mario Ross, Sgt Martineau, Sgt J.O.
"Rick" Limoges.
Centre Row: Sgt J.L.S. Gauvin, Sgt Smith, PO2 J.R. Michel Labossiere,
Sgt Alex D. Radzion, PO2 Jeff A. Collings, Sgt Glen B. Hupe, WO
Henry E. Doucette, Sgt J.J.L.L.P. Girard.
Front Row: WO Barry R. Eddy, Maj J. Michel Bédard, CPO2 Brian M.
Noble.

Militia TQL3 Course 9201.
Rear Row: Pte T.A. Whitehead, LFAA, Pte R.J. Vaughn, LFCA, Cpl
J.C. Whitman, LFWA, Pte Derrick D. Petrushko, LFWA, Cpl J. Fara-
gone, RHC (Black Watch), Pte M.M. Kuligowski, LFWA.
Front Row: Cpl Mark M. Emberly, LFAA, MCpl Michael C. Wagner,
LFAA, Capt C.W.E. Moor, LFCHQ, Capt Colin A.J. Kiley, LFAA, Lt
James Peter Terfry, LFAA, Sgt Wes E.B. Young, LFAA, Cpl Alan R.
Farquhar, LFAA.

Basic Classification Training Course 9201.
Rear Row: Cpl Mark M. Emberly, 2Lt Maddox, 2Lt S.J. McSherry, Lt
Chapman, MCpl J.P. Stéphane Lefebvre.
Front Row: Sgt Campbell, Capt R.A. Mader, Capt C. Moor, Sgt
Stéphane S. Auger.

## 1992, The Truth behind the Intelligence Section at Tunney's Pasture
### Extracts from an article by CWO Barry W. Sweeney

Years ago, Col By came to the area that is now known as Ottawa. At that time, Frank Tunney grazed his cattle and little by little the urban blight spread and Frank's pasture area became less and less. One day he opted to sell the land to the highest bidder with the stipulation that it retained his name. Thus was born the legend of Frank's Pasture and Grazing Area. Over the years, subtle changes took place. The government outbid all others and the name has been shortened to reflect the current Tunney's pasture.

The occupants of the basement Intelligence crew have rotated in significant numbers this year, with those departing including WO Collin Affleck heading for Kingston, WO William A. Mitchell (Petawawa), LS Veronica Marie Parolin (Calgary), PO2 David G. Maxim (Esquimalt), MCpl McDonnell (Petawawa), Sgt Kondejewski (Shilo), Capt John M. Heinrichs (NDHQ), Sgt Schuurhuis (CFLS Ottawa), Sgt Goetz (CFLS Ottawa), MS A. Bruce Fenton (CFLS Ottawa), Sgt Alex D. Radzion (Kingston), Capt Brad J. Smith (CFLS Ottawa), MS Jason S. Stewart (Petawawa), Capt Paul D. Johnston (DG Int Ottawa), MWO Armado Santos (Kingston), Sgt Misha L. Allen (ORAE Ottawa), and, MWO Joseph A. Michel White (CFSIS Borden).

Incoming personnel include Capt R.A. Mader, Capt Phil R. Coo, Lt (N) W.E. Miller, WO R.D. Dixon, WO W.J. Goodland, WO Dave D. Turner, PO2 Terry W. Fader, Sgt K.L. Dyer, MCpl Gamache, Cpl Cormier, Cpl Etherington, Cpl Tom J. Last, Cpl Daniel Francis McNeil, Cpl N.S. Robert, Cpl Jacques M.A.D. Verbrugge, Cpl Therrien, Cpl P.R. Gordon, Cpl Thomas L. Rea, and Cpl Campbell.[9]

## *1992, CISA AGM*

The CISA AGM was held at Longue Pointe Garrison, CFB Montreal, 17-18 Sep 1992. Present were: LCol Ian A. Nicol (1st VP). William "Bill" L. Watt (Past President, Director), Maj David A. Haas (Treasurer), Maj Nils E. Lindberg (Director), Lt E. Bruce Holmes, LCol Alf J. Laidler, LCol Ernest Skutezky, LCol Dale M. Watts (Director), Capt Peter T. Patton, Col A.H. Sam Stevenson (Director), Col Robert T. Grogan (Director), Maj L. Henderson, Capt M.A. Kulba, Maj Fred E.G. Jones (Director), Lt D.A. Stolovitch, 2Lt Paul R. Perchaluk, LCol Ed D. Sanford, LCol D. Southen, Maj Gary W. Handson, Capt W. Doug Whitley, Capt Doug R. Bennett, Maj Doris E. Guyatt (Director), Maj J.H. Mansfield, Maj Pat R. Ansell, Col Jeff S. Upton (Director), Capt C. Moor, Capt Russel H. Hensel, LCol Peter W.M. Wilson, Col Victor V. Ashdown, Lt Michael H. Hertwig-Jaksch, Maj Brian Kent, Maj Robert C. Dale (Director), Maj Franz F. Laizner (Director), Maj Frank Leigh, LCol Pierre J.F. Couture, Maj Richard J. Vella, Maj Bernie

9.   Intelligence Branch Association Quarterly Newsletter, Edition 3, 1992, p. 6.

Benoit, Maj John "Pappy" MacKinnon (Secretary), Capt C. Hug (Land Forces Command HQ Staff), MGen H. Wheatley (Observer), and LCol D. Jazey (Observer).[10]

During the meeting it was determined there was a need for a greater intellectual challenge to CISA members, with the essay competition being a modest beginning. In June 1992, the CDA Defence Policy Committee was created. It asserted that, "…CDA should not be seen as an extension of DND, but should speak with its own voice on matters of defence policy. For that voice to be respected, criticism has to be well founded and constructive." DND had recently commissioned MGen Howard Wheatley (Ret'd) to conduct a study into the relationship between CDA and DND. Some serving officers were very concerned about the impact which the Total Force Concept is having on the Militia. The Navy and Air Force seem to be integrating better. A CDA Task Force on the Reserves in the Total Force is studying this situation.

The CISA Dependent's Award went to Jennifer Leigh Commons of Russel, Ontario and the Serving Reserve Member Award went to Nancy L.Y. Mah of Edmonton, Alberta. The CISA Essay Competition was won by Lt Michael H. Hertwig-Jaksch his essay on "Roman Military Intelligence."

Col V.V. Ashdown made a presentation of Intelligence at CIS, and discussed the proposed Defence Intelligence Unit in the National Capital Area. LCol Wilson presented details on the current strengths of Militia and Regular Force units and what the end states would be under the Total Force Concept. Detachments could be set up in Canadian cities where no units were provided for. He also outlined the criteria proposed by LFC for the awarding of the Sir William S. Stephenson Trophy.[11]

Maj Ken Binda retired from the Regular Force and was nominated as the Reform party candidate in Carleton-Gloucester area of Ottawa. Capt Carl Ian Walker of Squamish, BC has written two books, one on Pipe Bands in BC and the second, Pioneer Pipers of BC. CISA member LCol Emile Berger was appointed the Honorary Col of the Medical Branch. Capt J.E.H. Bernard Lemieux reported on preparations for the 50th Anniversary of the C Int C at CFB Borden scheduled for 29-31 Oct 92.[12]

---

10. CISA Newsletter, Vol. 23, No. 1, Jan 1993, p. 4.
11. CISA Newsletter, Vol. 23, No. 1, Jan 1993, pp. 5-6.
12. CISA Newsletter, Vol. 23, No. 2, September 1992 (numbers out of sync), pp. 1-2.

## *Acorn INTREP 001*
## *Edited by Sgt Dan Bordeleau*

The Acorn INTREP was produced to mark preparations for the celebration of the 50th Anniversary Reunion of the Canadian Intelligence Corps, 29-31 October 1992. The committee included Honorary Chairman Reginald J.G. Weeks, MGen (Ret'd); Chairman Ray Bordeleau, Secretary Gary W. Handson; Old Comrades Coordinator J.E.H. Bernard Lemieux, Int Branch Rep J.R. Ray LeCavalier, and Members Rep W. Doug Whitley. 8 issues were produced up to September 1992. MGen Weeks wrote the introduction to the first issue, which reads as follows:

"I am pleased to give my support to the 1992 Committee which will help us all to mark, in an appropriate way, the 50th anniversary of the founding of the Canadian Intelligence Corps. Fifty years—half a century—is a long time for people, but a relatively short time for institutions

Those of us who were founder members of the C Int C, and those who became members over the years, can look back with pride and nostalgia on our efforts to promote and encourage Action from Knowledge; a motto which is as apt and as relevant today as it was in 1942. Our successors in the Intelligence Branch of the Canadian Armed Forces are carrying on the same tradition by their determination to develop and maintain skills, which bring light from darkness—E Tenebris Lux.

Together we serve, and have served the institution of the Military Intelligence, which, far from being a contradiction in terms, as some would have it, is an institution as old as the history of conflict. An institution that is so necessary, that if it did not exist would have to be constantly reinvented.

The theme of our 50th Anniversary, therefore, should not be one of noisy and exclusive nostalgia, but rather one of abiding satisfaction in a foundation which was well and truly laid and a future in which the institution of military intelligence will continue to merit the recognition and appreciation of those who need it and encourage the skills of those dedicated to the profession."

(Signed) Reginald J.G. Weeks, MGen (Ret'd).[13]

---

13.   Acorn INTREP 001, 15 Dec 1991, p. 1.

## Letter from the Minister of Veterans Affairs, C Int C 50<sup>th</sup> Anniversary

"My warmest wishes to all of you as the Canadian Intelligence Corps looks forward to its 50th Anniversary. By the very nature of your mission, much of the work you did in wartime went unpublicized. But there can be no doubt that the findings and input of the Canadian Intelligence Corps had a major influence on the conduct of many campaigns. I suspect that a number of veterans are probably alive today only because of your perseverance and knowledge.

That, in itself, is reason enough to celebrate the 50th anniversary of the founding of your Corps. I hope there is a fine turnout in 1992 and that you renew old friendships and make many new ones." Yours sincerely,

(Signed) Gerald S. Merrithew, P.C., M.P.[14]

## Notes from the far-flung Empire
## Extracts from a letter by W.H. "Bill" Kane

Very few of the original "Silver and Green" settled out west. This is a brief update on the whereabouts of former members of 1 Field Security Section (1 FSS):

Gordon Clark, last known to be a private eye in Philadelphia; Tony Daguisto, formerly with the Int Trg Coy in Winnipeg, last posting known to be Churchill; Bob Cardwell, wounded in action in Korea, later returned to Toronto to serve as a firefighter; John Morris, served in Japan, later returned to Winnipeg; Chuck Baine, Montreal; Larry Kingsland, Toronto, worked with Taverne magazine and Kingsland Press; Gordon "Bud" Elliott, Montreal, married a lady from Ste. Therese, North of Montreal, may have moved to the US; Lou Masse, worked for the Post Office; CSM Robert Henderson, career soldier; Jim Struthers, firefighter instructor in Toronto; Brian Swarbuck, TV interviewer in Toronto; Charles Webster, former Quartermaster, worked for TCA/Air Canada, last known to be in Fort Lewis; Eddie Corbeil, former CO of 1 FSS in Korea, compliments of 25th Brigade, may be managing an estate north of Toronto; Jim McDougall, 1 FSS in Korea, later commissioned and a career soldier, retired in the Ottawa area; Doug Reid, former members of No. 6 Group, Bomber Command along with Bill Kane during WWII. After

---

14.  Acorn INTREP 001, 15 Dec 1991, p. 2.

Korea, Doug was commissioned and transferred to Artillery, later retired in Ancaster, Ontario. Bernie Benoit, former CO 1 Int Trg Coy Montreal, later a sheep farmer in the Eastern Townships; George Youmatoff, a former Capt in the C Int C, later became a minister; Spurr Woodbury and Vince Mayhew were both with 1 FSS, but current location unknown.

Editor's note: Following his service in Korea, Bill Kane served with MI3. He was with Canadair during the shakedown and test flight operations for the F-86 Sabre and T-33 Silver Star.[15]

## More Notes from the far-flung Empire
## Extracts from a letter by William "Bill" M. Summersgill

Again, few of the "Silver and Green" members are in BC, but here is an update on a few of the retirees:

John I.R. Weller has been the director of security for Loomis in Vancouver since he left the service; WO2 William "Bill" C. Hargreaves and WO Ken W. Wishart are both happily retired and living in the Fraser Valley, Bill in Alder-grove and Ken in Chilliwack; Maj Stanley H. Winfield, former CO of No. 4 Int Trg Coy in Vancouver has retired as the legal counsel for the Insurance Company of BC. Stan stays active in the Int Association. Iain Brand, another former CO of No. 4 Int Trg Coy in Vancouver, moved his law practice to the Courtenay/Comox area, and was an officer with the Canadian Scottish Regi-ment; Norman Pope was living in Victoria; O. Bud Swanson is a firefighter in Langley with the Vancouver fire department. W. Richard "Dick" Ulm and Barry Toomer with the Int Branch live in Comox and Victoria respectively.

Editor's note: William "Bill" M. Summersgill worked for the BC govern-ment following his retirement in 1978, initially as a fraud investigator and for the last five years as an officer in the office of the BC Ombudsman.[16]

## In Profile, LCol (Ret'd) David W. Wiens
## Extracts from an article by Lenore Bordeleau

With the dramatic events of the past weeks in the Soviet Union, it is easy to remember that, at first, everyone greatly feared Glasnost was buried forever. On the morning when the West first learned of the coup attempt, LCol David

---

15. Acorn INTREP 001, 15 Dec 1991, pp. 3-4.
16. Acorn INTREP 002, Jan 1992, p. 2.

W. Wiens, former Commandant of the Canadian School of Military Intelligence at CFB Borden, remarked, "I always suspected something like this would happen. There are too many hard-line Communists left with jobs on the line." Although the coup was defeated, the Colonel's assessment was correct. In order to solidify his position, Mikhail Gorbachev was finally forced to disband the Communist party.

LCol Wiens received his own Intelligence training in England, beginning in 1942 where he attended school in Aldershot with Bob Raypoint. "I went overseas as an Armoured Corps officer and was sent on course. The Corps was just new then and I was convinced to change over and become one of the early members."

Among his particular areas of expertise, LCol Wiens gained knowledge of escape, evasion and interrogation procedures. Later, these were to form a major part of his contribution to the CSMI training. When asked what he considered his greatest accomplishment at the school, LCol Wiens listed these programs, but claimed that he was most proud of the Militia program begun by Robert H. "Tex" Noble, and widely developed during his own time as Commandant. "We had the Militia come in for a month in the summer for work in the field and in the classroom. We had such a fine team of instructors that these people left with a sense of enthusiasm about the subject."

Contributing to the sense of pride and esprit de corps were projects like the Corps Kit Shop. Remember "Sinister Sam," the small wooden cloaked figurine? That was LCol Wiens' contribution. "I ran into that carving at a store in Collingwood, Ontario. I found out that they were made in Quebec and got the name of the carver. We ordered thirty or forty of them and persuaded Maj Reginald R. Dixon to pay for the large statuette, "The Dixon Award" which was given to the best recruit at the school." The small wooden figures were sold at the Kit Shop, where Wiens remembered, "they sold like hotcakes."

Like the Corps flag, the Kit Shop and the Corps museum, Wiens believed these popular figures helped contribute to the "pizzazz" of the Corps, the feeling of pride and purpose that old members talk about.

The LCol's ability to call the situation accurately probably comes as no surprise to former students at the CSMI. As Commandant from July 1962 to July 1965, most new members of the Corps passed within his sphere of influence. Morale in the school and in the Corps was high. The future looked bright.

It ended, according to Wiens, with the integration of the Corps with the Military Police. "That hurt me deeply," he said. "Suddenly we were disbanded and left high and dry. There was no Corps to be proud of." The dissolution of the Intelligence Corps was, of course, a political decision. "In some ways," remarks the LCol, "it made sense. For example, in the Medical Corps. But not for us." Part of the problem stemmed from the relative sizes of the two Corps to be combined. LCol Wiens called the amalgamation, "a case of a lamb and an elephant. They were so much larger, things naturally went their way, not ours."

Perhaps the biggest regret Wiens had about the amalgamation was the fact that, as a Staff Officer at Headquarters, it was his responsibility to answer letters on behalf of the Chief of Defence Staff—justifying the decision to dissolve the Corps! "I couldn't believe it," he said, "its always been a sore point with me."

Perhaps the major loss, in Wiens' opinion, was the loss of good working relationships with the battalions and the Militia. "That was all destroyed overnight. It began to come back later, but it was a long time before it did."

Asked if the many changes had helped the Canadian intelligence business, Wiens replied, "Not at all, it there were a war, we'd be starting from scratch. It's now been so long that few knowledgeable people are left to train others."

After retiring as Commandant of the CSMI, LCol Wiens' duties varied and included Staff College in Kingston and duty Exchange Officer in Washington, D.C. "We were called Exchange Officers on Country Desks. I had Afghanistan. Looked after it beautifully too. Then I left and it all went straight to hell."

LCol Wiens retired from the military in 1971 and became a translator for DGIS, where he was promoted to Chief of Section. In 1981, he finally retired for good. He still translates for the Director of History and has worked on contract on a book about the U-Boat diaries, which he calls, "really fascinating."

Questioned about the future, for the military and himself, Wiens replied, "after seeing the Gulf War, I don't know if men with my background are qualified to talk much about it." Fascinated with the technology of the US forces, Wiens claimed that, "computers are the means of Intelligence skills now, and I don't think the people in the business are keeping up. We're still using map boards and coloured pencils."

When asked if these topics would be discussed at the reunion in Oct 1992, Wiens replied, "I think that if someone could go and speak to them about Electronic Warfare (EW) the old veterans would be very interested." LCol Wiens stated, however, that some important factors never change. He said, "accuracy, honesty and reliability are still important, but we need to teach peo-

ple to work with new tools. Of course, the reunion might be a bunch of old
boys talking about the glory days, especially if they all get a drink in their
hands."[17]

## 1992, Chatter Notes from the Old Comrade
## Extracts from articles by J.E.H. Bernard Lemieux

A new group of old comrades has appeared to us in the form of all ex-MI2
"No. 1 Discrimination Unit" members. Susanne Porter nee Day; MarGerry
(Bees) Alcock; and Margaret (Betty) Rose nee Barnett have all made contact
with the 50th Anniversary Committee.

Others who have checked in include Sgt Ernie Arndt; Capt Noel George
Ashby; Tommy Blood; Paul Bordeau; WO Jack A. Cuvelier; WO2 Norm C.
Dimmell; Maj Reginald R. Dixon; SSgt Larry H. Dyck; SSgt Warren A.
Gale; Capt Roy E. Girling; Frank Glover; Cpl Gordon B. Hardy; Maj Des-
mond F.G. Heffernan; William "Bill" H. Kane; HLCol Franz F. Laizner;
SSgt P. Gerry Martyn; Capt Jack B. Martin; Sgt Don P. Mattocks; Sgt Les
Peate; WO1 George L. Seguin; Maj Peter W. Sloan; Michael Stern; Sgt Wil-
liam "Bill" M. Summersgill; Maj Charlie I. Taggart; Col Jeff S. Upton; SSgt
Richard "Dick" C. Webster; Lt John I.R. Weller; LCol David W. Wiens; Maj
Willy Williamson; John Carreau; Bruno Vanier; Maj Alphee S. Bake; Maj
Ward I. Binkley; R.N. "Paddy" Bligh, ex OC of many wartime FSS.

Col Graham F. Blythe; Jock Cameron; Capt Hugh Campbell; Jack Car-
reau; Lou Charron; LCol Hugh D. Conover; Maj Eddie Corbeil; LCol G.
Cecil W. Dawkins; Capt William "Bill" L. Dickson; Maj G.E. Peter East-
wood; LCol George Wallis Field, formerly 2 Int Trg Coy; Bob Flaherty; Maj
Ian N. Fleming, former CO 1 Int Trg Coy; Leo Foucault; Col H. Thomas
Fosbery; Maj F. Gerry Fox, former CO of 1 Int Trg Coy; Maj John Allan
Gray, Sgt R. Bernie Gray; Capt Robert T. Greyeyes; HLCol Doris E. Guyatt;
WO2 William "Bill" C. Hargreaves; Maj Reg H. Haskins; LCol Hank H.
Hennie; Maj Ed H. Hollyer; SSgt Doug Hopkinson; Col Robert W. Irvine;
Maj Jan A. Jezewski, former OC of 1 Int Trg Coy; WO2 Don Johnson; Capt
Lawrie Kingsland, former OC of 2 Int Trg Coy; Col Charles D'Arcy
Kingsmill; Walter Kokotailo; Maj George D. LaNauze; Maj Wady Lehman,
formerly with No. 1 War Crimes Investigation Unit.

---

17.   Acorn INTREP 003, Feb 1992, pp. 5-6.

Allan Lytle; LCol George B. MacGillivray; Col Craig B. MacFarlane; Sgt John D. Mackenzie; Maj John "Pappy" MacKinnon; Maj H. Ian MacTavish, formerly with 2 Int Trg Coy; Jock McCormack; Maj Jim J. McDougall; LCol Al G. McMullan; LCol King G. McShane; Capt Eugene Morosan; WO W.M. "Doc" Moore; Justice Francis C. Muldoon, formerly with 5 Int Trg Coy; Burns Murphy, ex MI-9.

Maj John H. Newman; LCol Ian A. Nicol; WO R. Grant Oliver; LCol Jim E. Parker, formerly with 2 Int Trg Coy; Capt Peter T. Patton, formerly with 2 Int Trg Coy; BGen George C. Piercey, former CO of 3 Int Trg Coy; CWO James C. Poirier; Sgt George E. Potter; Capt Margaret R. Prentis, former 2 Int Trg Coy; Maj Wilf S. Puffer, formerly with 6 Int Trg Coy; Sgt G. Jerry Relf; William "Bill" Rempel; Sgt Arthur E. Roemer; Capt Harold F. Smith, formerly with 2 Int Trg Coy; Capt William "Bill" M. Strojich; Maj Herbert F. Sutcliffe; LCol William "Bill" Tenhaaf; Col Jeff S. Upton; Capt Victor G. Ursaki, formerly $1^{st}$ and $2^{nd}$ Corps HQ; Capt James P.K. Van Wynen, formerly with 1 Int Trg Coy; Capt Carl Ian Walker, formerly with 4 Int Trg Coy; Maj William "Bill" L. Watt; SSgt Richard "Dick" C. Webster; MGen Reginald J.G. Weeks; Maj Wilford C. Wheeler, formerly with 2 Int Trg Coy; Lt Keith J. Williamson; Maj Stanley H. Winfield, formerly with 4 Int Trg Coy; and Maj George Youmatoff.[18]

## *Acorn, the Origin of the Intelligence designation*

This is a word of explanation for those of you who are not familiar with the military use of the term "Acorn." It originated in the British Army during WWII, and later through the Korean conflict. It can be found in the Staff Duties in the Field, Canadian Army Manual of Training (CAMT) 2-36. A list of nicknames was published for use with voice procedure on radio nets. An example of these included Foxhound for Infantry; Watchdog for MPs; Bluebell for RCEME; Ironside for Armour; and Acorn for Intelligence. These are only a few examples, since most Army functions were included in the list of nicknames. Therefore, if you said, "Advise Acorn that Ironside is waiting for him at GR 298765," that meant that an armoured rep was waiting for Int staff at that location.[19]

18. Acorn INTREP 003, Feb 1992, pp. 7-8.
19. Acorn INTREP 003, Feb 1992, p. 7.

## 1992, Chatter Notes from the Old Comrade

As of 29 March 1992, the 50th Anniversary Committee had heard from the following Old Comrades of the C Int C: Capt William "Bill" M. Strojich; Betty Rose; CWO James C. Poirier; Bruno Vanier; Maj Eddie Corbeil; WO2 Cece G. Brown, the last person in the C Int C to hold the rank of IQMS; Ron Gebhardt, now Adjt of the West NS Regt; Capt David Rubin; Peter Catlender, formerly with 2 FSS, 27 CIB; Capt Herman J. Schneider, formerly with 4 CIBG; Maj Reginald R. Dixon; Maj Alphee Blake, formerly with 16 FSS; Capt Ken E.H. Smith, 3 Int Trg Coy; Maj Ian N. Fleming; Brian Johnston; SSgt Red J. Coppell; Rev Dave Dewar; Capt Eugene Morosan, formerly with 1 Int Trg Coy; Capt William "Bill" Allen, former Area Security Officer, Western Ontario Area; Capt William D. Ellis (age 96), retired Capt and ex member of No. 2 Detachment, Corps of Guides and later (1916), with 4th Divisional Cyclist Company. He was President of the Canadian Corps Cyclist Battalion 1937-39 and Editor of "Saga of the Cyclists in the Great War 1914-1918; Maj F. Murray Ball; Roy Whitten, formerly with Central Command; WO2 Jack Arthur Rahn; Bob Phillips, former member of Army HQ Int (b) in Holland, 1944-45; Sgt D. Wes Arnold; Maj S. Robert Elliot; Capt P.W. Clare Lagerquist, formerly with 1 and 2 Int Trg Coy; R.N. "Paddy" Bligh, formerly with Port Security in Amsterdam in 1945; and Capt Terry W. Sheardown, formerly with 5 Int Trg Coy.[20]

C Int C Old Comrades heard from included: Capt Pete Brooker; WO2 Jack Arthur Rahn, formerly with 1 FSS in 1941 and CSM with 3 FSS from 1943 to 1945; Susan Porter; Bruno Vanier; Capt Roy E. Girling; Capt George Parry, formerly with 2 Int Trg Coy from 1948 to 1951, then Regular C Int C from 1951 to 1959 with DMI and MI-8; WO (Ret'd) Josh Barry, formerly with 5 Int Trg Coy; Sgt Ernie Arndt; WO Ken W. Wishart; Maj Bernie Benoit, former OC 1 Int Trg Coy OC; HLCol Doris E. Guyatt; Lawrence A. Cullen, formerly with No. 1 Discrimination Unit; WO2 George F. and Betty Kelly; LCol William "Bill" Tenhaaf; Capt Victor K. Dailyde; Lt Don J. Davis; Maj Russ E. Knox; LCol R. John C. Rushbrook, PhD; Bob Anes, formerly with 3 Int Trg Coy; Maj Reginald H. Haskins; WO2 Art G. Nicholson; Jack Carreau; LCol Charlie Chaveau; Alex Draper, formerly with 1 Int Trg Coy; Capt Eugene Morosan; Capt William "Bill" M. Strojich; Capt

20.  Acorn INTREP 005, Apr 1992, p. 1.

Mike H. Armstrong, former Security Officer, Central Ontario Area; Col Graham F. Blythe; Clark Knowlton, formerly with No. 3 Reserve Det; Bruno Vanier; John "Dirk" Doerksne; Col Victor V. Ashdown, still serving with the current Int Branch; Peter and Shannon Smarz, former members of 5 Int Trg Coy;

In the Ottawa area, a C Int C Brunch held on 3 May 1992 at the Rockcliffe Officer's Mess included the following: Sgt Ray and Peggy Bordeleau; CWO J.R. Ray and Eleanor LeCavalier; Capt Les Peate; Capt Gil McDermott; Maj Ed and Eileen Hollyer; Sgt Danny and Lila Bordeleau; Capt Robert T. and Karin Greyeyes; SSgt John Butterworth; Maj F. Murray Ball; WO2 Art G. and Esther Nicholson; WO2 Norm C. Dimmell; LCol David W. and Betty Wiens; Maj Reginald R. and Grace Dixon WO2 Cece G. Brown; Capt Peter and Paula Patton; Maj John "Pappy" MacKinnon; Capt Eugene and Doris Morosan; Fred and Ann Pollack; Sgt George E. and Lady Potter; Sgt R. Bernie and Lady Gray; Capt J.E.H. Bernard and Marthe Lemieux.[21]

## Artillery Intelligence—An Important Tool of Combat Intelligence
### Article by W. Doug Whitley

In 1961, your scribe was assigned to Victor battery, 4th Regiment Royal Canadian Horse Artillery then stationed at Camp Petawawa, Ontario. The battery (bty) was composed of a headquarters, survey troop, sound ranging troop, meteorological (met) section and radar troop totalling approximately 150 all ranks. Earlier types of batteries included "flash-spotting" sub-units and later versions included remotely-piloted air vehicles. The bty was a unique organization in that when deployed, each sub-unit went off to do "its own thing" quite separate from each other. Why then, were they grouped into a bty?

With the exception of the survey Troop, the sub-units of the bty were the specialist eyes and ears of the artillery (no apology is made to those of air observation or forward observer lineage). The radar, sound ranging and met elements provided the only organic "over the horizon" (OTH) all-weather observation capability available to the tactical (divisional) commander. The survey Troops' connection to the other sub-units was that it provided an accurately-calculated position "fix" on the ground which all locating devices need.

---

21.  Acorn INTREP 006, June 1992, pp. 1-3.

Being an artillery resource, the only branch of the Army then concerned with the enemy's firepower located beyond the line-of-sight, the information collected went to the artillery staff located at the divisional headquarters. The staff was and is further sub-divided into various specialties. That sub-staff directly concerned with the information collected by the locating devices is the artillery intelligence (Arty Int) component. The training received by the Arty Int staff bears a strong resemblance to that received by intelligence specialists at large but is concentrated on the study of foreign artillery and the essential elements of information needed to neutralize that artillery.

The Arty Int staff's primary concern is locating enemy artillery for destruction by friendly artillery. Art Int collects, processes and disseminates information acquired not only by the locating devices but also by the extensive observation post system used by the gun batteries. The extensive communications network used by the artillery for the control of fire is ideally-suited for the rapid passage of other types of information as well. Most of the information collected is also of use to the general intelligence staff in determining the location, activities and intentions of the enemy as a whole. As a consequence, a good divisional intelligence staff will ensure that the Arty Int "types" are always invited to their social activities!

With the down-sizing of the armed forces since 1968, the artillery intelligence function in the Canadian Forces virtually became extinct as locating batteries were disbanded and Arty Int training disappeared; but the military intelligence professionals of today must remember that principles never change and a properly prepared Arty Int organization is an important tool of combat intelligence.[22]

22.  Acorn INTREP 007, July 1992, pp. 2-3.

# 11

## 1993, Intelligence Branch

### 1993, Chatter Notes from Old Comrades
### Notes from J.E.H. Bernard Lemieux

Old Comrades heard from during the run-up to the 8th and last issue of the 50th Anniversary issues of the Acorn INTREP included Capt Roy E. Girling; Maj S. Robert Elliot; Michael Stern; Capt David A. Rubin; Curly Carruthers; Ken Carter; Capt Phil E. Bachand; WO2 Harry Taylor; Sgt John T. Mansfield; WO1 J. McVeigh; Pete King; J.M.P. Lemire; Jock Cameron; Capt William D. "Dick" Ellis; HCol Franz F. Laizner; WO Stu E. Auld; Walter Kokotailo; Chief Justice Col Antonio Lamer; Mr. Justice Lt Francis C. Muldoon; Tommy Blood; Maj Wady Lehman, former war crimes investigator in North West Europe; Cpl Barry A. Boyce, formerly from DPIC (1964); and Maj John Allan Gray.[1]

There some funds left over from the reunion, it has been decided that they will be put towards the Sir William S. Stephenson Bursary Fund. This is a fund that was established by an endowment given by Ms Elizabeth Stephenson in memory of her father. The bursary is intended to provide financial assistance to dependants of members of the Intelligence Branch Association who are pursuing full-time post-secondary education.[2]

---

1. Acorn INTREP 008, September 1992, pp. 2-3.
2. Acorn INTREP 009, December 1993, pp. 2-3.

## 10/50 Anniversary
## Extracts from an article by LCdr M. Josh Barber,
## Anniversary Committee Chairman

Celebrations marking the 10th anniversary of the Int Branch and the 50th anniversary of the C Int C were successfully marked at CFB Borden by some 300 participants between 29 Oct and 1 Nov 1992. An excellent historical display was also shown on the main concourse of NDHQ and at Borden. Maj Don W. McVee, CFILO in Fort Huachuca, Arizona travelled the greatest distance to attend, but many other Branch members went considerable distances including those from Cold Lake, Bagotville, Valcartier, Moose Jaw and Winnipeg. Branch members on duty in Croatia forwarded messages, and a considerable reserve contingent showed up in Borden from Winnipeg and Toronto.

The organizing committee did a considerable amount of work to ensure the success of the event, including Lt (N) Shawn P. Osborne, Capt Jan L. Malainey, Lt Bob Martyn, CPO1 William "Bill" J. Lindsay, Sgt Phil Girard, MCpl Kris E. Pedersen, MCpl J.D. Pete Boutin, MCpl Phil Cooper, MS Dan Ash, LS Bob Given and Sgt Ray Bordeleau and J.R. Ray LeCavalier of the C Int C Association. Our thanks to all of them.[3]

## Message to the Int Branch from the Governor General of Canada, Ramon John Hnatyshyn

It is a great pleasure to extend my warmest greeting to everyone gathered for the 50th anniversary dinner of the Canadian Intelligence Corps.

This year is truly an historic occasion in the life of our country. While we join together with Canadians from every region to commemorate the 125th year of Confederation, many organizations such as the Canadian Intelligence Corps are also marking anniversaries. I am certain that all members of the Corps, be they newcomers or founding members, take great pride in the numerous accomplishments of Corps personnel throughout the past 50 years and look forward to many more years of exceptional service to Canada. Indeed, the activities of the members of the Canadian Intelligence Corps, and

3.   Intelligence Branch Association Quarterly Newsletter, Edition 1, 1993, p. 1.

their dedication to the values which are inherently Canadian, have become an invaluable part of Canada's proud military heritage.

As we take part in the ceremonies marking this milestone year, it is important that we pause to reflect upon those aspects of Canada which we most cherish and which have brought our country the respect and admiration of people throughout the world. Undoubtedly, the tradition of selfless valour and the time-honoured professionalism of our Armed Forces, both past and present, are among the noblest aspects of Canada which we are celebrating this year. This evening, it is my hope that you will also take a moment to remember the courageous spirit and commitment to duty of those not able to be with you; memories of whom, I am certain, inspire you in you daily lives.

As Governor General and Commander-in-Chief of the Canadian Forces, I am pleased to send my very best wishes for happiness and success to all members of the Canadian Intelligence Corps attending the 50th Anniversary Mess Dinner.

(Signed) Ramon John Hnatyshyn.[4]

## 1993, Letter from Croatia, 1993
## WO Marvin J. "Red" Hodgins

On behalf of the Int people here in Croatia, I wish those members present from the C Int C a very happy birthday. To those present from the Int Branch, our thoughts are with you tonight as you celebrate this momentous occasion. [On 29 Oct 1993] as you celebrate, we will raise a glass of local pivo in your honour. Have a good night and we will see you all on our return. Best Wishes.[5]

## 1993, Rwanda

After being plagued by racially motivated skirmishes at the beginning of 1993, Rwanda dissolved into an ethnic bloodbath after the death of its' President in a plane crash. 800,000 Rwandan Tutsis died at the hands of rival Hutus in a killing spree that lasted for months. Tutsi-led forces eventually regained con-

---

4. Intelligence Branch Association Quarterly Newsletter, Edition 1, 1993, p. 2.
5. Intelligence Branch Association Quarterly Newsletter, Edition 1, 1993, p. 2.

trol of the country. Thousands of Hutus fled to refugee camps in neighbouring countries to escape feared reprisals.

Between 1994 and 1995, Canada was involved in the UN effort to disengage warring Hutu and Tutsi factions in Rwanda. Both sides committed atrocities. Canadian Brigadier General Roméo Dallaire was the UN commander in Rwanda. Dallaire recognized that the genocide was occurring and pleaded for a stronger UN commitment. His pleas were ignored, and the Hutu murdered over 800,000 innocent Tutsi civilians. Dallaire subsequently testified before an International Criminal Tribunal revealing horrendous scenes of death and destruction. He passionately argued that had a firmer commitment for support been forthcoming, the worst could have been avoided. Returning from Rwanda, General Dallaire himself suffered from severe Post-Traumatic Stress Disorder (PTSD). He bravely brought the issue and reality of PTSD to the attention of the military and mental health communities, as well as the nation at large.[6]

The author has spoken with LGen Dallaire on several occasions, and with Capt Stewart G. Hamilton who served with him in Rwanda during the worst of the crisis, and he offered the following comments on the Int support that he received in theatre.

"In reference to our discussion on the quality and value of the Int briefs which we received while deployed as 95 Composite Mission Support Group on OP LANCE (Rwanda—Jun 95–Feb 96) I offer the following comments: Prior to deployment we received various Int brief on the current situation, what to expect, culture and traditions, and a handout with various simple phrases in the local language. While the initial Int briefs were extremely useful, I believe they did not fully prepare us (psychologically) for what lay ahead.

Once we were in theatre, we received Int briefs from our Int Ops in theatre as well as the UNMOs in the various sectors on a daily basis. From an administrative standpoint, the daily Int briefs were used as the basis for assessment of the Exceptional Hazard Allowance, which was at the highest rate. These Int briefs were not always current due to the ever-changing political climate and mistrust of the UN Forces in general by the local populace. Often, checkpoints would not be where they were reported to be, agreements between the factions would not be honoured, and we could not trust any of the RPA Commanders or soldiers. It seemed that Sector Commanders would do whatever

---

6.    Internet: www.thememoryproject.com.

struck their fancy, at any given moment. This resulted in a dramatic change to our rules of engagements (i.e. a round up the spout with safety on when leaving the Camp, not leaving the camp after dark, always traveling in pairs, transporting refugees or providing humanitarian relief under armed escort, etc.). What was supposed to be a peacekeeping (humanitarian) mission to help rebuild a country very quickly turned into a mission for survival. Tensions on all sides were extremely high and, quite frankly, we did not know what to expect at any given moment. This was especially true in the aftermath of the genocide and as more and more bodies and graves were discovered.

The Int briefs we received were as accurate as they could be; however, the Int situation was constantly changing, and it would have taken a miracle to have consistent, up-to-date, reliable Intelligence."[7]

Canadian Intelligence Branch personnel who served in Rwanda included Maj Ross L. Johnson, Capt Brian J. East, Sgt R. Hal Pugh and MCpl Alan W. Wilson.

## 1993, FG/CANR HQ Intelligence Section Update
## WO Carl Keenan

There are a number of newcomers to the Unit in North Bay, including Maj G. Al Grant, Capt Robert G. Nash, Capt Dave R. Hunt, Capt Rob Hogarth, and Lt Kerry T. Newton. All took part in a major NORAD/Fighter Group exercise recently, and pulled shifts on the Intelligence Watch Officer Duty. WO Marvin J. "Red" Hodgins has just returned from a six-week stint in Croatia, and is posted to Colorado Springs. Capt Ed C. Denbeigh is on near-permanent TD, and Capt Marcel Schreyer is attending the Staff School course in Toronto.

Air Reserve personnel working in the section include Maj Rudy Van Der Stoel, and Capt Fred L. Juett who has retired (again). WO Pete Demers and the Unit Admin clerk, Pte Brenda Lacombe make up the remainder of our hard-working staff.[8]

---

7. Dircon and E-mail, Capt S.G. Hamilton, LFAA HQ G1, Halifax, 23 Oct 03.

8. Intelligence Branch Association Quarterly Newsletter, Edition 1, 1993, Capt Don Cushman, Editor; MWO Ivor Schoots, Assistant Editor, p. 4.

## 1993, Sir William S. Stephenson Bursary Fund

The Branch Association will be offering a $500 bursary in honour of Sir William S. Stephenson for the first time this year. A bursary fund has been established from an endowment given by Ms Elizabeth Stephenson in memory of her uncle, Sir William S. Stephenson (Intrepid of WWII fame), and first Colonel Commandant of the Intelligence Branch. The bursary is intended to provide financial assistance to dependents of members of the Intelligence Branch Association who are pursuing a full-time post-secondary education.[9]

## 1993, LFC Update
## Extracts from an article by Sgt D.H. McLaren

1st Canadian Division Intelligence Company is the Int Branch's senior Int Unit within Land Forces Command (LFC) formerly known as the "Army." One third of the Company's strength is currently on UN deployments in the Former Yugoslav Republic and Somalia, and two more sorely needed bodies are in the final stages of preparing to rotate into the Balkans. Refresher training was recently conducted for our Op-tasked Reserves called Exercise Radical Assembly II.

In the fall, LFC formally tasked the Company with the responsibility to provide the Army with Intelligence on the situation in Yugoslavia. Although this quickly became our primary focus, it did not detract from other Unit tasks such as the provision of general Intelligence support to the Division Commander, incremental taskings in support of "the School," and Staff College exercises, conduct of general military training (i.e., the LFC battle fitness test, winter warfare, etc.), and of course sending personnel on course: MCpl Dave V. Morley and MCpl Connie Lancaster to the TQ6A and Sgt Dave Campbell to the Interrogation and SLC courses, all at CFSIS in Borden. Cpl Ernest S. Kuffner is on the Photo Interpreter course in England and Maj Gord P. Ohlke has gone to Staff College at Fort Frontenac, Kingston.

Cpl Charles A. Beattie, MCpl Dean G. Hyde and MCpl Randy Walton (Company Clerk), WO Barry E. Beldam and Capt Doug Mair are deployed to Mogadishu, while Capt W. Pat Grant heads up the Mil Info Cell in Camp Polom. WO Rick C. Nickerson and Sgt Dennis Roy are on their way to the Former Yugoslav Republic. For those remaining in Garrison, the Annual

9. Sinister Sam's Notebook, Edition 2, 1993, p. 1.

Technical Inspection (ATI) and the General Officer Commanding's Inspection are occupying much of their time.

Sgt Dave D. Campbell is posted to Halifax, WO Barry A. MacDonald is going to North Bay, Cpl Ernest S. Kuffner is bound for Cold Lake, and Maj Gord P. Ohlke is posted to LFWA HQ in Edmonton. Finally, SSG Ron Wines, attached to the Terrain Analysis Section, our West Virginian exchange Sgt, is on his way back to the USA.[10]

## 1993, LFC HQ Update
## Extracts from an article by WO J.H. Yves Labarre

Land Forces Command Headquarters G2 Branch is situated within the premises of CFB Montreal in St Hubert, La Belle Province. Departing members this summer include Maj Ron H.J. Ruiters, just back from a stint in Zagreb, heading for Kingston; Capt Chuck Moor, posted to Ottawa; Cpl Don J. Fougère is going to DIE, Capt D.D. Nickel is moving to become OC of one of the Western Reserve Int Coys, and MCpl G.M. Charbonneau (Clerk) is moving to NDHQ. Those remaining on station include LCol Peter W.M. Wilson, G2; Maj Gary D. Dover, Int Trg and Doc Section; Capt Eric E. Gjos; Lt Paul D. Johnston; WO J.H. Yves Labarre, and WO Arthur E.B. "Bert" O'Brien; CWO J. Ron Martin, MCpl J. François .J. Legér ; MCpl J.F. Gauthier; Sgt J.A. Chris Pelletier; Cpl K.J. Marchand; and Maj Ward A. Sweet, G2 Ops.

WO J.H. Yves Labarre was an instructor at CFSIS on the Interrogator's Course, and WO Arthur E.B. "Bert" O'Brien completed the TQ6B course at Borden. Capt Eric E. Gjos took the Intermediate Tactics Course (ITC) at Gagetown, and Cpl K.J. Marchand took a specialty course in England. Many have taken ADP introduction courses and a new Land Forces Information Search and Retrieval System (ISAR) is being developed under the direction of Capt D.D. Nickel, MCpl J. François .J. Legér , and a civilian ADP consultant, Mr. Jean Desjardins.[11]

---

10.   Sinister Sam's Notebook, Edition 2, 1993, p. 3.
11.   Sinister Sam's Notebook, Edition 2, 1993, pp. 3-4.

## 1992-1993, UNITAF, Somalia

From December 1992 to June 1993, Canada participated in the United States-led enforcement coalition called the Unified Task Force (UNITAF) in civil war and famine-ravaged Somalia. Members of the Intelligence Branch serving with the peacekeeping forces during this mission in Mogadishu included Maj Len E.N. Goski, Capt J.L. François Messier, Capt Doug M. Mair, WO Barry E. Beldam, Sgt Rick M. Chaykowski, MCpl Charles A. Beattie, Cpl J. Patrick A. Couture, Cpl Dean G. Hyde; and in Beletwane, Capt Paul Hope and Pat Couture.

## 1993, Somalia Notes
## Article by Sgt Rick M. Chaykowski

The Int staff from 1 Cdn Div HQ and Sigs Regt (literally, as we have two members from 2 EW Sqn, including myself and the other being MCpl Choquette, a 291er), send their greetings from lovely downtown Mogadishu. We have come to appreciate our Canadian way of life here and have also gotten a new perspective on our chosen field of employment. We all even miss the cold weather and snow (but not the shovelling). The heat here can be oppressive and the first few weeks of acclimatization were particularly difficult.

The job here in sunny Somalia encompasses almost all aspects of our trade. Although we do have some slow days, most days see us busy well into the late evening hours. The odd stand to at night in response to nearby bullets also help to keep us from being bored. The great weight loss program is in full swing with one meal per week being fresh rations (Saturday supper), with the rest of the week being IMPs. I have heard it said that we are trying to set a record.

The experiences being added up here will benefit the branch greatly. We have learned, in a very short time, how to conduct Intelligence in low intensity conflicts. The trade experiences being learned here can be passed through training aspects. The personal experiences will never be forgotten by any of us.

You can rest assured that we are doing the best job possible in some very trying circumstances. Best of luck to all of you and we hope to see you in the near future. On behalf of all members of the J2 staff in Somalia, Cheers, Sgt Rick M. Chaykowski.[12]

---

12.   Sinister Sam's Notebook, Edition 2, 1993, p. 5.

## 1993, OC Int Trg Coy, CFSIS

On 21 June 1993, the author put on his Major's slip-ons after serving as Chief Instructor at CFSIS. On 30 June 93, Major Michel Bédard and the author signed the handover scrolls for the transfer of the Int Company, with LCol Patricia M. Samson, Commandant of CFSIS, presiding over the ceremony making the author the Officer Commanding Intelligence Training Company, CFSIS.

## Message from the Branch CWO, CPO1 William "Bill" J.Lindsay

It is with great personal sadness that I report the passing of MWO J.R. Claude Morin on Monday 19 July 1993. The funeral took place on 23 July at Ste Victoria in Victoriaville, with interment at St Joseph cemetery. Le 12 Régiment Blindée du Canada from CFB Valcartier provided the Honour Guard and pallbearers. Honorary pallbearers consisted of eight members, two CWO from the Career Shop And six Int MWOs. Many other Int Branch personnel also attended the Service to pay their respects to a fallen comrade. His wife Ghyslaine and family survive MWO Morin.[13]

## Int OP Career Manager, MWO Ivo J.M. Schoots

MWO Ivo J.M. Schoots brings 25 years of experience into his new job as Int OP Career manager. He served with the Military Police in La Macaza, Quebec and North Bay, Ontario. As an Intelligence Operator, he began with 1st Canadian Signals Regiment (1 CSR) in Kingston, in the Task Force HQ. In 1975 he went to work for SSO I&S in FMC HQ, St Hubert, followed by three years in Tel Aviv, Israel. On return to Canada he was posted to 5e GBMC, Valcartier. After four years with 5e GBMC he came to Ottawa to work in DIE's Attaché Training Section which grew into the Interpretation and Training Section, until he became the Int OP CM. [14]

## 1993, Intelligence Personnel News

The following Int Branch personnel were promoted as of 1993:

---

13. Sinister Sam's Notebook, Edition 3, 1993, p. 1.
14. Sinister Sam's Notebook, Edition 3, 1993, p. 1.

Maj Richard A. Derkson, ATC HQ Trenton; Maj Ross L. Johnson, LFAA HQ Halifax; Maj Glen B. MacKay, DG Int/DDI-2 Ottawa; Maj J.L. François Messier, LFQA HQ Montreal; Maj Harold A. Skaarup, CFSIS Borden; and, Maj Brad J. Smith, UNPROFOR Yugoslavia; Capt Bill H. Becker, 4 Wing Cold Lake; Capt M.E. Louise Boutin, CSE LO Ottawa; Capt William "Bill" M. Glenfield, DG Int/DDI-4 Ottawa; Capt Eric P. Grehan, 416 Sqn Cold Lake; Capt R.B. Martyn, CCUNFICYP Cyprus; and, Capt Ed D.P. Rechnitzer, DG Int/DDI-5 Ottawa.

MWO George T. Izzard, 1 July; MWO Rolf F. Overhoff, 1 July; MWO David J. Whalen, 1 July; WO D.D. Campbell, 1 July; PO1 Jeff A. Collings, 1 July; WO Robert A. Deleau, 1 July; PO1 Terry W. Fader, 1 July; WO J.J.P.M. Fournier, 1 July; WO J.L.S. Gauvin, 1 July; WO Dave L. Howarth, 1 July; PO1 William D. Kean, 1 July; WO J. Pierre Murret-Labarthe, 1 July; PO1 J.A. Réjean Montmarquet, 1 July; WO R.G. Oliver, 1 July; WO Alex D. Radzion, 1 July; WO J.R.M. Ross, 1 July; WO Kevin N. Rowe, 1 July; WO Ronald K. Townsend, 1 July; Sgt J.D. Pete Boutin, 1 July; Sgt Trevor Cave, 1 July; Sgt J.R. Charles Conlin, 1 July; Sgt P.D. Cooper, 1 July; Sgt Mark J. Kelly, 1 July; Sgt Connie F. Lancaster, 1 Aug; Sgt Warren L. Lawrence, 1 July; WO Luc J.A.M. Leroy, 1 July; Sgt D.V. Morely, 1 July; Sgt J.C. Mario Roy, 1 Dec; Sgt Kevin Toomer, 1 July; Sgt J.F.J.M. Tremblay, 1 Aug; PO2 Donald R.A. Wagnell, 1 Aug; MCpl J. Patrick A. Couture, 1 Aug; MCpl Richard Lee Fletcher, 1 July; MS R.R. Given, 1 July; MCpl J. Paul Hodgins, 1 July; MCpl Serge Laforge, 1 July; MCpl Daniel Francis McNeil, 1 Aug; MCpl Dan B. McQuinn-Legér , 1 July; MS Veronica Marie Parolin, 1 July; MCpl K.B. Sanders, 1 July; MCpl John T. Smola, 1 May; and, MCpl Wayne D. Upshall, 1 Aug 93.[15]

## 1993, Basic Intelligence Officer Course

BIOC 9301 is scheduled to end 24 Nov 93, with the following candidates completing the course: Capt J.V. Gilles Clairoux, 5 Int Pl Valcartier; Capt Hugh A. Ferguson, LFCA HQ Toronto; Capt Pericles Metaxas-Mariatos, COS J3 Ottawa; Lt (N) Steve L. Neeb, DG Int Ottawa; Capt Robert "Bob" H. Smallwood, 1 Cdn Div Kingston; Lt D. Phil Forward, AIRCOM Winnipeg; Lt Kerry T. Newton, DG Int Ottawa; 2Lt M.J. Dow, ATG HQ Trenton; 2Lt William "Bill" R. MacLean, 410 Sqn Cold Lake; 2Lt J.F.J.D.

---

15.  Sinister Sam's Notebook, Edition 3, 1993, p. 2.

Massana, 433 Sqn/433e ETAC Bagotville; and, 2Lt Jean Jacques "J.J." Simon, 425 Sqn Bagotville.

Four Reserve Int officers also completed the BIOC: Capt Chuck Moor, Capt Liam Robertson, Capt Norman A. Sproll, and Lt Rick G. Stohner.

The following Int Branch personnel have taken their release: LCol A.G. McMullan, LCol K.J. Radley, Maj J. Mike Gauvin, Maj John W. Sullivan, Lt (N) Sam Cowen, Capt D.E. Davidson, and Lt (N) R. Bruce Millar.[16]

BIOC 9301, CFSIS, 14 Jul 1993.
Third Row: 2Lt W. "Bill" R. MacLean, 2Lt Jean Jacques "J.J." Simon, Capt J.V. Gilles Clairoux, Capt Chuck Moor, Lt (N) Steve L. Neeb, Lt D. Phil Forward, Capt Hugh A. Ferguson.
Second Row: Lt Rick G. Stohner, Capt Liam Robertson, 2Lt Marla J. Dow, 2Lt J.F.J. Dan Massana, Capt R. "Bob" H. Smallwood, Capt Norman A. Sproll, Capt Perry Metaxas-Mariatos.
Front Row: MWO H.H.W. Kuchler, Maj H.A. Skaarup, Lt (N) S.P. Osborne, WO Warren L. Lawrence.

16.  Sinister Sam's Notebook, Edition 3, 1993, pp. 2-4.

Intelligence Operator 6B Course 9301.
Rear Row: WO David D. Turner, WO Arthur E.B. "Bert" O'Brien, PO2 Darrell L. Gammon, Sgt D. Michael Donahue.
Centre Row: Sgt Lloyd D. Crosby, Sgt Keith M. Young, Sgt Darcy H. McLaren, Sgt J.G. Chartier, PO2 William M. Flanagan, Sgt Ed A. Knobelsdorf, Sgt Richard C. Gow, Sgt J.P.G. Vinetti.
Front Row: MWO Joseph A. Michel White, Maj J. Michel Bédard, WO E. Meril Crane.

Militia TQL3 Course 9301.
Rear Row: Sgt J.C. Marc Pozzo di Borgo, Cpl D.A. Rouselle, Cpl Benoit Themens, MCpl R.G. King, Pte S.T. Miskew, Pte N.M. Atkinson, Pte A.F. Blanchard.
Centre Row: Pte Bélanger, Pte Roy, Pte Martineau, Pte Joseph, Pte Greg I. Patterson, Pte Kenneth E. Johnson, Pte D.J. Rankin, Pte Beverly A. Kleckner.
Front Row: WO Martineau, Lt P. Michel Gareau, Maj Harold A. Skaarup, MWO Herb H.W. Kuchler, Sgt Glen A. McGuire. Missing Cpl R. Hugh.

Basic Classification Training Course 9301.
Rear Row: 2Lt D.L. Hughes, 2Lt Stubbert, Lt Cyopeck, 2Lt Giesbrecht, Capt Van Der Sluis.
Front Row: Sgt Michael C. Wagner, Lt James Peter Terfry, WO Tim G. Armstrong.

# 1993, 1 Canadian Division Intelligence Company

1 Canadian Division Intelligence Company, December 1993
Rear Row: WO Alex D. Radzion, WO Rick C. Nickerson, MCpl Walton, MCpl Kenneth E. Davies, MCpl Dean G. Hyde, Sgt Roy.
Centre Row: Sgt Connie F. Webb-Lancaster, WO J.S. Daniel St Pierre, MS J.U. Serge St Jacques, Sgt Nicholas R. Procenko, Sgt Rick M. Chaykowski, Cpl Charles A. Beattie, WO Dean E. Smith, SSgt Cruz (US Army).
Front Row: WO Barry E. Beldam, MWO R.D. Santos, Maj J. Michel Bédard, Capt Doug M. Mair.

# 1993, Changes in Staff at Tunney's Pasture
# CWO Barry W. Sweeney

Many changes in personnel have taken place at Tunney's Pasture. LCol Paul F. O'Leary has gone to London, England as the CFILO; Capt Mike H. Heitmann has moved to the NDIC; Sgt John A. Bain (Comox); Sgt R.G. Oliver (Borden); MCpl Tim L. Hagel (Winnipeg); WO F.V. Gordon (Edmonton); Sgt Robert A. Deleau (Kingston); WO Michael E. Malcolm (North Bay); MCpl Byron K. Mackenzie (Edmonton); Capt David R. Canavan (Calgary);

Cpl Pokorski (Gagetown); Sgt Mark P. Peters (Release); Sgt Calvert (Release); MWO Ivo J.M. Schoots (DGPCOR); Sgt G.D. Chaisson (Edmonton via Cyprus); and Cpl Mike H. Hurley (CFLS).

Incoming personnel include Cpl M.G. Denny, MS J.L. Dennis Goulet, Capt Perry R. Gray, Capt Sehgal, Cpl Don J. Fougère, Sgt J.G. Chartier, LS Dan C. Little, WO Al H. Dickie, MWO Rolf F. Overhoff, Capt Phil R. Moolenbeek, Lt Warren A. Rego, MCpl John T. Smola, Sgt Libby, WO J.L.S. Gauvin, and Ms. Robison in the video lab. LCol R. Geoff St John is the new Director at DBC.

Promotions at DBC this year included MWO David J. Whalen, PO1 Terry W. Fader, PO1 J.A. Réjean Montmarquet, Sgt P.D. Cooper, Sgt Kevin Toomer, Sgt J.D. Pete Boutin, MCpl Dan B. McQuinn-Legér , and MCpl M. Paul McNeil.[17]

## 1993, Sir William S. Stephenson Bursary Award
## Maj Rhedegydd ap Probert

Mr. Peter Jody Maillet, son of WO Peter and Heather Maillet, was recently selected by the CF Int Branch Association to receive the Sir William S. Stephenson Bursary for 1993-1994. Mr. Maillet is presently in his first year of studies at the University of New Brunswick in Fredericton, pursuing a Bachelor of Business Administration degree. WO Peter Maillet was posted to the G2 staff at the Combat Training Centre during July 1993. All members of the Int Branch extend best wishes to Mr. Maillet in his academic studies.[18]

## 1993, Report from Cyprus
## Extracts from an article by Capt R.B. Martyn

There are three Canadians still serving on UN duty in Cyprus at present. The Combat Int personnel with the UN continue to be designated "Ops Info" staff (there is officially no Intelligence in the UN). These Combat Int Troops may not have any previous G2 courses or experience, although most are keen and dedicated.

The Ops Info cell at UNFICYP HQ consists of Sgt G.D. Chaisson (departed in August, replacement TBD); MCpl J. Roch Guertin (left for Bag-

---

17.  Sinister Sam's Notebook, Edition 3, 1993, p. 5.
18.  Sinister Sam's Notebook, Edition 4, 1993, p. 1.

otville in September, replacement TBD); and Capt Rob Martyn. The section has a British LCpl Draughtsman (recently posted back to the UK, replacement TBD). A British Light Dragoon major on his third Cyprus tour, although new to the G2 world commands the section. A British Int Corps Sgt keeps busy with his own work plus that of the three personnel who have departed as well as keeping his two officers in line.

The UN has been involved with Cyprus for 29 years (six months 58 times) re-inventing the wheel with each Troop Rotation. The Buffer Zone between north and south Cyprus makes up 3% of the island, so a good rule-of-thumb is to refrain from dedicating more that 3% or your workload to it. Participation in the embassy/Defence Attaché circuit is a mandatory price demanded for Canada's continued involvement in the international Community.

Notwithstanding External Affairs pronouncements that "there are no more Canadian Troops in Cyprus," the mission remains an excellent posting. You develop A new appreciation for Canada and its place in the world (some sources will only talk to us because we lack an "imperialistic" history; a fact appreciated by our colleagues). Between personnel cutbacks and Cyprus' geo-strategic location, there is plenty of work (12-hour workdays can become common if you let them). For the sake of political correctness, I will avoid discussing Nissi Beach at Ayia Napa, but needless to say, I have a terrific tan. There is indeed no life like it. E Tenebris Brandy Sours.[19]

## 1993, 2 Intelligence Platoon Operational in Ottawa Extracts from an article by Capt Phil R. Berikoff

What started off as a concept has finally become a reality. In February 1993, the formation of Intelligence Units as part of the Land Forces was approved. Within Land Forces Central Area (LFCA), this comprised an Intelligence Company, as part of the infrastructure, and 2 Intelligence Platoon as part of the SSF.

2 Intelligence Platoon, a Total Force Unit, is comprised of both regular and reserve members. During APS 93, the Regular Force cadre positions for 2 Int Pl in Ottawa were manned. Overall commander of 2 Int Pl is Capt J.A.J.P. Cormier, located at CFB Petawawa; however, day to day operation of the Platoon is delegated to Capt Phil R. Berikoff, assisted by three Regular Force

---

19. Sinister Sam's Notebook, Edition 4, 1993, pp. 1-2.

members: Int Ops WO Kevin Row, MCpl Wayne D. Upshall, and admin clerk MCpl Heidi Vidler.

In this fiscal year, the platoon is authorized to recruit seven Class A reservists. Five of these positions were immediately filled with fully qualified Intelligence Branch personnel (Capt Paul G. Rivard, Lt Doug F. Agnew, Lt Karl F. Herman, Lt J.P. Stéphane Lefebvre, and MCpl Danny J. Palmer). The remaining two positions have tentatively been filled; however, members are still awaiting occupational transfers into the Branch, and thus, are not available to parade with the Unit. Consequently, this Total Force Unit now parades nine personnel in Ottawa at least once a week.

Beginning in FY 94, an anticipated ten new positions will be filled. The Unit is expected to be fully manned (43 pers) by 1997 and operational by the year 2000. Applications continue to arrive from all quarters of the Land Force Reserve, which keeps Capt Phil R. Berikoff busy assessing the best candidates for the job. With this Int support in Ottawa, it is our hope that deployments in support of SSF taskings are forthcoming.

What is "Total Force," and how does it apply to 2 Int Pl? Total Force is defined as "members of both the Regular and Reserve Force, who are serving together in the same Units or other elements in such numbers as are directed by the CDS, with each member of each such Unit or other elements retaining his or her distinctive terms and conditions of service."

Certainly the platoon falls under this definition, and the task of 2 Int Pl for FY 93 is to "recruit and train Intelligence personnel." Training within 2 Int Pl has concentrated on achieving the combat readiness standards as directed by MGen Vernon by implementing "The Warrior" program. This program is mandatory for all personnel in LFCA. Phase 1 of The Warrior training program will be completed by Dec 93.

Reserve support to the G2 staff has begun. Capt Paul G. Rivard and Lt Doug F. Agnew have volunteered to participate in Exercise PROUD FLAG scheduled for early December. Capt Phil R. Berikoff and WO Kevin N. Rowe have been tasked to work Higher Control, while MCpl Wayne D. Upshall will be with the G2. Other activities which will be undertaken by 2 Int Pl include the Militia Officers Staff Course (MOSC), a Liaison/Duty Officer (LO/DO) course, and further support to the G2 staff during an upcoming exercise in February.

After parade hours on Thursday nights, all Unit members have a mandatory activity of attending the 2 Int Pl adopted mess, the Mayflower Pub on Cooper Street.

Many an evening has been spent in a thrust of intellectual activity tempered with solid organization planning in a quiet corner of the spacious Mayflower. CPO1 William "Bill" J. Lindsay has often visited the 2 Int Pl crew (perhaps inspecting the activities below the ship's wheel). You are invited to join us on any of those late Thursday evenings for a little "Nacht Musik!"[20]

## 1993, Canadian Forces Intelligence Liaison Officer (CFILO) London
### Extracts from an article by WO Barry R. Eddy

CFILO (L), by agreement, acts as a two-way liaison office between the Defence Intelligence Staff (DIS) and our DCDS/DG Int since the DIS has no corresponding office at NDHQ. On 1 Jul 93, CFILO (L) was withdrawn from CDLS (L) and established as a detachment of DCDS/DG Int Group with its own UIC of 3207.

The CFILO (L) receives its administrative support from both the Canadian Forces Support Unit (Europe) and Canadian Defence Liaison Staff (London). We are a section of three, LCol Paul F. O'Leary (CFILO), Maj Lloyd W. Hackel (DCFILO) and myself, WO Barry R. Eddy, as Chief Clerk. In November 1992, CFILO (L) moved from the Metropole building into facilities in the Old War Office Building on Whitehall, where we are located with much of the UK Defence Intelligence Staff.

For those of you unfamiliar with London, we are located across the street from the Horse Guards, Trafalgar Square is to the North, and 10 Downing Street is across the street and south a few blocks. "Big Ben" is to our left and south about four blocks

The liaison function is a very demanding job, and contrary to popular belief, there is far more to it than attending social functions and enjoying the local culture, although the aforementioned are enjoyed and appreciated when the opportunity arises. Each day of the week is filled with an agenda for both officers, and my days are filled with mundane office routine such as courier duties, administrative concerns and ensuring the collection and distribution of Intelligence related material to Canada. Success of this job is relative to the professional as well as personal relationships developed between the DIS personnel, and ourselves, therefore a good "bedside Manner" is essential, along

---

20.  Sinister Sam's Notebook, Edition 4, 1993, p. 2.

with a good sense of humour. The good sense of humour is necessary to alleviate the boredom of riding the "tube" for two hours daily as well as putting up
with all the tourists and pollution to the downtown core. Overall, this is a
pretty decent job and a good place to work.

The LCol has moved into his permanent accommodation in St John's
Wood after a 2½-month stay in temporary quarters, and the diplomatic plate
is on the car. Maj Lloyd W. Hackel is coaching a women's hockey team (and
has to wear a blindfold during the post-game debriefing). Cheers.[21]

## 1993, UK Intelligence

British Intelligence Agencies include MI5—The Security Service; MI6—the
Secret Intelligence Service (SIS); and, the Government Communications
Headquarters (GCHQ). Britain's armed forces are supported by various ele-
ments of its military Intelligence Corps. The principal collection Agencies for
secret Intelligence are GCHQ and SIS. Their functions are set out in the
Intelligence Services Act 1994. The Joint Intelligence Committee (JIC) agrees
on the broad Intelligence requirements and tasking to be laid upon SIS and
GCHQ. These are reviewed annually in a process managed by the Intelligence
Coordinator. This combines a rigorous analysis of the need for secret Intelligence with extensive consultation with customer Departments and consideration of the financial and other resources required. The resulting requirements
are submitted to Ministers for approval.

The Intelligence requirements are ordered into three priorities according to
their importance to the national security and economic well-being of the
United Kingdom. They are further divided into matters on which secret Intelligence is actively sought, and those on which Intelligence should be reported
on an opportunity basis. Examples of high priority requirements would be
those dealing with terrorism, the proliferation of weapons of mass destruction,
and any other threats to the UK or to the integrity of British territory overseas.
At the end of each year the performance of the Agencies in meeting these
requirements is reviewed by the JIC and subsequently by Ministers. The Security Service has its functions set out in the Security Service Acts 1989 and
1996, and it contributes Intelligence on some of the JIC's requirements (for
example, terrorism).

---

21.  Sinister Sam's Notebook, Edition 4, 1993, Editor Capt Warren Rego,
      p. 3.

The Committee brings to the attention of Ministers and Departments, as appropriate, assessments that appear to require operational, planning or policy action. The Chairman is specifically charged with ensuring that the Committee's monitoring and warning role is discharged effectively. The Committee may constitute such permanent and temporary sub-committees and Working Parties as may be required to fulfill its responsibilities. The Committee reports to the Secretary of the Cabinet except that any special assessments required by the Chiefs of Staff shall be submitted directly to them in the first instance. Peter Ricketts is the Chairman, Joint Intelligence Committee and Intelligence Coordinator.[22]

## *1993, CISA AGM*

The CISA AGM was held at Longue Pointe Garrison, CFB Montreal, 16-18 Sep 1993. Present were: LCol Ian A. Nicol (President), Col Robert T. Grogan, Maj Fred E.G. Jones, Maj Doris E. Guyatt, Maj Gary W. Handson, Maj Franz F. Laizner, Capt Peter T. Patton, SLt (N) Richard Taylor, Maj Nils E. Lindberg, Lt Paul R. Perchaluk, Lt E. Bruce Holmes, Maj Robert C. Dale, Capt P.W. Clare Lagerquist, LCol Don R. Johnson, Lt D. Church, Capt W. Doug Whitley, Col A.H. Sam Stevenson, Col Al R. Wells, Col Victor V. Ashdown, LCol Peter W.M. Wilson, Capt David A. Rubin, Maj John "Pappy" MacKinnon (Secretary), and LCol M. Hind (CDA representative).[23]

President LCol Ian A. Nicol submitted the following Notice of Motion to be considered at the 1993 CISA AGM, scheduled for 16-18 Sep at Longue Point: "Whereas it is deemed desirable that the Association is restricted by by-law to those holding, or who have held, commissioned rank; be it resolved that, effective the 1993 AGM of the Association, the said by-law will be amended to expand membership to civilians and those not holding, or who have not held, commissioned rank, subject however, to the present approvals contained in the said by-laws."[24]

During the Fall 1993 CISA AGM, Col Robert T. Grogan spoke in honour of SLdr Bill McNair, a member who passed away during the past year. A minute's silence was observed in his honour.

22. Internet: http://www.fas.org, 2 Oct 2003.
23. CISA Newsletter, Vol. 23, No. 4, December 1993, p. 1.
24. CISA Newsletter, Vol. 23, No. 3, August 1993, pp. 1-2.

The 1993 CISA Academic Award was made to Mr. Dustin Johnson.

DG Secur, Col Al R. Wells, and Col Victor V. Ashdown (for DGIS) spoke on the operations of their respective Branches. Security Branch strength was relatively static, considering the force restructuring reductions, but more reductions are to be expected in the future. Col Victor V. Ashdown reported that progress on creation of a strategic Int Unit and a reserve Int Section had been delayed for financial reasons.

LCol Doug Southen was represented by LCol Peter W.M. Wilson, who reported on the Land Forces Development Plan, which would see an expansion in the number of Int Units in Canada. He reported that "some philosophical differences" were yet to be ironed out, re: the Sir William S. Stephenson Trophy, but a competition will take place in 1994, with the trophy to be awarded by CISA in September. Militia Int Units were examining terms of reference for the competition. Reports were given by Col A.H. Sam Stevenson for BC; by LCol Dale M. Watts for Prairie; by Col Robert T. Grogan for the National Capital Region; by Maj Fred E.G. for the rest of Ontario; and by Maj Robert C. Dale for the Maritimes. Report to follow from Maj P. Denis Pelletier in Quebec. All areas reported on social get-togethers etc.[25]

The Land Force Central Area Intelligence Company Standup is scheduled for 29 October 1993 at CFB Toronto.[26]

---

25.  CISA Newsletter, Vol. 23, No. 4, December 1993, pp. 1-6.
26.  Sinister Sam's Notebook, Edition 3, 1993, p. 5.

# 12

## *January 1994, Creation of the CFSIS Distance Learning Company*

The economic, political and overall world situation has changed drastically in the past few years. It appears that these changes will continue for a number of years to come. In such circumstances the CF, no doubt, will get smaller and will have to tighten its financial belt. Restructuring of the organization or parts thereof will be necessary to be efficient and effective.

The training environment will also have to change to meet the challenges of the future. The training paradigms of the 1960s and '70s must be transformed to suit the demands of the '90s and the next century. The current traditional methods and techniques of training may not be totally responsive to user's needs. The way training is delivered and the means by which students and trainees learn was, therefore, reviewed.

A restructure of CFSIS took place in January 1994, which focused on a new approach to instruction and training. CFSIS had been offering training to members of the CF/DND for many years by using traditional instructional techniques. Although this training was effective, it was assessed that it could be delivered more efficiently. A study of various CFSIS courses indicated that it costs approximately $20,000 overall to train a BIOC student during a 91-day course, not including student salaries and travelling expenses. In comparison it costs approximately $24,000 including room and board per year for a Grade 13 student to attend a Toronto area private school. With the advent of modern technology, however, training in the classroom is becoming obsolete.

In an attempt to stay current, CFSIS infused the traditional training methods with new material and techniques. This brought the school's material up to date, but without continued development, it was apparent that these methods would soon be surpassed. It had become necessary to enhance the school's methods of training by adding a new paradigm that would focus on distant learning (DL). The chief characteristic of DL is that communication between students and instructors is carried out through print and writing, various electronic devices, or a combination of these media. It is self-paced, can be responsive to the needs and mood of the learner, and can be used as an individual tutoring system. The new mode of training consists of Computer Based Training (CBT), Interactive Videodiscs (IVD) and Video Instructional Courses (VICs).

Various research data has shown that distant learning systems are effective in terms of student outcome and efficient in terms of outlays of time and money. Studies have shown that students who are individually tutored learn twice as much as students instructed in the conventional manner. Studies of student-paced instruction (vs. instructor-paced instruction) showed that students learn the same amount in 20% to 50% less time than when they are instructed in the conventional manner. It was assessed that the idea of using Distant Learning Courses (DLCs) to help in the training of Security and Intelligence personnel was feasible.

To enable CFSIS to meet the challenges of the 1990s and the next century, it was proposed that the school be restructured. The four-company organization was to remain, but the structure of the two companies was changed. The roles of the Intelligence and Military Police Training Companies were amalgamated to form one in-house training company. The other company focused on DLCs. The restructuring took place in January 1994, with a target date of September 1994 set for the dissemination of the first CFSIS DLC.[1]

---

1.  CFSIS Restructure Proposal, December 1993.

CFSIS Distance Learning Company, Jan–Jul 1994. The Originals.
Back: MCpl A. Scott, Sgt D. Gow, Sgt C. Cummings, Sgt A. Skoda, and
Cpl A. Cooke.
Front: WO C.P. Aucoin, WO M.R. Tracey, CSM MWO E. Aucoin, OC
Maj H.A. Skaarup, Coy 2IC Lt (N) S.P. Osborne, WO P.D. Eves.

## 1994, Intelligence Branch and Arms Verification Article by Capt Mike R.J. Ouellette

Following the signature of arms control treaties between NATO and the former Warsaw Pact, Canada has taken an active role in arms control verification. One of the main features of Canada's contributions to arms control consists of inspections of ground and Air Force Units in Eastern Europe.

Intelligence Staff take an active role in many aspects of arms control, including contribution to the planning and preparations of the inspections. Branch members are also involved on the ground as inspectors. This has given members of the Branch first hand experience in dealing with the Russians and Eastern European armed forces. Most importantly, these inspections have given us the opportunity to exchange different points of view and engage in discussions on tactics, exercises, the every day routine of our Troops, and comparing various types of equipment.

The interesting part of the arms control process is, of course, the actual inspection. Once the inspection team arrives at the Unit to be inspected, it is provided with a diagram of the site and a briefing on the equipment. The inspection team can then inspect the site, validating the accuracy of the information provided each year on 1 January.

The most recent example of a Canadian inspection took place from 9-11 March 1994, in Russia at Naro Fominsk, approximately 80 km south of Moscow. The Unit inspected was an elite Guards tank Regiment. After inspecting the equipment, which consisted of T-80 main battle tanks, BMP armoured infantry fighting vehicles, and 2S3 152-mm self-propelled artillery, members of the team were taken to the training area to drive the BMPs.

A number of interesting points were discussed during the inspection. These included our common northern heritage, including the cold climate and geography; news about Russian hockey players playing with the NHL teams; current conditions in each other's countries; and world issues, such as the fighting in Bosnia-Herzegovina. One particularly interesting point, which came out during the discussion, was the involvement of the Unit in the fighting for the Russian parliament in October 1993. We were told that the tanks firing on the "Russian White House," seen around the world on CNN, were in fact tanks from that Unit.

As can be seen from the above, a major by-product of the arms control treaties involves personal exchanges and confidence building. Not only do inspection teams confirm the accuracy of each other's arms control declarations, but also the personal contact between members on both sides is invaluable in decreasing the mutual suspicion which has built-up over the years. The Intelligence Branch has played an important role in all of this through its contribution to the training of inspectors, the background provided on the Units to be inspected, and the information provided to the arms control Community.[2]

2.    Sinister Sam's Notebook, Edition 1, 1994, pp. 1-2.

# 1994, 2 Intelligence Platoon, Ottawa
# Extracts from an article by Capt Phil R. Berikoff

Since the last report 2 Int Platoon in Ottawa has maintained its busy schedule. Following Exercise PROUD FLAG and completion of the Warrior Program in December, we began refresher training. Like the Combat Arms, Int types can never get too much practice. With red and blue markers in hand, training began in earnest. Under the guidance of WO Kevin N. Rowe, and MCpl Wayne D. Upshall, map marking skills, terrain analysis and Intelligence collection plans were quickly refined. In preparation for the 2 CMBG spring Command Post Exercise, Intelligence operations at brigade and divisional level were reviewed. Almost everyone involved in this year's exercise had to learn new orders of battle, enemy doctrine and even strange sounding place names. Previous years involved the Warsaw Pact swarming across the Inter-German Border (IGB), but the scenario for this conflict occurred in a fictitious locale known as karaoke and Chosan.

Capt Phil R. Berikoff's term as Course Officer on the Ottawa District LFC Driver Wheeled Course has been completed. WO Kevin N. Rowe spent three weekends employed as the Course WO for the pre-CLC/ISCC course. The militia officer's staff course is almost finished with Capt Paul G. Rivard and Lt Doug F. Agnew expected to graduate.

Welcome additions to the Platoon include: WO Robert A. Lavalle, now a reservist and wearing green; MCpl Mike Diamond, ex British Army, replacing MCpl Heidi Vidler as our Admin Clerk, and Cpl Rawl Hugh from the Governor general's Foot Guards. Despite their lack of paperwork, they have fit into the Unit very well.

Col Victor V. Ashdown, the Int Branch Advisor, visited the Unit in early February and following a "meet and greet" he spoke of his experiences as a Canadian Forces Attaché in Warsaw during the late 1980s. Col Ashdown also gave us an update on the current situation in Eastern Europe and around the world. He then challenged the Int Platoon to consider how the role of the government has changed with the rise of multi-national corporations and the advent of the information super-highway. The highlight of the evening occurred when Col Ashdown, much to everyone's delight and surprise, promoted Stéphane Lefebvre to the rank of Capt.

The next few months should prove equally busy. In addition to upcoming exercises, courses, and summer training, we have again begun our recruiting drive hoping by next September to have another ten people. 2 Int Platoon is very much alive. E Tenebris Lux.[3]

## 1994, CISA Member News

LCdr Sherry J.Y. Richardson retired from the Regular Force in 1991 and was rehired for REGOPs at her retirement party. She is serving as part of the REGHQ Component at Debert, NS, but will leave 1 Jul 94 after 40 years service. Brook Claxton was the Minister of Defence when she joined. LCdr Richardson wrote, "It's been a great experience, with tremendous comradeship and many, many changes." In her spare time she is a Lt on HMCS Sackville (a Museum Corvette in Halifax harbour), Secretary of NSNOA, Chester Legion, and St. Margaret's Arena Association, as well as being a Scouter with 1st Glenhaven Venture Company, and serving with the Glen Haven Rover Crew. "Doesn't leave much time to moulder," she says.

Maj P. Denis Pelletier reported from Beloeil, Quebec that he was working with the Canadian Space Agency (CSA), near CFB Montreal. MGen C. William "Bill" Hewson wrote he was serving as DG SIGINT Production at CSE. 2Lt John Hamilton has served six years as the Honorary Solicitor of the Royal Canadian Military Institute (RCMI). Lt Donald Mackenzie is now the Honourable Donald Mackenzie, working at the Court House in Brampton, Ontario.

Cdr Christopher S. Hordal was posted to the Directorate of NATO Policy, NDHQ, Ottawa. Capt Margaret R. Prentis reported she is enjoying her retirement. Major Peter W. Sloan reported on the inauguration of the new Int Coy in Toronto (2 Int Coy), with Maj Sandra L. Bullock as the first female CO of an Int Unit. Former members of No. 2 Int Trg Coy were also in attendance at the ceremony.

MGen Reg Weeks, Colonel Commandant of the Int Branch, nominated Maj Reginald R. Dixon to attend the 50th Anniversary of the D-Day landings in Normandy on 6 June 1944. Reg was an Int officer at the time. Capt David A. Rubin reported he had been awarded the long-service medal from the Order of St John of Jerusalem. Maj Hal A. Skaarup said he continues to find his job as OC Int Trg Coy, CFSIS, interesting. Lt the Hon Frank C. Muldoon reported he received the 125th Anniversary of Confederation medal. LCol King G. McShane is teaching law at Carleton University in Ottawa.

---

3.  Sinister Sam's Notebook, Edition 1, 1994, pp. 2-3.

LCol Ron J. Donovan is a managing partner in a high tech venture in vocational rehabilitation. Maj John J. Stonborough is mentioned, Col the Hon. John Matheson, one time IO RA, retired as a Justice of the Ontario Court, and had received an LLD degree (Honorius Causa) from RMC and delivered the Convocation address at its spring convocation.[4]

# 1994, CFSIS

Intelligence Operator 6A Course 9401.
Rear Row: MS W. Robert Murley, MCpl A.L. Pride, MCpl Ronald P. Walsh, MCpl Warren L. Lawrence, MS Cliff J. Boyechko, MCpl Dean G. Hyde, MCpl Kris E. Pedersen, MS Don S. Eenkooren.
Centre Row: MS J.U. Serge St Jacques, Sgt Phil D. Cooper, MS Richard Lee Fletcher, MCpl J.T. Serge Gagnon, MCpl Marie M. Hudson, MCpl Donald Bruce Warawa, MCpl François Leger.
Front Row: WO Rick G. Oliver, MWO Herb H.W. Kuchler, Maj W. Boone, Capt Pierre Michaud.

4.   CISA Newsletter, Vol. 24, No. 1, May 1994, pp. 1-3.

Intelligence Operator 6B Course 9401.
Rear Row: PO2 J.E. Paul Pellerin, Sgt G.D. Chaisson, Sgt J.D. Roy, Sgt
Gregory Charles Collins, Sgt J.A. Chris Pelletier, Sgt Peter G. Manuge,
Sgt J.M.R. Dan Jacques.
Centre Row: Sgt John Paul Michael Parsons, Sgt Nicholas R. Procenko,
PO2 B.D. Sammons, Sgt, Sgt Gary R. Hayes, PO2 J.R. François Bou-
chard, Sgt J.C.M. Roy, PO2 David H. Kushmier.
Front Row: MWO Herb H.W. Kuchler, WO E. Meril Crane.

## 1994, Arms Verification

Following the signature of arms control treaties between NATO and the
former Warsaw Pact nations, Canada took an active role in arms control verification. The main feature of Canada's contribution consisted of inspections of
ground and Air Force Units in Eastern Europe. Intelligence staffs worked in
many different aspects of arms control. They contributed to the planning and
preparation of the inspections. Intelligence Branch members are also involved
on the ground as inspectors. This activity gave many members first-hand
experience in dealing with the Russians and Eastern European armed forces.
These inspections gave Canadians an opportunity to exchange different points
of view and to engage in discussions on tactics, training, exercises, and the
everyday routine our Troops on both sides. The inspections also provided a

chance to compare various types of equipment. Three of the missions are OP PASSIVE SKIES; OP REDUCTION; and OP VERIFY (which involves CFE Treaty on Site Inspection).

A major by-product of the arms control treaties involves personal exchanges and confidence building. Inspection teams do not just confirm the accuracy of each other's arms control declarations; they establish personal contact, which is invaluable in decreasing the mutual suspicion, which has built up over the years. The Intelligence Branch played an important role in making the inspection teams function effectively, through its contribution to the training of inspectors, the provision of background on the Units to be inspected, and the information provided to the arms control Community.[5]

## *1994, CTC Tactics School, CFB Gagetown*

Posted to CFB Gagetown in July 1994, the author reported in for work at the Combat Training Centre (CTC) HQ and to the Tactics School as the G2/ Intelligence Directing Staff (DS). He met his new CO, LCol Don Peterson, along with MGen J.J.M.R. Gaudreau who had been the author's CO as the Col of the Airborne Regiment and as the BGen commanding 4 CMBG. There were many other familiar faces at CTC.

In August, the author had a long chat with LCol Kramers on the subject of Intelligence Preparation of the Battlefield (IPB). Later in the same month, the author was sent up to visit 1 Canadian Division Intelligence Company (1 Cdn Div Int Coy), where he spoke with Maj Ron H.J. Ruiters and his crew. He also ran into Capt Wes B. von Papineau and Maj A. George Johnstone, had lunch with them in the Signals Mess and then visited with the Int staff in 2 EW Sqn. Back in Gagetown, 5e Brigade came down from CFB Valcartier for field exercises. The author drove 40 km South into the base training area on 24 Aug to visit Capt J.I. Mike Beauvais and his 5e Brigade Int Section camped at Coote's Hill. They had great computer facilities and equipment considering they were in the field.

For the next few years the author participated in a large number of courses and training exercises scattered over many different areas in New Brunswick, and had the great good fortune to meet many of the CF's future military leaders who took part in the courses conducted by the Tactics School staff. It was a very great privilege to have been part of one of the most professional and

5.   Maj M. Ouellette, Sinister Sam's Notebook, Edition 1/94.

highly experienced Army training teams in the business. Many of our Int Capts will remember Ex RAPID RHETORIC I & II, held in -13º degree weather near the villages in Jacksonville and Lakeville, as well as the author's father flying over the class in his Challenger II ultra-light aircraft during Ex DANGEROUS DANCE on Flagstaff Hill. They will also remember how really deep the snow was, that seemed to be a permanent feature during Ex CRYSLER'S FARM and Ex CHÂTEAU GAI conducted near Jackson Falls. The snow was deep enough to require some serious use of our snow-shoes. Each student had to lay out an urban defence plan in the City of Woodstock during Ex URBAN FURY, not to mention planning a defence against an assault water crossing of the "Mighty Meduxnekeg River." They had to plan both the defence of a bridge in Woodstock and the destruction of another bridge at Marysville in Fredericton on Exercise ACADIAN BEA-VER, ending the course with Ex BEAU SABREUR, in order to complete the Intermediate Tactics Course (ITC).

In the spring the author had the incredible opportunity of being part of the enemy force working out of Petersville during the field exercises held in concert with the Combat Team Commander's Course (CTCC). It always seemed to start with a heavy snowstorm and finish in mosquito season. Another plus to being at CTC was the opportunity to participate in continuation parachute training, which gave the author the chance to make a number of military static-line jumps from a C-130 Hercules or the Iroquois helicopter onto the drop-zone at CTC Gagetown.

## 1994, CISA Member News

LCol H. John Wickey passed away in Lethbridge, Alberta at the age of 94. He was born in Lyons, France, and was raised and educated in Switzerland. He served with the French Foreign Legion in WWI, and received the French Medaille Militaire and the French and Belgian Croix de Guerre for bravery. Following service with the Legion in North Africa, he moved to New Zealand and then to Canada, where he was employed as a teacher. He served in WWII in many capacities including that of espionage agent parachuted into France before the Normandy invasion in 1944. He left the Service in 1946 in the rank of LCol. He then served with the Department of Justice in Winnipeg until his retirement.

FLt Eugene Morosan passed away in Belleville, Ontario, on 1 Apr 94. Gene was a former Air Force Flight Lt who had been working on a project that would recognize the part played by Air Intelligence in the past. He collected memorabilia and artefacts that could be placed in an Air Force or Int museum. Gene had a Ph.D. in Psychology from Syracuse University, was a teacher with the Hastings County Board of Education until his retirement in 1989; then set up his own marriage and family therapy business. He ran twice for Belleville city council, and twice provincially for the NDP. He was active as a director and member of many associations.

Maj Bernard Benoit passed away in Sutton, Quebec on 28 Apr 94. He was one of the few remaining original members of No. 1 Int Trg Coy, Montreal, and was its 2nd CO. During WWII, the then Capt Bernie Benoit specialized in psychological warfare. In later years he managed a very successful sheep raising operation in Sutton. Bernie was the husband of the famed culinary expert, Mme Jehanne Benoit, who predeceased him several years earlier.

Lt John A. Shirkie passed away in St. Catherine's, Ontario on 22 Nov 93. He was a member of the Int Reserve.

LCol Ronald E. Gladstone retired from the Senate, moved to Penticton and started a wing of the RCAF Association. He became President of the Pacific Group in Nanaimo. Maj (Dr.) Reg H. Haskins reported on his retirement in Saskatoon. Col the Hon John Matheson wrote from Rideau Ferry, Ontario, that he had been invested as an officer of the Order of Canada in 1994. He also mentioned that a number of strong nominations had been forwarded to the Secretary, the Order of Canada, Government House, Ottawa, asking that Mrs. Svetlana Gouzenko (widow of Igor) be considered for the Order of Canada. Maj Bruce K. Smith reported from Barrie, Ontario that he is still working in Japanese linguistics. Capt Merrick Jarrett, former member of No. 2 Int Trg Coy, C Int C, reported in from Kitchener. HCol Arnold B. Mottershead is serving as the Hon Col of 15 Edmonton Svc Ban. LCol Bernie N. Wright reported from Ottawa that he was working in the Defence 2000 Secretariat, the DND management renewal initiative. The intent of the program is to maintain operational capability at a time of shrinking resources.

Maj Dave Spilling reported on the closing operations at CFB Lahr and Baden-Söellingen, and Maj Harold A. Skaarup reported on the changes at CFSIS. Hal was posted to the Combat Training Centre at CFB Gagetown, NB, and Maj Rajeev G. Nath from North Bay moved into the Int Major's position to command the combined Int and Sec Trg Coy. Capt John M. Robertson retraced his wartime route from Juno Beach (D+10) to Oldenburg, Germany via Rouen, Ghent, Nijmegen, Kleve and Emmerich during a tour of the continent in June 93, accompanied by his wife who had served as a Nursing Sister in the RCAMC. Capt Robertson was an IO at HQ 1 Cdn Army in 1944, and then an IO at 2 Cdn Corps, then GSO3 (Int) at HQ 2 Cdn Inf Div.

Capt S.L. Spence, a parole office in civilian life, wrote from Mississauga about taking part in the start-up ceremony for the LFCA Int Coy (2 Int Coy) on 29 Oct 93. MGen J. Vernon and MGen Reginald J.G. Weeks were present to sign, along with Maj Sandra L. Bullock, the new CO of the Int Coy. Capt Charles B. Buffone, now on call-out as a staff officer at LFWA HQ, also attended the ceremony from Western Area. He had received his CD from Maj Bullock in Nov 93.[6]

Col the Hon B. Barry "Bud" Shapiro reported that after a long legal career, he had been appointed to the Bench in 1991, retiring in 1990. Since then, he has been practicing as counsel to a large Mississauga law firm. He retired from the Army Primary Reserve in 1978 after some 39 years association with the Militia and Active Force. He wrote, "I joined the University of Toronto COTC (NPAM) in 1939. Although there were breaks in the continuity of my 39 years, I did have overseas service in the C Int C during WWII in the UK, Italy and NW Europe. Post-war, I was one of the original members of No. 2 Int Trg Coy in Toronto, and at one time was 2IC. I also served 16 years as an ADC to three Lt Governors of Ontario."[7]

LCol Dale M. Watts reported he has been appointed Dean of the Mechanical-Transportation-Civil Engineering Technology Division of the Red River Community College in Winnipeg. LCol David M. Robb returned to Orleans Ontario with his wife Helena after serving as the CFILO in London. He was now running the current Intelligence operation at the National Defence Intelligence Centre in NDHQ. He also reported that Col Patrick D.R. Crandell has been the Canadian Forces Attaché in Belgrade since 1992, and has extended his tour to 1995. Capt Doug R. Bennett reports from Weston, Ontario and Maj Doris E. Guyatt, reported that WO Warren Grigg passed away in Aug 94.

Col Charles D'Arcy Kingsmill had been nominated by MGen Reginald J.G. Weeks to represent the C Int C at the 50th Anniversary of the Italian Campaign. He went to Sicily and Italy form 6-20 May 94, along with other veterans of that campaign. He wrote, "I was chosen because I was G2 Int at

---

6.     CISA Newsletter, Vol. 24, No. 2, August 1994, pp. 1-5.
7.     CISA Newsletter, Vol. 25, No. 1, May 1995, p. 1.

HQ 1 Cdn Corps during the whole of the Corps' tour of duty in the Mediterranean theatre (and later in Holland). Our party of 56 veterans, representing all ranks of Army, Navy and Air Force, visited cemeteries in Sicily and Italy, at each of which a ceremony and laying of wreaths was carried out under the direction of the Secretary of State, the Hon Lawrence MacAulay, PC, MP. I was impressed by two things: first, the number of Canadians who gave their lives in the Mediterranean Campaign, and second, the ages of those beneath the tombstones, mostly being in their 20s and early 30s." Col Charles D'Arcy Kingsmill added, "Although I have never been a member of the C Int C (being a gunner), in Jan 1948, under the late Col Peter E.R. Wright, I was one of the charter members of the CISA."

Maj Gary W. Beckman and LCol Ernest Skutezky are mentioned. Maj Wilf S. Puffer reported on the positive side of his retirement in BC, and Maj John Harrison reported from Nepean, Ontario that he is "the coordinator for a 2-year diploma program for Security management at Algonquin College in Ottawa. Capt Richard Leswick is working as a security management consultant with Assets Protection Management in Toronto. Lt Paul R. Perchaluk is working with the Freedom of Information Unit of the Waterloo Regional Police. LCol William "Bill" Tenhaaf is now a management consultant in organization and compensation in Ottawa.

Cdr John C. Macquarrie wrote that he had, "moved on to Director of Security and Military Police Plans Coordination," and that he had passed "command of the Special Investigation Unit to Cdr Paul H. Jenkins" that summer. Maj John "Pappy" MacKinnon ended his tour of duty as an Ottawa City and Regional Councillor on 30 Nov 94.

Maj Ian N. Fleming passed away on 2 Oct 94 in Saanichton, BC, where he and his wife Margaret had moved from Bermuda in 1992. Ian, originally with the Black Watch in Montreal, was the CO of No. 1 Int Trg Coy in Montreal from 1952-55. During WWII, Ian was a Photo Interpreter for some of the time at HQ 8th Army in Africa. Ian was a C.A. and had his own accounting firm in Bermuda.

## 1994, CISA AGM

The CISA AGM was held from 29 Sep to 1 Oct 94 at CFB Chilliwack, BC. 1st VP Maj Terry B. Kelly chaired the meeting in the absence of LCol Ian A. Nicol. BGen G. Silva, Vice-Chairman (Pacific) of the Conference of Defence Associations attended. Lt (N) Greg C. Walker, the Base Security Officer, welcomed everyone on behalf of the Base Commander. Those present included: Col Victor V. Ashdown, Capt Phil R. Berikoff, Lt H. Robin Bramall, Capt Beth Brown, Maj Hugh Campbell, Maj Robert C. Dale (Director), LCol Jack S. Dunn (Director), Capt Ted P. Ethier, LCol Ronald E. Gladstone, Maj Robert L. Grieg, Col Robert T. Grogan (Director), Maj D.E. Guyatt (2nd VP), Maj David A. Haas (Treasurer), Sgt John Cameron Hadden, Maj F.J. Hamlyn, Capt J. Humen, Lt David H. Hunt, Maj Terry B. Kelly (1st VP), Maj Franz F. Laizner (Director), LCol Frank Leigh, Maj Nils E. Lindberg (Director), Maj J.D. Mackenzie, Maj John "Pappy" MacKinnon (Secretary), Col P. MacLaren, Maj J.H. Mansfield, Maj David Olexa, Capt P. O'Sullivan, Capt George Parry, Capt M. Puffer, Maj W. Prentis, Capt Paul G. Rivard (Membership Secretary), Maj E. Short, BGen G. Silva (CDA Representative), Capt Don M. Stedeford, Col A.H. Sam Stevenson (Director), Lt (N) P. Walker, LCdr James Walton, LCol Dale M. Watts (Director), Maj Stanley H. Winfield, Capt R.H. Yeomans, and BGen Douglas Yuill.[8]

During the AGM, CISA chose to become a corporate member of the Canadian War Museum. BGen G. Silva spoke on CDA activities over the past year. He discussed CDA's response to the defence review, and the problems which DND has regarding the perception of the need for defence in the eyes of many in the general public.

Regional reports were presented at the AGM by: Maj Robert C. Dale for the Maritimes, Maj Franz F. Laizner for Quebec, Col Robert T. Grogan for the National Capital Region, LCol Dale M. Watts for Manitoba, and Col A.H. Sam Stevenson for BC. Capt Don M. Stedeford, Capt J. Humen and Capt Brown reported for Land Forces Western Area, and Capt Phil R. Berikoff reported for the new 2 Int Pl in Ottawa. Maj Franz F. Laizner noted that a new Int Coy (4e Cie de Rens) is to be created in Montreal, with a strength of 68 all-ranks, similar to the one now in existence in Toronto.

The CISA Academic Award for 1994 was awarded jointly to Erik David Olexa and Rosaleen Michelle Heffernan, with each receiving $600. Col Peter MacLaren, the incoming DG Secur and Col Victor V. Ashdown the DDI (for the DG Int Commodore Heath) made very interesting presentations on their areas of responsibility. BGen Douglas Yuill will succeed MGen Al Pickering as the Colonel Commandant of the Security Branch.[9]

---

8.    CISA Newsletter, Vol. 24, No. 3, December 1994, p. 3.

# 1994, *Acorn Intelligence Conference*

Acorn Intelligence Conference 1994 participants.
Fourth Row: MWO R.P. Jacquard, Maj J.M. Bédard, Maj G.C. Mayer, WO J.Y.H. LaBarre, Capt H.A. Ferguson, Capt R.S. W. MacAuley, Maj W.A. Sweet, OCdt S.P. Desjardins, Maj J.P.C.A. Langevin.
Third Row: Capt C.P. Cornect, WO D.A. Bishop, CWO V.J. Lefaive, WO J.Y. Leclerc, Maj R.H. J. Ruiters, Maj G.W. Jensen, WO J.A. Laforest, MWO R.J. Tervo, CPO1 W.J. Lindsay, Mr. G.L. Simard, MWO J.B. Germain.
Second Row: Capt E.E. Gjos, WO J. Pierre Turcotte, WO P.A. Maillet, Capt C. Doyle, MWO I.J.M. Schoots, Maj H.A. Skaarup, Maj C.J. Beamish, WO D.A. Gelsinger, Capt J.D. Villeneuve, Capt D.D. Nickel, Maj S.L. Bullock.
Front Row: Maj M.R. Rothschild, Capt J.I.M. Beauvais, Maj J.L.F. Messier, Maj R.L. Johnson, LCol J.M.R. Viens, LCol P.W.M. Wilson, CWO J.R. Martin, Maj M.J. Popovich, Capt C.B. Buffone, Maj G.D. Dover, Capt J.A.J.P. Cormier.

9.   CISA Newsletter, Vol. 24, No. 3, December 1994, pp. 1-6.

The annual Acorn Intelligence Conference was held at St Jean, Quebec, on 17 March 1994. Personnel in attendance but not in the photograph included: MGen J.J.M.R. Gaudreau, MGen (Ret'd) R.J.G. Weeks, BGen C.J. Addy, Capt P.D. Johnston, Capt P. Michaud, Capt M.R.J. Ouellette, Capt N.R. Ward, Lt B. Toomer, WO R.A. Deleau, WO Tom C. O'Brien, Sgt J.A.C. Pelletier, Sgt R.J. Wilson, MCpl J.H.D. Gauthier, and Cpl K.J. Marchand.

## 1994, Bosnia-Herzegovina

In February 1994, a Bosnia-Herzegovina Serb mortar attack on a Sarajevo market place killed 66 people and injured another 200. (At least that is how the incident was reported, although it is suspected that the Bosniacs fired the mortar on themselves to gain international sympathy). This act prompted NATO to threaten punitive bombing if the Serbs did not pull back from the city as directed. It is considered the day the Bosniacs "acquired an Air Force (NATO)." The Bosnia-Herzegovina Serbs then kidnapped UN Peacekeepers and used them as human shields to halt NATO air strikes. (One of these human shields was one of our Arms Verification Inspectors, Capt Pat Rechner).

A great number of CF Intelligence personnel have rotated through the various Int positions in Bosnia-Herzegovina. Each of them has a story to tell. As a Capt working as Contingent G2 Ops in Zagreb in July 1995, LCol Robert S. Williams reported that he "welcomed the arrival of Capt Phil R. Berikoff as the new G2 of Sector South in Knin, which was then Krajina in the Serb occupied sector of Croatia. All indications on the ground were that a Croatian offensive was likely in the near future. We agreed that I would visit Phil in Knin to help establish an Int cell. On 3 August I flew down to Knin on a UN Twin Huey with talc, maps and the usual Int misc. Phil greeted me and then we quickly toured the immediate area."

"At 0500 on 4 August we were awoken to the sound of heavy artillery fire on the town and bracketing our camp. 300 rounds landed in our vicinity in the first half hour and about 2,000 more came in during the day. The Croatian OP STORM (OLUJA) had commenced. The next few days were a blur of helping refugees (780 plus elderly Serbs), manning the gates to protect them, feeding them, picking up dead civilian bodies in the vicinity of the camp and trying to get word out in a coherent Int report fashion. All our soldier skills and Serb-Croat linguistic abilities were put to the test. Under the able leadership of BGen Alain Forand and Col Andrew B. Leslie, we 20 some odd

Canadians together with our Czech colleagues, but not some of the other nations based in Knin, safeguarded these civilians, both young and very old. A month later, they too went into exile in Eastern Slavonia, where many remain to this day. You never know what the day might bring for Int staff deployed."[10]

From Jan 93 to Apr 94 Maj Alex C. Chambers reported that he, "was the O I/C Yugo Crisis Cell, running the fusion centre for all military Int received on the Balkans War. Those were interesting & stressful times, when we had the equivalent of a Brigade in the field under fire. My team grew from five to 12 eventually, working 24/5 weekdays & 12 hrs on Sat/Sun. There are a lot of interesting stories from those days which we cannot publish."[11]

In the fall of 1993, Intelligence Officer Cdr M. Josh Barber was asked to be the Canadian member (and head) of the multi-national NATO Intelligence cell set up on board US Mount Whitney (flag ship of the US Navy's 2nd Fleet) for NATO Exercise Solid Stance 93. He spent about five weeks on board Mount Whitney in Aug/Sep 93 sailing out of Norfolk, Virginia and operating in the Norwegian and North Seas with visits to UK, Norway, and Germany. He headed the NATO cell, and was the primary briefing NATO Intelligence officer for Commander Second Fleet, VAdm William Flanagan, USN during the exercise.

The NATO cell consisted of Cdr M. Josh Barber and an officer each from the navies of UK, Germany, and Netherlands, plus USN personnel (officers and enlisted) from Mount Whitney's regular Intelligence staff. A Canadian team of Communications Researchers also participated in this exercise onboard Mt Whitney. The main significance of this event is that it was the first time a NATO (or any non-US, for that matter) Intelligence cell had been established in a US warship (as far as is known) and represented the first time that the USN was willing to integrate its Intelligence operations with its Allies at the operational level. The Intelligence integration was part of a larger exercise to trial having an integrated NATO staff onboard the flagship. This trial was to lead to the full time establishment of a NATO staff onboard Mount Whitney that now serves as the command platform for NATO's Combined Joint Task Force (CJTF) headquarters afloat. A Canadian Intelligence Officer, Maj J.A.J.P Cormier, has filled a permanent position as an integrated

10. LCol RS Williams, E-mail 10 Sep 2003.
11. Maj Alex Chambers, E-mail 5 Sep 2003.

Intelligence officer onboard the ship since the post was created in 1996/97. As
with many other NATO Intelligence positions, the professionalism of the
Canadian Intelligence Branch is very highly prized, as are our close ties to US
and UK Intelligence organizations and our facility in both of NATO's official
languages.[12]

Cdr M. Josh Barber spoke about other Canadian Naval Int activities, advis-
ing that officers who have participated in real live operations for the Navy
included: (then)—LCdr Darren W. Knight—head of Intelligence for the
Canadian Commander Middle East during the Gulf War; (then) Lt (N) Dan
P. Langlais—Canadian Task Force Intelligence Officer for the Gulf War
(deployed onboard HMCS Athabaskan at sea from Sep 90-April 91); Lt (N)
G. Reginald J. Quigley—deployed as Intelligence officer onboard HMCS
Huron in the Persian Gulf April–Oct (dates uncertain) 1991 in the immediate
aftermath of the Gulf War: (then)—Lt (N) Ivan Allain deployed at sea on
board HMCS Terra Nova as part of the operations enforcing sanctions
against Haiti. In 1992, Lt (N) Andrew W. Chester served in Cambodia as the
Intelligence officer for UN riverine operations/peace monitoring of the Cambodia Peace Agreement. Lt (N) Shawn P. Osborne: Flag Lt and Intelligence
Officer to RAdm Morse, CF, Commander of Standing Naval Force Atlantic
1999-2000. This was the first time that an Intelligence officer had been permanently deployed (and employed as such) as part of the SNFL staff. Both Lt
(N) Debra J. Mayfield and CPO1 Brian M. Noble were employed at times in
1994/95 at sea in the Adriatic as part of OP SHARP GUARD enforcing
sanctions against the Former Yugoslav Republic, aboard HMCS Protecteur.
Lt (N) Debra J. Mayfield was also the first Int Branch officer (and certainly
our first female Int officer) permanently posted to a seagoing billet when she
was posted to the staff of Maritime Ops Group 1 from 1996-99. Lt (N) Owen
J.W. Parkhouse was employed as the Intelligence officer onboard HMCS
Protecteur and ashore in East Timor supporting the Canadian Commander
(Capt (N) Roger Girouard) for OP TOUCAN in 1999-2000.[13]

## 1994, Haiti

On 19 September 1994, the US landed forces in Haiti and President Aristide
returned from exile in October of the same year. Between 1994 and 2000,

---

12.   Cdr M. Josh Barber, E-mails fall 2000.
13.   Cdr M. Josh Barber, E-mails fall 2000.

Canada participated in several missions to Haiti: the UN Mission in Haiti (October 1994-June 1996), UN Support Mission in Haiti (June 1996-July 1997), UN Transition Mission in Haiti (July 1997-November 1997), and the UN Civilian Police Mission in Haiti (November 1997–2000). The Haitian Community suffered from economic chaos and political instability, and therefore looked to the international Community to assist their government in maintaining internal security, to help it develop Transparent governance and policing practices, and to revive the nation's economy. The UN extended its mandate when President Preval was elected, and shortly afterwards, Canada took command of the UN contingent in Haiti as the US pulled out.[14]

LCol Mike R.J. Ouellette served in Haiti and reported, "After the collapse of the former Soviet empire, work for Intelligence officers became even more pressed as we then had to deal with not one known quantity, but with a myriad of smaller but no less dangerous situations developing across the globe. In my case, this involved three successive tours in Haiti as J2 from Mar 1996 to Jul 1997. Canada led this UN mission which, because of the asymmetric threat (although it was not called asymmetric at that time) enabled the Intelligence Branch to prove that Intelligence was critical to operations other than war. The Haiti mission was largely successful because of the Intelligence effort, which allowed us to marshal meagre UN forces in the right place at the right time in order to prevent insecurity and instability from getting out of hand.[15]

---

14. Internet: www.thememoryproject.com.
15. LCol Michael Ouellette, E-mail 29 September 2003.

# 13

## 1995, Intelligence Branch

### 1995, Bosnia-Herzegovina

In May 1995, NATO launched two days of air strikes in an effort to break a Serb blockade of Sarajevo. Bosnia-Herzegovina Serbs seized 400 UN peace-keepers and chained them to possible bombing targets to forestall further attacks. The hostages were gradually released throughout May and June. In July, the Bosnia-Herzegovina Serbs overran the UN safe areas of Srebrenica and Zepa and massacred most of the population and ethnically cleansed the rest. In August 1995, NATO resumed air-strikes in response to the shelling of Sarajevo. A ceasefire was established in October. In November, negotiators for all sides in the Bosnia-Herzegovina conflict met at Wright-Patterson Air Force Base in Dayton, Ohio, for a three-week planning session to hammer out a workable peace plan. By December, British and American military personnel were arriving in Bosnia-Herzegovina to assist in the implementation of the agreement. Canadian Intelligence personnel were part of the Peace Implementation Force (IFOR) and its follow on, SFOR, from the beginning.

OP Alliance involved the deployment of IFOR to Bosnia-Herzegovina as authorized by SACEUR from G Day (16 Dec 95). IFOR's forward HQ was located in Zagreb, with the ACE Reaction Corps (ARRC) HQ in the same location. The USA, the UK and France controlled three major zones. The 997-man Canadian Contingent initially came under the operational control of the Multi-National Division (MND) South West in the UK zone. Canada also provided an observer with the Organization for Security and Cooperation in Europe (OSCE), who was based in Sarajevo, and one Canadian Senior Staff Officer with UNMIBH. 5 Canadian Multi-National Brigade (5 CAMNB) had its HQ located in Coralici (north of the town of Bihac), while the National Support Element (NSE) was located in the town of Kljuc. One Canadian served as an UNMO in Montenegro, and another served in Macedonia.

In 1995, Croatia's President Tudjman allowed the UN peacekeeping mandate to lapse, and he renewed his region's battles with the Croatian Serbs. In August, Croatian Troops regained the territory in the Krajina region that had been lost to Croatian Serbs in 1991. In 1996, Sarajevo was handed over to the Bosnia-Herzegovina-Croat Federation. Public pressure forced the withdrawal of Radovan Karadzic, although he continued to direct political and criminal activities from his residence in Pale. IFOR became SFOR (Stabilization Force) in Bosnia-Herzegovina-Herzegovina.

## 1994-1995, Canadian Intelligence in the Former Yugoslav Republic
## Article by Col C.S. Hamel

*General.* If I was to contribute anything of some interest for other Branch members to share, it would be about three of the issues I became familiar with during my service with UNPF and UNPROFOR in the Balkans (June 1994–June 1995): the UN Military Information Office (MIO) concept in Zagreb, Croatia; the misconception of "safe duty" for headquarters personnel, as illustrated in Sarajevo, Bosnia-Herzegovina-Herzegovina; and the overall need to critically examine information received.

*UNPF HQ (Zagreb, Croatia) and the MIO Experience.* Military commanders involved in international stability operations need professional Intelligence support services to enhance their prospects for mission success. This need is readily apparent, and Intelligence assets readily available, in coalition operations. The same cannot be said of military peace support operations conducted on behalf of the United Nations (UN). This was the case for UNPF/UNPROFOR in the Balkans during the 1990s, when a MIO rather than a G2/J2 staff supported the senior UNPF military and political leadership in Zagreb, Croatia. MIOs can provide commanders situation awareness information concerning events that happened yesterday; they are not structured, suited or sufficiently supported to provide commanders with assessments of what will happen tomorrow.

*Intelligence Staff Presence.* Why an ABCA or NATO Intelligence staff would not support a major UN mission headquarters is explainable, even if not fully supportable. The "non-openness" of many Intelligence activities leads some observers to conclude that Intelligence work, by its very nature, serves to undermine efforts to achieve trust and foster harmonious relationships. Given the erroneous premise that Intelligence work is inherently hostile and not conducive to promoting peaceful resolution of conflict through openness and transparency, many host nations prefer not to have foreign Intelligence personnel operating in-country, perhaps targeting the host nation. The UN on occasion is thus deterred from having in its peacekeeping force headquarters a G2/J2 staff element. Moreover, it is deterred from having in its peacekeeping force an Intelligence line Unit and sophisticated information collection means to contribute to mission success and provide a much stronger force protection capability to help safeguard UN contingents against hostile threats in theatre.

*Access to NATO Intelligence.* Even if the presence of a very capable, professional ABCA/NATO Intelligence staff in a major UN mission HQ is desired by the UN General Assembly (UNGA) and permitted by the host nation, other impediments to full provision of Intelligence support during UN operations exist. In the interests of protecting national and alliance Intelligence capabilities, limitations and activities, NATO and its member nations have a natural reluctance to share Intelligence with non-NATO UN contingents, commanders and staff planners. If UN "mission Intelligence reports" were available to members of the UNGA, would anyone be denied access to NATO Intelligence included in these reports? Are security caveats, such as "UN CONFIDENTIAL-Official Use Only" meaningful and respected? These are not academic issues without practical consequence. In late 1994, to cite one example, UNPF MIO information was "leaked" and published on the front page of a major Croatian Newspaper. This incident highlighted UNPF's inability to protect its MIO information, let alone any NATO Intelligence that could have been included in MIO reports. It exposed the UNPF leadership to hostile criticism from the host nation media for the unacceptable information base upon which it was making decisions. In addition, it highlighted a problem of concern for professional Intelligence officers and NCMs working in this type of environment, namely: database creation, protection and access; dissemination and "need-to-know;" source protection; and "political sensitivity" when preparing MIO reports.

*Staff Skills*. If lack of Intelligence protection was a major problem in the UNPF HQ MIO experience, a belief by some that anyone can credibly perform "Intelligence work by another name" was another concern. There were committed and talented personnel on the MIO staff during 1994-95. Nonetheless, it was evident that apportionment of responsibilities and tasks within the MIO staff was disproportionate. This often resulted in long hours and seven-day workweeks for some—a situation that negatively affected staff harmony. Work in UNPF HQ's MIO during ARSK firing of long-range rockets into Zagreb was considered less stressful than attempting to meet some HQ staff expectations with limited MIO capabilities. Screening must be better to ensure that all members of a MIO staff have requisite language capabilities and general military knowledge. A small MIO staffed by personnel who lack necessary reading and writing abilities, experience in operational-tactical level Intelligence work, and basic map reading skills is not an acceptable substitute for a proper G2/J2 staff that can provide Intelligence to a UN mission's senior leadership, deployed contingents, and NATO support elements. Canadian Intelligence officers and NCMs deployed to a similar mission HQ in the future should not have to prepare lesson plans and teach the essentials of a basic Combat Intelligence course to other MIO personnel during an actual operation, as was the case in 1995.

*Insight and Accountability*. The high rate of turnover in any MIO staff leads to yet another issue: insight and accountability. As MIO personnel become familiar with assigned areas of responsibility, they are usually at the point where they are preparing for repatriation. This, coupled with inexperience developing databases and preserving records, usually leaves their successor in a "start-state" position to learn about the mission area, establish working contacts in the Headquarters and in the field, and too often learn the basics about Intelligence work. This common problem is one that all Canadian Intelligence officers and NCMs deployed in such environments must be accustomed to dealing with, particularly given the "spill-over" effect of having to handle some issues until the new replacement is comfortable enough to accept tasks.

*Summary*. In summary, absence of a skilled G2/J2 staff limits force commanders and operational planners in much the same way that peacekeeping Unit commanders would be limited if their soldiers were not provided weapons because such preparedness might be construed as aggressive. Without Intelligence, services to provide force commanders all-source analysis Intelligence assessments needed to develop Knowledge and understanding, commanders cannot be as pro-active in their negotiating efforts and force commitment to preserve peace. Lack of Intelligence support to force commanders not only threatens mission success. It has a serious impact on the ability of the commander to provide force protection in unstable environments where heavily armed warring factions may be using UN military presence as a shield or a means to gain time before renewing hostilities.

## UNPROFOR HQ, Sarajevo, Bosnia-Herzegovina, and the "Safe Duty" Misconception

The need for all Army personnel to be "warriors" first and "tradesmen" second has been highlighted on recent international stability operations, including the UNPROFOR mission in Bosnia-Herzegovina. In Sarajevo, a small G2 staff, rather than a MIO staff, supported Commander UNPROFOR. Several Canadian Regular and Reserve Force Intelligence members were routinely employed with NATO Intelligence counterparts on this staff. For these Intelligence personnel, and the other members of UNPROFOR HQ, "safe duty" for HQ personnel was a demonstrated fallacy. In a war zone, all staff personnel have to be prepared for dangerous duty and serve as trained soldiers.

Throughout the period that UNPROFOR HQ was located in Sarajevo, it was not uncommon for rounds from BSA indirect fire weapons and sniper rifles to be fired into the city, in near proximity to those working in UNPROFOR HQ or travelling in its vicinity. Nor was it uncommon for Intelligence personnel travelling into Sarajevo by the Mount Igman road to be exposed to sniper fire as their vehicle traversed "the run"—an open stretch of road littered with the remains of busses and trucks, victims of hostile fire and bad road conditions. Flying in and out of Sarajevo during the same time period was a challenge too, with passengers in flak jackets and blue helmets remaining behind sandbag walls until such time that C-130/Hercules and IL-76 transports arrived with their loads of relief goods and supplies. The sensation of helplessness experienced by those having their IL-76 struck by several bullets while taxiing to the runway for takeoff is one experienced by at least one Canadian Intelligence member, a "fact" made all the more real because it was (in UN vernacular) "UNMO verified" by an UNMO passenger.

Intelligence personnel who survived the run through "sniper's alley" as they entered the city from the airport were not immune from danger at "The Residency"—the UNPROFOR HQ compound adjacent to the American Embassy. A sign outside the compound warned locals of the danger of sniper fire in the area, and it was not uncommon to see bullet holes in the windshield of vehicles parked near the G2 office. Nor was it unusual to find shrapnel on the walkways of the compound after some periodic shelling incident. On one such incident in mid-1995, Cpl Mike H. Hurley, a Canadian Intelligence operator nearing the end of his tour in Sarajevo, was injured with several others when a mortar round struck a large tree near the door to one of the two sea containers housing the UNPROFOR G2 staff.

It did not help that the AbiH on occasion invited BSA fire into the city by positioning a multiple-rocket launcher system near UNPROFOR HQ at night, firing a few rounds, and leaving before BSA retaliatory fire arrived. It was also discomforting to know that an AbiH mortar pit was constructed near a building shared by UNPROFOR HQ and Bosnia-Herzegovina security forces. The loud sound of mortar impacts near the living quarters after finishing a duty shift at 0300 hrs left one questioning whether personal safety was more important than sleep deprivation. As incoming rounds got closer, desire for the former usually took precedence over the latter concern.

When the BSA siege of Sarajevo was enforced, food quality by Sarajevo standards was usually maintained. Access to basic supplies, computer parts, and "necessities" like Coke, toilet paper and writing paper, however, became a problem. During one extended period of siege in 1995, there was such a shortage of writing paper that the G2 staff submitted briefing notes for the Commander's attention on the back of used pieces of paper.

As Intelligence staff members, we learned to work through difficulties and maintain a sense of humour and camaraderie. It also helped to have great leadership—not only from the G2 (LCol Brian Powers, USAF) but from Commander UNPROFOR (LGen Rupert Smith, British Army) as well. LGen Smith took an active interest in Intelligence and the Intelligence staff, listening intently to Intelligence advice whether it came from the G2 or a Junior NCO on his staff. Aside from regularly inviting officers of all ranks to dine with him at his table, he also made the effort no matter how grave the situations he was dealing with to thank departing members of the HQ staff in his office. Leadership not only involves having clarity of vision, resoluteness and excellent management skills; it also involves having and demonstrating a genuine interest in the men and women who support the leader.

Critical Examination of Information Received. Intelligence work to "lift the fog of war," even in a Chapter 6 Peacekeeping operation, is not an easy endeavour. In the Balkans, establishing "fact" in an atmosphere of conflicting reports, inexperienced "Intelligence" personnel, political leanings of contributing nations and media editorial bias favouring one party or faction at the expense of others, "unexplainable" occurrences, and language difficulties made information gathering and Intelligence processing that much more difficult. Information collection and Intelligence sharing limitations, the large number and national diversity of UN contingents in theatre, the size of the area of operations, and warring faction activity under the cloak of darkness or beyond the line of sight of road barricades did not aid this situation. Indeed, these factors combined to highlight the importance of all-source analysis and critical examination of sources during the processing stage of the Intelligence cycle.[1]

## *A Word from Branch CWO Rick J. Tervo*

I would like to take this opportunity to say how honoured and pleased I am to have been appointed your Branch Chief. I am fully cognisant of the fact that I am stepping into some of the biggest "little" boots around in succeeding William "Bill" J. Lindsay, and will therefore try my best to live up to his fine example.

We have just finished going through a year of unprecedented change and turmoil. Almost 50% of our NCOs have been posted, and some of us are still fitting into, and learning our new jobs. Many of our comrades are serving, or have served in hazardous and difficult zones of conflict around the globe, and we also have learned to do more with less. By and large we have weathered the storm well. Yes, we have lost some positions, but we have also acquired new and more interesting ones. Yes, our pay and benefits are frozen, but we have also promoted over 14% of our ranks and opened up the trade to remuster. I am personally optimistic that 1995 will bring stability, better prospects and developments that are more favourable.

On another note, I am happy to report that the Branch number situation for the reserves has been resolved. After much discussion, it has been decided to continue the existing system rather than to issue separate numbers for the reserves. This is much easier to administer and it is anticipated that the first certificates will be out soon.[2]

1.   LCol C.S. Hamel, E-mail, Spring 2003.
2.   Sinister Sam's Notebook, Edition 1, 1995, p. 1.

# 1995, The Single Step, 2 Int Pl
# Article by Pte B. Young

Once, while I was reading the Chinese philosophy of Tao, I found a rather ageless extraction, "A thousand mile journey begins with a single step." I find this quite fitting in my situation. I have just recently remustered to the Intelligence trade from the Infantry, the Governor General's Foot Guards to be exact. The article that I am writing is to be a "newcomers" perspective on the Intelligence world. For the record, I should state that I am not a complete stranger to Intelligence, no pun intended. With my exposure limited to Intelligence briefings at my former Unit, integrating with my family's military background and personal interest in all things military, I saw 2 Intelligence Platoon as my opportunity to gain entrance to and become involved in the field of Military Intelligence. However, before I carry on, I should mention that I have just taken my first step of my thousand-mile journey.

My history with the Intelligence Trade is, well, limited. I have only been a member of the Intelligence Branch for a very short time, since late April 1994. However, I was aware of the desire of the Land Forces Command to develop And foster tactical Intelligence companies across Canada within the Militia areas back in the winter of 1993. I was interested from the word go. This was a chance of a lifetime. I must admit I am overwhelmed by my acceptance in 2 Int Platoon located in Ottawa.

It was with great desire and excitement that I requested my transfer to 2 Int Pl. From the eyes of a newcomer to the ranks, my perception of the Intelligence trade was quite different from what greeted me on my transfer into 2 Int Pl, a Total Force Unit, which has shown itself to be quite different from other reserve Units. The merging of the Regular Force and the Reservist together is nothing short of beneficial. The professionalism presented by the Regular Force members will be highly influential on me, the reservist, and my attitude towards the Trade. The following quote quite succinctly expresses my belief of the Intelligence Branch:

"What is called 'foreknowledge' cannot be elicited from spirits, nor from gods, nor by analogy with past events, nor from calculations. It must be obtained from men who know the enemy situation." Sun Tzu, The Art of War.

In turn, I believe the Reservist brings with them a sense of enthusiasm that injects a new and fresh outlook to the Unit. For me, this is new and exciting.

Some people who have been in for awhile might forget that feeling. To be completely and utterly honest, I have no complaints at all.

I fell that Intelligence is a dynamic, vibrant and innovative trade, and it is my goal to be part of it. With my background, interests and attitude, I know that I will measure up to the standards required by 2 Int Pl.[3]

## Reinventing Intelligence in the Information Age
## Article by Capt T.A. Quiggin

The rapid progress in information technologies is altering the very terrain upon which Intelligence organizations operate, whether or not they are aware of it or even concur with it. While the changes forced upon those organizations that deal with information are many and varied, two in particular are worth noting. The first issue, open source information, is intangible and it is often a process that is invisible to the Intelligence Community. The second issue is that of costs, a factor which is very tangible and painfully visible.

*Open Source.* Advanced nations that involve themselves in Intelligence activities are using mainly capabilities that deal with the industrial age and the Cold War. Lesser-advanced or minor nations are often dealing with Intelligence capabilities that are still behind the industrial age and focus upon internal security matters. Around all of them, however, is the commercial or Open Source Intelligence (OSINT). Frequently, the commercial capability is as good, or better, than the classified product and often it is the only source available.

One of the results of the explosion in information availability is the relative decrease in the value of classified Intelligence. Previously, being able to tell consumers what was happening, and where, was 'news' to them and was of value. Now, quite frequently the consumers of the Intelligence product know what has happened, where it happened, and who did it and they receive this in full colour video with commentary in real, or near real time.

In order to maintain, or increase, the value of Intelligence, particularly at the strategic level, the Intelligence analyst will have to raise the analysis up at least one level. The value will lie less in what happened, and more in why it happened, whom it will affect and what national or regional implications are involved. In short, the Intelligence analyst will have to be able to fit the event into its context locally, regionally and nationally.

---

3.    Sinister Sam's Notebook, Edition 1, 1995, pp. 3-4.

Further complicating the Intelligence problem for analysis is the fact that current conflicts are becoming more complex. During the Cold War analysts only had to deal with two main categories of players: them and us. Furthermore, there was only one type of conflict to be considered, that being high intensity, and the conflict could be assumed to operate at one level only, that being the nation state. This, if nothing else, made the bounds of the playing field clearly definable. Current conflicts are less neat in their organization. Instead of two main blocks, there are now literally dozens of players who can affect ongoing conflicts. Fighting ranges from high intensity to low intensity. Conflicts are occurring at several different levels, those being nation state, sub-state, communal and personal, with each level of conflict having its own dynamics and affecting the situation in a different way.

In order to maintain the value of Intelligence in the Information Age, the analyst needs skills in several different areas. In addition to the traditional ability to assess various sources (COMINT, ELINT, IMINT, TECHINT, DOCINT, HUMINT etc.), the analyst must also have ready access to OSINT and the ability to extract value from it.

The most important analytical skill in this complex area is to be able to view the arguments and positions of others and deconstruct them to see if their arguments are logical and defendable. Following this, the analyst must be able to construct logical and conceptually clear arguments or their own which will place the conflict or situation in a context that is useful to the consumer.

*Costs and Budgets.* Information is a replacement for time, money, labour and space. Those organizations with timely access to accurate information will expend less on unnecessary efforts and more on endeavours that actually related to the mission. Current budget trends dictate that there will be less money and fewer personnel to get the job done. Current security trends worldwide and particularly where Canada has interests suggest that the missions will get more complex and difficult. Intelligence organizations have no control over these two divergent trends, but both of them directly affect the Intelligence function.

By being able to clearly identify trends, identify important events, and place emerging conflicts into context for consumers, Intelligence organizations will save resources. This will be most pronounced in money and personnel, but it will also be felt in effort and time spent dealing with otherwise vague issues.

*Moving Ahead.* These divergent trends, together with the revolution occurring in OSINT, are an opportunity for Intelligence organizations to make themselves more valuable to their consumers. This will come at a cost, however, and may not be painless. It may mean a shift to gap driven collection and analysis rather than priority driven efforts. This will reduce repetitive work against the same target and fill in gaps in other areas. It may also mean more hiring of short-term contract employees to fulfil specific taskings and fewer employees with long term tenure who have only narrowly defined skills that may no longer be needed. The ability to produce clearly written arguments in an effective manner is a function of both education and regional experience. Intelligence organizations will have to hire away or invest their own resources in producing these types of skills, either of which will require medium to long term planning and investment. Intelligence organizations may also have to face competition from private sector firms that can effectively produce useful Intelligence in a timely manner using only OSINT.

Responding in an aggressive manner to the issues raised by the information revolution and budget problems will mean future Intelligence organizations that provide a high level of value-added product. Failure to do so will mean a low level of value added work and competition from other sectors.[4]

## 1995, CISA Member News

LCdr Sherry J.Y. Richardson has been appointed CO of HMCS Sackville, a Canadian Navy memorial, but still a commissioned warship. She is the first female to command a Canadian warship.[5]

---

4.    Sinister Sam's Notebook, Edition 1, 1995, pp. 4-5.

Capt John M. Robertson revisited European battlefields in the summer of 1994. His group received a civic reception near Dieppe in the village of Les Quatres Vents, which he helped liberate on 30 Aug 1944, while serving as an IO at 2 Cdn Corps. Capt Robert T. Greyeyes is enjoying his retirement in

5.   HMCS Sackville is a dauntless fighting ship that has become a symbol for the Canadian Navy. It is not a more conventional or recognizably fast and heavily armed warship, but a vessel evolved from peacetime sea-going endeavours, born of necessity and named "Corvette." 123 corvettes were built in Canada for service in WWII. They became the workhorses of the North Atlantic, escorting convoys and fighting submarines. Ten were lost in action. HMCS Sackville is the last of the Flower Class corvettes. The Saint John Shipbuilding and Dry-dock Company built HMCS Sackville in the spring of 1941 as hull number 11. In late summer of that year, Sackville was launched and then commissioned on 29 December. She would be one of only three built in the Maritimes. The ship began active operations as soon as working up exercises were completed in the spring of 1942 carrying out convoy escort duties from St. John 's, Newfoundland to Iceland. By the end of the year she was steaming all the way across the North Atlantic to Londonderry in Northern Ireland. While escorting an eastbound convoy on 3-4 August 1941, Sackville engaged three German U-boats in foggy weather over a 36-hour period. One U-boat was seriously damaged, another was hit by shellfire from the ship's 4-inch gun and the third was shaken up in a depth charge attack. The Capt, Lt Alan Easton, RCNR, received the DSC and other members of the ship's company were also given awards for their part in these actions. Sackville sailed to Galveston, Texas, in early 1944 where the forecastle was extended at Todd Shipyards. Returning to convoy duty in mid-1944, she made only one ocean crossing before a ruptured boiler retired her from active war service. After a short time as a training ship for HMCS Kings, Sackville was designated to replace an aging cable ship, and in September work began for conversion to a controlled loop layer. As it turned out, this would save her from general disposal when WWII ended. Sackville served until late 1946 recovering harbour defence installations at Sydney, Halifax and Saint John, NB. After serving on both naval and civilian auxiliary duties until 1982, Sackville was retired and assigned to the care of the Canadian Naval Corvette Trust, which has completed the ship's restoration. It serves as a national naval memorial and floating museum in Halifax. Intelligence Branch Journal, Number 1–1985, p. 14.

Orleans and is involved in a number of volunteer activities. Maj David Spilling is posted to Atlantic Det SIU and is anticipating release through FRP in Jul 95.

Lt Dennis Souder of Toronto and Lt the Hon. Justice Frank C. Muldoon of the Federal Court reported in, along with LCol Jean Laporte of Ste-Foy, Quebec. Cdr Christopher S. Hordal has been seconded from DND to the Intelligence Assessment Secretariat (IAS) of the Privy Council Office. Maj John H. Newman is currently Director of the Ontario Cattlemen's Association. Maj Stanley H. Winfield reported he had been appointed Chairman of the New Westminster Court of Revision for 1995.

Col John P. Page wrote, "In Sep 1994, I was presented with the USSR Order of the Red Banner, originally awarded in May 1945 at Halle, Germany, for cooperation with the Russian Forces. Lt Don M. Fowler wrote from Brockville, Ontario, that he was coordinating the "Canada Remembers" return to Holland for several WWII comrades, spouses, etc., via the Phillips Electronics Ltd., sponsored "Thank You, Canada" Foundation National Committees invitation. This commemorates the 50th anniversary of the liberation of the Netherlands.

BGen Douglas Yuill, who was appointed Col Comdt of the Security Branch on 1 Oct 1994, wrote about his military background: "While I was successively a Sapper, a Cpl and later an Infantry Officer, I served from 1977 to 1981 as Director of Defence Intelligence in NDHQ and, according to Sam (Col A.H. Sam Stevenson) and many other Security and Intelligence friends, that qualifies me for membership in CISA."

Capt Phil R. Berikoff and guests presided over the inauguration of 2 Int Pl in Ottawa on 8 Apr 1995. Col Patrick D.R. Crandell reported on the Yugoslav "roller-coaster" he and his wife have been riding for the past 2-½ years in Belgrade, Serbia. Pat returns to Ottawa from his posting as Canadian Military Attaché in Aug 1995. Maj Robert C. Dale in Halifax retired from the Militia. Capt Ted Ether spoke of his retirement in Nanaimo.

MGen Reginald J.G. Weeks reported that the Dieppe Decoration is available to eligible recipients through Veterans Affairs.[6]

---

6.    CISA Newsletter, Vol. 25, No. 1, May 1995, pp. 1-4.

# 1995-1997, 2 Int Platoon, Ottawa

The Sir William S. Stephenson Trophy (SWST) was awarded to 2 Intelligence Platoon, for both the 1995-1996 and 1996-1997 training years. Capt J.P. Stéphane Lefebvre was the Acting Commanding Officer for both years, during which 2 Int Pl was the first Unit to be awarded trophy. The SWST Trophy is awarded to the reserve Intelligence Unit adjudged to be the most proficient overall during the course of a training year (1 June-31 May).

Capt J.P. Stéphane Lefebvre, CD, retired as Deputy Commanding Officer of 2 Intelligence Platoon in July 2001. During his service he has been an Intelligence officer, Headquarters, Secteur de l'Est (Milice) (1987-1989); Intelligence officer, Headquarters, Land Force Central Area (1991-1992); Intelligence officer and second-in-command, Training Company, 4th Battalion, Royal 22e Régiment (Châteauguay) (1992-1993); Training Officer, 2 Intelligence Platoon (1993-1995); Acting Commanding Officer, 2 Intelligence Platoon (1995-1996); Deputy Commanding Officer, 2 Intelligence Platoon (1996-1999); Acting Commander Officer, 2 Intelligence Platoon (June 1999-January 2000); and, Deputy Commanding Officer, 2 Intelligence Platoon (January 2000-June 2000), with release procedure stating at that point.

On 17 Sep 1996, MGen B.E. Stephenson, CD, presented Capt J.P. Stéphane Lefebvre with the "Commander Land Force Central Area Commendation." The Commendation in part "Capt J.P. Stéphane Lefebvre is hereby awarded the Commander LFCA Commendation in recognition of his outstanding motivation, dedication and service to 2 Intelligence Platoon during his appointment as Acting Commanding Officer 15 July 1995 to 5 August 1996, in the absence of both the Regular Force Commanding Officer and Second In Command.[7]

---

7.   E-mail, Capt Lefebvre, 25 Nov 2003.

# 1995, CFSIS

Intelligence Operator 6A Course 9501.
Rear Row: MCpl John P. Kubryn, MCpl Serge Laforge, MCpl W.E. Webb, MCpl Norman F. Wilhelm, MCpl Wayne D. Upshall, MCpl Alex D. Mackenzie, MCpl Philip E.D. Nicholson, MCpl J. Patrick A. Couture.
Centre Row: MCpl Daniel Joseph Garant, MCpl Dan B. McQuinn-Legér, MS Thomas E. Scott, PO2 J.L. Dennis Goulet, MCpl J.H.D. Gauthier, MS Richard A. Fisher, MCpl M. Paul McNeil, MCpl John T. Smola.
Front Row: Capt Derek V. Marchbank, MWO Herb H.W. Kuchler, Maj Nancy Larivière, WO Rick G. Oliver.

Intelligence Operator 6B Course 9501.
Rear Row: Sgt Donald M. Gallaher, Sgt Byron K. Mackenzie, Sgt J.M.A.
Stéphane Chartrand.
Centre Row: Sgt Reginald J. McAuley, WO Peter A. Maillet, Sgt J.
Patrick D. Knopp, Sgt J.J.J. Brun, WO Al H. Dickie, Sgt R. Jack Wilson,
Sgt J.S. Daniel St Pierre.
Front Row: MWO Herb H.W. Kuchler, Capt Derek Marchbank, WO
Rick Oliver.

Basic Classification Training 2 & 3 Course 9501.
Rear Row: 2Lt David Travers, Lt Zwarg, 2Lt Bramhill, 2Lt Norman, 2Lt Perler, Capt Ngo, 2Lt Hilfor, Frederick Paradie.
Front Row: Capt André. F. Berdais, Maj Nancy Larivière, Sgt Glen A. McGuire.

## 1995, CISA Member News

LCol J.W.G. "Bud" MacDougall wrote about his return to Holland with veterans in May 1995, stating they had a "Wonderful welcome by grateful people in Breskins Packet, where Canadians fought hard in Sep-Oct 1944 to open the Scheldt River to gain use of the port of Antwerp. I was in Army Int then in Antwerp." LCol William "Bill" Tenhaaf also visited Holland 27 Apr-17 May 95, and wrote, "Did not see any Int personnel and only a few Provost. This was my first celebration of this kind. Hospitality overwhelming; could not have been better." LCol Hank H. Hennie was also in Holland 1-11 May as part of the DVA delegation of representatives of Units that helped to liberate Holland. Hank served as a Field Security Officer in North West Europe, and after the War, headed the security detail for British PM Clement Atlee and his delegation at the three-power Potsdam Conference in Jul 1945, where the post-war boundaries of Eastern Europe were decided. Back in Canada, Hank served as a staff officer in the C Int C, and was Commandant of the CSMI at CFB Borden from 1955 to 1959.

Honorary Col George B. MacGillivray passed away on 22 Sep 94. As a Major, George served in North West Europe as one of the "originals" of the C Int C, and returned to Canada for health reasons, then served on the directing staff of the wartime Intelligence courses at RMC in Kingston. Post-war, he was one of the founders of the CMIA in Toronto, and then he moved to Thunder Bay to become the publisher of the local newspaper. He was a dynamic person and will be very much missed.[8]

## 3 Int Coy Unit History

Although the formation of a Militia Intelligence Unit in Halifax is a post WWII event, this unit owes its conception to wartime situations and events. During the First World War, there were numerous reports on scouts and agents obtaining information about the enemy. In Aug 1950, the Department of Defence formally authorized the formation of a number of Militia Intelligence Training Companies. The following six came into existence between 1948 and 1950:

a.   1 Int Coy—Montreal,

b.   2 Int Coy—Toronto,

c.   3 Int Coy—Halifax,

d.   4 Int Coy—Vancouver,

e.   5 Int Coy—Winnipeg,

f.   6 Int Coy—Edmonton.

The aim of these newly formed Intelligence Companies remained much the same as it is today: to provide a pool of trained manpower to augment the Regular Force when needed.

---

8.   CISA Newsletter, Vol. 25, No.2, July 1995, pp. 1-2.

On 15 Nov 1950, HQ Eastern Command authorized the formation of 3 Intelligence Company. 3 Intelligence Training Company was given the important role of being the Intelligence Unit responsible to Group HQ. Also, the responsibility of providing Intelligence Training to the Battalions and Support Units of the Group was laid upon them. These appointments encompassed the following aims/goals:

a.  to aid both in the security of Group HQ and security training of units within the Groups,

b.  to keep the Group Commander informed on Intelligence matters,

c.  to provide and maintain a high standard of Intelligence Training within the Company personnel, and

d.  the provision of Intelligence products within the Group as required (i.e. Intelligence Summaries (INTSUMS), Intelligence Reports (INTREPS), etc.).

To command and set any new company on the right path, an officer of experience, initiative, and skill was and still is required; such a man was Maj Edward Fairweather Harrington. Maj Harrington had World War II experience in the Intelligence Field. This Maj possessed both the traits, and skills required to take command of this new Intelligence Company. Maj Harrington was transferred from Halifax Rifles (23rd Armoured Regiment) to the Canadian Intelligence Corps (C Int C), on 15 Nov 1950. Maj Harrington was born in New York. He spent his early years in Hampton, New Brunswick and he eventually graduated from Hampton Consolidated School. It was not until 1945 that he moved here to Halifax. Maj Harrington served with the Royal Flying Corps during the First World War and went on to serve with the C Int C in the Second Word War.

3 Intelligence Company was established at the Queen Street Armouries by Maj Harrington on 7 February 1951. This new company office was located on the corner of Queen and Spring Garden Roads. The site is now less than two blocks from the former Intelligence Company quarters at Royal Artillery Park (RA Park).

Maj Harrington was immediately authorized to start transferring/recruiting personnel. The first people enrolled in the Company included Capt G.C.

Piercey, Capt A.P. McCarthy, and Capt R.V.A. Swetnam. All three of these men had served with the C Int C during World War II. (At a later date both Captains Piercey and Swetnam held the honour of commanding the Unit).

The first enlisted personnel who transferred in and became part of the new unit were Pte G.P. Ehler, and Pte R.A. Cox. Among the first recruits of 1951 were: Privates Ken Lord, Sherman Veinotte, and Sam Gaskin. (In years to follow, Lord and Veinotte went on to command the company.) The initial surge of recruiting resulted in a staff of 7 officers and 18 men.

During the 1950s both the newspaper and paper media played an important role in the recruiting process. Sending out flyers was one of the main methods of bringing the Unit's vacancies and attributes to the Public Notice. Today, people can find out about various vacancies and attributes in several ways. First of all, a person can contact the Intelligence Company or Unit of interest and drop off a current resume. Another option is for the person to visit the local recruiting centre to find out about trades and options.

The role of 3 Intelligence Training Company encompassed a wide number of subjects/topics including:

a.   the monitoring of the enemy order of battle,

b.   equipment recognition,

c.   training in interrogation of POW,

d.   Security training,

e.   Air Photo Interpretation,

f.   Foreign Languages Training, and

g.   map provisioning.

Most intelligence training in the 1950s and 60s was conducted at the Canadian School of Military Intelligence, which was initially based at Camp Petawawa, and then at Camp Borden CFSMI from 1953 and later CFSIS. These schools were a training centre for Corps members; both Regular and Reserve Forces. Over the years the unit would continue to attend this, and other schools to train and reinforce skills already learned. There were courses for trade specialties—plus exams to write to qualify for "specialty rating" as well as "specialty pay." Some of the courses taught were:

a.  photo reading,

b.  photo interpretation,

c.  Intelligence Investigator,

d.  Counter Intelligence, and

e.  Russian Language Training.

In the years between 1953, and the integration of the Canadian Armed Forces in 1968, competitions at the school would play a large part in the unit's life. These competitions were a method of measuring, by direct comparison, the knowledge and skill levels of all Militia Intelligence Units. Various Militia trophies for proficiency in intelligence were awarded during these years. 3 Int Trg Coy did well and won many awards.

The Insinger Trophy was established in 1953 in memory of Capt Ted Insinger who was killed in action during the Dieppe Raid of 19 August 1942. This trophy was awarded annually to the Intelligence Training Company which achieved the greatest overall progress in comparison to their previous year. 3 Int Trg Coy was awarded the Insinger trophy that same year, as well as in 1955, 1961, 1963, and 1966.

The Jock Murray Memorial Shield was first awarded in 1957, and again annually to the Intelligence Company that won the softball tournament during the summer camp. Since the Shield was in memory of Col Jack Murray, the first Director of the Military Intelligence in the Canadian Army, competition was limited to Intelligence Trg Coys only. 3 Int Coy, of Halifax, won this trophy in 1968.

The CMIA Imagery Interpretation trophy was awarded annually to the Intelligence Unit that set the highest standard of proficiency in an Imagery Interpretation Exercise. The Canadian Military Association donated this trophy. To ensure uniformity, the Defence Photographic Interpretation Centre prepared a Photo Interpretation Exercise. This exercise was sent to each Int Trg Coy in November of the year. Each company was required to complete the exercise and return it to the DPIC by 15 March of the next year. DPIC would mark the exercise and select the Int Trg Coy with the highest proficiency in Basic Imagery Interpretation. 3 Int Coy won this trophy in its inaugural year of 1964.

The Crerar trophy, which was also established in 1953 by the Canadian Military Intelligence Association, was presented to the Int Trg Coy which had the highest efficiency rating in the training year. 3 Int Trg Coy won this trophy in 1956, and again in 1966.

The Van der Vliet trophy was awarded annually to the person/unit, who attained the highest proficiency in Russian Language Training. 3 Int Coy won this trophy in its first year, 1954.

The George MacGillivray trophy, also known as the 3D trophy because of its term of reference, was awarded to the Intelligence Company which set the highest standard of dress, drill, and deportment. This was determined by an inspection by Head of Corps, at the unit's home location, and marks were awarded by the Inspecting Officer. 3 Int Coy won this trophy in 1966, and again in 1968.

In its lifetime, the Intelligence Section has had many homes. Initially 3 Intelligence Training Company was housed in the Queen Street Armouries at the corner of Queen Street and Spring Garden Road. The first move took place in 1952 when the unit moved to the Barrington Street Armouries. The next move was in 1958. The Armouries at the Corner of Cunard and Maynard Streets was the location that was to last for 14 years. Another move came in 1972, when the unit once again took up and moved to Building 3 Ahern Avenue. This building is located at the base of the Citadel Hill. This location was good for another 14 years. In 1986, the unit moved to Building 1 on Ahern Avenue. In 1991, with the implementation of Land Forces Atlantic Area HQ, the Intelligence Section (Platoon) moved to the old MARCOM Building located at the corner of South and Barrington Streets. From the MARCOM Building the Intelligence Unit moved to Building 6 RA Park in 1995. IN the summer of 2002, 3 Int Coy moved to its present home at Windsor Park in Halifax.

Officers Commanding 3 Int Coy have included:

a. Maj E.F. Harrington        15 Nov 1950 to 30 Sep 1954

b. Maj G.C. Piercey          1 Oct 1954 to 30 Sep 1958

c. Maj R.V.A. Swetnam        1 Oct 1958 to 30 Sep 1961

d. Maj C.R.R Douthwaite    1 Oct 1961 to 1 Jan 1965

e. Maj W.A. Landry         1 Jan 1961 to 1 Sep 1969

Officers Commanding the Atlantic Militia Area (AMA) Int Section have included:

a. Maj Ken N. Lord         1 Sep 1969 to 1 Sep 1973

b. Maj Sherman R. Veinotte  1 Sep 1973 to 1 Sep 1978

c. Maj Robert C. Dale      1 Sep 1978 to 1 Jan 1995

Officers Commanding 3 Int Coy include:

a. Capt Colin A.J. Kiley (acting)   4 Nov 1995 to Sep 1996

b. Maj Ross L. Johnson     4 Nov 1995 to 11 Jun 1997

c. Maj Rick A. Mader       11 Jun 1997 to 1 Sep 2003

d. Maj Colin A.J. Kiley    1 Sep 2003 to Present

During the history of 3 Int Coy and its predecessors, many Regular Force Members have been attached to the Unit in an Advisory and or Support position ranging from one year to three years, including the following:

a. S/Sgt Rollie Unstill              1951 to 1951

b. S/Sgt Jack Bishop                 1952 to 1955

c. S/Sgt W. (Bill) Heargreaves       1955 to 1958

d. S/Sgt James C. Poirier            1961 to 1963

e. S/Sgt Ken Young                   1963 to 1965

f. Sgt M. Al Smith                   1967 to 1970

g. Vacant                            1970 to 1975

h. Sgt M. Al Smith                   1975 to 1978

i. Sgt Robert W. Churchill                    1978 to 1980

j. Sgt Ron J. Herman                          1980 to 1985

k. Sgt Robert G. Bowins                       1985 to 1986

l. Sgt Pierre Murret-Labarthe                 1986 to 1988

m. Sgt Robert R. Belliveau                    1988 to 1990

n. WO Matt G. McCann                          1990 to 1992

o. Sgt Eric Oblenis                           1992 to 1995

p. Sgt Frank Davis                            1995 to 1996

q. Sgt John H.F. Debison                      1996 to 1998

r Sgt Lana Desilets                           1998 to 2001

s. Sgt Charlene M. King                       2002 to 2004

t. PO1 J.R. François Bouchard                 1997 to 2001

u. MWO D.B. Powers                            1997 to 2004

v. PO1 Robert W. Murley                       2001 to 2004

Many members of 3 Int Coy have transferred to the Regular Force including the following who went to the Intelligence Branch: Capt Hal Skaarup, Sgt Barry A. MacDonald, Sgt R. Hal Pugh, 2Lt Barrett, Sgt Peter G. Manuge, Pte Tony Manuge, and Lt Wes B. von Papineau. Others joined the Regular Force to serve in other elements, including Pte Ebony Nash in Air Traffic Control, Capt Lorne Cooper in the Artillery, Capt Ian Alexander in Air Logistics, Cpl Greg Patterson in the Artillery, and Cpl Richard Vacheresse who joined the Navy.

Numerous members of 3 Int Coy have had the opportunity to travel and gain experiences on call-outs at a National Level including the following:

a.   Sgt Wes E.B Young. was deployed on OP DANACA from 15 May–15 Dec 1978

b.   Cpl Craig J. Tudor. was deployed on OP HARMONY from 21 Mar–5 Nov 1993

c.   Cpl Onik B. Papazian was deployed on OP MANDARIN from 15 Aug 94–15 Feb 95

d.   Major Ross L. Johnson, MCpl Alan W. Wilson, and WO R. Hal Pugh were deployed on OP LANCE from 7 Jul 95–25 Jan 96.

e.   WO R. Hal Pugh was deployed on OP PALLADIUM from 8 Aug 97–20 Feb 98.

f.   Sgt Michael C. Wagner was deployed on OP PALLADIUM from 19 Jan 97–15 Aug 97.

g.   Capt Andrew G. Morrison was deployed on OP PALLADIUM from 8 Nov 97–8 Aug 98.

h.   Maj R.A. Mader was deployed on OP PALLADIUM from 26 Dec 97–8 Aug 98

i.   Sgt. Craig J. Tudor was deployed on OP PALLADIUM from 24 Feb 98–24 Sep 98

With the stand-up of 3 Intelligence Company on 4 Nov 1995, a proud tradition is once again revived. To a large extent this is only possible due to the number of unit personnel who remained with the Atlantic Militia Area Intelligence Section, the successor 3 Intelligence Training Company in 1968, and the Land Forces Atlantic Area Intelligence Platoon (later company), in the years between then and now. These personnel preserved the proud tradition of the Intelligence Training Company through some very difficult years. To many, it is not just a rebirth, it is a justification for the perseverance and confidence they have shown in Reserve Intelligence Training.

3 Intelligence Company is identified in the Intelligence Master Development Plan (IMDP), as both a national and regional Intelligence augmentation unit. Its role, as it was for 3 Intelligence Training Company in 1951 is training. This role in many ways embraces many of the same themes as the former company. E Tenebris Lux.[9]

3 Int Coy, 4 Nov 1995.
Back Row: Sgt Frank J. Davis, Cpl Alan R. Farquhar, Sgt Michael C.
Wagner, MCpl Gordon A. Watson, Pte Warren A. Watson, Pte Richard
A. Vacheresse, Sgt Anthony G. Kiley, Cpl Kyle W. MacLean, MCpl Alan
W. Wilson.
Front Row: Lt Paul Stubbert, Capt Clark P. Cornect, Capt Colin A.J.
Kiley, WO J.J.P. Mike Fournier, Lt Andrew Morrison.

## 1995, Inauguration of 3 Int Company

On 4 Nov 1995, the author headed off from Fredericton to Halifax for the inauguration of 3 Int Coy (the author's former unit). He stopped in New Maryland to pick up WO Peter A. Maillet, and continued on to arrive just in time for the stand-up parade of 3 Int Coy near the old library building in Royal Artillery Park, downtown Halifax. There were many past and currently

9.   Cpl Jennifer Vacheresse and Pte Daniel Fishman, *Our Moment in Time, a history of 3 Int Coy*, March 1999, pp. 1-15.

serving members and guests attending to mark the occasion, including LCol Greg W. Jensen, Capt Ed D. Kirby, Maj Hal Skaarup, Capt Robert J. McCutcheon, Capt and Mrs Capt Ken E.H. Smith, Sgt Robert R. Belliveau, Maj Robert C. Dale, BGen George C. Piercey, LCol W.A. Landry, Cpl Alan R. Farquhar, PO1 Don B. Powers, Sgt Wes E.B. Young, and OCdt Mike Craig. Present from the Company were Sgt Frank J. Davis, Cpl Alan R. Farquhar, Sgt Michael C. Wagner, MCpl Gordon A. Wilson, Pte Warren A. Wilson, Pte Richard A. Vacheresse, Sgt Anthony G. Kiley, Cpl Kyle W. MacLean, MCpl Alan W. Wilson, Lt Paul Stubbert, Capt Clark P. Cornect, Capt Colin A.J. Kiley, WO J.J.P. Mike Fournier, and Lt Andrew G. Morrison.

## 1995, Intelligence Personnel News

The following Int Branch personnel have been promoted:

Col Gordon S. Graham, LCol G. Al Grant, LCol Pat A. Renaud, Maj J.R.Y. Mike Foucreault, LCdr R. Paul Grimshaw, Maj Chione M.B. Hughes-Robinson, LCdr J. Doug Schweyer, Maj Brian E. Watson.

WO Jack G.W. Campbell, WO Lloyd D. Crosby, WO D. Mike Donahue, WO Donald M. Gallaher, PO1 J.R. Michel "Mike" Labossiere, PO1 William M. Flanagan, WO Richard C. Gow, WO John Paul Michael Parsons, PO2 Richard A. Fisher, Sgt Tim L. Hagel, Sgt Philip E.D. Nicholson, Sgt W.E. Webb, Sgt Marie M. Hudson, Sgt Rick F. Luden, Sgt J. François .J. Legér , PO2 Veronica Marie Parolin, Sgt K.B. Sanders, MCpl Charles A. Beattie, MCpl Tom J. Last, MCpl Mark P. Peters, MCpl J. Duncan Ralph, and MCpl Vaughn C. Simpson.

The following personnel have or will have taken their release by the end of 1995:

Maj Don W. McVee, Capt T.A. Quiggin, CWO Rick J. Tervo, MWO A. Paul Grant, WO J.G. Callin, PO1 Harry V. Delorey, PO1 J.O. "Rick" Limoges, WO M.G. McCann, WO Rick M. Milne, WO J.E.M. Riberdy, WO R.G.G. Fournier, WO David A. Gelsinger, WO W.J. Goodland, WO William E. Hamilton, WO V.S. Keefe, WO G. Wayne Ivey, Sgt W. Robert "Bob" Murley, Sgt Gary R. Hayes, Sgt John L. Henderson, Sgt R. Hal Pugh, Sgt J.P.G. Vinetti, Sgt Keith M. Young, MCpl Ian K. Hargrove, and MCpl Dean G. Hyde.[10]

---

10.   Sinister Sam's Notebook, Edition 2, December 1995, pp. 3-4.

## *Message from the Colonel Commandant*

On the occasion of the Intelligence Branch Seminar, held in Winnipeg, Manitoba 5-8 Dec 1995, I would like to single out MWO Batchelor and PO1 William "Bill" M. Flanagan, who have been named for appointment to the Order of Military Merit, as well as 14 Wing Intelligence, Maritime Air Group, which received a formal Commander's commendation.

These awards do not surprise me, because I know the quality and value of the work done in Canada and overseas by the Service Intelligence Community. You can all be proud and confident that this is more and more widely recognized and appreciated throughout the Armed Forces. I want you to know that I share your pride and congratulate the individuals and the Unit who have brought us these honours.

(Signed) Reginald J.G. Weeks, MGen (Ret'd), Int Branch Colonel Commandant[11]

---

11.   Sinister Sam's Notebook, Edition 2, December 1995, p. 4.

# 1995, Acorn Intelligence Conference

Acorn 95 participants.

The 1995 Acorn Intelligence Conference was held in Halifax, Nova Scotia, with the following personnel participating: MGen Reginald J.G. Weeks; Col Gordon S. Graham, DIPCD; LCol Greg W. Jensen, LFCHQ; LCol W.D. Kuebler, LFWA HQ; LCol M.C. Maurer, 1 Cdn Div; LCol K. Watkin, AJAG Halifax; Maj Sandra L. Bullock, LFCA HQ; LCdr D. Rick Douglas, MARCOM; Maj Gary D. Dover, LFC HQ; Maj I. Hope, LFC HQ; Maj Ross L. Johnson, LFAA HQ; Maj Gerry C. Mayer, Cdn LO, Ft Huachuca; Maj Don W. McVee, DLR NDHQ; Maj Mike J. Popovich, LFCA HQ; Maj Terry W. Procyshyn, AIRCOM; Maj Ward Sweet, LFC HQ; Capt Roy C. Armstrong, LFCA HQ; Capt J.I. Mike Beauvais, 5 CMBG; Capt Phil R. Berikoff, 2 Int Pl; Capt Charles B. Buffone, LFWA HQ; Capt Clark P. Cornect, LFAA HQ; Capt Don Cushman, SSF HQ; Capt Phil J. Drew, 2 EW Sqn; Capt C.J. Doyle, LFCA HQ; Capt Hugh A. Ferguson, LFCA HQ; Capt Eric Gjos, 1 CMBG; Capt W. Pat Grant, 1 Int Coy; Capt Richard

MacRae, LFCHQ; Capt Rob Martyn, Cdn AB Regt; Capt D.D. Nickel, LFWA Int Coy; Capt Mike R.J. Ouellette, LFQAHQ; Capt John Robertson, 2 Int Coy; Capt Keith Sutton, DLFD NDHQ; Lt Paul Stubbert, LFAA HQ; CWO Ron Martin, LFC HQ; CWO Rick J. Tervo, DIPCD; WO David J. Whalen, 1 Cdn Div; WO Barry E. Beldam, 1 Int Coy; WO F.V. Gordon; PO1 William "Bill" D. Kean, 1 CMBG; WO Peter A. Maillet, CTC Gagetown; WO D. McLaren, LFCA HQ; WO William A. Mitchell, SSF HW; WO Kevin N. Rowe, 2 Int Pl; MCpl L. Monette, LFC HQ; Mr J. Kiras, Pearson Peacekeeping Centre; Mr. G.L. Simard, LFC HQ; and, Dr. David A. Charters, Centre for Conflict Studies (UNB).

Subjects under discussion included DLFD: The Future of the Army; Manoeuvre Warfare; The Op Sabre Platoon; The Law and Peacekeeping; Meteorological Applications to Intelligence; RV 95 and Joint Exercises; Air Support to Joint Force Operations; Intelligence and Low Intensity Conflict; Intelligence into the 21st Century; and concluding remarks by MGen Weeks, Int Branch Col Comdt.[12]

## 1995, LFWA Report

The Regular Force staff at LFWA HQ G2 includes Major Gord P. Ohlke and WO F.V. Gordon. Reserve members include Sgt Steve J. Goronzy, MCpl Warwawa, Cpl N. Beauchemin and Cpl Derrick D. Petrushko. Int support is also provided to LFWA by 6 Int Coy in Edmonton, with its three detachments located in Edmonton, Vancouver and Winnipeg. The Int personnel with 1 CMBG in Calgary round out the rest of the Army Int personnel west of Thunder Bay.[13]

## 1995, SQFT Report

The Int function at SQFT has been making steady strides ahead because of the efforts of the various branch personnel who are posted here. Maj Michael R.J. Ouellette, who serves as the G2 Ops, heads the G2 Branch. Maj Ouellette assumed the helm on promotion this last summer, following the departure of Maj J.L. François Messier to command 1 Cdn Div Int Coy. SQFT staff includes Lt Stephen P. Desjardins (Domestic Ops) and Lt Jim D. Gode-

12. Acorn 95 Reference Notes, p. 3.
13. Sinister Sam's Notebook, Edition 2, December 1995, p. 5.

froy (les jumeaux), who handles training. Steve recently returned from the FRY, where he served as PA and personal IO to MGen Baril, Comd SQFT. The General requested Steve specifically, another sign of the recognition our function has earned. Jim spent three weeks in Gagetown with 2 CMBG as they exercised for the COP COBRA task. He served as the Int LO between 2 Bde and the higher US formation, and found the experience very professionally rewarding.

Lt Stephen P. Desjardins is ably supported by WO John Paul Michael Parsons, who is finally getting over the shock of serving in an Army HQ. Paul supervises the work of Cpl Yannick Martineau and Cpl Benoit Themens, two members of 4e Cie de Rens detached to the HQ who do the Lion's share of the day-to-day work. Paul also saw a short-lived involvement in COP COBRA, trading his Air Force blues for combats during the pre-deployment training phase of the operation in Petawawa.

The G2 Section gets able assistance from our G2 Coord, WO J. Eric C. Savoy, and MCpl Reine St Jean, the section clerk. Eric and Reine are responsible for budgets, tasks, admin and all the other essentials which keep our wheels on track.

The Area Int Coy's acting DCO, Capt P. Michel Gareau, finds himself short-staffed at present as no less than seven of the personnel from the Company (4e Cie de Rens) are serving in the FRY. These include Capt J. Daniel Villeneuve, Capt N. Bruno Vanasse, Sgt J.C. Marc Pozzo di Borgo, Sgt François Maheux, Sgt Marc-André Lefebvre, Cpl J.L. Richard, and Sgt Stéphane S. Auger, who just returned. Area Int staff have made a strong contribution to operations, and continue to view the support of ops as a priority.[14]

## 1994-1995, Somalia, A Sailor's Saga
## Article by William "Bill" J. Lindsay

When I was asked to submit an article on recent experiences in Somalia, I suppose I should have done so immediately. Instead, I have waited almost six months, and, as anyone who has been to that country can tell you, that puts me very much out of touch with the situation. I apologize from the beginning to those who have been to the area if I make some observations that to you will seem all too obvious.

---

14.   Sinister Sam's Notebook, Edition 2, December 1995, pp. 5-6.

Shortly after my retirement from the military, the United Nations Development Program (UNDP) hired me as a "consultant". The job was entitled "Deputy Field Security Officer." Basically, it was to monitor the security situation in the various areas of Somalia where UN Agencies were conducting their respective programs. Duties included the preparation of emergency evacuation plans, representation at the various inter-Agencies' meetings with regard to security aspects, pass and security guard control, and report writing. Another significantly large part of the job entailed ensuring the UNDP and other Agencies' International employees (i.e. non-Somali) stayed out of harm's way, while trying to conduct their business. This last duty was to prove one of the most frustrating and hair-raising of the lot.

I make no claim to understand the structure of the UN. I can only outline what was presented to me as the UN involvement in Somalia. UNOSOM II was the controlling factor in the country during my short stay. Its mandate was to establish an atmosphere wherein the various national parties could reach a consensus on the formation of a new government. It further was to provide military protection to UN Agencies and Non Government Organizations (NGOs) such as the International Red Cross, OXFAM, etc., in their efforts to deliver aid and relief and in the implementation of the various programs. The record of UNOSOM II has been widely discussed, including the UN's announcement that the mission was unable to successfully bring the opposing parties together. UNOSOM II withdrew from Mogadishu, its last geographical position inside Somalia in early March 1995.

Therefore, you have UNOSOM II, seven different UN Agencies and dozens of NGO groups, all desperately trying to help rebuild a country that had and still has no government to be helped. There were many small successes, such as water wells for small towns, 4-6 room schoolhouses being rebuilt, and various agricultural projects. Unfortunately, these could not justify the many millions that were being spent. UNOSOM II alone reportedly poured 2 ½ million US dollars per day into the country.

There is no complete story to Somalia, certainly not from me. Perhaps, for those of you who did not have the opportunity to visit the area, the best feeling of the nature of the economic, social and political conditions would come from a few short recounts of incidents that, more than anything, will give you a feel for the situation and the frustrations that all those concerned feel in the attempts to salvage what many believe to be unsalvageable.

In December of 1994, there was a significantly fierce firefight in the close proximity (next door) of the then UNDP Residence and Offices. The

Murisade Clan had been pushing the Abgal Clan slowly away from the area and taking over traditional territory. One morning the Abgal launched a fierce counter-attack and by the end of the day had driven the Murisade completely from the area. In the next few days, the fighting moved to another contested area, commonly known as "Bermuda" (for its triangular shape) and continued between the two factions.

Alliances change rapidly in the area. The Murisade, who had once been allied with the Abgal, were in this case aligned with another enemy of the Abgal, the Haber Gedir. It seems that after two days of fierce fighting in the 20-square block area, the Abgal were losing ground to the Murisade, mainly due to the Murisade having more Technical vehicles (trucks sporting .50 cal, recoilless rifle, etc.).

I have no reason to disbelieve the reports we received that the Abgal entered into secret negotiations with their enemies, the Haber Gedir, to rent 12 Technical vehicles with which they subsequently drove the Murisade from the contested area. Apparently, business is business.

On another occasion, a man who claimed to be the landlord of the compound occupied by the UNDP announced that he could get no satisfaction from the recognized landlord as to the payment of rents and allowed us 48 hours to vacate the building, at which time he was going to "blow it up." He even signed it, "for your kind consideration." This was not a city where such a notice could be taken lightly. We managed to placate the individual for the time being, but within a week or two had to leave the compound and relocate to another, which brings me to another story.

On deciding to leave the compound in question, we ran into more problems. Firstly, whose trucks should we use to haul the sea containers of equipment down to the Seaport? If we were to use Clan A, then Clan B would most certainly intercept the cargo and "confiscate" it. Secondly, would our Mad Bomber allow us to leave without his particular agenda being settled? Thirdly, there was the small matter of a group of young, poorly controlled militiamen on the rooftops directly across from us who pointed their AK-47s and M-16s in our direction and, as the occasion suited them, fired into our compound.

The first question was the most pressing. I must say that I admired the reasoning of our Logistics Officer, a South African. He hired a Clan who we had contacted once before, but whom we had not yet paid. In his words, "if they want to get paid for the first job, they had best not lose the second." In the end, we managed, between we four internationals and our Somali workers, to remove 98% (approximately $1,000,000 US at the time), of the UNDP property to safety and eventually to Mombassa Seaport. At one point we were surrounded on three sides by different factions all demanding something. The oddest was a group leader, carrying a hand-held rocket launcher, who wanted us to pay money because the container trucks were making too much noise and disturbing "the neighbourhood."

With a three-month contract completed, a month break back in Canada and an additional three months' work, I was beginning to tire. Meanwhile, February 1995 was ending and so was my contract. I had arranged for my wife Carol to fly over to Kenya so that we could have a small vacation. If the organization wished to continue my employment, I would be available. Otherwise, it would be Carol and me on our way back home.

I was set to fly out of Mogadishu to Nairobi on 23 February. On 22 February, I made what I considered my final trip to the UNDP Compound from the safer confines of the UNOSOM-controlled Airport. After about two hours of sending out messages to our office in Nairobi and gathering up some last minute records and supplies, our little convoy started back to the Airport main gate, a distance of 7-8 blocks away.

I should mention that it was standard procedure that no International travelled in the area with less than two vehicles; one van with a driver and two armed guards and a second vehicle, usually a small pick-up with a driver and two armed guards. On this occasion a third van belonging to UNHCR was tagging along, so in fact we had six armed guards, and additional 8-10 UNDP Somali employees and me. It was not enough.

We pulled away from the compound and onto the Airport road, but had only gone about a block when we could see some vehicles approaching from the Airport entrance at high speed (even for Somalis). As they closed on us, two small pick-ups crossed to our right and then one veered left to catch us in a wedge. I remember watching four or five armed men alighting from each of the vehicles even before they had completely halted, and thinking, "oh darn, shucks," or something like that before making a dive for the floor. Imagine my surprise when I found one of the Somalis had beaten me to it. So there I was, my bottom half on top Of some fellow's back and my top Half sprawled along the seat. The bad guys yelled something, our guys yelled something back, and then all hell broke loose.

The entire fracas probably lasted a minute or two. I was later asked if our guards returned fire, and the answer was an obvious yes, as otherwise, why would there have been so much shooting? Of course, you must remember that at that time I was desperately trying to turn myself into a seat cover and was in no mood to cover the play-by-play of the situation. The shooting would stop, there would be a brief stillness, and then more bursts of fire. There must have been some blackout time involved, as I remember looking out of the van's side door and seeing two men who I did not recognize with weapons levelled in our direction. The next time I looked up, one of our own was crouched near the door. I asked what I now consider to have been a stupid question, "is everything OK!" I received a semi-affirmative nod and started searching for my hand-held radio on the floor.

It was about then that I became aware that my Somali associate was gone from beneath me and that I was bleeding from my right hand. It later transpired that the bad guys were probably intending to take an International hostage to give themselves bargaining power with a rapidly disappearing UN. When they saw that I was wounded, and probably thought it was worse than a slight hand wound, they took the man underneath me, assuming he was an International, as he was considerably lighter-skinned than the average Somali. I think this bears out, as a few minutes down the road, they apparently discovered their mistake and unceremoniously threw him off the pick-up. He showed up a little later, relatively unharmed except for a very bad case of nerves.

After contacting UNOSOM Security via radio, we decided to make our way on foot back to the Compound, where we had an infirmary. Our non-injured loaded the serious casualties in the guard pick-up and sped away to the Somali hospital. We left our van, every window shot out, and quickly returned to the Compound. I though that it was a little ironic that in six months I had not walked on a public street in Mogadishu because it was considered too dangerous, and here I was, front and centre on Airport Road.

At the Compound infirmary, I received quick attention and very shortly, UNOSOM Security forces showed up to escort me back inside the Airport. As we prepared to leave, our van was being towed in. I was quite upset to find that my Toronto Maple Leaf hat was no longer on the van floor. I think at the time I was more peeved over that than anything else.

Within a few minutes, I was inside the Airport and being attended to by the Pakistani Contingent field hospital. Two hours later, I was on a flight to Nairobi, and by six o'clock that evening I was quite comfortably ensconced in the Aga Khan Hospital. Carol arrived in Nairobi shortly after, having been intercepted in Frankfurt to ensure she was aware of the incident, as it was apparently on European TV. A specialist performed a procedure on the hand the next day.

The good part of all this is that we did get to spend a few days watching lions on the plains before it was decided that I should return to Canada for any further treatment. After three months of physiotherapy in Kingston, the hand was pronounced as good as it would ever get, which is pretty good. At the same time UNDP informed me that it was policy not to return employees to an area where they had been involved in an accident of this type. As there was nowhere else to send me, I am essentially between contracts, and await their call.

It did seem odd that on the very day of the incident, 22 February, I marked 32 years completed military service and was two days short of finishing my retirement leave. 32 years, and never anything worse than a few good bruises; how odd.

The final count? I was never able to find out if any of the bad guys were shot. My driver, whom I was situated directly behind, died of his wounds at the scene. A guard in one of the other vehicles was also killed. My real guard was seriously wounded, as was another guard. There certainly were bullets enough to go around for everybody. As for me, the hand is fine except for the occasional sharp twinge or ache when the weather changes. Just as a gentle reminder of what could have been had there not been a very active Guardian Angel looking over me. William "Bill" J. Lindsay.[15]

## 1995, Air Transport Group, Versatile and Ready Extracts from an article by Capt Peter J. Scales

Air Transport Group (ATG) is currently involved in the Balkans, Rwanda, India/Pakistan, CFS Alert, Haiti, Russia and 40 other countries. ATG is headquartered at 8 Wing Trenton, and operates strategic and tactical missions worldwide. It also conducts search and rescue flights from 30W to 141W and from Pelee Island to the top Of Ellesmere Island. There are nine Int Branch personnel and one Admin Clerk directly supporting the day-to-day operations of ATG.

From the offices overlooking the scenic Bay of Quinte, ATG HQ Int provides Global Monitoring services to the commander and his staff. Cpl J.G. Sylvain Lefebvre maintains an all-source collation system based largely on 150

15. Bill Lindsay left Canada on 1 Dec 1995 for a tour in Georgia as a UN Security Officer. He and his wife later retired to a new home in Nova Scotia. Sinister Sam's Notebook, Edition 2, December 1995, pp. 6-10.

country files, while Sgt George Gillingham produces summaries on countries of direct interest to ATG, does all of our Internet research and makes all of the slides for the duty briefers. PO1 Jeff A. Collings is the primary Global Monitor who researches every stop On every ATG overseas flight, and produces a paper briefing for the crew.

Sgt Gillingham is in Ancona, Italy, where he works in the Joint Air Ops Cell (JAOC) with American, German, British and French Intelligence people in support of AIRBRIDGE, the UN humanitarian airlift into Sarajevo. Long workdays in theatre are spent producing current threat briefings as well as in-depth aircrew briefings and debriefings, and keeping up with the rapidly changing Balkan situation.

MWO Ivo J.M. Schoots is the unit POC for all Joint issues and exercises, and for all training issues. He has been seconded to CFSIS for a few months, writing various course documents. Capt Peter J. Scales runs projects as diverse as Intervention Force (IFOR) planning, re-engineering (OP TRANSPORT GENESIS), support to Ancona, and special briefings. MCpl Sharon Cain, a Class B (annotated A) Admin Clerk, does all of the mail and works as the SMP Clerk.

Maj Robin Bradley heads the section, coordinates all intelligence and support and develops intelligence plans and policy for ATG. Across Hwy 2 from ATG HQ is the cramped office of 8 Wing Int. Capt Marla Dow, Sgt Mark Frigge and MCpl Vaughn C. Simpson provide support to five Trenton squadrons, including ten tactical airlift exercises (TALEXs) per year, briefings to the Wing Commander (WComd) and to the Tactical Airlift School. MCpl Simpson, a linguist, is on the Canadian team for the Arctic Search and Rescue Exercise (SAREX) series. Arctic SAREX involves Russia, the USAF and Canada, and exercises our ability to respond to major air disasters in the Arctic.

Each of the five squadrons in Trenton has a secondary duty Int Officer, usually a pilot or navigator. Ideally, they will have attended the Unit Air Int Officer (UAIO) Course at CFSIS before taking on the secondary duty, but none of the five UAIOs has this training.

In Winnipeg, 435 Sqn does not have an Int staff, and it therefore relies on Trenton Int personnel for briefings before their long-range training flights. When 435 Sqn aircraft are carrying out air-to-air refuelling, Fighter Group (FG) Int personnel support them. In Greenwood, 413 Sqn relies on the local Int personnel for extraordinary support.

There has been a great shift in the importance of Int in ATG during the past five years. Although ATG aircraft and crews have operated in hostile theatres ever since 1950, it is only since 1990 that ATG has been relying on Int as an integral part of all operations and plans. In the Balkans, Rwanda and other hot spots, Int pers are there, doing the job to make the mission safe and effective.

"Versatile and Ready" is the motto of Air Transport Group. The same may be said for the Int Branch personnel of ATG.[16]

## 1995, LFAA G2 and 3 Int Coy

The Int staff at LFAA HQ (Fall 1995), include the G2, Maj Ross L. Johnson; the G2 Ops, Capt Robert J. McCutcheon; the G2 Ops WO, PO1 Don B. Powers; Int Ops Sgt Wes E.B. Young, MCpl Andrew J. MacFayden, Cpl Alan R. Farquhar and Cpl Lindsay C. Young, and Sgt Frank J. Davis doing double duty as the G2 Chief Clerk and the Coy Clerk.

The Int staff provided support for the Halifax Summit (G7 Conference) and to Roto II of OP LANCE (Rwanda). The LFAA contribution to OP LANCE Info Ops Section included Maj Ross L. Johnson, as well as WO R. Hal Pugh and MCpl Alan W. Wilson from 3 Int Coy. The team provided graphic accounts by phone of the horrific activities ongoing in Rwanda during the appalling genocide that had taken place there. Capt Clark P. Cornect and WO J.J.P. Mike Fournier round out the regular forces members of 3 Int Coy.

3 Int Coy moved from the old Maritime Command HQ buildings which pre-dated WWI into new quarters situated in Royal Artillery Park. Even though this old brick building possibly predated the founding of Halifax (not really) it is in much better condition than the old one on Ahearn Avenue. The Coy is to formally stand up on 4 November 1995.[17]

## 1995, CISA Member News

Maj Franz F. Laizner informed CISA that the Chief Justice of Canada, the Right Honourable Antonio Lamer, had been a Lt in 1 Int Trg Coy in Montreal. Capt Gerald "Gerry" A. Mendel visited Holland with his wife to attend the 50th Anniversary of the Liberation, and marched in the parade in Apel-

16. Sinister Sam's Notebook, Edition 2, December 1995, pp. 10-11.
17. Sinister Sam's Notebook, Edition 2, December 1995, p. 16.

doorn. He wrote, "It was an unforgettable experience! What hospitality, what enthusiasm, what organization on the part of the Dutch!"

Capt Phillip A. Dawes reports he "was commissioned Capt and appointed Commander of the Winnipeg Det, Land Forces Western Area Int Coy in May 1994. I enrolled as a Pte Int OP In the Winnipeg Int Section in Oct 1976, and went from Pte to MWO in the Winnipeg Int Det, then became CWO (RSM) at 17 Svc Bn."

On 12 Nov 1995, Maj Russ E. Knox, a former Int Corps officer and staff officer at the CSMI at CFB Borden was killed in a 2-car collision in Ottawa. Col Jeff S. Upton, Col Robert T. Grogan, LCol William "Bill" Tenhaaf, and Maj John "Pappy" MacKinnon attended his funeral.

## 1995, CISA AGM

The CISA AGM was held in the RCAF Officer's Mess, Ottawa, 31 Aug to 2 Sep 1995. Those in attendance included: Maj Terry B. Kelly (President), Col Victor V. Ashdown (Int Branch Advisor), LCol Emile Berger, Maj Robert C. Dale (Director), Col Ron J. Donovan (Director), LCol Jack S. Dunn (Director), Capt Don M. Fowler, Capt Mike Gelinas, Col Robert T. Grogan (Membership Secretary), Maj Doris E. Guyatt (1st VP), Maj David A. Haas (Treasurer), Maj Gary W. Handson, Lt E. Bruce Holmes (Director), SLdr Richard "Dick" J. Jordan, Maj Brian Kent, LCol Alf J. Laidler, Maj Franz F. Laizner (Director), Capt Stéphane Lefebvre, LCol Frank Leigh, Maj Nils E. Lindberg (Director), LCol John B. Long, Maj John "Pappy" MacKinnon (Secretary), Capt Robert A. McColgan, Col Peter MacLaren (Security Branch Advisor), Maj Howard Mansfield, Maj John H. Newman, LCol Ian A. Nicol (Past President), Capt Peter T. Patton, Lt Paul R. Perchaluk (Director), Capt Paul G. Rivard (Director), Col A.H. Sam Stevenson (Director), LCol William "Bill" Tenhaaf, Lt (N) Richard Taylor, Capt James P.K. Van Wynen, MGen Reg Weeks (Col Comdt Int Branch), BGen Douglas Yuill (Col Comdt Security Branch) and LCol Tony Battista (Comdt, CFSIS.[18]

The CISA AGM held in the RCAF Officer's Mess in Ottawa was the first held in the National Capital, and the first away from a Canadian Forces Base. A minute's silence was observed for Hon Col George B. MacGillivray, Maj

18. CISA Newsletter, Vol. 25, No. 3, December 1995, p. 5.

Ian N. Fleming and Capt Noel George Ashby who had passed away since the last meeting.

The SSO Int LFHQ reported presentation of the Sir William S. Stephenson Trophy was awaiting completion of establishment of the new Int Coys, now that the terms of reference for the competition were in the course of finalization. LCol Vic Coroy, the Executive Director of the Conference of Defence Associations spoke on the major role CDA had to provide support to DND. He noted that the "peace alliance" continued to be very vociferous in its push to cut defence expenditure in favour of social programs. A result of this pressure was the reduction in the grant to CDA, which led to a corresponding reduction to CDA's allocation to member associations including CISA.

LCol Greg W. Jensen, SSO Int LFHQ, spoke on the Canadian Army Intelligence Support Concept, which was approved in 1994. He pointed out that over half of Int personnel are in the Army, and by 1997, 60% of Int personnel will be reservist, as part of the Total Force Concept. Militia Int consists of four Reserve Int Coys, with 3 Int Coy in Halifax, 4e Cie de Rens in Montreal, 2 Int Coy in Toronto, and 6 Int Coy in Edmonton and 2 Int Pl (Reserve) in Ottawa. LCol Greg W. Jensen reported that the amount and quality of Int training at CFSIS for the Militia is under study, as is the preparation of Int personnel for roles that they are to carry out under combat conditions, which Military Police are doing in peacetime.

The CISA Academic Award for 1995 will go to Michael David Spilling, a BA/Social Sciences student at the University of Calgary; son of Maj David Spilling of Security Branch. The Academic Award for a serving member of the reserves was also made to Cpl Greg Hill, an Int OP In 2 Int Pl. Ottawa, and a BA History student at the University of Ottawa.

Col Victor V. Ashdown, Int Branch Advisor, DDI, gave an interesting Int briefing on the situation in Russia, the Former Yugoslav Republic, and the rest of the world, and explained the DG Int Order of Battle. He is moving from DDI to a planning position, but will remain as Int Branch Advisor.

Reports were presented by Regional Directors, Maj Robert C. Dale for Atlantic Canada; Maj Franz F. Laizner and Lt E. Bruce Holmes for Quebec; Col R.J. Donovan for the National Capital region, assisted by Capt J.P. Stéphane Lefebvre; Lt Paul R. Perchaluk for the rest of Ontario; Maj Nils E. Lindberg assisted by Capt Paul G. Rivard (on behalf of LCol Dale M. Watts) for the Prairies; and Col A.H. Sam Stevenson for BC. LCol Ian A. Nicol, the Director of Policy, made a number of suggestions for increasing the effectiveness of CISA.[19]

## *1996, CISA Member News*

Plans have been made for the first presentation of the Sir William S. Stephenson Trophy at the CISA AGM, CFB Borden, September 1996. Dedication of a new CFSIS building will also take place.

LCol David M. Robb retired after 35 years with the Artillery and Int Branches. LCol Ernest Skutezky, LCol Jean Laporte and Capt Richard Waremere are mentioned. reports that he is still involved with Canadian Executive Service Overseas, most recently working in the Ukraine.

Col the Hon John R. Matheson was part of the Canadian delegation of the Institute of Strategic Studies sessions in Nov and Dec 1995 in Brussels, where there were briefings on the European Union and at the Maastricht Institute at Geilenkirchen. BGen Jim Hansen escorted them. Jim took them to a number of military bases and provided a series of excellent lectures on modern European history.

Maj Reginald R. Dixon and Capt Don M. Fowler are travelling to England for a presentation and unveiling of a commemorative plaque to the Stormont, Dundas and Glengarry (SD&G) Regiment. Reg was the D-Day IO for the SD&G, and then became the 9th Bde IO, then IO of 3 Cdn (Assault) Div. Following WWII, Reg remained in Military Int, and has worn "several hats" in the 1st Bn SD&G Highlanders Association, including its honorary chairman and editor of the Associations" publications.

Maj George D. LaNauze, Maj Ward I. Binkley and Capt Doug R. Bennett passed away since the last report.

Col John Matheson and Maj Stanley H. Winfield attended the elections in Bosnia-Herzegovina in early Sep 96 as official UN Observers.

LCol D.H. Neil Thompson reports that 1996 is the 20th anniversary of the National Defence Intelligence Centre (NDIC), and that he is preparing a brief historical summary of the NDICs operations.[20]

---

19.  CISA Newsletter, Vol. 25, No.3, December 1995, pp. 1-6.
20.  CISA Newsletter, Vol. 26, No.1, May 1996, pp. 1-5.

# 14

# 1996, Intelligence Branch

## 1996, Retirement of MGen Weeks, Colonel Commandant

It is with much regret that MGen Weeks relinquished his appointment as Colonel Commandant of the Intelligence Branch, effective 3 May 1996. MGen Reginald J.G. Weeks has served as the Colonel Commandant since 1 Oct 1985. Throughout his long tenure, he most capably represented the Intelligence Branch at the highest levels. Because of his dedication and effort, he has become widely respected throughout the Branch, most notably for his sympathetic ear and sound counsel. He will be sorely missed by all.[1]

## 1996, Farewell from the Branch Advisor, Col Victor V. Ashdown

The following comments mark a "double farewell.' I handed the Branch Advisor reins to Col Patrick D.R. Crandell on 1 Apr 96, and I plan to start retirement Leave on 21 May.

I find that reminiscing becomes a natural pastime at this stage of my career and that 'numbers' seem to dominate my memories, numbers such as: 35 years' service; 10 years in the rank of Col; 33 years in the Canadian Intelligence Corps, Security Branch and Intelligence Branch; 13 years total at NDHQ; nine years as Branch Advisor; and best of all, 70% pension! The latter number

---

1. Sinister Sam's Notebook, Edition 1, May 1996, p. 1.

explains why I have decided to try more leisurely pursuits. After all, I've spent over 2/3 (numbers again!) of my life in the service of Canada and the Forces. It seems to me that it's time for a break. Also, the difference between pay and pension, after taxes and work expenses, is a surprisingly small amount.

Reminiscing also makes you ask yourself if you've learned anything over the past three-plus decades and what 'gems of wisdom' (if any) you might wish to bequeath to the next generation. My answer to these questions is simple. At the end of the day, when you pull your finger out of the glass of water and observe the fleeting consequences, the only aspect that endures is your personal relationships with the people that matter—your colleagues, your family, your relatives, your friends, your neighbours, and, above all, yourself. When you're talking about people who have retired, what do you remember most about them—what they did, or what they were like? Exactly! Who cares to remember the ones who reached the higher ranks on the backs of their colleagues? No one!

Unfortunately, sometimes we are forced to remember such individuals. There have been public accusations of "careerism" in today's CF. There is some truth in those accusations, and not only in the more senior ranks. When I joined the Canadian Army, I learned that the senior officer present took responsibility (especially when things went wrong!) and that when things went well, the soldiers received the credit. Does that concept sound foreign to you? It shouldn't, but I expect it does at a time when 'managers' have become 'micro-managers,' afraid to allow their subordinates the freedom to grow by making mistakes, and when so-called leaders insist on having the best people, not for the good of the organization or the well-being of their subordinates, but to make themselves look good. It is easy to win the tournament if your team is all super-stars—the true coach (leader) is the one who wins by motivating players to play like a super-star team!

The solution is relationships—be fair to your co-workers, trust your subordinates, balance your time between your work relationships and those involving family, friends and neighbours, be completely honest with everyone—especially yourself—and never use your rank or position for personal gain. Follow these principles and try to convince (by example) your fellow members to do the same, and the word 'careerism' will never again be used in the same breath as 'Canadian Forces.' Furthermore, you will be admired and respected, even by people you hardly know, the person you live with will still be your best friend and lover, not a stranger, and you will always be able to look in the mirror and like what you see. Remember, 'success' is fleeting at best—it means nothing if there is no one to share it with you. I must add a caution—building positive relationships demands honest effort and constant attention. However, the rewards last forever.

You can learn a lot in 35 years (if you pay attention) and there are may other 'gems' I could pass on. However, relationships dominate all else—if you establish those, everything will fall into place. I'm sure most of us know this, deep down, but it becomes particularly apparent when you finally select a retirement date. At that point in life, you realize that many of the relationships that you have established and nurtured over many years can no longer be fully sustained. That is my only regret as I approach the end of my military service.

I have had the immense good fortune to have served with some of the finest people in the Forces—in fact, there have been days when I wondered whether the Forces realized the importance of the vital contribution being made by our little band of Intelligence professionals. As your Branch Advisor, I found that the Intelligence Team had few 'average' players and a disproportionate share of super-stars. The remarkable performance of the Branch over the past 13-plus years resulted from the dedication and excellent performance of each of you. For that you have my eternal gratitude—I feel honoured and privileged to have had the opportunity to serve as your leader. Your support and loyalty made my job easy.

To each of you, I wish success, long life, happiness, a little prosperity, and the continuing joy of meaningful relationships. E Tenebris Lux. Col Victor V. Ashdown, Branch Number 21.[2]

## 1996, Remarks from the Branch CWO, CWO J. Ron Martin

I would like to begin by expressing how proud I am of having been asked to serve as your Branch CWO. I am committed to serve with all my energy and experience to provide support and assistance to all members of the branch. I would also like to express my appreciation to our former Branch CWO, Rick J. Tervo. Again, Rick, thank your for the dedication and hard work during your tenure in these rapidly changing times—I wish you and your family the best in all future endeavours.

I have, over the last year, had the privilege of visiting all the Command HQs as well as all the Army Intelligence Regular and Total Force Units. After

---

2.　Sinister Sam's Notebook, Edition 1, May 1996, pp. 1-2.

meeting with many Int OP NCOs and their leaders, I am impressed with the total commitment and professionalism that the men and women of our Branch demonstrate at all times. Although our Int Ops face challenges that are increasingly complex, they nonetheless 'charge on' in the finest tradition of the Intelligence branch and our predecessors, the Canadian Intelligence Corps.

I also had the pleasure of attending the graduation ceremonies of the TQ5 Int OP Course—the first in almost six years. I cannot overstate how proud I was to meet and talk with these new Int Ops. The candlelight dinner and graduation parade, organized by the Intelligence Company of CFSIS was nothing short of sensational!

Bravo Zulu to the graduates, the staff of the school, as well as the various incremental staffs from all Commands in accepting the challenge and successfully bringing to term a newly overhauled course. Our most hearty welcome to all new Intelligence Operators. As 'information warriors' they are a welcome addition as we enter the 'information age,' with new war fighting concepts such as 'information warfare.'

As the new Branch CWO, my greatest concern right now is our junior personnel. During these times of a high operational tempo, personnel and fiscal constraints as well as the troubling situations which we read and hear about on a daily basis, it is imperative that we keep our focus on the task at hand. It is critical for officers and we, the Senior Non Commissioned Officers, to accept our responsibilities and exercise the principles of leadership which is the basis of our being. It is so easy for one to be absorbed by the mission and forget the well-being of the soldier, as well as ensuring he or she possesses all the right tools to perform his or her duties. There is an old motto that describes how I believe leadership works and that is: "Take care of the soldiers, and the soldiers will take care of you." E Tenebris Lux.[3]

## 1996, Intelligence Personnel News

The following Int Branch personnel have been promoted in 1996 to the rank indicated:

Col R. Geoff St John, DIE; LCol Jean E.T. Bigras, CFCSC Toronto; Maj Robert J. McCutcheon, LFAA Halifax; Maj J.A.E. Kent Dowell, DG Int/NDIC; CWO Rolf F. Overhoff, DG Int/J2 Plans, Ottawa; WO J.M.A.

---

3.    Sinister Sam's Notebook, Edition 1, May 1996, p. 3.

Stéphane Chartrand, CFA Warsaw; WO G.R.A. Gauthier, CFA Beijing; WO J. Patrick D. Knopp, DG Int/DIE Ottawa; WO Manuel A. Thibault, Haiti; Sgt Daniel Joseph Garant, 3 Wing Bagotville; Sgt Tom J. Last, DG Int/DIE Ottawa; and, MCpl W. Paul Wehmeier, 1 Cdn Div HQ Kingston.

Graduates of the TQ5 9601 course have been assigned to the following locations:

Cpl Ronald K. Bell, 1 Bde HQ, Calgary; Cpl W.T. Bill, LFWA 6 Int Coy, Edmonton; Cpl Chris K. Buczynski, 2 EW Sqn, Kingston; LS R.J.F. Daigle, MARLANT HQ, Halifax; Cpl Paul E. Gagnier, CFEWC (EWOSC), Ottawa; Cpl J.A.M. Eric Gagnon, 5e Bde HQ, Valcartier; Cpl D.T. Gauthier, 1 Cdn Div Int Coy, Kingston; Cpl R. Steven M. Gingras, DG Int/DDI, Ottawa; Cpl Al J. MacDonald, 2 Bde HQ, Petawawa; Cpl Donald W. Rowe, DG Int/DIE, Ottawa; Cpl Dale G. Sonstenes, 1 Cdn Div Int Coy, Kingston; Cpl J. Paul St Laurent, 3 Wing, Bagotville; Cpl Kurt A. Trebels, DG Int/DIE; Cpl Angela L. Unger, LFC HQ, Montreal; and, Cpl Roy Vandenberg, 2 EW Sqn, Kingston.

The following personnel will take their release in 1996:

Maj Len E.N. Goski, DG Int.DDI-6; Lt (N) Andy Nafekh, DG Int; CWO Jean G. Charette, CFB Moose Jaw; and, Sgt Joseph Jean Pierre Paquette, DG Int/NDIC.[4]

## 1995-1996, CFSIS News
### Article by Maj Robert G. Nash, OC Int Trg Coy

On 13 Oct 1995, 12 of 14 CFSIS Int personnel were re-concentrated to create the Intelligence Training Company under the command of Maj Robert G. Nash. Capt Pierre Michaud and MCpl G. Bruce Scott remain employed in key support functions within the HQ Company. This was just one of many changes made to the CFSIS organization by the new Commandant, LCol Tony Battista, to posture the Unit for the future.

The driving force behind this change was the incredible effort required to renew Int training to meet the requirements of the Int Branch and the Commands. During 1995, LFC rewrote all Militia Training Standards (TS), from QL3 to ACT; the Regular Force Int OP QL5A TS and Training Plan (TP) were rewritten; a new Unit Air Int Course (UAIC) TP was written; the Int Officer Integrated Occupation Specification (IOS) was finalized; and a new

---

4.  Sinister Sam's Notebook, Edition 1, May 1996, pp. 3-4.

Basic Intelligence Officer Qualification Standard (QS) was written. A proposed Advance Intelligence Officer QS is currently being circulated for comment—approval is anticipated in early 1996. While all this was happening, we managed to graduate the following courses: BIOC, PRes BCT, RegF QL6B, Pres QL6B Pt 1, and Adv Cbt Int. It has been a very busy year! Throughout, incremental support was provided by all Commands to augment the CFSIS Int training and Standards staffs.

The first, new and improved RegF Int OP QL5A course will run from 8 Jan to 4 Apr 96. With the assistance of MWO Ivo J.M. Schoots, CPO2 Brian M. Noble, and most of the LFCA and LFWA Int communities, Capt Derek Marchbank, WO Richard C. Gow and the rest of the Int Trg Coy staff have, in less than four months, put together a very promising course. During the same time, under the guidance of MWO Herb H.W. Kuchler and WO Rick Oliver, Sgt Rick F. Luden, MCpl Charles T. Scott and Cpl Raymond M. Kruger started the work necessary to revitalize the Collation Section so that they can effectively support our training requirements. Also, with the assistance of Capt Chuck Moor, WO Vance Gordon, and Sgt J.B. François Allard, WO Cyril P. Aucoin ran a very successful Adv Cbt Int course—with the assistance from LFC he will run another starting in Jan 96. Sgt Glenn McGuire was on the O2 curse in England from Jul to Nov and missed most of the fun, but his new skills will be put to good use during the QL5A course. Unfortunately, despite the best efforts of both CFSIS and ATG Int staffs, we ran out of time and people to finish the preparations for and run the UAIC scheduled for the Fall.

During the Fall of 95, the Int Standards staff, Lt (N) Doug C. Jantzi, WO Mario Ross and Sgt Greg S. Smith, was very busy with the Int Officer QS, the QL5A and UAIOC TPs and course preparation, and providing Standards support to Cyril's Adv Cbt Int course. It will only get busier in 1996. Between Jan and May we will be convening TP Writing Boards for the BIOC, the Pres QL6A and QL6B, and, once approved, the new Advance Int Officer Course (AIOC); converting the RegF QL5A and Pres QL3 and QL4 into an integrated QS; and supporting the QL5A, QL6B and Adv Cbt Int course. In the Fall, we will combine the Pres QL6A and QL6B TS with their RegF equivalents to create integrated QS. Throughout 96 the Int Standards staff will be extensively involved in preparations for both the BIOC and AIOC currently scheduled to start in Jan and Mar 97 respectively.

Our course schedule for 1996 includes: a RegF QL5A and QL6B; Pres QL6A, QL6B, BCT and ACT; a UAIC; an Interrogator course and two Adv

Cbt Int courses. The QL6A and BIOC originally scheduled for the Fall have been rescheduled to the first half of 97 in consultation with the Career managers and the Branch CWO. The requirement for an additional RegF QL5A course has yet to be finalized. The Interrogator course remains in doubt pending the final legal decision regarding the legitimacy of the training requirement and course content. We will probably have to find the time and people to conduct both QS and TP Writing Boards before we run the next course. Finally, the Adv Cbt Int course scheduled for Apr–Jun 96 and the ICT scheduled for the Summer training period have been cancelled in consultation with LFC to ensure adequate resources can be applied to the accomplishment of their priority training objectives. An LFC-led review of both Basic and Adv Cbt Int training will probably lead to additional QS, TP and courseware preparation activity.

In accordance with the wishes of the Branch and Commands for updated training, which is relevant to the world of the 90s, our training plan for 96 is very ambitious. We will not accomplish it without extensive support. Our QS and TP writing boards will require substantial Command representation to ensure all Int Branch and Command requirements are satisfied. At the Int training Steering Committee meeting on 14 Dec 95, the Command Seniors committed themselves to providing the support they can, in these incredibly busy times, to facilitate Int training during 1996.[5]

---

5.   Sinister Sam's Notebook, Edition 1, May 1996, pp. 4-5.

# 1996, Intelligence Branch

## 1996, West Coast Report
## *Extracts from an article by PO2 Richard A. Fisher*

PO2 Richard A. Fisher reported from Maritime Forces Pacific Headquarters Intelligence Section in Victoria BC. The section is commanded by LCdr Ted Parkinson, and includes Lt (N) Ivan Allain, PO2 Richard A. Fisher, and MS Cliff J. Boyechko. Also under the Intelligence umbrella are EWAT and CDSE.

The Section was very busy over the past year with WESTPLOY 95 (a three-month deployment to Australia and the Far East); UNITAS (another three-month deployment, this time to Central and South America); OP TRANQUILLITY (HMCS Calgary's six-month around the world deployment to the Arabian Gulf and the Adriatic); and MARCOT 2/95 (one-month exercise with the US, Chile, and Australia). In addition, the section completed full country studies, threat assessments, and recce packages for each port that is to be visited, and then monitored the ship's progress continuously throughout their deployment, while keeping up with the day-t-day staff job of briefing the Admiral and his staff, collation and ADP.

For 1996, a major renovation has begun on the section building, in a reconstruction project called NEPTUNE, which will give the section an enhanced Intelligence capability (BALESHARE System) as well as a limited capability for 24/7 operations. It is also expected that another ten Int Ops and six 291'ers will be added to the establishment. BALESHARE/ADNATE/JDISS/ JMCIS systems (too many acronyms to define here) are being added. At the end of February, the Section will be hosting delegates from Australia, Canada, the USA and the UK at the ASPACMIC (Asia-Pacific Maritime Intelligence Conference). Shortly afterwards, another WESTPLOY and RIMPAC will be conducted. MARPAC is expected to reorganize and adopt the "J" system, once it is approved by MARCOM.

Members of the Section have produced deployment packages for HMC Ships on CD-ROM, which saves on paper and bulk packaging. Much of the information is also being passed via the Internet, (including a brief country study on Thailand, for example), to the Admiral while he was on TD. Cheers from the Rainy West Coast.[6]

## 1996, LFWA HQ report
### Extracts from an article by WO F.V. Gordon

Many changes have taken place in LFWA, with Maj Gord P. Ohlke as the OC, Capt Brian E. Hamilton G2 Ops and WO F.V. Gordon as the Int WO. Capt Charles B. Buffone, a reserve Int Officer on Class B has gone to a civilian job as a computer analyst but intends to stay in touch with 6 Int Coy. The remaining Reserve staff includes Sgt Steve J. Goronzy, Sgt D. Bruce Warawa, Cpl Derrick D. Petrushko and Capt Wallstern. Cpl Nancy Beauchemin (Mah) has been in Yugoslavia for a three-month tour and is now back in 6 Int Coy.

LFWA Int Coy officially became 6 Int Coy at the end of October 1995. This event was celebrated with a parade, a mixed dining-in and other activities. The company's Regular Force staff consists of Capt D.D. Nickel, WO Robert W. Moug, WO Dan J. Haslip and PO1 J.R. Michel "Mike" Labossiere. WO Haslip is the IO of the Winnipeg Detachment, and PO1 Labossiere holds the position in Vancouver. The Coy HQ in Edmonton also has a Met WO and Sgt Clerk.

The Brigade Int Section has been undergoing a great number of personnel changes, with a Capt, WO Donald M. Gallaher, Sgt Charles T. Scott, PO2 Veronica Marie Parolin, PO2 Brian A. Trager, MCpl Byron K. Mackenzie and a few others TBC. WO F.V. Gordon is off to CFSIS Int Trg Coy in Borden as incremental staff on a second Combat Int course, this time for two officers and six NCOs, following one run in Oct-Nov 95 for the officers.[7]

## 1995, Intelligence and the UN Lessons from CANBAT 2 in Bosnia-Herzegovina
### Article by Capt J. Daniel Villeneuve & Sgt Marc-André Lefebvre

The use of Intelligence in peacekeeping operations has always been a sensitive prospect. Peacekeeping operations are defined as military operations conducted for the purpose of maintaining and restoring peace other than by the application of force, which is only to be used under extreme circumstances. On

---

6.  Sinister Sam's Notebook, Edition 1, May 1996, p. 6.
7.  Sinister Sam's Notebook, Edition 1, May 1996, pp. 6-7.

the face of it, contingents participating in a UN mission are neutral and have no enemy. Therefore, there should be no need for Intelligence in such an operation. The reality on the ground, however, is quite different, as recent experiences in the Former Yugoslav Republic have demonstrated. A UN mission remains a military operation, and as with any military operation, there is a requirement for Intelligence support.

This article summarizes some of the particularities I encountered with respect to the employment of Intelligence in a UN operation. I served as the Intelligence officer for the 3ième Bataillon, Royal 22ième Régiment (a French-speaking Canadian infantry battalion), which was deployed in Bosnia-Herzegovina from 30 April to 30 October 1995.

Background. My battalion formed the lion's share of the battle group known as CANBAT 2 (Canadian Battalion 2, CANBAT 1 being located in Croatia), and was deployed at Visoko, 30 km North West of Sarajevo, in central Bosnia-Herzegovina. The Unit, with some 825 members of all ranks, had an area of responsibility (AOR) of approximately 900 square kilometres.

In the AOR, the Unit found itself dealing with all three factions, with observation posts (OP) deployed on the Bosnia-Herzegovina Serb side of the confrontation line (the only UN Unit in Bosnia-Herzegovina doing so). Part of the 20 km total exclusion zone (TEZ) surrounding Sarajevo was inside the AOR, and the area was located along some of the main north-south communication routes of central Bosnia-Herzegovina.

The mission of the Unit was:

a.  To maintain the freedom of movement required for the delivery of humanitarian aid;

b.  To help preserve the Bosnia-Herzegovina Muslim-Croat federation (an agreement between the Bosnia-Herzegovina Croats and the Bosnia-Herzegovina Muslims); and,

c.  To freeze the confrontation line between Bosnia-Herzegovina Serb and Federation forces.

To accomplish its mission, CANBAT 2 manned a series of Ops on both sides of the confrontation line, as well as a series of checkpoints along the main lines of communication. The Unit also patrolled throughout the AOR, maintaining liaison with all three factions.

A basic concept I observed in peacekeeping operations is that the longer the warring factions do not fight each other, the more opportunities they have to talk. The more numerous these opportunities, the more likely a compromise solution becomes. The UN forces are there to help the factions maintain the cease-fire and to prevent or resolve disagreements. If this concept is to succeed, there is a need for the warring factions to cooperate, both between each other and with the UN.

CANBAT 2 started its tour employed in a typical peacekeeping role. Less than a month after their arrival in theatre, however, the situation stated to deteriorate. The warring factions were not yet ready to negotiate, still considering the military option to be a better solution to their problems. The first crisis the Unit was involved in was the Bosnia-Herzegovina-Serb hostage taking of UN personnel following NATO air strikes at the end of May. CANBAT 2 had 53 members taken hostage; the last of these were not safely released until 17 June. No sooner had the hostage crisis ended than the Unit found itself in the middle of a major Bosnia-Herzegovina Muslim-Croat Federation offensive to open Sarajevo. This offensive, which started on 15 June, lasted approximately one month. Although the offensive was a failure, it did cause CANBAT 2 to lose its freedom of movement for approximately 10 days, followed by a slow return to normal by the beginning of August. While the AOR was quiet during the last three months, the UN/NATO air strike campaign against the Bosnia-Herzegovina Serbs in September kept the Unit on its guard, with the potential for renewal of hostilities always present. The air offensive resulted in a cease-fire at the beginning of October, with the Dayton Peace Accord following by the end of the month.

Intelligence Becomes Military Information. As I discovered in Bosnia-Herzegovina, the UN tacitly acknowledges that there is an operational requirement for Intelligence support of a military Unit deployed on a mission. To reduce the negative impact attached to the word "Intelligence," however, the term "military information" is used instead. My title in Bosnia-Herzegovina, for example, was Military Information Officer (MIO); Intelligence summaries (INTSUMs) became military information summaries (MILINFOSUMs), etc. Warring factions 'or belligerents' replaced the term 'enemy'. Despite these cosmetic changes, the Intelligence process remains unchanged. The UN does require, however, that the collection be done with more discretion, and that only overt means be used.

Role of CANBAT 2 military Information Cell. As with any tactical military operation, the role of the Intelligence function in a UN context is to advise the commander on how the warring factions, the ground and the weather could affect the accomplishment of the mission.

During the training phase prior to deployment, the basic concept the battle-group developed for the employment of Intelligence to support its mission saw the section given the task of establishing what was the normal state of affairs, if any, in the AOR. The idea was to determine a baseline for the area in terms of warring faction's deployment, movements, firing incidents and so on. Once established, all events could then be compared to this baseline to determine if there was a threat to the cease-fire or not. The rationale behind this was to have as much warning as possible of impending events in order to be pro-active instead of reactive. This concept was based on the static nature of the operations both in terms of the non-changing AOR and the reduced level of military action expected when the concept was being developed. As previously mentioned, the rapid and active evolution of military events during the tour prevented the full application of this concept.

The main tasks of the section were as detailed below:

*Indicators and warning.* The first task was to predict potential crisis situations inside the AOR before they occurred. We sought to give as much time as possible to the battle group to diffuse situations before they led to incidents. It is always easier to prevent then to patch up afterward.

*Situation development.* The Intelligence section was tasked to follow the evolution of events both tactically inside and around the AOR and strategically/politically throughout the Balkans, with the aim of keeping the Unit informed of the evolution of events. Once again the aim was to put the events occurring inside the AOR in context.

Threat assessment. The situation throughout the AOR was continually monitored to determine the level of threat against the UN and to immediately inform the Unit of any changes. The threat came mainly from modifications in the warring factions' attitudes, the presence of mines or the effects of weather on the road conditions.

*The Intelligence Cycle.* The following are some observations I made with respect to the employment of the Intelligence cycle in a peacekeeping operation. The first thing I would like to mention is that the cycle is very flexible, lending itself easily to adaptation to any situation. At least half a dozen contingency plans were developed during the tour to deal with the different crises which confronted the Unit. In some cases, the level of conflict went from low to almost mid-intensity overnight. Some of the contingency plans were directed against potential actions of particular warring factions, which could have put us in direct confrontation with that faction had it been necessary to execute the plan. Being in a peacekeeping context does not obviate planning for a worst-case scenario. Flexibility is very important.

In the Direction phase of the cycle, the main problem which faced us was the lack of Order of Battle information and tactical templates of the different warring factions in the AOR. This resulted in difficulties with the IPB process. The only way to make up for these shortfalls was to create our own Orders of Battle and tactics for each of the warring factions. This approach took time, however, and a continuous effort was required to keep the information up to date. We learned that all possible efforts should be made to compile as much data as possible while the opportunity is there. When a crisis occurs, it is generally too late.

Another problem that confronted us on many occasions was a limit to reconnaissance possible on the ground due to movement restrictions imposed on the Unit. When this occurred, the manoeuvre Troops turned to the Intelligence section for support. The presence of a Terrain Analysis Team (TERA) with the Unit was a significant help, and went a long way towards making up reconnaissance shortfalls. TERA products were produced to provide answers to specific questions, and to respond to Intelligence requirements with respect to the terrain and the combined effects of terrain and weather on military operations. Periods of movement restriction also demonstrated the priceless value of the Unit database of air photos and route studies. The photos must be of a very large scale in order to show useful detail of ground characteristics. It is recommended that studies of the main communication routes in the AOR as well as the area of potential crisis should be done on air photos prior to deployment.

In the Collection phase of the cycle, the main source of information was limited almost exclusively to HUMINT sources. The numerous contacts that a Unit has with the warring factions on an almost daily basis must be put to good use, as excellent information can be gathered by exploiting this source. The Troops must be taught that information can be gathered from different levels, and sensitised to the role that they can play in building the Intelligence picture. Information could come from the Unit commanding officer meeting one of the warring factions' local commanders, from a liaison officer meeting a belligerent counter-part, from a soldier on an OP Talking with a local soldier performing the same boring guard duty. A good debriefing process must be in place to gather this information.

In addition to the warring factions, numerous other sources and agencies could provide information. I was in regular contact with the flanking military contingents in regard to the action activities in their specific areas. The UN political affairs officer was a good source for the overall political picture and the detailed particulars of the Unit AOR.

During the operation we found that HUMINT sources could be very good; we noted, however, that they also had the potential to offer bad or misleading information. All information received from this type of source must be corroborated by other sources. We received numerous reports that later turned out to be false. I learned, as a result, to be very careful with single source information.

Processing is the phase of the cycle that was the least affected by the situation. Information must be analyzed and put into context to make sense of it, even in a peacekeeping operation. We learned that a good collation system is essential if you hope to avoid being lost in the mass of data received almost daily. Vetting of files on a regular basis is also important. I found a good rule of thumb was that if you were in doubt about keeping something, throw it out.

Analyzing and interpreting what was left became easier, and was very important. It put things into context, and gave them significance. As obvious as this might seem, our section was actually doing something new. Too often, I found that mostly unanalysed data was passed through the UN Intelligence chain, leading to potential misinterpretation of the situation. Dissemination of the information was done using UN report formats. I discovered that sensitive information should not be put on wide distribution, as numerous leaks exist in the UN system and there was a good chance that the information could end up in the hands of the warring factions. This could result in the Unit losing its impartiality in the eyes of one or all of the warring factions. Sensitive information was disseminated on a need-to-know basis, avoiding large distribution channels.

I also tried, as much as possible, to protect the source.

A good way of exchanging information is to develop a good liaison visit program. With face-to-face discussions, the potential for better exchange of information is improved. Another good way that was used was to have conferences on a regular basis with all the parties involved in the information business. With this, information is exchanged, but above all, good contacts are established. In a UN operation, rotation occurs every six months and the turnover of personnel is very large. Basically, you almost end up with a new crew every six months. With these meetings, it gives you the opportunity to know the persons with whom you are dealing.

In conclusion, a peacekeeping mission remains a military operation and Intelligence has an important role to play. During the tour in Bosnia-Herzegovina, the numerous crises the Unit faced provided a constant challenge to the Intelligence section, as we worked to provide the commander with the information he required.[8]

## *1996, IFOR, Bosnia-Herzegovina, The Gates of Madness*
## *Article by Capt Phil R. Berikoff, 2IC CANIC, Sarajevo, Bosnia-Herzegovina*

"Dobar Dan, welcome to the "Gates of Madness" the aircraft pilot should announce as the C-130 Hercules rapidly descends onto the tarmac of the Sarajevo International Airport. Instead, graffiti (poorly painted) proudly adorns a wall of a war-torn building along the road to the city centre—Welcome to Sarajevo.

Nearly four years ago, Sarajevo was being ripped apart by shell and sniper fire from besieging Serbs. The city was dotted with fires burning out of control. Rows of mature trees still graced the parks and cemeteries before they were cut down for firewood. Few imagined four years of fighting lay ahead.

The 4th March of the Bosnia-Herzegovina war finds the country quiet following the signing of the Dayton Peace Accord in Paris on 14 Dec 1995. Shabby, shrapnel-pitted and shorn of most of its trees, Sarajevo now stands awkwardly between war and peace. As you wander through the Lion's Cemetery where many of the city's 10,500 war dead are buried, you finally realize that for the first time since 1992, there may be a possible end to this nightmare.

The scale of rebuilding will be awesome. In many towns throughout the country, about 80% of the dwellings are uninhabitable, their interiors stripped of plumbing and wiring by looters and their wooden frames turned to ashes by arsonists. While streets stand ghostly and silent, lined with the shells of abandoned homes.

---

8.   Sinister Sam's Notebook, Edition 1, 1996, pp. 7-10.

For some refugees returning to their homes has reopened old wounds and rekindled hatreds dampened by distance. It will be difficult to appease the bitterness of hundreds of thousands of ordinary people for whom the war has brought much loss and no gain. The theory is "time will heal and the passion for revenge will fade," with NATO Troops giving the peace process a year's start. Whether its war or peace, the people of Bosnia-Herzegovina will have a lot to explain to their children.

Currently within the Implementation Force (IFOR), there are approximately 52,000 Troops from NATO countries and other participating signatories. Their mandate is to enforce the military aspects of the Dayton Peace Accord. So far, the military aspects are considered to be successful and on schedule. However, the civilian aspect of the accord is causing major concerns. For example, there may be a delay in the up-coming election process and only about one-third of the UN police force is in place. As well, it appears that the Croat-Muslim Federation is not proving to be successful and will probably take longer than a year to be resolved. There

is growing concern throughout the international Community that some type of military force will have to replace IFOR if a long-term peace agreement is to be achieved.

Canada has about 1,000 military personnel in Bosnia-Herzegovina-Herzegovina. 22 are located in Sarajevo. The Canadian National Intelligence Cell (CANIC) Sarajevo was established in Dec 95 by the DCDS. It was initially staffed with two officers, LCdr Dan P. Langlais and Capt Phil R. Berikoff; two WOs, WO Tom C. O'Brien and WO Randy Maltais. As well, the cell has two Sgts, Sgt François Maheux and Sgt Brian Mullin. Since our initial deployment we have bid farewell to WO Tom C. O'Brien and wish him well in Kingston, and welcome WO Jerois Gagné from Bagotville to the cell.

The mission of the CANIC is to provide Intelligence support to NATO/IFOR through the HQ ARRC Main, the Commander Canadian Contingent in-theatre (CCIFOR), and to any national decision-making with regards to the Former Yugoslav Republic.

Like all deployments in the military, CANIC wasn't any different. Capt Phil R. Berikoff who was in-theatre and working as G2 Ops at HQ UNPROFOR Sarajevo, became the advance party and moved from the HQ in the city to establish CANIC's presence within the HQ AARC Main complex at Ilidza, a former Serb suburb of Sarajevo. WO Tom C. O'Brien joined him later in January.

Frustrations and setbacks were too numerous to count. The on-again off-again scenario was played over and over. Finally, the go ahead was given and on 29 Jan 96 the CANIC main body arrived in Zagreb; albeit without vehicles or communications. Eventually the vehicles arrived. On 15 Feb, the CANIC convoy, consisting of an Iltis (Sarajevo Sarah) and two MLVWs with trailers began its infamous 12-hour trip to Sarajevo. Numerous breakdowns and a tour of the country saw the CANIC arrive three days later (a story of its own!). LCdr Dan P. Langlais was not impressed.

It has now been a month since the CANIC became fully operational. Since that time, numerous contacts have been established throughout the NATO/IFOR Intelligence Community and the working relationship with the Yugoslav Crisis Cell at NDHQ has been super. Valuable lessons have been learned on both sides of the ocean. The Post Mission Report at the end of this tour should prove interesting.

With only three months left before CANIC staff rotates, the cell is looking forward to seeing more of the country, taking some well-deserved leave, and to continue supporting the mission as best we can. Until next time, "Dovid-jenja."[9]

## 1996, 4ième Compagnie du Renseignements, acquires a Russian T-72 Tank
### Extracts from an article by Cpl J.J.F. Bruno Asselin

On 2 Feb 1996, a Russian T-72 tank was delivered to the military tank park/museum at Long Pointe, Montreal, outside the offices of 4e Cie de Rens. The Unit felt it needed a full-scale vehicle for identification training, and liaised with DREV at CFB Valcartier to arrange for one that had been used for test and evaluation to be moved to Montreal after its testing phase was complete. Armed with a 125-mm cannon, the T-72 was a replacement for the T-64. It is a welcome addition to the Unit, and represents a major element of the Cold War era on display in Quebec.

There are only a few Russian T-72s on display in Canada, one is in front of the CFB Gagetown Museum, and one other is on display at CFB Borden Museum, alongside a pair of T-62s. The Canadian War Museum has a T-34 in working condition. Other former Warsaw Pact vehicles have been brought

9.   Sinister Sam's Notebook, Edition 1, 1996, pp. 10-11.

to Canada, but destroyed in anti-tank missile tests in accord with of various Arms Verification Control agreements.[10]

## 1996, SQFT Intelligence
## Extracts from an article by Lt Jim Godefroy

On 19-20 March 96, a number of personnel from different Units and organizations with SQFT assembled at the MegaPlex in Saint-Jean, Quebec to participate in the 2nd SQFT Intelligence Conference (the 1st was conducted in 1994) conducted by the G2 Branch of the Land Forces Quebec Area. A variety of interesting topics were covered during the conference, including the situation in Haiti, the Former Yugoslav Republic (FYR), a number of hot-spots in Africa and in the Middle East. The presentations were primarily given Int representatives from NDHQ in Ottawa, assisted by staff from the Int Section at St Hubert. The conference was well-received and it is planned to make it an annual event.[11]

## 1996, Enemy Force for the Combat Team Commander's Course

Late in April 1996, the Tactics School Directing Staff conducted a recce of the Lawfield training area for the Combat Team Commander's Course (CTCC). The students and instructors moved into Petersville on 5 May and got off to an early start at 4 AM, with the two groups of seven enemy force vehicles marked with red tape and red flags moving off in a light snow fall to take up defensive positions "somewhere downrange." The author lucked in with a well-experienced crew working in the command APC, call-sign 52C. Our team defended five positions, and then spent the evening in a cabin at the Lawfield Observation Post (OP). The crew had another 4 AM start the next morning and again set off in two groups of seven enemy force vehicles, each group defending five positions during the day's training.

The same pattern was followed for the next few days, although there were some night positions that had to be defended as well. In some cases, the team slept in their defensive positions, and sometimes it was just too wet, so all crammed into the APC. The fast pace of training continued through 11 May,

---

10. Sinister Sam's Notebook, Edition 1, 1996, pp. 11-12.
11. Sinister Sam's Notebook, Edition 1, 1996, pp. 12-13.

with a full Battle Group assault in heavy thick fog and rain. The enemy force defended three different positions on the way down the corridor, then four separate positions back to the Lawfield OP, then finished it up with a night assault until 5 AM when all returned to Petersville. The final part of the course involved a major assault on Bell Bridge at 0600 on 13 May 96. Quite the experience being on the receiving end of attacks, and seeing a complete combat team do what they do best.

## 1996, CISA Member News

Capt Doug R. Bennett, CD, of Weston, Ontario, passed away on 15 Mar 1996. Doug served in the 48th Highlanders of Toronto before WWII, and when war came, he went overseas with them. He transferred to Intelligence as a Photo Interpreter, and became an expert in this field, both in his work for the Ontario Government and with No. 2 Int Trg Coy post war. He served as the Membership Secretary of the CMIA and was one of the organizers for many CISA events. He served on the Board of Directors of the Ontario Association for Cerebral Palsy and for one of the residences for those afflicted.

Maj George D. LaNauze, CD, of Ottawa, passed away on 9 Jan 1996. George came up through the PPCLI and served as a Battalion Int NCO in the 1950s in Korea, then became a Guards officer in Petawawa, an Int Staff Capt at Eastern Ontario HQ in Kingston, and Chief Instructor at the CSMI at CFB Borden.

Maj Ward I. Binkley, CD, passed away in May 96 in Herefordshire, England, where he lived after his retirement from the Regular Force. Ward began his Military Intelligence career as a Lt in 12 Field Security Section (12 FSS) in Aldershot early in 1945. Back in Canada, he assisted in the debriefing of Canadian prisoners-of-war. After WWII he served as the Commandant of the CSMI from 1958 to 1962, and in various other duties elsewhere in Canada. He took part in the formation of the CMIA in 1946.[12]

## 1996, Bosnia-Herzegovina, On, Off, and On Again

On 12 September 1996, the author was warned that he would be going to Bosnia-Herzegovina within a week. On 13 September, the Bosnia-Herzegovina deployment was cancelled. On 14 September, it was back on. On 18 Sep-

---

12.   CISA Newsletter, Vol. 26, No.2, August 1996, pp. 1-4.

tember, he visited CTC stores and drew his flak vest, flak blanket and Kevlar helmet and kit for Bosnia-Herzegovina. On 19 September, he was informed "for sure," that Bosnia-Herzegovina was back on. He collected a number of needle injections, did a bit of the pre-deployment administration, and flew to Kingston to take the pre-deployment course. One of the people on the same course was LCol Peter Devlin, with whom the author would later cross paths again when he was Brigade Commander, KMNB, ISAF in Kabul, Afghanistan in 2003-04.

The course was very well conducted, and things had gone well. On the last day of the course, the author walked over to the hospital to receive the last two big haemoglobin shots in my butt. As he walked back into the school, the Chief Instructor handed him a FAX from the J3 Shop In NDHQ informing him that the mission had been cancelled and that he could go home. LCol Devlin gave the author a lift to Toronto. He flew back to Fredericton, and shortly afterwards, he was informed that he would most likely go on a six-month deployment to the CANIC in June. He was eventually deployed as the Commanding Officer of the Canadian National Intelligence Centre (CANIC) with the Canadian Contingent of the NATO led Peace Stabilization Force (CC SFOR) in Sarajevo, Bosnia-Herzegovina-Herzegovina from 21 June to 30 December 1997.

## 1996, Vice-Admiral L.E. Murray

On 1 Oct 1996, our Minister of National Defence (MND), Mr David Collenette resigned. A few weeks later the author flew off to Ottawa to participate in a conference on ethics in the military. On 24 Oct 96, the author had the privilege of meeting a very honourable man, acting Chief of Defence Staff (CDS) Vice Admiral L.E. Murray. He also spoke with Col Patricia M. Samson, who was at that time the CF Provost Marshall, and would later earn the rank of BGen and DSecur, followed by a tour of duty as DG Int. The author also ran into Cdr Paul H. Jenkins, Maj Paul Duff, and Maj Ed Haskins. He also met with BGen (later LGen) Roméo Dallaire, who spoke about his experiences in Rwanda at the conference.

# Message from the Intelligence Branch Advisor, Col Patrick D.R. Crandell

In this my first newsletter contribution as Branch Advisor, I want to share some of my thoughts with you on a number of subjects. As I indicated in my introductory message to the Branch, I hoped to visit all Intelligence Sections and Staffs during my first year in the chair. To date I have visited MAR-LANT and LFAA, 1 Cdn Div Int Coy, 2 Int Pl, 5 CAMNB HQ in Coralici Bosnia-Herzegovina and have a two hour session with all the Int Ops in the Intelligence Division. The Branch Chief and I hope to do a Western swing late this year or early next year.

On the evening of 17 Oct we gathered at the NDHQ Sgts and WOs Mess for a mixed dining-in to recognize those who had retired from the Branch during the past year and to say good-bye to Col (Ret'd) Victor V. Ashdown and MGen (Ret'd) Reginald J.G. Weeks. Thanks to the outstanding efforts of the Organizing Committee of Maj Ron H.J. Ruiters, Capt J.A.J.P. Cormier, WO Barry R. Eddy, WO J.V. William "Bill" Leclair, WO Ron T.A. Wulf, Sgt Tom J. Last, Sgt J.A. Chris Pelletier, and Sgt Ronald Richard Patrick Walsh, the evening was an outstanding success. Farewell remarks to all those retiring and the responses of the two guests of honour were from the heart. In the case of Col Victor V. Ashdown and MGen Reginald J.G. Weeks, it was difficult to say good-by to two individuals who have done so much for the Branch and who have been both my masters and mentors through the years. Good luck, good health, and God's speed to all retirees; we your successors thank you and on behalf of the CF, I thank you.

The Branch Senate meeting, which I said I would hold, was held in Ottawa on 18 Oct 96. The Senate is comprised of the Branch Cols and LCols and the Branch CWOs. The Senate touched on Many issues. Although Minutes will be promulgated in due course, I want to share two points with you at this time.

*New Colonel Commandant.* Many of you have asked about our new Colonel Commandant. I am happy to tell you that the Senate has selected a person whom we believe will best satisfy the needs of the Branch over the next three years. The name of our new Colonel Commandant will be announced as soon as Ministerial approval is received.

*The Future of CFSIS.* As many of you are aware, there was a proposal to split CFSIS and move the Intelligence portion to Kingston. This proposal was studied by the CFRETs consultant team who concluded that a good business case for splitting the school did not exist. This study was flawed and CFRETS has agreed to re-examine the proposal in light of continuing re-engineering of CFRETS Schools and Security and Intelligence functions at NDHQ. Pending the outcome of these deliberations, I want everyone to know that the Intelligence Training Company is very much back in business. The new Heritage room has been opened and displays professionally the history of both Branches. The Commandant is committed to maintaining a robust Intelligence training capability commensurate with our needs. If the School remains together, I have indicated that we want to fill the Commandant and RSM positions on an equitable rotational basis.

Intelligence R-engineering efforts at NDHQ have entered a new phase. Having re-engineered the Intelligence Process and not achieved anticipated PY savings, DG Int has been given approval-in-principle to conduct a contracted feasibility study of establishing a Strategic Intelligence Line Unit/Centre. Conceptually, this organization would include all of J2 Ops, part of theJ2 Plans distribution centre, the CF Photo Unit, and MCE. The feasibility of combining this Unit with the METOC, CFSRS, and CFSIS may also be considered. You will be advised when the study commences.

The annual cycle of promotion boards has been completed. For those of you who have never taken part in a promotion board, I want to assure you that every time I do one (and I did two this year); it reinforces my faith in our personnel evaluation system. Promotion boards are fair! Indeed, it is uncanny to see just how few discrepancies there are between board members on the scoring of each file. Having said that, I want to emphasize several points that I noticed from the boards in which I participated. I should emphasize, however, that members of all the boards that were held share these views. The Branch Chief addresses similar concerns in his letter to the Branch.

*Inflation*. Despite high score controls there were still instances where most of the persons in a particular organization were "water walkers." Notwithstanding that the Branch has a lot of very good people, such a situation is unrealistic and much more importantly, it undermines the credibility of PERs from that organization. Supervisors do not do their personnel any favours by inflating scores and do a disservice to the CF.

*Second Language Scores*. Those persons who are not bilingual are throwing away 25% of the 'potential' scoring that determines who will be promoted. The message is clear: if you expect to progress, become functionally bilingual. What amazes me is that becoming bilingual is something over which each member has some control, yet it is shocking the number of members who are not bilingual, or worse, have not bothered to go for testing/re-testing.

*OPDP.* I was heartened to find that a number of our NCMs have written OPDP exams and done exceedingly well. To each of you, congratulations. However, I was equally disheartened to find a number of officers who had not completed their OPDP. Successful completion of OPDP not only contributes to 'potential' scoring but also is a prerequisite for attendance at Kingston, Winnipeg, and Toronto Command & Staff Courses. Again the message is clear: if you want to progress, you have to satisfy CF training requirements.

The next issues I want to discuss are intertwined and are vital to our continued existence. Since taking over, I have discovered to our collective detriment that we are neither thinking nor acting as a family. No one element of the family (and we are a family of a sort), is more or less important than any other and it is essential that all members realize and accept this. The posturing must stop; it is divisive and counter-productive! As our Branch is made up almost exclusively of reclassifications and remusters, it is essential that Branch values, ethos, and traditions be taught to and accepted by all members. It would be unheard of for a member of a Regiment to show up at a regimental function sporting the accoutrements of their previous Regiment, yet this happens in our Branch. Personally I am disappointed when I see this, as it indicates that the wearer's allegiance is not this, as it indicates that the wearer's allegiances not to the Branch. If we are going to survive, we must start thinking and acting as a family. Personnel who want to be part of something else should leave.

In the context of the foregoing, we need to revisit the rationale for and purpose of the Branch Association, which is simply "to foster, maintain, and promote the tradition and well-being of the CF Intelligence Branch." As such, I believe the Association fills a vital role…My aim is to develop A Branch that is healthy, happy, close knit, and capable of providing the full range of military Intelligence support required in peace and war at all levels of command. I care about this Branch and expect no less from the rest of the family.

As I finish this letter, Branch personnel have been and are deploying on yet another overseas operation—this time to Zaire. To all who are involved in the mission, Good Luck! I know you will all do an outstanding job. E Tenebris Lux.[13]

---

13. Sinister Sam's Notebook, Edition 2, November 1996, pp. 1-3.

## *Branch Chief's Message, CWO J. Ron Martin*

CWO J. Ron Martin has been in NDHQ since 3 Sep 96 and has participated in a number of Branch functions. He wrote, "In September I attended the inauguration of the new CFSIS building, previously known as the Dieppe Building (WOs and Sgts Mess) just up the hill from CFSIS. This included the official opening of the "CFSIS Heritage Room" as part of the Dieppe building. This exhibition of MP and Intelligence historical memorabilia is done with exceptional good taste and professionalism. The Commandant of CFSIS, LCol Tony Battista and his staff, in particular WO Vance Gordon, are to be commended for the conception and design of the various exhibits." While in Borden, both CWO J. Ron Martin and Col Patrick D.R. Crandell spent time visiting with the students of the in-house QL 6B Course.

On 14 Sep 96, CWO Martin attended the 10th Anniversary celebrations of the Reserve EW Sqn at CFB Kingston. The Unit was very well turned out for the parade. On 30 Sep CWO Martin attended part of the TQ 6A/6B CTS writing board. Full time members of the board were CPO2 Brian M. Noble from MARCOM, WO Don B. Jorgensen from AIRCOM, WO Tim G. Armstrong, LFCA, WO Cyril P. Aucoin from CFSIS Standards who also acted as the secretary, and MWO Ivo J.M. Schoots, Board Chairman. The board achieved excellent results, and CWO Martin wrote, "I believe this type of training will sustain the momentum that the Int Training Company at CFSIS has [initiated]. Future attendees of these courses will be better challenged and subsequently better trained as Senior NCOs of the Int Branch, ready to bring us into the next century. I realize that Commands and Units are hard-pressed to release their personnel to attend these writing boards, but if we are to retain or enhance the quality of Senior NCOs in the Branch, we must pay the bill. I would like to thank Maj Robert G. Nash and his staff for their continued support during my visits over the last year. I sensed a high level of excitement as the rejuvenation of the Intelligence Company makes itself felt."

On 3 Oct 96, I accompanied the Colonel Commandant, MGen Reginald J.G. Weeks, and the Int Branch Advisor, Col Patrick D.R. Crandell, to the presentation of the Sir William S. Stephenson Trophy. This trophy is, as of this year, presented annually to the best Reserve Intelligence Unit in Canada. This year's deserving Unit is 2 Intelligence Platoon of Ottawa. As a member of the judging committee, I can assure you that the competition was very close. Notwithstanding, I would like to congratulate Capt J.P. Stéphane Lefebvre, the reserve and Regular Force members of this Unit on their unique achievement. The atmosphere and camaraderie that is evident amongst members of this Unit helps explain why this Unit was successful over the last year. I would also like to congratulate the Regular Forces support staff, in particular Sgt Ronald Richard Patrick Walsh and the Unit Clerk, MCpl Woermke, for their work during what was for the Unit a difficult year due to operational taskings.

On 17 Oct 96 most of the Senior Intelligence Officers and MWOs from the various commands were in town for various Intelligence Conferences (Intelligence Training Steering Committee, Senior Military Intelligence Officer Conference, etc.), which permitted a large attendance of Int Branch personnel at the celebrations for the 14th Anniversary of the Branch. Those present included MGen Reginald J.G. Weeks, Col Victor V. Ashdown, CWO Rick J. Tervo, Sgt Rick Marleau from Bagotville, and no less than 118 participants. Congratulations to Maj Ron H.J. Ruiters and his committee for a job well done.

During the week of 21-25 October, I participated in the NCM Merit List Board for 1997. Most of the PERs are being well-written; however, I will restate the important factors that assessors should keep in mind when writing these evaluations. Keep to the facts, the board wants to know what the person has done and how. As far as the NCM is concerned, it is critical that they get tested on second language capabilities. It is crucial that their personal records are kept in order, and it is important that we as supervisors check our personnel's files at least once a year and advice our subordinates as required. It is critical to everyone's careers that this information is kept up to date.

It has been most rewarding to see our Branch thrive through these hard times. I cannot begin to tell you how proud I am when, as it has happened recently, I hear from various Senior Officers and CWOs of this and other HQs who have visited the Troops in the various operations, tell me how impressed they were by the professionalism and dedication of our Intelligence Personnel. Well done ladies and gentlemen. E Tenebris Lux.[14]

---

14.  Sinister Sam's Notebook, Edition 2, November 1996, pp. 3-4.

## 1996, 3 Wing Report from Yenisehir, Turkey
## Extracts from an article by PO1 J.R. François Bouchard,
## 433 Sqn/433e ETAC

3 Wing Int Section is participating in a NATO exercise while operating from a temporary base in Turkey under the command of 6 ATAF. Our hosts have welcomed us with outstanding hospitality Sgt J.R. Marc A. Paradis found the local driving habits particularly interesting. At home in Bagotville, the past year has seen the Unit involved in numerous Sunday exercise deployments, a successful Air Show, a major flood disaster, a crash (no loss of life), and the ongoing NATO exercise. Personnel departing this year include Sgt J.J. Rick Marleau and MCpl John T. Smola.

Incoming personnel include newly trained Int Ops from the most recent TQ5 course, Cpl J. Paul St Laurent in April, and Cpl Angela L. Unger who arrived in August. Within two weeks of his arrival, Paul was dispatched to CFB Cold lake for the annual MAPLE FLAG Exercise. Angela (the first female Int OP At 3 Wing) deployed to Turkey with 433 Sqn/433e ETAC within two weeks of her arrival. MCpl Onik B. Papazian is due in from Ottawa and will be working with the 425 Sqn Int Det.

Capt J.G. Yves Forcier returned in May from a six-month tour of duty in Haiti; Capt Jean Jacques "J.J." Simon has been in Vicenza, Italy since June; Sgt J.R. Marc A. Paradis returned from Turkey; and, Sgt Daniel Joseph Garant may have acquired the reputation of being the most deployed Int OP Of 3 Wing, if not NATO.

Sgt J. Guy Foisy made us proud when he assisted in the safe removal of a driver of a diesel fuel tanker and also the driver of a car. This exploit occurred on 18 Aug at about 2245 hours when Guy and his family, returning from vacation, witnessed an accident between a diesel fuel truck and a passenger car. As Murphy would have it, the truck spilled its content and burned. The engine compartment of the passenger car also caught fire and the driver was stuck, hurt, and needless to say, panicking. Sgt Foisy quickly assessed the situation and after being given a fire extinguisher, proceeded to put out the fire in the engine of the car. After the fire was out, Sgt Foisy and another civic-minded individual were able to free the driver from under the steering wheel and from the tangle of her seat belt. By then, the fire from the diesel spill had grown in both size and intensity. A local newspaper later reported the flames reaching as high as 35 feet. Fortunately the driver of the tanker was ejected from the burning wreck into an area away from the flames where he lay in a state of semi-consciousness. Sgt Foisy assisted him to get away from a potential danger. A local radio station interviewed Sgt Guy the following day—we can all justifiably be very proud of him.[15]

## 1996, G2 Cell, 5 Canadian Multi-National Brigade, Coralici, Bosnia-Herzegovina
### Extracts from an article by WO John Paul Michael Parsons

The members of the G2 Cell for 5 CAMNB have been in the Bihac area of Bosnia-Herzegovina since early July 1996. We have an excellent team providing the Commander with Intelligence, although we also have a very large area of operations to cover, stretching from Velika Kladusa at the NW corner of Bosnia-Herzegovina, down to Bosanski Petrovac in the south and past Banja Luka in the east. There is a great deal of work for all, because 5e GBMC's mission with IFOR is, in many ways, unconventional by military standards.

The Brigade G2 is Capt J.V. Gilles Clairoux, who is also the G2 with 5e Bde when it is back in Garrison at CFB Valcartier. In-theatre, he maintains close links with the Bde Commander, BGen Christian Couture, as well as with our many sources and agencies. He often spends time doing personal reconnaissance analyzing the information gathered and briefing the Commander and the rest of his staff. WO Dan J. Haslip, who was posted to the Int Coy from Winnipeg shortly before we deployed to Bosnia-Herzegovina, is the Senior Political Analyst. He monitors trends and developments relating to the Dayton Peace Accord's mandated elections. On the other side of the Shop, WO Neil Gordon, hailing from Vancouver, is our only Militia member. He is also our Senior Military Analyst who is tasked with deciphering the wealth of military issues involving the three former warring factions within our AO. The assistant political and military analysts are PO2 Don S. Eenkooren and Sgt J.T. Serge Gagnon, respectively. Don, like the other members of the FIST, comes to us from the Int Coy in Kingston, while Tony is an original member of 5e Bde from Valcartier. The final member of the FIST and, of course, he also come to us from Kingston, is recently promoted MCpl Rob J. Lindsay, our collator and personalities analyst.

15. Sinister Sam's Notebook, Edition 2, November 1996, pp. 5-6.

Sgt Kris E. Pedersen deployed with the Unit at the beginning of July, doing extremely good work as Assistant Military Analyst until a back injury necessitated his repatriation back to Kingston in early September. To fill the ranks Cpl Darren Gauthier, also from Kingston, will shortly join us. I am WO Paul Parsons, attached to 5e Bde from SQFT in Montreal, and my job is to provide coordination with the G2 Cell, both with administration and support functions on the camp, as well as with outside Units and agencies, through the preparation of collection plans, patrol task tables and Intelligence requests, etc.

The team is solid and morale is high. We took over from 2 CAMND in early July 96, and we are scheduled to return to Canada some time in late December. During our stay the level of violence in Bosnia-Herzegovina has been down to its lowest level in five years. We are quite fortunate to have access to almost every type of source possible. It is also an interesting experience working with our multi national brigade members from the Czech Republic, the UK, the USA and France. Intelligence in the IFOR context is both challenging and rewarding, and the Unit will be returning to Canada having returned some semblance of stability to north western Bosnia-Herzegovina, an area of the country with unique and complicated problems.

We also devote an important part of our time and effort to force protection. For a multitude of reasons, there are a number of local elements that would like to see IFOR either embarrassed or hurt. As so—we must remain vigilant to ensure that our soldiers return home at the end of their tour and that our mission is ultimately and absolutely successful. We, as part of IFOR's continuing mission, can visibly see that we have managed to harness the FWF and put a stop To the dreadful war which has so utterly shattered this beautiful country. E Tenebris Lux.[16]

## 1996, 2 EW Sqn Report

Over the past two years, 2 EW Sqn has been undergoing a complete overhaul of equipment and capabilities. When this overhaul is completed in 1998, the Sqn will be equipped with the very best tactical Electronic Warfare equipment available.

The upgrading of 2 EW Sqn has brought the squadron into a position where it can fight and survive on the 21st century battlefield. Most noticeable to the average person is the incorporation of the Bison AVGP into the squad-

---

16. Sinister Sam's Notebook, Edition 2, November 1996, pp. 7-8

ron lines. This vehicle, with its armour and excellent off-road capability, will help the squadron to deploy into areas which were previously inaccessible to our wheeled vehicles, and will provide an element of survivability to our very vulnerable artillery targeting devices (AKA jammers). A total of 16 Bisons will be delivered to the squadron by the summer of 1997.

Over the past year the squadron received the new AERIES direction finding system. This Bison-mounted system is operational and has performed extremely well in field exercises, producing DF results that are nothing short of incredible. When the input from the AERIES is fed to the analysis section in the Computerized Electronic Warfare Operations Centre (CEWOC), it doesn't take too long for the target to disappear under a cloud of hot lead.

This winder the squadron will be receiving the new Tactical Radar Identification and Locating System (TRILS). This system will provide the squadron with a new capability to identify and locate tactical radars including SAMs, locating radars, ground surveillance radars, and of course, those ever elusive OPP cruisers. We are looking forward to using this system to look for the armour's new Coyotes, as they try to sneak about the battlefield. Later in the year we will be taking delivery of our new jammers as part of the Jammer Under Armour (JUA) project. While this will not give us a new capability, it will definitely increase the mobility of our jammer detachments and substantially increase their life expectancy as they sit on the FEBA trying to knock the enemy off the air.

In 1988 the squadron is expecting delivery of the Electronic Warfare Coordination and Analysis Centre (EWCAC). This improvement to the already excellent capability offered by CEWOC will enhance the ability of the squadron to move information quickly to whichever formation it is supporting.

The squadron currently has 11 Intelligence Branch personnel in its establishment, ranging in rank from Cpl to Capt. If you're physically fit, up to the challenge of working in a field environment, and you want to work in NATO's most advanced Electronic Warfare Unit, come and give us a try![17]

## 1996, Canadian Forces Photographic Unit

The Canadian Forces Photo Unit (CFPU) is a new addition to the J2 Division, located on the Montreal Road Campus of the National Research Council (NRC). The CFPU's mission is to support military operations and defence

---

17.   Sinister Sam's Notebook, Edition 2, November 1996, pp. 8-9.

Intelligence through the provision of Imagery services, and test and evaluation services of imaging systems. We are very proud of recent significant strides made in the realm of digital imaging, some of which have been battlefield tested. An invitation is extended to all J2 personnel to visit the CFPU and see what we really do.

Recent recipients of the CD in the CFPU include Cpl Lucie Breton, Cpl Carole Morissette, and Cpl Chris Provost. Cpl Morissette has also been named NDHQ female Athlete of the Year.[18]

## 1996, CANIC, Sarajevo, Observations
### Article by Lt Jim D. Godefroy

I've noticed that most people who serve in the Int Branch seem to have a bias towards one particular aspect of our work, as a result of their background or formal training. As a Lt who has received very little formal training (BIOC), and as the G2 Trg for SQFT, my bias tends to be towards Intelligence training issues. As a result, I've decided not to write about the weather, or the scenery, or any other superficial aspect of our deployment here in Sarajevo. Instead, I've decided to write about how my training, and that of my soldiers, has and has not prepared us for our mission. This deployment has been a fantastic opportunity to actually do Intelligence work, and as I've worked my way through the daily problems, I've found that I've learned a great deal.

The first CANIC rotation arrived on the ground on 16 June, replacing personnel who had been here since January. Our staff consists of Maj W.A. "Tony" Rennett (OCO0, Lt Jim D. Godefroy (2IC), WO Rick Dennique (CI/LO), Sgt B. Shawn Mootoo (Int Sgt), PO2 René McMullan (Communicator), and Sgt Sylvain Lambert (Site Administrator/Communicator). WO Joris Gagné was the first CANIC CI/LO and was replaced by WO R. Dennique just last month.

One thing became obvious to me soon after our arrival. We all tend to be a product of our training, our experiences, and our attitudes. Any one of these things can make or break our ability to do our jobs. Maj W.A. "Tony" Rennet's approach to his role was an example of how all these factors come into play. His background includes experience as CFILO to DIA in Washington, DC. This shaped his approach to the CANIC function. Maj Rennett made a point of networking and developing contacts in Canada before departure. He

---

18.   Sinister Sam's Notebook, Edition 2, November 1996, p. 9.

sought and received very clear guidance on his role, and established permission for direct liaison with all agencies at home. This pre-deployment groundwork was vital. Once on the ground, he made a point of conducting ruthless liaison with the other Intelligence staffs, and building personal and professional relationships. He determined what information requirements existed, and used this analysis to develop Areas in which CANIC could contribute unique national products. This became my first observation on understanding of how the Canadian Intelligence system works is vital; and cannot be gained from a couple of months of PJT, a formal lecture, or an office tour. The exploitation of our national capabilities must be trained and exercised. How many people regularly use the services of J2 Ops, J2 Imagery, or J2 Geomatics? An understanding of how it all works, who does what, and where to go to get something is vital.

My second observation concerns the importance of training on the systems we deploy with. CANIC staff came to theatre with only limited contact training on the various systems we would use in theatre. We spent a lot of time after arrival becoming familiar with these systems and exploring their capabilities and limitations. This time was taken away from liaison and analysis work. None of the CANIC staff had ever used LOCE or JC2IS beyond the limited introduction given in Ottawa. At least one CANIC staff member had limited experience with computers. These limitations hindered our ability to get things running smoothly as quickly as we might have. When you only have six months on the ground, every day wasted getting up to speed counts. There is no period when the flow of Intelligence produce is less vital. Critical incidents can and do occur during the transition period or beginning of mission, and missing or misreporting them cannot be mitigated by the fact that you are new and busy learning systems.

My third observation was that we don't learn enough about the doctrine and capabilities of our allies. Canadian Intelligence personnel receive little formal instruction or training on this subject. It seems to be something that we pick up, if we are fortunate, by working with other nationals, or participating in operations. All Canadian Intelligence staff would be well advised to learn as much as possible about our allies' systems. The hardware, doctrine, organization structures and collection capabilities of our allies are all critical elements of understanding which we must bring with us to operations.

A fourth observation concerned the classification of Intelligence product. Before arriving in theatre, I had yet to routinely produce Intelligence and assign it a classification in the course of my daily duties. All of my training had centred on plotting data from reports, or cutting and pasting various reports into consolidated documents. In Sarajevo, I suddenly found myself receiving raw reports, DOCINT and other information, which I had to evaluate, classify and report. This skill is not practiced or taught nearly enough in Canada, and is something we would be well advised to train. Reasons for classification need to be emphasized. At ARRC HQ, the CANIC works within a multinational environment which includes materials with varying levels of security clearance and access. There is always a fine line to walk between protection of sources and methods, and getting the right information to the right decision-maker in the timeliest fashion. The Intelligence professional needs to know where that line is, and who can help him or her stay on the right side of it.

The importance of being a soldier first is another observation. This one seems obvious, and yet we still don't seem to get it right. In a nutshell, the soldier skills or training that CANIC staff brought with them to the theatre were almost entirely the product of their experiences before they joined the Branch. It is natural that any Unit will have a blend of personnel with different strengths and skills. The IBTS initiative is an example of trying to qualify what an Intelligence soldier should be able to do at each rank level. We need to go even further, however, and train branch members to a minimum level of soldier skills as well. Int Branch NCOs need to know how to drive and maintain vehicles. They need to know how to light a Coleman stove, how to start a generator and how to read a map. Int Branch officers should also be able to drive, read a map, and use a compass. These requirements should seem obvious, and yet the fact that any of the CANIC crew could do any of these things was purely incidental and in no way the result of anything but past experience.

As final observation must be made on the value of professional contacts. CANIC works very closely with 5 CAMNB G2 staff and their FIST support element from 1 Cdn Div Int Coy. We also provide administrative support to all Canadian Forces personnel in the Sarajevo area, to our peers from J2 Geomatics who have worked on the IEBL survey as part of the Geographic Support Group (GSG) in Kiseljak, and to individuals from as far away as Mostar and Tuzla. This aspect of our job has been both a pleasure and a reward in itself. I think what has impressed me most is the professional manner in which all Canadian J2 personnel in theatre have worked together. When 5 CAMNB FIST's LOCE was done, we faxed them the reports they required. When they had early warning of some event of potential interest to AARC, they passed it to us, in addition to their Division, as a courtesy. Small acts like these grew over time into a Unity of purpose, and the end result has been a success, which the Intelligence Branch can look to with pride.[19]

## 1996, 1 Canadian Division Intelligence Company (Spearhead of the Formation)

1st Canadian Division Intelligence Company is a military Unit synonymous with Combat Intelligence. This is the ability to provide a supported commander with a clearer picture of the enemy, terrain and weather, using various computer and communications capabilities.

The role of this unique organization is to provide a deployable, all-source, multi-discipline combat Unit capability to support 1st Canadian Division HQ in all its roles, or any other formation as directed by the Commander. Presently the Unit is training and organizing itself to be able to carry out its mission of deploying by air, sea or land anywhere in the world with 14 days notice, ready to provide the Combat Intelligence support of 1st Cdn Div or any other formation to accomplish its mission.

The goal of being fully combat-ready in the event of war or in support of operations other than war is reflected in the organization's training plan. Within the Int Coy, each section develops its expertise, either through individual training or section exercises. In Ex RADICAL ASSEMBLY, 11-16 Aug 96, the sections were brought together to walk through the IPB process, where coordination is essential to produce the Intelligence required by the Commander.

Ex RITE BASIC, 26-30 Aug 96 was a command post exercise in which the Int Coy rehearsed what was learned in Ex RADICAL ASSEMBLY, as an organization supporting the G2, within the architecture of divisional headquarters. As well, this exercise aims at educating divisional staff to a standard level of interoperability, i.e., the ability to function on the IT IS net, communicating information through messages, documents or on Battlefield Graphics.

In Ex CASCADE MIST and CASCADE PEAK, 1 Cdn Div Int Coy, like RITE BASIC, rehearsed its support within the Intelligence Collection and Analysis Centre, through continuous IPB process and collection management. In these exercises, 1st Cdn Div HQ aims at improving operational capa-

---

19.　Sinister Sam's Notebook, Edition 2, November 1996, pp. 9-11.

bility under combined command. In this case, with its American, Australian and British partners.

As a combat Unit, 1ˢᵗ Cdn Div Int Coy trains to be combat ready by meeting the Army standards as directed in the Warrior program. Three exercises are a part of the training cycle, including Ex POLAR DAGGER, Ex WARRIOR SPEAR, and Ex WARRIOR STALKER.

Committed to enhancing the knowledge of its profession, the Int Coy has a professional military education program. Professional studies of history, new technologies, regional conflicts, and current operations strengthen operational proficiency and provoke thought and discussion. In Ex TENEBRIS WARRIOR, 24-27 Jun 96, the Int Coy went to Quebec City to do a battlefield study of a landmark in our nation's history, from an Intelligence perspective. This gave the Company the opportunity to see the theatre of operations from a bird's eye view, as well, through the eyes of Louis-Joseph, Marquis de Montcalm-Gozon, Seigneur de Saint-Véran, and General James Wolfe, and their respective armies.

In maintaining relations with the US military Intelligence Units, educational exchanges are often made with 110 MI Battalion at Fort Drum. Besides their participation in Ex TENEBRIS WARRIOR, they have also invited personnel to partake in their HUMINT courses. In Ex SONORA MAPLE, 10-17 Jun 96, 1 Cdn Div Int Coy and members of associated Units, were able to tour the facilities of the US Military Intelligence School at Fort Huachuca, as well as being briefed on some of the US collection management capabilities. In Jan 97, the Int Coy will train in a joint and combined environment with 1ˢᵗ Surveillance Recon Intelligence Group (1 SRIG), 1ˢᵗ Marine Expeditionary Force (1 MEF), during Ex SEMPER STAR at Camp Pendleton.

1 Cdn Div Int Coy is a dynamic organization. In light of Canada's increasing participation in joint and combined taskings, Combat Intelligence is essential in keeping the divisional staff on a functional level with its partners, and more importantly, in keeping Canada's Troops alive in the theatre of operations. E Tenebris Lux.[20]

## 1996, LFAA G2 and 3 Int Coy Report

In Atlantic Canada, the Army Int Community has been busy supporting domestic operations with police and security liaison and a federal penitentiary

20.   Sinister Sam's Notebook, Edition 2, November 1996, pp. 11-12.

threat update. WO J.J.P. Mike Fournier has done route/ground recce as well as air recce (compliments of 403 Sqn) of the four federal institutions in Nova Scotia and New Brunswick. His final product will be produced on CD-ROM by Base Photo, complete with hand-held ground and aerial views of the institutions, along with text and maps. This is LFAA G2's first attempt at a completely digitized product and we are obviously anxious to view the final product and see how our "customers" receive it.

We are also busy planning for our move to collocate with MARLAN-THQ/N21. The move is tentatively scheduled for early Jan 97. The move is coincidental with Area restructuring which will have some impact on our eventual configuration. The collocation should benefit both LFAA and MARLANT. LFAA will have access to a great deal of sophisticated equipment and MARLANT will have access to Army Intelligence.

3 Int Coy has been busy integrating its Warrior training with its trades training. They had a busy summer with individuals away on trades training and augmenting CFSIS. As well, the culmination of training was the Annual Area Reserve Concentration (ARCON) '96 in August. All reports indicate that 3 Int Coy personnel did the Branch proud in both individual and collective training. Due to the financial constraints facing this Unit as with the rest of the Forces, training will have to be very focused and the Company is concentrating on developing its ICAC Platoon. Capt Colin A.J. Kiley and WO R. Hal Pugh are devising a new and innovative approach to make this training year a huge success.

3 Int Coy is already planning for ARCON 97, where they will face new challenges with a higher tempo exercise planned. The theme of ARCON 97 will be "Fighting through the Objective." Sgt Michael C. Wagner had his team are currently Flocarking the area of operations with the Commander's mission as their direction, beginning the IPB process.

LFAA consists of Maj Ross L. Johnson, Capt Rick Mader, WO J.J.P. Mike Fournier, Sgt Wes E.B. Young, MCpl Andrew J. MacFayden and Cpl Alan R. Farquhar.

LFAA's mission is to:

a. Support Comd LFAA in his mission, both regionally and nationally;

b. Support CTC HQ G2, who in turn support CTC, 2 RCR, and 4 ESR;

c. Support 3 Int Coy, who in turn support LFAA Trg Bde; and

Provide Comd and Branch heads with daily Int products.[21]

# 1996, CFSIS

Intelligence Operator 6B Course 9601.
Rear Rank: Sgt J.R. Charles Conlin, Sgt Connie F. Webb-Lancaster, Sgt
J.L. Ivan Dellaire, WO G.R.A. Gauthier, Sgt Brian K. Mudge, Sgt Trevor
Cave, Sgt Mel A. Wilkerson, Sgt George P. Houston, Sgt Mark H. Figge,
WO Ron T.A. Wulf, Sgt Dennis G. McNulty, Sgt Glen A. McGuire, Sgt
Richard E. "Dick" Hurst, Sgt Kevin Toomer, Sgt Phil D. Cooper, Sgt
J.F.J.M. Tremblay.
Front Rank: MWO Ivo J.M. Schoots, CWO Delage, LCol Battista, Maj
Robert Glyn Nash, WO Rick G. Oliver.

During the summer months of 1996, the Int Trg Coy at CFSIS underwent
the usual rotation of personnel while continuing with training and the re-
engineering of some courses. Changes of Int Branch members at CFSIS during APS 96 include the departure of Capt Pierre Michaud to SQFT, Montreal; MWO Herb H.W. Kuchler and WO Mario Ross to J2, Ottawa; and the
retirement of Sgt Greg S. Smith. In their place, the Int Trg Coy received Capt
J.I. Mike Beauvais from UNFICYP in Cyprus; MWO Ivo J.M. Schoots from
ATG HQ, Trenton; WO F. Vance Gordon from LFWA, Edmonton; and
Sgt W.E. Webb from 1 Cdn Div Int Coy, Kingston. The Coy is also employing two reservists from LFAA, Halifax, Capt James P. Terfry and MCpl

<hr>

21.  Sinister Sam's Notebook, Edition 2, November 1996, pp. 15-16.

Craig J. Tudor, who will assist with reserve training until at least Spring 97. The other members of the Int Trg Coy include Maj Robert G. Nash, Lt (N) Doug C. Jantzi, WO Cyril P. Aucoin, WO Richard C. Gow, WO Rick G. Oliver, Sgt Rick F. Luden, Sgt Glenn A. McGuire and Cpl Raymond M. Kruger. There are also two Branch members, Capt Derek Marchbank and MCpl G. Bruce Scott, who are currently employed at CFSIS HQ.

In August, four Int Branch reservists completed their Basic Classification Training: Capt Brant Jolson from LFWA HQ, Edmonton; SLt Marc-André Meunier and SLt John Parsons from Cie Rens, SQFT, Montréal, and SLt Anyk Nusbacher from 1 Cdn Div HQ, Kingston. SLt J.A. Parsons finished as the top Student. Two other students completed one phase of the course and will return in the future to complete their training.

The Int Trg Coy launched into the Fall 96 training period by conducting a QL 6B course in September. Sixteen branch members graduated from the course, which focused mainly on analytical work and "threat papers." The TOP Student was Sgt Phil Cooper from Petawawa. Coincidentally, Sgt Cooper was awarded the "Dick Bushe Memorial Trophy" for his leadership skills and potential. The Coy is now gearing up the Unit Air Int Course scheduled for 30 Oct-27 Nov. This course is intended for non-Branch pers, such as flight crew, who perform Intelligence functions within their Units. After the Christmas break, the Int Trg Coy will be very busy conducting both an Advance Combat Int Course and the Basic Intelligence Officer Course (BIOC).

The BIOC has undergone significant changes to reflect the changing times and "customer" needs. Rather than the old four phases (Strategic, Land, Air and Naval), the new course will be divided in three parts. In the initial "core" phase, students will acquire their basic skills to function in most Int jobs within the Branch. This phase also emphasizes Intelligence at the Strategic level, so that students will have the right tools to perform immediately within the J2 staff. The second phase will focus on specific skills, such as IPB and OPFOR organization, equipment and tactics required by students to function within their respective elements. The last part of the course is the "Joint" phase in which students will gain further knowledge on Int support to other types of ops in addition to lessons learned during recent deployments (Bosnia-Herzegovina, Rwanda, Haiti, etc.). The course is certainly different from previous ones and should yield a better product.

Following QL6B 9601, a Qualification Standard Writing Board was held for both the QL6A and QL6B. It was chaired by CFSIS and had the assistance of MWO Joseph A. Michel White, J2 Imagery; CPO2 Brian M. Noble, MARCOM; WO Tim G. Armstrong, LFCA; and, WO Don B. Jorgensen, AIRCOM. The Board completed the review and rewrite of all Int OP Employment and training. This endeavour started with the rewrite of the QL5A and all Pres Int OP R111 Qualifications in 1995. The result will be a significant improvement in Int training to meet the needs of the Int Branch and the CF.

Other significant activities at CFSIS over the past few months include the initiation of the Heritage Project on 12 Sep 96 and the dedication of the Dieppe Building as part of CFSIS. The Heritage Room, located in the Dieppe Building, holds many historical items from both the Security and Military Police, and the Intelligence Branches. On the Intelligence side, there are items covering the three main periods: the Corps of Guides, Canadian Intelligence Corps, and the current Intelligence Branch. CFSIS also hosted the CISA AGM, which culminated with an excellent and extremely well-attended Mess Dinner on 14 Sep 96.

Finally, Int Trg Coy is also continuing the efforts to improve its Information Technology (IT) capabilities. Several projects, such as the addition of Internet, Reuters Business Brief and the future acquisition of JC2IS and LOCE, are underway to provide quality training to Int Branch members. Every effort is being made to have Internet access and Reuters in place in time for BIOC 9701. In closing, the School Commandant, LCol Tony Battista, the School CWO, SCWO Delage, the OC Int Trg Coy, Maj Robert G. Nash, the Int Trg Coy CSM, MWO Ivo J.M. Schoots, and all Intelligence staff at the "Home of the Branch" send their best wishes. We hope to see you at CFSIS in the near future.[22]

## 1996, 10 Tactical Air Group Report
## Extracts from an article by Capt David R. Canavan

The following is an update of changes to 10 TAG now underway. The introduction of the CH-146 Griffon and the re-engineering presently underway in the Air Force has changed the face of 10 TAG somewhat. The plus side of the change is that there will be an increase in the level of Intelligence support within the group.

---

22.  Sinister Sam's Notebook, Edition 2, November 1996, pp. 16-17.

As a result of the introduction of the Griffon utility helicopter, the Group has phased out the CH-136 Kiowa and is still in the process of phasing out the CH-135 Iroquois (Twin Huey). The retirement of the Kiowa has left 10 TAG without a dedicated LOH platform. While this resulted in the elimination of a collection asset to the land force brigades, the CH-146 introduced a capability that neither the CH-135 nor the CH-136 offered. The electronics support package on the CH-146 includes a Radar Warning Receiver, and a Missile Warning System. In addition to the FLIR capability, these assets have the potential to provide a new spectrum of ELINT data to land and Sqn Int staffs.

Recent discussions indicate the LOH function may be re-introduced, and incorporated into the six 10 TAG CH-146 equipped squadrons. The Group has gone through some reductions. The air reserve wings in Montreal and Toronto as well as 450 Sqn in St Hubert have been eliminated. The six remaining Sqns are 403 Sqn, Gagetown; 430 Sqn, Valcartier; 438 Sqn, St Hubert; 427 Sqn, Petawawa; 400 Sqn, Borden; and 408 Sqn, Edmonton. The next major change will occur in APS 97 when 10 TAG disbands in St Hubert and 1 Wing stands up in Kingston.

17 Reserve Intelligence Class A positions have been created across the Group, with the exception of 403 Sqn in Gagetown. A MCpl and Cpl will go to both 400 Sqn and 438 Sqn; a Sgt, MCpl and two Cpls will go to each of 408 Sqn, 427 Sqn and 430 Sqn; and one WO will go to 1 Wing HQ.

With the Army's creation of three Light Infantry Battalions, and the increased attention air mobility operations will receive as a result, an increased Intelligence capability at the Sqn level is required. Sqns are already showing an interest in filling the Reserve Int OP Positions. For those looking at posting choices for next year, these are bound to be challenging and rewarding positions. For the Group/Wing, the future is promising.[23]

# *1996, Air Command Report*
# *Extracts from an article by LCol Susan F. Beharriell*

Down-sizing, Operations, Re-engineering, CHANGE, Business Planning, Vicenza, Alternate Service Delivery, Flight Plan '97, Blue Flag, Deployments, New Think, Red Hat Comments, Drug Busts, Zagreb, Air Component Commander's HQ, Ground School, Fish Wars, CHANGE, Continuous

---

23. Sinister Sam's Notebook, Edition 2, November 1996, p. 17.

Improvement, targeting, SAREX '96, Multi-skilling, Joint Maple Flag, Devolution, Haiti, closures, Wing Self-Assessment, Ancona, OPRAM, Out-of-the-Box Thinking, Joint Air Intelligence Link, Terms of Accountability, Empowerment, and Inclusion.

If you have had any contact with the Intelligence staffs across the Air Force these days, you have probably heard at least some of these new realities, projects and activities. If you haven't seen much of us lately, let me set the scene.

To start with, as of summer 1996, the Air Force will be 45% smaller than it was only two years ago. That is quite a downsizing! Also this summer, all five Air Force HQ will close. 50% of the positions will be cut completely. A handful of the remainder will be sent to detachments on each coast to support maritime air operations, a larger handful will support the Chief of the Air Staff in Ottawa, and the rest will staff the new 1 Canadian Air Division/Canadian NORAD Region HQ (1 CAD/CANR HQ) in Winnipeg. Needless to say, we will carry on doing everything we used to do, but with half the people.

Work Smarter, Not Harder. Do more with less. Yes, there certainly are buzzwords around and flavour-of-the month methods. But the fact remains that we must change the ways we do things and we must change them now. So we at Air Command HQ decided that the best way to sort out all the cuts and changes was to re-engineer—to shut down for a week, bring in NCMs and officers from every wing and Group, and put ourselves in the hands of an experienced consultant and the Air Force "Change" Guru.

Re-engineering was a mystery to all of us and no one had any idea where it would take us in the end. We began by throwing our all our sacred cows, mad cows and excuses that "we must do it this way because that's the way we have always done it," etc., and started with a blank sheet of paper. Everyone pitched in, brought their experience to bear, worked very hard, really used their imaginations and developed logical, workable solutions. While it certainly would have been easier to complete all this with no constraints, reality and the Commander's direction did place limits on some of the creative, "out-of-the-box thinking" which took place. But in the end people were satisfied that they had done the best they could, and that they had created the groundwork for Air Intelligence support for the future.

Part of the re-engineering process is to produce Mission and Vision statements. Some of you may wonder why such things are even necessary, but they do provide a useful focus for not only our own staff, but also for the operators we all support. The mission of 1 CAD/CANR HQ Intelligence Centre is "to provide timely, accurate and relevant Intelligence support to Air Force operations." Our vision is" Focused Intelligence Through Flexible Teamwork.

One of the significant tasks, which will come to Winnipeg, is the responsibility for the Canadian NORAD Region. Under the guidance of newly retired Mr. J. Kent Peebles, the staff here is ploughing through lots of reading material and preparing for the rapidly approaching training exercises.

One of the significant changes at the Wing level is that Wings will be responsible for planning, mounting and sustaining Intelligence support to Contingency Operations. Command and Group HQs used to play a major role in these activities. With the imposed cuts to HQs, however, the tasks and the resources with which to carry them out will devolve to the Wing level. As part of our re-engineering efforts, each Wing and Group submitted its manning requirements to meet these new tasks.

All well and good, you may say, but where are you going to get more positions in these days of cuts/Independent of our re-engineering efforts, the Air Force ops research experts devised a model (OPRAM) which determined the total number of each MOC required to carry out the Air Force obligations to support CF Plans. They even factored in the chances that Plan A and Plan B might be activated at the same time. Much to everyone" satisfaction, the manning requirements identified will nearly double the number of Intelligence personnel at the tactical level! The PYs will come from the thousands of other MOC PYs, which are being cut. What was also satisfying to see was that the numbers submitted to the Wing staffs were practically identical to the OPRAM numbers. This certainly helps validate both processes. A mass ECP is being prepared in Winnipeg and our Career Managers will start to fill the new positions this APS. Yes, these are significant and positive changes!

As part of the re-engineering we set up the Transition Team here in Winnipeg and an Implementation Team across the Air Force. Members of both teams have used conference calls to good advantage, sorted out OPIs and milestones, drafted guidelines for Wing Self-Assessment, determined the legal requirements for archiving certain materials, written master Implementation Plans to cover closing down and standing up of old and new HQs and moved ahead by leaps and bounds.

In the meantime our people have been deployed all over the world supporting our aircraft and aircrews. The Commander's Flight Plan '97 way ahead is an ambitious vision for the future, which entails seamless transitions in an atmosphere of increasing operational activities. From identifying Battle Damage on the side of a C-130 Hercules and debris on the Arctic ice, to analyzing potential SAM launchers on the flight path into Sarajevo, unknown radars off the coast of the Former Yugoslav Republic, and barbed wire "helicopter traps" in Haiti, Intelligence personnel are certainly proving their worth every day.

The significant new task of Targeting has now become part of Air Intelligence duties. Previously Canadians did not perform this task because we always operated in an Allied environment, such as NATO, in which we were on the receiving end of Air Tasking Orders. Canadians have not played a significant role in the production of these ATOs. Now, however, with the increasing role of coalition and other cooperative operations, Canadian Air Force personnel are training to augment coalition air operations centres. This augmentation will require Int personnel to be full players in the development and execution of the Air Component Commander's Battle Plans. A handful of Int personnel have received basic targeting training in Germany and first hand experience as part of the NATO Combined Air Operations Centre (CAOC) in Vicenza, Italy. Others are gaining valuable training through participation in the Air Force's most important exercise, Ex Joint Maple Flag, held annually each spring in Cold Lake. Yes, an introduction to targeting will be included on the next BIOC course and plans are in the works to assess a USAF targeting course for possible follow-on training.

On top Of this, our spaces here in the Air Intelligence Centre will soon be ringing with the sounds of construction workers, saws and hammers. We are expanding a bit within the shielded area in order to accommodate the new NORAD equipment and role. If all goes according to plan, we should have all the sawdust swept away by the end of February.

All this should help to bring you up to date on just what we Int folks across the Air Force have been up to lately. These are exciting and certainly turbulent times. But we are rising to the challenge and forging on.[24]

## 1996, Catch the Wave! The Info Age Wave
## Extracts from an article by Cpl Angela L. Unger, 433 Sqn/433e ETAC Bagotville

CFSIS graduated 15 new Int Ops with QL5A Course 9601 on 4 Apr 1996. The course began on 8 Jan 96, and was completed by the following new additions to the Int Branch: Cpl Ron Bell, Cpl Bill Bill, Cpl Chris K. Buczynski,

---

24. Sinister Sam's Notebook, Edition 2, November 1996, pp. 17-19.

LS Roger Daigle, Cpl Paul Hagnier, Cpl J.A.M. Eric Gagnon, Cpl Darrin Gauthier, Cpl R. Steven M. Gingras, Cpl Al J. MacDonald, Cpl Donald W. Rowe, Cpl Dale G. Sonstenes, Cpl J. Paul St Laurent, Cpl Kurt A. Trebels, Cpl Angela L. Unger, and, Cpl Roy Vandenberg.

The influence of Information Technology in the world of Military Intelligence was the main theme of this QL5A course. The course subjects included map reading and plotting, collating, Imagery, research techniques, tactics (Army, Navy and Air Force), information security, exposure to JDISS, equipment training, current Intelligence and country briefings.

The course began with software training on WP Windows and Harvard Graphics 4.1 to bring all students to the same minimum level of expertise. This initial introduction to Information Technology allowed us to surpass all the instructors' expectations. Our equipment and Current Intelligence briefings were spectacular, colourful and very effective. Computer problems (crashing) did cause some concern, as the age of Information and Technology is not without its difficulties.

Students worked in syndicates of three or four students, rotating and undergoing evaluation of a number of different jobs such as logging, collating, plotting, writing messages and giving both impromptu and planned briefings. Practical research projects were conducted from open sources at Barrie's Public Library and College facilities. During the end-course exercise, students were exposed to and evaluated on a combination of Arm, Navy and Air Force tactics. The exercise took place in the imaginary countries of Desertia and Kubat, situated in the areas of Iraq and Kuwait. Saudi Arabia, Canada and the USA were coalition partners operating as a joint task force with Kubat.

Our course was challenging with its share of both fun and frustration and many late nights in the classrooms of CFSIS. When the course ended, not only were we proficient in our Intelligence duties, but also we were all able to better appreciate the role and influence of information technology in the life of an Int Op. I wish all my new "Int Brothers" an interesting and challenging career.[25]

## 2 Int Coy Unit History

2 Intelligence Company formally returned to the Canadian Army's Order of Battle on 29 Oct 1993 as land Force Central Intelligence Company. It

---

25. *Sinister Sam's Notebook*, Edition 2, November 1996, p. 19.

regained its historic designation on 19 May 1995. 2 Int Coy perpetuates the presence of a military intelligence unit in Toronto that can be traced back to the original No. 2 Mounted Guides Company that was formed in 1903.

As mounted units, Guides Companies were tasked to survey their respective regions as well as to collect information of potential value to military intelligence. With the onset of the First World War, Guides personnel were reassigned to other duties. This was due to the fact that there was no establishment for intelligence units in the British divisional structure on which the Canadian Expeditionary Force was based. However, Guides personnel did serve in intelligence capacities at corps, division and brigade level throughout the war.

Following the end of the First World War, units of the Corps of Guides were restructured as Cyclists and a company assigned to each Military District. On 15 Dec 1921, the company in Toronto was re-designated No. 2 Cyclist Company. As divisional troops, these units were tasked to conduct reconnaissance and force protection.

The 1920s, however, were lean times for military intelligence and on 31 Mar 1929, due to extreme financial constraints, the Corps of Guides was disbanded. If the 1920s were difficult for Canadian military intelligence, the 1930s were utterly devastating. Military intelligence was virtually ignored, so that when Canada entered the Second World War it had no officer or man trained in "field intelligence." It was not long though, before the military disasters of Hong Kong and Dieppe highlighted the need for accurate, timely collection and dissemination of intelligence.

The Canadian Intelligence Corps was formed on 29 Oct 1942. Overseas, the Corps grouped together several specialist units as well as all personnel employed in intelligence duties at various headquarters, but did not include senior staff officers or intelligence officers at brigade and battalion level. Within Canada, Canadian Intelligence Corps units were responsible for training of specialist personnel, performing signals intelligence and censorship duties as well as conducting counter-intelligence. One of the latter units was No. 2 Intelligence Section, which operated in Toronto from 1 April 1942 until 27 February 1946.

The need to train officers and men without wartime experience was recognized quickly after the end of the Second World War and reserve intelligence companies were established across the country. In Toronto, No. 2 Intelligence Company was formed on 4 Sep 1947. Training was provided in combat intelligence, air photo reading, field security, and languages. With the 1960s and integration, the amalgamation of the Regular Force intelligence component with the Provost Corps inevitably led to a concurrent amalgamation of their militia counterparts. On 1 Feb 1970, No. 2 Intelligence Company was reduced to a section within the Military Police Platoon of the Toronto Service Battalion. This is where military intelligence until there was again a recognized need for an intelligence line unit to be responsible for recruiting, training and preparation of specialist combat support personnel.

2 Int Coy currently participates in training in all aspects of the modern combat intelligence system. The Company is involved in the conduct and support of collective training exercises from unit to formation level. In addition to its training mandate, 2 Int Coy has actively supported Canadian Forces operations at home and abroad.[26]

## 1996, 2 Intelligence Company News
## Extracts from an article by Maj Doris E. Guyatt

2 Int Coy moved into new quarters in the Federal Building at 4900 Yonge St., North York, Toronto. 2 Int Coy will have its change of command on 16 Nov 1996, with Maj Roy C. Armstrong taking over command from Maj Sandra L. Bullock.

## 1996, 2 Intelligence Platoon Report
## Extracts from an article by Sgt Ronald Richard Patrick Walsh

On 3 Oct 1996, 2 Intelligence Platoon paraded in the Cartier Square Drill Hall for the inaugural presentation of the Sir William S. Stephenson Trophy. This trophy, named after the first Colonel Commandant of the Intelligence Branch, is presented annually to the top Reserve Intelligence formation in the country. Selection criteria for the award is based on Warrior Individual Combat skills results, number of personnel who have augmented the Regular Force on Exercise and operations, individual results on career courses, and overall performance.

The parade was attended by MGen R.G.J. Weeks (Ret'd), who had served as an Intelligence Officer with the 3rd Canadian Infantry Division during the

---

26.  Maj Liam Robertson, CO 2 Int Coy, 2 Intelligence Company Smartbook, Intelligence Operators Field Manual, 2001, pp. 5-6.

Normandy campaign; Col the Honourable Judge J.R. Matheson, who served as the Flotilla Intelligence Officer during the invasion of Sicily and was wounded at Ortona; Col Patrick D.R. Crandell; LCol Greg W. Jensen; the new CISA President, Major Doris E. Guyatt; Major John "Pappy" MacKinnon (Ret'd) from CISA; Maj Rhedegydd ap Probert ; Capt Peter T. Patton; Lt (N) Richard Taylor and CWO Rolf F. Overhoff from the Director Land Force Readiness (DLFR); and CWO J. Ron Martin. MGen Reginald J.G. Weeks and Col Patrick D.R. Crandell inspected the Unit, and Major John P. MacKinnon presented the Sir William S. Stephenson Trophy to the Unit.

During the parade, Col Patrick D.R. Crandell commissioned 2Lt Lisa Elliott, and promoted Cpl M.J. Ford to MCpl, while LCol Greg W. Jensen had the honour of presenting MCpl P.S. Blaber with his CD. After the parade, all retired to the Unit lines, where MGen Weeks presented 2 Int Pl with his CF tunic, complete with undress ribbons. He was presented with a plaque from 2 Int Pl by MCpl J.E. DeBruijn on behalf of all platoon soldiers in appreciation of his continuing support of the Unit. MGen Weeks, Col J.R. Matheson and Maj John "Pappy" MacKinnon all gave a speech to the members present.

Capt Robert S. Williams, the Unit OC, called upon Capt J.P. Stéphane Lefebvre, who was acting OC for most of the period the Unit was assessed for the Trophy, to receive it. The ceremony took place in the Unit lines, where then OCdt now 2Lt Lisa Elliott, an Economics student at Carleton University in Ottawa, was presented with a certificate to commemorate her winning the CISA Academic Award for a Serving Member.

MGen Reginald J.G. Weeks donated his Major General's uniform to 2 Int Pl for display purposes, as he had resigned as Colonel Commandant of the Int Branch. He spoke eloquently of the spirit of support that exists within this Unit. Col J.R. Matheson also added his encouragement.

The members of 2 Int Pl take great pride in their achievements over the past year and are continuously striving to improve themselves, to fulfill the role of providing the nucleus for the Intelligence Collection and Analysis Centre (ICAC) for a contingency brigade ready to deploy anywhere in the world. 2 Int Pl has already set its sights on next year's award and will endeavour to repeat as the nation's best Int Unit. E Tenebris Lux.[27]

---

27. Sinister Sam's Notebook, Edition 2, November 1996, pp. 6-7.

# 1996, CISA AGM

The CISA AGM was held at CFSIS, CFB Borden, 12-14 Sep 96. Those in attendance included: Maj Terry B. Kelly (President), Maj Roy C. Armstrong, Capt John Anderson, LCol Tony Battista, Maj Sandra L. Bullock, Capt J.D. Baxter, Capt J.I. Michael Beauvais, Col Patrick D.R. Crandell, Capt Luc Cyr, Col Ron J. Donovan, Maj Gary D. Dover, Maj Robert C. Dale, LCol Jack S. Dunn, LCol G. Wally Field, Maj Doris E. Guyatt, Col Robert T. Grogan, Capt Don M. Fowler, Lt E. Bruce Holmes, Lt George F. Holdron, LCol Don R. Johnson, Maj Fred E.G. Jones, Capt P.W. Clare Lagerquist, Maj Nils E. Lindberg, Capt J.P. Stéphane Lefebvre, Maj J. Legére, LCol Frank Leigh, FO Ian B. Carruthers, Maj Franz F. Laizner, Capt Rob B. Martyn, CWO D.H. McLaren, Col Craig B. MacFarlane, Maj Robert G. Nash, Capt Peter T. Patton, Lt Paul R. Perchaluk, Capt Mike Motyl, LCol Greg W. Jensen, MGen Al Pickering, LCol Jim E. Parker, Capt J. Perron, Capt Dennis H.S. Rowden, Capt John M. Robertson, Lt K. Rowcliffe, Maj Bernie A. Richardson, Mrs Genevieve Richardson, Capt Eugene Slonetsky, Capt Herman J. Schneider, Maj J. Simpson, Capt Paul Thobo-Carlsen, LCol William "Bill" Tenhaaf, Lt (N) Richard Taylor, Col A.H. Sam Stevenson, Capt David A. Rubin, Maj Merrick K. Szulc, Capt James P.K. Van Wynen, LCol Dale M. Watts, Maj William "Bill" L. Watt, Capt Robert S. Williams, Col Andrew F. Ritchie, BGen Douglas Yuill, Maj John "Pappy" MacKinnon, and guest BGen Paul Hayes.[28]

Outgoing CISA President Maj Terry B. Kelly, CFB Borden Base Commander Col Ian Nicholls and CFSIS Commandant LCol Tony Battista welcomed CISA members to the base for the AGM. Tribute was paid to members who had passed away by Col Robert T. Grogan. To LCol Reg Bornor; by Maj D.E. Guyatt to Maj Ward I. Binkley, Lt E.R. Milne, Maj George D. LaNauze, and Capt William D. "Dick" Ellis; and by Capt David A. Rubin to Capt Doug R. Bennett and LCol Bob Hillier. A minute's silence was observed in their memory.

Col Patrick D.R. Crandell provided a detailed analysis of the various flashpoints around the world, with particular reference to Bosnia-Herzegovina. BGen Douglas Yuill made a presentation on the status of the Security Branch.

---

28. CISA Newsletter, Vol. 26, No. 3, November 1996, p. 3.

The winner of the Essay Competition was Capt Mike Motyl, MP Operations Officer at Land Force Central Area HQ, for his essay "Canadian Forces Role in Drug Interdiction." An honourable mention was awarded to Cpl Joe Faragone, for his essay "Intelligence and Operations Other Than War." A cheque for $400 was presented to Capt Motyl at the meeting.

LCol Tony Battista spoke on the CFSIS Heritage Project, speaking on the assembly of Security and Intelligence artefacts and the naming of buildings after those who had made a great contribution to Intelligence and Security in the Canadian Forces. LCol Greg W. Jensen, G2 Land Forces Command HQ, spoke on the work of the Int organization within Army Command in Canada. The HQ had just moved to Ottawa from St-Hubert.[29]

## Branch Advisor's Message, Col Patrick D.R. Crandell

It is with great pleasure that I announce the appointment of MGen (Ret'd) J.E. Pierre Lalonde, CD2, as the new Colonel Commandant of the CF Intelligence Branch. MGen J.E.P. Lalonde brings with him a wealth of experience gathered over 33 years in both the Canadian Army and the Canadian Forces. His experience in the Intelligence function includes having served as the DG Int at NDHQ, and as Assistant Chief of Staff for Intelligence at SHAPE. MGen Lalonde's extensive background in both operations and staff functions can only serve to benefit all members of the Int Branch. He is looking forward to visiting Int Branch staff wherever they may be during the term of his appointment. On behalf of the Branch, I would like to formally welcome MGen Lalonde.[30]

## 1996, DLFR Report
## Extracts from an article by CWO Rolf F. Overhoff

Army HQ returned to Ottawa on 3 September 1996, and is now located on the top Three floors in NDHQ's North Tower. The Commander of the Army remains Commander LFC and he is served by his "Land Staff." The Commander's G2 staff is now officially known as Director Land Force Readiness 4 (DLFR 4). The staff consists of LCol Greg W. Jensen, Maj Rhedegydd ap Probert , and CWO Rolf F. Overhoff. The mission of DLFR 4 is "to provide

---

29. CISA Newsletter, Vol. 26, No.3, November 1996, pp. 1-6.
30. Sinister Sam's Notebook, Edition 1, March 1997, p. 4.

dedicated Army Intelligence resource management support and advice to the Army Commander, Land Staff, and Intelligence staffs at subordinate headquarters." This Intelligence staff is committed to:

a. Providing the Army Commander, Land Staff, and subordinate headquarters' Intelligence staffs with clear advice and guidance; and

b. Ensuring that Army elements deployed on operations and training exercises in Canada and abroad are provided with tailored Intelligence support. This includes the provision of highly trained Intelligence personnel, and material resources, as well as the provision of timely, relevant and accurate Intelligence products from appropriate Intelligence agencies.

As, well, DLFR 4 staff will continue to provide "Corps" advice in the development and refinement of Army Intelligence doctrine and training procedures in coordination and consultation with CLFCSC and CTC. Finally, the staff is also the conduit for Army Intelligence advice to the J2 staff.

In light of the current fiscal climate and reduced staff size, the G2 staff must provide Army Intelligence services by implementing more efficient processes and procedures, and making the best use of available resources. For example, DLFR 4 staff is not in the business of producing Intelligence. The J2 staff is now providing the Intelligence products for the Commander and his staff. In most cases the Land Staff needs can be met without significant additional burden to the J2 staff.

Other Intelligence Branch members with the Land Staff in NDHQ include: DLFR 4-7 Maj J.A.E. Kent Dowell; DLFR 4-10 Capt Phil J. Drew; Director Land Concepts (DLC) 4-3 Maj Clark J. Beamish; Director Land Personnel (DLP) 3 LCol Jean E.T. Bigras; and outside this region are: Maj Gord P. Ohlke with Director Army Doctrine in Kingston; and Capt Phil R. Berikoff with Director Army Training in Gagetown.

Major issues, which will be addressed by DLFR 4 over the next 12-24 months, include:

a. The Army Intelligence Support Concept (AISC), the Army Met Support Concept (AMSC), and coordination and implementation of the Intelligence Master Development Plan (IMDP);

b. Command and Control Warfare (C2W)/Information Operations (impact on training, organizations, and concepts);

c. Land Staff processes with respect to NDHQ/J2;

d. Information technology issues (ATISS, JDISS, etc.);

e. Intelligence and Electronic Warfare (IEW) (proposal for rationalization of collection processing assets);

f. Command and Control of 2 Int Pl, Ottawa;

g. Land Force Reserve Restructure (LFRR);

h. Training, including the Joint School of Intelligence and Security (JSIS) issue and Advanced Classification Training (ACT) for Army Reserve personnel and the Advanced Intelligence Officers Course for Regular Force personnel; and

i. Branch "housekeeping."

DLFR welcomes the move to Ottawa and a cordial relationship with the J2 staff. The relocation of the Environmental Chiefs of Staff to Ottawa signals a new era for everyone in NDHQ. DLFR 4 is open for business and we welcome all personnel to our new location on the 19th floor of the Pearkes Building.[31]

## *1996, Acorn Intelligence Conference*

Acorn Intelligence Conference 1996 participants.

Personnel in attendance at the 1996 Acorn Intelligence Conference included: MGen R.J.G. Weeks, Col Comdt; BGen Ken C. Hague, DG Int; BGen MacDonald, Res Adv LFCHQ; Col Vic Ashdown, Int Branch Advisor; Col Pat Crandell, J2 Ops; Col Gord Graham, J2 Plans, LCol Greg

---

31.   Sinister Sam's Notebook, Edition 1, March 1997, pp. 5-6.

Jensen, LFCHQ; LCol M.C. Maurer,, 1 Cdn Div; Maj Rhedegydd ap Probert , LFCHQ; Maj Michel Bédard, DGLFD; Maj Sandra Bullock, LFCAHQ; Maj Don Cushman, 2 CMBG; Maj Gary D. Dover, LFCHQ; Maj Len Goski, J2 Ops; Maj Ross Johnson, LFAAHQ; Maj Gerry Mayer, Cdn LO, Ft Huachuca; Maj François Messier, 1 Int Coy; Maj Rob Nash, OC Int Coy CFSIS; Maj Gord Ohlke, 6 Int Coy; Maj Mike Ouellette, LFQAHQ; Maj Paul Rivest, 2 EW Sqn; Maj Ron Reuters, 1 Cdn Div; Maj Christian Rousseau, J2 Plans; Maj Hal Skaarup, LFAA/CTC; Maj Bob Stedeford, 6 Int Coy; Maj Ward Sweet, Int Career Manager; Capt Michel Clairoux, 5 CMBG; Capt J.A.J.P. Cormier, J2 Plans; Capt Eric Gjos, 1 CMBG; Capt Brian Hamilton, LFWAHQ; Capt Jim Hill, J2 Plans; Capt Stu MacAulay, 2 EW Sqn; Capt Richard MacRae, LFCHQ; Capt Rob Martyn, 2 Int Coy; Capt Rob McCutcheon, LFAAHQ; Capt John Robertson, 2 Int Coy; Capt Norm Sproll, LFCAHQ; Capt Keith Sutton, DLR; Capt Dan Villeneuve, 4 Int Coy; Capt Chris Wallace, J2 Ops; Capt Kent Dowell, Lt Stephen Desjardins, LFQAHQ; Lt Jim Godefroy, LFQAHQ; Lt Andrew G. Morrison, 3 Int Coy; Lt Cody Sherman, 2 Int Coy; CWO Lefebvre, LFCHQ; CWO Ron Martin, LFCHQ; MWO Rolf Overhoff, J2 Plans, MWO Dan Galley, 1 Cdn Div; MWO T. Kozak, 6 Int Coy; MWO Herb Kuchler, CSM CFSIS; MWO David Whalen, 1 Int Coy; WO Tim Armstrong, LFCAHQ; WO Don Gallaher, 1 CMBG; WO Darcy McLaren, 2 Int Coy; WO Robert Moug, 6 Int Coy, WO Pierre Murret-Labarthe, 5 CMBG; Sgt Ronald Richard Patrick Walsh, 2 Int Pl; MCpl A.N. Mannie, LFCAHQ; Mr Brookmyre, RCMP Supt Ret'd; Mr Graves, CSE; Mr Hansen, Ottawa; Mr Richardson; and Mr Waarbroek, CASIS.

# 15

# 1997, Intelligence Branch

## 1997, Combat Training Centre, Gagetown
## Extracts from an article by Maj Harold A. Skaarup

There have been a lot of changes in CF organization and establishments recently, and the subsequent downsizing has hit the CTC at CFB Gagetown relatively hard this year. At present the Int Section is co-located with the Tactics School and consist of two personnel, Maj Harold A. Skaarup and WO Peter A. Maillet. We share the instructing duties and tasks, with WO Maillet teaching the majority of the AFV and aircraft recognition classes and providing operational deployment briefings, while the G2 instructs on the bulk of the lectures on enemy force tactics.

Intelligence appointment titles have changed, with the G2 now the Tactics School Intelligence Directing Staff officer. He spends most of his time with the Intermediate Tactics Course, Level II (all Army officers are required to take ITC II before attending CLFCSC in Kingston). WO Maillet is the CTC Int WO. The most interesting stage of the school training curriculum comes in the spring when the courses move outdoors and change from "tactics on paper" to field exercises conducted for the Combat Team Commander's Course. The CTCC commits a minimum of a squadron of Leopard tanks from the 8th Hussars and a Company of Infantry from 2 RCR, along with the required Engineers, Artillery, Recce, TOW, CSS vehicles etc., against an enemy force which consists of a platoon of AFVs (numbers vary depending on serviceability). The RED force under the Int DS has the privilege of losing some 32 battles while defending various positions spaced at intervals up and down the Lawfield corridor on the base. From an Int perspective, it is an exciting and challenging job, observing and reporting on the levels of success of aggressive and extremely well-trained new combat team commanders. The CF will be well served by the course graduates—they truly have to have their act together to coordinate a successful attack, (and by the time a candidate has been selected for this course, he usually does).

Capt Phil R. Berikoff is the newest Int member in residence in Gagetown. He is set up in the new Air Defence Building and will likely be participating in a number of Int taskings at CTC, when the Div permits. CTC is rapidly becoming the home of the majority of the Army's advanced schools, with the new CFSEME building nearing completion next to J-7, where the Tactics School is located. (J-7 itself may well be one of the largest buildings in the Maritimes). The anomaly is that in spite of reductions, there is more work and there will be more schools to service for the Int staff at CTC. It is an interesting place to be. (It would be even better if they could just get those CH-146 Griffon helicopters functioning so that we can collect come jump pay!).[1]

## 1997, Developments in LFC
## *Extracts from an article by CWO Rolf F. Overhoff*

There have been some very positive developments in the past month in several Army Intelligence organizations. These developments mean that now, instead of taking a loss in PYs, Army Intelligence will have achieved a modest increase in positions.

Perhaps the most significant development is in 6 Int Coy, LFWA. Earlier in the year the Company had lost five RSS positions, including the WO position in each of the company's three detachments. LFWA has very recently agreed to retain the WO positions in both Vancouver and Winnipeg for at least the next two years. The Regular Force positions in Vancouver and Winnipeg are considered vital to these two detachments. The loss of these positions probably, over time, would have spelled the end of these detachments.

There have also been changes in three of the four Area headquarters. LFWA G2 increased its establishment by three PYs: one Capt, one Sgt, and a Cpl. LFCA G2 also increased by three PYs: one Sgt, One MCpl and a Cpl. SQFT G2 added a second WO position.

---

1.   Sinister Sam's Notebook, Edition 1, March 1997, pp. 6-7.

With the graduation of a TQ5 course later this summer, the intake of several reservists, and some creative personnel management, most of these positions will be filled this APS. Several holes will remain, however, but these will be filled as personnel become available.

While some might question why the Branch is growing during a period of overall CF downsizing, initial results of the Intelligence Branch MOS Review clearly show that our Branch is under strength. Any new positions can only help to alleviate this situation.[2]

## 1997, Changes at CFSIS Int Trg Coy
## Extracts from an article by WO F. Vance Gordon

A number of major structural changes have recently been made in the School lines. The Library (O-77), MP Trg (O-78) and the Field Stores (O-93) buildings have been razed to make way for the new CFSIS Campus. A new addition to the School lines is the Dieppe Mess. The WO and Sgts Mess has been renovated into the MP Training and Field Stores building. Also included in this building is the CFSIS Heritage Hall, which is located in what used to be the casual bar area. It is now an Annex of the Base Borden Museum and serves as a display area for: Corps of Guides, C Int C, Intelligence Branch, Provost Corps, Military Police Branch, CFSIS and other Canadian Int and MP historical memorabilia.

The main drawback to the Heritage Hall is that a majority of the items are only on a short-term loan from the Base Borden Museum, and are subject to recall at any time. As of this date, several items have already gone back or are on the recall list. Fortunately, we are receiving several items from the Old Guard under the stipulation that the articles be displayed in the Heritage Hall and not the Base Museum. We have received uniforms, publications, maps, personal papers and items of kit from MP, Int and Security Branch members, both retired and currently serving.[3]

---

2.   Sinister Sam's Notebook, Edition 1, March 1997, p. 7.
3.   Sinister Sam's Notebook, Edition 1, March 1997, p. 7.

## A Challenge for the Intelligence Branch
## Article by BGen Ken C. Hague, J2/DG Int

*Introduction.* Confucius once stated, "May you live in interesting times." I am not sure if the great philosopher meant this pronouncement as a curse or a wish; however, it certainly has applied during my 18 months as J2/DG Int. The hallmark of the CF, and by extension the Intelligence Branch, has been turbulence, constant change, and uncertainty for the past several years. R-engineering, personnel and budget reductions, rapid advances in information technology and management (IT/IM), social change, media attention, and numerous other factors have influenced our military culture and mores, some would argue, more than at any other time in the history of the Canadian Forces.

In addition to experiencing this change phenomenon, we have also been the subject of an extraordinary volume of operational and professional challenges, which have taxed our diminishing resources to the limit: Bosnia-Herzegovina, Haiti, Zaire, Guatemala, greater Int opportunities, increased demand and requirements, more sophisticated clients who are product smart, and increased demands on fewer managers.

For you in the Intelligence Branch, what do these changes and challenges mean? What will be the future consequences on you as individuals and as a collective group? I would like to address the issues I believe will affect you the most.

*Training.* The single most asked question of me as J2/DG Int relates to the question of training, about which there are several aspects. The first question concerns formal training conducted by the Intelligence Training Company at CFSIS. Recent graduates and supervisors at all levels receiving the graduates, are frustrated by their inability to walk immediately into the work place and operate the IT/IM and communications equipment. In recent years, the School has not been able to keep pace with emerging technology. School staff is addressing this problem, and we will see the results on the next series of courses. However, these changes will only incorporate current equipment. The next generation is already being procured: therefore, the School has a significant challenge to work with NDHQ J2 Plans and Policy staff to ensure the latest information technology developments are discussed early, including their application and affect on policy and doctrine. A proactive approach to keeping ahead of the IT/IM power curve is essential.

An additional aspect to the training problem is the introduction of new IT equipment into the workplace without incorporating an accompanying refresher-training program. We have been short-sighted in the past in our equipment procurement policy. The emphasis has been on the hardware and software, while ignoring the professional development of our personnel. Within my own Division, this myopic approach has led to considerable frustration by both military and civilian personnel. While we have taken steps with DISOA to alleviate this problem, individual refresher training must be planned, funded and conducted as mandatory steps for all future IT/IM equipment purchases. Supervisors must find the time to send their staff on this training when it is scheduled. It is a leadership responsibility.

*Lessons Learned.* Similar to all combat functions, Intelligence activities must be modified and improved based on lessons learned from operational deployments. I will give two examples. The missions in both Haiti and Bosnia-Herzegovina confirmed the invaluable role played by human Intelligence (HUMINT). Eighty percent of all Intelligence used by commanders in these missions was derived from HUMINT sources. The Army should insist, and the Intelligence Branch must respond, that HUMINT training be instituted at CFSIS, that HUMINT sections be formed at brigade level, and that these sections be employed each and every time the CF deploys on peace operations. The second example is the National Intelligence Cell (NIC) concept utilized primarily in Bosnia-Herzegovina. NICs have proven extremely beneficial to both NATO commanders and home nations. The concept is now accepted as fundamental doctrine for NATO. The Army and Air Force should also accept it and ensure that NICs are part of the force structure each time a Canadian commander is deployed on operations. It is the only means by which we will guarantee that such commanders will receive the full range of Intelligence products required to execute their tasks.

*Harnessing Brainpower.* We cannot help but be impressed with the equipment and computer software being developed to assist in all facets of our profession. My fear is that we will expect these innovations to accomplish all our thinking for us, and that we will become complacent in searching for imaginative and creative solutions to every day problems. Our challenge must be to exploit each and every new gadget and tool to the fullest by looking and thinking outside the box of conventional operational practices. This challenge is not a simple or easy one. It requires inquiring minds at the coalface, and encouragement and recognition by supervisors.

*Essentiality.* You all understand the severe personnel and fiscal restraints under which we must now operate. The bottom line of these restraints is clear—all work must be prioritized, with essential requirements being executed first. I have issued clear instructions to my Directors: if an operator, Group Principal or Ally has not requested the work, do not do it. The perception of Intelligence staffs producing self-generated products must be eradicated. The requirements process must drive all Intelligence activity. In that regard, one prerequisite is necessary—you must seek direction from commanders at all levels regarding priorities of effort. I have not been particularly successful in this regard at the strategic level, but the situation is improving. For example, we instituted for the first time in 1996 an annual national Intelligence priorities determination process, which requires ministerial approval. We fully intend to follow this first step with a means of meeting regularly with Environmental Chiefs of Staff beginning in Sep 97 to regularly solicit their direction.

*Conclusion.* I have only touched on a few issues. There are many others at the national level including increased synergy between Geomatics, photography, and Intelligence, instituting a formalized feedback system on Intelligence products from commanders, and initiating a feasibility study on the formation of a national Intelligence line Unit in the Ottawa region. I hope the subjects I did address will provide the basis for discussion among Branch members. In addition, I encourage you to respond to the challenges we all face by committing yourself to continuous self-improvement, to exploiting IT/IM to the fullest, and to search for methods of maximizing the return on Canada's investment on the military Intelligence function.[4]

# 1997, LFAA G2, Halifax
## Extracts from an article by Capt Rick Mader

Greetings from LFAA HQ G2 and 3 Int Coy. Here in Atlantic Canada, the Army Int Community has been busy supporting domestic ops with police and security liaison and a federal penitentiary threat update. WO J.J.P. Mike Fournier has done route/ground recce as well as an air recce (compliments of 403 Sqn) of the four federal institutions in Nova Scotia and New Brunswick. His final product will be produced on CD ROM by Base Photo, complete with hand-held ground and aerial views of the institutions, along with text

---

4. Sinister Sam's Notebook, Edition 1, March 1997, pp. 8-10.

and maps. This is LFAA G2's first attempt at a completely digitized product and we are obviously anxious to view the final product and see how our customers receive it. We are also busy planning for our move to collocate with MARLANT HQ/N21. The move is tentatively scheduled for early January, but timelines could be moved either way. The move is coincidental with Area restructuring which will have some impact on our eventual configuration; once again it's a watch and shoot situation. We are now very much looking forward to the move and feel that collocation (with the emphasis on collocate vice amalgamate) will benefit both LFAA and MARLANT. LFAA gets access to a hockey sock full of sophisticated equipment while MARLANT finally gets some Intelligence!

3 Int Coy has been busy integrating its Warrior training with trades training. They had a busy summer with individuals away on trades training and augmenting CFSIS. As well, the culmination of annual training was the Annual Area Reserve Concentration (ARCON) 96 in August. All reports indicate that 3 Int Coy personnel did the Branch proud in both individual and collective training. Due to financial constraints facing this Unit, as with the rest of the Forces, training will have to be very focused and the Company is concentrating on developing its ICAC Platoon. Capt Colin A.J. Kiley and WO R. Hal Pugh are devising a new and innovative approach to make this training year a huge success.

3 Int Coy is already planning for ARCON 97 where they will face new challenges with a new, higher tempo exercise planned. The theme of ARCON 97 (and the Commander's mission) will be "Fighting through the Objective." Sgt Michael C. Wagner and his team are currently Flocarking the area of operations with the Commander's mission as their direction. IPB has begun.

The LFAA staff currently consists of Maj Ross L. Johnson, Capt Rick A. Mader, WO J.J.P. Mike Fournier, Sgt Wes E.B. Young, MCpl Andrew J. MacFayden, and Cpl Alan R. Farquhar. The Unit's mission is to support Comd LFAA in his mission both regionally and internationally; support CTC HQ G2 who in turn supports CTC, 1 RCR and 4 ESR; and support 3 Int Coy, who in turn support LFAA Trg Bde. 3 Int Coy's daily activities include: training reserve Int Personnel; providing geo support to LFAA; support to LFAA G2, and Warrior training.

In closing it should be noted that contrary to press reports, morale in LFAA is high. We work in a happy HQ that lives in an area whose residents still regard the profession of arms as honourable and feels privileged to have those of us in uniform live amongst them. In short, there isn't enough artillery left in the CF to move us out of here![5]

## 1997, A Leap into the Future
## Extracts from an article by MWO Joseph A. Michel White, DG Int/J2 Imagery

J2 Imagery (formerly DIE) is undergoing renovation and construction to make room for computer equipment designed to take the Unit into the computer age. Miles of fibre optic cables have been laid, computers installed and many of the light tables have disappeared as more of the work here is being done digitally. While the work is progressing, the Interpretation/Attaché Training Cell is still busy scanning the complete Imagery library into the Imagery Search and Retrieval System (IMSRS) computer, making hand-held Imagery more accessible to the analysts and better able to fulfil other Units' requirements for Imagery. At present, most of the older Imagery has been scanned and any coming in is done on receipt.

Local products are quickly worked up digitally on our new Restricted Access System (RAS) by our analysts using the Digital Imagery Exploitation and Production System (DIEPS) Imagery software. These products are then sent out on our in-house systems such as JDISS and LOCE so that both our own Troops and NATO allies can be in possession of the Imagery along with the write-up within minutes.

The big problem now is room. With all these systems in operation, as well as the older ISVIS still around, analysts are plagued with an overabundance of computer terminals, scanners, printers and, sometimes, computer experts in their work areas. Still, the work is done and done well. Everyone knows that this is only a transition phase which will allow our Imagery analysts to better manage the modern tools of our trade and keep up with the digital times.[6]

## 1997, Combat Training Centre, NDIC and RMC

On 14 March 1997, the Tactics School staff took the students on the ITC II course in Gagetown for a road run at 0600 hours. Getting up early to go in for the run, the group saw the comet Hale-Bopp at 0510 AM. It was a very clear

---

5. Sinister Sam's Notebook, Edition 1, March 1997, pp. 12-13.
6. Sinister Sam's Notebook, Edition 1, March 1997, pp. 14-15.

night and the comet was easily visible to the right of Cassiopeia, looking north on the horizon. Later in the day the staff attended a seminar on Domestic Operations, with excellent speakers from NDOC, CSIS, the RCMP and the OPP (represented by Inspector Jim Potts, a Mohawk with 36 years in the RCMP and 3 years in the OPP). On 18 March, the Tactics School began an ITC II class, which was joined by three officers from Caribbean nations, including one from Jamaica, one from Trinidad and one from Guyana.

## 1997, War Studies, RMC, and Preparations for Deployment to Bosnia

On 21 March 1997, the author visited RMC in Kingston to be examined for his master's Thesis in War Studies. At 0800, Professor Joel Sokolsky did some "role playing" with the author before the board session (basically a trial of questions and answers). The author was led into the "Chamber" at 1000 hours by Capt Schmidt-Clever, and discovered that the room was laid out like a court, with the author in the witness chair. He introduced himself to Professors Tredenick, Bland and Gagnon. Prof Joel J. Sokolsky chaired the board. Two solid hours of questions later, the author was directed to wait outside. Ten minutes later they all trooped out and offered congratulations on the strong defence of his thesis. The thesis needed a few changes, as the board indicated they would like to see more of the author's personal observations and examples included within the text of the paper, much of which the reader will find in this history. The author then went over to sit in on the ongoing history seminar. Professor Barry Gough was there from the author's first year course, along with Maj Bob Graydon, Maj E. Wayne Boone, Terry Copp and many others encountered or known from recent courses and general history discussions. The author also spoke with Professor Ronald G. Haycock (about Sir Sam Hughes among other subjects); and with Prof Marc Milner who was one of the Professors at UNB.

On 11 May 1997, the author flew up to Ottawa for his pre-Bosnia-Herzegovina briefings, and on 12 May visited the National Defence Intelligence Centre (NDIC) to speak with LCol D.H. Neil Thompson, Maj A. George Johnstone et al. He met Sgt Byron K. Mackenzie and the crew he would be working with in Bosnia-Herzegovina, and spoke with Maj Rhedegydd ap Probert , Capt Paul Johnson, Capt Kathryn B. Clouston, Capt M.E. Louise Boutin. On 13 May, all took part in additional briefings, and the author spoke with LCol Greg W. Jensen and the crew in the Army Shop. The author ran into a lot of familiar faces, and met some new ones including the US DIA LO, LGen (Ret'd) Charles Cunningham, to discuss the War Studies program, and US Capt (N) Vaughn, en route to the NDIC. On 14 May the crew on this rotation visited Tunney's Pasture to meet with Colin Buckett, Maj J.P. André Tremblay, Maj Robert "Bob" H. Smallwood, and a number of other very familiar faces with the DIE crew. The author later visited CSE, and Col Patrick D.R. Crandell, at that time the J2 Ops. He introduced the author to his UK counterpart and added some details to the in-theatre mission requirements. In the evening the author's wife Faye and sons Jonathan, and Sean arrived in Ottawa, to join him for the trip to Kingston.

On 16 May 1997, the author and his family drove from Ottawa to Kingston to attend his graduation ceremony at RMC at 12:30 hours. The 3½ hour ceremony saw 26 successful candidates receiving Master's degrees including Capt Ed C. Denbeigh (a fellow Int officer), LCol Paul Taillon (now with CSIS and a fellow officer cadet when they were in the Reserves together at CFB Shilo, Manitoba, in 1973), and Maj J.G. Savard (a Security Officer from CFSIS). The group marched into the Auditorium carrying their red hoods over their left arm. As Professor Ronald G. Haycock read out each name, the graduates marched forward one at a time to present themselves to the Dean, where he placed the hood over each degree recipient's head, conferring the degree of Master of Arts War Studies on each. Each graduate then took one step backward, saluted, made a right turn and marched off. The author now had an MA, some 23 years after earning his BFA degree at NSCAD.

## *1997, CISA Member News*

Penelope Noble, widow of LCol Robert H. "Tex" Noble completed a biography entitled "Tex—A Memoir, 1933-1947," chronicling Tex's activities in Intelligence before and during WWII, and post-war in Germany, before his return to the C Int C in Canada.

Capt J.P. Stéphane Lefebvre, 2 Int Pl Ottawa, was presented the Commander LFCA Commendation in recognition of his outstanding motivation, dedication and service to 2 Int Pl during his appointment as Acting CO from 15 Jul 95 to 5 Aug 96.

LCol John Cruse is being awarded the OMM. Maj John Brian Brooks reported from Winnipeg where he and other members of the Int Branch are working on the Red River Flood control force.

The CDA AGM took place in Ottawa 22-25 Jan 97, with Maj Doris E. Guyatt and Maj Fred E.G. Jones attending on behalf of CISA. Col Patricia M. Samson of the Security Branch and Col Patrick D.R. Crandell of the Int Branch also attended, along with Col Ron J. Donovan, LCol Jack S. Dunn, LCol Earnest Skutezky, Maj Terry B. Kelly, and Maj John "Pappy" MacKinnon. A Special Advisory Group on Military Justice and Military Police Investigation Services was announced at the meeting, to be chaired by the Right Honourable Brian Dickson. Col R.J. Donovan, assisted by LCol Jack S. Dunn served on the group's advisory committee and input was drawn from members BGen Douglas Yuill, Col Patricia M. Samson, LCol Tony Battista and others. Col Samson spoke to the CISA AGM on the concerns of the Security Branch, principally on the future of MPs in the CF. Col Patrick D.R. Crandell spoke about the main problem for the Int Branch—too much work for too few people, a problem shared by Col Samson's Branch.

Col Craig B. MacFarlane passed away in Burlington, Ontario, on 23 Jan 1997. He was appointed the first patron of CISA in 1981, and had been an honorary life member of the association. Col MacFarlane had been an Attaché with the Canadian Embassy in Moscow.

Col John Pemberton Page of Waterdown, Ontario, passed away on 16 Feb 1997. John served in the CF, Regular and Reserve for 50 years in many capacities. As a Maj, he was appointed G3 Int at CMHQ in London, England, in Nov 1940. One of his first aims was to evaluate Canadian Army Int and to promote the idea that the Canadian Army should have its own Int Corps, such as the British Army had. He pursued this aim relentlessly by a reasoned, logical study of the background, problems and possible future trends of Int. His efforts eventually bore fruit, and the C Int C was formed on 29 Oct 1942. Maj S. Robert Elliot stated in S to G, "if anyone can claim to be the Father of the Corps, it is Col John P. Page." Maj S. Robert Elliott described him as "a brilliant administrator," whose work at CMHQ was "outstanding." He took part in the planning of the North Africa and Normandy landings, and postwar served as co-administrator of the War Crimes Section of the Canadian Army. Among his decorations are the Croix de Guerre with Rubies from France, the Bronze Star from the USA, and the Order of the Red Banner from the USSR for his work in the exchange of Canadian and Russian POWs. After WWII, he resumed his pre-War teaching career at several colleges. A keen educator, he and his associates researched and initiated many new programs in the early days of the Community college movement. He was also actively involved in cadet training, and his Unit won the Earl Grey Trophy for the best in Canada.

Capt Ben Kuban passed away in Vancouver on 29 Jan 1997 at the age of 69. Ben was born in Turkey and served in the Israeli Security and Intelligence apparatus before immigrating to Canada in 1966. He worked in Vancouver as an accountant and in management before retiring in 1992.

Maj Stanley H. Winfield, a former President of CISA, was posted as an RCAF Sgt (Int) to 84 Gp HQ RAF at Celle, Germany in May 1945. Celle, a town with a history dating back to 990 AD, is about 20 km from the notorious Bergen-Belsen Concentration Camp, which had been overrun by 11 British Armd Div in Apr 45. Stan returned to Belsen for the 50th anniversary of the Camp's liberation as a guest of the Government of Lower Saxony, on 25 Apr 1995.[7]

## *1997, Air Intelligence, Trenton*

Major Alex C. Chambers reported that he, "arrived at 8 Wing Trenton in July 1997. With an establishment of eight personnel, we were constantly deploying on Ops & exercises. Following 9/11/01, the Comd 1 CAD, with "prodding" from LCol J.R.Y. Mike Foucreault, recognized that the under-strength Air Force Int cadre could not support all the deployments & activities being demanded of it. He therefore authorized an increase of 54 PYs across the Air Force, with 16 of those new positions coming to 8 Wing so we could perpetually support our own Tactical Airlift Ops, continue to perform normal duties at home, & allow time for professional training."[8]

Ice Storm, Ontario and Quebec, 1997

## *1997, Ice Storm, Quebec*

Intelligence was also of critical importance when the ice storm hit Quebec in 1997, knocking out power in large parts of the province. LCol Mike R.J. Ouellette had the following comments on the situation. "I was able to put together a 40-pers Intelligence section from elements of my G2 staff, the 4e Cie de Rens and 1 Cdn Div Int Coy in Kingston and we did IPB on the areas which were out of power, areas which were considered critically short of elec-

7. CISA Newsletter, Vol. 27, No.1, May 1997, pp. 1-6.
8. Maj Alex Chambers, E-mail 5 September 2003.

tricity, and those areas which were coming back on line etc. Through this work, the Intelligence section was able to accurately brief the Commander on the situation on the regions most badly hit and in need of help. The popularity rating of the CF shot up with this operation, as the CF were seen to be in control of the situation and providing service personnel and resources (providing firewood, shelters, generators, water etc) to over 1.5 million people in dire need. The efforts of the Intelligence section was recognized by the Comd when I was presented with the LFQA Area Commander's Commendation."[9]

## June to December 1997, Sarajevo, Bosnia-Herzegovina, CO CANIC

The author was mugged out of the Tactics School on 19 June 1997 and on 21 June headed overseas to Bosnia-Herzegovina to be the CO CANIC, CC SFOR in Sarajevo. The flights took him from Fredericton to Boston, then on to Frankfurt, Munich, and Zagreb, Croatia. He checked in with the Canadian administrative centre at Pleso near Zagreb airfield, and spent the night in the Holiday Hotel in Zagreb—pretty much the standard in-clearance procedure for new arrivals in theatre.

The next morning the author drew his Kevlar helmet, flak jacket, 9mm pistol, two magazines with ten rounds each, a comfortable shoulder holster, and was issued his rules of engagement (ROE) card. On his way back to Zagreb airport he took note of the five Russian-made Mi-24 Hind helicopters on the tarmac. While waiting for the Greek C-130 Hercules flight into Sarajevo, he observed a Russian-made Mi-17 Hip helicopter flying in. This was the first time the author had seen either of these helicopters after several years of teaching "Red Force" aircraft recognition to various Intelligence students. He also took particular note of several well-marked minefields, sealed off with barbed wire along the pathway to the flight line.

During the Hercules flight into Sarajevo, the author spoke with Brigitte Duschene, a Canadian UNCF Area Information Officer for the FYR also based in Sarajevo. She had remained in the city throughout the shooting war, and based on her experience and observations, firmly believed the upcoming elections in Bosnia-Herzegovina would not go ahead in September 97. Most SFOR personnel believed otherwise.

---

9.    LCol Michael Ouellette, E-mail 29 September 2003.

On arrival at Sarajevo's heavily damaged airport, the author was met by Maj Robert J. McCutcheon and Sgt Michael C. "Skippy" Wagner from 3 Int Coy in Halifax. The author's kit was quickly loaded into the CANIC's Mitsubishi truck and they headed off to Camp Ilidza. Although the city is surrounded by beautiful high mountains, the considerable battle damage done to the city during the war was heavily evident along the route to Ilidza. French VAB and AMX-10RC armoured vehicles were stationed at close intervals nearby to provide security, along with a number of US HUMMVs and a variety of multi-national forces patrolling various key routes. Although Sarajevo sits at a high elevation in the mountains, the atmosphere was very humid. The author toured the CANIC and met PO André Gibeault again, as well as his new 2IC, Capt David B. Owen, WO Byron K. Mackenzie and MCpl Ian Steel.

CANIC, Sarajevo, Bosnia-Herzegovina, 1997.
Front row kneeling: Capt David B. Owen, MCpl Ian Steel, PO André Gibeault.
Rear row standing: WO R. Hal Pugh, Maj Harold A. Skaarup, Sgt Michael C. Wagner, WO Byron K. Mackenzie, Capt Al Haywood, PO1 William D. Kean

Within the SFOR compound at Ilidza on the west end of the city, bunk space was extraordinarily difficult to come by. There was only enough space for a one-for-one exchange of personnel, four to a room. This meant all new-comers were bunked temporarily in the empty beds while other SFOR personnel were away or on leave. In the evening he met Turkish Officers who worked with the Turkish NIC (TUNIC). They had a very long chat about the Kurds, Bosniacs, Saladin, the Ottoman Empire and Turkey. The author spent his first night in Sarajevo in the top Bunk in a room in the Srbija Hotel, where four people were crammed in a room about the same bathroom-sized one the author had for just himself at the Ledra Palace in Cyprus.

There were 13 National Intelligence Centres (NICs) in the NIC village located inside a secure compound on the Western end of Sarajevo in the sub-urb of Ilidza. The Americans worked out of the USNIC in a central com-pound with lots of security guards and MPs (50-100 people). The British worked across from the Canadians in the UKNIC (11 pers), just behind the SFOR helicopter landing pad. The Turkish NIC (with 5 or 6 pers) was to the immediate right of the CANIC, not far from the Spanish NIC (six pers), the Swedish NIC (4 pers), the Italian NIC (up to 3 pers), the Norwegian NIC (1 here and 11 in the Norwegian garrison up North), the German NIC (about 13 people), the Danish NIC (six people), the French NIC (seven people) and the Dutch NIC (with 3 pers). There was also a group with the Deployed Security Force (DSF) made up with representatives from four nations (UK, US, FR & GE). The Swedes, Danes and Norwegians eventually combined to form a Scandinavian NIC called the "SCANIC" in January 1998. The Portuguese, Belgians and Romanians also began working with us to establish NICs within our intelligence community).

The author began making the rounds to meet the various organizations the CANIC worked in concert with to support the SFOR mission, beginning with MWO Penley with the Mapping Engineers. Rob and the author then drove down to the Holiday Inn which served as the press conference centre for most Public Affairs and media activities in Sarajevo), to meet with Ms Dus-chene. Brigitte had remained in the city throughout the fighting and carefully pointed out several battle positions and sniper sites she had seen in use during the war. The remains of war damage were evident everywhere in the city, with 20 and 30 story buildings burned out or partially gutted, although some of the lower stages were already under repair. The newspaper office seemed to be the most heavily damaged (and photographed), because it had been on the front line and took a lot of serious hits from tank rounds. Shell strikes could be seen on most of the buildings in the city.

The Int Majors returned to Camp Ilidza, which is essentially a five-hotel complex that used to have thermal baths (badly damaged now). The Archduke Franz Ferdinand and his wife Sophie stayed there the night before their assassination by Gavrilo Prinzip on 28 June 1914. The spot where Prinzip stood when he fired his "shot heard around the world," had been marked with a plaque, but the markers in downtown Sarajevo were eradicated not long after the author's arrival, because Prinzip had been a Serb. The citizens of Sarajevo, particularly the Bosniacs, were decidedly unhappy with the treatment and shelling meted out to them during the war by the Serbs. Helicopters constantly churned into the heliport alongside the CANIC with the first one the author observed being a Royal Navy Sea King helicopter peculiarly decked out with an arctic "zebra-stripe" winter camouflage pattern, since it had just returned from the Falkland Islands.

The author was introduced to Wendy Gilmore, from the Canadian Office of the High Representative (OHR). Wendy worked for the Canadian Department of Foreign Affairs and International Trade (DFAIT) in Sarajevo. The OHR is actually senior to SFOR. The three had an interesting chat about the politics and personalities in Bosnia-Herzegovina. The two Majors went for a brief walk downtown, with the "Newbie" feeling odd being armed at the time, although it was normal for all military personnel there. There were lots of young people strolling around the pedestrian mall area, and there were many shops open at ground level. The war damage however, was evident everywhere, in the form of multiple mortar splashes in the pavement underfoot to the scores of burnt out stories and wings of buildings. Some repairs were underway, but it appeared that it was going to be a long slow recovery process before the city was restored to its pre-Olympic stature.

The author met with Canadian Public Affairs Officer (PAFFO), LCdr Denise LaViolette, who had driven up from Mostar where she worked with the headquarters of the French-led Multinational Division South East (MND (SE)), and then visited the UK NIC to meet their CO, Maj Andrew Perry. They also spoke with the GCHQ LO, Dewi Blythe. Both men were two of the finest one could know in theatre. In the evening the author was invited to visit the TUNIC where Capt Fikret Guzeller introduced the author to the CO of the TUNIC, Col Celic, and his NIC staff.

The HQ staff and senior NIC personnel attended a video tele-conference (VTC) each day at 0800 hrs. These conferences were chaired by a British officer, BGen Simon Munro (who had attended Toronto Staff College), and were a regular feature of the CANIC daily routine. The conference was primarily for the commanders of the three MNDs (N, SW & SE) with SFOR in Bosnia-Herzegovina. This was followed by several briefings covering the American-led Train and Equip (T & E) program (which a number of SFOR participants had some serious heartache with), which was also held in the Srbija Hotel. The author met US LCol Washington (J3 Coord), and later met with the CANUKUS Intelligence Community at the UKNIC. These became the most interesting and valuable meetings of the week. The author also met a British Analyst, Maj Julian Moir, who was wearing a uniform he acquired on a previous overseas tour in Cambodia. Julian wore a black patch over one eye, to cover an injury he had sustained after accidentally striking unexploded ordnance (UXO) during a training exercise in Suffield, Alberta. Maj Andrew Perry, CO of the UKNIC, and Maj Rick Gallegos, DCO of the USNIC also participated in these meetings. LCol Robert M. Parsons (who worked for CJ2 and had been designated as the Canadian Army G2) and a crew of 20 Int people from all three countries sat in on the verbal free-for-all. There were excellent and productive round-table discussions on every subject of intelligence interest concerning Bosnia-Herzegovina.

The two Majors visited the Canadian Embassy, where they met with Ms Kati Csaba, Deputy to the Ambassador. Kati had been in the city of Kiev, in the Ukraine prior to being posted to Sarajevo, and spoke some Russian as well. She introduced us to Ambassador Serge Marcoux. The three engaged in a long and useful chat on the history of the Balkans and on possible future developments in the area. They returned to the CANIC for an evening farewell BBQ party at the UKNIC for all the departing NIC crews rotating out. Capt Eric E. Gjos, the Int officer in Coralici dropped in to visit with his crew.

The author signed off the Board of Inquiry for the CO's handover, and on 27 June Rob and the author signed the CANIC Change-of-Command certificates for the handover, and then went through some more indoctrination. At 1030 hours, Capt Eric E. Gjos gave an Int briefing to the collected SFOR staffs. His presentation went over very well and he made the Canadian Int Branch look good.

The CANIC team attended meetings at the Canadian Camp in Velika Kladusa on a monthly basis. The route averaged several hundred kilometres, and to maximise the opportunity, we drove a different route each time. During each of the trips we took along our helmets, flak jackets, pistols, kit-bags and lots of water. At the end of June, Sgt Michael C. Wagner drove Rob and the author in the Mitsubishi over to the site of the former Olympic ice-skating stadium at Zetra to pick up LCol Robert M. Parsons. This is the same Olympic stadium where Canada's Gaetan Boucher won two gold medals in 1984. The stadium looked like it was nearly ready to collapse, although it was probably a lot like the Aitken Centre in Fredericton before it was shelled. Although we assessed that it would likely have to be torn down and rebuilt because of the amount of damage it had sustained, it was eventually repaired and SFOR was required to "move out." The US Embassy, which was nearby, was very heavily sandbagged and protected with armoured Bradleys. The group drove out of the city at a hair-raising pace on what turned out to be a very hot day.

They passed by a fair number of German LUCHs and French VAB APCs along the way. (Earlier, one of the LUCHs crews had accidentally electrically discharged five 20mm rounds from the Rarden cannon mounted on his LUCHs into the vehicle ahead, killing two of his German colleagues). They continued on South West, passing an old Roman bridge just outside the Ilidza defensive compound. It is not far from one of the 25 lodges (this one had been destroyed) that Tito used to maintain for himself and his party officials. The scenery is fantastic with beautiful tree-lined valleys, but far too many damaged and ethnically cleansed (EC) homes were in evidence everywhere. (The UN reports the destroyed houses number over two million in BiH alone).

The group drove past the garrison town of Bradina where the author observed a pair of Sherman tanks, some home-made APCs and several tubes of artillery (105mm and 120mm) parked out front. At Jablanica they drove by a Ukrainian Airborne unit equipped with BTR-70s, guarding a bailey type bridge. Signs indicated that the French Foreign Legion (FFL) built the bridge. They drove past some major battle damage near Potruci and on to the city of Mostar. It is very heavily damaged, but the saddest view was of the remains of the beautiful old bridge the city of Mostar is famous for (Most means bridge), which formerly spanned the Neretva (Ar) River. The Mostar Bridge was built in 1566 by the Turks, but was destroyed by a Croat tank in 1993. There is a rough suspension bridge hanging in its place, and SFOR engineers have constructed other bridges over the river to restore the flow of traffic.

The crew crossed through the Bosnia-Herzegovina-Croatian border checkpoint, where they were waved through without any formality due to the SFOR sign on the truck. They had to remove and stow their pistols as they are now out of their jurisdiction in Croatia. They drove north along the Adriatic coast to the touristic city of Split, and then began the uphill climb through mountain roads passing bare and ragged looking white rock which rose several thousand feet up from the coast. They dropped off LCol Robert M. Parsons at Trogir airport. They followed the coastal route to Sibenik, noting several radars and an old round tower (possibly WW II era) and forts sitting high in the hills. They then turned inland to Benkovac, passing countless numbers of wrecked and unoccupied homes. As far as the eye could see, all electricity lines were down and power poles had been destroyed. There were many villages with 20 homes where the locals had blown up seven or eight of their ethnically incorrect neighbours. Continuing overland to Obrovac, the crew observed entire villages with 50 to 60 homes abandoned or looted, all now ghost towns. Lots of them…far too many of them…and always more of them.

They skirted around a lake at Novigradska More, and then drove down a steep valley passing a strategically sited medieval castle ruin which had a long defensive wall running down to the river. Crossing the river, they followed seemingly endless hairpin switchbacks more than 5,000' up over the mountains. They kept passing a great number of villages entirely abandoned. It is a grim sight when you come from the farm country the author calls home in New Brunswick and see the countless number of ancient farms not being tended, and no signs of life or livestock for very long distances. In over 100 kms along this route, there were only a few goats seen along the way. They drove down the other side of the mountain to Gracac, where there were many more damaged homes, although some seemed to be occupied. Half the village of Gracac seemed to be abandoned; the other half seemed to be barely functioning.

At Prijeboj they turned east and zig-zagged up the mountains to Bihac. They crossed the border at Petrovno-Selo, where the first visibly noticeable and instant change was the sight of well-cultivated, thoroughly well-cared for farms and fields bursting with ripe crops. It reminded the author of southern Germany in prime harvest season. There were new mosques and minarets everywhere. Every field seemed to be well tended and groomed, hay mows were stacked by hand, corn, wheat, wall-to-wall crops could be seen, and an enormous contrast of green compared to the route we had taken thus far. There was a very "middle-European" appearance to the place. At this point, however, the reality check set in, and all of us put our weapons back on.

Bihac is a very prosperous and modern-looking town, somewhat like Lahr. The northern end of the city had suffered some battle damage, however. The town is taking care of itself and there was a lot of reconstruction evident on mosques and minarets with shiny new copper roofing. On the way up the hill towards Cazin the crew passed a local police checkpoint (likely unauthorized), and a man roasting what must have been a goat (the group at first thought it was a dog) on a spit.

Above Cazin they came upon a very well restored late medieval castle with three turrets and a long stone curtain wall. Its wooden roof had been restored, and the castle was strategically placed to overlook the valley near Coralici. They arrived at the Headquarters for the Canadian Contingent (CC) SFOR, a logistics camp at Velika Kladusa (VK), after covering 600 km of some very rough terrain. There were two Czech Mi-17 Hip helicopters in grey and white tiger stripe camouflage parked in the centre of the camp. The author met Col J.J. Selbie and his staff and then toured the excellent facilities they have set up in an old farm implement factory. Col Selbie gave Rob and the author CO's rooms (a single CORIMEC trailer to ourselves). The author slept like a king.

Early the next morning, the author seized the opportunity to spend an hour inside one of the Mi-17 Hips chatting with the three-man crew of the Czech helicopter, followed by a 3½ hour staff meeting. Col Selbie presided over Rob's and the author's Change of Command of the CANIC. After supper it grew very hot and muggy. Rob and the author walked about 9 km (4.5 km each way) to an old castle with three towers including a very high one in stone with a restored wooden roof. They stopped to chat with a German speaking Bosnia-Herzegovina family on the way back, and learned that the family was afraid of what will happen when SFOR leaves.

The next day Rob was dropped off in Zagreb and the author and "Skippy" headed back to Sarajevo, driving along a long winding road along a green river valley, with lots of zig-zagging through the towns of Potok, Tounj, Josipdol, passing a lot of well-groomed farms. Josipdol was the first town they encountered with significant war damage that appeared to have involved an equal amount of ethnic cleansing. Seven homes were destroyed, 25 were still occupied. Along the coast they passed by an empty Croat Naval and Air Base with a destroyed Mi-8 Hip helicopter (Blue and White colours) occupying a deserted compound on the inland side.

They drove past more wrecked buildings just 2 km north of Krisac, and then on to Tribanj, right on the water, where they observed several homes that had been cleansed (dynamited) on the shore north and south of Paklenca. 8 or 9 homes had been destroyed in the village of Murvika, then a whole series of groups of homes and buildings were observed that had been demolished beyond salvage, with everything flattened. As they drove into Zadar, they passed by countless numbers of more wrecked homes. Many more had suffered light damage from shell fragments but new construction and repairs seemed to be underway. The shell fragments seemed to do less damage than the ethnic cleansing. Lights were blown out, and many buildings were burned out on the north edge of town. In several cases, huge amounts of explosives must have been required to flatten the large numbers of stone and concrete buildings in this area. Driving south towards Sibenik they passed a large Marina at Sukosan. A few buildings had artillery shell holes, but no demolition had taken place to finish them off. In Vodice there was a large observation post with flags flying and scaffolding to shore up its reconstruction on a hill on the north end of the town. Strangely, there was no apparent damage in Sibenik.

It was dusk as they reached the border. They continued back up the Neretva River valley and were back into Ilidza just past the 11 PM curfew. The Norwegian guard gave them a bit of "stick," but eased up when he recognised Sgt Michael C. Wagner. ("Skippy" must have been the best-known Canadian in Bosnia-Herzegovina, because of his friendly demeanour and the fact that he said hi and spoke to everybody).

On 3 July the CANIC crew participated in an interesting CANUKUS "Three-eyes" meeting. They sent off some useful data to the Yugoslavia Crisis Cell (YCC), later renamed the Bosnia-Herzegovina Intelligence Cell (BIRT), in Ottawa. The author met the CO of the GENIC and the new CO of the USNIC. Cdr Larry Ash during the USNIC change of command ceremony. The author also spoke with the Hellenic NIC (Greek) and FRNIC COs, and later met LCol Møller-Peterson, the Danish Ops O and members of the ITNIC and SPNIC. The CANIC staff visited LCol Kjell Eriksson, the CO of the Swedish NIC (SWENIC) and had a "two-eyes" meeting with his staff.

At 0800 on 10 July 1997, the morning video teleconference at SFOR HQ in Sarajevo was very calm. At 0900 hours the CANIC Int staff attended the weekly three-eyes meeting in the UKNIC. During the discussions, a CH-147 Chinook helicopter lifted off from the helipad beside them, and then a Sikorsky CH-53 Super Stallion lifted off behind it. These are all heavy lift helicopters, and it was very unusual for them to be on the pad at the same time. Moments later, Cdr Ash, the USNIC CO was pulled from the meeting. Shortly afterwards, Capt Eric E. Gjos called from the Canadian Battle Group in Coralici to tell us "heads up—something is in the wind."

About 0900 hours the SAS/SFOR moved to arrest Simo Drljaca, as Bosnia-Herzegovina Serb Person Indicted for War Crimes (PIFWC) and former police chief of Prijedor in the RS. He pulled out a pistol and shot one of the British soldiers in the leg during the arrest. They promptly ventilated him with about five rounds, killing him on the spot. At the same time, another PIFWC, hospital director Milan Kovacevic as well as Drljaca's brother in law and Drljaca's son, were also seized and taken to the Hague for trial. There was of course, a lot of associated intelligence activity. (Drljaca's son and brother-in-law were released the next day).

The author visited the Canadian Embassy to meet with Kati Csaba and Guy Archambault for an interesting discussion. OHR/DFAIT representative Wendy Gilmore called, and so did UN information officer Brigitte Duschene. The senior OHR representative Mr Carlos Westendorp arrived just as the author exited the Srbija/SFOR HQ. There were a lot of plain-clothes security personnel around, all wearing earphones and carrying heavy weapons. This was the largest turnout of interested participants the author had seen to date for the daily 17:30 hours Joint Operations Centre (JOC) conference. The mood in the UK/US community was very upbeat (unlike the 36 other nations in SFOR that felt they had been left out of the loop).

On 8 July members of the CANIC crew headed off north to Doboj in heavy rain, intending to loop over to visit the US camp at Tuzla. They drove the SFOR routes Finch, Dove, Skoda and Lada, 79 km to Zenica were there was very heavy damage to the factories and train stations visible along the way, along with dozens of shattered villages north of Sarajevo. A beautiful river coursed along the route between very steep hill sides and heavily wooded valley walls and with the roads in fairly good shape. Every village had its share of ethnically cleansed homes, most of which appear to have been destroyed by their own neighbours. The large autobahn bridge at Visoko was blown up by the locals during the Canadian occupation of the town in 1993. There is a bailey bridge over the river and a large detour around it, but the road is good beyond it for highway travel. A German LUCHs guarded the bridge crossing site.

Although Canada had occupied the town of Visoko during the war, there were no Canadians based there in 1997. The bulk of the 1,300 Canadian forces in Bosnia-Herzegovina were located in Coralici and Velika Kladusa, with about 50 personnel in the Sarajevo area, including the six in the CANIC. A man walking his cow or goat is a very common sight here. There are so many uncharted minefields that livestock must be herded carefully to keep them from being blown to pieces. In the Bosnia-Herzegovina Muslim areas, the Serbs Orthodox Christians have mostly been cleansed, although some of the victims may have been Catholic Croats. Serb homes have a single two sided peak roof over them, Bosnia-Herzegovina homes have four-sided square roofs, and Croat homes have a small gable on each end of a peaked roof, much like Black Forest homes. You could quickly tell who the victims were and therefore who were the most likely perpetrators by the shape of the damaged and destroyed homes.

During the trip the crew noticed a Czech SFOR Mi-17 Hip flying low through the wet weather over the river valley beside them—quite a site when one remembers all those recognition lectures every Int person has had. The crew observed a lot of damage in the Croatian pocket at Maglaj, and clear evidence of heavy ethnic cleansing and shellfire damage on the south edge of the city as well. They passed by a number of SFOR groups of vehicles escorting ARBiH Troops through the area, as well as many more signs of ethnic cleansing. There was a large resort style hotel completely burned out sited on the north side of town. Dutch Troops were examining an ARBiH truck near Trgvina. Just south of Doboj they came upon two destroyed T-55 tanks and a wrecked BVP M-60 APC. The wrecked tanks and APCs are technically in no-man's land, between the two factions.

The Danes and the Dutch manned the checkpoint at the Bailey bridge in a heavily defended SFOR position on the internal unofficial border between the Federation and the RS. There was a lot of shell damage apparent at Rasadnik. They passed by a Danish SFOR Camp just south of Doboj and another one run by Finland. The scenes of damage gradually disappeared as they crossed the river and headed east to Tuzla on a yellow SFOR route.

The crew pulled into the United Nations International Police Task Force (UNIPTF) HQ to meet RCMP Inspector Chris Bothe. He supervised 500 monitors in the Tuzla area, plus anther 259 in Brcko. His IPTF officers were from 28 different countries (although only a few of them served in SFOR). The CANIC staff had a good chat with Chris and he introduced them to his Russian deputies and some members of the force from Nepal. After a brief stop at the US Task Force Eagle base, they headed south, encountering Russians, Swedes, Turks, Norwegians, Brits and American SFOR Troops everywhere. Following Ostrich route they headed west to Zivinice, which had a very narrow and extremely winding route back, with major parts of it under construction. They continued on through a very narrow valley with steep sides and the road cut into the mountain walls and hard rock above the river. They continued passing a number of ethnically cleansed restaurants and homes high in the mountains.

From Kladanj, a lumber mill town, they continued back up more winding routes past some seriously damaged buildings, where everything seemed to have been demolished in small communities of a dozen or so homes. All of the single dwellings and restaurants every few km on the winding roads had been destroyed. The letters "SDA" were spray painted on many of the wrecked buildings. The crew estimated that 50% of the buildings they saw along this route had been destroyed as they neared the Stupcanica lumberyard. Heavier damage was sustained by the factories and apartments in Olivo.

Signs everywhere indicated that Brcko is "the key." It is a small town on the Sava river of importance to all factions, and was the most contested site in Bosnia-Herzegovina up to that time. Whoever gets control of it has serious economic power, and all three sides want it, hence the continuing tension in the area. There were lots of large but totally devastated farms in view on the northern edge of Ivanica. GDS and SDA signs have been spray painted on the wrecked buildings. The CANIC crew crossed over a bailey bridge dubbed "Edith Bridge" just before driving into Srednije. They followed very steep mountain roads to Semizovac, where they observed several Egyptian APCs and soldiers guarding a railway station checkpoint. There were lots more wrecked buildings all the way down the mountain road to Sarajevo.

On a return trip to VK, they passed through Klenovic, and found evidence of severe ethnic cleansing, with lots of damage everywhere. There were dozens of wrecked farms, and no occupants could be seen, although there were a few fresh haystacks (very few). It was the same in Bravsko. Ethnic cleansing to the nth degree. They drove past more large open fields and pastures, rolling foot-hills with small farms, all trashed. Passed a crashed DC-3 Dakota that appears to have been mounted on concrete pylons to preserve it as a memorial out in the middle of nowhere. Apparently there is (or was) an airstrip nearby that had been heavily fought over during the war. It sits in a barren area just south of Vtroce. The town of Ripoc appears to be more than 90% destroyed due to both battle and ethnic cleansing. The CANIC crew pulled into the city of Bihac. They passed by an M53/59 twin 30mm SPAAG (Czech & Yugo made), burned out on the edge of the road just south of Ripoc.

The crew continued on to the Canadian camp at Coralici, with its gate on the West side of the road and well marked. The gate guard on duty had been in 2 Commando when the author was in Cyprus in 1986-87. The crew visited Capt Bob Martyn, the Battle Group Int Officer. He had a nine person Int

Section (including Private Hereford from 6 Int Coy in Edmonton. The LdSH and the PPCLI make up the bulk of the battle group in Coralici. The crew continued on to VK where they met their new CO (Admin), Col M.D. Capstick. It had taken roughly eight and a half hours of mountain driving to cover the 359 km between Sarajevo and VK.

The next morning the CANIC crew drove 2-3 km into Croatia and north to Mihojska. Here one could see homes where people had returned and repaired their homes with new glass (a figure S is marked on the glass in soap), only to have it smashed out again, probably by the same neighbours who did it in the first place. The message was very clear, they don't want these people to move back. They drove south to Jovov, Dunjak, and Donja Busovaca and then looped back to Krstinja. Everywhere you looked there were shot up farms. They noticed that the gravestones of Serbs had been shot up with pistol rounds. The Croat and Bosnia-Herzegovina ethnic cleansing of Serbs and their homes was just as intense here as what was observed on the other side. The crew headed back to VK, and in the afternoon, the Canadian Ambassador, Serge Marcoux, visited the camp and addressed the conference. Maj Richard Round gave a really good briefing on the OSCE and the September elections coming up. The crew headed back to camp (it was not a place one would really want to spend a lot of time in, let alone six months. We were glad to be working in Sarajevo).

The desolation and destruction throughout the country makes one think of the scorched earth policy in place during Napoleonic times. In many cases, every building, no matter how remotely situated, had been destroyed. The crew found a UNIPTF station in Lusci Patanka sited in a town that was completely wrecked. There were people carrying out repairs in the towns of Fnjtovici and Kamengrad (about 50% destroyed). They passed by a number of British AS-90 155mm self-propelled guns in an SFOR camp at or near Sanski Most ("Most" means bridge). Then they came upon a Czech recce platoon (the real thing), with three BMP-2 APCs and supporting SSVs, just like what Int staff have been teaching from the books on Fantasian and Generic Enemy forces.

The road running into Kljuc on Bluebird route was very rough. They found a lot of damage in Komar, and a patrol of Dutch M-113s on the route into Travnik. Here there were lots of buildings undergoing repairs and a good road to Kakanj. They took a major detour through Visoko. The main highway bridge here had been blown down during the war and the site was still causing a major detour, although SFOR engineers were working on cutting the mess up and putting a bailey type bridge across the river. The crew arrived back into Sarajevo after a 400 km return trip in eight hours.

On 30 Jul 97, there was a US four-star change of command ceremony, with Gen Crouch handing over the command of SFOR to Gen Eric K. Shinseki. Gen Wesley K. Clark from SACEUR presided over the ceremony. Just before the ceremony, the author ran into Gen William W. Crouch and spoke briefly with him about the situation in theatre. The author also spoke with the SFOR Political Advisor, Ms Mette Nielsen about Madame Plavsic, one of the Serb leaders invited to the ceremony but who didn't show up. The Generals in charge of each of the three MNDs also changed command, with MGen LeChatelier handing over to MGen Christian Delanghe in MND SE, MGen Montgomery C. Meigs handing over to MGen David L. Grange in MND N, and MGen Ramsay taking over in MND SW.

On 11 Aug 97, a CANIC Brainstorming session was held for all NICs. This was the first regular meeting with members of the CANIC, NONIC, TUNIC, SWENIC, and UKNIC (GCHQ). A second meeting for the CANIC, ITNIC, NLNIC, SPNIC and CO UKNIC took place in the after-noon. The author had dubbed these meetings think-tank sessions, and advised all participants to bring an argument. They also had to bring a flak jacket if they felt that their particular opinion was the only correct one, since each par-ticipant had to leave his rank and flag at the door. Also, everyone had to have a cup of coffee if they came in (the theory being it is hard to be disgruntled with a cup of coffee in your hand). Major disagreements were to be taken out to the penalty box (an outdoor shed roofed over and wired with a stereo sys-tem above the bench built by the CANIC crew). The Germans dubbed the meetings "brainstorming" sessions, and the name stuck.

In August the crew visited HQ MND SE at Camp Ortijes on the east side of the Neretva river. The French, Spanish, Moroccans, Germans and three Canadians occupy this Camp. They also visited the AMIB team in Camp Ortijes.

On another trip they drove north to Tuzla and on into the Serb Republic. At the IEBL they came upon the infamous "Arizona Market" with a prolifer-ation of vendors selling watermelon, cassette tapes, car parts and just about anything legal or illegal one could think of on the regular as well as the black market in this "no-man's land" between the Federation and the RS. Just past the Arizona market, the devastation began again. The farms are not worked for about four km, then suddenly the view changes and there are fields of corn, ploughed fields and freshly painted Serb homes, although they were still on Arizona route. They turned and drove east to Brcko on Texas route. Brcko is a beautiful little town on the Sava River, and the site of the most controversy between the three factions in Bosnia-Herzegovina-Herzegovina. It is locked up tight by the US, and as they entered the shot up area of the city, a Black-hawk helicopter constantly hovered overhead. (Three days later the RS organized a "spontaneous" demonstration that led to the burning of 40 vehicles belonging to members of the IPTF in Brcko).

Heading south, the crew stopped to eat in a restaurant at Vlasenica. The owner was reluctant to let armed soldiers in ("it is bad for business," he explained in German), but he agreed to let them eat outdoors where he served them "deer medallions." As they ate, they noticed some very interested visitors inspecting their Mitsubishi. In fact, too many and too often the same swarthy individuals for their comfort. They paid their bill and hauled freight up the mountains, driving back to Sarajevo in the dark via the Pale overpass. An Italian Centauro (an eight wheeled AFV armed with a 105mm gun) and an American convoy passed them on the way, both very reassuring).

On 28 Aug 97, Brcko exploded in the morning. Organized "demonstrators" were bussed in by the Pale faction of the RS to harass and intimidate the UN IPTF. SFOR does not supposed to fight unarmed civilians. Civil matters are handled by the police. These demonstrators however, destroyed police cars at the station, then "cleansed" the station itself, then walked to the specific homes of the IPTF and burned their vehicles there as well. At least 40 were torched during the demonstration. The Canadian RCMP representative, Duncan, was one of the few who stayed to monitor the situation in the city throughout the crisis. The regular three-eyes meeting was interesting. A long period of writing reports followed. By about 3 PM the show was over, and the spontaneous demonstrators in Brcko were paid and driven back to their homes in time for supper.

At the evening video-teleconference (VTC), BGen Simon Munro tried to lighten up the atmosphere by bemoaning the lack of music. The author went back and got the CANIC miniature tape recorder and taped a bit of "Monty Python" music to have for the next morning's VTC. The next morning, at the 0800 VTC he waited until the Brigadier marched in and as he came by he hit the tape. The Italian beside him jumped away to distance himself from the author, but the Brigadier's aide, a Scottish major flashed him a big grin and a thumbs up. The Brigadier hollered, "that's not my regimental march," but then smiled and sat down. (The Scottish major later went one better, and did the same thing only with the correct march. The author spent weeks trying to find a real piper to see if he could one up him again, but both were posted out. There is no point in letting everyone get bored).

The crew had a very good all-NICs meeting at 0930. The author had a very long chat with the Turkish NIC CO, Col Celik. Col Celic took out a red-ribboned gold medal that his father had earned during the Turkish war of Independence during the 1920's. As a serving member of the Turkish Army, this was the one day he is permitted to wear it on his father's behalf. He invited the author as his guest to the Turkish Victory Day celebration at the Army Hall in downtown Sarajevo. He picked the author up in his land rover and then drove to the hall with flags flying. The guests observed a promotion ceremony for three Turkish officers, two of whom the author knew. One was promoted to LCol and one to Maj. The recipients were bussed on both cheeks in the same manner as the French officers. Very interesting evening.

On 30 Aug 97, WO Byron K. Mackenzie and the author headed up Finch route to Visoko en route to Banja Luka and VK. They still had to detour around the destroyed bridge near the former Canadian camp at Visoko, but there was a lot of reconstruction underway. They crossed the IEBL into the RS on good roads with little traffic.

Banja Luka is a city with lots of trees lining the streets, and no visible damage. With lots of shops and large department stores, it looked like a thriving city. (How did it escape the war?). They passed by the parliament buildings, which were guarded by the only soldiers in the RS permitted by SFOR to carry rifles—very unusual. They drove north to the UNIPTF camp and then west to the MND SE HQ camp where they stopped for lunch at British PX restaurant called Echos. A large VRS military camp was sited very close to the UN camp and not far from the SFOR HQ. From MND SE HQ, they headed straight west to Prijedor.

As they neared the Croatian border, the ethnic cleansing became evident again with a vengeance. By the time they hit the town of Osaka situated on a beautiful river, the entire area appeared to have been smashed. The bridge had been blown and a bailey bridge had taken its place. The heavy damage appeared to be due to shellfire, with the mosque minarets blown off, although parts of the town appeared to be undergoing repairs. They followed the river to the RS border, marked by a black market for cars (most of which were likely stolen as the licence plates represented nearly every member of the EC). They made a brief stop At the Canadian camp in Coralici to visit Capt Rob Martyn and his Int staff, and then headed on up to Velika Kladusa. That evening in camp, we learned that Diana Princess of Wales was killed in a car crash in Paris, when the Mercedes she was being driven in hit a concrete barrier at 120 kph. They were in a tunnel in Paris being pursued by Paparazzi when it happened about midnight. What a waste.

The following day the crew headed south to Coralici and dropped in on Capt R.B. Martyn for a longer visit. Arrangements were made to bring a few of his Int Ops down to Sarajevo for some OJT (and a change). They drove on to Bihac and circled through the town on the way. There was a very impressive castle on a hill just south of Bihac, but it was obscured by villages that had suffered some very heavy ethnic cleansing. They continued south on Bluebird route to Bosanski Petrovac, passing long expanses of abandoned, trashed and neglected farms in large open plains. They also passed a wrecked DC-3 Dakota memorial near Vitoce, then turned south on Emu route and drove up over the mountains towards the town of Drvar. On the way they passed a large stand of tees planted on a bare hill spelling out Tito's name. They drove up past a ski resort that had serious damage and the Croatian flag flying everywhere, and then down the other side of the mountain into Tito Drvar.

The town had suffered a lot of damage, but it was decked out with a lot of political posters. The town falls under the Canadian Area of Operations (AOR) and is continuously bubbling along with violent demonstrations and confrontations. There were a good number of HVO troops everywhere. They continued on North to Zablace and got back on Bluebird route, heading East to Mrkonjic Grad, then South to Jezero and on to Vulture route to Sipovo. They stopped for break at the UK SFOR base in Sipovo (King's Royal Hussars equipped with Scimitars).

They drove back up into the mountains again and headed south on Parrot route, noting a major change in the terrain as they ascended. The saw lots of stone and thicket walls and fences along the way, until they arrived at what appeared to be a ghost town on the IEBL, and then a wide bare plain at 5,000' stretching out to the mountains on the far horizon. It was hard to believe they were in the same country. Right in the middle of the most remote stretch of plain with every house and farm within 50 km destroyed, they came upon "Ice Station Zebra", a former Canadian Checkpoint. It was manned by Malaysians, and there could not have been a more remote or bleak Observation Post (OP) in the country (although some of the Czech camps come close). They drove on into the severely damaged town of Kupres and back into Federation territory with Croatian flags flying everywhere (not the new approved Federation flag, or even the Bosnia-Herzegovina flag). They headed North on Gull route to Donji Vakuf, where British engineers were putting a new bailey bridge across the river. They zig-zagged again over the high volcanic peaks with a fine sunset over the mountains behind them, taking the main route back into Sarajevo.

While on a four day pass from his tour of duty with SFOR in Sarajevo, the author took a German Transall transport aircraft flight to Ramstein AFB, Germany, where he rented a car and explored familiar parts of Germany, heading southeast to see what had changed since the closure of CFE. He visited the former Canadian base at Baden-Söellingen and discovered that it was now a commercial airpark. The old green air traffic control tower that he used to skirt while coming in to land with his parachute had been painted a bright white and is used for the commercial airport on site. The remainder of the base is not well used and much of it was locked up. He drove a very familiar autobahn route south to Lahr, pulling into the former Canadian base, which sat under the Schutterlindenburg.

The airport theatre is now an indoor-outdoor skate-board centre. The old fire hall had been turned into a Gasthaus style No 2 Royal Canadian Legion. The only airplane on the base was a two-seat MiG-15 parked down in the old Service Battalion lines. The NBCW building is now the Video 8 Discotek. The green Catholic church is now cream coloured and is called the Flugplatz Kirke. Lahr itself does not appear to have changed much. He drove by 101 Schwarzwald Strasse (where the author and his family lived from 1989-92), the Bank of Montreal (now a Turkish Market), and the former PMQ area (where the author lived from 1981-83). The Kaserne where the Brigade Int Section and the Int Section at HQ CFE were located now had the appearance of a tumbleweed-like ghost town, very sad. The Black Forest Officer's Mess (BFOM) was now painted white and is used as a hotel for family members visiting people in the hospital, which is well used and a going concern.

The author drove up to the castle ruins of Hohengeroldseck, which hasn't changed much since it was burned by the French in 1689, then back through Lahr, looping around some of the streets, very familiar and much the same as when the Canadians left it. He took the autobahn back to Baden-Baden, and while downtown, went for a two hour soak in the Caracalla baths, thoroughly enjoying every second of it. He spent the night in the Hotel Schwann near the base in Baden—Söellingen after a brief walk around town.

In November the CANIC crew drove down the Neretva River valley to visit MND SE HQ in Mostar, with plans to travel over the mountains to visit the pilgrimage town of Medugorje. The author went into the cathedral with Sgt Free, and walked around to view the mountains from the back in very heavy rain, thunder and lightning. There was an unusual "feeling" to the place. Not long afterwards, WO J.L.A. Martineau had a car smash his vehicle mirror just beside the shop the crew was in, attracting their attention (another unusual coincidence). He took the crew up into the mountains where his AMIB unit is located. The site overlooks Medugorje, and is not far from where six children believe they were (and continue to be) visited by an apparition of the Virgin Mary. It is quite a remarkable place, with lots of Italian soldiers visiting the site. The crew drove on down to Caplina with its fortified monastery and then back into Mostar, then headed back up the Neretva valley passing the battlefields and heavy damage one never gets used to seeing.

On 15 Nov 97 the CANIC staff set off on a trip to Trebinje. It was cloudy with a few rays of sunlight and fog. Sgt Mario Paris was at the wheel of the Mitsubishi, and Sgt Chris W. Free had his rifle ready. They drove past Butmir downhill along a broad beautiful mountain and river gorge. They passed in and out of the IEBL and through the Gorazde corridor, noting several TD type tanks in the RS at Brod. They crossed a bailey bridge laid alongside the large concrete ruins of the bridge at Brod. The RS town of Trnovo seemed to be very badly shot up, but there were a large number of homes partly repaired and smoke coming out of their chimneys. They drove up through thick fog high into the mountains, and then crossed a bailey bridge from route Tuna to route Viper heading south. On the way they met a "professional" VRS (Serb) soldier while pausing to change drivers. There were a few patches of sun, and then the crew had a near miss with a bulldozer blade on a flatbed passing too close on a narrow road along the Drina River. They drove past snow covered mountains on the route near Suhe, then passed by a very unusual memorial at Tjentiste. The memorial looked like some kind of ski-lift or resort marker.[10]

They had a beautiful drive high up in the mountains. The sun came out at Cemerno, lighting up the snow and fog-capped peaks. A cold but clear beauti-

10.   Tjentiste was the site of a major WW II battle in which Tito was wounded. 15,000 partisans including 4,000 wounded broke out of an encirclement by 117,000 enemy forces. The monument is a symbolic representation of the breakthrough.

ful blue sky opened up over them as they crossed over the top of the mountains at Vrba. They zig-zagged past the Motel Klinje and drove down to Gacko with its large conical coal-fired power plant. They passed by a Spanish SFOR camp on the hill above the eastern edge of Gacko. Following along a low flood plain, they came off the mountain roads in very bright sunshine. Cattle, pigs and sheep were being dressed by local farmers. Troops manning Spanish APCs were observing an RS political rally in Avtovac. They followed a straight route (very unusual in Bosnia-Herzegovina) along low scrub and rock, then found themselves on a moderately winding route to the large town of Biljeca. This town had a fair sized VRS Army base with several museum pieces on display, including an RPU-32, an old M-46 gun and a BTR-50 CP intact in the camp on the south edge of the town. There was a large old stone fort overlooking the reservoir on the south side of the town. There were a lot of low stone walls and old stone buildings partially submerged in the reservoir. They drove into the beautiful town of Trebinje with a very fine old multiple-arched stone bridge, and then on through the IEBL, stopping to take pictures of a badly shot-up BVP-M-80 APC. This was a very rough road, and they paused to examine it before proceeding. Just then, an Italian Carabinieri vehicle arrived, and after a brief chat, escorted them through and guided them down to the road to Dubrovnik high above the Adriatic coast. The mountain ride was incredible, and the view of the Adriatic sea leaped up at them as they crested the last mountain. What a change from wet and snowy Sarajevo. (The route they took from Sarajevo to Broad to Trebinje to Dubrovnik was 286 km. Their return route via Mostar would be 274 km).

The following day they continued up the North West Coast, then North on Pacman route, stopping into MND SE HQ and stopping for lunch in Mostar. They spoke with Capt Andrew G. Morrison, (a 3 Int Coy officer serving with the AMIB Det in Medugorje and LCdr Denise LaViolette, (Canadian PAFFO in Mostar). They also contacted the CANIC for a SITREP. It seems that the Serbs had been acting up and tried to take over the Mount Trebevic radio tower (1629m high). Butmir was also being blockaded (it figures, leave for one day and the dust hits the fan).

On 16 Dec 97, Capt Bob Martyn and Sgt Ollia Kitash from the LdSH BG came down to Sarajevo for a visit from Coralici. The CANIC crew took them for a tour of the battle damage in Sarajevo under a heavy snowfall, and then went up to the Turkish fort and out to Butmir.

On 20 Dec 97, the CANIC crew set out on a mission to Bugojno. They checked out two Galeb aircraft and an old Dragonfly helicopter (museum pieces) at the ARBiH Camp at Pazaroc. Continuing on to Tarcin, under a bright double rainbow, with the weather alternating wet and then turning to heavy rain for the rest of the day. An SFOR BRDM-2 (Ukrainian) guarded the tunnel exit. They passed by a pair of TD tanks at Bradina, plus a home-made APC and several small AT guns. There were quite a few Federation Troops on parade. It rained heavily as they drove over to view a wrecked WWII memorial bridge with several small trains parked nearby. This site is one of Tito's memorials to a successful partisan breakout at Jablanica. They continued on Opal route North West. They drove by a big dam on the Rama River just six km west of Jablanica, then ran into more rain and fog all the way up into the mountains, through the town of Gracac and up to the Croat town of Prozor. They made a brief stop for lunch at the King's Royal Border Regiment Camp (MND SW) in Gorni Vakuf. There was very heavy battle damage throughout the area. They continued on to Bugojno to view the munitions factory which was the object of the trip, which was 162 km each way. It poured rain all the way down the mountain. They arrived back in Sarajevo by 1700 hours.

On 26 Dec 97, the author spent his last morning in Sarajevo. His first stop was to see the CJ2, BGen Isler. The General surprised the author by presenting him with an NSA bronze coin. Most of his colleagues in the other NICs had already rotated out. He dropped in to say farewell to the residents of the USNIC, DANIC, GENIC, NLNIC, the FRNIC, the Hellenic NIC, the ITNIC, the SWENIC, the SPNIC and the TUNIC. The CO of the TUNIC paraded all six personnel, Col, LCol, 2 Capts, 2 Sgts, to say goodbye. The author presented them with a book on the province of New Brunswick to keep as a souvenir, then visited the UKNIC and finally stopped at the CANIC. Capt Al Haywood had organized the crew and turned them out on parade, a very decent and greatly appreciated gesture. There were many more thank yous and goodbyes. They were an excellent crew to work with. Maj Rick Mader would be arriving with a good team waiting for him.

They headed north with Sgt Mario Paris driving and accompanied by Maj Louis Garneau (PAFFO) en route to Zagreb at 09:30 hours, just as the fog began to lift. The huge blown down bridge at Visoko had almost been restored. They passed through a Turkish checkpoint guarded by modified M-113 and BTR-80 APCs near Zenica. The crew drove along a very long route lined with wrecked and destroyed homes, some battle damaged, most ethnically cleansed, all the way north to Bosanski Brod, passing by a horse-drawn funeral cortege en route. The destruction just got worse, and the amount of it, even at this late date, proved very depressing to view. They crossed a checkpoint manned by Americans on the river to Slovanski Broad on the Croatian side.

They continued along highway 180 to Zagreb, noting an immense change in the villages and the scenery along the way. They were back in central Europe. They zig-zagged through the 900-year old but very modern city of Zagreb to the Holiday Hotel. They had to stay in an executive suite with its own living room and two bathrooms (oh dear). They enjoyed a great meal in the hotel. The last few days of late nights caught up with them and all zonked out, although there was a lot of "pre-New Year's Eve" gunfire outside. The author repacked some of his kit, then the next day the crew drove back out to the airport to pick up Maj Rick Mader, the author's replacement and incoming CO of the CANIC, at 15:30 hours. They took him to Pleso to clear in, then had supper in the hotel, lots of chat and hand-over notes. It was still raining, and there was more gunfire all night.

On 28 Dec 97 they set out from Zagreb with Mario, Louis and Rick en route to VK, driving through Karlovac via the autobahn, then South to VK in BiH. This was the first view of the typical urban damage in the area for Rick. They toured Velika Kladusa camp, then met with Col M.D. Capstick, who conducted the formal hand-over, Board of Inquiry (BOI) and presided over their official change of command. Both Majors were presented with handover scrolls from CC SFOR. Rick was given a briefing by Capt Bob Martyn and WO Jack W. Campbell from the LdSH BG. At 15:30 hours they headed back to Zagreb, had supper in the hotel, and did some final repacking. The gunfire never let up, which made the author decide to sleep on the floor. On 29 Dec 97 they went over to Pleso to turn in the last of his kit. The author handed over his pistol to Rick (all rounds still intact). He also handed in his flak jacket, gave his helmet to Louis, and then said good luck and goodbye. Not long afterwards, the author found himself on his flight home and the end of his SFOR tour in Bosnia-Herzegovina Herzegovina.

# *1997, Safe Roads, Bosnia-Herzegovina-Herzegovina Observations*

The collection of information in the field of duty is important because many lives depend on it, more so now than at any time since WWII. A great leader once said, "I would trade all the sophisticated Intelligence collection apparatus available for one good spy in the enemy camp." Machines can't read minds and get into the psyche of the person or group that potentially poses a threat. More importantly, the threat to one man or group of people may not be of concern to another. The best way to illustrate this is by describing an experience that members of our CANIC team had in Sarajevo.

One of the constant factors about being on duty in a country that has been at war is the concern with the safety of the routes one must take to get from point A to point B. In order to determine which roads were safe and which were not, we did our best to find and make use of at least five reliable sources of information to confirm the best route to take. The "HUMINT" method of Intelligence gathering often involved sitting down with people from different countries on a one on one basis, and having a cup of coffee with them.

On more than one occasion we would be asked if a particular route was safe, most often by someone who was about to take a convoy from point A to B along that route. We would tell the people requesting the information that we would do what we could to find out, and in this particular instance, I began the process by visiting the commander of a middle-eastern contingent, whose area the route went through. The Muslim commander insisted on having a cup of coffee (you may know the kind I mean, it seems like it consists of 50% thick sludge, and 50% raw caffeine, and with one sip your eyeballs are "THIS BIG" for three days). When I asked the question about whether the route being considered was safe, he responded by asking about what the weather had been like. My first impression was that he was trying to change the subject, but after a chat about family, our tour of duty in Bosnia-Herzegovina and the situation in general, we eventually came back to discussing the subject of the safety of specific routes.

He explained that the types of mines that were in use by the local belligerents weren't usually laid under the pavement of the roadways because it was impractical to do so. However, because the most common type of landmine in use in the area was about the size of a hockey puck, it could easily be planted in the dirt banks on the high side of the road. When it rains heavily, as it does in the mountains at the time of year we were concerned with, the mud washes down onto the road, bringing the mines along with it. This meant that if the weather had been bad for the past few days, the road was unlikely to be safe. Even if you weren't on a foot patrol, hitting one of these anti-personnel mines with a soft-skinned vehicle could cause you to blow off a tire on a particularly nasty stretch of steep mountain road, and of course, the mine would be sited to ensure there was a long drop off on the opposite side of the road. If the weather had been good for more than a week and others had travelled on the road in the same period, the odds were relatively good that the road was comparatively safe to take. On the other hand, the Muslim commander did point out and recommend the use of a longer although somewhat more difficult route that was used by his Troops to travel from point A to B all the time.

I then visited with the commander of a European Unit to get his opinion of the route in question. He was of an Orthodox religion, and they don't often share their views with other contingents, let alone the Muslims. However, with the ever present (one might say absolutely necessary) cup of very strong coffee in hand, he listened to my question attentively, and then asked me if there were any Dutchmen in the convoy. I responded yes, the ambulance crew was from the Netherlands. He suggested that this might pose a problem, because a number of Bosnia-Herzegovina "war heroes" had been arrested and taken from a particular village along the route. These individuals had then been sent to "The Hague" in the Netherlands and were presently standing trial as a "war criminals." If the local villagers happened to see the Dutch vehicle, they would stone the convoy at the very least. He recommended a detour through another specific route, which interestingly enough was the same route the Muslim commander recommended.

I then visited the commander of a North European nation and asked him the same question about the safety of the route in question. He in turn warned me that one of the vehicles from the country mounting the convoy had accidentally backed over a small car in another village near the route chosen a few weeks ago, and in the process accidentally killed a woman and her child. He strongly recommended that another route be taken if they didn't want to have a hostile encounter.

Word also passes quickly on the military "grapevine," so most of us were well aware of incidents involving Troops from another country we worked with that were new to the business of keeping the peace in Europe, (and we were part of a group of 39 different nations in the Peace Stabilization Force known as SFOR). One or two of these "newbies" had severely strained their relations with the local people along the route by dumping garbage anywhere they felt like it, which is not a common thing in Europe. I would have recommended against anyone taking a convoy through a route where the locals were inordinately hostile to members of contingents who had made themselves unwelcome in their area. No one needs unnecessary grief. There were also other so-called allies whose off-duty activities in the black-market made them unwelcome in certain sectors. One Eastern-based SFOR group had a few representatives who took up the practice of charging "tolls" to local vehicles transiting past their camp. Members of this particularly enterprising group took to shooting at passing local vehicles when they didn't pay the tolls. This is not the kind of activity that will endear you to the people you are supposedly there to protect.

This still left a good number of other nations to consult, and as mentioned, I usually liked to check in with five for good measure. The lead liaison officer of another contingent that I visited to gather information about the route indicated to me in no uncertain terms after I asked the question, that, "of course the route was safe." I asked him how he knew this to be so, in light of the information I received from other solid sources that indicated otherwise, and his response was, "because our state department says so." I did not find that kind of qualification to be very reassuring, particularly when it was highly likely that I might have to make use of the route myself. Based on the simple interactive discussions with the representatives of the other nations I've just described, I would have to get down to "brass tacks" and ask key questions, such as: "Would you want to travel up an uncertain route just on the say so of any one particular country, particularly if they do not have "eyes on the ground?" For that matter, do you specifically distrust the word of colleagues and observers who seem to know more about the route than you do?" I think not.

Eventually, I would connect with a group of like-minded people from many of the 39 different countries involved in the mission, not necessarily the same ones each time because people, contingents and routes change. I would then compile a list of the routes that were assessed as safe to take, and we would advise allied contingents whose representatives would in turn advise their convoy commanders accordingly. Quite often the safety of a number of these routes is not in accord or agreement with the assessments provided by state departments of other nations. However, I believe our Intelligence Section had a more than reasonable degree of certainty as to where it was safe to drive and where it was not. It was a formula that worked well for us, and I felt that it might have applications elsewhere.

The bottom line about information gathering is, if it involves the safety of my life and yours, I want to know for sure that any route we may have to travel on is safe, before we let a convoy go anywhere over there, wherever "over there" may be. That principle has to be applied to any of the numerous deployment sites such as Afghanistan, Ethiopia, Rwanda, the Golan Heights, the Democratic Republic of Congo and other areas our government is arranging to send us. As you can see, information gathering from as many sources as possible is worth its weight in lives. All-source Intelligence specifically includes the "HUMINT" factor. Radar and Satellite imaging in conjunction with electronic and communications Intelligence are only a few of the current examples of very necessary tools in our information-gathering toolbox. It is, however, equally necessary to be speaking with the people on ground in the location of interest, and specifically with someone who has been there and knows what he is talking about, before assuming the risk of sending someone along a route he might not come back from. In the end, if you can't get the information with technology, you may have to go and look for yourself. A very old military rule is that time spent on reconnaissance is seldom wasted—even if it is rarely recovered.

The essential ingredient to the business of information gathering in the kind of environment one finds oneself in while on duty in places like Bosnia-Herzegovina is the need for continuous human interaction with all of our allies. A great deal of patience and the ability to engage people in a meaningful dialogue with practical social skills are necessary elements in the business of information gathering. The ability to work with the disgruntled is necessary when dealing with more than just the obvious belligerents. One learns quickly that there are representatives from more than a few theoretically "friendly" countries, who seem to go out of their way to make themselves unwelcome with an attitude of "We are here to sort you out and you had better be grateful or else." By example, I have seen representatives from Country A treat everyone like dirt and so no one wants to deal with him or her. The representative from Country B doesn't seem to speak English in a form that anyone else can understand (no names, no pack drill here please). The crew from Country C seems to take a "religious" view on every task it is assigned. Country D has to put a political spin on things. Country E is only there for the money, black-market and otherwise. Some countries actually want to make a difference—and in that, we are almost unique.

The only way to make that difference is to educate the people who send us on these missions about what the environment is like in the theatre we are going into, and what is reasonably possible to accomplish once we get there. It is very important to know what the exit strategy is before we go in. The Intelligence team has to be in the loop from the commander's direction downwards, on what constitutes the "mission accomplished" End State. The soldiers understand why you need information and what to do with it on the ground (and the more you have in advance, the better), but one is left with the impression that sometimes, the politicians that put us in these places are slightly "less well-informed," on the risks we are exposed to, to put it in politically correct terminology.

Our job is to gather information about those who pose the threat to the Troops on the ground and get it to them in a timely and useful manner. Those we work for need to instruct our political masters on the important (and potentially life-threatening) aspects that they need to know about the situation they intend to put us in and why it is the way it is. As we begin to deploy on even more dangerous missions to unstable and highly volatile nations, (within the classic "three-block war" scenario now part of Army doctrine), we need to be better prepared with people who know how to gather the information and get it to those who need to make the best use of it. It has never been more important.

There is a great need in our service for people with language training, overseas experience, and human interactive social skills who can be employed to conduct long-term interactive liaison and intercourse with target nations. A number of our members have excellent skills, such as having an Interrogation course qualification. Attendance on Kinesiology courses can be useful as well (this is the business of studying a person's face and body language to read whether or not they are telling the truth).

Traditional Intelligence briefing and debriefing of patrols is still necessary. Making direct personal contact with our Intelligence counterparts in theatre on a continuous basis is absolutely necessary. It involves a degree of "showing the flag" but also lets others know we are there to get the job done and to make a difference, by building trust. Being inside the "grapevine" or Community information loop can also be useful in increasing one's sense of well being and can reduce the chances of being on the receiving end of unwelcome surprises. These activities have always been a necessary part of our world, although they are not always applied universally across the board. The best preparation for conducting operations involving information gathering in the field is good solid basic Army training. The most important ingredient for success is the use of common sense based on practical experience, something our Intelligence personnel have bags and bags of, as I have been privileged to observe in the field.

The bottom line is this: Don't accept everything you hear as being absolutely true, make use of all sources, be discerning, and most importantly think for yourself. If you are not going to do that, then stay out of it. Sometimes when things are at their darkest, you have to be the light, and that is essentially what this report is about—the right people being in the right place at the right time, so that the rest of us can sleep soundly at night. E Tenebris Lux.

## Message from the Branch Advisor
## Col Patrick D.R. Crandell, CD, J2 Operations

I want to start this pot pourri of thoughts with a BZ to those who were involved in OP ASSISTANCE and to those who have served and are serving now with SFOR, Haiti, and Cyprus. You have all done a magnificent job and the Branch is proud of you!

MGen (Ret'd) J.E. Pierre Lalonde, CWO J. Ron Martin and I have had the great privilege of attending the graduation ceremonies for BIOC 9701 in June and those of the TQ 5 and Reserve TQ 6 course on 1 August 1997. When I saw and talked with the graduates, I was impressed with the calibre and dedication of these newest members of the Branch. Because of their individual abilities and collective teamwork, and the superb efforts of CFSIS personnel, we have graduated some exceptionally well-trained personnel. To the recent graduates: "Well done" and once again, welcome to the Branch. To members of CFSIS, and the staff of the Intelligence Training Company in particular, you did a superb job.

By now you are aware of the Minister's Direction that the SI/CI functions of DG Security and Military Police be transferred to J2/DG Int. The transition is proceeding smoothly with "Security Intelligence" now under the control of J2 Operations, "CI doctrine and planning" under J2 Plans and Policy, and the 40-person National Counter Intelligence Unit (NCIU), under the command of Maj Olson, reporting directly to J2/DG Int. NCIU Headquarters will be located in Ottawa, and NCIU detachments/sections will be located in Halifax, Montreal, Kingston, Toronto, Edmonton, and Esquimalt. This is an interim posture and may be modified at a later date. To the Security Branch officers and Military Police investigators who have joined the Intelligence Division and the NCIU: I extend a very warm welcome and request that every Int Section across the CF extend friendship and full support to members of the NCIU. The job they have to do is equally important and we are stronger together as a team than we are apart.

In wrapping up this quick note, I would be remiss if I did not recognize the efforts of those members of our Association Executive Committee who are leaving or have departed already. These personnel have given selflessly of their time and we, the members of the Association, owe them a debt of gratitude. I want to particularly recognize LCdr Dan P. Langlais' contribution as our past President. Dan, you and your team did an outstanding job and we thank you for your efforts. The new President is Maj Robert S. Williams of J2 Operations.

For those of you who have been on Summer leave already, I hope you and your families had a great holiday. For those of you who have yet to go, have a safe and relaxing time! For those of you starting new postings—good luck! E Tenebris Lux.[11]

## 1997 Winner of the Sir William S. Stephenson Bursary

The Executive Committee is pleased to announce the winner of the 1997 Sir William S. Stephenson Bursary is Ms Annie Montmarquet, daughter of PO1 J.A. Réjean Montmarquet, who is currently working with 4e Cie de Rens, Montreal. Annie Montmarquet is 17 years old and intends to pursue her second year of studies at the Collège de l'Outaouais in Hull in the field of Bureautique.[12]

## Branch CWO Corner
## CWO J. Ron Martin, J2 Plans 2-3

Once again it is a privilege to speak to you on various activities underway in this ever-changing Branch. Many things have happened since my last letter to you. We have just graduated another QL 5 course of 17 new Int Ops; we have a new Colonel Commandant; we have completed and have almost put to bed our MOS study; we have a new staff in the Career Manager Shop, and finally we have gone through another Annual Posting Season (APS).

To begin with, I would like to wish all of those branch members listed in this edition who have recently elected to take their retirement: all the best be it in their second careers or in any undertaking they may be headed for. It has been a privilege to serve with you all, and I hope that you remain in contact with the Branch. I would also like to welcome the new Int Branch officers and NCOs who have just recently graduated from their respective courses. I had the privilege to attend both graduations, as did the new Colonel Comman-

---

11.  Sinister Sam's Notebook, CMIBA, Edition 2, August 1997, pp. 1-2.
12.  Sinister Sam's Notebook, CMIBA, Edition 2, August 1997, p. 2.

dant, MGen J.E. Pierre Lalonde, and the Branch Advisor, Col Patrick D.R. Crandell. I am pleased to report that we continue to attract what I believe to be amongst the best personnel out there.

Our Career Manager Shop Has recently gone through a fairly important transformation. CPO1 Gord Kelsey is going on to bigger and better things and is being replaced by not one, but two persons. I would like to welcome his replacements, CPO1 Bob Salomon and MWO Donna Dixon. MWO Dixon is the Career Manager for the Photo Technician trade and will also have our files in her capable hands. In the name of all Int Ops, I would like to thank Gord for the work he has done for us. With all the changes that we have gone through over the last few years, it has I know been quite a challenge for him. All the best in your new job—I'm sure you won't find it as exciting as being our CM.

Finally, I would like to take this opportunity to thank our outgoing Int Branch Association President LCdr Dan P. Langlais for his contribution to the Association. I believe LCdr Langlais, through perseverance and long hours, has succeeded in advancing the cause of the Association enormously. Our Newsletter had become a huge success, the Bursary fund is on track, the membership is up and he has succeeded in initiating a new sense of participation and involvement in the Association by its members. We are fortunate that he will remain involved as Editor of the Newsletter—thereby insuring its ongoing success. Again thank you, Sir. E Tenebris Lux.[13]

## 1997, J2/DG Int Turnover

The current Director General Intelligence, BGen Kenneth C. Hague, was relieved by BGen Robert "Bob" G. Meating on 11 Aug 1997. After two years in the J2/DG Int chair, BGen Hague is now moving on to Kingston to assume the position of Commandant of the Royal Military College.

## 1997, Historical News

The Historical Rep acquired a large WWII terrain model, by anonymous donation. This was the original terrain model of the West Coast of Dieppe used for the planning of the 1942 raid. It will be placed on display in the CFSIS Heritage Hall at CFB Borden.

---

13.  Sinister Sam's Notebook, CMIBA, Edition 2, August 1997, pp. 2-3.

On 22 February 1997, Mrs. Audrey Davie donated a collection of 150 scratch-built models and a display case. The models portray ground equipment types dating from WWII to the present. The collection was built by her former husband, LCol Tom F. Davie (Ret'd), who was a member of the C Int C and CF Int Branch. LCol Davie passed away in 1987.[14]

## 1997, Award of MAG Commander's Commendation to 14 Wing Int Section
### Extracts from an article by WO Roderick L. Gill

The Commander Maritime Air Group (MAG) Commendation was awarded to the 14 Wing Intelligence Section on 9 June 1995 by the (then) Commander Maritime Air Group, BGen B.C. Horseman. This Commendation was awarded in recognition of outstanding service during OP OCEAN VIGILANCE. The details of the actual operation are sensitive, although the citation is on display in the 14 Wing Greenwood Int Section. The citation includes the following remarks, "The dedication and expertise demonstrated by the Wing Intelligence Section had significant impact on planning for OP OCEAN VIGILANCE. Their commendable efforts were in keeping with the highest standards and goals of 14 Wing." (Signed) BGen B.C. Horseman, Comd MAG, 9 June 1995.

The members of the 14 Wing Intelligence Section during Operation OCEAN VIGILANCE were: Capt Al Haywood (Wg Int O); Capt C. French (ANAV); Sgt J.R. Charles Conlin; MS Dan J.M. Ash; MS Richard Lee Fletcher; MCpl Andrew J. "A.J." Krause; and Cpl D.A. Daneliuk.[15]

## 1997, NORAD, Florida
### Extracts from an article by Maj Brian E. Watson, 1st Air Force, Tyndall AFB

The Chief, Intelligence Operations, 1st Air Force (AF)/Continental NORAD Region (CONR), Tyndall AFB, Florida exchange position has been occupied by an Air Force CF Intelligence Branch Major since its inception in 1988. I

---

14.  Sinister Sam's Notebook, CMIBA, Edition 2, August 1997, p. 7.
15.  Sinister Sam's Notebook, CMIBA, Edition 2, August 1997, p. 7.

have had the opportunity to be assigned to Tyndall AFB since 1 August 1996. To situate you, Tyndall AFB is located on the Florida panhandle and is between Pensacola and Tallahassee on the Gulf of Mexico. Tyndall AFB is the home of the 325th Fighter Wing, flying F-15 Eagles, and 1 AF/CONR.

The Canadian Intelligence Officer at 1 AF/CONR wears two hats. The officer is the Deputy Chief, Intelligence and Operations Officer for the Directorate of Intelligence. The Director, Intelligence (IN) is a USAF LCol. As deputy Chief, Intelligence, I am responsible for the Directorate in the absence of the IN. The IN presently has a staff of 11 personnel, with an expected increase to 20 personnel in the near term. The IN presently has a staff of 11 personnel, with an expected increase to 20 personnel in the near term. The IN is responsible to provide direct support to the Commander 1 AF/CONR, a USAF MGen. In addition, the IN supports three NORAD Sector Air Operations Centres (SAOC); the NE Air Defence Sector (NEADS) at Rome, NY; the Western Air Defence Sector (WADS) at McChord AFB, WA; the SE Air Defence Sector (SEADS) at Tyndall AFB, FL; and ten fighter wings located around the periphery of the continental USA.

The IN has two branches—operations and unit support. The Unit Support Branch is responsible for providing unit support through a vigorous Staff Assistance Visit (SAV) program to all 1 AF/CONR units. These inspections are in support of Operational Readiness Inspections. The Operations Branch, for which I am responsible, provides analytical support to the IN, Commander and Units in the field. My branch is divided between strategic and counter-drug analysis. We provide briefings to the Commander, produce a weekly intelligence cable, a monthly counter-drug forecast and liaise with higher commands, providing support for strategic exercises and scripting all 1 AF/CONR exercises.

Like units in Canada, we are also given ancillary taskings. In the past, we have provided personnel for missions in Saudi Arabia, Italy, Iceland and Panama. We are also presently pursuing an exciting new mission. We are in the final stages of accepting responsibility for an Information Operations (IO) mission. This will include an increase in staff of nine persons from AIA and the creation of an IO Flight within the IN.

As you can see from this brief description, the mission here is busy and very challenging. This assignment provides a unique opportunity to work with our American allies and a chance to work in and observe the operations of another nation's intelligence organizations and Air Force.[16]

## 1997, Operation ASSISTANCE—Air Component A2 Extracts from an article by Maj Richard A. Derkson, CFSAS Winnipeg

On 25 April 1997, the Directing Staff (DS) at the CF School of Aerospace Studies (CFSAS) finalized the last-minute details for the Advanced Aerospace Operations Course (AAOC), slated to commence 30 April. Shortly afterwards, Air Command cancelled the AAOC to prepare for operational and accommodations requirements for OP NOAH (renamed later that day to OP ASSISTANCE), the CF operation to battle the Red River Flood.

As one of the DS, I did not expect to be designated the A2 for the Air Component HQ, especially considering all of the expertise resident across the runway at AIRCOM HQ. As DS, we taught Joint Operations on the AAOC, but few of us had any experience in the conduct of actual joint ops. Would what we taught in theory work in practice?

On 26 April, planning commenced in earnest for the stand-up of an Air Component HQ (ACHQ) to support the Joint Force. The ACHQ was to be set up in the syndicate rooms of the AAOC in the CFSAS basement, with the Joint Forces HQ (JHQ) occupying the upper floors.

Over the next few hours, the manning requirements for the A2 organization took shape. The ACHQ would need Int officers and Int Ops for 24/7 operations, and Int support had to be provided to the two subordinate units that were being formed—the Composite Aviation Unit with eight Griffon, six Jet Ranger, three Sea King and three Labrador helicopters; and the Fixed-Wing Aviation Unit with Hercules, Aurora, Dash-8 and additional assets from other government departments. It was determined that a total of three officers and eight Int Ops would be required to support the operation, and the need for augmentation became apparent. A staff check with AIRCOM's subordinate units in advance of the formal tasking message revealed an abundance of Int personnel ready to support the operation. Within 30 minutes A2 staff could pencil in those who would deploy to Winnipeg, some of whom would arrive less than 20 hours later.

Augmentation for OP ASSISTANCE A2 staff came from the AIRCOM Int Centre (Capt D. Phil Forward, WO Dean E. Smith, WO Ronald K. Townsend and Cpl D. Bruce Warawa); FG/CANRHQ (Sgt Lynn J.

---

16. Sinister Sam's Notebook, CMIBA, Edition 2, August 1997, pp. 7-8.

Brooks),14 Wing Greenwood (MCpl Richard Lee Fletcher); 3 Wing Bag-otville (PO1 J.R. François Bouchard); 4 Wing Cold Lake (WO D. Garry Kohinski); and 19 Wing Comox (MCpl Norman F. Wilhelm). Within a short period, they had coalesced into an effective team; one which brought praise from the Chief of Staff and Air Component Commander (ACC), Col Sharpe, for its effectiveness and professionalism.

OP ASSISTANCE was not a traditional type of operation from an Int perspective, but the concepts and principles with which we are familiar proved to be very effective. Priority Intelligence Requirements (PIRs) and Int Requirements (IRs) were identified, a Collection Plan prepared, and a "Target List" (Named Areas of Interest) was produced. The "enemy" was the advancing floodwater, with the "targets" being areas where the floodwater would breach or end-run the dikes, wash out roads and bridges, etc. The A2 staff prepared a daily INTSUM, provided three update briefings every day (two to the ACC and staff, and one to the ATO board), and input into the ACHQ Daily SITREP. The Int Ops at the tactical level briefed and debriefed aircrew, and fed the results up to the ACHQ so that the ACC and staff were kept up to date. Their efforts were recognized by the ACC, who commented that he felt the information being provided by the A2 staff was more accurate and detailed than that of any other source. It is interesting to note that once Int Ops began briefing and debriefing the aircrews, the flow of information more than doubled from the highest previous level.

OP ASSISTANCE provided the Air Int community with the opportunity to showcase its ability. Despite being employed in a non-traditional type of operation, the personnel quickly demonstrated their value and adaptability. Some of the operators were initially quite sceptical of the utility of Int personnel for the operation, and in particular at the numbers of augmentees being deployed to support the ACHQ. The professionalism, enthusiasm and work ethic displayed by all the Int staff quickly convinced the unconverted. From a personal point of view, the performance of those working with me during OP ASSISTANCE reaffirmed my conviction that the Int Branch is composed of highly-skilled and dedicated personnel. Those involved should be justifiably proud of their efforts.[17]

---

17. Sinister Sam's Notebook, CMIBA, Edition 2, August 1997, pp. 8-9.

## 1997, LFWA HQ G2
### Extracts from an article by Sgt Steve J. Goronzy

There has been a flurry of activity in Western Canada surrounding the flood situation in Manitoba. A number of Int Ops from LFWA were deployed to assist command staffs controlling the CF effort, including WO Donald M. Gallaher, Winnipeg Det of 6 Int Coy. His hard work along with that of other Int Ops deployed later, proved beyond a doubt the value of deploying Int personnel in support of domestic ops.

The current focus of operations within LFWA is support to the amphibious portion of the upcoming MARPAC naval exercise, MARCOT 2/97. Concurrently, planning and support is being given to the CF Joint Task Force, which is supporting the upcoming Asia Pacific Economic Cooperation (APEC 97) conference scheduled for November in Vancouver.

During the last year a number of changes have occurred that have affected the Int structure within LFWA. The primary change has been the concentration of 1 CMBG units in Edmonton. This has had the effect of positioning all but a few of Western Canada's Army Int personnel in one location—Edmonton Garrison (formerly CFB Edmonton, Lancaster Park). Currently the only Int staff not located in Edmonton are 6 Int Coy, which still maintains its dispersed disposition with the Coy HQ in Edmonton and Dets in Vancouver, Edmonton and Winnipeg.

The last posting season (APS 96) saw a number of changes in the personnel of the LFWA HQ G2 Branch. Current manning is: LFWA HQ G2, Maj Robert J. McCutcheon; G2 Ops, Capt Brian E. Hamilton; OIC ICAC, vacant; G2 I & W, WO Dave D. Turner; G2 Domestic Analyst, Sgt Steve J. Goronzy; G2 International Analyst, Sgt P. Scott Peters; and, G2 Data Management, Cpl Derrick D. Petrushko.

Maj Robert J. McCutcheon has just returned from a six-month tour of duty with SFOR in Bosnia-Herzegovina, and PO2 H.W. Glover (from 6 Int Coy) is being posted in this summer.

By the end of the Summer, the G2 Branch will have a manning strength of nine, four of whom will be Reservists. Experience at this HQ has shown that the total force concept works. Reservists, filling Class B/A positions for 3-4 years, constitute 40% of the Branch's manpower. Without them, the Branch would be hard pressed to complete all task given to it. For the Reservists, this time period is extremely valuable, exposing them to knowledge and training they would not normally get in the Reserve world. This experience can then be transferred to the Reservist's home unit once he completes his employment. At times the learning curve for both Regular and Reserve members can be almost vertical. However, once both are familiar with the "peculiarities" of the other, an effective team can be developed.

Personnel posted out of the unit included Maj Gord P. Ohlke, posted to Army Staff in Kingston; WO F. Vance Gordon posted to CFSIS; and Cpl D. Bruce Warawa, who transferred from the Reserves to the Regular Force and is posted to AIRCOM HQ in Winnipeg.

At present, LFWA HQ is to remain in its current location, the Gault Building, Griesbach Barracks. New computer systems, including JDISS are coming on line and the acquisition of digital cameras will give the unit a limited Imagery capability.[18]

## 1997, CFB Comox Assists in Stopping High Seas Driftnetter (HSDN)
### *Extracts from an article by Capt Gord Dow, 19 Wing Comox*

Driftnet fishing, sometimes referred to as "the wall of death," was made illegal in 1993 by the United Nations. Multinational agreements are in place to share the workload of enforcing the ban on this type of fishing. Canada's contribution is six deployments a year to the North Pacific, with about 250 hours of patrol time per deployment.

On 26 June 1997, a CP-140 Aurora Long Range Maritime Patrol Aircraft from 407 Sqn, Comox, located and took Imagery of a vessel suspected of driftnet fishing east of Japan. Analysis of that Imagery by 19 Wing Intelligence confirmed that the vessel was indeed in violation of international law. The Imagery was forwarded to the USCG for use in prosecuting the vessel and crew. In the meantime, Canadian and American air assets were used to maintain contact with the suspect vessel until a USCG ship arrived on the scene. After 14 days and numerous attempts, the USCG managed to stop and board the suspect vessel, which was believed to be of Chinese origin. It contained in excess of 11 NM of gillnet and 120 tons of fish parts—mostly albacore. The crew and vessel were taken to Guam to face legal prosecution.[19]

---

18. Sinister Sam's Notebook, CMIBA, Edition 2, August 1997, pp. 10-11.
19. Sinister Sam's Notebook, CMIBA, Edition 2, August 1997, pp. 11-12.

## 1997, Intelligence Personnel News

*Order of Military Merit (OMM)*, 47th List. Recent appointments to the Order as listed in the Government House Press Release of 17 Dec 96 include: LCol J.F. Cruse, Grade of Officer, for service in DISOA, currently serving as J2 Imagery; Capt R.A. Mader, Grade of Member, for service in DIE, currently serving with LFAA/G2; and, Capt Wes B. von Papineau, Grade of Member, 1 Cdn Div HQ.

*Meritorious Service Medal (United States)*. Maj Brad J. Smith, for outstanding accomplishments while serving as an exchange officer at DIA from July 94 to July 97. Currently posted to 4 Wing, CFB Cold Lake.

*DCDS Commendation* Presentation, ZIRT (Commanders Group Commendation). From 11 November 1996–31 December 1996, a number of DG Int Division personnel were assigned to the Zaire Intelligence Response Team (ZIRT) to support OP ASSURANCE. Personnel from organizations external to the Ottawa area also augmented the ZIRT. In recognition of their outstanding performance, the ZIRT was presented a Group Deputy Chief of the Defence Staff Commendation. The following DG Int and Command personnel participated: LCol D.H. Neal Thompson, Maj Mike R. Rothschild, Maj Ron H.J. Ruiters, Capt Marla J. Dow, Capt Brian J. East, Capt Rajeev G. Nath, Capt Robert "Bob" H. Smallwood, Capt Bev F. Toomer nee Baker, Capt G.F. Dow (19 Wing Comox), Lt (N) Mike F.H. Arnoldi (MARCOM HQ Halifax), Lt J.F.J. Dan Massana (12 Wing North Bay), WO J.V. William "Bill" Leclair (CFSIS Borden), WO William A. Mitchell, WO J.R.M. Ross, WO Ron T.A. Wulf, Sgt Charles A. Beattie, PO2 J.L. Dennis Goulet, Sgt Byron K. Mackenzie, WO J.L.A. Martineau, Sgt Daniel Francis McNeil, Sgt Dennis G. McNulty, Sgt Patrick M. Palahicky, Sgt J.D. Roy, Sgt K.B. Sanders, Sgt Kevin Toomer, MCpl D.A. Daneliuk, MS L.M. Madore (AIRCOM Winnipeg), Cpl Kurt A. Trebels, and Cpl Jacques M.A.D. Verbrugge.

J2/DG Int, BGen Ken C. Hague, hosted the awards ceremony at the NDHQ WOs and Sgts Mess on 16 May 1997. The A/DCDS, MGen R.R. Henault, conducted the presentation.

*DCDS Commendation*, DIE FWD (Commanders Commendation). In February 1996, DIE Detachment (DIE FWD) was awarded the DCDS Commendation for distinguished performance of duty and meritorious achievement while deployed to the LOCE Correlation Centre, RAF Molesworth, UK. Ten Imagery analysts (IAs) deployed to the LOCE CORCEN to provide near real-time Imagery Int support to CCUNPF in the Former Yugoslav Republic. Members of the detachment included: WO Collin (Ed) Affleck, (12 Aug–19 Nov 95); WO Dave D. Turner (5 Jun-10 Jul 95); Sgt Joseph Yvon Alain Bilodeau (3 Jul-21 Aug 95); Sgt J.D. Pete Boutin, 1 Cdn Div HQ, (3 Jul–24 Aug 95); Sgt Tom J. Last, (5 Jun–5 Jul 95); Sgt Daniel Francis McNeil, (24 Aug-8 Nov 95); PO2 J.L. Dennis Goulet, (24 Aug-8 Nov 95); MS Mark H.C. Herrndorf, (12 Aug-8 Nov 95); MCpl Richard M. Clowater, (3 Jul-8 Nov 95); and, MCpl S.E. Porter, (12 Aug-8 Nov 95).

*MARCOM Commendation* (Commanders Commendation). Lt (N) Andrew W. Chester, MARLANT HQ Halifax, (Awarded 17 April 1997, for development and implementation of CANMARNET). LCdr Dan P. Langlais, J2/DG Int, (Insignia awarded retroactively for 1990/91 Persian Gulf War service).

*AIRCOM Commendation* (Commanders Commendation). LCol Ray J. Taylor, CFILO (W), (Insignia awarded retroactively for services rendered to AIRCOM HQ, effective 1993). Maj Terry W. Procyshyn, J2 SRA, (Insignia awarded retroactively for services rendered to AIRCOM, effective 1995).

*DCINC NORAD Commendation* (Commanders Commendation). Maj J.P. André Tremblay, J2 Imagery, (Insignia to be awarded retroactively, effective 1989). Capt J.R.R.R. Sylvain Robidoux, J2/DG Int, (now Major), (Insignia to be awarded retroactively, effective 15 May 1992). MWO W. Ken Spike, J2 STI, (Insignia to be awarded retroactively, effective 1992).

*Somalia Medal.* This operational service medal recognizes service with the Canadian Joint Force providing military humanitarian relief in the Somali Democratic Republic from 16 November 1992–June 1993. Members of the parallel UN Operation in Somalia (UNOSOM) are recognized by their own distinct and separate UN Medal. The medal is awarded to: Maj Len E.N. Goski (Ret'd), Maj François Messier, Capt Paul W. Hope, Capt Doug M. Mair, WO Barry E. Beldam (now MWO), Sgt Rick M. Chaykowski (now WO), MCpl Charles A. Beattie (now Sgt), MCpl J. Patrick A. Couture, and MCpl Dean G. Hyde (now Cpl, after re-enrolment).

*MARLANT Commander's Bravo Zulu Award.* PO2 Thomas E. Scott, MARLANT HQ Halifax, (Awarded April 1997 for significant contributions to operational support within the Command).

*BIOC 9701 Graduates.* Congratulations to the 17 new Int Branch Officers who graduated from the 9701 Edition of the Basic Intelligence Officers Course at CFSIS. Graduation ceremonies were held at CFB Borden on 6 June 1997, and were presided over by the new Branch Colonel Commandant, MGen J.E. Pierre Lalonde (Ret'd). The graduates include: Lt Roger C.

Bowden, Air, AIC 1 CAD/CANR Winnipeg; Capt Doug R.E. Bugeaud, Land, NDIC; Lt Joe V. Churman, Air, 4 Wing Ops/CFB Cold Lake; Capt Tom G. Gilchrist, Air, 4 Wing Ops/CFB Cold Lake; Capt J.H.K. Pierre Lamoureux, Land, J2 SRA; Lt (N) Kevin S. Luke, Sea, J2 Imagery; Lt (N) Dean Martins, Sea, MARLANT HQ Halifax/N21; Capt Phil R. Moolenbeek, Land, J2 Plans Pol; Lt (N) J.N. Guy Morissette, Sea, J2 SRA; 2Lt J.M.J. Stéphane Neveu, Land, SQFT/G2 Ops; Lt (N) Owen J.W. Parkhouse, Sea, MARLANT HQ Halifax/N21; Lt (N) Kent R. Pendleton, Sea, MARPAC HQ Esquimalt/N21; Lt Tico Louis Remillard, Air, Escadron 433 Sqn/ 433e ETAC Bagotville; Capt Ron A. Roach, Land, Posted as G2, 2 CMBG; Capt Robert E. Rogers, Land, 2 EW Sqn Kingston, (promoted to current rank while on BIOC); Lt Dave Travers, Land, RSSO 6 Int Coy/CFB Edmonton; and, Lt (N) Troy D. White, Sea, J2 Plans (Maritime)/1 Cdn Div HQ Kingston.

*Educational Upgrading*. Congratulations to Capt Ed C. Denbeigh of J2 Ops and Maj Harold A. Skaarup of CTC Gagetown for completing Master of Arts (War Studies) Degrees. Both officers pursued their degrees part time through the newly established Continuing Education Program at RMC. Convocation ceremonies were held at RMC 16 May 1997.

## 1997, Intelligence Personnel News

The following officers have been posted, promoted or are retiring: Col R. Geoff St John, posted to CFA Rome; LCol Jean E.T. Bigras posted to AFNORTH WEST HQ, UK; LCol Greg W. Jensen, posted to CFILO London; LCol Paul F. O'Leary, retiring; LCol Robert M. Parsons, posted as Land Staff/DLFR-4, Ottawa; LCol Christian Rousseau, posted to SHAPE, Belgium; LCol Peter W.M. Wilson, posted to CFCSC Toronto, (DISTAFF); Maj Rhedegydd ap Probert , posted to CFLS Ottawa; Maj Clark J. Beamish, moving with Land Staff/DLC to CFB Kingston; Maj J. Michel Bédard, posted to J2 Ops; Maj Robin Camkin, posted to 1 CAD, Winnipeg; Maj Alex C. Chambers, posted to 8 Wing, Trenton.

Maj J.A.J.P. Cormier, posted to COMSECONDFLT, Norfolk, VA (a seagoing billet); Maj Phil J. Drew, leaving the Branch to attend MLTP; LCdr D. Rick Douglas, posted to J2 Ops; Maj Hugh A. Ferguson, posted to 1 Cdn Div Int Coy as CO; LCdr R. Paul Grimshaw, posted as MARPAC HQ Esquimalt/N21; Maj Lloyd W. Hackel, posted to J2 Ops; Maj Ross L. Johnson, posted to CFLO Fort Huachuca, AZ; Maj A. George Johnstone, posted to DIA Washington, DC; LCdr Dan P. Langlais, posted as MAR-LANT HQ Halifax/N21; LCdr W. Burns MacDonald, posted to J2 Plans & Policy; Maj Rick A. Mader, takes over as LFAA HQ/G2; Maj Glen B. MacKay, posted to 21 AC&W Sqn, North Bay; Maj Gerry C. Mayer, posted to CFSIS as OC Int Trg Coy; Maj J.L. François Messier, posted to DISOA.

Maj Robert G. Nash, posted to AIRCENT HQ, Ramstein, Germany; Maj Mike R.J. Ouellette, returns to SQFT as G2 after Haiti tour; LCdr Ted Parkinson, posted to CINCEASTLANT, UK; Maj Terry W. Procyshyn, posted to CFCSC Toronto; Maj J.R.R.R. Sylvain Robidoux, posted to 3 Ere, Bagotville; LCdr Andrea L. Siew, posted to CFCSC Toronto; Maj Robert "Bob" H. Smallwood, J2 Imagery; Maj Brad J. Smith, posted to 4 Wing, Cold Lake; Maj Ward A. Sweet, posted to CFILO London; Maj J.P. André Tremblay, moves to Air Staff, Ottawa; Maj Chris J. Wallace, posted to Land Staff, Ottawa (DLFR-4); Maj Robert S. Williams, posted to J2 Current/YCC; Lt (N) Mike F.H. Arnoldi, to release, Dec 97; Capt M.E. Louise Boutin, posted to ANR, Elmendorf AFB, Alaska; Capt David R. Canavan, posted to LFCA HQ, Toronto.

Lt (N) Andrew Chester, posted to ONI, Washington, DC; Capt Phil Coo, retiring to pursue a medical career; Capt Clark P. Cornect, retired; Capt Don J. Cushman, posted to J2 Ops; Capt Ed C. Denbeigh, moves to J2 SRA; Capt Boris A. Fedoruk, moving to Land Staff, Ottawa/DLR-10; Capt J.G. Yves Forcier, posted to J2 Plans & Policy; Capt J.C. Chris Gagnon, posted to 1 Cdn Div HQ, Kingston; Capt Eric E. Gjos, posted to CFLS Ottawa; Capt Jim D. Godefroy, posted to J2 Ops; Capt W. Pat Grant, posted to J2 Plans & Policy.

Capt Perry R. Gray remains in Cyprus, the position is now a 2-year accompanied tour; Capt Eric P. Grehan, posted to 1 CAD, Winnipeg; Capt Paul W. Hope, posted to 2 Int Pl, Ottawa; Capt R. Stu W. MacAulay, at CLFCSC Aug-Dec 97 from LFAA; Capt Barry A. MacDonald, posted to J2 Ops; Capt R.B. MacRae, to release Dec 97; Capt D.M. Mair, moves to 1 Wing, Kingston; Capt Jan L. Malainey, posted to 19 Wing, Comox; Capt J.F.J.D. Massana, moves to 21 AC&W Sqn, North Bay; Lt (N) Debra J. Mayfield, moves to MOG 1, Halifax; Lt (N) Jamie G. Miller, retired; Capt D.D. Nickel, posted as G2, 1 CMBG; Capt Robert J. O'Gorman, taking his release.

Capt Wes B. von Papineau, posted to LFAA HQ; Lt (N) G. Reginald J. Quigley, posted to MARLANT HQ, Halifax; Capt Ed D.P. Rechnitzer, moves to SO to J2 Ops; Capt Marcel H. Schryer, posted to 14 Wing, Greenwood; Capt Tim Walser, posted to 1 Cdn Div HQ/G2 Ops; A/SLt Norman B. Everett, posted to BTL for OJT (MARLANT HQ); 2Lt Melissa J. Olegario, posted to BTL for OJT (LFWA); OCdt Kirk D. Bland, posted to BTL for OJT (Shearwater);OCdt Steve Bramhall, posted to BTL for OJT (1 Cdn Div Int Coy); and, OCdt Fred J. Curson, to PG Training, 2 years at UNB.[20]

## 1997, Int Branch NCM News
### Extracts from an article by CWO Rolf F. Overhoff, Land Staff, Ottawa

The Career Manager, CPO1 G. Kelsey had forecast a total of four promotions, but there have been at least eight unforecast retirements, mostly at the MWO/WO rank this year. These retirements have resulted in countless changes to the posting plot, many promotions, numerous farewells, and now a manning shortfall across the country. Even with the graduation of QL5 9701 on 1 August, the Branch faces a shortage of at least 10 Regular Force NCMs. The QL5 will not be run until April 1998. This means that recruiting is required.

MWO Donna Dixon is the new Int NCM CM, at least until next summer. MWO Dixon will be responsible for the Career Management of the Int Ops and Photo Techs. MWO Dixon previously worked in J2 Imagery. The Branch extends a sincere welcome to Cpl D. Bruce Warawa, Cpl Stéphane Vézina-Gaudreault, and Cpl Éric J.M. Brillon, who recently accepted Component Transfers into the Regular Force side of the Int Branch.

## 1997, Intelligence Personnel News

The following Int Branch members have, or will be retiring in 1997: MWO Herb H.W. Kuchler, J2, NDHQ Ottawa; MWO George T. Izzard, J2, NDHQ Ottawa; MWO David J. Whalen, 1 Cdn Div Int Coy, Kingston; WO J.J.P. Mike Fournier, LFAA HQ, Halifax; WO Donald M. Gallaher, 6 Int Coy, Winnipeg Det; WO J.H. Yves Labarre, 4e Cie de Rens, Montreal; WO Rick C. Nickerson, CF Northern Region HQ, Yellowknife; WO J. Eric C. Savoy, J2, NDHQ Ottawa; and Sgt Brian K. Mudge, 2 EW Sqn Kingston.

The following NCMs have been promoted to the rank shown: MWO Barry E. Beldam, CFLS Ottawa; MWO Marvin J. "Red" Hodgins,

---

20.  Sinister Sam's Notebook, CMIBA, Edition 2, August 1997, pp. 13-17.

NORAD, Colorado; WO Rick M. Chaykowski, CFA Prague; WO J.L. Dellaire, NDHQ Ottawa; WO Byron K Mackenzie, J2, NDHQ Ottawa; WO J.A. Chris Pelletier, J2 NDHQ Ottawa; WO Jorg K. Adler, 2 CMBG, Petawawa; PO2 Cliff J. Boyechko, MARPAC, Esquimalt; Sgt J. Roch Guertin, J2, NDHQ Ottawa; Sgt John P. Kubryn, J2, NDHQ Ottawa; Sgt Larry E. Neilson, 2 EW Sqn, Kingston; Sgt Vaughn C. Simpson, CFB Trenton; MCpl W.T. Bill, 6 Int Coy, Edmonton; MCpl Chris K. Buczynski, 1 Cdn Div HQ, Kingston; MCpl L.A. Clarke, J2, NDHQ Ottawa; MS R.J.F. Daigle, CFB Greenwood; MCpl David T. Fields, J2, NDHQ Ottawa; MCpl Paul E. Gagnier, CFEWC, Ottawa; MCpl J.F. Gauthier, 1 Cdn Div Int Coy, Kingston; MCpl R. Steven M. Gingras, J2, NDHQ Ottawa; MS Mark H.C. Herrndorf, J2, NDHQ Ottawa; MCpl Mike H. Hurley, MARLANT HQ, Halifax; MCpl Raymond M. Kruger, CFSIS, Borden; MCpl J. Paul St Laurent, CFB Bagotville; MCpl Dale G. Sonstenes, 1 Cdn Div HQ, Kingston; MCpl J.J.P. Trudeau, NDHQ Ottawa; MCpl R. Vandenberg, 1 Cdn Div HQ, Kingston; MCpl Timothy A. "Jake" Winslow, J2, NDHQ Ottawa.

The following NCMs are posted in APS 97: MWO Barry E. Beldam, 2 EW Sqn, Kingston; MWO Dean J. Dunlop, J2, NDHQ Ottawa; MWO J. Dan Galley, 1 Cdn Div Int Coy, Kingston; MWO Marvin J. "Red" Hodgins, 1 Cdn Div HQ, Kingston; WO Collin (Ed) Affleck, CFLS, Ottawa; WO Tim G. Armstrong, 2 Int Coy, Toronto; WO J.R. François Bouchard, LFAA HQ, Halifax; WO Rick M. Chaykowski, 1 Cdn Div Int Coy, Kingston; WO Jeff A. Collings, J2, NDHQ Ottawa; WO Robert A. Deleau, NORAD, Colorado; WO D. Mike Donahue, J2, NDHQ Ottawa; WO Steve R. Fader, CFB Trenton; PO1 William "Bill" M. Flanagan, CFSIS, Borden.

WO Dan J. Haslip, 2 EW Sqn, Kingston; WO Don B. Jorgensen, CFB Cold Lake; WO J. Patrick D. Knopp, 1 Cdn Div Int Coy, Kingston; WO D.H. McLaren, LFCA HQ, Toronto; PO1 J.A. Réjean Montmarquet, 4e Cie de Rens, Montreal; WO Robert W. Moug, Belgium; WO R.G. Oliver, 1 Cdn Div Int Coy, Kingston; WO John Paul Michael Parsons, J2, NDHQ Ottawa; WO J.A. Chris Pelletier, CFILO Washington; WO Kevin N. Rowe, CF Northern Region HQ, Yellowknife; WO Dean E. Smith, AIRCOM Winnipeg; Sgt P.D. Cooper, Cyprus; Sgt Kenneth E. Davies, CFB North Bay; PO2 Richard A. Fisher, CFSIS, Borden; Sgt J. Guy Foisy, CFEWC, Ottawa; PO2 H.W. Glover, LFWA HQ, Edmonton; Sgt T.D.G. Graham, J2, NDHQ Ottawa; Sgt K.J. Marchand, U2 Staff, Haiti; Sgt J.M.R. Dan Jacques, CFA Belgrade; Sgt D.R. Kell, 1 CMBG, Edmonton; Sgt Mark J. Kelly, CFB North Bay; Sgt J. François .J. Legér , CFA Prague.

Sgt G.A. McGuire, CFLS, Ottawa; Sgt M. Paul McNeil, 1 Cdn Div Int Coy, Kingston; Sgt Peter G. Manuge, 1 Cdn Div Int Coy, Kingston; Sgt W. Robert "Bob" Murley, CFA Moscow; Sgt Patrick M. Palahicky, AIRCOM Winnipeg; Sgt Veronica Marie Parolin, J2, NDHQ Ottawa; Sgt J.E. Paul Pellerin, J2, NDHQ Ottawa; Sgt Barry Toomer, CFLS, Ottawa; Sgt J.P. André Tremblay, 5 CMBG, Valcartier; Sgt Ronald Richard Patrick Walsh, CFLS, Ottawa; Sgt R. Jack Wilson, 1 Cdn Div Int Coy, Kingston; Sgt B. Young, CFB Comox; MCpl W.T. Bill, LFWA HQ, Edmonton; MCpl David T. Fields, CFB Cold Lake; MCpl Don J. Fougère, CFB Cold Lake; MCpl R. Steven M. Gingras, CFB Trenton; MCpl J.F. Gauthier, CFB Bagotville; MCpl Rob J. Lindsay, AIRCOM, Winnipeg; MCpl W.P. Wehmeier, CFB Comox; and MCpl Raymond M. Kruger, CFB Shearwater.

The following new Branch members are graduates of QL5 9701, who completed their course on 1 August 1997: LS H.C. Anderson, CFB Greenwood; Cpl Jeffrey R. Blair, CFSIS Borden; Cpl J.Y. Stéphane Cotnoir , CFB Bagotville; Cpl A.K. Denner, J2, NDHQ Ottawa; Cpl Gary C. Dulong, J2, NDHQ Ottawa; Cpl Scott A. Erskine, J2, NDHQ Ottawa; Cpl Christina T. Franklin, J2, NDHQ Ottawa; Cpl J. Alain B. Gendreau, J2, NDHQ Ottawa; Cpl Michael J. Hague, CFB Cold Lake; Cpl Dean R. Hancock, CFB Greenwood; Cpl Kenneth E. Johnson, J2, NDHQ Ottawa; Cpl Norbert A. Kausen, J2, NDHQ Ottawa; MS Warren M. Lepine, MARPAC, Esquimalt; Cpl J.K.C. Ng, LFCA HQ, Toronto; Cpl Trevor R. Palmer, 1 Cdn Div HQ, Kingston; Cpl Kenneth G.J. Pedde, 2 CMBG, Petawawa; and Cpl Charles "Chuck" D. Widenmaier, 1 CMBG, Edmonton.[21]

## 1997, CISA Member News

Col Bruce Mackedie passed away. Bruce, a former Artillery officer, had been a Brigade Intelligence Officer before becoming a member of 1 Cdn Army Photo Interpretation Section. After WWII, he rose to the rank of Col in the Militia.

Late in May 1997, MGen J.E. Pierre Lalonde was appointed Colonel Commandant of the Intelligence Branch. He had a long and varied military career before he became DG Int at NDHQ in 1991. Promoted to Major General in 1992, he was appointed Assistant Chief of Staff for Intelligence at SHAPE, a position he held until his retirement in 1994. Since then, he has

21.   Sinister Sam's Notebook, CMIBA, Edition 2, August 1997, pp. 17-19.

been Vice-President, Strategic Planning and Corporate Marketing at Computing Devices of Canada Ltd.[22]

## Winter 1997-1998, CISA Member News

Capt Ed D. Kirby, 2IC of the Halifax Intelligence Company passed away in the Fall of 1997 at the age of 60. Before he became a Capt, he had served as the District RSM and the Area RSM.

Maj Charlie I. Taggart died at the age of 84 on 7 Nov 97. During WWII, he served with the RCE and the C Int C, and was renowned for his expertise as a Photo Interpreter. He served in Korea and as a Canadian delegate to the International Truce Commission, and in Indo-China 1958-59. After his retirement from the military in 1964, Charlie joined the National Research Council and later other atmospheric environment firms and pioneered developments in satellite data imaging and interpretation.

## 1997, CISA AGM

The CISA AGM was held at CFSIS, CFB Borden on 25 Sep 97 chaired by the President, Maj Doris E. Guyatt. Those present included: Maj David A. Haas (Treasurer), Col Robert T. Grogan (Membership Secretary), Col Jeff S. Upton, LCol Dale M. Watts (2nd VP), Maj Robert C. Dale (Director), Maj Gary W. Handson, LCol Don R. Johnson, Lt E. Bruce Holmes (Director), Lt Paul R. Perchaluk (Director), BGen Douglas Yuill (Security Branch Col Comdt), MGen J.E. Pierre Lalonde (Int Branch Col Comdt), Maj A. Wayne Kendall, Capt David A. Rubin (Director), Capt P.W. Clare Lagerquist, Col Ron J. Donovan, Maj Peter W. Sloan, Maj Franz F. Laizner (Director), Capt James P.K. Van Wynen, Capt Harold F. Smith, Maj William "Bill" L. Watt, LCol King G. McShane, Maj Brian Kent, LCol William "Bill" Tenhaaf, Lt George Holdron, LCol Tony Battista (CFSIS Comdt), Capt Mike Motyl, MGen Al Pickering (Past Col Comdt, Security Branch), Col Patrick D.R. Crandell (Int Branch Advisor and Director, Operational Int), Maj John "Pappy" MacKinnon (Secretary). Guests: MGen Nick Hall (Vice Chair CDA)), Dr Tim Smith (CSIS), LCol Robert M. Parsons (DLFR4, NDHQ), Col W.C. Thompson (Comd, Training Schools, CFB Borden), and several members of CFSIS staff who assisted LCol Battista in his presentation.[23]

---

22. CISA Newsletter, Vol. 27, No.2, August 1997, pp. 1-3.

The former Commandants of CFSIS as well as the Colonel Commandant of the Security Branch, BGen Douglas Yuill and the Colonel Commandant of the Intelligence Branch, MGen J.E. Pierre Lalonde attended the AGM. Col Patricia M. Samson of the Security Branch and Col Patrick D.R. Crandell of the Intelligence Branch provided briefings during the conference.

Tribute was paid to members who had passed away since the last meeting, including Col Craig B. MacFarlane, Col John P. Page, Capt Ben Kuban and Col Bruce Mackedie. A minute's silence was observed in their memory.

Maj William "Bill" L. Watt and Maj Eddie Corbeil were put forward to the Colonel Commandant of the Int Branch as nominees to attend the 55th anniversary trip for survivors of the Dieppe Raid. Col Patrick D.R. Crandell provided a detailed explanation of the work of DG Int, Unit by Unit, and answered questions.

Capt Sylvie Beaudry detailed the progress on the CFSIS Heritage Hall project, including the naming of buildings and training rooms as part of the Base Borden Museum. Dr. Tim Smith of the Canadian Security and Intelligence Service (CSIS) spoke on the subject of terrorism, internationally and in Canada. During the mess dinner after the conference, 2 Int Pl of Ottawa was awarded the Sir William S. Stephenson Trophy for the second time. MCpl J. Faragone of 2 Int Pl was declared the winner of the CISA Essay Competition for 1997.

LCol Robert M. Parsons, the senior Int officer on the Army Staff at NDHQ, spoke on his organization and its responsibilities, and answered questions. Col R.J. Donovan spoke on the "Report on the Somalia Enquiry" and the "Report of the Special Advisory Group on Military Justice and Military Police Investigation Services." He described the developments in the Somalia Operation chronologically, noting the problems of discipline, training and leadership.[24]

## 1997, A Farewell to Haiti
### Article by Capt J. Daniel Villeneuve, UNTMIH/U2 Haiti

From March 1995 until the end of November 1997, the Canadian Forces have deployed Troops in Haiti as a participating nation to the United Nations mis-

---

23. CISA Newsletter, Vol. 27, No. 3, Winter 199-98, p. 2.
24. CISA Newsletter, Vol. 27, No.3, Winter 1997-1998, pp. 1-5.

sion in that country. Among the deployed forces was a significant contribution from the CF Intelligence Branch. Intelligence was an integral and important part of the mission, and the good work of Branch members were consistently recognised by all. In the words of BGen Pierre Daigle (former Force Commander, who mentioned this on many occasions) Intelligence played a key role in the success of operations in Haiti.

Haiti was anything but a typical United Nations mission. There were no warring factions and the problem was an internal one to Haiti. Officially, the UN was there to help restore democracy in the country. This effort started with a massive US (almost) invasion in September 1994 to establish the conditions for the return of President Aristide one month later. In February 1995, the UN took over and its presence was intended to maintain stability while the new Haiti National Police (HNP) was being put in place. The HNP was envisioned as a replacement for the former Forces Armées d'Haiti (Ex-FAD'H) that had then just been disbanded. In reality, Haiti was becoming a major burden for the US. Under American influence, the UN got involved to help restore some order in this problematic area. The Haiti mission was marked throughout by numerous mandates that were decided at the last minute (from UNMIH to UNSMIH and finally to UNTMIH) and by a constant reduction in forces. Despite all these changes, Haiti was in essence a military operation and, like all military operations, there was a need for intelligence support.

Upon my arrival in Haiti at the beginning of July 1997, I discovered to my great pleasure a U2 Branch that was well organized and that was running a smooth and efficient intelligence operation. I was the first of a group of intelligence personnel that was arriving in replacement of those already in theatre—some of whom had been in-country for close to 18 months. At that moment, the military mission was composed of Canada and Pakistan—the only remaining nations of the somewhat dozen that were initially involved. Both contingents were located in Port au Prince, with their assigned mission being to patrol the whole country.

The set-up of the intelligence organisation of which I was a part was established in March 1996 with the arrival of Major Mike R.J. Ouellette and his crew (Capt J.C. Chris Gagnon, WO Manuel A. Thibault and MCpl J.F. Gauthier, who were later augmented by Capt D.D. Nickel and Sgt K.J. Marchand). They are the ones who accomplished the outstanding work of setting up the ensuing intelligence operation, and we cannot overlook their good work in silence.

The U2 Branch was by far the busiest Branch of the Force Headquarters. This was demonstrated by the fact that despite numerous reductions in personnel throughout the duration of the mission, the U2 Branch remained untouched. The Branch was organised in the following way. It was under the command of Major J.R.Y. Mike Foucreault from Winnipeg. By the way, it is important to mention that the Major quickly discovered that the only way to survive driving in Haiti is to drive like the Haitians themselves. He soon became an expert at this game. The Branch administration was under the responsibility of Sgt Ishaq from Pakistan, a first class clerk who impressed everybody with his diligent good work. Under Major J.R.Y. Mike Foucreault were two Sections: operations and analysis.

The Operations Section was under my control. With me was Sgt J.P. André Tremblay, freshly posted in from Ottawa to Valcartier. He did not even have time to unpack before leaving again for Haiti. Our main task was to coordinate the mission collection of information effort. This was done by means of a weekly patrol coordination meeting. On a weekly basis, the UN was patrolling over twenty locations all over the country, under the direction of the U2 Branch. It is interesting to note that the UN was the only agency able to maintain a countrywide collection of information effort, and for this reason our Allies maintained close liaison with us. The Operations Section was also responsible for coordinating the activities of the Field Information Section. Composed of eight Military Police members (from the former SIU), most of them qualified in CI, the Section was able to field four teams of two. Those teams were essentially HUMINT debriefing teams. Two of these teams were responsible for the Port au Prince area, one for covering the North of the country, and the last for covering the South. The Field Information Section, directly under the control of the J2, was a great asset in the collection effort. The Section was headed by MWO Lachance and was composed of PO2 Knight, Sgt Labrie, PO2 McGilvery, MCpl Gulbord, Cpl T.P. Ethier, Cpl Lampron and Cpl Wright.

The Analysis Section was under the control of Capt Daniel Massana from North Bay. After the initial shock of working in an Army environment, he quickly adapted to the mission tempo. He was responsible for long-term assessments of the situation. With him was Capt Babar from Pakistan, who was the current situation analyst. Working for the first time in an intelligence cell, Capt Babar demonstrated superior aptitude for his tasks. Sgt K.J. Marchand from Ottawa was also part of the analysis team, responsible for tracking of local gangs when not busy trying to get broken computers or trucks fixed.

Having stayed one year in Haiti, Sgt K.J. Marchand played a key role as the Section corporate memory. Cpl M.R. Huot, a reservist from Toronto's 2 Int Coy, was the collator. He maintained the well-established reputation that reservists can do an excellent job. He is thinking about transferring to the 4ième Compagnie du Renseignement in Montreal, as he had moved there shortly before his deployment to Haiti. Due to the frequency of criminal activities and the need to work closely with the CIVPOL, Constable Michel Ranger of the RCMP was also attached to this Section for liaison and as a criminal analyst. Michel had an outstanding sense of humour, which helped maintain a relaxed working environment.

Working in an operational environment under the UN was an interesting and personally rewarding experience. On a daily basis, we maintained close contact with both National contingents, the CIVPOL, the UN administrative support staff, MICIVIH, the US Support Group and other agencies such as the different embassies. We were at the forefront of knowledge on the situation, and it was challenging to maintain an accurate picture of what was happening. Haiti was not a traditional military mission as we knew them, and the U2 was involved in a special context, with HUMINT playing a key role in the information gathering process. This new environment broadened our horizons and demonstrated the flexibility of our intelligence system, in that it can be adapted to almost any situation.

Haiti will be remembered for its excursions to Club Med on Sundays, the endless barbecues with the Americans, the good restaurants of Petionville, the warm and nice weather and the cooperative work environment. There was also the frustrating driving conditions, the ever-present poverty and misery of the population, the dirt and smell of Port au Prince and the long working hours. Nevertheless, everybody is returning home with the feeling of a job well done. In a few years from now, we will remember our experience as the good old days![25]

---

25. The Intelligence Journal, Volume 1, Issue 1, March 1998, pp. 2-5.

# A Brief History of the Canadian Forces School of Intelligence and Security (CFSIS)
## Lt (N) Doug C. Jantzi

In August 1966, the Royal Canadian Air Force (RCAF) Police School, Borden, merged with the Canadian Provost Corps School, Borden. The C Pro C School and the Canadian School of Military Intelligence, Borden, were subsequently amalgamated to form the tri-service Canadian Forces School of Intelligence and Security (CFSIS), CFB Borden, on 18 September 1967. The formation of CFSIS took place as a result of the unification of the Canadian Navy, Army and Air Force into the Canadian Forces.

Today, CFSIS comprises a Headquarters Coy, an Intelligence Training Coy, a Security and Military Police (SAMP) Training Coy and a SAMP Operations Coy. CFSIS is tasked to train officers and non-commissioned members in basic, advanced and specialty courses in Military Police, Security, and Intelligence skills to support operational requirements of the CF in all environments. In addition, the School provides security, ADP security, and Base Auxiliary Security Force training courses to other members of the CF, as well as Reserve Security and Military Police and Intelligence personnel training. CFSIS also provides training to Military Police from six Caribbean countries, and is the sponsoring Training Establishment for many other government agencies. These latter include the OPP, CISO, Correctional Services, 99 RC (Air) Cadet Sqn in Orillia, and the COPS (Army) Cadet Corps in Mississauga. Training at the School is conducted in both official languages. CFSIS offers 36 separate courses to an annual student population of approximately 700. In 1994, when the SAMP Operations Coy joined the unit, CFSIS also assumed an operational role: that of providing SAMP services to CFB Borden and Commander CFRETS.

All courses are constantly reviewed to ensure that training is consistent with operational requirements. In the past year, much emphasis has been placed on the upgrading and modernization of CFSIS training facilities, equipment and training aids. This progressive approach has clearly established the high standard and direction that both the Intelligence and Security Branches will require to serve effectively the CF of the future.

As a final note, CFSIS is the "professional home" of both the Intelligence and the Security and Military Police Branches.[26]

# 1997, Notes from the Reserve Electronic Warfare Squadron (RESEWSQN)
## Extracts from an article by Capt Gary R. Hayes

This year the RESEWSQN paraded 122 personnel (LEME, Int, Sigs, Log, Admin) and averaged 80-90 members on parade nights and weekends, in addition to 25-45 personnel to support Regular Force units during the school year.

Many Int members of the I&A Troop Have been with the unit for ten years—and the unit is only 11 years old. A number of ex-Regular Force 291 tradesmen, NES Ops and about 15 Int Ops are joining the unit. Most of the members have degrees and computer science backgrounds and are cross-trained as Rad Ops, Fin Clerks, etc. Combined with civilian skills and can-do attitudes, they provide a well-rounded group to the EW world.

Some of the major exercises we attended in 1997 were Ex Frozen Gun in March and Ex MARCOT in June, with elements of 2 CMBG and 5 CMBG. As well as these exercises, we conducted EW School again in conjunction with 2 EW Sqn in our building, confirmation training, and call-outs with UN Ops/NATO. Between May and September, employment reached 90%. This does not include the numerous functions and displays such as the UK Chief of Signals, Brigadier Woods, who visited us in July.[27]

# 1997, 3 Intelligence Company Branch Anniversary Gathering
## PO1 Don B. Powers

On the occasion of the 15th Anniversary of the CF Intelligence Branch, Members and spouses gathered at the WOs and Sgts Mess at the Halifax Armouries to celebrate. 3 Int Coy, Halifax, hosted the gathering with other members coming from LFAA G2 and MARLANT/N21. As well, a number of retired reserve and Regular Force members from the area were in attendance. These included Maj Robert C. Dale, Capt Ken E.H. Smith, MWO M. Al Smith, MWO Rose M. Sutherby, WO Stu E. Auld, WO J.J.P. Mike Fournier, WO Tom W. Pieroway and Sgt Robert R. Belliveau. All, renewing old friendships

---

26. · The Intelligence Journal, Volume 1, Issue 1, March 1998, p. 4.
27.   The Intelligence Journal, Volume 1, Issue 1, March 1998, pp. 4-5.

and catching up on past news, had a good time. Maj Rick A. Mader and WO Stu E. Auld were almost inseparable in trying to catch up on the past 20 years since they had seen one another.

In other news, 3 Int Coy participated in Remembrance Day ceremonies at Mahone Bay, NS. The local Legion provided light refreshments after the parade and members of the Coy had ample opportunity to mix with the local Veterans. These included BGen (Ret'd) Amy, who once commanded Western Area (when we had an Army).

These past several months witnessed the safe return (from CANIC Sarajevo) of Sgt Michael C. Wagner and the departure for Bosnia-Herzegovina of (newly promoted) Capt Andrew G. Morrison and the venerable WO R. Hal Pugh (his third tour). Shortly to hit the road for Bosnia-Herzegovina are the CO (Maj Rick Mader) and Sgt (also newly promoted) Craig J. Tudor. Both are serving with the CANIC. Meanwhile, PO1 J.R. François Bouchard will be deploying with the RCR Battle Group on ROTO 3. Capt R. Stu W. MacAulay has been off languishing in Kingston at "Foxhole U" and will be back by Christmas. Also promoted was Sgt Alan W. Wilson. Cpl Richard Vacheresse and Pte Jennifer George were married, and are also the proud new parents of a baby girl, Briuana Marie Vacheresse, born 8 November 1997. 3 Int Coy suggested, "the official history of the Branch should reflect this blessed event as the first baby born to a couple that were both serving members of an Intelligence Company." (So noted, and included).

On a sad note, Capt Ed D. Kirby passed away in October 1997. Ed Kirby had 34 years service with the Militia and Reserves. He joined No. 3 Int Trg Coy in the late fifties and served until CRA in 1992. During his years in the Reserves he rose to the rank of WO within 3 Int Trg Coy, before transferring to the Nova Scotia Militia District. There he served as District RSM until he was transferred to Area Headquarters as Area RSM under BGen Peter Lloyd. After having served with great distinction in that capacity, he was commissioned as a Capt and returned to the Area Intelligence Unit, which was by then the Atlantic Militia Area Intelligence Section. There he served as DCO of the Section, until his retirement in 1992.

Capt Ed D. Kirby also had 30 years service with the Ports Canada Police, retiring in 1993 with the rank of Inspector. At the time of his death, Ed served on the Board of Directors of the Halifax Port Corporation. He was also a member of the Royal Canadian Legion, Branch 162 and Sackville Masonic Lodge 137; was Chairman of the Cobequid Economic Development Association; a member of the Board of Directors of the Halifax Regional Development Agency; and Chairman of the Orchard Beach Estates Homeowners Association.

Ed was a distinguished member of the Atlantic Area. As District and Area RSM he exerted a positive and lasting influence over all that worked with him. Within the Intelligence Unit in Halifax, he was a role model and mentor for both NCOs and officers alike. His passing is a great loss for the Intelligence community in Halifax and the Branch as a whole.[28]

## OP RAMPART—EX MARCOT 2/97
## Lt (N) Shawn P. Osborne MARLANT/N23-1

As part of the seagoing staff for MARCOT 2/97 on the West Coast last October, I was able to experience first hand the challenges faced by Int officers at sea providing direct support to the Maritime Component Commander (MCC). In this case, I was employed as a member of Commodore Buck's team as part of the staff of the Commander, Canadian Fleet Pacific. This staff was responsible for the development and implementation of the operational plan in support of OP RAMPART, a UN embargo operation being conducted in the entrance to the Straits of Juan de Fuca south of Vancouver Island. In addition, an Int staff under Capt Brian E. Hamilton, deployed to Nanoose to support an amphibious landing by "C" Coy, 3 PPCLI. Because of the geographic dispersion of the Land Component Commander (LCC) and the MCC, there was little opportunity for interaction between us.

Initial integration of the TG staff went well, with good support being provided by all MARPAC Int staff. Prior to the submission of the OPTASK Int for review, none on the TG staff had seen one. This necessitated the requirement to provide instruction to the staff about the role of an Int officer at sea, and the Int function.

Daily activity included provision of Int assessments based on incoming data, initially from JFC information and later from all-source analysis. The most important assessment related to the MCC Concept of Operations for OP RAMPART. This required a significant effort in conjunction with the MCC Combat Officer throughout the course of the training phase of the exercise. Of note, the MCC placed a very high level of importance on this and

---

28. The Intelligence Journal, Volume 1, Issue 1, March 1998, pp. 10-11.
Capt Ed Kirby was truly one of those of whom one could say, "I had the privilege to have served with him." Author.

all other intelligence assessments. In addition, the MCC IO produced morning SITREPs, OPNOTE reports using the Navy's Joint Maritime Command and Information System (JMCIS) (vice slower message reporting), daily briefings and INTSUMs. Daily briefings were also provided to ship's company through an on-board TV network.

The value of having an intelligence officer embarked lay in the ability of the IO to absorb large amounts of information and turn it around quickly in an easily digestible format. Experience in HQs where rapid turn around is required was very useful. In addition, the thought process for assessments had to be clear and logical, and any reports generated had to be concise. A high degree of literacy was essential to enhancing credibility and presenting information in an easily absorbed format.

The IO had to be more than just an IO. On a staff where each member takes up valuable bunk space, it was critical that the IO accepts jobs not strictly Int related. For example, I wrote daily SITREPs, and assisted in the development of ops plans, etc. It wasn't essential that every moment be spent in the Ops Room, but participation in as many staff meetings as possible, and situational awareness in the broader sense, was critical. Ship and squadron staffs have plenty of experience and knowledge about the specifics of their trade. The Io advantage lies in not being as involved in the details of the operation but in looking at things in a more general way. This allows for freer thinking and more time for analysis. Acting as a sounding board for TG Staff helped, as did prior experience as a MARS officer. In fact, the latter was critical to comprehending the requirements of the Staff.

Staffs from PALANTIR II, USS OLDENDORF and HMCS HURON took part in the final stages of the pre-deployment phase. PALANTIR II deployed a Det to Nanoose to support the amphibious operation. The Cryptologic Direct Support Element (CDSE) is now an integrated part of the HMCS HURON ship's company. The MCC was very happy with CDSE, in no small part due to some timely reports issued by the team during the initial surface engagement.

In general, the deployment was an excellent opportunity for all elements of the intelligence team to demonstrate their capabilities. As TGIO, it provided me the chance to observe first hand the severe limitations of our on-board communications systems, and the 'work-arounds" associated with this shortfall. JMCIS proved its worth; sometimes being the only effective means of rapid communication other than INMARSAT. Although new to the CDSE game, the team in HMCS HURON proved their worth to the CTG, despite experiencing some significant communications problems.[29]

## Int Advisor to the Chief of Air Staff at NDHQ Ottawa Maj J.P. André Tremblay, CSA Ottawa

It was a significant turning point in 1997 for the Air Force with the disbandment of four Air Groups, the closing of the Command HQ, the formation of the Air Staff in NDHQ as well as 1 Canadian Air Division and Canadian NORAD Region (1CAD/CANR) HQ in Winnipeg. The tempo of operations has been high, both overseas and at home. Major activities included OP CONSTABLE (Haiti), OP BISON (Italy), OP MIRADOR (Bosnia-Herzegovina), and OP ASSISTANCE (Manitoba flood). I started my new job as the Intelligence Advisor for the Chief of the Air Staff at the end of July 1997. This is also when the Air Staff was activated.

First, let me tell you what the Air Staff is all about. It is basically a strategic level headquarters for the Air Force. The Chief of the Air Staff (CAS) is LGen Al DeQuetteville. His staff is divided into three major components: plans & requirements, materiel, and personnel. I come under the first component headed by the Assistant CSA MGen R.R. Henault, under the Directorate of Air Force Employment (D Air FE). It is interesting to note that there is a considerable Reserve force component integrated within the CAS structure. The total number of personnel is 194.

D Air FE is a staff organization that has the mandate to influence strategic level decisions on the provision and utilization of Air Force resources. The Directorate keeps the Commander informed on current air operations and force employment issues as required. This is primarily done through close liaison with 1 CAD/CANR HQ as well as the NDHQ Joint (J) Staff. It should be noted that this function is simply the provision of timely and pertinent information, and it is not intended to mirror or parallel the activities of an operation centre. The Directorate also serves as the main focal point for exerting Air Force influence on strategic force employment decisions, including post-operations issues requiring strategic level action. For joint and/or combined operations this will require liaison with my colleagues at the Chief of Maritime Staff (CMS) and the Chief of Land Staff (CLS) as well as the NDHQ J Staff. To this end, the Director of D Air FE, as J3 Air, sits as a

29. The Intelligence Journal, Volume 1, Issue 1, March 1998, pp. 11-13.

member of the Joint Staff Action Team (JSAT) chaired by COS J3. JSAT is a virtual team composed of all J Staffs in NDHQ. They normally meet once a week and control all operations. The Directorate also carries out essential liaison activities with organizations and agencies external to the Canadian Forces. For example, these include the National Search and Rescue Secretariat, Transport Canada, NAVCAN, and foreign Air Forces where appropriate. Finally, D Air FE functions as a centre of excellence for the study and analysis of issues pertaining to the operational posture and employment of the Air Force of the future.

My responsibilities are directly related to D Air FE mandates. My primary area of responsibility is to provide intelligence advice to assist in defining the Air Force posture for operations and influencing national force employment decisions. I work closely with both the DCDS J Staff and the staff of the CMS and CLS at NDHQ, as well as with the staffs of 1 CAD. In addition, I work closely with the other Directorates within the CAS on various procedural, policy, doctrinal and force employment issues.

Here are my terms of accountability:

a. To provide advice to the CAS, the Air Staff and subordinate formations on Int issues;

b. To influence national Int procedures, policies and doctrine. Produce strategic level air Int doctrinal inputs in coordination with 1 CAD A2 & D Air FE;

c. To coordinate strategic Int input into contingency planning;

d. To participate in strategic/mission analysis and long-term planning; and,

e. To conduct liaison with other environmental staffs, NDHQ staffs, OGDs & foreign intelligence agencies.

I hope I was able to give you a flavour for what I do. It is very interesting, challenging and rewarding. I am presently involved in various projects associated not only with Doctrine and Policy, but also with Space, Information Operations, UAVs, Int Function Automation, Reserves, SIGINT, various Int Boards, etc. My office is located on the 12th floor, North Tower, NDHQ.[30]

---

30. The Intelligence Journal, Volume 1, Issue 1, March 1998, pp. 13-14.

## 1997, CFSIS Intelligence Training Company
## Capt J.I. Mike Beauvais, Int Trg Pl Comd, CFSIS

This year is the 30th Anniversary of CFSIS, marking the fact that more than 2,000 staff have worked there and more than 30,000 graduates have received course training at the school since its inception.

The Reserve Intelligence Advanced Classification Training (ACT) Course was conducted between 22 September and 3 October 1997. While a number of Basic Classification Training (BCT) and Intermediate Classification Training (ICT) Courses have been conducted over the years at CFSIS, this was the first ever ACT. The Course Officer was Maj G.D. Dover (R82). The course WO was PO1 William "Bill" M. Flanagan. The graduates of this course were: Maj Don M. Stedeford, 6 Int Coy Det Vancouver; Capt P. Michel Gareau, DREV Valcartier; Capt Gary R. Hayes, Res EW Sqn Kingston; Capt Dave R. Hunt, 6 Int Coy Det Vancouver; Capt Colin A.J. Kiley, 3 Int Coy Halifax; and, Capt N. Bruno Vanasse, 4e Cie de Rens Montreal.

Maj Gary D. Dover was awarded the first ever Commander's Commendation for his tremendous efforts, not only in the preparation and conduct of the ACT, but also with regards to his efforts as the Course Officer for the ICT which was conducted during the Summer. While attending the 1 Canadian Air Division Air Intelligence Symposium on 2 Dec 1997, MWO Ivo J.M. Schoots was awarded the "Air Commander's Commendation" by MGen George E. MacDonald, the Commander of 1 Canadian Air Division. The Commendation was in recognition of MWO Ivo J.M. Schoots 'outstanding dedication during the development and delivery of Air Intelligence Reserve Officer and non-commissioned officer classification and trades training. Over the course of several months in 1996 and 1997, MWO Ivo J.M. Schoots distinguished himself through admirable commitment, keen understanding and perception exemplifying the Air Force values of professionalism, excellence and teamwork. He was commended for his principal role in accomplishing these tasks in a way that reflected positively on the training community and on the Air Force.[31]

---

31. The Intelligence Journal, Volume 1, Issue 1, March 1998, pp. 16-17.

## The Intelligence Branch "State of the Union" Address Col Patrick D.R. Crandell, NDHQ Ottawa J2 Operations and CF Int Branch Advisor

Col Patrick D.R. Crandell gave a snapshot overview of the Int Branch community at the 1997 CISA AGM at CFB Borden 24-28 September 1997. He reported that the Regular Force Intelligence Branch provided the Army with 102 personnel, while the Reserve Component of the Branch contributed 150 personnel. The figures provided broke down as follows: 82 Regular Force personnel were on Operational tours; 63 Reserve personnel were on Operational tours; 127 Reserve personnel provided augmentation to CPX/FPX; 9 Reserve personnel provided UN Backfill; and 30 Reserve personnel were on callouts and providing support to G2 Staff.

The Navy has two coastal formations: MARLANT and MARPAC. There are 12 Intelligence Branch personnel serving in MARLANT and five in MARPAC. These totals include one Maritime Air Component Intelligence officer for each coast. As the intelligence and operations functions are very much integrated in the Navy, there are actually a large number of non-Int Branch personnel supporting the Int function.

The MARLANT N2 organization is outlined as follows: N2 works directly for N3. Under N2 are three sections. The first is N36/N21, which is the Maritime Operations Centre (MOC). The OIC of the MOC is a MARS officer—N36. He is the Current Operations Support Officer and Administrative CO of the N3 Branch. Working as his 2IC and Current Intelligence Support Officer is N21—an Int Branch LCdr. The second section is N22, which encompasses Information Management, Collation and the Formation Photographic Services. A USN LCdr Int exchange officer from ONI currently fills this billet. The third section is N23, which covers plans and Policy, doctrine, C2W, training and SIGINT/Cryptologic support. N23 is a MARS officer. The Maritime Air Component (Atlantic) Intelligence Officer, an Air Element Capt, works directly within the MOC and acts as the Surveillance Officer—a critical position within the combined current Ops/Int support organization. Co-located with the MOC is a SIGINT Support Element (SSE), which is subordinate to CSE and is integrated with the MOC 24/7 watch. There are three SSEs in Canada.

In MARLANT, N2 is subordinate to the Plans and Operations Branch (N3) and operators and intelligence personnel man the MOC jointly. This centre is under the direction of the N2. About 75 personnel support the N2 organization. A similar scheme is under development in MARPAC with slightly fewer numbers envisaged.

Naval Intelligence has undertaken a number of initiatives this past year, which include the following:

a.   Integration of Ops/Int personnel in the Ops Centre;

b.   Amalgamation of the Base Photo Section into the N2 organization (as part of collation/information management);

c.   Development of techniques to exploit web-based computer technology for Int processing and dissemination;

d.   Embarkation of a Task Group Intelligence Officer (an Int Branch Lt (N) as a permanent member of the afloat staff;

e.   Establishment of a permanent Cryptologic Direct Support Element (consisting normally of 4 X Communications Research personnel) in the flagship;

f.   Designation of a Command and Control Warfare staff position in the N2 organization; and,

g.   Creation of an in-house training organization.

Elements of the Air Force Intelligence Community and their respective personnel strength are as follows: 1 CAD has 6 officers and 10 NCMs; 8 Wing has 2 officers and 6 NCMs; 21 AC&W Sqn has 2 officers and 6 NCMs; 3 Wing has 4 officers and 8 NCMs; 1 Wing has 1 officer and 1 NCM; 14 Wing has 2 officers and 11 NCMs; 19 Wing has 2 officers and 5 NCMs; 12 Wing has 1 officer and 2 NCMs; MACs has 2 officers; CAS has 1 officer; for a total of 28 officers and 60 NCMs, equalling 88 Int Branch personnel. Many of these units are also short of their personnel-manning establishment.

The Air Force has been considerably involved in operations over the last year. Air Int staff have provided (or are still providing) support (both in personnel and Int products) to CF-18 operations in Bosnia-Herzegovina; NATO transport crews in Italy flying into FRY from Rimini; the CANIC in

Sarajevo; the new NORAD Region Battle Staff and to the flood relief efforts during OP ASSISTANCE.

The Air Force also faced a turbulent year from within. 50% of HQ staffs were cut, all five Air Force HQs were closed, the Chief of the Air Staff was moved to Ottawa, and 1 Canadian Air Division HQ was formed in Winnipeg. As a result, the intelligence process within the Air Force has been re-engineered. The following changes have been instituted:

a.   Planning, mounting and sustainment of intelligence support to contingency operations has been devolved to the wing level;

b.   The number of intelligence staffs at the tactical level has almost been doubled; and,

c.   New concepts of operations and terms of reference are being drafted.

In addition, the new Air Force command and control system, a fibre-optic high-speed trunk that will link all the Wings together and permit common access to classified databases, is in the process of being implemented.[32]

---

32.  The Intelligence Journal, Volume 1, Issue 1, March 1998, pp. 1-5.

# Epilogue

"Know the adversary and know yourself, and in a hundred battles you will never be in peril. When you are ignorant of the enemy but know yourself, your chances of winning and losing are equal. If ignorant of both your enemy and yourself, you are certain in every battle to be in peril.[1]

Sun Tzu

---

1.   Sun Tzu, _The Art of War_, 400-320 BC, quoted in JP 2.0, p. IV-4.

# About the Author

## *Vitae*

Major Harold Aage Skaarup was born in Woodstock New Brunswick 8 Aug 1951. He joined the Reserves in Feb 1971, being taken on strength with 56 Field Sqn, RCE in St. John's, Newfoundland. In Sep 1971 he transferred to 723 Comm Sqn in Halifax while attending the Nova Scotia College of Art & Design, where he graduated with a Bachelor's degree in Fine Arts in 1974. He was enrolled as a Reserve Officer University Training Plan cadet in the fall 1972 with the HQ Mil Area Atlantic Int Sect. From 1977 to 1979 he was a member on the CF Parachute Team in Edmonton. From 1979 to 1981 he was a member and AOC of the HQ Northern Alberta Mil Dist Int Sect and while working for an Aerial Survey firm. Between 1981 and 1983 he served as the Class C Reserve SO3 Int Officer at HQ Canadian Forces Europe in Lahr, Germany.

In July1983, he transferred to the Regular Force, and attended the BIOC at CFSIS, CFB Borden where he later served as an instructor. Posted to Ottawa in March 1984 he served as an Attaché trainer and Int Analyst in DDI-6 at Tunney's Pasture. From 1986 to 1989, he was the Regimental Int Officer for the Canadian Airborne Regiment based at CFB Petawawa, and took part in a 7-month deployment on UN duty in Cyprus from Aug 86 to Feb 87. He attended Staff School in Toronto and Army Staff College in Kingston, as well as courses in Electronic Warfare and Psychological Operations in the UK. In June 1989 he was posted back to Lahr, Germany, where he served three years as the G2 Operations officer in the HQ and Signals Squadron, 4 CMBG.He participated in Arms Verification Control tasks in Germany and Iceland, and took courses in Advanced Electronic Warfare in Germany, and Interrogation in the UK.

In 1992 Capt Skaarup was posted to back to CFSIS, CFB Borden to serve as an Instructor, and on promotion to Major in 1993, became the Officer Commanding the Intelligence Training Company, and later the officer commanding the Distance Learning Company. In 1994, he was posted to the Tactics School at the Combat Training Centre in Gagetown, where he served as the Intelligence Directing Staff officer, and Base G2. In May 1997, he was awarded his Master's degree in War Studies at RMC, Kingston. From 23 June to 30 December 1997, Major Skaarup served as the CO of the CANIC with the NATO-led Peace Stabilization Force in Bosnia-Herzegovina.

From 1998 to 1999 he attended the Land Forces Technical Staff Officer's Course at RMC, and following completion of the course, he was posted to the J2 Exercise Section at NORAD HQ in Colorado Springs. In 2003, Major Skaarup was posted to LFAA in Halifax where he is the area G2. From January to July 2004, he served as the Deputy G2 and Chief Assessments on the staff of the Kabul Multinational Brigade, ISAF, in Kabul, Afghanistan, returning to LFAA in August 2004. Hal is married to Faye and they have two sons, Jonathan and Sean. Their home is in Fredericton, New Brunswick.

# APPENDIX A

## *Intelligence Branch Badge and Customs*

The Intelligence Branch Badge design shown on the cover of this book is a 16 point silver compass rose representative of the North Star. It was authorized in March, 1982 and the description and significance is as follows:

*Description*: Party per bend vert and gules, charged with a bendlet argent. In front a four point star with 12 rays argent; and;

*Significance*: The colours scarlet, dark green and white denote the evolution of the Int Branch from the Canadian Corps of Guides, the C Int C, and the CF Security Branch, respectively. The star is based on the silver North Star symbol embodied in the C Int C badge and thus further preserves historic ties. It is configured in the shape of a compass rose to draw notice to the worldwide scope of the Branch responsibilities.

These attributes make it an appropriate symbol for the Int Branch of the Cdn Armed Forces. It is an attractive badge, distinctive in appearance, has historical significance and is identifiably Cdn.[1]

*Design*: The design of the badge was begun before the Int Branch came into being. LCol Victor V. Ashdown discussed the subject with Director Ceremonial (DC), Mr. Buckingham, who offered some design assistance. The Int

---

1. The angle of the bandlet is 123.25 degrees. The ratios of the lengths of the star, rays and recesses; from the centre, in order of longest to shortest are, 6:5:4:3.

Branch CWO, LCol Ashdown 's staff and many other Int Branch members in the Ottawa area assisted in the selection of the design.

There is no official "shape" for a Branch badge (unlike bases, stations, ships, etc). Therefore, a badge outline was chosen using cardboard cutouts for comparison. It was decided that an oval shape was more "pleasing" than a circle. In order not to be too "radical," a "surround" of maple leaves with the crown above a central oval was selected. The next item was to choose the standard 10 maple leaves (as in the CF badge and many other Branch badges) or 14 leaves as in the Security Branch badge. The 14-leaf" surround was selected because it gave a better sense of proportion between the crown and the rest of the badge, it was less "common" in that only one other Branch (Security) uses it (the Legal Branch has similar proportions but only 10 leaves), and it provided a subtle historical link to the Security Branch. The scroll was deleted since it was considered unnecessary—the word "Intelligence" would be redundant while a motto would be so small on a hat badge that it would be unreadable from any distance. DC suggested a motto could be included on a scroll under the badge, but not as part of the badge. Since this idea allowed greater flexibility, it was accepted.

What to place within the oval proved to be a more difficult question. Many members suggested a Tudor rose, mainly because it is used by the US, UK, and Australian Intelligence Corps. A number of sketches were produced for consideration. The rose was considered appropriate because it supposedly means "secrecy" in heraldic terms. Research into heraldry revealed that this connotation was probably based on the Latin term "sub rosa" meaning "in confidence." This play on words appeared secondary to the traditional attributes of the rose, i.e. beauty, love, friendship—admirable qualities to be sure, but not all that appropriate. Furthermore, the rose had no historical connection in Canada. Although the badges of HMCS York and the Royal Canadian Hussars use the white rose of York, it was noted that the Admiralty had furnished the HMCS York design and authority for its use.

Other ideas suggested for the Int Branch badge included a sphinx, a lamp of knowledge, a unicorn, etc. The star idea was drawn from the original Corps of Guides and C Int C true North Star. WO R.M. Gray submitted a design incorporating an eight-pointed star symbol, with all points of the star equal. Superimposed on this Silver Star was a red Tudor rose, and, in turn, a tiny gold lamp of knowledge was superimposed on the lower portion of the rose. The design was attractive, but overly complex.

Since the rose and lamp options had been discarded, LCol Victor V. Ashdown concentrated on the star, which in heraldic terms signifies supremacy. It was also an obvious historical link to the Intelligence Corps and the old Corps of Guides and, since it was meant to represent the North Star on those badges, had a Canadian flavour as well. It was unacceptable as it was because it looked very much like the Royal Canadian Regiment badge (less the Royal Cipher).

LCol Ashdown designed an eight-point start with narrow points and the four cardinal points longer than the others. He then modified it to a 16-point star, and in so doing realized he had arrived at a shape very similar to a compass rose (found on old maps and having from 4 to 64 points). The only difference was that his star had all points joined to the centre, while a true compass rose is built in layers with the four cardinal points in front. The symbol was therefore doubly appropriate since it incorporated both the North Star and the compass rose shape as well. The compass rose is a well-known symbol (the NATO "star" is really a four-point compass rose; the CIA badge incorporates a 16-pointer), and several Canadian military badges use it (CFB Trenton, CFB Winnipeg and HMCS Mackenzie, for example). It is also used on the armorial bearings of the North West Territories.

The choice of whether to use a silver star on a dark green background or a gold star on a dark blue background was resolved by Maj Darcy J. Beatty, who pointed to a copy of Maj (Ret'd) S. Robert Elliot's "Scarlet to Green," and stated "there are your two colours."

In heraldic tradition, a metal line or "dyke" is required between solid colours on the field of a badge. A thin white line was incorporated, with the object of representing the history of Canadian Military Intelligence in colours, with scarlet for the Corps of Guides, dark green for the C Int C, and white for the Security Branch.

The badge is 50mm overall in height, 39mm wide and the Silver Star is 27mm in diameter, both horizontally and vertically. The collar badges and belt buckle stars are identical to the star on the badge.

Since the long cardinal points on the star already divide the field into quadrants, rotating the white line to either the vertical or the horizontal positions proved unsuitable. The "eleven o'clock to five o'clock" declination was selected because it is almost identical to the position of the magnetic north needle represented on the former C Int C badge. The white line therefore served a dual purpose. In honour of the title "Scarlet to Green," the scarlet sector was placed on the left and the dark green on the right. Int Branch members proved to be pleased with the design, artwork was sent to DC for official painting, and the Branch had its badge.

The painting of the Int Branch badge was approved by ADM (Per) and the CDS, and Her Majesty Queen Elizabeth II signed it in Mar 1982.[2]

The first hat badges were metal. A loom-embroidered badge in coloured thread followed and is worn by all-ranks. The third badge is metal and thread embroidered, worn optionally by officers and CWOs on the forage cap or wedge cap.

## Intelligence Branch Motto

The officially approved and registered Intelligence Branch Motto is 'E Tenebris Lux'—'Light out of Darkness'. Over 2000 mottoes in all were selected and reviewed to see if it had any applicability to the Int function or the branch badge. This resulted in an intermediate list of about 180, and then a short list of five. E Tenebris Lux was the motto selected.[3]

## Intelligence Branch Flag

The Intelligence Branch flag has a white line about the centre until it corresponds to the inclination of the 'Bendlet' on the badge. It has a dark green colour above the line and scarlet below with the star superimposed in the centre.[4]

## Intelligence Branch Birthday

The Intelligence Branch birthday, although officially established on 01 October 1982, has its birthday on 29 October 1982. It is significant in that 29

---

2. Col (Ret'd) V.V. Ashdown, letter, 17 Aug 1982, pp. 12-17.
3. The other top Four were:
   APPARET QUOD LATEBAT (What Lay Hidden Appears)
   MONITUS, MUNITUS (Forewarned, Forearmed)
   I SHINE UNSEEN
   NON FALLOR (I am Not Deceived)
4. LCol Dendy provided the idea of rotating the diagonal clockwise about the centre of the star until it corresponded to the inclination of the "bandlet" on the badge, using trapezoids instead of triangles.

October is also the birthday of the former Canadian Intelligence Corps, thereby maintaining historical ties.

## Intelligence Branch March

The approved title of the Intelligence Branch March is the branch motto, "E Tenebris Lux." The director of the Central Band arranged the march based on the "Allegro" from "Serenade No. 13 in G-major, 'Eine Kleine Nachtmusik'" (A Little Night Music). It is one of Mozart's most well known compositions.

(Maj Peter W.M. Wilson asked MWO Gossip of the Central Band to score a military march based on the Allegro. The march was approved on 17 Aug 1982).

## Intelligence Branch Traditions

The night of the first mess dinner convened following the inauguration of the Intelligence Branch on 29 October 1982, all candles and lights were extinguished part way through the playing of the Intelligence Branch March. Moments later, all candles and lights were simultaneously relit on cue, to "demonstrate the illuminating power of Intelligence," E Tenebris Lux—Out of darkness—Light! This Intelligence Branch Tradition is continued at all mess dinners where Intelligence Branch members are present.[5]

---

5.   LCol Susan F. Beharriell, 04 May 2000.

# APPENDIX B

## *Intelligence Branch Numbers*

Since the reformation of the Intelligence Branch in 1982, all Regular Force members of the Branch have been allotted an Intelligence Branch Number. For the record, the numbers currently stand at over 1300, and include those presently serving or recently retired.

Since its inception, the honour of Intelligence Branch No. 1 has been reserved for the Honorary Colonel Commandant. Sir William S. Stephenson was the first to hold the number in 1982. MGen (ret') Reginald J.G. Weeks held the number from 1990 to 1997. MGen J.E. Pierre Lalonde held the number from 1997 to 2002, when MGen C. William "Bill" Hewson was appointed.[1]

Reserved: No. 1. Colonel Commandant

**1982:** No. 2. CWO Mervin B. Michener; 3. Sgt R.J. Herman; 4. WO J.R. Haché; 5. Capt J.E.H. Bernard Lemieux; 6. Col Jeff S. Upton; 7. CWO J.R. Ray LeCavalier; 8. WO R.M. Gray; 9. Capt Don L. Browne; 10. Capt J.R.G. Cossette; 11. Maj Gary W. Handson; 12. Capt Robert T. Greyeyes; 13. CWO W. Richard "Dick" Ulm; 14. Capt Fred L. Juett; 15. LCol Thomas F. Davie; 16. WO Mel C. Barlow; 17. Maj John H. Newman; 18. WO Robert M. Steedman; 19. Sgt D.A. Butt; 20. Col George L.R. Bruce; 21. Col Victor V. Ashdown; 22. Maj J. Michael Gauvin; 23. Col Robert W. Irvine; 24. Maj

---

1.   *Reserve Intelligence Personnel in service on 29 Oct 1982 who have not been accorded an Intelligence Branch number:* LCol Ian A. Nicol; LCol Dale M. Watts; Maj Desmond F.G. Heffernan; Maj Elaine E. Mellor; Maj Wilf S. Puffer; Maj Sherman R. Veinotte; Capt I.M. Alexander; Capt P.A. Dent; Capt G.C. Lonsdale; Capt J.L. Owen; Capt G.A. Roebuck; Capt C.W. Moor; Capt S.L. Spence; Capt F. Michael Halloran; Lt P.I. Jackson; Capt Ed D. Kirby; Capt M. Leroux; Capt Stephen D. Moody; Capt Kostas P. Rimsa; Capt Ken E.H. Smith; Capt Kelly E.M. Stone; Lt Brian A. Werner; Lt P.G. Allen; Lt S.L.A. Abbot nee Gordon; Lt W.H. Black; Lt B. Boily; Lt Judi Hastings; Lt K. Gehmann; Lt D.W. Phillips; Lt T.J. Riley; Lt A. White; Lt M. Ziviski; 2Lt J. Mullen; 2Lt A. Schaldemose; 2Lt S.I. Squire; 2Lt R.D. Waite; 2Lt D.M. Watters; 2Lt P.A. Wilson; OCdt M.S. Craig; OCdt E.N. Emas; OCdt M. Metcalfe; MWO J.T. Friedrich; MWO J.H. Jones; MWO M. Al Smith; MWO Rose M. Sutherby; MWO S. Troche; WO R. Bowin; WO W.F. Conabree; WO J.L. Dawes nee Titus; Sgt Adye; Sgt R. Cipro; Sgt J.B. Erlandson; Sgt G.W. Graffman; Sgt C. Dave Graham; Sgt R.A. Stott; Sgt Pauli; Sgt D.M.R. Pellerin ; Sgt M.V. Hubley; MCpl R.T.F. Annesley; MCpl E.M.R. Appleby; Cpl J.K. Boutin; MCpl J.F. Cliffe; MCpl H.J. Devlin; MCpl J.W. Felch; MCpl G.M. Gagné; MCpl Renan Garfinkle; MCpl McCarry; MCpl N.S. Whitley; Cpl L.J. Begin; Cpl G.D. Dubyna; Cpl E.G. Jolda; Cpl D.G. Knodel; Cpl G.R. Leeson; Cpl Maestri; Cpl G.J. McClur; Cpl F.F. Morris; Cpl R.D. Newman; Cpl G.J. Pederson; Cpl D.G. Rogers; Cpl M.A. Slade; Cpl J.A. Smith; Cpl J.M. Soulieres; Cpl Williams; Cpl L.C. Young; Pte R.M.S. Churburski; Pte T.A. Gordon; Pte Y.G. Groleau; Pte E.J. Langston; Pte N.S.M. Skapski; Pte R.G. Scheller; and Pte David H. Schimmelpenninck van der Oye.

G.G. Rowlandson; 25. MWO R.A.T. Hawkins; 26. Capt W. Doug Whitley; 27. LCol Al G. McMullan; 28. MWO D.W. Renwick; 29. WO W.R. Jones; 30. LCol K.A. Peter Mackenzie; 31. Capt William L. Dickson; 32. Sgt John T. Mansfield; 33. WO D.E. Richardson; 34. CWO Jean G. Charette; 35. Sgt F.O. Barrett; 36. CWO Barry W. Sweeney; 37. WO Earl H. Brogan; 38. LCol John O. Dendy; 39. LCol W.R. Vallevand; 40. CWO Barry Toomer; 41. MWO J.P.A. Norm Lefebvre; 42. WO Tom R. Campbell; 43. Capt Jean Guy H.E. Martineau; 44. MWO Herb H.W. Kuchler; 45. Maj Gerry C. Mayer; 46. Maj Alexander George Johnstone; 47. Sgt Gary E. Fox; 48. Capt Alan W. Catherwood; 49. Col Patrick D.R. Crandell; 50. Maj Len E.N. Goski; 51. Cdr Christopher S. Hordal; 52. Maj Ron W. Huntley; 53. WO J. Roy Shaver; 54. WO Pete B. Demers; 55. WO Trevor R. Palmer; 56. MWO Richard "Dick" K. Bushe; 57. WO John E. Cranston; 58. WO A.C. Lawrence; 59. CPO1 William J. Lindsay; 60. Sgt Ed S. Burke; 61. Sgt J.G. Daniel Berrigan; 62. LCol Ray J. Taylor; 63. Maj Gary W. Beckman; 64. MWO David James Sundberg; 65. WO Tom H. Maddox; 66. Maj Rudy Vanderstoel; 67. LCol Darcy J. Beatty; 68. LCol David M. Robb; 69. WO Jim R. Fysh; 70. Sgt Robert G. Bowins; 71. MWO Joseph A. Michel White; 72. WO John G. Callin; 73. WO Roger E. Oderkirk; 74. MWO Art E. Sibley; 75. Sgt Herb C. Bond; 76. MWO Arthur E.B. "Bert" O'Brien; 77. WO Rick J.J.R. Marleau; 78. CWO Dean J. Dunlop; 79. Sgt Robert Hutchison; 80. CPO2 Brian M. Noble; 81. Capt J.J.P. Rose; 82. Sgt D.R. Cole; 83. WO Hans J.G. Kroemer; 84. WO William J. Goodland; 85. WO Carl R. Keenan; 86. WO Michael V. Marsh; 87. MWO Robert A. Lavalle; 88. Sgt Gary Rung; 89. WO J. Charles Cotton; 90. MWO Ivo J.M. Schoots; 91. Sgt Kenneth J. Radley; 92. Sgt Robert A. Churchill; 93. Sgt J.P. Bissonette; 94. Maj Rick A. Mader; 95. CWO Rick J. Tervo; 96. Sgt M.R. Hayes; 97. WO William E. Hamilton; 98. WO Jean Pierre Caron; 99. WO Barry R. Eddy; 100. WO Yves Lévesque; 101. Sgt J.T. Serge Gagnon; 102. Maj J.P. André Tremblay; 103. MWO Paddy Hatfield; 104. WO J.G. Nadeau; 105. Sgt J.G. Malenfant; 106. CWO J. Ron Martin; 107. MWO A. Paul Grant; 108. MWO Barry M. Gardner; 109. MWO J.V. William Leclair; 110. WO Steve R. Fader; 111. Col Richard Geoff St John; 112. Maj Ivan J. Ciuciura; 113. MWO Terry J. Thompson; 114. Maj Don W. McVee; 115. Maj John Brian Brooks; 116. Capt D. Pat Wieshlow; 117. WO R.T. Dicks; 118. Sgt A.A. Hiscock; 119. MWO Marvin J. "Red" Hodgins; 120. WO Rick M. Milne; 121. WO R.G. King; 122. Sgt Brian D. "Jake" Gallipeau; 123. Sgt John L. Henderson; 124. MWO Don B. Powers; 125. WO J.H. Yves Labarre; 126.

Sgt Roy H. Belanger; 127. WO John A. Bain; 128. Sgt J.E.M. Riberdy; 129. WO J. Eric C. Savoy; 130. Sgt Ed J. Granger; 131. PO2 S.B. "Subby" Calford; 132. Capt D.G. Carr; 133. Maj John "Jack" W. Nixon; 134. Capt John Antaki; 135. WO David A. Gelsinger; 136. Maj John W. Sullivan; 137. Sgt H.P. Blois; 138. Capt Russel H. Hensel; 139. Col Gordon S. Graham; 140. Maj Alex C. Chambers; 141. LCol Susan F. Beharriell; 142. LCol Jean E.T. Bigras; 143. Sgt V.H. Vouriot; 144. LCol Peter W.M. Wilson; 145. Sgt J.R. Gibson; 146. MWO George T. Izzard; 147. Sgt M. Paul McNeil; 148. Maj Dick A. Dirkson; 149. WO J.P.R. Goguen; 150. MWO W. Ken Spike; 151. MWO J.R. Claude Morin; 152. WO Joe V. Million; 153. Maj William H. Becker; 154. WO Cyril P. Aucoin; 155. MWO J. Dan Galley; 156. WO J.J. Claude Fradette; 157. Maj H. Wayne Nightingale; 158. WO Dave J. Bruton; 159. Sgt Robert R. Belliveau; 160. Capt Richard "Dick" A. Anslow; 161. LCdr W. Burns MacDonald; 162. LCol Paul F. O'Leary; 163. WO R.G.G. (Bear) Fournier; 164. Maj Barry A. MacDonald; 165. Maj Robert J. McCutcheon; 166. Capt Tom C. O'Brien; 167. WO Vince S. Keefe; 168. WO Dean E. Smith; 169. PO1 Charlie T. Scott; 170. MWO David J. Whalen; 171. WO M. Brian Mahoney; 172. WO Michael E. Higgins; 173. WO Robert A. Deleau; 174. WO Rick C. Nickerson; 175. Capt Dave R. Hunt; 176. Capt Ed C. Denbeigh; 177. WO J. Pierre Murret-Labarthe; 178. MWO F. Vance Gordon; 179. Capt Phil R. Berikoff; 180. MWO Jim H. Rasmussen; 181. WO E. Meril Crane; 182. Sgt Steve Mercer; 183. WO J.A. Réjean Montmarquet; 184. Sgt J. Michael Poulin; 185. LCol Pierre Michaud; 186. Sgt C.K. Hansen; 187. PO2 Dan A. McCoy; 188. Maj Gordon P. Ohlke; 189. Maj Ken F. Binda; 190. LCol John F. Cruse; 191. LCol Donald H. Neil Thompson; 192. Maj Stanley L. Carr; 193. LCol Pat A. Renaud; 194. CWO Rolf F. Overhoff; 195. WO Tom W. Pieroway; 196. PO1 Harry V. Delorey; 197. Sgt Richard E. "Dick" Hurst; 198. WO William A. Mitchell; 199. CWO Collin Affleck; 200. Sgt R.O. Hill; 201. WO Lynn J. Brooks; 202. WO Lloyd D. Crosby; 203. Capt Robert N. Cooper; 204. Sgt R.W. Estes; 205. WO G. Wayne Ivey; 206. WO Peter A. Maillet; 207. PO1 J.O. "Rick" Limoges; 208. CWO Armado Santos; 209. WO Robert W. Moug; 210. MWO Dan J. Haslip; 211. Sgt J.F. Gauthier; 212. WO J.M. Letellier De St Just; 213. MWO Michael E. Malcolm; 214. Sgt J.R.J. Martineau; 215. WO J.J. Dionne; 216. WO Michael R. Tracey; 217. MWO Bruce E. Smith; 218. Sgt D.W. Jokela; 219. Sgt W.W. Walker; 220. LCol Greg W. Jensen; 221. LCdr D. Rick Douglas; 222. LCol Robert M. Parsons; 223. Maj Brad N. Hall; 224. Capt Chris J. Dodd; 225. Capt Roy C. Armstrong; 226. Capt Robert T. Stranks; 227. Sgt D.A. Lehman; 228. Sgt M.P. Paquin; 229. PO2 A. "Tony" Wyver; 230. WO J.J.P. Michael Fournier; 231. WO Tim G. Armstrong; 232. WO Rick L. Gill; 233. Sgt R.B. Adye; 234. Sgt Ed A. Knobelsdorf; 235. Capt Henry E. Doucette; 236. Sgt Keith M. Young; 237. MWO Barry E. Beldam; 238. PO2 Jeff A. Collings; 239. WO Matt G. McCann; 240. Sgt Glen B. Hupe; 241. WO Ray O. Toovey; 242. WO Don B. Jorgensen; 243. Sgt J.R.P. Turcotte; 244. Sgt T.J. Fraser; 245. WO R.K.H. Wood; 246. Sgt J.P.G. Vinetti; 247. Sgt G. Bruce Scott; 248. Sgt D.B. Smith; 249. Sgt J.R. Marc A. Paradis; 250. Sgt J.J.L.L.P. Girard; 251. Sgt Ken L. Dyer; 252. Lt (N) Richard L. Gustafson; 253. Sgt J.P. Gauthier; 254. Sgt J.E. Coté; 255. Sgt I.G. Cowan; 256. WO Nick R. Procenko; 257. Sgt Robert P. Conway; 258. Sgt Greg S. Smith; 259. Sgt D.D. Campbell; 260. Capt Robert J. O'Gorman; 261. Sgt W.C. Campbell; 262. WO Kevin N. Rowe; 263. MCpl S.R. Hedges; 264. Sgt F.B. Lavigne; 265. PO1 Terry W. Fader; 266. MWO D. Garry Kohinski; 267. Sgt W.A. Morgan; 268. WO Dave D. Turner; 269. Sgt Joseph Jean Pierre Paquette; 270. Sgt K.S. Rankin; 271. WO Al H. Dickie; 272. MWO John G. "Jack" W. Campbell; 273. MCpl K.P. Connors.

**1983**: No. 274. MCpl L.W. Bradt; 275. MCpl Bruce A. Hubbard; 276. Sgt George D. Chaisson; 277. MWO J.L.A. Martineau; 278. Sgt E.L. Larocque; 279. PO2 Darrell L. Gammon; 280. MWO Ron K. Townsend; 281. PO1 William D. Kean; 282. WO Rick M. Chaykowski; 283. WO J.L.S. Gauvin; 284. WO Manuel A. Thibault; 285. Capt Gordon R. Teale; 286. LCol G. Allan Grant; 287. Maj J. Kent Peebles; 288. Maj Lloyd W. Hackel; 289. Col J.G.A.J. Christian Rousseau; 290. Maj Clark J. Beamish; 291. Capt Tim A. Larson; 292. Capt Jay G. Mercer; 293. Maj Larry T. Grandmaison; 294. Maj Brian E. Hamilton; 295. LCol Michael R.J. Ouellette; and 296. Maj Harold A. Skaarup.

**1984**: No. 297. PO1 H.W. Glover; 298. WO Byron K. Mackenzie; 299. PO1 J.R. Michel Labossiere; 300. Sgt Chuck J. Spillane; 301. WO Alex D. Radzion; 302. MWO Rick G. Oliver; 303. MCpl B.I. Schimmens.

**1985**: No. 304. Lt (N) Frank W. Keating; 305. Capt J.M. Richard Larchevesque; 306. Capt C.J. Forrest; 307. Capt (N) Darren W. Knight; 308. LCol J.R.R.R. Sylvain Robidoux; 309. Maj Robin R. Camkin; 310. Capt Gary R. Hayes; 311. Sgt Patrick D.R. Cost; 312. Maj Eric P. Grehan; 313.

Capt J.P.S. Knight; 314. Sgt T.D.G. Graham; 315. CPO1 J.R. François Bouchard; 316. WO Dave L. Howarth; 317. PO2 Daryl W. Monk; 318. WO J.D. Roy; 319. WO J. Patrick D. Knopp; 320. Sgt J. Guy Foisy; 321. WO R. Hal Pugh.

**1986**: No. 322. LCol Terry W. Procyshyn; 323. Capt Barry S. Alexander; 324. Lt (N) Sam Cowen; 325. Capt Perry R. Gray; 326. Capt Lois J. Hart; 327. Capt Tim E. Walser; 328. Lt (N) R. Bruce Millar; 329. LCol Bradley J. Smith; 330. Maj Linda P. Knie; 331. Capt (N) Andrea L. Siew; 332. LCol Brian E. Watson; 333. LCol J.L. François Messier; 334. MCpl P.W. Young; 335. WO J.R.M. Ross; 336. MCpl J.G. Chartier; 337. WO Donald M. Gallaher; 338. CWO Darcy H. McLaren; 339. MCpl G.R.A. Gauthier; 340. Sgt J.P. Tetu; 341. MCpl T.P. Farnel; 342. MCpl J.S. Daniel St Pierre; 343. MCpl J.A. Carr; 344. MCpl M.W. Greenwood; 345. Capt William M. Flanagan.

**1987**: No. 346. WO J.B. Franck Allard; 347. WO Richard C. Gow; 348. Cpl Jacques M.A.D. Verbrugge; 349. MWO Ron T.A. Wulf; 350. WO Mel A. Wilkerson; 351. Sgt P.M. Palahicky; 352. Sgt Rick F. Luden; 353. PO1 David H. Kushmier; 354. CPO1 J.E. Paul Pellerin; 355. MCpl D.H. Mitchell; 356. Capt J.A. Chris Pelletier; 357. MCpl Luc J.A.M. Leroy; 358. Sgt Dennis G. McNaulty; 359. MCpl G.M. Charbonneau; 360. Maj J.B. Pierre Trudeau; 361. Maj Ward A. Sweet; 362. LCdr J. Doug Schweyer; 363. Maj Alan G. Barnes; 364. Capt John M. Heinrichs; 365. LCol Rhe Ap Probert; 366. Maj Michael R. Rothschild; 367. Maj Ross L. Johnson; 368. Cdr Daniel P. Langlais; 369. Cdr Maitland Josh Barber; 370. Capt Peter J. Scales; 371. Maj Westley B. von Papineau; 372. LCol Chione M.B. Hughes—Robinson; 373. Maj Paul W. Hope; 374. WO D. Michael Donahue; 375. WO John A. Dooley; 376. WO J.J.L. Dennis Chercuite; 377. WO R. Jack Wilson; 378. Sgt Kris E. Pedersen; 379. MCpl J.A.N. Tremblay; 380. MCpl P. Murray Campbell; 381. MCpl Dan B. McQuinn-Legér; 382. WO Alex D. Mackenzie; 383. Sgt Brian K. Mudge; 384. Sgt Michael H. Hurley; 385. Sgt Tim L. Hagel; 386. Lt (N) A. Bruce Fenton; 387. WO John C. Penner; 388. Lt J.L. Ivan Dellaire; 389. CWO J.M.A. Stéphane Chartrand; 390. MCpl B.D. Sammons.

**1988**: No. 391. MCpl F.J.A. Arseneau; 392. Maj Ronald H.J. Ruiters; 393. Maj Michael J. Popovich; 394. Maj W.A. "Tony" Rennett; 395. Maj J.

Michel Bédard; 396. Capt Dan A. Climo; 397. Capt J.C. Hill; 398. Maj Robert Glyn Nash; 399. LCdr Frederick Parkinson; 400. LCdr David S. Peterson; 401. Capt Sean R. Bruyea; 402. Capt K.A.V. Sutton; 403. LCdr R. Paul Grimshaw; 404. Maj Phil J. Drew; 405. MWO John Paul Michael Parsons; 406. WO Dean G. Hyde; 407. WO J.C. Tony Gagnon; 408. Sgt George P. Houston; 409. MCpl J.G.H. Jodoin; 410. WO J.M.R. Dan Jacques; 411. WO J.F.J.M. Tremblay; 412. Sgt Gregory Charles Collins; 413. WO Glen A. McGuire; 414. PO2 David G. Maxim; 415. Capt Reginald J. McAuley; 416. WO Mark H. Figge; 417. Sgt Marie M. Hudson; 418. MCpl William "Bill" R. Lorimer; 419. WO Peter G. Manuge.

**1989**: No. 420. LS Dan C. Little; 421. Lt M. George Gillingham; 422. PO1 Richard Lee Fletcher; 423. WO Neil M. Fletcher; 424. WO J.R. Charles Conlin; 425. PO1 Donald R.A. Wagnell; 426. PO1 Thomas E. Scott; 427. WO Kenneth E. Davies; 428. PO2 R.R. Given; 429. PO1 W. Robert "Bob" Murley; 430. Sgt Sean T. Dutrisac; 431. Sgt J.J. Jean Brun; 432. PO2 Don S. Eenkooren; 433. PO2 J.U. Serge St Jacques; 434. PO1 J.L. Dennis Goulet; 435. WO Luke A. Clarke; 436. Cpl C.M. Fleming; 437. PO1 Cliff J. Boyechko; 438. WO J.C. Mario Roy; 439. Sgt Lawrence M. Tierney; 440. WO Connie F. Webb; 441. MCpl D.F. McDonald; 442. MCpl John T. Smola; 443. WO Wayne D. Upshall; 444. Sgt Ernest S. Kuffner; 445. Sgt J.L.R. Pelletier; 446. WO Kevin Toomer; 447. WO Serge Laforge; 448. WO Daniel Joseph Garant; 449. WO Ronald Richard Patrick Walsh; 450. Sgt J.D. Peter Boutin; 451. Capt T.J. O'Toole; 452. Capt G.F. Dow; 453. Maj Boris A. Fedoruk; 454. Maj Chris J. Wallace; 455. Capt D.D. Nickel; 456. Capt Rajeev G. Nath; 457. Maj J.C. Chris Gagnon; 458. Capt Derek V. Marchbank; 459. Capt J.E.S. Lesage; 460. Lt (N) Doug C. Jantzi; 461. Capt Mike H. Heitmann; 462. Capt Kathryn B. Clouston; 463. Capt R. Stu W. MacAulay; 464. Maj Al Haywood; 465. LCdr Shawn P. Osborne; 466. Maj William "Bill" M. Glenfield; 467. Maj P.M. Kelly; 468. Lt (N) W.E. Miller; 469. Capt Phil R. Coo; 470. Maj David R. Canavan; 471. Maj J.A.E. Kent Dowell; 472. Sgt J.H.D. Gauthier; 473. Sgt A.L. Pride; 474. PO1 Daniel J.M. Ash; 475. Cpl R.M. Prenger; 476. Sgt Dave V. Morley; 477. MWO J. Paul Hodgins; 478. WO Trevor Cave; 479. PO2 Veronica Marie Parolin; 480. Sgt Tom J. Last; 481. Sgt Michael J. Martino; 482. Sgt W.T. Gordon; 483. Capt John P. Kubryn; 484. Sgt J.G. Sylvain Lefebvre; 485. Capt Marcel H. Schryer; 486. LCol J.R.Y. Mike Foucreault; 487. Maj Glen B. MacKay; 488. Capt G. Reginald J. Quigley; 489. Capt Clark P. Cornect.

**1990**: No. 490. Lt (N) Andy Nafekh; 491. LCdr Ivan Allain; 492. Capt M.E. Louise Kane née Boutin; 493. Capt M.P. Boudreau; 494. Capt R.B. MacRae; 495. Lt (N) Mike F.H. Arnoldi; 496. Sgt J. François J. Legér; 497. WO John Duncan Ralph; 498. Sgt R.S. Wilkie; 499. MWO Mark J. Kelly; 500. Sgt D.S. Phillips; 501. WO Warren L. Lawrence; 502. WO Phil D. Cooper; 503. Sgt Don J. Fougère; 504. Capt Philip E.D. Nicholson; 505. WO Mark S.R. Bourdon; 506. WO Andrew J. "A.J." Krause; 507. PO1 Brian A. Trager; 508. Sgt Larry E. Neilson; 509. Sgt Norman F. Wilhelm; 510. WO J. Roch Guertin; 511. Capt D.E. Davidson; 512. Capt Robert B. Martyn; 513. Capt Brian J. East; 514. Maj Nick R. Ward; 515. Maj J.I. Mike Beauvais; 516. LCol J. Daniel Villeneuve; 517. Maj Paul D. Johnston; 518. Capt David B. Owen; 519. LCdr Andrew W. Chester; 520. Maj Don J. Cushman; 521. Maj Ed D.P. Rechnitzer; 522. Capt Jan L. Malainey; 523. Capt J.L.C. Bienvenue; 524. Capt M.R.C. Larocque.

**1991–1992**: No. 525. Sgt S.E. Porter; 526. Sgt Richard M. Clowater; 527. Sgt J. Patrick A. Couture; 528. WO Charles A. Beattie; 529. WO W.E. Webb; 530. WO Jorg Kurt Adler; 531. WO Mark P. Peters; 532. WO K.B. Sanders; 533. PO2 Mark H.C. Herrndorf; 534. Sgt Debbie B. Watkin; 535. Sgt B. Wilson; 536. MCpl I.K. Hargrove; 537. WO Robert J. Lindsay; 538. MCpl D.A. Daneliuk; 539. MCpl Onik B. Papazian; 540. Capt Doug M. Mair; 541. LCol Robert S. Williams; 542. Maj J.A.J.P. Cormier; 543. Capt T.A. Quiggin; 544. Maj Eric E. Gjos; 545. Maj J.G. Yves Forcier; 546. Maj Warren A. Rego; 547. Sgt W.P. Wehmeier; 548. WO Joseph Yvon Alain Bilodeau; 549. Sgt Malcolm G. Denny; 550. WO D.R. Kell; 551. WO Thomas L. Rea; 552. PO1 Richard A. Fisher; 553. Sgt Kelly J. Marchand; 554. PO2 Raymond M. Kruger; 555. WO J.J.P. Trudeau; 556. WO Timothy A. "Jake" Winslow; 557. WO Vaughn C. Simpson; 558. Sgt David T. Fields.

**1993-1995**: No. 559. Capt Kerry T. Newton; 560. Maj W. Pat Grant; 561. Capt Bev F. Baker; 562. Capt Jamie G. Miller; 563. Lt (N) Debra J. Mayfield; 564. Capt D.G. Mountain; 565. Capt J.F.J. Dan Massana; 566. Maj Pericles Metaxas-Mariatos; 567. LCol Hugh A. Ferguson; 568. Maj J.V. Gilles Clairoux; 569. Capt Jean Jacques "J.J." Simon; 570. LCol Robert "Bob" H. Smallwood; 571. Maj William "Bill" R. MacLean; 572. Maj D. Phil Forward; 573. LCdr Steve L. Neeb; and 574. Capt Marla J. Dow; 575. WO Ed M. Dziepak; 576. WO T. Kozak; 577. Capt Phillip A. Dawes; 578. Sgt Wes E.B. Young;

579. MWO Neil L. Gordon; 580. Maj Robert C. Dale; 581. Cpl J.B. Eriandson; 582. Cpl J.M. Lauziere; 583. Cpl Lindsay C. Young; 584. Sgt P. Scott Peters; 585. WO K.D. Zoroneck; 586. Lt Anthony G. Kiley; 587. Capt J.P. Stéphane Lefebvre; 588. Maj Norman A. Sproll; 589. Capt Paul G. Rivard; 590. Maj David A. Haas; 591. Cpl D. Hinds-Hueglin; 592. Cpl C.B. Temple-Unger; 593. Capt André. F. Berdais; 594. Maj Colin A.J. Kiley; 595. Capt Arnold S. Neumann; 596. Cpl C.E. Pauls; 597. LCol Don M. Stedeford; 598. Cpl R.G. Herderson; 599. Lt Karl F. Herman; 600. MCpl Danny J. Palmer; 601. MCpl J.S. Amorin; 602. Sgt Daniel J. Topolinski; 603. WO Steve Mullins; 604. Cpl P.D. Eves; 605. Cpl L.D. Robertson; 606. Capt Charles B. Buffone; 607. WO B. Shaun Mootoo; 608. Cpl R. Hugh; 609. Cpl S.J. McSherry; 610. Cpl R.C. Jones; 611. Capt Doug F. Agnew; 612. Lt Don J. Davis; 613. Cpl O.M. Kitas; 614. Cpl L.F. Spence; 615. Maj P. Michel Gareau; 616. Cpl K.N. Gehman; 617. Sgt N.L. Mah; 618. Sgt Steve J. Goronzy; 619. SLt Michael C. Wagner; 620. Sgt J.J. Maheux; 621. WO Stéphane S. Auger; 622. Lt David H. Hunt; 623. Capt N. Bruno Vanasse; 624. Capt Rick G. Stohner; 625. WO Chris W. Free; 626. Cpl M.J. Ostafichuck; 627. Sgt Marc-André Lefebvre; 628. Capt Michael H. Hertwig-Jaksch; 629. Cpl L.J. Underwood; 630. Cpl Mark M. Emberly; 631. Capt James Peter Terfry; 632. Cpl Jason W. Schleich; 633. MCpl Derrick D. Petrushko; 634. Cpl T.R. Whitman; 635. Cpl L.G. Willet; 636. Cpl C.J. Maddock; 637. MCpl Andrew J. MacFayden; 638. Sgt Alan R. Farquhar; 639. WO Alan W. Wilson; 640. Cpl S.T. Miskew; 641. Cpl D.J. Bowie; 642. Cpl P.N. Kissoon; 643. Sgt Craig J. Tudor; 644. Cpl V.M. Bradshaw; 645. Cpl Richard A. Vacheresse; 646. Cpl J.J. Johnson; 647. Sgt A. Kurt Sinclair; 648. Cpl S.C. Wong; 649. Cpl M. Vandertoon; 650. MCpl Karl E. Martin; 651. Sgt D.J. Rankin; 652. Capt Gordon A. Watson; 653. Cpl A.C. Glazin; 654. Capt Beverly A. Kleckner; 655. Cpl L.M. Rusnac; 656. Cpl M.N. Duff; 657. Cpl A.F. Blanchard; 658. Cpl M.R. Huot; 659. MCpl M.S. Phoenix; 660. Cpl E.C. Jacksh; 661. Cpl J.A. Chateher; 662. Lt Greg I. Patterson; 663. Cpl V. Wallsten; 664. Cpl R.G. Prox; 665. Cpl D.B. Purdy; 666. Cpl Dan D. Medeiros; 667. Cpl N.M. Atkinson; 668. Cpl D.C. Collins; 669. Cpl Mylemans; 670. MCpl K.E. Clasper; 671. Cpl M. Barnwell; 672. Sgt B. Young; 673. Cpl C.B. Kyle; 674. Cpl M.C. Yoblonski; 675. Cpl M.R.W. Hall; 676. Cpl P.T. Edwards; 677. MCpl J. Faragone; 678. Capt Lisa Elliott; 679. MCpl M.J. Ford.

**1996**: No. 680. WO Ronald K. Bell; 681. Sgt Bill T. Bill; 682. WO Chris K. Buczynski; 683. PO1 R.J.F. Daigle; 684. Sgt Paul E. Gagnier; 685. MCpl

J.A.M. Eric Gagnon; 686. WO R. Steven M. Gingras; 687. Sgt Al J. Mac-Donald; 688. Sgt Donald W. Rowe; 689. Sgt Dale G. Sonstenes; 690. PO2 J. Paul St Laurent; 691. Sgt Kurt A. Trebels; 692. Sgt Angela L. Unger-Temple; 693. Lt Roy Vandenberg; 694. WO Darren T. Gauthier; 695. WO J.C. Marc Pozzo di Borgo; 696. Lt Donald Bruce Warawa; 697.Cpl D.A. Rouselle; 698. Capt Frederick Paradie; 699. Maj Sandra L. Bullock; 700. Sgt E.G. Pinto; 701. Cpl C.J. Doyle; 702. Cpl P.F. Robinson; 703. Lt Paul R. Perchaluk; 704. Capt D.L. Hughes; 705. Capt Cody D. Sherman; 706. Cpl A.L. Harrower; 707. Cpl D.W. Harder; 708. Cpl A.M. Prusila; 709. Cpl L.K. Murray; 710. Cpl A.N. Mannie; 711. Cpl M. Moricz; 712. Cpl M.A. Tramontin; 713. Cpl J.A. Chatelier; 714. Cpl S.A. Hughes; 715. Cpl T.W. Hoemke; 716. Cpl E. Nitsopoulos; 717. Cpl M.B. Wadden; 718. Cpl M. Boyne; 719. Cpl A.D. Bilc; 720. Cpl S.F. Dwyer; 721. Cpl E.G. Wright; 722. Cpl A. Shaldemose; 723. Cpl W.N. Peeler; 724. Cpl S. Sauvé; 725. Cpl A.P. Skiba; 726. Cpl B. Thiessen; 727. Cpl J.C. Whitman; 728. Cpl R.R. Padua; 729. Cpl D. Heglin; 730. Cpl J.N. Kaduck; 731. Cpl P. Irwin; 732. Cpl J.J.F.B. Asselin; 733. Cpl J.A.M. Fontaine; 734. Maj James D. Godefroy; 735. Cpl Sabine Hey; 736. Sgt F. Maheux; 737. Cpl Yannick Martineau; 738. Cpl Marc-André Meunier; 739. Cpl J.F. Ordonez; 740. Lt John A. Parsons; 741. Cpl J.L. Richard; 742. Cpl J.F. Rodgers; 743. Capt D.M. Sforza; 744. Sgt Benoit Themens; 745. Sgt Stéphane Vézina-Gaudreault; 746. Cpl K.E. Barr; 747. MCpl P.S. Blaber; 748. Cpl D.D. DeBruijn; 749. Cpl M.M. Wambera; 750. Cpl P.F. Battey-Pratt; 751. Cpl J.J.M. Berzenji; 752. Cpl S.J. Ciufo; 753. Cpl A.P. Debrie; 754. Cpl J.M. Donnelly; 755. Cpl J.A. Fong; 756. Cpl S.G. Herbold; 757. Cpl R.M.J. Hick; 758. Cpl Kyle W. MacLean; 759. MCpl S.A.L. McFadden-Davies; 760. MCpl Howard Paul F. Mooney; 761. Cpl S.T. Russell; 762. Cpl M.M. Santschi; 763. Cpl T.A. Shorman; 764. Capt F. Quiroz-Borrero; 765. Cpl A. Amine; 766. Cpl J.G.C. Bourgois; 767. Sgt Éric J.M. Brillon; 768. Sgt Sébastien R.B. Godefroid; 769. Cpl P. Chevalier; 770. Cpl J.M. Hudon; 771. Cpl H.J. Kim; 772. Cpl M.M.R. Petit; 773. Sgt J.C.R. Tardiff; 774. Cpl J.L. Theriault; 775. Cpl K.F. Varasisky; 776. Cpl G.M. Hill; 777. Cpl K.A. Dowell; 778. Cpl L.A. Windsor.

**1997**: No. 779. Capt Roger C. Bowden; 780. Capt Douglas R.E. Bugeaud; 781. Capt Joseph Victor Churman; 782. Capt Thomas G. Gilchrist; 783. Maj J.H.K. Pierre Lamoureux; 784. LCdr Kevin S. Luke; 785. LCdr Dean Martins; 786. Capt Phil R. Moolenbeek; 787. Capt J.N. Guy Morissette; 788. Maj J.M.J. Stéphane Neveu; 789. LCdr Owen J.W. Parkhouse; 790. LCdr Kent

Roscoe Pendleton; 791. Capt Tico Louis H. Remillard; 792. Maj Ron A. Roach; 793. Capt Robert E. Rogers; 794. Maj David Travers; 795. LCdr Troy Donald White; 796. SLt Heather C. Anderson; 797. Sgt Jeffrey R. Blair; 798. Sgt J.Y. Stéphane Cotnoir; 799. Sgt Axel K. Denner; 800. Sgt Gary C. Dulong; 801. Scott A. Erskine; 802. WO Christina T. Franklin; 803. Sgt J. Alain B. Gendreau; 804. Sgt Michael J. Hague; 805. Sgt Dean R. Hancock; 806. WO Kenneth E. Johnson; 807. Sgt Norbert A. Kausen; 808. PO2 Warren M. Lepine; 809. Sgt J.K.C. Ng; 810. Sgt Philip Steven Palmer; 811. Sgt Kenneth G.J. Pedde; 812. Sgt Charles "Chuck" D. Widenmaier.

# APPENDIX C

*Colonel Commandants of the Intelligence
Branch, 1982-1997*

*Sir William Samuel Stephenson, CC, MC, DFC
First Colonel Commandant Canadian Forces
Intelligence Branch (1982-1985)*

William Samuel Stephenson was the first Intelligence Branch Colonel Commandant. Sir William was the son of an executive in the lumber business, born at Point Douglas, near Winnipeg, Manitoba on 11 January 1896. At the outbreak of the First World War, he enlisted in the Royal Canadian Engineers, saw service in France from mid-July 1916. he was wounded and gassed shortly after his arrival, and returned to England to convalesce at Sherncliffe. He trained near Oxford and Exeter College while recovering. During that time he took courses in the theory of flight, internal combustion engines, communications and navigation. Stephenson was promoted to acting Sergeant in September 1916, and later became a full Sgt. In April 1917, he joined the Cadet Wing of the Royal Flying Corps for flight instruction. He trained near Denham, and received his wings at an RFC field at South Carlton, Lincolnshire. He returned to France with the RFC in February 1918, reporting for duty with No. 73 Sqn. During the war, Stephenson was a boxer, and won the featherweight championship of the Inter Allied Games held in Amiens. In March 1918, Stephenson's Sopwith Camel was attacked by two enemy aircraft and severely damaged and he was nearly killed. He climbed into another machine and shot down two German aircraft the same day. He was awarded the Military Cross in April 1918, the Distinguished Flying Cross in August 1918, and, the Croix de Guerre avec Palme by the President of the French Republic. According to the *Cross & Cockade International*, a WWI Aviation Society, Stephenson shot down a total of 12 aircraft. The French paper *Avion* reported that he had shot down 18 aircraft and two kite balloons. On the afternoon of 28 July 1918, Stephenson shot down three German aircraft during a large air battle, only to be mistakenly downed in turn by a "French reconnaissance machine." He was wounded in the leg by the French air gunner, then again by a German gunner on the ground in the same leg, before he was captured and held prisoner at Holzminden.[1]

Stephenson had become a flying "Ace" with [five confirmed and up to] 27 victories to his credit.[2] Following his capture and internment by the Germans, Stephenson made a successful escape back to France in 1918.[3]

1. Bill Macdonald, *The True Intrepid, Sir William Stephenson and the unknown agents*, (Surrey, BC: Timberlane Books Ltd., 1998), pp. 53-54.
2. Burnelli, Vincent and Nan, *Spy/Counterspy, An Encyclopaedia of Espionage*, (Toronto, McGraw-Hill Book Company, 1982), p. 305.
3. H. Montgomery Hyde, *The Quiet Canadian, The Secret Service Story of Sir William Stephenson*, (London: Hamish Hamilton, 1962).

Following the War, Stephenson married Mary Simmons of Tennessee, and became a successful entrepreneur and financial speculator. He was in Berlin in 1933 when the Nazis staged their notorious book burning. He reported his impressions of the growing military might of Germany under the leadership of Austrian-born Nazi leader Chancellor Adolf Hitler (1933-1945), to Winston Churchill. His far-flung business interests, contacts in the British Secret Service (SIS), and Great Britain's need to strengthen Anglo-American relations after Hitler's conquest of France led to Stephenson's rise to prominence. Appointed as an SIS station chief in April 1940, Stephenson operated from his headquarters in Room 3603 of the RCA Building in New York to counter threats against British war supplies. His operation was renamed British Security Coordination (BSC) in 1941.[4] BSC became responsible for sorting and disseminating SIGINT intercepts to Canadian, British and American authorities, and for assisting in the coordination of allied Intelligence efforts.[5]

Codenamed "Intrepid", Stephenson had links to SIS, as well as the national leaders of the United States and Great Britain, the British Home and Foreign Offices, the British War Cabinet and Joint Intelligence Committee, the British Security Service (MI5), and the British Special Operations Executive (SOE).[6]

The SOE also appointed Stephenson to recruit agents for its sabotage and subversion operations in Europe, and in Central and South America. At "Camp X", a BSC-administered special-operations training school near Whitby, Ontario, Americans were instructed in the British arts of secret warfare, "Station M" faked documents, and top-secret communications were

4.    Maj S.R. Elliot, *Scarlet to Green: Canadian Army Intelligence 1903-1963*, (Toronto: Canadian Intelligence and Security Association, 1981), p. 427.

5.    John Bryden, *Best-Kept Secret: Canadian Secret Intelligence in the World War II*, (Toronto: Lester Publishing, 1993).

6.    A number of books on Intrepid have been written, including *Room 3603*, by Montgomery Hide, Dell Publishing Co. Inc. This book was first published in England under the title "*The Quiet Canadian*," with a foreword by Ian Fleming. According to the author, Bill Stephenson received no remuneration for his activities, and when peace came, he had spent close to one million dollars of his own personal fortune on the operation and organization of BSC. Canadian Intelligence Quarterly, Vol. 3, No. 3, July 1965, p. 21.

transmitted from "Hydra" across the Atlantic.[7] Stephenson also managed the numerous SIS stations throughout Latin America, and for a time took on some of the tasks assigned to MI5. He also assisted in the development of the Office of Strategic Services (OSS), the American independent secret Intelligence and special operations agency (and forerunner to the CIA).

At the onset of the Cold War, Stephenson played an influential role in the handling of the defection in Ottawa of the Russian cypher clerk Igor Gouzenko.

Stephenson was knighted by King George VI in 1944, awarded the Order of Canada and the William J. Donovan Award, and became the first non-American to receive the Presidential Medal of Merit, that country's highest award for a civilian, awarded by President Franklin D. Roosevelt in 1945. The BSC. Like the OSS, was disbanded in 1946.

Stephenson went back to business, some of it in partnership with Gen W.J. Donovan, and settled in Jamaica. In 1985, he was appointed the Intelligence Branch Patron, after serving as the inaugural Intelligence Branch Colonel Commandant from 1982 to 1985. Sir William S. Stephenson passed away at his home in Bermuda in January 1989, after a career dedicated to ensuring Canada's place in the North Atlantic Intelligence alliance.[8]

---

7.    David Stafford, *Camp X, SOE and the American Connection*, (Toronto: Lester & Orpen Dennys Ltd, 1986).

# Major-General Reginald John Weeks, CD
# Colonel Commandant Canadian Forces Intelligence Branch (1985-1997)

8. Sir William Stephenson, personal biography, courtesy of the Canadian Forces Intelligence Branch. He was 86 at the time of his appointment. The idea of choosing Sir William originated with LCol G.L.R. Bruce. Ministerial approval of the appointment was required and given. On 1 June 1982, the CDS sent a letter to Sir William informing him of the appointment. Sir William accepted with the following reply:
Bermuda 82/80 11 1108
TO NDHQ OTTAWA/CDS
ATTN GENERAL RAMSAY M WITHERS
CHIEF OF THE DEFENCE STAFF CANADIAN ARMED FORCES
THANKS YOU LETTER FIRST JUNE STOP I AM MOST PLEASED AND GREATLY HONOURED TO ACCEPT THE APPOINTMENT OF COLONEL COMMANDANT OF THE INTELLIGENCE BRANCH OF THE CANADIAN ARMED FORCES STOP MY GRATEFUL THANKS TO YOU SIR FOR YOU EVIDENT CONFIDENCE IN MY ABILITY TO BE OF CONTINUING SERVICE TO CANADA STOP YOURS EVER. WILLIAM STEPHENSON. TELEX INTER 3261 BA BERMUDA

Major-General Reginald J.G. Weeks was born in Yorkshire, England, 22 April 1922. He was educated in Great Britain, the United States, Germany, and Canada. Major-General Weeks enlisted in the Lorne Scots as a private soldier in 1941.

Commissioned in 1942, he attended the War Intelligence Course at the Royal Military College, Kingston, Ontario. In 1943, as an Intelligence officer, he served with the 3rd Canadian Infantry Division, during the D-Day landings in Normandy, and throughout the campaigns in North West Europe. Subsequently, he held a similar appointment with the Canadian Army Occupation Force in Germany.

On his return to Canada in 1946, Capt Weeks was appointed a general staff officer, grade three, in the directorate of military Intelligence at Army Headquarters, Ottawa. In 1951, he became an exchange officer in the war officer in Britain and, on completion of the Canadian Army Staff College course in 1954, became resident staff officer at the University of Saskatchewan.

In August 1960, he joined the Canadian Army Staff in Washington, DC. In July 1963, he returned to Canada and became military secretary in the office of the minister and associate minister of National Defence. LCol Weeks was appointed Canadian Forces Attaché to Bonn, Germany, and was promoted to the rank of Col in August 1968.

In August 1972, he was appointed Director Intelligence Production and was promoted to Brigadier-General in September 1972. In November 1972 after the NDHQ restructuring, he was appointed Director General Intelligence and Security (DGIS). Brigadier-General Weeks was promoted to the rank of Major General on 01 September 1975.

On 15 August 1977, he was assigned to NATO Headquarters as Director Intelligence Division and Assistant Director of the International Military Staff in Brussels, Belgium. Major-General Weeks retired from the Canadian Forces on 30 December 1980. He served as the Intelligence Branch Honorary Colonel Commandant in an exemplary manner until his second "retirement" in the spring of 1996.[9]

---

9.    MGen Reginald J.G. Weeks, Letter, Sep 1999.

# APPENDIX D

## Senior Canadian Directors of Intelligence, 1964-1997

### Senior Int Appt, Army HQ 1903-1964 (abolished in 1964)

First DG Int—BGen Lloyd E. Kenyon (1964-1968)
DGIS—BGen Norman H. Ross (1968-1970)
DGIS—MGen A. Jim Tedlie (1970-1971)
DGIS—MGen Roland A. Reid (1971-1972)
DGIS—BGen Reginald J.G. Weeks (1972-1977)
DGIS—BGen Walter J. Dabros (1977-1978)[1]
DGIS—Cmdre John Rodocanachi (1978-1980)
CIS—RAdm John Rodocanachi (1980-1982)
CIS—MGen Al Pickering (1982-1985)

    DG Int—BGen R. Percival Pattee (1983-1985)

CIS—MGen C. William "Bill" Hewson  (1985-1988)[2]

    DG Int—Cmdre J.C. Slade, DG Int (1985-1987)

    DG Int—Cmdre J.B. O'Reilly, DG Int (1987-1988)

---

1. BGen W.J. Dabros was a Military Police Officer.
2. MGen C.W. Hewson went to SHAPE as ACOS (I).

CIS—MGen R. Percival Pattee (1988-1989)[3]
CIS—RAdm J.C. Slade (1989-1991)
DCDS ISO—MGen Paul G. Addy (1991-1992)

DG Int—BGen L. Doshen, DG Int (1991)

DG Int—BGen J.E. Pierre Lalonde, DG Int (1991-1992)

J2/DG Int—Cmdre Ted Heath (1994-1995)
J2/DG Int—BGen Ken C. Hague(1995-1997)
J2/DG Int—BGen Robert "Bob" G. Meating (1997-2001)

---

3.   MGen R.P. Pattee went to SHAPE as ACOS (I), and was replaced in that post by MGen J.E. Lalonde in 1992.

# Biographies

## *Brigadier-General Lloyd Everett Kenyon, Director General Intelligence, 1964-1968*

BGen Kenyon was born on 9 June 1915 in Waterloo, Ontario. He enrolled in the 10th Field Battery, RCA (Militia) in 1935, and was commissioned during the winter of 1938/39. At the outbreak of WWII his battery became part of the 2nd Field Regiment, RCA Recruiting. Shortly afterwards, his unit moved overseas to Aldershot, England, where they began intensive training. Kenyon attended the first Canadian staff college course in January 1941, prior to being posted as a Staff Captain to the 3rd Canadian Infantry Brigade.

Capt Kenyon was later appointed to Canadian Corps headquarters, where he was involved in the planning of operations for the Mediterranean Theatre. Promoted to Major, his next appointment was as the officer commanding 12th Battery, 7th Army Field Regiment (later designated the 7th Medium Regt RCA). In May 1943, Maj Kenyon was posted to a personnel job at Aldershot in the UK. In January 1944, he was sent to Corps Headquarters in Italy, and then to the 5th Canadian Armoured Division as a Grade II staff officer. In 1945, he moved to Belgium with the Corps. At the end of the war, Maj Kenyon returned to Canada and was posted to the Army Staff College for a year as one of the directing staff. From there he went to Ottawa, to work in the Directorate of Military Intelligence. In 1951 Kenyon was posted as a Military Attaché in Yugoslavia.

During his tour in Yugoslavia, LCol Kenyon reported on the visits of foreign heads of state, including the Soviet Union's President Nikita Khrushchev. Kenyon returned to Canada in 1955, and was stationed in Regina (Prairie Command), before becoming the chief of staff in Winnipeg. He attended a tactical nuclear course in the United States. He was promoted to full Colonel and in 1958, and participated in brigade exercises, in which much of the training was focused on Civil Defence.

Col Kenyon was appointed to Ottawa, where he was involved in the planning of exercises and Army organization in response to nuclear war. Shortly afterwards, he was posted to NATO, and served in Paris as part of the international staff in the position of Civil Defence Advisor. Following his tour with NATO, Col Kenyon returned to NDHQ in Ottawa. In Sep 1963 he was posted to Vietnam, with the International Control Commission (ICCS), working closely with representatives from Vietnam, India, Poland, and Canada. During his tour he visited Hanoi, and he was in Saigon during the South Vietnamese coup in 1963, which he described as being "virtually bloodless."

On his return to Ottawa, Col Kenyon was sent to Planning and Intelligence where he became Director of Intelligence. Kenyon commanded the military funeral of General H.D.G. Crerar, the C Int C's first Honorary Colonel Commandant. He encouraged his staff and others to "think intelligence" and widened participation within the organization. He took part in Cabinet briefings and of the Minister of External Affairs, and gave informal briefings to the CDS, to the Minister of Defence, Paul Hellyer, and to Prime Minister Trudeau. He also too part in the discussions to justify the existence of the Intelligence Branch while steps were being taken to integrate the Canadian Forces. BGen Kenyon retired after 33 years of service, and was succeeded in position by MGen. Norman Ross.[4]

## Major-General Norman H. Ross, Director General Intelligence and Security, 1968-1970

MGen Ross was born on 5 June 1915 in Winnipeg and went to school there. While attending the University of Manitoba, he was enrolled in Canadian Officer Training Corps (COTC), and joined the Cameron Highlanders as a second lieutenant. In 1939 he was offered a Permanent Force commission, but decided to stay with the Cameron Highlanders because of the approaching war. Mobilization and direct recruiting took place in Sep 1939. He spent his first winter spent on basic training and then moved with his Battalion to Camp Shilo in late spring, 1940. On 5 June 1940 he took his unit's advance party to England. While in England, he became a Staff Captain (learner) at 2nd Division headquarters administration staff school at Oxford University. He served as the Administration officer at a bomb reconnaissance school. In 1942, he was promoted to major and officer commanding A Company in the Cameron Highlanders.

Capt Ross took part in combined operations training on the Isle of Wight in preparation for the raid on Dieppe. The main task of his battalion was to pass through other troops and capture German documents. He felt that prep-

---

4. Extracts from the Internet, William S. Thackray edited by William S. Thackray and Chris Petter © University of Victoria Libraries, 1997, ISBN 1-55058-125-2.

aration for the raid was thorough. After a false start in July, the raid took place in Aug 1942. The Camerons landed at Pourville and were to through the South Saskatchewan Regiment. Heavy defensive fire caused these plans to be altered. They moved well inland against increasing resistance, but were ordered to withdraw, and were pinned down on the beach for a while. Eventually evacuated, Capt Ross had to swim to a landing craft assault. He and his men "returned to Newhaven to a well-organized reception," where they spent "several days sorting out troops, intelligence reports, etc." By the summer of 1943 they had replaced casualties and were again well-trained.

Capt Ross attended senior officers school and then was made second-in-command of the battalion. In 1944 he became the commanding officer. At that time, the Camerons were part of the 2nd Canadian Infantry Division became part of the deception force deployed opposite Calais prior to D-Day. Ross landed in Normandy on 8 July 1944 as part of the 6th Infantry Brigade commanded by BGen Hugh Young. He took part in his first action after passing through Caen, and reported having excellent artillery support and engaging enemy tanks close to the Orne River. He was badly wounded in the leg when his jeep was destroyed by German shellfire. He was operated n at British field hospital, and then evacuated by hospital ship to a civilian hospital in England. After about a month he was returned to a hospital in Winnipeg. While in the hospital he volunteered to work for local military headquarters. Following a review board in Ottawa, he was accepted by the Permanent Force and went to Staff College.

LCol Ross served in an administrative job in Ottawa before being posted to Washington, D.C. for four years as a general staff officer, grade I. He was a Liaison Officer to the Pentagon during the Korean War. On his promotion to Colonel he became Director of Manning at a time when it was difficult to maintain the strength of the army. He served three years as a Military Attaché in Tokyo, followed by a tour of duty as the chief of staff, Western Command. Promoted to BGen, he became the Area Commander, New Brunswick. He attended the Imperial Defence College, and then became the Deputy Chief of General Staff. From 1968 to 1970, he commanded the intelligence and security branch where he was quite independent. BGen Ross felt that this service had done well under unification. MGen Tedlie succeeded him.[5]

## *Major-General Alfred James Tedlie, DSO, Director General Intelligence and Security, 1970-1971*

MGen Tedlie was born of Irish parents on 20 March 1916 in Montreal, where he was also educated. In Oct 1939, he joined the 17th Duke of York's Royal Canadian Hussars. In 1940 he transferred to the Royal Montreal Regiment, where he was commissioned. During his service he commanded an army demonstration team, touring Ontario and Quebec, before going overseas, where he took command of a machine-gun platoon.

Lt Tedlie's regiment became the 32nd Reconnaissance Regiment, and utilized armoured cars. He was promoted to Captain. In March 1944 the regiment was disbanded and Capt Tedlie was transferred to the British Columbia Regiment (BCR), making a complete change for him to tank warfare. The BCR came under the 4th Armoured Brigade and landed in Normandy in July 1944, where Tedlie was in command of the tank delivery squadron specifically for the use of his regiment. The unit suffered heavy tank casualties in Aug 1944, at which time he brought the entire squadron forward. He was in action on 13 Aug 44 during Operation Tractable, taking part in a battle where most of his squadron was lost, including his own tank.

Promoted to Major in Sep 1944, he continued to command his squadron until the end of the war, except for a few weeks when he commanded the 4th Armoured Division training school for tank commanders. Major Tedlie was awarded the Companion of the Distinguished Service Order for action in Feb 1945 in Hochwald Forest. At the end of the war he administered a German town for a short time before being promoted to Lieutenant Colonel, and placed in commanded of the Cameron Highlanders of Ottawa who were serving as occupation troops in Wilhelmshaven, Germany.

Becoming a member of the Permanent Force, LCol Tedlie attended the 1946/1947 Army Staff College course at Kingston, Ontario. Following ASC, he was placed in command of the winter experimental station at Fort Churchill, Manitoba. In 1954 he was sent to Vietnam to take part in the International Commission for Control. He was established at a base in Hanoi in Aug 1954, where he was in command of fifty-three officers and men, deal-

---

5.    Extracts from the Internet, William S. Thackray edited by William S. Thackray and Chris Petter © University of Victoria Libraries, 1997, ISBN 1-55058-125-2.

ing with violations of the Geneva Convention together with Indians and Poles. During his tour of duty, he worked with Gen Giap, and met Ho Chi Minh, monitoring the withdrawal of the French army from Hanoi. LCol Tedlie attended the National Defence College in 1955/1956.

Following NDC, he was promoted to Colonel, and became the Chief of Staff, Saskatchewan Command. He next served as Director of Armour, then of Combat Development, where he took part in frequent meetings to plan military doctrine, in consultation with the Americans and British. He was promoted to Brigadier, and sent to command 2nd Canadian Infantry Brigade. BGen Tedlie went directly from 2 CIB to command the international peace-keeping force in Cyprus, which was at that time composed of soldiers from Canada, Finland, Denmark and Britain. BGen Tedlie noted that the force lacked an intelligence organization, and observed that military intelligence was unknown in the United Nations. He felt that much self-reliance was required of the individual soldier on the spot in Cyprus.

In 1964 BGen Tedlie was appointed commander of the 4th Canadian Infantry Brigade Group in Europe, an appointment he held for two years. He was then posted to Training Command in Winnipeg. Promoted to Major General, he became the Deputy Chief of Staff for Force Development. MGen Tedlie retired in 1971 after thirty-two years of service.[6]

# Major-General Roland A. Reid, CM, CVO, MC, CD, Director General Intelligence and Security, 1971-1972

MGen Reid was a veteran of the Normandy campaign and after retiring from the CF became one of the directors of the Canadian Battlefields Foundation. As the founding President he led commemorative activities in Caen, speaking to students in Normandy about his personal memories as a CANLOAN officer.

---

6.  Extracts from the Internet, William S. Thackray edited by William S. Thackray and Chris Petter © University of Victoria Libraries, 1997, ISBN 1-55058-125-2.

# Brigadier-General Walter J. Dabros, Director General Intelligence and Security, 1977-1978

BGen Dabros was born 26 Feb 1933 in London, Ontario. After initial service with the Canadian Army Reserve, he transferred to the Regular Force to serve with the C Pro C as a private in 1951. On completion of basic training, he was selected to attend the Officer Candidate School, Camp Borden, Ontario, and was commissioned 2Lt on 27 Jan 1952.

BGen Dabros served in a variety of junior officer appointments during the next 17 years, including Commander Provost Detachment in Valcartier (1952-53), Asst Chief Instructor C Pro C School in Shilo (1956-59), Commander Provost Detachment Central Ontario Area in Toronto (1961-63), and Executive Asst to Commander Canadian Defence Liaison Staff, Washington, D.C. (1966-67). From Jul 1969, when he was promoted LCol to Apr 1970, he served with the UN peacekeeping force in Cyprus as both Force Provost Marshal and Commanding Officer of the Military Police Company.

Following his tour of duty in Cyprus, BGen Dabros was assigned to Canadian Forces HQ, Ottawa, as a section head in the Directorate of Security. In Aug 1971, he was seconded to the Department of the Solicitor-General, Ottawa, as Chief, Analysis and Information Development section. On promotion to Col in Jul 1973, he was appointed Director of Security at NDHQ.

In Jun 1974, BGen Dabros was selected to attend the Federal Government Bilingual and Bicultural Development Program at Quebec City. One year later he returned to NDHQ as Director of Defence Intelligence. He was promoted BGen in Aug 1977 and assumed the position of Director General Intelligence and Security.

BGen Dabros attended National Defence College, Kingston, in 1978-79 and in Aug 1979, was appointed Chief of Staff, Administration at Mobile Command, St Hubert, QC. His last appointment was Canadian Forces Military Attaché in Washington, D.C., in 1983. BGen Dabros retired from the Canadian Forces on 7 Jul 1990.

BGen Dabros was the first ex-C Pro C officer to attain general officer rank. An excellent rapport existed between the DGIS and CISA largely due to BGen Dabros' candour and energy. He was succeeded by Capt (N) J. Rodocanachi.

# Rear-Admiral John Rodocanachi, Chief of Intelligence and Security, 1980-1982

Born in England, RAdm Rodocanachi joined the Royal Navy from Rugby School, where he underwent the normal junior officer training, and then specialized in submarines. In 1957 he transferred to the Royal Canadian Navy, and, during a distinguished naval career, served inter-alia as Commanding Officer of three submarines, a destroyer and a destroyer squadron. Among his various staff appointments, he was a director in NDHQ when he drafted and received approval for the requirements for the new Canadian Patrol Frigates. Later he was Chief of Intelligence and Security for the Canadian Forces for four years and subsequently Chief of Intelligence and Counter Intelligence for the Supreme Allied Commander in Belgium for three years, the first Canadian to hold the position.

On retirement from the Navy he completely re-organized transport security for Transport Canada for eight years as its first Director General of Security and Emergency Preparedness. On final retirement in 1995 he became active in the Municipality of Oak Bay, where he rewrote the Municipal Emergency Plan while a member of the Emergency Planning Executive Committee, and was a member of the Oak Bay Volunteers, including service on the Board and participating in the Volunteer Income Tax program for lower income Canadians. RAdm John Rodocanachi, RCN (Ret'd) passed away in Victoria, BC at the age of 71. His wife Dorothy, four children and one grandchild survive him.

# Major-General A. Pickering, Chief of Intelligence and Security, 1982-1985

MGen Pickering was born in Wimbledon, England in 1929. He graduated from RMC in Kingston in 1953, and obtained a Bachelor of Science degree in Mechanical Engineering from Queen's University in 1954.

He completed pilot training during the summers he attended RMC, receiving his wings in July 1951. After graduation from Queen's, he completed operation and instructional tours in Air Transport Command on C-119 Flying Boxcars, North Star and Yukon transport aircraft. During this time he served seven months with the United Nations Emergency Force flying personnel and supplies into Egypt in C-119 aircraft. In 1962 he was posted to the

USAF Systems Division in Los Angeles, California. He served for one year as Project Officer for the NASA Ranger (Lunar) and Mariner (Mars) Programs, and was then appointed Chief of the Engineering Division, Agena Target Vehicle for the Gemini Program.

In 1965, MGen Pickering returned to Canada and studied at the RCAF Staff College in Toronto. In 1966, he was posted to RMC where he served first as Air Force Staff Officer, and on promotion to Wing Commander in 1967, as Director of Cadets and military Training. He was appointed Commanding Officer of VP 404 Maritime Patrol Squadron in Greenwood, NS, in July 1969 and three years later he became Base Operations Officer. In 1973, MGen Pickering attended the United States navy War College in Newport, Rhode Island. On graduation in 1974, he returned to CFB Greenwood, where he became the Base Commander. In 1976 he joined the CP-140 Aurora Program as Commander of the CF Detachment at the Lockheed Corporation Plant in Burbank, California.

On 31 July 1979, BGen Pickering assumed command of the Maritime Air Group with Headquarters in Halifax, NS. He was promoted to MGen on 01 July 1982 and assumed the post of Chief Intelligence and Security shortly thereafter.

## Brigadier-General R. Percival Pattee, CD, Director General Intelligence and Security, 1983-1985.

MGen R.P. Pattee was born 9 Dec 1934 in Montreal. He enrolled in the RCAF in 1953 and trained as a pilot. During the late 1950s he served four years in France flying Canadair F-86 Sabres with 439 Sqn and then as an intercept controller with 63 Air Control and Warning Squadron. Upon his return to Canada he instructed at RCAF Station Moose Jaw, Saskatchewan, flying the Harvard and Tutor aircraft. His next assignment was to the Officer Selection Unit at RCAF Station Centralia, Ontario. He was subsequently senior personnel selection officer at the Personnel Selection Unit, CFB St Jean, Quebec.

MGen Pattee has held staff positions in operations and in training at both 1 Canadian Air Group and Air Command levels. He was the senior staff officer operations and training at 10 Tactical Air Group Headquarters, senior staff officer fighters at Air Command, and assistant Chief of Staff, Plans and Policy at Allied Air Forces Central Europe Headquarters in the Federal Republic of Germany (FRG). MGen Pattee has served at each level of command from flight commander to air group commander. He was the squadron commander of 433 Sqn/433e ETAC, Base Commander of CFB Lahr, FRG, Deputy Commander of Air Reserve Group, Commander of 14 Training Group, Director General Organization and Manpower, and Director General Intelligence, in the Intelligence and Security Branch at National Defence Headquarters. In 1985 he was appointed Assistant Chief of Staff, Intelligence Division at Supreme Headquarters Allied Powers Europe in Belgium. On 22 July 1988, he assumed the position of Chief, Intelligence and Security.

During his service, MGen Pattee has participated in the full range of military professional training, including Staff School, Staff College, and National Defence College. He has a BA in political science, an MSc in International Relations and is a Ph.D. candidate at the University of Manitoba in an Interdisciplinary Program in Strategic studies. He and his wife Joan have two sons.[7]

## *Commodore J.C. Slade, CD, Director General Intelligence and Security, 1985-1987*

Born in Portsmouth, UK of a naval family, Rear-Admiral Slade completed his high school at Lisgar Collegiate, Ottawa, before being accepted for the Regular Officer Training Plan and attending the Royal Military College of Canada in 1955.

After graduation in 1959, Rear-Admiral Slade attended the University of Toronto for a further year to complete his degree in Electrical Engineering. This was followed by the completion of junior officer courses and a first seagoing appointment on HMCS Ottawa in January 1961. His next series of seagoing appointments included a stint as the Navigating Officer of HMCS Saskatchewan in 1963, Operations Officer of HMCS Yukon in 1965, and Executive Officer of HMCS Terra Nova in 1969. These seagoing tours were interspersed with a one-year Operations "long course" in 1964, and a one-year post-graduate course in Operations Research, again at the University of Toronto, in 1966. The latter was followed by a tour in the Operations Research Establishment, Ottawa and by participating on the 1968 Officer Development Board, chaired by MGen Roger Rowley.

---

7. Intelligence Branch Journal Number 7, Fall 1988, p. 5.

Following his service on HMCS Terra Nova, RAdm Slade spent two and a half years ashore in Halifax, working first in the Operational Test and Evaluation Force office, then as the Maritime Command Coordinator for the DDH 280 program. His only "foreign" posting occurred for a six-month period in 1972 when he attended the Armed Forces Staff College, Norfolk, Virginia, before returning to his previous appointment in Halifax.

In 1973, as a LCdr, RAdm Slade was appointed to be in command of HMCS Gatineau in Esquimalt, BC, and was promoted Commander shortly before returning to Halifax as Senior Staff Officer, Sea Systems Readiness, in 1975.

In 1976, RAdm Slade took command of HMCS Athabaskan for two years, prior to spending two years at NDHQ in the Directorate of Maritime Requirements as Section Head of the command, control and communications section. In 1980 he was promoted naval Capt and was appointed to command the Second Canadian Destroyer Squadron in Esquimalt. This was followed in 1982 by another tour in Halifax as Deputy Chief of Staff Plans on the Maritime Commander's staff, and one year later, he returned to NDHQ as the Executive Assistant to the Chief of the Defence Staff.

In 1985 RAdm Slade was promoted Commodore and was appointed as the Director General Intelligence. On 21 Sep 1987 after promotion to his present rank, he assumed the position of Chief, Maritime Doctrine and Operations. On 28 Jul 1989, RAdm Slade was appointed as Chief of Intelligence and Security.[8]

## Commodore J.B. O'Reilly, CD, Director General Intelligence, 1987-1988

Commodore J.B. O'Reilly was born 7 August 1937 in Cornwall, Ontario. He joined the Royal Canadian Navy in Sep 1955. Upon completion of junior officer training in 1959, he served in Her Majesty's Canadian Ships Crusader, Buckingham, and Chaleur, prior to attending the Fifth Weapons Officer's Course in HMCS Stadacona from January to October 1964.

Following a 30-month tour as Weapons Officer in HMCS St Croix, Lt O'Reilly served for three years in NDHQ Ottawa. During this posting Lt

---

8.    Intelligence Branch Journal, Number 8, Fall 1989, p. 4. (Last of eight editions of the IBJ)

O'Reilly attended CF Staff School in Toronto. In 1970 he assumed command of the minesweeper HMCS Miramichi and was promoted to Lt-Commander. Following one year as Executive Officer of HMCS Qu'Appelle and one year as Executive Officer of HMCS Kootenay, he was promoted to Commander and assumed command of HMCS Terra Nova. Commander O'Reilly attended the United States Armed Forces Staff College in Norfolk, Virginia in 1976 and then became Senior Staff Officer Naval Weapons in the Canadian Defence Liaison Staff at Washington.

In July 1978, Commander O'Reilly assumed command of HMCS Athabaskan. Following that posting he spent one year as Senior Staff Officer Combat Systems Readiness in Maritime Command Headquarters, Halifax. Commodore O'Reilly was promoted to Capt (N) in August 1981 and became the Director maritime Operations, Plans and Reserves. He held that position until July 1983 when he assumed command of HMCS Preserver. In January 1985 Capt (N) O'Reilly was appointed Naval Advisor in CDLS London and CFA The Hague.

In 1987 Capt O'Reilly was promoted to his present rank and was appointed as the DG Int. Comdre O'Reilly is married and has two children who are serving officers in the Canadian Forces.[9]

## *Major-General Paul G. Addy, Deputy Chief Defence Staff Intelligence Staff Officer, 1992-1993*

From June 1992 to January 29,1993, MGen Addy was the Deputy Chief of the Defence Staff, Intelligence, Security and Operations (DCDS (ISO)). He was the principal staff officer for operations of the Canadian Forces (CF) and, additionally, for the period of deployment of the Canadian Joint Force Somalia (CJFS) to the date of relinquishing his appointment, he was the commander of a command positioned in the chain of command between the Chief of the Defence Staff (CDS) and Commander CJFS.

His responsibilities included intelligence, security, and operations. The major responsibilities of the position included advising on and promulgating operational direction to the CF and monitoring CF activity; establishing standards for and monitoring the effectiveness and efficiency of the CF intelli-

---

9.    Intelligence Branch Journal Number 6, Spring 1988, p. 4.

gence, security, and operations activities; maintaining an operational readiness system on a forces-wide basis to indicate the operational effectiveness of the CF relative to approved missions and tasks; acting as a commander of a command for all peacekeeping units/formations; and developing and recommending operational training standards for all environments and services in joint operations.

## *Brigadier-General Larry T. Doshen, Director General Intelligence, 1991*

BGen Doshen is the author of the Intelligence Support and Guidelines handbook. In 1995, he was retained by the CF to prepare a study on issues of morale and leadership in the CF, culminating in a report he wrote entitled, "Report on the Study of Mechanisms of Voice/Complaint Resolution in the Canadian Forces."[10] He followed this report with a second calling for an implementation plan for an organizational ombudsman. On his retirement from the CF, he worked in Canadian Animal Health Emergency Management.

## *Commodore Ted Heath, OMM, CD, J2/Director General Intelligence, 1994-1995*

Cmdre Thomas C. "Ted" Heath, was Director General Intelligence in National Defence Headquarters from 1994-95 and Assistant Chief of Staff Intelligence SHAPE HQ, Mons, Belgium from 1995-1998 where he was heavily involved in the planning and execution of the NATO Implementation Force/Stabilization Force (IFOR/SFOR) and planning for Kosovo.

## *Brigadier-General Kenneth C. Hague, Director General Intelligence, 1995-1997*

Ken Hague was born in Thunder Bay and attended university from 1967 to 1972 at both le College Militaire royale de St Jean, Quebec and Royal Military College in Kingston, Ontario. After graduating with an Honours BA in Economics and Commerce, he was posted to le 5e Regiment d'Artillerie légère du

10. BGen Larry T. Doshen, *Report on the Study of Mechanisms of Voice/Complaint Resolution in the Canadian Forces*, 30 November 1995.

Canada in Valcartier, Quebec in May 1972 as a Lieutenant in the Artillery. He spent the next 28 years primarily in operational assignments across Canada and abroad.

His main appointments from 1972 to 1995 include Battery Commander and Regimental Second-in-Command with le 5e Regiment, Commanding Officer of 2nd Regiment, Royal Canadian Horse Artillery in Petawawa, Ontario, Deputy Chief of Staff of the Army Reserves in St Hubert, Quebec, and Deputy Commander of the Combat Training Centre at CFB Gagetown, New Brunswick. In 1994, he served as a peacekeeper in Croatia for seven months.

He was promoted to Brigadier General in 1997 and was appointed Director General Intelligence at National Defence Headquarters in Ottawa. After two years in the J2/DG Int chair, BGen Hague moved to Kingston to assume the position of Commandant of the Royal Military College. BGen Hague was relieved by BGen Robert "Bob" G. Meating on 11 Aug 1997.

BGen Hague retired from the Canadian Forces in June 2000 and moved to Vancouver. He became a volunteer Loaned Representative with United Way of the Lower Mainland for 16 weeks that fall and was hired by United Way as a full-time fundraiser in April 2001. In January 2003, he was appointed Director Resource Development, and in April 2004 was appointed Vice President, Resource Development with United Way of the Lower Mainland.

Ken is an avid golfer and would like to spend considerably more time on the links. In winter, he skis with his son Aaron at Whistler. He is married to Wendy Hague, also from Thunder Bay, and currently lives in Vancouver.

## *Brigadier-General Robert "Bob" G.Meating, OMM, CD, MSM,, Director General Intelligence, 1997-2001*

BGen Robert "Bob" G. Meating was born in Saint John, New Brunswick, in May 1946. He enrolled in the Canadian Army in 1965 as an Armoured Officer and served with the 8th Canadian Hussars in Petawawa, Ontario, until 1968 and in Soest, Westphalia, until 1970 as a Troop Leader.

Promoted to Capt in 1970, he moved with his new regiment, The Royal Canadian Dragoons, from Northern Germany to Lahr, in the Schwarzwald, that same year. He remained with the Dragoons as a Troop Leader until 1972, when he returned to Toronto, Ontario, with the assignment of Area Cadet

Staff Officer 1972-75. In 1975, he returned to Toronto, Ontario, with the assignment of Area Cadet Staff Officer 1972-75. In 1975, he returned to his Regiment in Germany and, in the following three years, occupied the positions of Squadron Battle Capt and Regimental Operations Officer. In 1978, he was posted to CFB Chilliwack, BC, as an instructor and Company Commander at the Canadian Forces Officer Candidate School (CFOCS).

While at CFOCS he was promoted to Major and posted as the Commanding Officer, Canadian Contingent Administrative Unit Middle East (CCAUME), serving in both Ismalia, Egypt, and the Golan Heights, Israel. After completing his United Nations tour, he attended the Canadian Forces Command and Staff College, Toronto, during 1980-81. Between 1981 and 1983, Major Meating commanded the independent tank squadron (C Squadron, The Royal Canadian Dragoons) in Gagetown, New Brunswick. He led the squadron through two annual operational flyover deployments in Germany in 1981 and 1982.

In 1986, Lt-Col Meating assumed command of Canada's NATO-deployed tank and armoured reconnaissance regiment, The Royal Canadian Dragoons in Lahr. During his tour as Commanding Officer (in 1987), he moved the Regiment from Lahr to Petawawa, Ontario. In July 1988, he gave up command in Petawawa and returned to Lahr and the Headquarters, 4 Canadian Mechanized Brigade Group, as the Brigade Senior Staff Officer Operations/Chief of Staff. He held this position for two years until July 1990.

Promoted to Col in July 1990, he assumed a new post with the Headquarters, 1st Canadian Division, as Chief of Staff (Division Forward) in Lahr. In June of 1992, Col Meating was appointed Commander, 4 Canadian Mechanized Brigade, during its last year of active service to NATO and to Canada. When the task of closing 4 Brigade and its operational commitments was completed in July 1993, Col Meating was assigned as Base Commander, CFB Petawawa.

On promotion, BGen Meating took command of 1 Canadian Mechanized Brigade Group, headquartered in Calgary, in early June 1995. In July 1997, he relinquished command of 1 CMBG to take up his new assignment in Ottawa as Director General Intelligence.

In July of 1992, in the rank of Col, BGen Meating was awarded the United States of America Meritorious Service Medal (MSM) for his personal, extensive work with VII (US) Corps. Later in the fall of the same year at Rideau Hall, Ottawa, he was invested as an Officer in the Order of Military Merit (OMM).

BGen Meating is married and has two daughters.[11]

---

11. Sinister Sam's Notebook, CMIBA, Edition 2, August 1997, p. 5.

# APPENDIX E

## Intelligence Branch Advisors, 1982-1997

Col Victor V. Ashdown (1982-1983)
Col Robert W. Irvine (1983-1984)
LCol David M. Robb (1984-1985)
Col George L.R. Bruce (1985-1986)
LCol David M. Robb (1986-1989)
Col Victor V. Ashdown (1989-1996)
Col Patrick D.R. Crandell (1996-2001)

# APPENDIX F

## *Senior Intelligence Officers, CSMI, CFSIS and CFSMI, 1949-1997*

Throughout the evolution of the Canadian School of Military Intelligence and the Canadian Forces School of Intelligence and Security (and on to CFSMI), there has been at least one Intelligence Major at the school. The following is a chronological list of these personnel.

LCol Robert "Bob" L. Raymont, CD, MBE, CSMI Commandant, 1949–1950
LCol Craig B. MacFarlane, CD, CSMI Commandant, 1951–1952
Maj Robert H. "Tex" Noble, CSMI Commandant, 11 Mar 1952–31 Oct 1955
Maj Hank H. Hennie, CSMI Commandant, 01 Nov 1955–09 Aug 1959
Maj Ward I. Binkley, CSMI Commandant, 10 Aug 1959–31 Jul 1962
Maj David W. Wiens, CSMI Commandant, 01 Aug 1962–31 Jul 1965
Maj R. Hal Murphy, CSMI Commandant, 01 Aug 1965–31 Jul 1969.
In the fall of 1967, CSMI integrated with the C Pro C and AFP School and formed into CFSIS. The Intelligence Commandant became the Officer Commanding the Intelligence Division, CFSIS.
Maj Jeff S. Upton, OC Int Div, CFSIS, 01 Aug 1969–1973. In 1973, Maj Upton was promoted to LCol, and became the CFSIS Commandant, 1973–31 Jul 1976

Maj Tom F. Davie, OC Int Trg Coy, CFSIS, 01 Aug 1976–31 Jul 1974
Maj K. George Wolf, OC Int Trg Coy, CFSIS, 01 Aug 1974–31 Jul 1975
Maj William "Bill" L. Watt, OC Int Trg Coy, CFSIS, 01 Aug 1975–31 Jul 1976
Maj Len E.N. Goski, OC Int Trg Coy, CFSIS, 01 Aug 1976–31 Jul 1979
Maj Al G. McMullan, OC Int Trg Coy, CFSIS, 01 Aug 1979–31 Jul 1982
LCdr Christopher S. Hordal, OC Int Trg Coy, CFSIS, 01 Aug 1982–31 Jul 1985
Maj John H. Newman, OC Int Trg Coy, CFSIS, 01 Aug 1985–31 Jul 1987
LCdr W. Burns MacDonald, OC Int Trg Coy, CFSIS, 01 Aug 1987–31 Jul 1989
Maj Robert M. Parsons, OC Int Trg Coy, CFSIS, 01 Aug 1989–31 Jul 1990
Maj J. Michel Bédard, OC Int Trg Coy, CFSIS, 01 Aug 1990–31 Jul 1993
Maj Harold A. Skaarup, OC Int Trg Coy, CFSIS, 01 Aug 1993–01 Jan 1994. On 1 Jan 1994, the Intelligence Training Company was amalgamated with the MP Training Company. The OC Int Trg Coy became the OC Distance Learning Company.
Maj Harold A. Skaarup, OC DL Coy, CFSIS, 01 Jan 1994–31 Jul 1994
Maj Robert G. Nash, OC DL Coy, 01 Aug 1994–31 Jul 1997
Maj Gerry C. Mayer, OC DL Coy, 01 Aug 1997–31 Jul 2000

# APPENDIX G

## *4 Canadian Mechanized Brigade Group Intelligence History*

4 Canadian Mechanized Brigade Group (4 CMBG, later 4 CMB) Intelligence Section traced its history back to the formation of 27 Canadian Infantry Brigade (27 CIB) in 1951. No. 2 Field Security Section (2 FSS) C Int C was formed 7 May 1951 to support 27 CIB with NATO in Europe. No. 1 FSS, which was formed on 16 Nov 1950, was already serving with the Canadian Contingent, United Nations Forces in Korea. 2 FSS went overseas from Montreal under Capt W.E. "Bill" Blanc, and its first task was to teach security to 27 CIB. 27 CIB was Garrisoned in Hannover in the British occupied zone of Germany, and came under the command of the British Army of the Rhine (BAOR).

The 1st Canadian Infantry Division was created in 1953, and 1 Canadian Infantry Brigade Group (1 CIBG) then replaced 27 CIB in November 1953. On 1 Feb 1964, 2 FSS was renumbered No. 1 FSS, because the designation had become vacant when the original 1 FSS had returned from Korea and was disbanded on 15 Dec 1951.

1 FSS remained at full establishment with 1 CIBG in the Soest area in northern Germany, although over the next six years it was progressively reduced in strength until it became a small Detachment headed by an officer, and then part of a combined Police Unit.

2 CIBG replaced 1 CIBG in Nov 1955, keeping 1 FSS under its command until it handed over to 4 CIBG in 1957. In 1960, 1 FSS was incorporated into the Brigade HQ. 4 CIBG was renamed 4 Canadian Mechanized Infantry Brigade Group (4 CMIBG) in 1968. Shortly afterwards, the Infantry designation was dropped, creating 4 CMBG.

Between 7May 1951 and 31 Oct 1957, 2/1 FSS, C Int C was commanded in turn by Lt J.E. Martin, Capt William Blane, Capt Dave M. MacAulay, Lt Leo J. Durocher, Capt George Youmatoff, Lt Ken J. Hope and Capt Raymond S. Shelley. Approximately 50 other ranks were recruited, badged as C Int C, and received some training. Not all went overseas, and many were rotated. With the changes in Unit strength after 1957, the Intelligence duties appear to have been taken over by 4 CMBG HQ staff.

The Brigade Intelligence Officer (G2) was usually a combat arms major. The following officers served as the Bde G2: Maj K.D. Brigden, 1979-80; Maj. H.E. De Coste, 1980-82; Maj M.J. Tanguay, 1982-83; Maj Mike K. Jeffery, 1983-84; Maj D.S. Moreside, 1984-86; Maj R.J.M. Selman, 1986-87 (also served as the first 1 Cdn Div G2); Maj G.E. Thompson, 1987-88; Maj Dan Redburn, 1988-89; Maj F. Paul Crober, 1989-90; Major J.H. Jacques Levesque, 1990-91; and Maj J.W. Georges Rousseau, 1991-92.

The G2 Operations (G2 Ops) officer was C Int C, and an Intelligence Branch officer held the position until the disbandment of 4 CMB in 1993.

On 1 Feb 1968, the Canadian Army, the Royal Canadian Navy (RCN) and the Royal Canadian Air Force (RCAF), became the unified Canadian Forces (CF). HQ Canadian Forces Europe (CFE) was created and on 1 Oct 1970, 4 CMBG was moved to CFB Lahr in the Black Forest region of South Western Germany. In making the move, 4 CMBG was renamed 4 Canadian Mechanized Battle Group, marking its reduction in size, and was operationally tasked to HQ Central Army Group (CENTAG), on 1 Dec 1970. The G2 Ops at this time was Capt G.E.D. Wolf, who held the position from 1969-72. Capt Len E.N. Goski, from 1972-75 followed him in turn. In 1973, the Battle Group was renamed 4 Canadian Mechanized Brigade Group (4 CMBG). The practice of bringing over a major Unit to do a three-year tour was abandoned and replaced with the practice of rotating man-for-man, with the exception of 3 RCR and 2 PPCLI, who rotated between Baden-Söellingen and Winnipeg in 1984 and 1988. The remainder of the Units existing in the Battle Group in 1970 stayed in CFE up to 1993.[1]

G2 Ops since 1975 have been Capt J. Mackenzie, 1975-79; Capt John "Jack" W. Nixon, 1979-83; Maj A. George Johnstone, 1983-85; Capt Robert M. Parsons, 1985-86; Capt J. René Gauthier, 1986-1989; and Capt Harold A. Skaarup, 1989-1992.

Capt John "Jack" W. Nixon was in charge of the members of the Int Branch participating in the inauguration ceremonies at CFB Lahr on 29 Oct 1982. This event brought together Int Branch personnel from HQ CFE and CFB Baden-Söellingen, and led to annual commemorative events such as mess dinners and the Norm Lefebvre Int Branch Bonspiel. MWO Lefebvre was a former Int Member of the 4 CMBG FSS.

On 30 Nov 1989, 1st Canadian Division was inaugurated; with 4 CMBG losing its "Group" status and being renamed 4 CMB. During the change, the FSS became the 1 Canadian Division Forward (1 Cdn Div Fwd) Counter Intelligence (CI) Section, and moved into the 1 Cdn Div Fwd HQ in the Lahr Kaserne.

The last members of the 4 CMB Int Section to serve included WO J.M. Letellier De St Just, Sgt Rick M. Chaykowski, Sgt J.R. Marc A. Paradis, MCpl J.C. Mario Roy, and Cpl K.E. Davies. Within 4 CMB, 4 Service Battalion had its own Int Op, Cpl Marie M. Hudson. WO G. Forcier provided graphics support for both the Div CI and Bde Int Sections.

The last few years of 4 CMB's service were unprecedented in the number of political and military changes that took place in the European theatre. The Berlin Wall fell in October 1989, and late in 1990/early 1991, the Brigade prepared to be deployed to participate in the Persian Gulf War. It was planned that 4 CMB would join two British Brigades to form a Commonwealth Division. The government of Canada chose instead to send primarily air and naval elements and approximately 1,000 ground Troops in supporting roles early in 1991. Throughout the rapidly changing world scene, the 4 CMB Int Section kept the Brigade and Division elements in CFE abreast of continuing developments. Its members also took part in several major exercises, Arms Verification Inspections of British, German and American equipment in theatre, ran a Combat Int course, did the usual Army fitness 2 X 16 km hikes with the 4 CMB HQ & Sig Sqn, and participated in Professional Development training which included battlefield tours of Verdun and Normandy. All of the 4 CMB

---

1.    Excerpts from *Canada's NATO Brigade, a History*, 1983.

Int jobs provided challenges and good experience in Combat Intelligence operations and training.

The 4 CMB Units under the command of BGen J. Clive Addy included a Headquarters and Signals Squadron, the 8th Canadian Hussars Armoured Regiment equipped with the Leopard tank, the 1st Battalion R22eR (based in Lahr) and the 3rd Battalion RCR (based in Baden-Söellingen. In his dual role as Deputy Commander, BGen J. Clive Addy also had charge of the Forward Divisional Units of the 1st Canadian Division, headquartered in Kingston, Ontario.

The 1st Cdn Div Units in Lahr included 1 Royal Canadian Horse Artillery, equipped with M-109A2 155mm self-propelled guns, 4 Canadian Engineer Regiment, equipped with the Leopard ARV and the AVLB, 4 Service Battalion providing recovery, repair and maintenance as well as general service support to the Division, 4 Field Ambulance Battalion providing Medical support, 4 MP Platoon providing traffic control and police support, and 444 Tactical Helicopter Squadron equipped with the Kiowa light observation helicopter (LOH). 1st Cdn Div had additional Units located with 5e Brigade Mechanisé du Canada based in Valcartier, Quebec. The main elements of 4 CMB also relied on 127 Air Defence Battery, 4 Air Defence Regiment, CFE, equipped with ADATs and Blowpipe air defence weapons systems.

During its annual training program, 4 CMB worked with Allied elements of II German Corps and with the VII US Corps, particularly during the FALLEX exercise period. When the 1st Cdn Div Fwd elements in Germany were grouped together, the resulting Brigade Group (4 CMB+) was comprised of approximately 4,000 officers and Troops. When all Divisional elements were combined, 1st Canadian Division had approximately 12,500 Troops who were well equipped to provide a solid force within a NATO Corps formation.

In the fall of 1990, 4 CMB HQ staff was tasked to prepare plans for the brigade to deploy to the Persian Gulf, but time and space prevented the full brigade's departure. As a result, Units and personnel were deployed piecemeal to support the operation. These included elements of both the 3 RCR and 1 R22eR Infantry Battalions, tasked to protect the Canadian CF-18 Hornet fighter aircraft sent to the Gulf, and various brigade support personnel such as engineers, communications and repair personnel, cooks and chemical decontamination Troops.

With the reductions in tensions in one part of the world, the brigade became part of the national program of force reductions and last elements returned to Canada in 1993.

Close cooperation was maintained between 4 CMB Int Staff and the 1 Cdn Div Fwd CI Section. The OC was Maj Clark J. Beamish, and WO G. Wayne Ivey, Sgt J.P. Gauthier, Sgt J.L.A. Martineau, Sgt J.R.M. Ross manned his section, along with Div Staff members Sgt Dave L. Howarth and Cpl L.A. Clarke. The Intelligence material received from HQ CFE was voluminous and indispensable, thanks to the work of Maj G. Al Grant (LCol Ret'd) and Capt Ron H.J. Ruiters (Maj) and the HQ CFE Int Section which included PO William "Bill" M. Flanagan, MS T.J. Farnell, Cpl Neil M. Fletcher, LS Dan C. Little, and Cpl R.S. Wilkie, also located in the Lahr Kaserne.

Within 4 CMB, a former C Int C member, Capt William "Bill" L. Dickson, held the G5 position. Bill reported that before 4 CMBG arrived, Int personnel from 1968 to 1970 had conducted Mission Planning and Photo Interpretation for 1 Wing in Lahr. In Oct 1968, the First Int James Bonspiel in Lahr was organized by Sgt Gary W. Handson (Maj Ret'd), Sgt Ernie Arndt, Sgt Arthur E. Roemer, Sgt Brian Johnston, Cpl Robert "Bob" M. Steedman, and Bill.

Int Branch Air Int officers serving with 1 CAD included Capt Richard A. Derkson (Maj Ret'd). At CFB Lahr the 3 Wing Base Int Section with Capt Dan A. Climo, WO W. "Bill" Goodland, Sgt John A. Dooley and MCpl D.G. McNulty.

MGen J.J.M.R. Gaudreau commanded 1 Cdn Div, BGen J. Clive Addy commanded 4 CMB 9 Apr 1991 until it was reduced in strength and placed in the hands of the last commander, Col Robert "Bob" G. Meating (MGen and future DGIS) who closed the Brigade's service in Germany in 1993.

# Appendix H

## Canadian Airborne Intelligence History

### 1st Canadian Parachute Battalion

Enemy, weather and terrain. These three things are of paramount concern to any Airborne organization preparing to deploy on operations. The Intelligence Branch and its members within all past Canadian Airborne formations is the primary provider of these key pieces of information. Former members of the Canadian Airborne Regiment's Intelligence Section can trace their history back to the original 1ˢᵗ Canadian Parachute Battalion (1 Can Para Bn) and the First Special Service Force (FSSF) formed during World War Two. 1 Can Para Bn was established on 01 July 1942 and began its training in Fort Benning, Georgia. It later moved to the then newly established Parachute Training Centre in Shilo, Manitoba. A review of the flight manifests from these early years reveals that three chalks of six Int Operators (Int Ops) and one Intelligence Officer (IO) made up the 1 Can Para Bn Int Section of 17 personnel. According to the War Diaries of the battalion, it would appear that Lt D.S. MacLean was the battalion's first IO.[1]

Early in July 1943, 1 Can Para Bn was sent on active service overseas to England where it joined the 6ᵗʰ British Airborne Division (6 Brit AB Div). Its' service in the European theatre included the Airborne invasion of Normandy on the night before D-Day, 6 June 1944. Capt D.S. MacLean was apparently killed

---

1.   John A. Willes, *Out of the Clouds*.

on the night of the drop on Normandy, although his body wasn't found until some weeks afterwards. Lt R.D.J. Weatherbee was therefore appointed on the ground to be the IO. He held this position until he was wounded and taken out of action in January 1945. Lt M.A.F. Mountain took his place until Lt (later Capt) J.A. Rossiter replaced him, as 1 Can Para Bn's last wartime IO.

1 Can Para Bn participated in a short reinforcement stint in Belgium and Holland before it participated in the Airborne crossing of the Rhine. It continued on through Germany to Wismar where the battalion met the Russians. The battalion returned to Canada in June 1945 and was disbanded at Niagara-on-the-Lake. Capt J.A. Rossiter remained with 1 Can Para Bn until it disbanded, then joined the post-war Army and served with DND until his death in 1954.

## First Special Service Force

In the Brigade sized combined Canada-United States First Special Service Force (FSSF), which operated in Kiska and in Italy, the Unit Intelligence Officer was an American, Maj R.D. Burhans, throughout the Unit's WWII service. Maj Burhans worked in the Army Intelligence Section in Washington before being promoted and becoming the FSSF G2 in July 1942. His Intelligence Assistant was Lt Finn Roll. When the FSSF disbanded, Maj Burhans went back to an American Unit. Maj Burhans is also the author of the history of the FSSF.[2]

## Canadian Airborne Intelligence during World War II

There have been a few interesting weapons and equipment changes for Intelligence paratroopers and their modern day counterparts over the years. During the war, the officers of 1 Can Para Bn carried a .45 cal pistol and a .30 cal M1 carbine. The Int Ops carried a .30 cal M1 with two magazines. They also worked with scouts and observers who carried the .30 cal M1, the .30 cal Model 1903, or the .45 cal Thompson sub-machinegun (SMG). While on operations in Europe, each paratrooper carried a fighting knife, toggle rope, escape kit (with French currency), and two 24-hour ration packs. With his additional standard equipment, the paratrooper's workload added up to approximately 70 pounds.

2.   Robert H. Adleman & Col George Walton, _The Devil's Brigade_, (Toronto: Bantam Books, 1966), p. 43.

They also used an aircraft called an Albemarle, as opposed to the Dakota that they had trained on in Canada. For the Rhine Crossing (Operation Varsity), they were airlifted in 38 C-47 Dakotas, three of which were also towing gliders. The gliders carried jeeps and trucks.

The operational directives given to the paratroops on the night prior to the Normandy invasion were straightforward and to the point: a) Speed and Initiative on the part of all ranks is the order of the day; b) Risks will be taken; and c) The enemy will be attacked and destroyed wherever he is found.

The Normandy drop Took place between 0100 and 0130 on D-Day, 6 June 1944. With the casualties 1 Can Para Bn took throughout the night, it is hardly surprising that there were many "instant" job changes. With Capt D.S. MacLean missing and presumed dead, Lt R.D.J. Weatherbee found himself as the new IO conducting a recce of the town of Varraville with two men. He was tasked to check on the condition of the bridge crossing located there, and to get back with a report on the situation while the remainder of the HQ Company, along with an assortment of other Units...set out for the crossroads located at Les Mesnil. His party then came under sniper fire. The Brigade Int Officer then arrived along with Capt Griffith and set up a temporary defensive position to hold the bridge at Dives Crossing until the bridge was blown. At 1200 hours on the 7th of June, he came to guide the party back through the lines. Lt R.D.J. Weatherbee was wounded the first time on the 28th of June when a German artillery shell landed on the Battalion HQ.

Lt R.D.J. Weatherbee had some colourful other ranks serving with him. On 2 June 1944, in preparation for the invasion, the Brigade Commander was briefed by members of the 1 Can Para Bn. He commended the Int Section on their briefing preparations and stated that "they were the best in the Division." The Int Section had constructed very detailed models for these briefings. Modeling of drop Zones and target areas was an activity that continued with 1 Can Para Bn's post war counterparts in the CAR until its disbandment in 1995.[3]

The Int Ops who served with the Int Section of 1 Can Para Bn provided some interesting stories. While the Unit was in Tourgeville, France, on 23 August 44, Pte W. Blanchard was dispatched by the Int Section to St Gatien on a motorbike to determine if the Germans had withdrawn from the town. On his arrival, seven German soldiers ran out to meet him, and surrendered. When he

---

3.  1st Canadian Parachute Battalion War Diary, 1942-1945, (CFB Petawawa).

returned with his prisoners, the battalion proceeded into the town, only to be met by shellfire from a German self-propelled gun. There were no casualties, but needless to say, the recce had been incomplete.[4]

The paratroopers were sent back to England to get ready for the next operation and took part in a number of exercises, including Ex Eve and Ex Acorn, which involved several night jumps. 1 Can Para Bn eventually arrived in Holland, and one of the first patrols sent out by the Int Section consisted of Privates W. Blanchard and F.T.J.B. Kelly. Their orders were to set up an observation post (OP) in a building about 100 metres ahead of the battalion lines to observe German activity along the front. It was Private Kelly's first time into action with the Normandy-seasoned veteran Blanchard, and he expected that their move out to the building would be according to the military textbook procedure. Instead, the two men walked out to the building in the early morning just before sunrise. On their arrival, Blanchard hammered on the door with the butt of his STEN-gun and hollered, "you in there Jerry?" When they received no reply, Private Blanchard pushed open the door and entered, with Private Kelly close at his heels.

1 Can Para Bn moved to Marche on 5 January 45 on foot for most of the way, and for all ranks including the officers, it was a long and tiring trip. Along the way, the battalion's Adjutant, Capt Simpson, noticed that the padre was quite thirsty. Capt Simpson turned to the Int Section's Private Kelly and told him to offer the Padre a drink of water from his canteen. Private Kelly was reluctant to do so, because he had filled his canteen with wine before he set out on the march. With some hesitation, but at Capt Simpson's insistence, Private Kelly offered his canteen to the Padre with the words, "its pretty good water, Padre." The Padre raised the canteen and drank, then without the slightest indication that the canteen contained anything but water, pronounced that it was "good indeed." On 28 March 1945, Private Kelly jumped with the battalion on the Rhine Crossing. He later managed to gather 15 or 16 people together that had been scattered on the drop And took them to the battalion HQ.

On 14 April 1945, the 1 Can Para Bn Int Section was sent as an advance party to recce the town of Celle, northeast of Hanover in Germany. It was the first Unit to enter the town, and upon finding that the Germans had withdrawn, they proceeded to build a bridge across a small creek in the town. The bridge was

---

4.   John A. Willes, *Out of the Clouds*.

christened the Pokmouche Bridge, the name of the hometown of Private "Blackjack" Blanchard, by now a well-known member of the Int Section.

Although various Units conducted parachute-training activities in Canada after the war, the Airborne Intelligence Section did not return until the formation of the Canadian Airborne Regiment in Edmonton, Alberta on 8 April 1968.

## Canadian Airborne Regiment

Until its disbandment, the Canadian Airborne Regiment was composed of five Units. The infantry element included three airborne commandos (1e Cdo from the R22eR, 2 Cdo from the PPCLI, and 3 Cdo from the RCR); combat service support provided by Airborne Service Commando; and an Airborne HQ and Signals Squadron, which included the four-man Regimental Intelligence Section. The total strength of the regiment in peacetime was approximately 750 all ranks.

Capt K.A. Peter Mackenzie was the first Regimental Intelligence Officer (R Int O) of the new regiment. (He retired from the Intelligence Branch as a LCol). Capt Bob Mahar (also retired as a LCol); then Capt Ian A. Nicol (retired as a reserve LCol in Edmonton) followed him in turn. The next IO was Capt Robert M. Parsons (retired as LCol). In succession, Capt D. Pat Wieshlow (Ret'd), Capt Jean Dextraze (Ret'd) followed as R Int Os. Capt John Cruse (retired as LCol) and Capt Greg W. Jensen (retired as an Int Branch LCol) were followed by Capt Tim Larson (retired, now works with CSE), Capt Harold A. Skaarup (now a Major), Capt Chris J. Wallace (retired as a Major), Capt Paul W. Hope (now a Major), and Capt Robert "Bob" B. Martyn (retired).

Intelligence Operators who served with Airborne Int Section include WO Ken W. Wishart, WO J.A. Cuvelier, WO Dan Maddox, Sgt Gerry Gosselin (Photo Tech), WO R. Grant Oliver, Sgt Stu E. Auld, Sgt Jules Knuyver (MP), Sgt Hugh Conway, MWO Brian Johnston, MCpl J.P. André Tremblay, MCpl Rick Mader (Maj Ret'd), Sgt Duke Aulenbach (MP), Sgt Bill Pruski (MP), Sgt Jerry Gallagher, Sgt E. Bruce Hayes, WO William "Bill" L. Dickson, Cpl Henry E. Doucette, WO John E. Cranston, Sgt G.S. Kohinsky, MCpl Manuel A. Thibault, MCpl R.C. Nickerson, Sgt J. Dan Galley, WO Brian M. Noble, Sgt Barry E. Beldam, Sgt Rick Burns (CWO MP Ret'd), Cpl Richard A. Derkson (Maj Ret'd), Cpl Everett Summerfield (MP Ret'd, now RCMP Inspector/Superintendent, Yellowknife), Cpl Clem LeMay

(MP), Cpl J.S. Daniel St Pierre, Sgt Richard C. Gow, WO Dean J. Dunlop, MCpl Chuck J. Spillane, MCpl Rick G. Oliver, and Sgt M. Paul McNeil. Photographers MCpl John Rodger, Cpl Dale Southward, and Sgt Denis Mah also served in the Airborne Int Section.

The Airborne Int Sections were involved in numerous operational activities after the war. The CAR was deployed to St Hubert during the October Crisis of 1970, providing air and mobile response teams to deal with potential problem areas. The Intelligence Section of the Canadian Airborne Regiment was involved in many interesting activities during the Regiment's Edmonton existence and deployed to areas as varied as Alaska, Jamaica, Mojave Desert and Cyprus.

The Regiment's Int Section was particularly active during the 1974 brew-up in Cyprus. The R Int O and Int Ops in Nicosia assisted the Regimental Commander with daily briefings and analysis of the situation ongoing between the Turk and Greek combatants on the island. The situation on the island continues to be highly volatile, and in fact, there are still one or two Canadian Int personnel serving with the island's HQ staff some 39 years after the initial deployments of Canadians to Cyprus. A lot of patrolling was conducted during the Airborne's many tours there.

The Regiment was also deployed to provide security for the 1976 Olympics in Montreal. In this instance, the Int Section supported the operations and duty staff for the RHQ. Members of the Airborne Int Section have been deployed to Somalia and Rwanda. Many past serving Cdn AB Regt Int personnel have gone on to the Former Yugoslav Republic (FYR) with deployments with the Canadian Battle Group in Coralici in Bosnia-Herzegovina. The Canadian Contingent of the NATO led Interdiction Force (IFOR) followed by the Peace Stabilization Force (SFOR) in Bosnia-Herzegovina was and still is supported by members of the Canadian National Intelligence Cell (CANIC) in Sarajevo, and a few are still serving in Afghanistan.

The primary role of the Canadian Airborne Regiment was to provide a quick reaction force in support of national security, North American defence and international peacekeeping. Jumps were conduced in areas as far north as Inuvik and Coppermine. The Int Section also lent support to the Toronto Summit and Militia training at CFSIS, while maintaining its own special brand of rigorous training.

Exercise Pegasus Venture, held in May 1988, was typical of Regimental activity. The Int Section along with the HQ & Sigs Sqn drafted, reviewed and revised the Intelligence scenario based on the Regimental Commander's direction. Air photo mosaics, map enlargements and terrain models were constructed in detail for each of the drop Zones and target areas and these were used in extensive briefings and debriefings. Late at night, the Regiment boarded fleets of buses for a three-hour drive to Trenton, where 450 men with weapons and equipment boarded 12 Hercules aircraft (with two more on standby as backup). The fleet of Hercules conducted the mass drop in four flights of three aircraft each approaching from a different direction within minutes of each other, over the target DZ at CFB Borden with few casualties (in spite of a number of landings on the base runway).

The Int Section was tactically loaded with each man on a different aircraft, just in case one went down or became N/S. Most of the Int Section members hit the runway after the drop. We then rendezvoused with RHQ and continued to monitor the battle for the Regimental Commander, assisted by the RMPs in processing prisoners and checking the released hostages. Within two hours of the drop, the Hercules returned, landed, taxied down the runway, lowered the ramp, turned around without stopping, loaded Troops and evacuees on the run, and then took off without ever stopping the aircraft in motion. All personnel were off the ground and en route back to Petawawa within four hours of the initial drop. Back in Camp, the Int Section participated in the debriefings and post-exercise reports—a worthwhile exercise for all concerned. Not all exercises come off with so few glitches. The Regiment lost more than two-dozen people in a Hercules aircraft crash while on a winter exercise shortly afterwards, in Alaska in 1989.

The present day Canadian Forces Intelligence Branch still has a significant number of personnel who served in or with the Canadian Airborne Regiment. They also continue to serve the CF with skill and professionalism, carrying on the traditions of a long line of airborne military Intelligence personnel who have served Canada.[5]

With the disbandment of the regiment, it will be some time before there are officially others to follow in their footsteps.[6] There is a very strong need for

---

5.   The author served as the Regimental Intelligence Officer, Canadian Airborne Regiment, 1986-1989.

6.   Against the advice of the Chief of the Defence Staff, the Minister of National Defence, the Hon. David Collenette, announced the disbandment of the Canadian Airborne Regiment on 24 January 1995. The CAR was disbanded on 05 March 1995

a Unit of its kind, and when it is reformed, there are many members of the Int Branch ready to be part of it.

## Joint Task Force 2

Canadians served with distinction in several types of Allied Special Forces units during the Second World War. One such unit was the legendary Canadian and US combined 1st Special Service Force or, as it was commonly known, "the Devil's Brigade." It achieved a sterling combat record despite overwhelming odds. While tactics, weapons and technology have changed, today's Joint Task Force 2 (JTF 2) soldiers are perpetuating the basic qualities that define such units.

JTF 2 was created on 1 April 1993, when the Canadian Forces accepted responsibility for federal counter-terrorism operations from the RCMP. Since its inception, the unit has continuously evolved to meet modern-day threats. As the events of 11 September 2001 have shown, the threat of terrorism comes from an elusive, sophisticated and determined enemy. In order to maintain an edge in this operational environment, JTF 2 is continuously developing new capabilities, technologies, and tactics.

The year 2001 marked an important milestone in the history of JTF 2. The unit was committed to the international Special Operations Forces coalition in Afghanistan, completing its operations there in November 2002. This deployment was the first time JTF 2 was used in a major combat role outside Canada. The unit played a critical role in coalition Special Operations Forces and earned the respect of Canada's allies for its professionalism.

JTF 2 is a unit of the CF and is subject to exactly the same code of conduct, military discipline and overriding Criminal Code statutes as any other military unit. Due to the strategic nature of its operations, the unit answers directly to the Deputy Chief of the Defence Staff in the chain of command. This allows for very timely command and control, access to strategic intelligence, and the oversight considered essential for military operations undertaken to meet national objectives. The Deputy Chief of the Defence Staff is accountable to the Chief of the Defence Staff who, in turn, is responsible to the Minister of National Defence.

Like other units of the CF, JTF 2 follows Rules Of Engagements (ROE) authorized by the Chief of the Defence Staff. Its members are entitled to the same support and health services as other service members, they are accountable to the military and civilian justice systems, and they must follow the same regulations and orders as the rest of the CF. Like any other CF unit, internal over-sight bodies such as the Chief of Review Services, the Military Police Complaints Commission, the Pay and Allowances Review Board, the Access to Information Office and the CF Ombudsman all have access to JTF 2, if required, to carry out their duties.

JTF 2 is comprised of CF members employed in assaulter and supporter roles. All members are carefully screened for service in the unit but it is the assaulters who undergo a selection and training regime for eventual service in the fighting arm of the unit. Any Regular Force member of the CF can apply to become a member of JTF 2 after completing 2 years of service and meeting other initial entry requirements. Members of JTF 2 are highly motivated, dedicated, mature, mentally robust and physically fit. Potential assaulters are carefully screened to ensure that they meet these criteria and are the type of team-ori-ented and highly-skilled professional soldier, sailor or airman that can effec-tively function in this high stress environment. The CF's strongest asset is the people that fill its ranks across the country. Many of these service members have tried out for the JTF 2 selection process but, on average, only two in ten candi-dates that arrive at the unit for final selection will actually become a JTF 2 assaulter.

The standards established for selection and employment with the unit are scientifically designed and validated at the CF Dwyer Hill Training Centre in order to ensure that the members selected will be capable of accomplishing all tasks assigned to the unit. These standards are not just limited to physical abili-ties. High standards are also required for professionalism, integrity, psychologi-cal profile, mental aptitude, discipline, and maturity. These standards are required of all unit members, are tested regularly, and are an integral part of the JTF 2 ethos.

JTF 2 is subject to very stringent security procedures in order to protect the unit and its mission. Indeed, the type of operations assigned to JTF 2 naturally captures the interest of the public but there are many risks involved with infor-mation disclosure. The CF recognizes the need to inform Canadians about the measures put in place by their Government to protect them against the threat of terrorism. Since its creation, JTF 2 has conducted numerous capability demon-strations for appropriate authorities that need to be aware of unit capabilities as part of their position or appointment. Such audiences include the CF chain of command, Members of Parliament, government officials and police authorities. The Government has also informed Canadians about JTF 2 by notifying the public about its creation in 1992, its expansion following 11 September 2001, and the JTF 2 commitment to Afghanistan in 2001, as well as by responding to media questions about the unit within the limits of the security policy. However, being open and transparent about certain aspects of the unit could seriously compromise the effectiveness of Canada's counter-terrorism capability. History has shown only too clearly that terrorist organizations will use information about a unit's personnel, weapons, tactics and procedures to great effect by modifying their methodologies to counter the very forces designed to defeat them.

JTF 2 has established itself as a well-regarded Special Operations Forces unit. It has done so over its short history because of the outstanding quality and ability of its members, its proven operational effectiveness and its stringent operational security policy. This reputation has allowed the unit to develop strong relationships with its allied Special Operations Forces counterparts, relationships built on trust and confidence. These relationships assist JTF 2 in providing the best possible counter-terrorism defence for Canada. The CF security policy for JTF 2 is primarily based on Canada's situation, and is designed to safeguard information sharing and most importantly to protect Canada's counter-terrorist capability.

The Federal Budget of December 2001 allocated approximately $120 million over six years to expand unit capabilities, as part of the Government of Canada's overall plan to enhance security for Canadians following the attacks of 11 September 2001. Since then the unit has embarked on a program of expansion and capability enhancement while at the same time maintaining its high operational and training standards.

JTF 2 must be ready to respond immediately to any task assigned by the chain of command at home or abroad. The unit maintains the highest operational readiness standards in order to defend Canada against terrorism. On land, at sea and in the air JTF 2 challenges itself to ensure it's ready to defeat a multitude of potential threats. Canadians can take great comfort in the knowledge that this Special Operations Force is standing on guard 24 hours a day to defend Canadians, and Canadian interests at home and abroad.[7]

---

7.    Internet: http://dcds.mil.ca/units/jtf2/pages/about_e.asp.

# Abbreviations

| | |
|---|---|
| A2 | Air Staff Intelligence Officer |
| ACID | Air Command Intelligence Daily |
| ACIS | Automated Combat Information System |
| ACOUSINT | Acoustic Intelligence |
| AMIB | Allied Military Intelligence Battalion |
| ANR | Alaska NORAD Region |
| ASCC | Air Standardization Coordinating Committee |
| ASIC | All Source Intelligence Cell |
| ATIC | Air Tactical Intelligence Centre |
| BARSTA | Battlefield Surveillance, Reconnaissance and Target Acquisition |
| BIOC | Basic Intelligence Officer's Course |
| BSA | Basic Standardization Agreement |
| CANIC | Canadian National Intelligence Cell |
| CANR | Canadian NORAD Region |
| CAOC | Combined Air Operations Centre |
| CBRN | Chemical, Biological, Radiological, Nuclear |

| | |
|---|---|
| CCIFOR | Canadian Contingent Interdiction Force |
| CCIR | Commander's Critical Information Requirements |
| CCIRM | Collection, Coordination and Information Requirements Management |
| CEWOC | Computerized Electronic Warfare Operations Centre |
| CFILO | Canadian Forces Intelligence Liaison Officer |
| CFIUSS | Canadian Forces Integrated Undersea Surveillance System |
| CFJOG | Canadian Forces Joint Operations Group |
| CFMPSA | Canadian Forces Military Police and Security Academy |
| CFNCIU | Canadian Forces National Counter Intelligence Unit |
| CFSMI | Canadian Forces School of Military Intelligence |
| CIC | Combined Intelligence Centre |
| CIFC | Combined Intelligence Fusion Centre |
| CMNB | Canadian Multi-National Brigade |
| CONR | Continental USA NORAD Region |
| CSCE | Committee of Security and Cooperation in Europe |
| DCIS | Deputy Chief Intelligence and Security |
| DDI | Directorate of Defence Intelligence |
| DDR | Disarmament, Demobilization and Reintegration |
| DFLR | Directorate of Land Forces Requirements |
| DGIS | Director General Intelligence and Security |

| | |
|---|---|
| DGMI | Director General Military Intelligence |
| DIAC | Defense Intelligence Analysis Center |
| DIE | Directorate of Imagery Exploitation |
| DIEPS | Digital Imagery Exploitation and Production System |
| DOCINT | Document Intelligence |
| D Space D | Directorate of Space Defence |
| DSI | Directorate of Strategic Analysis |
| DSTI | Directorate of Scientific and Technical Intelligence |
| EWCAC | Electronic Warfare Coordination and Analysis Centre |
| EWCC | Electronic Warfare Coordination Centre |
| FIST | Field Intelligence Support Team |
| FYR | Former Yugoslav Republic |
| G2 | Army Staff Intelligence Officer |
| HUMINT | Human Intelligence |
| HWC | Heavy Weapons Cantonment |
| IAC | Intelligence Assessments Committee |
| IAS | Intelligence Assessment Secretariat |
| ICAC | Intelligence Collection and Analysis Centre |
| ICSI | Interdepartmental Committee on Security and Intelligence |
| IFOR | Implementation Force |
| IMINT | Imagery Intelligence |
| INTWP | Intelligence Interservice Working Party |

| IPB | Intelligence Preparation of the Battlefield |
|---|---|
| IPG | Intelligence Policy Group |
| IRC | Intelligence Requirements Committee |
| IRIWP | Imagery Reconnaissance Interpretation Working Party |
| IRT | Intelligence Response Team |
| ISAF | International Security Assistance Force |
| ISTAR | Intelligence, Surveillance, Target Acquisition and Reconnaissance |
| KFOR | Kosovo Force |
| KMNB | Kabul Multi-National Brigade |
| MASINT | Measurement and Signature Intelligence |
| MNF | Multinational Force |
| MOSART | Military Occupation Structure Analysis, Redesign and Tailoring |
| N2 | Naval Staff Intelligence Officer |
| NCIU | National Counter Intelligence Unit |
| NDCC | National Defence Command Centre |
| NDIC | National Defence Intelligence Centre |
| NDOC | National Defence Operations Centre |
| NEADS | North East Air Defence Sector |
| OCIPEP | Office of Critical Infrastructure Protection and Emergency Preparedness |
| OSG | Office of the Solicitor General |
| OSINT | Open Source Intelligence |

| | |
|---|---|
| OMF | Opposing Militant Forces |
| OSINT | Open Source Intelligence |
| PCO | Privy Council Office |
| PIFWC | Person Indicted for War Crimes |
| PIR | Priority Intelligence Requirements |
| PTSD | Post-Traumatic Stress Disorder |
| RFI | Request for Information |
| RGV | Remotely Guided Vehicle |
| ROE | Rules of Engagement |
| RPV | Remotely Piloted Vehicle |
| SAOC | Sector Air Operations Centre |
| SCIF | Secure Compartmentalized Intelligence Facility |
| SEADS | South East Air Defence Sector |
| SEWOC | Signals and Electronic Warfare Operations Centre |
| SFOR | Stabilization Force |
| SIGINT | Signals Intelligence |
| SLNDIA | Senior Level National Defence Intelligence Authority |
| SPARG | Security Planning and Research Group |
| STANAG | Standing NATO Agreement |
| TCCCS | Tactical Command, Control and Communications System |
| TECHINT | Technical Intelligence |
| TERA | Terrain Analysis |

| | |
|---|---|
| TFK | Task Force Kabul |
| TRILS | Tactical Radar Identification and Locating System |
| UAV | Uninhabited Air Vehicle |
| UASTAS | Unmanned Airborne Surveillance and Target Acquisition System |
| WADS | Western Air Defence Sector |
| WMD | Weapon of Mass Destruction |

# Bibliography

ABCA Memorandum For Record, 7<sup>th</sup> Meeting of the Quadripartite Working Group on Intelligence. (26-30 Aug 1996).

Acorn INTREP 001, 15 Dec 1991; Acorn INTREP 002, Jan 1992; Acorn INTREP 003, Feb 1992; Acorn INTREP 004, Mar 1992; Acorn INTREP 005, Apr 1992; Acorn INTREP 006, June 1992; Acorn INTREP 007, July 1992; Acorn INTREP 008, September 1992; and, Acorn INTREP 009, December 1993. (Ottawa).

Air Command Intelligencer. (Edition 1, Volume 1, 17 March 1991; Edition 2, Volume 1, July 1992).

American, British, Canadian, Australian Armies' Standardization Program, Memorandum For Record, Seventh Meeting of the Quadripartite Working Group on Intelligence. (Fort Huachuca, Arizona, August 1996).

ANGELL, David J. R. "NORAD and Bi-national Nuclear Alert: Consultation and Decision-making in the Integrated Command," article, Defence Analysis, Vol. 4 (June 1988).

BERCUSON, David. Continental Defense and Arctic Sovereignty, 1945-50: Solving the Canadian Dilemma, article, The Cold War and Defense, edited by NEILSON, Keith and HAYCOCK, Ronald G. (Praeger, New York, 1990).

BRYDEN, Earl. Chief Warrant Officer. History of Canadian Military SIGINT. (Minute Sheet of Major Dave Lawrence, OC E Sqn, Kingston, File No 1326-1, 15 Apr 1991).

BRYDEN, John. **Best-Kept Secret: Canadian Secret Intelligence in the World War II**. (Toronto: Lester Publishing, 1993).

Canada, Department of National Defence, **1994 Defence White Paper**. (Ottawa: DND, 1994).

Canada, Department of National Defence, **Challenge and Commitment: A Defence Policy for Canada**. (Ottawa: DND, 1994).

Canada, Parliament, Senate, Standing Committee on Foreign Affairs, Sub-Committee on **Security and National Defence**. (Ottawa: 1992).

Canadian Department of Foreign Affairs and International Trade, **Treaties and Acts with the United States of America**. (Internet: www.dfait-maeci.gc, 20 May 1996).

**The Canadian Intelligence Community, Report of the Auditor General, November 1996, Chapter 27**. (Internet: *http://www.oag–bvg.gc.ca*).

**Canadian Military Intelligence Association Newsletter**. Vol. 14, No. 1, January 1983; Vol. 14, No. 2, June 1983; Vol. 14, No. 3, August 1983; Vol. 14, No. 4, December 1983; Vol. 15, No. 1, June 1984; Vol. 15, No. 2, August 1984; Vol. 15, No. 3, December 1984; Vol. 16, No. 1, May 1985; Vol. 18, No. 1, June 1987; Vol. 18, No. 3, August 1987; Vol. 18, No. 4; Vol. 19, No. 1, April 1988; Vol. 19, No. 2, July 1988; Vol. 19, No. 3, December 1988; Vol. 20, No. 1, May 1989; Vol. 20, No. 2, July 1989; Vol. 20, No. 3, December 1989; Vol. 21, No. 1, June 1990; Vol. 21, No. 2, August 1990; Vol. 21, No. 3, December 1990; Vol. 22, No. 1, March 1991; Vol. 22, No. 2, July 1991; Vol. 22, No. 3, December 1991; Vol. 23, No. 1, June 1992; Vol. 23, No. 2, September 1992 (numbers out of sync); Vol. 23, No. 3, August 1993; Vol. 23, No. 4, December 1993; Vol. 24, No. 1, May 1994; Vol. 24, No. 2, August 1994; Vol. 25, No. 1, May 1995;Vol. 24, No. 3, December 1994; Vol. 25, No. 1, May 1995; Vol. 25, No.2, July 1995; Vol. 25, No.3, December 1995; Vol. 26, No.1, May 1996; Vol. 26, No.2, August 1996; Vol. 26, No.3, November 1996; Vol. 27, No.1, May 1997; Vol. 27, No.2, August 1997; Vol. 27, No.3, Winter 1997-1998.).

CLAUSEWITZ, Carl von. **On War**. (London: Penguin Books, 1957, 1992), [Vom Kriege, 1832].

**Combat Intelligence** (First Draft), Department of National Defence Publication, B-GL-315-002/FT-001. (FMC HQ, July 1988).

COX, David. **The Guide to Canadian Policies on International Peace and Security**. (Kingston, Ontario: Canadian Centre for Global Security, 1994).

CRITCHLEY, W.H. "**Civilianisation and the Canadian Military**". Article, HUNT and HAYCOCK (Eds.) **Canada's Defence: Perspectives on Policy in the Twentieth Century**. (Toronto: Longman Co., 1993).

CROSBY, Ann Denholm. **The 1996 NORAD Renewal Agreement**. (Department of Political Science, York University, Internet: www. Math.yorku. 20 May 1996).

**Defense Intelligence Agency**. (Internet: http://www.dia.mil [DIA Home Page], 2004).

**DND Intelligence Link Commonwealth AUS/CAN/UK/US *(INTELINK-C)*.**

**DND Maritime Command**. (Internet: www.marlant.halifax.dnd. ca/marcom.html).

**DND Canadian Navy Homepage**. (Internet: www.marlant.halifax.dnd.ca/ marcom.htm).

**DND White Paper 94, Chapter 4, Protection of Canada**. Internet: www.cfcsc.dnd.ca/white/four.html).

**DND, White Paper 94, Chapter 5, Canada-United States Defence Cooperation**. Internet: http://www.cfcsc.dnd.ca/white/five.html).

**Department of Foreign Affairs and Trade, News Release No. 44, Canada and the United States to Renew Defence Agreement**. Internet: www-uvi.eunet.fr/ armament-and-disarmament/nuke/disdi596.html).

DOBSON, Brigadier-General (Ret'd) Robert. "<u>Canada's other Military Responsibilities to the World</u>," article, <u>Canadian Forces Roles Abroad</u>, CDAI Eleventh Annual Seminar, edited by COLE, David E. and CAMERON, Ian. (Ottawa: Conference of Defence Associations Institute, 1995).

DYER, Gwynne, and VILJOEN, Tina. **The Defence of Canada , In the Arms of the Empire**. (Toronto: McClelland and Stewart, 1990).

ELLIOT, Stuart Robert, Major. **Scarlet to Green: Canadian Army Intelligence 1903-1963**. (Toronto: Canadian Intelligence and Security Association, 1981).

**FMCO 25-1, (Force Mobile Command Order 25-1)**. (St Hubert, Quebec, 1985).

GAFFEN, Fred. **In the Eye of the Storm: a history of Canadian Peacekeeping**. (Toronto: Deneau & Wayne, 1987).

GRANATSTEIN, Jack L. and STAFFORD, David. **Spy Wars: Espionage and Canada from Gouzenko to Glasnost.** (Key Porter Books, Toronto, 1990).

GRANATSTEIN, Jack L. **Yankee Go Home, Canadians and Anti-Americanism**. (Toronto: Harper Collins Pub Ltd., 1996).

HANDSON, Major Gary W. **Standardization**, article, Intelligence Branch Journal. (Number 7, Ottawa, Fall 1988).

**THE HOLY BIBLE**, King James Version. (Camden, New Jersey: Thomas Nelson Inc., 1970).

HUGHES-WILSON, Colonel John. **Military Intelligence Blunders and Cover-Ups**. (London: Robinson, 2004).

HUNT, B.D., and HAYCOCK, R.G., editors. **Canada's Defence: Perspectives on Policy in the 20th Century**. (Toronto: Copp Clark Pittman, 1993).

**Intelligence Branch Journal**. (Number 4, Spring 1987; Number 5, Fall 1987; Number 6, Spring 1988; Number 7, Fall 1988; and, Number 8, Fall 1989).

**Intelligence Branch Association Quarterly Newsletter**. (Edition 1, 1992; Edition 2, April 1992; Edition 3, 1992; Edition 1, 1993).

**Intelligence Journal**. (Volume 1, Issue 1, March 1998)

**Intelligence Branch Association Newsletter**. (Edition 2, November 1996; Edition 2, 1999).

**Intelligence Branch Association Journal**. (Millennium Issue 1, 2000; Issue 2, 2000; Issue 1, 2001; Issue 1, 2002, 20th Anniversary Edition; Issue 1, 2003).

**The Intelligence Branch Association Professional Review**. (Volume 1, 2001).

JOCKEL, Joseph T. **Security to the North: Canada-U.S. Defence Relations in the 1990s**. (East Lansing, Michigan: Michigan State University Press, 1991).

**Journal of Conflict Studies**. (Fredericton: Journal of the Centre for Conflict Studies, University of New Brunswick, Spring 1996).

**Journal of Discussions and Decisions for the 197th Meeting of the Permanent Joint Board on Defence held at Fort Monroe, Virginia, 02-04 April 1996**. Assistant Deputy Minister (Policy and Communications). (Ottawa, Ontario, NDHQ, 1996).

LANGILLE, Howard Peter. **Changing the Guard: Canada's Defence in a World in Transition**. (University of Toronto Press, 1990).

LEDGER, Don. **UFO Files: Personal accounts from actual Military and RCMP Documents**. (Halifax: Nimbus Publishing Limited, 1998).

LEYTON-BROWN, David. **Canada-U.S. Relations and the Quandary of Interdependence**. (Article, Canadian Forces College, Strathrobyn Papers, December 1996).

**MacLean's, Canada's Weekly Newsmagazine**. (Toronto: Brian Segal Publisher).

MALONEY, Sean M. **War Without Battles, Canada's NATO Brigade in Germany, 1951-1993**. (Toronto: McGraw-Hill Ryerson Limited, 1997).

MARITIME COMMAND. **The Naval Vision: Charting the Course for Canada's Maritime Forces into the 21 st Century**. (Halifax, 1994).

MIDDLEMISS, Danford W., and SOKOLSKY, Joel, J. **Canadian Defence, Decisions and Determinants**. (Toronto: Harcourt Brace Jovanovich, 1989).

NEILSON, Keith and MCKERCHER, B.J.C., editors. **Go Spy the Land, Military Intelligence in History**. (Westport, Connecticut: Praeger Publishers, 1992).

**NATO, United States Security Strategy for Europe and NATO, Looking to the Future**. Internet: http://www.dtic.mil/defenselink/pubs/anada/chapter_5.html, 2004).

**NATO, The North Atlantic Treaty Organization, NATO Integrated Data Service**. Internet: www.NATO Home Page, 2004).

**NORAD Renewal Steering Group. Options for Canada-US Cooperation in Aerospace Defence**. (Ottawa/Washington, 1994).

**NORAD, Canada's CIRVIS Reports**. Internet: http://www.schmitzware.com/IUFOG/Foia/Canada-janap1.html, 2004).

**NORAD, Colorado Springs Military Community, Fort Carson, The Peterson Complex, U.S. Air Force Academy, Cheyenne Mountain Air Force Base, and Falcon Air Force Base**. Internet: *http://www.databahn.net/galleria/orgs/cscc/military.html*, 2004).

**NORAD, USAF Fact Sheet 95-04, Air Combat Command**. (Internet: www.Dtic.mil/Air Forcelink/pa/factsheets/Air_Combat_Command.html, 2004).

NORAD Renewal Steering Group. **Options for Canada-US Coop in Aerospace Defence**. (Ottawa/Washington, 1994).

**The North Atlantic Treaty Organization**. (NATO Integrated Data Service, INTERNET, 11 Dec 1996).

**Ottawa Citizen**, 18 Jan 2004.

REHBEIN, Robert E. **Informing the Blue Helmets: The United States, UN Peacekeeping Operations, and the Role of Intelligence**. (Kingston, Centre for International Relations, Queen's University, 1996).

RUDMIN, Floyd W. **A Cognitive History of Canadian Avoidance of American Threats, 1910-1990**, (Psychology Dept., University of Tromsø, Tromsø, Norway, Internet article, 13 Dec 1996).

SCHEURWEGHS, Chris. **NATO World Wide Web Interface**. (Internet, scheurwe@hq.nato.int, 21 April 97).

**Sinister Sam's Notebook, Canadian Military Intelligence Branch Association Newsletter**. (Ottawa: Edition 2, 1993; Edition 3, 1993; Edition 4, 1993; Edition 1, 1994; Edition 1, 1995; Edition 2, December 1995; Edition 1, May 1996; Edition 2, November 1996; Edition 1, March 1997; Edition 2, August 1997).

SKAARUP, Harold A. **Siegecraft—No Fortress Impregnable**. ( iUniverse.com, Lincoln, Nebraska, 2003).

SOKOLSKY, Joel, J. and JOCKEL, Joseph T., editors. **Fifty Years of Canada-U.S. Defense Cooperation: The Road From Ogdensburg**. (Lewiston, New York: The Mellen Press, 1992).

SOKOLSKY, Joel, J. **The 1996 Renewal of NORAD**. (Kingston: NDHQ Discussion paper, 1996).

STAFFORD, David and JEFFREYS-JONES, Rhodri, eds. **American-British-Canadian Intelligence Relations 1939-2000**. (London: Frank Cass, 2000).

THOMPSON, John, H. and RANDALL, Stephen, J. **Canada and the United States: Ambivalent Allies**. (Kingston, Ontario: McGill-Queen's University Press, 1994).

TUMMERS, Cdr Ed. **Undersea Surveillance Systems: Part of a Balanced Maritime Force**. (Working papers No. 2, June 1995).

TZU, Sun. The Art of War. Translated by Thomas Cleary. (Boston: Shambala, 1991).

**U.S. Military Intelligence Sites**. (Internet: www.loyola.edu/dept/politics/milintel.html, 24 February 1997).

WHITAKER, Reg. **The Canadian Intelligence Archives**, (paper presented to the International Studies Association, London, England, 23 March 1989).

# E Tenebris Lux

## (Out of Darkness—Light)

## Volume 2

# Index

Air Command Intelligence 51, 52, 53, 54, 55, 182

Air Intelligence 31, 32, 118, 210, 263, 352, 354, 431

Airborne Int 83, 106, 495, 496

AIRBRIDGE 308

AIRCOM 30, 31, 52, 208, 240, 336, 350, 408, 411, 412, 417

Alcock
   M. 226

Alexander
   Capt B.S. 38, 116, 450
   Capt I.M. 446

Allain
   LCdr I. 203, 270, 320, 452

Allard
   WO J.B.F. 82, 154, 203, 214, 318, 450

Allen
   Capt W. 228
   Lt P.G. 446
   SSgt M.L. 219

Altherr
   Capt A.E. 12

amalgamation 18, 225

Amine
   Cpl A. 454

Amorin
   MCpl J.S. 179, 453

Ancona 308, 352

Anderson
   Capt J. 359
   SLt H.C. 418, 455

Andrew
   Maj H.F. 11, 175

Anes
   R. 228

Annesley
   MCpl R.T.F. 446

ANR 415, 501

Ansell
   Maj P.R. 198, 199, 219

Anslow
   Capt R.A. 448

Antaki
   Capt J. 39, 448

Appleby
   MCpl E.M.R. 446

Archambault
   G. 385

Arms Verification 174, 190, 194, 207, 260, 268, 330, 437, 487

Armstrong
   Capt M.H. 229
   Maj R.C. 24, 39, 300, 357, 359, 448
   WO T.G. 62, 178, 213, 244, 336, 350, 363, 417, 449

Arndt
   Sgt E. 226, 228, 489

Arnold
   Sgt D.W. 228

Arnoldi
   Lt (N) M.F.H. 169, 203, 412, 415, 452

ARRC 272, 328, 344

Arsenault
   Capt D.J. 117
   MCpl 32

Arseneau
   MCpl F.J.A. 450

ASCC 110, 111, 113, 114, 501

Ash
   Cdr 384.
   Cdr L. 384
   MCpl K.J. 204
   PO1 D.J.M. 214, 232, 406, 451

Ashby
   Capt N.G. 226, 311

Ashdown
   Col V.V. 4, 7, 12, 50, 145, 146, 147, 174, 175, 200, 202, 219, 229, 251,

Bothe
Inspector C. 386
Bouchard
CPO1 J.R.F. 116, 154, 260, 295, 338, 409, 417, 426, 450
MCpl J.D. 62
Boucher
BGen P. 69
Boudreau
Capt M.P. 203, 452
Bouillé
Capt D. 191, 192
Bourdon
WO M.S.R. 452
Bourgois
Cpl J.G.C. 454
Boutin
Capt M.E.L. 240, 372, 415, 452
Cpl J.K. 446
MCpl K. 33
Sgt J.D.P. 124, 154, 187, 232, 240, 246, 413, 451
Bowden
Capt R.C. 414, 454
Bowie
Cpl D.J. 453
Bowin
WO R. 446
Bowins
Sgt R.G. 295, 447
Boyce
Cpl B.A. 231
Boyechko
PO1 C.J. 154, 259, 320, 417, 451
Boyne
Cpl M. 454
Bradley
Maj R. 308

Bradshaw
Cpl V.M. 453
Bradt
MCpl L.W. 88, 449
Bramall
Lt H.R. 266
Bramhall
Capt S. 416
Brand
Capt I. 223
Brcko 386, 387, 390
Breton
Cpl L. 342
Brigden
Maj K.D. 486
Brillon
Sgt E.J.M. 416, 454
British Army of the Rhine 485
Brogan
WO E.H. 39, 447
Brooker
Capt P.F. 228
Brooks
Maj J.B. 373, 447
MWO L.J. 14, 409
WO L.J. 62, 448
Brown
Capt B. 266
WO2 C.G. 228, 229
Browne
Capt D.L. 446
Bruce
Col G.L.R. 12, 27, 28, 34, 38, 39, 40, 44, 48, 57, 58, 61, 62, 64, 82, 145, 446, 481
Brun
Sgt J.J.J. 154, 187, 287, 451
Brunsuum 5, 102, 173

Church
Lt D. 251
Churchill
Sgt R.A. 447
Sgt R.W. 295
Sir W. 50, 459
Churman
Capt J.V. 414, 454
CI 5, 17, 43, 109, 112, 158, 342, 403, 422, 487, 489
CIA 7, 18, 441, 460
CIC 209, 502
CIFC 502
CINCHAN 108
Cipro
Sgt R. 63, 446
CIS 6, 27, 40, 48, 52, 53, 54, 57, 72, 82, 90, 91, 138, 167, 199, 203, 209, 463, 464, 473, 474
CISA xvii, 7, 11, 12, 15, 25, 27, 70, 82, 90, 91, 118, 141, 142, 166, 167, 175, 181, 199, 206, 220, 252, 258, 262, 266, 282, 288, 309, 312, 358, 374
CISA Academic Award 4, 70, 82, 90, 137, 167, 175, 199, 252, 266, 311, 358
CISA AGM 198, 219
1983 11
1984 24
1985 39
1986 68
1987 88
1988 136
1990 174
1991 198
1992 219
1993 251
1994 265
1995 310
1996 359
1997 419

CISA Essay Competition 206, 420
Ciuciura
Maj I.J. 64, 447
Ciufo
Cpl S.J. 454
CJTF 269
Clairoux
Maj J.V.G. 240, 241, 339, 363, 452
Clark
G. 222
Gen W.K. 389
R.O. 175
Clarke
WO L.A. 154, 417, 451, 489
Clasper
MCpl K.E. 453
Claxton
B. 258
Clemis
Maj D.E. 167
CLFCSC 72, 83, 94, 141, 143, 144, 361, 364, 415, 437
Cliffe
MCpl J.F. 446
Climo
Capt D.A. 105, 117, 173, 451, 489
Clouston
Capt K.B. 154, 208, 372, 451
Clouthier
Maj P. 69, 89, 90
Cloutier
E. xx
Clowater
Sgt R.M. 413, 452
CLS 429, 430
CMHQ 9, 10, 374
CMNB 502
CMRB 103, 104
CMS 429, 430

Cousineau
  Capt J.A.Y. 4, 16
Couture
  LCol P.J.F. 11, 25, 69, 89, 219
  MGen C. 339
  Sgt J.P.A. 240, 286, 413, 452
Cowan
  Lt (N) S. 176
  Maj B. 90
  Maj C.N. 69
  Sgt I.G. 449
Cowen
  Lt (N) S. 241, 450
Cox
  BGen J.S. xix, 65, 67
  Pte R.A. 291
CP-140 Aurora 411
Craig
  OCdt M. 298
  OCdt M.S. 446
Crandell
  Col P.D.R. xix, 11, 23, 24, 81, 203,
    264, 284, 313, 333, 336, 358, 359,
    360, 362, 373, 374, 403, 405, 419,
    420, 432, 447, 481
Crane
  MWO E.M. 117, 213, 242, 260, 448
Cranston
  WO J.E. 14, 136, 447, 495
Crerar
  Gen H.D.G. 26
Crerar Trophy 26, 27
Croatia 232, 233, 235, 268, 273, 322, 381,
  388
Crober
  LCol F.P. 165, 173, 486
Crosby
  WO L.D. 38, 169, 242, 298, 448
Crouch
  Gen W.W. 389

Cruse
  LCol J.F. 166, 203, 373, 412, 448, 495
CSA 258, 429
Csaba
  K. 380, 385
CSCE 195, 502
CSE 166, 203, 240, 258, 373, 432, 495
CSIS 16, 372, 373, 420
CSMI 16, 146, 224, 225, 289, 310, 331,
  424, 483
CTC 72, 124, 150, 203, 246, 261, 262,
  263, 332, 347, 361, 364, 365, 370, 371,
  414
CTCC 262, 330, 364
Cullen
  L.A. 228
  Lt J.L. 137
Cummings
  Sgt C. 255
Cunningham
  LGen C. 373
Curson
  Capt F.J. 416
Cushman
  Maj D.J. 300, 363, 415, 452
Cuvelier
  WO J.A. 226, 495
Cyopeck
  Lt 244
Cyprus 20, 35, 65, 68, 86, 138, 166, 208,
  240, 246, 247, 348, 378, 387, 403, 415,
  417, 496
Cyr
  Capt L. 359

# D
D Space D 503
Dabros
  BGen W.J. 118, 463, 470

Dendy
  LCol J.O. 7, 447
Denner
  Sgt A.K. 418, 455
Dennique
  WO R. 342
Denny
  Sgt M.G. 246, 452
Dent
  Capt P.A. 446
Depew
  Capt J. 27
DeQuetteville
  LGen A. 429
Derkson
  Maj R.A. 38, 117, 173, 208, 240, 408,
    489, 495
Desilets
  Sgt L. 295
Desjardins
  Capt J. 188
  J. 237
  Maj S.P. xix, 267, 301, 302, 363
Detweiler
  LAC D. xx
Devlin
  BGen P. 332
  MCpl H.J. 446
Dewar
  Sgt D.A. 228
Dextraze
  Capt J. 495
DFAIT 379, 385
DFLR 502
DG Int 5, 20, 37, 57, 72, 96, 103, 145,
  175, 199, 203, 204, 208, 219, 240, 249,
  266, 311, 316, 317, 332, 334, 360, 367,
  403, 405, 412, 413, 418, 420, 463, 464,
  473, 474, 477, 478
DG Secur 72, 252, 266, 403

DGIS 252, 462, 463, 470, 489, 502
DGMI 503
DIA 8, 18, 342, 373, 412, 415
DIAC 8, 81, 208, 503
Diamond,
  MCpl M. 257
Dick
  Col M. 34
Dickie
  WO A.H. 32, 38, 88, 95, 246, 287, 449
Dicks
  WO R.T. 39, 447
Dickson
  B. 374
  Capt W.L. 10, 12, 13, 14, 117, 173,
    191, 226, 447, 489, 495
DIE 72, 86, 111, 114, 174, 237, 239, 316,
  317, 371, 373, 412, 503
Dieppe 206, 283, 284, 350, 366, 405, 420
DIEPS 371, 503
Dimmell
  WO2 N.C. 226, 229
Dionne
  WO J.J. 10, 14, 153, 448
DIPCD 211
DIPD 72, 110
Directorate Intelligence Plans, Coordination
  and Doctrine 211
Dirkson
  Maj D.A. 448
DIT 147
DIWO 210
DIWP 147
Dixon
  CWO R.D. 219
  Maj R.R. 198, 224, 226, 228, 229, 258,
    312
  MWO D. 405, 416
Dixon Award 224
DLCIS 111, 113

LCol G.A. 12, 13, 153, 173, 235, 298, 449, 489
LCol J.A. 38
Maj R.S. 87
Maj W.P. 236, 300, 415, 452
MWO A.P. 95, 298, 447
Gravelle
  Sgt G. 105
Gray
  Capt P.R. 246, 415, 450
  Maj J.A. 226, 231
  Sgt R.B. 226, 229
  WO R.M. 440, 446
Graydon
  Maj R. 372
Great War
  1914-1918 228
Green Paper 40
Greenwood
  MCpl M.W. 450
Grehan
  Maj E.P. 62, 95, 117, 240, 415, 449
Greyeyes
  Capt R.T. 36, 174, 186, 204, 226, 229, 283, 446
Grieg
  Maj R.L. 266
Grigg
  WO W. 264
Grimshaw
  LCdr R.P. 117, 120, 298, 414, 451
Grogan
  Col R.T. 11, 24, 39, 40, 68, 89, 136, 138, 186, 198, 219, 251, 252, 266, 310, 359, 419
Groleau
  Pte Y.G. 446
Guatemala 367
Guertin
  WO J.R. 246, 417, 452

Gulbord
  MCpl 422
Gulf War 181, 183, 225, 270
Gustafson
  Lt (N) R.L. 449
Guyatt
  HLCol D.E. 11, 25, 89, 90, 137, 138, 174, 198, 219, 226, 228, 251, 264, 266, 310, 357, 358, 359, 374, 419
Guyon
  Maj M.L.T. 25, 40, 68
Guzeller
  Capt F. 378, 379

**H**
Haas
  Maj D.A. 126, 166, 167, 174, 186, 198, 219, 266, 310, 419, 453
Haché
  WO J.R. 446
Hackel
  Maj L.W. 12, 13, 115, 126, 153, 165, 168, 249, 250, 414, 449
Hadden
  Sgt J.C. 266
Hagel
  Sgt T.L. 88, 177, 245, 298, 450
Hagnier
  Cpl P. 355
Hague
  BGen K.C. 362, 367, 405, 412, 464, 476
  Sgt M.J. 418, 455
Hahn
  Maj J.E. 142
Haier
  Maj R.P. 83
Haiti 270, 271, 307, 317, 330, 338, 349, 352, 354, 367, 368, 403, 415, 417, 420, 421, 422, 423, 429
Hall
  Col A. 25

Maestri
Cpl 446
MAG 53, 131, 132, 208, 299, 406
Mah
N.L.Y. 220
Sgt D. 496
Sgt N.L. 153, 188, 453
Mahar
LCol R. 495
Maheux
Sgt F. 188, 302, 328, 454
Sgt J.J. 453
Mahoney
WO M.B. 14, 24, 62, 178, 203, 448
Mailhot
Lt 90
Maillet
P.J. 246
WO P.A. 14, 38, 153, 246, 267, 287, 297, 301, 364, 448
Mair
Capt D.M. 236, 238, 245, 413, 415, 452
Malainey
Capt J.L. 203, 232, 415, 452
Malcolm
MWO M.E. 10, 88, 245, 448
Malenfant
Sgt J.G. 154, 447
Maloney
Capt S.M. 169
Maltais
WO R. 328
Mannie
Cpl A.N. 454
MCpl A.N. 363
Mansfield
Maj J.H. 4, 11, 25, 27, 39, 40, 68, 70, 82, 88, 89, 91, 136, 137, 138, 174, 219, 266, 310
Sgt J.T. 168, 231, 447

Manuge
Pte T. 295
WO P.G. 94, 117, 154, 187, 204, 260, 295, 418, 451
Marchand
Sgt K.J. 237, 268, 417, 421, 422, 423, 452
Marchbank
Capt D.V. 208, 286, 287, 318, 349, 451
MARCOM 15, 30, 31, 53, 102, 128, 129, 130, 131, 133, 200, 203, 320, 336, 350, 412
MARCOT 132, 133, 320, 410, 425, 427
Marcoux
S. 380, 388
Marion
E. 4
Maritime Intelligence Conference 320
Maritime Warfare Centre 131
MARLANT 317, 333, 347, 370, 413, 414, 415, 417, 425, 427, 432
Marleau
WO J.J.R. 337, 338, 447
Marlowe
Sgt 33
MARPAC 31, 53, 61, 102, 128, 129, 130, 203, 320, 410, 414, 417, 418, 427, 432, 433
Marsh
WO M.V. 24, 32, 35, 62, 117, 447
Martin
Capt J.B. 83, 90, 137, 226
CWO J.R. 24, 32, 51, 153, 237, 267, 301, 336, 358, 363, 403, 404, 447
Maj J.E. 486
Maj R. 105
MCpl K.E. 453
WO J.R. 153
Martineau
Capt J.G.H.E. 14, 38, 55, 447

CWO D.L. 363
WO D. 301
McLellan
M. 24
McMullan
LCol A.G. 169, 203, 227, 241, 447, 484
PO2 R. 342
McNair
SLdr W. 18, 251
McNaulty
Sgt D.G. 450
McNeil
Sgt M.P. 154, 246, 286, 418, 448, 496
WO D.F. 154, 219, 240, 412, 413
McNulty
Sgt D.G. 82, 489
WO D.G. 154, 187, 203, 348, 412
McQuinn-Legér
MCpl D.B. 88, 240, 246, 286, 450
McShane
LCol K.G. 227, 258, 419
McSherry
Cpl S.J. 453
Lt S.J. 179, 218
McVee
Maj D.W. 232, 298, 300, 447
McVeigh
WO1 J. 231
Meating
MGen R.G. 208, 405, 464, 477, 479, 489
Medeiros
Cpl D.D. 453
Meigs
MGen M.C. 389
Mellor
Maj E.E. 11, 25, 39, 68, 83, 446
Mendel
Capt G.A. 141, 309

Mercer
Capt J.G. 12, 13, 51, 82, 449
Sgt S. 153, 178, 448
Merrithew
G.S. 222
Messier
LCol J.L.F. 63, 74, 90, 95, 150, 153, 240, 267, 301, 363, 413, 415, 450
Metaxas
Maj P. xx
Metaxas-Mariatos
Maj P. 240, 241, 452
Metcalfe
OCdt M. 446
Meunier
Cpl M.A. 454
SLt M.A. 349
Mi-17 Hip 376, 383, 386
MI2 226
Mi-24 Hind 376
MI3 223
MI5 250, 459, 460
MI6 250
MI-8 228
Mi-8 Hip 383
MI-9 227
Michaud
Maj P. 10, 39, 203, 259, 268, 317, 348, 448
Michener
CWO M.B 62, 446
Millar
Lt (N) R.B. 241, 450
Miller
Capt (N) D.E. 132, 133
Capt J.G. 415, 452
Lt (N) W.E. 154, 219, 451
Million
WO J.V. 55, 117, 448

Mottershead
  LCol A.B. 263
Motyl
  Capt M. 198, 199, 359, 360, 419
Moug
  WO R.W. 10, 14, 62, 88, 94, 123, 124,
  125, 126, 321, 363, 417, 448
Mountain
  Capt D.G. 452
Mountbatten
  Lord Louis 7, 15
MP 407 132
MTC 153
Mudge
  Sgt B.K. 88, 154, 177, 203, 348, 416,
  450
Muldoon
  Lt F.C. 27, 186, 227, 231, 258, 284
Mullen
  Lt J. 39, 446
Mullin
  Sgt B. 328
Mullins
  WO S. 179, 453
Mulroney
  Prime Minister B. 115
Munro
  BGen S. 380, 390
Murley
  PO1 R.W. 295
  PO1 W.R. 154, 259, 298, 418, 451
Murphy
  B. 227
  Maj R.H. 483
Murray
  Cpl L.K. 454
  VAdm L.E. 332
Murret-Labarthe
  WO J.P. 10, 62, 178, 240, 295, 363, 448

Museum 189, 258, 329, 366
Mylemans
  Cpl 453

**N**

N21 347, 370, 414, 425, 432
NACSI 111
Nadeau
  WO J.G. 24, 447
Nafekh
  Lt (N) A. 317, 452
Nash
  Maj R.G. 117, 173, 235, 317, 336, 348,
  349, 350, 359, 363, 415, 451, 484
  Pte E. 295
Nath
  Capt R.G. 154, 208, 263, 412, 451
NATO 55, 85, 111, 134, 138, 155, 255,
  260, 268, 269, 272, 274, 275, 276, 323,
  328, 329, 332, 338, 341, 354, 368, 371,
  425, 433, 437, 438, 441, 462, 478, 485,
  488, 496
NATO Advisory Committee on Special
  Intelligence 111
Naval Intelligence 31, 61, 128, 129, 131,
  433
NCIU 403
NDC 473
NDHQ 5, 28, 31, 36, 37, 48, 52, 53, 54,
  57, 78, 84, 96, 97, 102, 128, 147, 161,
  162, 163, 183, 184, 200, 211, 212, 219,
  232, 237, 249, 264, 284, 313, 329, 330,
  332, 333, 334, 336, 342, 360, 361, 362,
  367, 412, 416, 417, 418, 420, 429, 430,
  462, 471, 473, 474
NDIC 8, 147, 208, 212, 245, 312, 316,
  317, 371, 372, 414, 504
NEADS 407, 504
Neeb
  LCdr S.L. 240, 241, 452
Neilson
  Sgt L.E. 169, 417, 452

Rechner
  Maj P. 191, 192, 268
Rechnitzer
  Maj E.D.P. 240, 415, 452
Redburn
  LCol D.M. 486
Rego
  Maj W.A. 246, 452
Reid
  D. 222
  MGen R.A. 463, 469
Reilly
  Lt T.J. 11
Relf
  Sgt G.J. 227
Remillard
  Maj T.L. 414, 455
Rempel
  W. 227
Renaud
  LCol P.A. 62, 81, 298, 448
René
  Capt Y.S. 174
Rennett
  Maj W.A. 28, 117, 134, 139, 155, 165,
    342, 450
Renwick
  MWO D.W. 39, 447
RESEWSQN 31, 73, 202, 425
RESO 124
Reuters
  Maj R.H.J. 363
RGV 505
Riberdy
  Sgt J.E.M. 298, 448
Richard
  Cpl J.L. 302, 454
  K. 90
  WO R.L. 90

Richardson
  G. 359
  LCdr S.J.Y. 11, 25, 258, 282
  Maj B.A. 359
  WO D.E. 7, 447
Ricketts
  P. 251
Riley
  Lt T.J. 446
Rimsa
  Capt K.P. 11, 15, 63, 446
Ritchie
  Col A.F. 11, 39, 174, 359
Ritgen
  Col H. 144
Rivard
  Capt P.G. 83, 89, 90, 125, 136, 138,
    166, 174, 198, 199, 248, 257, 266,
    310, 311, 453
Rive
  LCol 202
Rivest
  Maj P. 363
RMC 142, 259, 289, 371, 372, 373, 414,
  438
Roach
  Maj R.A. xx, 414, 455
Robb
  LCol D.M. 21, 25, 27, 29, 35, 44, 56,
    62, 69, 70, 89, 94, 101, 118, 137, 145,
    264, 312, 447, 481
Robert
  Sgt N.S. 219
Robertson
  Capt J.M. 263, 283, 301, 359, 363
  Capt L. 241
  Cpl L.D. 453
  LCol S. 23
  Maj L. 151, 152, 241

UNTSO 62
Upshall
  WO W.D. 154, 240, 248, 257, 286, 451
Upton
  Col J.S. xix, 34, 39, 40, 68, 82, 138,
    219, 226, 227, 310, 419, 446, 483
Ursaki
  Capt V.G. 227
USS Intrepid 7, 15
USSPACECOM 209
UTPM 39, 72, 119

# V
Vacheresse
  B.M. 426
  Cpl R.A. 297, 426, 453
  Pte R.A. 298
Vallée
  2Lt J. 89
Vallevand
  LCol W.R. 12, 447
Van Der Sluis
  Capt 244
Van Wynen
  Capt J.P.K. 11, 25, 39, 68, 89, 90, 137,
    174, 198, 227, 310, 359, 419
  S. 175
Vanasse
  Capt N.B. 302, 431, 453
Vandenberg
  WO R. 317, 355, 417, 454
Vanderstoel
  Maj R. 136, 447
Vandertoon
  Cpl M. 453
Vanier
  B. 226, 228, 229
Varasisky
  Cpl K.F. 454

Vaughn
  Capt (N) 373
  Pte R.J. 217
Veinotte
  Maj S.R. 4, 11, 16, 25, 39, 68, 88, 90,
    118, 137, 153, 446
Veinotte Memorial Trophy 153
Velika Kladusa 339, 383, 385, 391, 397
Vella
  Maj R.J. 11, 25, 39, 69, 174, 219
  V. 4
Verbrugge
  Cpl J.M.A.D. 82, 219, 412, 450
Vernon
  MGen J. 248, 264
Vézina-Gaudreault
  Sgt S. 416, 454
Vicenza 338, 351, 354
Vidler
  MCpl H. 248, 257
Viens
  LCol J.M.R. 267
Vietnam 105
Villeneuve
  LCol J.D. 267, 302, 321, 363, 420, 452
Vimy 165
Vinetti
  Sgt J.P.G. 39, 117, 242, 298, 449
Visoko 322, 385, 388, 391, 396
Vitae 437
Vladivostok 176
von Papineau
  Maj W.B. 15, 25, 32, 33, 39, 62, 166,
    174, 261, 295, 412, 415, 450
Vouriot
  Capt W.H. 117
  Sgt V.H. 448

1510065

Made in the USA